Democracy in
Developing Countries

LATIN AMERICA

Democracy in Developing Countries

LATIN AMERICA

Second Edition

edited by
Larry Diamond, Jonathan Hartlyn,
Juan J. Linz, and Seymour Martin Lipset

LYNNE
RIENNER
PUBLISHERS

BOULDER
LONDON

Published in the United States of America in 1999 by
Lynne Rienner Publishers, Inc.
1800 30th Street, Boulder, Colorado 80301

and in the United Kingdom by
Lynne Rienner Publishers, Inc.
3 Henrietta Street, Covent Garden, London WC2E 8LU

Library of Congress Cataloging-in-Publication Data
Democracy in developing countries. Latin America /   edited by Larry
    Diamond . . . [et al.].—2nd ed.
        p.   cm.
    Includes bibliographical references.
    ISBN 1-55587-798-2 (pb. :   alk. paper)
    1. Democracy—Latin America. 2. Latin America—Politics and
government—1980– I. Diamond, Larry Jay.
JL960.D46   1999
320.98'09'049—dc21   99-24155
                                                                  CIP

British Cataloguing in Publication Data
A Cataloguing in Publication record for this book
is available from the British Library.

Printed and bound in the United States of America

⊗   The paper used in this publication meets the requirements
    of the American National Standard for Permanence of
    Paper for Printed Library Materials Z39.48-1984.

    5 4 3

CONTENTS

Preface   vii

Map of Latin America   xiv

1   Introduction:
    Politics, Society, and Democracy in Latin America
    Larry Diamond, Jonathan Hartlyn, and Juan J. Linz   1

2   Argentina: Capitalism and Democracy
    Carlos H. Waisman   71

3   Brazil: Inequality Against Democracy
    Bolívar Lamounier   131

4   Chile: Origins and Consolidation of a
    Latin American Democracy
    Arturo Valenzuela   191

5   Colombia:
    The Politics of Violence and Democratic Transformation
    Jonathan Hartlyn and John Dugas   249

6   Peru: Precarious Regimes, Authoritarian and Democratic
    Cynthia McClintock   309

7   Venezuela: The Character, Crisis,
    and Possible Future of Democracy
    Daniel H. Levine and Brian F. Crisp   367

8   Costa Rica: The Roots of Democratic Stability
     John A. Booth   429

9   The Dominican Republic:
     The Long and Difficult Struggle for Democracy
     Rosario Espinal and Jonathan Hartlyn   469

10   Mexico:
     Sustained Civilian Rule and the Question of Democracy
     Daniel C. Levy and Kathleen Bruhn   519

     List of Acronyms   575
     The Contributors   581
     Index   585
     About the Book   594

PREFACE

This second edition of our book has been produced at a very different moment in the life cycle of democracy in Latin America and the world. When our project began in the mid-1980s with a conference on twenty-six developing countries, the "third wave" of global democratization had not yet been named or clearly identified, and the return of democracy to Latin America was still somewhat new and uncertain. This extensively revised collection appears exactly ten years after the first, and much has changed over the past decade. What is most important, however, is what has not changed: ten years later, none of our cases of democracy in Latin America has yet broken down—though Peru suffered a serious interruption in the early to mid-1990s and at most only a partial reequilibration. And our only case of a nondemocracy, Mexico, is now moving toward a genuine electoral democracy.

The story of the past ten years, however, is not only one of progress. As we document in our introduction, and as is apparent from many of the chapters, a number of our country cases have struggled with serious problems of democratic decay and malfunctioning, including human rights abuses and the resurgence of undemocratic styles of politics and governance. We felt that this remarkable record of progress and decay required serious empirical treatment and analytical and theoretical reflection.

We do not attempt here to recapitulate the intellectual history of comparative democratic studies, or of the project that produced the three original volumes on Africa, Asia, and Latin America, as well as two comparative collections. For that, we refer the reader back to the longer preface in the original volume on Latin America, which also discusses the comparative logic and case selection of that twenty-six-country project.[1] Rather, here we want to explain the structure of our case study chapters and to offer an updated treatment of how we conceptualize democracy and related regime types and conditions.

THE STRUCTURE OF THE CHAPTERS

As in the first edition, each country chapter follows a similar organization. After an introductory overview, a first section provides a political history that examines the country's major experiences with democratic and non-democratic governments and explains the fate of each regime (especially each democratic one), why it persisted or failed or evolved as it did, and why successive ones emerged as and when they did. A second section offers a summary theoretical judgment of the factors that have been most important in determining the country's overall record with democracy—to abstract across the various regimes and events the most consistently significant and salient factors from among the inventory of variables presented in the project outline (and others that may have been neglected). A final section then explores the current challenges and future prospects for democracy.[2]

Some authors also assess the country's overall experience with democratic government, using a six-point scale developed for the initial project. The points on this scale were (1) *high success*—stable and uninterrupted democratic rule, with democracy now deeply institutionalized and stable; (2) *progressive success*—the consolidation of relatively stable democracy after one or more breakdowns or serious interruptions; (3) *mixed success*—democratic and unstable (i.e., democracy has returned following a period of breakdown and authoritarian rule, but has not yet been consolidated); (4) *mixed success*—partial or semidemocracy; (5) *failure but promise*—democratic rule has broken down, but there are considerable pressures and prospects for its return; and (6) *failure or absence*—democracy has never functioned for any significant period of time and there is little prospect that it will in the coming years.

CONCEPTS, DEFINITIONS, AND CLASSIFICATIONS

There has been considerable conceptual and theoretical work on democracy and democratization since the first edition was published. In general, there has been an increasing acceptance of the value of a conceptualization of political democracy that focuses on procedural issues rather than substantive outcomes, and that does not conflate democracy with social and economic dimensions; this is the perspective on political democracy presented in the first edition and continued in the second. At the same time, there have been fruitful discussions regarding the limits of narrow types of procedural conceptualizations. Before turning to a brief discussion of these, it is worth repeating the view of democracy and the classification of regimes advanced in 1989.

Democracy—or what Robert Dahl terms "polyarchy"—denotes a system of government that meets three essential conditions: meaningful and extensive *competition* among individuals and organized groups (especially political parties) for all effective positions of government power, at regular intervals and excluding the use of force; a highly inclusive level of *political participation* in the selection of leaders and policies, at least through regular and fair elections, such that no major (adult) social group is excluded; and a level of *civil and political liberties*—freedom of expression, freedom of the press, freedom to form and join organizations—sufficient to ensure the integrity of political competition and participation.[3]

Countries that broadly satisfy these criteria nevertheless do so to differing degrees. In fact, none do so perfectly, which is why Dahl prefers to call them polyarchies. Furthermore, the boundary between democratic and nondemocratic is sometimes a blurred and imperfect one, and beyond it lies a much broader range of variation in political systems. In the first edition and now, we readily concede the difficulties in classification this variation repeatedly causes. Even if we look only at the political, legal, and constitutional structure, several of our cases appear to lie somewhere on the boundary between democratic and somewhat less than democratic. The ambiguity is further complicated by the constraints on free political activity, organization, and expression that may often in practice make the system much less democratic than it appears on paper. In all cases, we have tried to pay attention to actual practice in assessing and classifying regimes. Yet, for several countries, including Colombia in 1989 and several more of the Latin American cases today, the decision as to whether these may be considered full democracies is replete with nuance and ambiguity.

We have alleviated this problem somewhat by recognizing various grades of distinction among less-than-democratic systems. While isolated violations of civil liberties or modest and occasional vote rigging should not disqualify a country from broad classification as a democracy, there is a need to categorize separately those countries that allow greater political competition and freedom than would be found in a true authoritarian regime, but less than could justifiably be termed democratic. Hence, we classify as *semidemocratic* those countries where the effective power of elected officials is so limited, or political party competition is so restricted, or the freedom and fairness of elections so compromised that electoral outcomes, while competitive, still deviate significantly from popular preferences; and/or where civil and political liberties are so limited that some political orientations and interests are unable to organize and express themselves. Still more restrictive is a *hegemonic party system,* like that of Mexico in 1989, in which opposition parties are legal but denied—through pervasive electoral malpractices and frequent state coercion—any real

chance to compete for power. Descending further on the scale of classification, *authoritarian* regimes permit even less pluralism, typically banning
political parties (or all but the ruling one) and most forms of political organization and competition, while being more repressive than liberal in their
level of civil and political freedom. Paying close attention to actual behavior, one may distinguish a subset of authoritarian regimes that we call *pseudodemocracies,* in that the existence of formally democratic political institutions such as multiparty electoral competition masks (often, in part, to
legitimate) the reality of authoritarian domination—Cynthia McClintock
makes this case for Peru (Chapter 6).

The "dependent variable" of the study was concerned not only with
democracy, but also stability—the persistence and durability of democratic
and other regimes over time, particularly through periods of unusually
intense conflict, crisis, and strain. A *stable* regime is one that is deeply
institutionalized and consolidated, making it likely to enjoy a high level of
popular legitimacy. *Partially stable* regimes are neither fully secure nor in
imminent danger of collapse; their institutions have perhaps acquired some
measure of depth, flexibility, and value, but not enough to ensure the
regime safe passage through severe challenges. *Unstable* regimes are, by
definition, highly vulnerable to breakdown or overthrow in periods of acute
uncertainty and stress.

RECENT CONCEPTUALIZATIONS

We will not attempt a full review and discussion of a growing literature on
conceptual issues regarding political democracy. Rather, we want to underscore that there is now greater sensitivity to the need to pay attention to a
broader set of institutions and factors than those simply associated with
free elections, including a coherent state, effective and democratic accountability and rule of law, and civilian control over the military.

What this has meant is that more minimalist definitions of what might
be termed an "electoral democracy"—that is, a civilian, constitutional system in which the legislative and chief executive offices are filled through
regular, competitive, multiparty elections with universal suffrage—have
been amplified by what David Collier and Steven Levitsky have termed
"expanded procedural" conceptions.[4] For example, in their conceptualization of democracy, Jonathan Hartlyn and Arturo Valenzuela, in addition to
the criteria of contestation and inclusiveness, also explicitly incorporated
the rule of law as a third dimension of democracy.[5] In turn, Juan Linz and
Alfred Stepan noted that "no modern polity can become democratically
consolidated unless it is first a state," and then focused on five crucial arenas necessary for democratic consolidation. They argued that three of them,
"a lively and independent civil society, a political society with sufficient
autonomy and a working consensus about procedures of governance, and

constitutionalism and a rule of law . . . are virtually definitional prerequisites of a consolidated democracy," while underscoring the importance of the other two, a functioning state apparatus and an institutionalized market economy.[6]

Further, Larry Diamond draws a distinction among electoral democracy, intermediate conceptions, and liberal democracy.[7] He argues that, in addition to the elements of electoral democracy, liberal democracy requires, first, the absence of reserved domains of power for the military or other actors not accountable to the electorate, directly or indirectly. Second, it requires the horizontal accountability of officeholders to one another; this constrains executive power and so helps protect constitutionalism, legality, and the deliberative process.[8] Third, it encompasses extensive provisions for political and civic pluralism, as well as for individual and group freedoms—of belief, opinion, discussion, speech, publication, assembly, demonstration, and petition—so that contending interests and values may be expressed and compete through ongoing processes of articulation and representation, beyond periodic elections. Freedom and pluralism, in turn, can be secured only through a "rule of law," in which legal rules are applied fairly, consistently, and predictably across equivalent cases, irrespective of the class, status, or power of those subject to the rules. Under a true rule of law, all citizens have political and legal equality, and the state and its agents are themselves subject to the law.[9]

In the chapters that follow, as the authors have analyzed trends of progress and decay, they have frequently considered issues associated with these expanded conceptualizations of democracy.

*   *   *

This second edition of *Democracy in Developing Countries: Latin America* was made possible by a grant from the Carnegie Corporation of New York to the research and publications program of the International Forum for Democratic Studies of the National Endowment for Democracy. We are grateful for the support of the Carnegie Corporation and the International Forum, neither of which has any responsibility for the factual assertions, theories, and interpretations advanced in these pages. We thank in particular Marc F. Plattner, Larry Diamond's codirector at the International Forum, and Art Kaufman, the Forum's senior program officer, for their encouragement and cooperation.

We also want to acknowledge several people who helped us considerably with research assistance, as well as with the editing, coordination, and production of the book manuscript: Jonathan Hartlyn thanks Alec Ewald, Claudio Fuentes, and especially Merike Blofield at the University of North Carolina; and Larry Diamond thanks Marguerite (Petie) Kramer at the Hoover Institution.

We would like to express gratitude to our contributors, both those who agreed to undertake the very considerable effort to revise the chapters they had originally published in 1989, and those who joined us anew as coauthors of several of the case studies. We have been privileged to work with such an innovative and energetic collection of scholars, who have also proven once again to be generous and considerate colleagues.

Finally, we wish to remember here an extraordinary young scholar, Charles G. Gillespie, who coauthored our original chapter on Uruguay and passed away in 1991. Charles was not just a trenchant student of Uruguay; he was a comparativist with great theoretical insight and promise. We learned much from our interaction with him during the first phase of this project. His loss is not only a personal one, but a tangible one for the discipline.

—The Editors

NOTES

1. See Larry Diamond, Juan J. Linz, and Seymour Martin Lipset, eds., *Democracy in Developing Countries: Latin America* (Boulder, CO: Lynne Rienner, 1989), and the preface on pp. ix–xxvii; see also, by the same editors and publisher, *Democracy in Developing Countries: Africa* (1989); *Democracy in Developing Countries: Asia* (1989); *Politics in Developing Countries: Comparing Experiences with Democracy* (1990); and *Politics in Developing Countries: Comparing Experiences with Democracy,* 2nd ed. (1995).

2. Because of Chile's long history with democracy prior to the 1973 coup, that chapter provides a theoretical treatment of democracy prior to examining the reasons for the breakdown of democracy, the authoritarian period from 1973 to 1990, and the recent transition to democracy.

3. Robert Dahl, *Polyarchy: Participation and Opposition* (New Haven: Yale University Press, 1971), pp. 3–20; Joseph Schumpeter, *Capitalism, Socialism, and Democracy* (New York: Harper and Row, 1942); Seymour Martin Lipset, *Political Man* (New York: Doubleday & Co., 1960), p. 27; Juan J. Linz, *The Breakdown of Democratic Regimes: Crisis, Breakdown, and Reequilibration* (Baltimore: Johns Hopkins University Press, 1986).

4. See David Collier and Steven Levitsky, "Democracy with Adjectives: Conceptual Innovation in Comparative Research," *World Politics* 49 (April 1997): 430–451, for a presentation and analysis of these. For a useful critique of a minimalist conceptualization and presentation of an "expanded procedural" one, see Philippe C. Schmitter and Terry Lynn Karl, "What Democracy Is . . . and Is Not," *Journal of Democracy* 2, no. 3 (1991): 78.

5. Jonathan Hartlyn and Arturo Valenzuela, "Democracy in Latin America Since 1930," in Leslie Bethell, ed., *Latin America Since 1930: Economy, Society, and Politics, Vol. VI, Part II of Cambridge History of Latin America* (Cambridge: Cambridge University Press, 1994).

6. Juan Linz and Alfred Stepan, *Problems of Democratic Transition and Consolidation: Southern Europe, South America, and Post-Communist Europe* (Baltimore: Johns Hopkins University Press, 1996), quotes from p. 7, p. 10; see also their definitions of democratic transition and democratic consolidation on pp. 3–7.

7. This draws from Larry Diamond, *Developing Democracy: Toward Consolidation* (Baltimore: Johns Hopkins University Press, 1999), chapter 1.

8. For the political quality of democracy, the most important additional mechanism of horizontal accountability is an autonomous judiciary, but crucial as well are institutionalized means (often in a separate, autonomous agency) to monitor, investigate, and punish government corruption at all levels. On the concept of lateral, or horizontal, accountability and its importance, see Richard L. Sklar, "Developmental Democracy," *Comparative Studies in Society and History* 29, no. 4 (1987): 686–714; Richard L. Sklar, "Towards a Theory of Developmental Democracy," in Adrian Leftwich, ed., *Democracy and Development: Theory*

and Practice (Cambridge: Polity Press, 1996), pp. 25–44; Guillermo O'Donnell, "Delegative Democracy," *Journal of Democracy* 5, no. 1 (1994): 60–62; Andreas Schedler, Larry Diamond, and Marc F. Plattner, eds., *The Self-Restraining State: Power and Accountability in New Democracies* (Boulder, CO: Lynne Rienner, 1999). Sklar terms the lateral form "constitutional democracy" and emphasizes its mutually reinforcing relationship to vertical accountability.

9. For an important explication of the rule of law and its related concepts, see Guillermo O'Donnell, "Polyarchies and the (Un)Rule of Law in Latin America," in Juan Méndez, Guillermo O'Donnell, and Paulo Sérgio Pinheiro, eds., *The (Un)Rule of Law and the Underprivileged in Latin America* (Notre Dame: University of Notre Dame Press, 1999).

LATIN AMERICA

1

INTRODUCTION:
Politics, Society, and Democracy
in Latin America

Larry Diamond, Jonathan Hartlyn & Juan J. Linz

This volume is being published one decade after the first edition.[1] Democracy in Latin America is now of even greater relevance; there is no longer any dispute that issues regarding democracy in the region are of real concern to political and social actors within each of these countries and not arbitrary impositions by ethnocentric foreign scholars. At the same time, there continue to be strong debates regarding appropriate conceptualizations of democracy or relevant causal factors. We provide our conceptualization of democracy in the preface; in the following pages, we examine arguments about why and how different types of causal factors are important. Rather than provide a reductionist and artificially elegant model, for which many of our country cases would have to be considered exceptions or outliers, we have opted to retain a broader, more comprehensive explanatory focus. Our chief aim is to identify the factors whose influence and interplay are most important in explaining the varied experiences with democracy of our nine Latin American cases. We highlight in particular past historical experiences and sequences and political-institutional factors in the democratic evolution of these countries.

As noted in the first edition of this book, with the exception of the United States, the countries of Latin America are by far the oldest of the "new nations" that have broken free of European colonial rule in the past two centuries. Thus, their experiences with alternative regimes—democratic, proto-democratic, semidemocratic, military, populist-authoritarian, bureaucratic-authoritarian, and so on—are considerably longer, and more numerous than those of the Asian and African cases examined in this comparative project.[2] This has imposed an especially difficult challenge upon our contributors, who have had to compress a century and a half of postindependence political evolution (not to mention several centuries of colonial rule) into a chapter-length treatment. Theoretically, it has also complicated the quest for causal explanations: there is in each of our nine cases here not only a longer past experience with regimes (and typically more regime change) to explain, but also therefore more potential for the past to weigh upon the present in various ways. The challenge has been even greater in our second edition, as the authors have balanced the need to maintain the depth of historical presentation necessary to understand path dependence with the close examination of recent political developments necessary to assess the character, quality, and stability of democratic regimes that are, in most of our nine cases, at least twice as old today as they were when our first edition was published.

However, this second edition also presents us with distinctive opportunities for explaining why democracies emerge, mature, consolidate, break down, and reemerge—and why some countries have greater overall success with democracy than others. Because the countries in this volume are more alike in some respects than those examined in the volumes on Asia and Africa, some variables are more or less constant across the cases. In addition to their similar age of nationhood (though by no means consolidated statehood), there is the obvious fact that all our cases share a long tradition of Iberic (and more specifically, in every case save the Brazilian, Spanish) colonial rule. This common cultural heritage may enable us to evaluate more systematically the thesis that the failure or instability of democracy in Latin America has a deeply rooted cultural component. In addition, the much greater length of the postindependence political histories enables us to examine time itself as a potentially important variable in several respects. Thus, we are interested to see here how the democratic prospect is affected by the sequence of historical developments, and how political struggles, choices, and outcomes at one point in time may shape, constrain, or facilitate political evolution well into the future, while also considering such issues as the phases or stages of a country's socioeconomic development, the shifting models or pressures in global political culture, and the changing conditions in the world economy.

The cases in this volume include the seven most populous countries in Latin America and two of the most theoretically interesting smaller ones, Costa Rica and the Dominican Republic.[3] They encompass the most stable democratic regimes in the region, the most successful cases of democratic development historically, and also the longest standing undemocratic regime, Mexico, which has made important strides toward democracy in recent years. But it is important to appreciate that they are not representative of the full range of historical political variation in Latin America, and that this skewing of our sample may give an overly optimistic impression of both the past and the future of democracy in the region.

Our work excludes many of the countries that until the most recent period have not experienced prolonged periods of at least modestly stable democracy, such as Bolivia, Ecuador, Paraguay, and four of the Central American republics. Nor have we included Haiti, where a tenuous democracy is currently attempting to take root under very difficult circumstances. The case of Cuba would have to be analyzed separately in the broader context of the path dependence and particular dynamics of United States–Cuban relations in the post–Cold War era.

There has been an unmistakable and truly historic movement toward democracy in recent years, though it has been neither complete nor unilinear. If by democratic consolidation we mean that democracy has become the only legitimate form of government in a country, that all significant political actors, including broadly the mass public, reject any alternative form of government and accept the existing constitutional rules and procedures as the only legitimate means for contesting for power and pursuing their interests, then it may be argued that only Costa Rica among our nine cases, and Uruguay, among the "third wave" democratic regimes of the region, may be considered consolidated democracies, though others, such as Argentina, have moved in this direction.[4] Chile has also followed a regularized, institutionalized path since the removal of General Pinochet from the presidency, though undemocratic elements remain tenaciously enshrined in its constitution (and in some segments of public opinion as well), and, as indicated by the intense controversy over the arrest of General Pinochet in Britain in October 1998, the country remains bitterly divided over its past. Our other seven cases have all confronted significant economic crises, political violence, state deterioration, or a combination of these, with ultimately some degree of institutional disruption and democratic decline. Specific incidents that lie behind this assertion include, in Peru, an *autogolpe* or presidential coup followed by only partial reequilibration; in Brazil and Venezuela, severe economic turmoil, charges of corruption, and presidential impeachments and convictions; in Venezuela (as in Argentina a few years previously), several military uprisings that ultimately failed; in Colombia and Mexico, the assassination of presidential candidates, and the penetration of organized crime (based on drug trafficking) into politics and government; and in the Dominican Republic, accusations of fraud forcing constitutional reform and shortening a president's term in office.

Of course, in contrast to a serious military coup attempt or an *autogolpe,* a presidential impeachment or assassination, or a corruption scandal or period of economic turmoil, do not in themselves signal the nonconsolidation (or *de*consolidation) of democracy. Over its long history, the United States has suffered all of these while maintaining the stability of its constitutional system. However, when these traumas are accompanied by other evidence that some significant political actors are not constrained by the rules of the democratic game, and that a significant portion (i.e., a third or more) of public opinion doubts or rejects the legitimacy of democracy, then consolidation has yet to be achieved.[5] These circumstances apply to most of our cases, even though several (such as Argentina and Brazil) have made notable democratic progress. However one assesses their degree of progress toward consolidation, our nine cases encompass sufficient variation in democratic histories, current status, and future prospects to provide a rich ground for comparative analysis.

THE IMPERATIVE OF CONSOLIDATION

The most common criticism of the theoretical introduction to our first edition, and to the related theorizing from our project, was that we did not provide an integrated model or establish some clear hierarchy of importance among our variables. As we have already indicated, a parsimonious model may aid in theorizing about relationships, but at the expense of fully comprehending why democracy took the course it did in one country as opposed to another. Explanation demands a more comprehensive theoretical architecture, and we believe we have identified below the theoretical variables that matter consistently across our cases (and others in Latin America and the developing world), even though some variables may be of only marginal salience in some cases. There is also the problem that different variables would have to be weighted differently in different cases; there is no hierarchy of causal influence that can apply uniformly across all cases.

Nevertheless, this does not reduce our effort to a mere inventory of causal factors. With the exception of the military—which can undermine or constrain democracy somewhat independently of what the rest of society thinks and wants—all of our variables affect the stability of democracy through one common intervening variable that lies very much at the heart of our stories: political legitimacy. Stable democracy requires that the broad mass of the public and all significant political actors (at the level of elites and organizations) believe that the democratic regime is the most right and appropriate for their society, better than any other realistic alternative they can imagine.[6] This is the core condition for consolidation: that political leaders, parties, social organizations, and the mass public come to manifest both an attitudinal, or normative, and a behavioral and constitutional commitment to democracy, and to its rules and restraints.[7] But in this respect (and, we think, many others) consolidation is the mirror image of breakdown. Just as consolidation requires broad and deep legitimation, so the process of breakdown begins with the unraveling of political legitimacy as key organizational and elite actors manifest what Linz called "disloyalty" to the democratic system: a willingness to use force, fraud, or other illegal means to acquire power or influence policies; "knocking at the barracks" door for military support in a political struggle; a refusal to honor the right to govern of duly elected leaders and parties; the abuse of constitutional liberties and opposition rights by ruling elites—in short, an unwillingness to be constrained by the rules of the democratic game. This unraveling of democracy may be further indicated by "semiloyalty": intermittent or attenuated disloyal behaviors; a willingness to form governments and alliances with disloyal groups; or a readiness to encourage, tolerate, or cover up their antidemocratic actions.[8]

This is why we take so seriously the character and quality of political leadership. The choices that key political leaders make in managing crises or constructing the patterns and parameters of a political system have a powerful influence on whether the legitimacy of democracy will be established, maintained, or squandered. We do not think that the choices elites make, and the strategies they pursue, are merely given by the historical or structural situation. Any comparison of Menem in Argentina and Cardoso in Brazil would fail if it neglected the normative and ethical as well as the political and strategic dimensions of national leadership.

Neither can a largely voluntarist reading of Latin American (or any other) history stand up to close scrutiny. As the recent setbacks to democratic advances in countries like Brazil and Colombia have highlighted, there is a risk to an excessive political voluntarism which considers that democracy will be successfully achieved (or consolidated) if political actors are sufficiently committed to it. We seek (as do most scholars in our field these days) to avoid either the structuralist or the voluntarist extreme, examining a limited (if still substantial) set of factors we believe are important, and which the authors evaluate in each of their country chapters.[9]

In each of our cases, the prospects for democracy have been more or less substantially constrained and shaped by structural factors and, as we will shortly emphasize, earlier historical paths and choices. Do some of these structural factors weigh upon legitimacy more heavily than others? In the early life of a democracy, in particular, we give more weight to the importance of political factors, in particular, getting the institutions right and making them work. A growing amount of research suggests that people may put up with considerably disappointing social and economic performance in the short run, so long as they perceive that democracy delivers on its political promise of freedom, transparency, and accessibility to power.[10] The perception that democracy is working *democratically*, and that it is at least capable of formulating solutions to the problems confronting the society (system efficacy), may be enough in the short run to begin to generate legitimacy, or to sustain and refashion the legitimacy that a system inherits by default—by virtue of the fact that it is not the hated previous dictatorship.

In the medium to long run, democracy must come to grips with the substantive problems confronting the society, and in Latin America this means poverty and inequality. After a generation of miserably failed revolutionary experiments and dreams, Latin Americans no longer expect miracles. But they do believe that steady incremental progress is not unreasonable to expect. Significant time has been bought, and political legitimacy accumulated, through the conquering of hyperinflation in a number of Latin American countries, including Argentina, Brazil, Peru, and Bolivia. For this reason, and because of world trends, in many of the countries in the region there is a new societal willingness to consider, if not entirely accept, neoliberal policy directions. But neoliberal reforms must eventually bring the social and economic, not just formal political, incorporation of vast marginalized populations, or democracy in many of our cases could once again become vulnerable to new movements that challenge the prevailing consensus on the legitimacy of democracy. We treat state structure and strength prominently below not only because they may bear directly on the "democraticness" of the regime, but because they may bear indirectly on its legitimacy through their effect on economic and social performance. We take civil society as important not only because of its increasingly central role in expanding participation, voice, and access to power, but also because in doing so it can help to forge more broadly consensual, and therefore legitimate and sustainable, substantive policies.

Ultimately, successful economic and social policy requires effective governance to forge a broad course through consultation and consensus and to sustain it over time, which brings us back to political institutions. If democracy is to work, it requires a party system that is capable of forming a government that can mobilize support in the congress for its policies while voicing and aggregating societal preferences. An institutionalized party system, based around two or a few cohesive parties with broad support in society, is not an absolute requirement for democratic consolidation or stability, but it clearly helps, as it may facilitate some of the other conditions for stable democracy (such as successful economic reform and social policy, and a broad normative commitment to and involvement with democracy). Democracy also requires a constitutional system that can structure choices, manage conflicts, and constrain power while avoiding political crisis and deadlock. Many types of constitutional frameworks may suffice, but some are clearly better than others, and certain institutional combinations appear fraught with danger.

Democratic consolidation requires balancing elements of democracy with elements of institutionalization. Institutions channel conflict, lengthen the time horizons of actors, and promote governability by facilitating the search for consensus. The exercise of democracy, though, involves the expression of multiple interests and thus of conflict. There is thus an unavoidable tension when we talk about *democratic institutions*. On the one hand, democracy involves participation and empowerment, and on the other, functioning institutions must be not only representative and accountable but also efficient and authoritative. In our view, developing institutions that are both effective and democratic requires construction from "above" and "inside" as well as pressure from "below" and "outside." State and regime actors must work to enhance basic democratic governing institutions and decisionmaking, even as civil society must organize to seek and to demand it.

What follows is a survey of the theoretical dimensions that have guided our authors and that we believe offer some insights into the question that continues to motivate this study: What explains the widely varying experiences with democracy of these (and other) developing countries?

SOURCES OF DEMOCRATIC PROGRESS AND FAILURE

Historical Legacies, Paths, and Sequences

The nine cases in this volume share the common legacy of long periods of colonial rule by Spain or Portugal. Many students of Latin American politics attribute to this colonial rule a homogeneous authoritarian legacy, since the metropolis ruled the colonies through a centralized, bureaucratic state structure as part of a patrimonial monarchical state pursuing mercantilistic policies. However, neither the colonial experiences nor the colonial legacies were uniform. Where mineral resources were particularly abundant and indigenous populations large, as in Peru and Mexico, or where slaves were imported for hacienda agriculture, colonial rule was especially harsh and exploitative; steep, severely polarized class divisions developed that would impact on social and political life well into the future. The tremendous inequality that became embedded in the social and economic structures of these countries remains to this day one of the primary challenges impeding democratic development and consolidation in countries such as Mexico, Peru, and Brazil. In Peru, this structural legacy is overlapped and compounded by bitter ethnic cleavage, as the memory of Spanish betrayal of the Incan king and the crushing of the Indian rebellions reinforces (four centuries later) the indigenous peoples' feelings of exploitation and exclusion. In general, Chile and Argentina did not have economies based on a large indigenous labor supply. Costa Rica, the Dominican Republic, and Venezuela were all relatively unimportant colonial backwaters.

In contrast to the contemporary decolonization of Asia and Africa, independence was not gained by Native elites against outside colonial administrators who transferred power to nationalist leaders and returned to the metropolis, but by a Creole, culturally Spanish, or (at the most) mestizo elite against the officials sent by the crown to rule and administer the "Indics." The indigenous population played no role in the struggle for independence, except, perhaps, in Mexico, where a more popular revolution was led by the priest Hidalgo, succeeded by the soon-to-be-defeated Morelos. These were settler colonies, transplants of European societies in

some cases imposed on large Indian or black slave populations, or occupying (as in the Plata region) poorer and emptier outposts. Independence,
therefore, was more similar to that of the North American colonies or, in
the cases of Argentina and Uruguay, to that of Australia or New Zealand.

To be sure, the Spanish and Portuguese empires ruled over their overseas territories differently than England ruled over its thirteen North
American colonies, with their complex constitutional structures, their char-
ters and assemblies. In continental Europe in the eighteenth century, the
liberal revolution had not yet been consolidated, though liberal revolutionary ideas were being received in the colonies from the metropolis.
Undoubtedly, the political change in England before its colonies achieved
independence left a different legacy from that of continental absolute
monarchies with their patrimonial bureaucracies. Yet the local Creoles of
Spanish America did participate in government through such institutions as
the *cabildos* (city governments), in a way that could be compared to the
participation of the local Hong Kong population in government when it
was, until recently, a Crown Colony.

The independence of Spanish America coincided with a political
change toward liberalism in the metropolis with the approval of the 1812
constitution in Spain, but before its consolidation. Independence was not so
much a revolt against the crown, but the result of a power vacuum generated by Napoleon's occupation of the metropolis and resistance against the
rule of his brother, appointed king. Initially, as in Spain, juntas emerged
representing the privileged groups of colonial society (with the exception
of Mexico) and assuming power in the name of the imprisoned Bourbon
king. However, some Creoles, such as Simón Bolívar and Francisco de
Miranda, inspired by the U.S. example and the ideas of the French
Revolution, made a republic and independence their goal. The occupation
of Spain created a legitimacy crisis that in the case of Brazil was avoided,
since the king of Portugal moved to the colony until the throne in Lisbon
was recovered. Conflicts between liberals and absolutists prevented Spain
from sending reinforcements to reassert its authority and support those in
the Americas loyal to the crown, such as the authorities in Peru.
Independence, therefore, had many elements of a civil war among Creole
leaders. In contrast, the Brazilian independence process involved a peaceful
transfer of power from the Portuguese king to the new emperor, Dom
Pedro, thus avoiding a crisis of legitimacy that might have resulted from an
abrupt break with existing institutions.[11]

The colonial legacies were also not uniform. It is important to recall
that the wars of independence and then the subsequent wars between the
emerging states destroyed the continuity of most political and administrative institutions. This contrasts sharply with the continuity of institutions
and boundaries in the thirteen colonies of what became the United States

after the displacement of the British king and his representatives. It is very likely that in many of the Spanish colonies the institutions that had provided some minimum protection of the Native populations against landowners, mine operators, and local oligarchies disappeared or were weakened in the process of independence.

It is also important to appreciate that in the course of the nineteenth century, different countries followed markedly different paths of political development. Costa Rica, the Dominican Republic, and Venezuela were isolated outposts of the Spanish empire. The first two lacked great agricultural or mineral wealth and were bypassed as sites for hacienda agriculture, with a relatively small (and quickly decimated) indigenous population. Yet, Costa Rica ultimately benefited from what John Booth in chapter 8 terms "the leveling effect of poverty and isolation," evolving some form of limited, oligarchical semidemocracy in the nineteenth century, as did Chile, Uruguay, and Argentina. An explanation for why the Dominican Republic did not similarly benefit from its poverty and isolation, as argued by Rosario Espinal and Jonathan Hartlyn, requires an understanding of historical events in the nineteenth century rather than simple extrapolation from the colonial period. Further, as Arturo Valenzuela notes for the case of Chile, the institutions of limited democracy were forged in that country by breaking to some considerable degree with the colonial cultural and institutional legacy, rather than by building upon it as was done in the United States and Canada. This difference between North and Latin America, and that among Latin American countries with a common colonial heritage, must give pause to those who would cite the colonial legacy as a decisive factor in explaining Latin America's subsequent experience with democracy.

The prominent role of postindependence immigration raises further questions about the effect of Spanish colonial heritage on political culture. In a number of Latin American countries the descendants of the colonizers are today a minority. For example, Argentina in 1850 had 1,000,000 inhabitants, and between 1857 and 1920 received 5,741,000 immigrants of which only 1,853,000 were Spaniards and 2,718,000 were Italians.[12] Nor should we ignore the contribution to many countries made by immigrants from other parts of Europe, their prominent place in the elite, and the number of authoritarian leaders of neither Spanish nor Portuguese descent.

Without denying the importance of the colonial experience and the obstacles it may have raised for subsequent democratic development in the region, the different circumstances surrounding the achievement of independence and subsequent events should be taken into account. When one looks for the roots of authoritarianism in at least some Latin American societies, one has to turn to the political, social, and economic developments of some seventy-five years of independence before 1900.

Postindependence politics and state building. The abrupt and violent manner in which Latin American countries seized or gained their independence is of theoretical interest. Not only did these bloody independence wars disrupt existing institutions and heighten the violently conflictual nature of the struggle for power, but in many Latin American countries they also gave rise to lengthy periods of civil war and instability that destroyed the wealth and infrastructure of the colonial period, enervated nascent state structures, obstructed state building, and enhanced the importance of military prowess in the pursuit of political power.

The obstacles to state building during this century and their negative relationship to democracy form an important theme in many of our chapters; indeed, nearly all of them highlight how central the issues of coherent, accountable, and democratically controlled states are to contemporary struggles for democratic consolidation. Our ensuing discussion only highlights the need for further study of how political development in Latin America has been shaped by the many difficulties in the process of creating modern states—establishing an effective rule of law, delegitimating private political violence, making constitutional provisions effective, and ensuring honest elections. Latin American countries have also had to contend with the rise of military leaders to political power and the expanding role of armies in politics.

All of the cases in this volume emphasize the political turmoil in the nineteenth century (and, in the cases of the Dominican Republic and Venezuela, well into the twentieth century) that made continuous, measured progress toward constitutional, stable government and ultimately democratization so difficult in Latin America. Those crises have to be seen in the perspective of a state-building process in countries that initially were artificial in their boundaries. The difficulties in state building and the recourse to force in the process show some analogies to the decolonization in Africa, with some significant differences due to the lack of an international guarantee of the existing boundaries and the much greater difficulties in establishing control, given the military and communication resources of the nineteenth century. Shifting the problem from the instability of governments and ultimately constitutional rule to an analysis of the difficulties of state building modifies our thinking about the historical process of democratization in Latin America in ways that resonate with more and more scholars as well as international funding agencies.[13]

Spanish America—there is a fundamental difference with Brazil— faced the problem of decapitating a legitimate structure of central authority (whatever its limits and weaknesses) represented by the crown in Spain; it also faced the impossibility, given the size and geographic dispersion of its territories, of creating even a weak central authority. The failure of Bolívar's attempt to create a larger confederation of the newly independent colonies, and even the failure of his Gran Colombia (which broke up into

Venezuela, Ecuador, and Colombia), stand out in contrast with the initial capacity of the thirteen colonies to unify and ultimately create the United States.[14] A look at the map would show the difference in scale of the task. One could speculate on how much more difficult it would have been to unify the United States had its territory included Florida, Louisiana, and the Midwest, not to mention Texas and California, at the turn of the nineteenth century. The geography of Latin America and the importance of a limited number of urban centers of the colonial administration and economy generated a large number of independent states. In addition, some of the key centers, such as Peru, were initially not committed to independence, but were liberated by outside armies. The military character of the independence process generated a whole new type of leadership—the *caudillos*—and a symbolism, which would not disappear, of the military strongman creating the nation.

The destruction of the centers of authority and the constant conflicts between centers and peripheries in each of the emerging republics complicated the process of state building for decades, and had sometimes incalculable human and economic costs. The struggles between centralists and federalists dominated the nineteenth-century history of Spanish America and very often led to questioning the emerging constitutional structures. Those conflicts were complicated by the fact that within the new republics there were relatively few secondary centers outside of the coastal capitals or a few urban centers of Spanish administration in the interior.[15] Thus, a strictly equal federal structure like that existing among the North American colonies was difficult to establish. Federalism did not pit multiple economically comparable centers of power against each other, but rather counterposed a predominantly rural, large landowning interior against coastal cities of commercial elites who—with the disruption of trade caused by independence—generally had no resources with which to assert their authority. The answer to this crisis of authority between center and periphery was either efforts to dominate the interior by force, resulting in civil wars and fights among *caudillos,* or in some cases the abdication of central authority to local notables who governed their regions in patrimonial fashion, undermining the progress of constitutional government and the rule of law.

In addition, the cultural homogeneity among the Spanish colonies made it difficult to define the boundaries between emerging republics. The administrative boundaries between viceroyalties and *audiencias* of the Spanish administration served as a nucleus for the building of new states, but those boundaries were not always well defined and did not respond to the resources of the new states. One of the results was that ever since, there have been boundary conflicts leading to a number of wars and to claims that remain unresolved to this day. Some claims were settled only in the twentieth century and left deep scars in the national consciousness. The

War of the Pacific (1879–1884), in which Chile gained large areas of Bolivia and Peru, was not finally resolved by treaty until 1929. Other important conflicts included the great Chaco war (between Paraguay and Bolivia, 1932–1935); Paraguay's earlier War of the Triple Alliance (1864–1870) with Brazil, Argentina, and Uruguay; the conflicts among Colombia, Ecuador, and Peru; Bolivia's difficulties in state building in its struggle with Chile and Peru to maintain access to the sea; and the conflict over Uruguay between Argentina and Brazil until 1851.

These interstate wars (whose cost in human lives, economic destruction, resources, and disruption of political processes, like the internal wars of the late twentieth century, deserves more systematic analysis) had consequences for the processes of political institutionalization reflected in our different chapters. They legitimized the importance of the army in state building and the claim of the armed forces to resources that otherwise would have been devoted to other tasks. They gave popularity to successful army commanders in the victorious countries. And they delegitimized governments and regimes that lost wars. We tend to think of Latin American militarism today almost exclusively in terms of its role in controlling "internal subversion" and social conflict, forgetting how important armies were in those international wars and the surviving animosity and fear among Latin American republics. Contemporary Latin American armed forces seek not only adequate equipment for internal war but sophisticated weapons of international warfare—fighter jets and submarines, for example. It is easy to think of these weapons as expensive toys or as an ideological justification for the military; however, we should not ignore the real concern of some of the military about the security of their borders based on the historical legacy of distrust between states, even if this legacy is considerably less than in other world areas. It is also significant to note how those nineteenth-century conflicts generated a nationalism that remains politically potent, as became apparent during the Malvinas-Falkland crisis.[16] The distinct combinations of nationalism and insecurity bred in Mexico and the Dominican Republic by the loss of territory or occupation by the United States had similarly negative consequences for democratic construction. In general, the nationalism bred by this legacy of insecure statehood and interstate conflict also facilitated some of the populist mobilization linked with anti-imperialism and anti–United States leftism in the Cold War era.

A very different legacy was left in Brazil, where the slow evolution and peaceful transition from colonial rule to independence through the imperial period, the avoidance of military secessionist efforts in the nineteenth century, the maintenance of the unity of the vast country by accommodation within a complex set of compromises in the federal structure, and the alliance between São Paulo and Minas Gerais assured the unity of the country. As Bolívar Lamounier highlights in chapter 3, this legacy has favored compromise and negotiation among multiple centers of power, particularly the central government and the powerful governors. In contrast to Spanish America, it yielded notably more peaceful and complex politics, and not merely in the nineteenth century. Even the difference between Brazil's Gétulio Vargas (who emerged out of a school of state politics to become dictator) and Argentina's Juan Perón (who emerged from the nationalist military to become dictator), as well as their different legacies, can be understood in this perspective.

Historical sequences. One of the features that distinguishes some of our Latin American cases from the others in this volume and from our Asian and African cases is their evolution during the nineteenth century of competitive, representative political institutions, which became increasingly inclusive and democratic over time. Chile, Argentina, Uruguay, and Costa Rica all began evolving by the mid-nineteenth century some form of competitive oligarchy or "aristocratic democracy." In Colombia this process was delayed and truncated by recurrent civil strife, but flowered in the early twentieth century, while in Brazil an even more limited parliamentary monarchy developed during the period of the empire (1822–1889).

The early development of a partial, elite democracy, however tentative and flawed, contributed to the ultimate development of full democracy. Of those countries in Latin America that have had the most overall success with democracy historically, or that now have liberal democracy, only Venezuela failed to develop an early elite democracy. By contrast, those countries that have had the least success with democracy in the past few decades—including, in our study, Mexico, Peru, and the Dominican Republic—are also those that were unable to develop and institutionalize some kind of partial oligarchical democracy in the nineteenth century.[17]

The protodemocracies of the nineteenth century were hardly exemplary models of free and fair competition for power. Fraud and force figured more or less prominently in each electoral system, diminishing more quickly and substantially in some cases (such as Chile) than in others. But these experiences involved the establishment of important democratic institutions—elected presidents and congresses, political parties—and at least some degree of meaningful competition for and rotation of state power. And the most successful of these experiences—in Chile, Argentina, Uruguay, and Costa Rica—also involved the gradual and continuous expansion of the boundaries of competition, incorporating ever larger proportions of the population (first middle-class groups, then workers and peasants) through peaceful political reforms extending suffrage and access to public office.

This path of political development had several positive implications for democratization. First, even where (as in Brazil) they did not produce lasting democratic institutionalization, these elite settlements on peaceful competition for power at least resolved (or preempted) the violent, chaotic conflict of the early postindependence period, permitting the process of state building to proceed.[18] Over the past decade scholars have reemphasized the importance of these historical processes due to the centrality of functioning state institutions to political democracy. Second, even where (as in Costa Rica) they were frequently interrupted, the oligarchical democracies produced political parties and other democratic institutions that took root in the society and provided the political infrastructure around which democracy could grow and mature. Third, regular elections through constitutional procedures gave competing elites valuable experience with democratic competition and permitted the gradual evolution of trust between contending parties and factions. Over time, the integrity of political competition improved and its arena widened to incorporate more and more social groups. Fourth, because this process of incorporation was gradual and regulated by elites, with institutional continuity and political learning on all sides, mass political participation—signaling the transition to a fuller democracy—could be accommodated as socioeconomic pressures for it crystallized without elites fearing mortal damage to their interests. Thus, wider democratic competition, when it came, was more subdued and less polarized than it would otherwise have been.

Theoretically, then, our cases give strong support to Robert Dahl's thesis that the most favorable path to polyarchy has been one in which political competition preceded the expansion of participation. The result is that "the rules, the practices, and the culture of competitive politics developed first among a small elite, and the critical transition from nonparty politics to party competition also occurred initially within the restricted group."[19] At the same time, there are parallels in other countries (e.g., Uruguay or in the context of a much weaker state, Colombia) to Lamounier's admonition that in Brazil this seemingly beneficial pattern was somewhat overshadowed by a state structure that was excessively strong vis-à-vis civil society, fostering clientelist rather than citizen ties while also perhaps yielding an excess of elite conciliation. Overall, the cases also support, as Valenzuela observes, theories that posit an optimum sequence that begins with the emergence of national identity, followed by the establishment of legitimate and authoritative state structures, only after which does the "crisis" of participation crystallize and find resolution in the expansion of citizenship rights to non-elite elements.[20] Thus, one of the most crucial historical variables in our Latin American cases is the way in which ruling elites responded to pressures for increasing mass participation in the polity. Where the elite made room gradually for autonomous institutional expressions of new popular interests, democracy developed, though not, in most cases, sturdily enough to withstand the pressures of the Great Depression. Where it resisted incorporation and inclusion, adaptation and political reform, the result was the radicalization and polarization of mass politics, as in Peru. Where reform through brief democratic experiments failed or was blocked, and elites later pursued strategies of mass incorporation from above in the absence of any existing democratic institutions, the result was the most stable undemocratic regime in independent Latin America: Mexico. Where ruling elites panicked in the face of the challenge of mass political incorporation, abandoning democratic institutions for exclusionary or corporatist strategies of inclusion, the result, as Carlos Waisman demonstrates in chapter 2, was the tragic and sweeping reversal of development that plunged Argentina into decades of praetorian instability. Finally, where elites feared mass mobilization in the absence of mediating institutions and following long periods of authoritarian rule, democracy was aborted (as in Venezuela in 1948 and in the Dominican Republic in 1962).

We find, then, that the past does weigh heavily on the present in Latin America, but it should be viewed in a path-dependent fashion as it is mediated and can be renegotiated by elite strategy and choice. These choices, in turn, may themselves have consequences for democratization, positive and negative, deep into the future.

State Structure and Strength

A democratic regime requires—indeed, it presupposes—an authoritative, effective state. A major theme of recent scholarship on comparative democratic development is that democracy is threatened as much by the absence of such a state as it is by the presence of excessively dominant state institutions.[21] For much of the nineteenth century, Latin American countries were challenged more by the former problem. In much of the twentieth century, an overweening state has been the threat to democracy, but even in these instances some basic state functions have still not been performed in a competent fashion. As the region moves into a new century, a central question for many countries is whether previously overextended states that entered into crisis in the 1980s and 1990s will be able to restructure themselves in ways that enhance a democratic rule of law, effective policymaking and service delivery, and civilian control over the armed forces. Thus, the theme of state building remains of central theoretical concern.

The historical evolution of our cases shows quite dramatically the tension between stateness and statism, a tension that could also be characterized as one between authority and control, or between domination and capacity. In the process of state building in Latin America, there has been a strong tendency on the part of weak and insecure state elites to substitute control for authority and domination for effective policy. A similar tension arises between the need for the state to maintain order and the inclination to do so by blunt, violent, repressive, and undemocratic means. Not unrelated to these tensions is how best to achieve democratic control over the armed forces, as well as the constant tug and pull between the attractions of centralization for a weak, bedeviled state and the need for some vertical distribution of power to ensure democratic vitality and responsiveness.

Historically, as we have already suggested, democracy was more likely to evolve and take root where, as in Chile, early progress was made toward the establishment of an authoritative state able to maintain order and territorial integrity. Where this challenge persisted unresolved into the twentieth century, it pressed toward centralist, authoritarian, and repressive state-building projects like those of the Partido Revolucionario Institucional (PRI) in Mexico, Gómez in Venezuela, Trujillo in the Dominican Republic, and Leguía in Peru.

The capacity of the state to maintain political order and, at the same time, a rule of law has been an important determinant of democratic stability. Declines in such state capacity, as indicated by growing political violence and terrorism, commonly by both state and nonstate actors, played a large role in the breakdowns of democracy in Colombia in 1949, Uruguay in 1973, and Argentina in 1976, as well as in the 1992 *autogolpe* in Peru. In the late 1990s, such state decay continues to threaten seriously the regime in Colombia, where armed guerilla insurgencies, paramilitary squads, drug trafficking, terrorism, and anarchic, criminal violence have spawned human rights violations, increasing military autonomy and restlessness, and mounting public unease and despair. As Jonathan Hartlyn and John Dugas show in chapter 5, the decay has been particularly prolonged and alarming in previously stable Colombia, where the drug traffic has corroded the integrity of vast sectors of the state and society. Latin America's recent history demonstrates that democracy cannot long survive such increasing ungovernability. Other countries may not face as severe a threat as Colombia, but issues of growing crime and insecurity have drawn more and more attention to the fact that effective police and judicial institutions are largely absent in many countries in the region.

The crisis of state expansion and economic intervention. The growth in crime and insecurity on the continent has been linked not only to drug trafficking, but also to the high costs of introducing market-oriented economic reforms to the continent, which at least in the short term have exacerbated poverty and inequality in many countries.[22] Indeed, another important dimension of state structure is its degree of economic intervention and control, as well as its sheer size. Certainly the European experience shows that democracy can be compatible with a sizable welfare state and extensive state intervention in and regulation of the economy. But the effect of such state expansion on democracy seems to depend significantly on historical timing. Where representative institutions became entrenched and strong, and autonomous structures of civil society developed before (or at least concurrent with) the construction of a large state bureaucracy for public welfare and economic production and regulation, this state expansion does not appear to have damaged democracy (at least not directly). Rather, as in Chile, Uruguay, and Costa Rica, strong political and social institutions were able to subject the expanding state to democratic accountability and control, and different social groups were able to articulate their interests autonomously. But as Arturo Valenzuela observes in chapter 4, where such democratic infrastructure was not in place, the expansion and bureaucratization of state power tended to produce authoritarian and corporatist patterns of interest representation. Dismantling the institutional legacies of state corporatism, and reducing economic control by bureaucratic forces not accountable to public opinion, have been vital to building viable democracies in Argentina, Brazil, and Mexico.

Increasingly in the 1980s, especially as the region's debt crisis helped generate a severe fiscal crisis, statism came to be viewed as a problem for democracy as well as for economic growth and stability in Latin America. Large, inefficient state structures, with extensive state ownership over vast sectors of the economy and huge state bureaucracies, were increasingly understood to be hampering economic efficiency, constituting major obstacles themselves to the renewal of economic dynamism. Throughout the region, in countries as varied as Argentina and the Dominican Republic, Mexico and Peru, the extensive losses of state enterprises heavily contributed to mushrooming fiscal deficits. The swelling of civil service and public-sector employment as a result of patronage-intensive politics was, Charles Gillespie has argued, "a major cause of the mounting inflation and slumping investment" that plunged Uruguay into economic crisis after 1957.[23] In Costa Rica, as in many other countries, there was growing criticism of statism for fostering inefficiency, corruption, and inequality and hindering investment and growth. At the same time, globalization has weakened the state's autonomous capacity for making economic and social policy.

The consequence in most of the countries discussed in this volume— especially Argentina, Chile, Mexico, and Peru—has been a dramatic restructuring of the economy, involving an extensive process of state shrinking and reorganization through privatization and cuts in state spending. These reforms have helped reduce fiscal deficits, control inflation, generate massive inflows of foreign investment, and rekindle growth (though sometimes, as in Mexico, in uneven and turbulent fashion). The central debate regarding market-oriented reforms of this nature is whether or not they are in fact critical over the medium term for democratic consolidation because they establish the bases for successful, sustained economic growth that would not otherwise be possible; because they provide for the diffusion of economic resources both away from the state and more broadly throughout society; and because they permit the reconstitution of a capable state.[24] Liberalizing reforms have brought steady economic growth and state strengthening to Chile. In Argentina and Peru, they have also strengthened the state and stabilized the economy, laying a new foundation for economic growth. Elsewhere (e.g., in Costa Rica and Brazil) they have helped stabilize economies without yet demonstrating clearly their abilities to create stronger (if "leaner") states. Increasingly, international financial institutions as well as domestic actors have recognized that if market-oriented reforms are not complemented by important state reforms—enhancing regulatory and judicial mechanisms, delivering basic education and health more efficiently, and making state structures more accountable and transparent—the outcome could be states that are less responsive to and engaged with their citizens, unable to monitor much less affect basic economic and social processes in their territories.[25]

Centralization and decentralization. One of the most important intellectual shifts throughout the region in the recent past has been one toward a belief in the political, socioeconomic, and administrative benefits of decentralization. For many years, it was believed that having a powerful central government would help produce economic growth, redistribute resources, and relieve the huge social and economic problems accumulating in the mushrooming cities. Increasingly, though, as this view has been called into question, momentum has gathered behind the alternative argument that devolution of power is necessary to enhance participation, deepen democracy, and stimulate development in the periphery. This has led to significant decentralizing reforms, both fiscal and political, in such countries as Brazil, Chile, Colombia, and Venezuela, with results that to date have been mixed.

Historically, intellectual and political thinking in the region has leaned heavily toward the imperatives for centralism. Many analyses have focused on the negative consequences of clientelistic networks and of the unwillingness of Congress—representing narrow local interests, against the rationality of the presidential central government and its teams of expert advisers linked with international planning agencies—to relinquish its influence on policies. Some of that debate, however, ignores the role that conservative provincial, notable networks can play and have played in distributing resources, if not to the most needy, certainly to the periphery. The delegitimation of those nonmodern forces by much of the centralizing democratic progressive perspective in Latin America may well have ignored their latent functions in the democratic process, as well as the symbiotic relationship that often existed between purportedly democratic forces in the center and provincial forces capable of delivering clientelist votes. At the same time, they may have underestimated the extent to which a rational central government—rather than being able to do more for the development of the interior than backward political forces—would be forced to respond to the pressures from the masses of impoverished people in the big urban centers that threaten public order.

Yet, the mixed results of current decentralizing reforms also show the risks of a somewhat naive view that devolution of power to the regions should automatically enhance participation and responsiveness. In Brazil, as Lamounier underscores, the constitution fostered a perverse form of decentralization devolving programs to the regions, but not the commensurate responsibility of assuring their funding, tremendously complicating issues of governance. In other countries, such as Colombia and Mexico, without appropriate mechanisms of state oversight and control (which require adequate expenditures in personnel and equipment) and without independent organizations in civil society, decentralizing reforms in some areas of the country have degenerated into localized corruption and mismanagement.[26] At the same time, in other regions of these countries, and in countries like Venezuela and Uruguay, the popular election of mayors and governors and other decentralizing reforms have provided an important space for opposition parties to gain offices, and thus the political and administrative experience to contest at higher levels. The reform that permitted the landmark election in 1997 of Cuauhtémoc Cárdenas, leader of the opposition PRD (Partido de la Revolución Democrática), to be mayor of Mexico City should have a similar effect in that country.

The military. One of the most crucial dilemmas that confront all democracies is how to ensure civilian democratic control over the state security apparatus. A full and secure democracy requires a professional, partially insulated force that will respond to civilian democratic control, neither seeking power directly nor serving the personalistic dictates of a president bent on usurping power or abusing the constitution. More specifically, as Felipe Agüero articulates it, "civilian supremacy" gives democratically elected government unquestioned authority over all policy arenas, including defining the goals and overseeing the organization and implementation of national defense. In such a system, the military role is constrained to matters of national defense and international security, the military is removed from all responsibility for internal security, and governmental structures (such as a civilian ministry of defense) exist to enable civilians to exercise effective oversight and control of the military (as well as the intelligence services).[27] With the exception of Costa Rica, which abolished its armed forces in 1949, and of Mexico—which established civilian supremacy in the absence of democracy—none of our other Latin American cases have come close to achieving civilian supremacy over the military, though many have made substantial progress in recent years. All the authors of our case studies refer, within the limits of space they confronted, to the civil-military relations in the historical past, to the military regimes that interrupted the evolutionary process of democracy, to the military doctrines and role expansion that established the armed forces as "privileged definers and guardians of the national interest" (to quote Carlos Waisman on Argentina),

and nowadays to the legacy of military rule and the problems facing democratically elected governments in achieving a proper relationship with the
military and its subordination to civil authority.

This volume does not include discussion of country cases where full
praetorianization of politics was historically the norm (such as in Bolivia or
some Central American republics). These were cases where the army as an
institution was highly divided into politicized factions, which in turn had
strong ties and alliances with political and social forces, and where it was
very difficult to talk about civil-military relations, or about periods of civilian or military rule. It is also important to keep in mind the distinction
between a military presence in the political process—the exercise of influence and even veto power over certain decisions by the military—and a
military regime, in which the leadership of the armed forces collectively
and in the name of the institution exercises power. In many of the countries
included in this volume, the military have long cast their shadow over
democratic politics, but periods of strictly military rule have been limited
and, one could argue, exceptional.

We further emphasize the difference between a military regime and a
regime led or inaugurated by a military officer. A military officer at the
head of the regime does not always mean that the military as an *institution*
exercises power. In spite of his close ties to the military until near the end
of his regime, neither Perón's first nor his second presidency can be understood as a military dictatorship or regime. In a very different way one can
question if the power of Trujillo in the Dominican Republic was based on
the army as an institution or if instead he had created a praetorian guard as
his personal instrument, which did not function as a professional armed
force, in his sultanistic type of regime.[28] As Valenzuela highlights in chapter 4, General Pinochet developed a personal power base and tight control
over the armed forces, reducing the political role of the armed forces by
emphasizing continuously his authority as president according to the 1980
constitution and the need for depoliticization of the armed forces. Of
course, as events since the transition to democracy have further demonstrated, this did not mean that the armed forces and those who were involved in
the coup and the repression did not identify strongly with Pinochet.

A military threat to democratic rule is not inevitable anywhere, and is
lower throughout Latin America today than perhaps at any time in the modern era. Nevertheless, the military factor remains in most of our cases a
confining condition for democracy, and in many countries one that can only
be ignored by democratic rulers at their peril. In much of South America in
particular, repeated interventions in politics over decades have shaped the
mentality of military officers and the formal role conception and organization of the armed forces in ways that generate a higher probability of political intervention (of which a coup is only one form). This underscores the
need for democratic leaders to move at an early stage to circumscribe and

professionalize the military role, though as Argentina under Menem and the Dominican Republic under Guzmán indicate, greater civilian control is sometimes achieved at the price of diminished respect for the rule of law. Certainly, the purging of disloyal elements among the officer corps—as in Venezuela after 1958, Mexico during the 1920s, or the Dominican Republic in the late 1970s—would seem to be a necessary element in an overall strategy of subordinating the military. So would the termination of military control over important economic and administrative institutions not strictly related to national defense, which in fact has been one of the consequences of the implementation of market-oriented reforms in Argentina and other countries. But it is difficult to generalize about how far and fast democratic leaders should move toward these goals, or how much (if at all) military funding should be cut, or to what extent amnesty or accountability is the best policy for past military crimes and abuses against society.

Part of the dilemma is that those cases where subordination and even punishment of the military are most needed also tend to be those where such decisive moves by democratic leaders would be most likely to precipitate a military coup; as Manuel Antonio Garretón has argued, an ethical-symbolic logic that fears the costs of forgetting and impunity confronts a politico-statist logic that is haunted by concerns of authoritarian regression.[29] Soon after taking power in Argentina, the new democratic administration of Raúl Alfonsín retired most top officers, reduced the military budget significantly, removed many firms and agencies from military jurisdiction, and tried the top leaders of the military regime for human rights abuses. However, military rebellion and intimidation forced the granting of an amnesty to lower-level officers. As Waisman notes, under Menem the top leaders were pardoned (though it was stated this did not imply absolution) and in return the military relinquished their historic claims of autonomy. Menem also substantially reduced the size and budget of the armed forces, while also terminating controversial nuclear and missile programs. Yet issues of human rights violations are not simply disappearing; they are tending to reemerge years later when military prerogatives are not as strong, civilian groups are more emboldened, and judicial systems less open to coercive pressure, or through the creative use of increased international judicial activism.[30]

The conflict between the military and democracy has to be seen as a result of a broader set of problems and constraints in the consolidation of democratic regimes. The conflicts derived from the legacies of the past are likely to continue to generate serious tensions in some countries. However, a fundamental backdrop to eroding military influence in many Latin American countries in recent years has been the decline in the support for military intervention both by the United States and by key societal actors within each country. The military's growing realization of its incapacity to govern in an era of globalization is another factor; military officers do not have the experience to manage the difficult task of economic reform, and global markets and financial institutions are less and less likely to repose confidence in soldiers overseeing a diversified, globally integrated economy.

Still, there are worrisome obstacles and countertrends. Militaries have found new internal missions in combating the drug trade and to some extent crime more generally, and these new missions, touching anew on domestic security and politics, have won the approval and even active support and collaboration of the United States and other international actors.[31] As Pion-Berlin notes, recent military adherence to legal norms and the absence of coups are not the same as civilian control, which requires a change in the values of the military so that their compliance is internalized. As the failed military uprisings in Venezuela and (unconsummated) military coup plotting in Colombia under the scandal-plagued Samper administration indicate, many within the armed forces continue to view their compliance with civilian authority as contingent.[32] The incapacity of democratic regimes to deal successfully with widespread violence, guerrilla warfare, drug trafficking, urban terrorism, and other forms of violence makes the military a much more relevant political actor than in more pacified and stable societies.

Ultimately, the capacity and willingness of the military to intervene is a function of the overall legitimacy, efficacy, and effectiveness of democratic rule. However, the ability to improve civilian control over the military is one dimension of the effectiveness of a democratic regime, and possibly a means for it to establish or deepen its legitimacy. Where the military as an institution has a long tradition of political intervention and retains extensive political and economic prerogatives, new democracies face a particularly difficult and dangerous challenge. In such circumstances, establishing civilian supremacy is a complex and typically protracted process, requiring many of the factors that promote democratic consolidation in general: skilled political leadership, unity among civilian political forces (across partisan and other divides), and civilian expertise (both in and outside government) on national security matters—as well as luck (in the form of divisions within the military, and military rebellions too partial and inept to succeed).[33]

Successful reform also requires a long-term policy vision, driven by political leadership.[34] The military must be steadily removed from the political realm, including such nonmilitary responsibilities as rural development, "civic action," domestic intelligence, policing, and participation directly in the cabinet. Such involvement in domestic affairs—even in worthy goals such as developing the hinterland—erodes the military's distinct professional role as a defense force and immerses it in political conflicts and concerns.[35] Reorientation to a more narrowly defined mission of external defense takes time—to prune a bloated officer corps, to reduce the size of the military (and hence its capacity to seize and exercise political power), to devise new missions and doctrines, to revise long-standing programs of military officer training and education, and to reorganize force structures around more modern weaponry better suited to performing the military's essential mission of defending the country's borders, air space, and sea lanes (as well as ancillary functions, such as giving assistance in times of national emergency or natural catastrophe). These legitimate missions involve international peacekeeping as well.

Democratic consolidation typically requires a strategy by which military influence over nonmilitary issues and functions is gradually reduced and civilian oversight and control is eventually established over matters of broad military and national security policy as well (including strategy, force structure, deployment, expenditures, and—if armed conflict should come to pass—rules of engagement). Unless the military has somehow been defeated or shattered, as with the transition in Argentina or the U.S. invasions of Panama and Haiti (where outright elimination or complete reorganization of the army then becomes possible), this strategy will usually have to pursue reforms incrementally through bargaining, dialogue, and consensus building rather than blunt confrontation. The risks of military reaction can be reduced in the process if civilians always accord the military a position of respected status, honor, and income, never use the military as a power resource in political competition, avoid political interference in routine promotions, and avoid highly conflictual trials for crimes committed under authoritarian rule. Yet even when amnesty is accompanied by a detailed accounting of past crimes, it leaves a legacy of impunity and deeply felt injustice that can also plant seeds of future political instability. Samuel P. Huntington is no doubt right that in many new democracies, "the least unsatisfactory course may well be: do not prosecute, do not punish, do not forgive, and above all, do not forget."[36] But the need to prevent military rebellion must also be weighed against the need—not simply ethical but political—to establish a new set of expectations grounded in lawfulness and accountability. Amnesty for past human rights violations by military rulers can only be justified on pragmatic political grounds, and thus the case for it becomes weaker as the power of the military erodes and the social and political distance widens between the new generation of commanding officers and those officers who were responsible for abuses under military rule.

Political Institutions

The fundamental thread that runs like a silver lining through the political history of Latin America, and consequently through all of our chapters here, is the early option for an institutional design derived from constitutional thinking, with such features as the rule of law, representative institutions, elections, modern legal systems, and political freedoms. The dramat-

ic story told in all the chapters is how difficult it was for that commitment
to overcome the many obstacles that the social and economic structure, the
personalities and ambitions of political leaders, and deep conflicts about
the good society posed to its realization. However, this should not lead us
to ignore the fundamental fact that in the last 150 years no other institutional arrangements have been able to gain full legitimacy in Latin America.
There have not been and are not now monarchs claiming the divine right to
rule. There have not been mass-mobilizing single parties claiming a revolutionary legitimacy unrelated to constitutional procedures (with the exception of Cuba, though Mexico did achieve revolutionary legitimacy for
decades, largely with one-party dominance and with only marginal dependence on the legitimacy of democracy as defined in this volume). While
fascism left its imprint on some of the populist movements in the 1930s and
1940s, particularly in Brazil and Argentina, the leaders of those movements, Vargas and Perón, manipulated and controlled existing institutions,
rather than creating new institutions breaking with Western constitutionalism. More recently, the military rulers of Brazil could not ignore, as
Lamounier shows, the constitutional tradition of two houses and regular
elections. Ultimately, the weight of that tradition led them to the *distenção*
and *abertura,* and ultimately devolution of power to civilian leaders.

In Uruguay, the tradition of a fair electoral process was able to resist
military ambitions to constitutionalize authoritarian rule in the 1970s and
1980s. Ultimately, a restoration of democratic institutions and the preexisting party system became unavoidable despite the legitimate criticism that
those traditions deserved. Even the most authoritarian of contemporary military rulers, Pinochet, did not talk in a new political institutional language,
but legitimized his personal rule by constant references to a constitution he
made and got approved in a referendum, and which ultimately served as the
instrument to oust him from the presidency. One can say that the hypocriti-
cal and even cynical manipulation of that institutional tradition is the price
that vice pays to virtue. Ultimately it made impossible the institutionalization and legitimation of nondemocratic rule.

Thus, the constitutional, liberal, and democratic idea delegitimizes the
authoritarian realities of power in Latin America. However, this fact has
another side that has been and continues to be less promising for democracy. Many countries, particularly some of the Andean countries and even
more in Central America, have lived with regimes purportedly governed
under liberal democratic constitutions, but which in fact have been hypo-
critically and often brutally distorted, perverted, and manipulated.
Therefore, *ruptura*—the break with that authoritarian past—has not been
symbolized by a change from authoritarian institutions like those of Italian
fascism, Franco's organic democracy, or António de Oliveira Salazar's corporatist Estado Novo to new institutions. It can always be argued by those
who are defeated that things have not changed when democratization is

attempted. As the chapters highlight, throughout their history in many countries individuals became so distrustful of institutions that they turned to arms, guerrilla resistance, or death squads rather than trust in the outcome of formal political processes. In the contemporary period, the primary challenges in most of our cases have been different: to reverse the decline in the ability of political parties to channel conflict and construct consensus, and to infuse formal political institutions with meaning, substance, and predictability, thereby overcoming the historic pattern of weak institutions that are routinely manipulated or modified as part of the struggle for power and resources.

Parties and party systems. Political parties play a critical role in political democracy.[37] They organize electoral challenges to authority. They serve as key links between political elites and the citizenry, mobilizing participation, articulating demands, and aggregating political interests. Thus, the process of party formation, the particular role that individual parties play at different moments, and the overall strength and viability—institutionalization—of parties and party systems are important factors in understanding historically the success or failure of democracy. A central feature differentiating across our cases has been the strength and principal characteristics of their party systems. With the exception of the highly articulated single party in authoritarian Mexico for so many decades, the strongest and most cohesive parties and party systems have tended to be found in countries with the longest trajectory of elections and democratic alternation in power (Chile, Uruguay, Colombia, Costa Rica, and Venezuela). Weak and diffuse parties have been more prevalent in countries where frequent military coups and authoritarian interludes have interrupted party continuity and undermined efforts to develop organizational coherence and leadership development (Peru and Brazil).[38] In the Dominican Republic, a surprisingly strong party system was forged from dictatorship, and the struggle against it, including civil war and a brief foreign intervention.

Several of the countries examined here experienced some form of the conservative-liberal political cleavage in the nineteenth century. Conservatives tended to defend centralization of power and the privileges of the Catholic Church and oppose free trade; liberals sought a more secular, decentralized, and market-oriented order. However, regional, family, and personalistic struggles for power often overshadowed the apparent ideological differences. Only in Chile and Colombia did these "parties of notables" approximate modern parties by the end of the century, as inter-elite competition expanded from the legislative arena through networks of regional and local elites, eventually yielding mass-based party organizations.

Although the conservative-liberal cleavage affected most countries to a greater or lesser extent, subsequent waves of party formation were much more deeply affected by national experiences, including the path and extent of industrialization and urbanization, the resulting class conflict, the degree of competitiveness of the political system at the time of the expansion of mass suffrage, and the response of traditional parties and leaders to the challenges of creating political movements that went beyond coteries of notables to incorporate the middle class, and subsequently the working class, into the political system. Thus, Chile was unique in developing a multiparty system that incorporated both communist and socialist parties. In Colombia, in turn, the traditional parties were able to maintain their dominant position for much of the twentieth century. In other countries, the established order was challenged not only by parties of the left but also by populist parties and movements. Those populist parties that maintained themselves over time—such as the Acción Democrática (AD) in Venezuela, the Partido de Liberación Nacional (PLN) in Costa Rica, the Alianza Popular Revolucionaria Americana (APRA) in Peru, and the Peronists in Argentina—usually moderated their radical rhetoric, reached out to a greater variety of social groups, sought to institutionalize (although, sometimes only minimally) their party structures, and reduced (even if partially) the charismatic and emotional nature of their appeals. In Venezuela and Costa Rica, the populist parties that emerged at the end of World War II— AD and PLN—became electorally predominant and key institutional actors in their respective democracies. Elsewhere, populist parties either established themselves as only ambiguously democratic actors in hostile environments (Argentina and Peru) or never fully institutionalized themselves (Brazil). In addition to leftist and populist parties, from the late 1940s, a number of parties inspired by Catholic social doctrine began to emerge in Latin America. Christian Democratic parties became especially influential in Chile, in Venezuela, and eventually in Costa Rica.

Yet as the checkered history with democracy of countries like Chile and Uruguay in the 1970s and 1980s, and of Colombia and Venezuela more recently, indicates, it is not simply that institutionalized party systems are insufficient for maintaining democracy in the face of other severe challenges; certain kinds of party institutionalization may become problematic for democracy over time. Political parties and party systems are stronger to the extent they include broad sectors of the population, preferably relying on a mix of appeals. Parties that rely purely on ideological or programmatic appeals may encourage an excessive sectarianism and polarization in society (as did Chilean political parties during the fateful years under President Salvador Allende, 1970–1973). Yet those that rely almost exclusively on clientelism or specific material benefits may ultimately breed excessive political corruption and cynicism. In the years prior to 1973, the Uruguayan parties approximated this, as have the traditional Colombian parties into the present.

If excessive polarization and extreme ideological incoherence and clientelism can be problematic, so can very rigid party structures. Hartlyn and Dugas show how Colombia's traditional political parties deliberately sought to dampen conflict by *not* expressing social cleavages or political demands, but rather by constraining participation, by relying on and even seeking to foster a persistently weak civil society. Ultimately, they helped to invite the sort of reaction from society that institutionalized party systems are presumably intended to avert. As Daniel Levine and Brian Crisp explain in chapter 7 on Venezuela, excessively centralized and disciplined party organizations, which at first may appear beneficial for democracy, may over time obstruct or erode democratic consolidation and governability.[39] This underscores the wisdom of viewing adaptability as an important dimension of genuine institutional maturity and strength.[40]

Although what some have called "overinstitutionalized" party systems[41] create serious problems for democracy, the costs to democracy of weak, poorly institutionalized, incoherent political parties have almost certainly been higher. One factor in the instability of competitive politics in Argentina for half a century from 1930, Waisman argues, has been the fragile and penetrated character of political parties, relative to powerful, politicized, and autonomous interest groups. The diffuse character of the Peronist party, containing numerous undemocratic and mutually contradictory tendencies, historically was especially damaging. The political insecurity of economically dominant groups, who lacked a viable conservative party and also wielded little influence in other "catch-all" or middle-class parties, has often been noted as a factor explaining their frequent support for military coups. The debacle of the last military regime and the dramatic changes in the Peronist party over the 1980s and 1990s have finally changed that situation in the country. The breakdown of democracy in Brazil in 1964 is partly traced by Lamounier to the "de-institutionalization" of the party system that began in the mid-1950s, fragmenting or dividing each of the major parties and subjecting the system overall to "increasing radicalization." Decreasing coherence and political capacity diminished the ability of the main parties to implement needed socioeconomic reforms, which failure reduced their popular support at the same time that social change was also eroding traditional political ties. The inability of weak parties to adapt to and harness changing social and economic forces finally proved fatal in 1964. Equally if not more so in Peru, the historically shallow and loose character of political parties that were lacking in structural depth and excessively dependent on personalities (except for APRA, which was not a consistently pro-democratic actor) has made for weak democracy. We thus find it difficult to quarrel with Lamounier's conclusion that stable democracy in Brazil, and throughout the region, requires the construction of "organized and minimally ideological parties," which have the coherence, strength, and will to institute necessary but politically difficult policies for economic stabilization and reform.

A review of the experiences of these countries over the last two decades (or since their most recent transition to democracy) also suggests that it has been extremely difficult to construct strong party systems where none previously existed in the face of new economic challenges, social demands, and campaign technologies. Brazil and especially Peru have been marked by extraordinary electoral volatility along with the decline and emergence of new parties. Along with the at least initial economic and political success of a reformist, institutionally minded president, Fernando Henrique Cardoso, electoral volatility has now been attenuating in Brazil, at the very time that two countries with historically solid party systems, Colombia and Venezuela, have experienced growing electoral volatility and party system instability. As Levine and Crisp note, the decline of Venezuela's once dominant parties and the emergence of new alternatives are partially products of democracy itself, signaling the ability of a vastly changed and more dynamic society to respond to economic crisis and decline in new ways as the established political parties remain mired in stale patterns of control, caution, and corruption.

Yet, the Venezuelan and Peruvian cases highlight the dangers of the rise of antiparty politicians and discourse. This is an increasingly global phenomenon, driven by such common influences as the growing pervasiveness and competitiveness of the mass media, the decline in the ideological function of parties due to the end of the Cold War and the narrowing of policy choices in the face of globalization, and the consequent growing detachment of voters. In Latin America, the effects of managing economic crisis (which had devastating—though not in all cases irreversible—electoral consequences for the Radicals in Argentina, the Partido Revolucionario Dominicano (PRD) in the Dominican Republic, the PRI in Mexico, the APRA in Peru, and the AD in Venezuela), and the impact of these crises in altering the social bases of numerous parties and increasing the size of the informal sector, may well have exacerbated the disrepute of parties and the rise of antiparty movements and discourses.[42] One can view these changes as enhancing choices for voters at the same time that the growing strength and diversity of nongovernmental organizations enhances pluralism in civil society. However, as the logic of our theoretical arguments suggests, and as Levine and Crisp argue for Venezuela, the decay of parties may mean that groups and individuals are set adrift with fewer resources to represent their interests, leaving them easier prey to manipulative leaders and personalistic movements. As Cynthia McClintock notes in chapter 6, independent candidates were the norm in the most recent Peruvian elections, and the "deinstitutionalization of Peru's political parties is one of the most serious obstacles to democratization in the country."[43]

Democracy can work with many kinds of party systems and degrees of institutionalization. However, the deeper the social cleavages and conflicts are that must be reconciled in the political arena, and the narrower and more shallow the legitimacy of democracy, the more democratic stability requires political parties with some organizational coherence and effective linkages to the most important social groups and constituencies (which in turn requires the ability to adapt to social change and so to represent newly emerging interests). Democratic stability requires some measure of balance between consistency and change, between conflict and consensus, and between governability and representativeness.[44] In the tension between governability (which seeks to maximize efficiency in decisionmaking) and representativeness (which involves the expression of and negotiation among diverse multiple interests), political institutions and especially political parties are intended to serve as both channelers of demands and forgers of compromise. Today in Latin America, political institutions do not appear to be instruments of polarization in society, as they were for some countries in the past. The greater risk has been that they would be circumvented by plebiscitarian leaders or abandoned by alienated voters, in either case becoming irrelevant, at great cost to democracy.

Constitutional structure. Among the political institutions common to all Latin American countries, one of the most striking is the almost universal option for a presidential rather than parliamentary type of democracy. In comparative terms, this option certainly stands out. Most of the successful European democracies have parliamentary systems, as does the largest democracy in Asia, India, and the other democracies of the British Commonwealth (including, in the Americas, the Anglophone Caribbean states). Latin America is, with the United States and a few Asian countries, the only part of the world in which democracy has been institutionalized (or even repeatedly attempted) in the form of presidentialism. Surprisingly, however, in the debates about the causes of democratic failure, no attention has been paid until very recently to the role of presidential government, perhaps because it was so successful in the United States. Latin American republics had simply transferred the North American institutions, so it was tempting to attribute much less successful performance to other political, social, and economic factors. This focus obscured the role of specifically political institutions: the presidency, the congress, the relationship between congress and president, federalism, centralism, the role of local governments, and, until recently, even parties and party systems. One of the promising intellectual consequences of the recent authoritarian periods and the search for stable democratic frameworks has been renewed attention (reflected in our chapters) to political institutions, including issues of constitutional structure and efforts of constitutional reform in a number of countries.[45] Although these have led to a surprising and somewhat unexpected flurry of political and electoral reforms, these have largely not touched the presidency.

We cannot restate here all of Linz's arguments about the problems of presidentialism and the advantages of parliamentarism for a great many polities.[46] But it is worth highlighting the considerable evidence from our cases showing how presidentialism has facilitated and exacerbated crises of democracy, especially in the situation of multiparty polarized politics of Chile. Valenzuela demonstrates the lack of fit between a highly polarized and competitive multiparty system—which, because it could not generate electoral majorities, necessitated bargaining and coalition making—and a presidential system of centralized authority, zero sum outcomes, and fixed terms. Presidents, he notes, "felt responsible for the national destiny as the embodiment of popular sovereignty," and yet they represented only a third or so of the electorate and could never count on strong legislative support. In this context, "the fixed terms for both president and Congress contributed to an atmosphere of ungovernability and a feeling of permanent crisis." Increases in presidential power only aggravated the inherent strain in the system and reduced the scope and incentives for accommodation, creating a tendency to polarization and stalemate that finally "came to a tragic head in the Allende years." Valenzuela's counterfactual speculation on the difference a parliamentary system would have made has relevance well beyond the Chilean case and bears recapitulation here:

> A parliamentary system of government would have defused the enormous pressures for structuring high-stakes coalitions around a winner-take-all presidential option, which only reinforced political polarization. At the same time it would have eliminated the stalemate and confrontation in executive-legislative relations. . . . Allende's government might have fallen, but democracy would have survived. (See chapter 4)

Chile continues to face certain risks because of the combination of presidentialism with the danger of a fragmented party system. However, with moderate, prudent leadership (especially in the presidency) and an overarching pact in Chile between center and left parties, there is no reason to forecast a breakdown, especially in the current international conjuncture.

Our case studies of Argentina, Brazil, the Dominican Republic, Peru, and Venezuela show that since the mid-1980s, other democracy institutions have often been marginalized by the presidency, short-circuited by direct plebiscitary appeals and executive decrees, though Brazil and the Dominican Republic have moved in more institutional directions under Cardoso and Leonel Fernández, respectively. The malfunctioning of parties and party systems interacted with socioeconomic and state crises to concentrate power in the hands of a president who was able to act with little accountability or checks on his power.[47] Even in Costa Rica, Booth indicates, the president increasingly usurped economic policy powers through executive decrees as the country lost autonomy over its economic destiny due to the consequences of the debt crisis and associated problems.

In several countries, the debilitating rigidities of presidentialism became manifest in the 1980s as presidents such as Alfonsín in Argentina and García in Peru—whose programs had failed catastrophically and whose political support had evaporated—limped through the rest of their terms in office with virtually no capacity to respond effectively to the deepening economic and political crises. Their successors, in turn, were able to win reelection after engineering constitutional reforms permitting immediate (and thus their own) presidential reelection, highlighting how voters rewarded economic stability or enhanced security, albeit in conditions strongly manipulated by the governing parties. The dramatic failures of men like Alfonsín, Jorge Blanco, García, and Collor de Mello, on the one hand, and successes of individuals like Menem and Cardoso, on the other, underscore the highly personalized nature of political leadership in presidential systems. To be sure, personalization has hardly been absent from European parliamentary democracies (particularly in the era of mass media), but presidential elections inevitably focus on individual candidates to the detriment of parties and lower-level leaders.

Some of the initial literature on democratic transitions viewed that moment as a privileged one for legal-institutional change and reform. However, over the past several years (well beyond the period of transition) most of our cases have undertaken extensive constitutional, institutional, and electoral reforms. This underscores how political actors have extended their struggle over power and the control of resources to the manipulation of formal democratic rules. Three countries enacted substantially altered constitutions in specially convened constitutional assemblies or conventions (Argentina in 1994, Colombia in 1991, and Peru in 1993), and all the others except Costa Rica carried out constitutional, judicial, or electoral reforms of differing magnitude (Brazil, Chile, Dominican Republic, Mexico, and Venezuela). Three countries modified their constitutions to permit immediate presidential reelection (Argentina, Brazil, and Peru), and one did so to prohibit it—and thus to facilitate the removal of a president believed to have regained office through fraud (the Dominican Republic). All eight countries (Costa Rica was again the exception) substantially revised their electoral laws, modifying the formula by which congressional representatives are elected or the timing of congressional elections relative to the presidential one. Some strengthened independent electoral oversight agencies or instituted other reforms to increase the likelihood of free and fair elections (Dominican Republic and Mexico). Others instituted elections for subnational officials, such as governors or mayors (Chile, Colombia, Mexico, and Venezuela). Colombia (in 1991) and Argentina and the Dominican Republic (1994) joined Brazil, Chile, and Peru in requiring a second-round presidential election if no candidate wins a majority on the first round. The results to date have been varied. In Mexico, institutional changes have clearly fortified democracy; in Peru under Fujimori, they have not had that intended effect; and in Colombia, their democratizing effects have largely been overshadowed by other societal or state crises.

There have also been limited inroads in the realm of gender equality on a political-institutional level in many countries since their democratic transitions. One innovation has been the passage of quota laws requiring that a certain percentage of candidates for different electoral posts be women. Of the countries included in this volume, Argentina, Brazil, Costa Rica, the Dominican Republic, and Peru have all passed some form of quota law, though its effectiveness in increasing the presence of women in elected posts has varied depending particularly on the percentage of positions required to be set aside for women, the nature of the country's electoral system, and the willingness of individual political parties to support their women candidates. Nevertheless, by 1998 women held an average 15 percent of legislative seats across Latin America, up from 4 percent in 1970. Nearly all Latin American countries have also established women's agencies in recent decades, with the ones in Chile and Peru having ministerial rank.[48]

Our cases offer many other lessons about constitutional structure, but we will only briefly mention some elementary ones here. A further weakness of democratic experiences in Latin America (not wholly unrelated to the problem of presidentialism) has been the lack of power and effectiveness of legislatures, which often must live in the shadow of extensive presidential decree powers and sharp constraints—de facto if not always de jure—on their authority to budget and investigate. In many countries, congresses have been hampered by their incapacity or unwillingness to provide themselves with professional staffs and serious investigative and reporting abilities. They have been much more capable of obstructing than of generating active agendas or entering into constructive collaboration with, admittedly, often equally uncompromising executives. Thus, congresses have often lacked the institutional resources and structures necessary not only to check but also to balance executive power by proposing constructing alternatives and seeking compromise, as well as by the ability to oversee and monitor executive bureaucracies.[49]

A corollary proposition can be offered for the judiciary, which has been subject throughout the region to political manipulation, corruption, intimidation, and underfinancing, while also suffering—even in cases not as marked by the previous traits, such as Chile—from excessive isolation and formalism. A confluence of forces in the region has focused new attention on the importance of the judiciary and the rule of law. International financial institutions and foreign investors have been concerned about property and intellectual rights and contract enforcement; middle-sector groups have become increasingly concerned about corruption; and with the transition to democracy, human rights organizations in several countries have focused attention on the rights of the accused and on the multiple problems with the criminal justice system. Indeed, several of these countries (Argentina, Chile, Colombia, Costa Rica, Dominican Republic, and Venezuela) have enacted substantial judicial reforms, regarding such features as the organization or funding of the country's judicial system, constitutional oversight by judicial powers, or how supreme court, constitutional tribunal, or other judges would be named. However, implementation has sometimes been poor or overshadowed by other circumstances. Thus, in Colombia, judges and increasingly the entire legal structure have become targets of coercive manipulation by drug traffickers, paramilitary groups, terrorists, and even actors within the state. In Argentina, in spite of the reforms, the judicial branch has been subject to manipulation or coercion by the executive under Menem; Waisman writes of the presidency as "monarchic" and the rule of law as unstable and conditional. A similar statement can be made of Peru under Fujimori. Furthermore, the blatant disregard of basic due process by special courts in Colombia and Peru and the willingness of elected leaders in countries like Brazil to countenance official brutality in the face of soaring crime rates highlight the tensions between democracy (in which a majority of the public may acquiesce in, if not clamor for, harsh measures to control crime and violence) and the rule of law. The difficulties of constructing a democratic and liberal rule of law in these countries are numerous and complex.[50] Needless to say, consolidated democracy requires some kind of effective division and balancing of power, and also a rule of law. Of the nine countries discussed in this volume, only in Costa Rica do both of these institutional conditions clearly obtain today.

Political Leadership

From the above, it is already apparent that the skills, values, strategies, and choices of political leaders figure prominently in our explanation of the enormously varied experiences with democracy in Latin America. At a general level, we might reiterate two of our themes above. First, the style of political leadership is quite crucial. A flexible, accommodative, consensual leadership style is more successful in developing and maintaining democracy than a militant, uncompromising, confrontational one (though sometimes, as we will see, at the price of not accomplishing needed reforms). Shifts in political leadership strategies and styles from consensus to confrontation, from accommodation to polarization, have been visible in the breakdowns of most of Latin America's long-standing democratic regimes. Second, the effectiveness of democratically elected or oriented leaders in state building and economic development is clearly associated with the success or failure of democracy over time. As the history of the Dominican Republic illustrates, where democratic or protodemocratic leaders have repeatedly proven weak and inept, especially in contrast to authoritarian rulers, democracy has been unable to develop institutional strength and popular support. And Daniel Levy and Kathleen Bruhn show in chapter 10 that Mexico demonstrates a corollary rule: where leadership has been skilled and effective over time but undemocratic in its values and intentions, the result is a stable but undemocratic regime.

More specifically, four elements of political leadership choice and skill stand out in Latin America's political development: (1) the decisions, initiatives, and behavioral styles of political leaders in founding or extending democratic regimes; (2) the ability of democratic leaders to adapt and enlarge the political system to satisfy expanding demands for participation; (3) the responses of democratic leaders to economic crises; and (4) the responses of democratic leaders to crises of political polarization and stalemate. The second element is a matter of crisis avoidance, and the latter two, which are sometimes closely interrelated, involve the challenge of crisis management and resolution.

Founding democratic leadership. As Seymour Martin Lipset has demonstrated for the United States, the period in which a new democratic regime is founded and begins to function provides a particularly wide scope for political leadership to shape the actual character of politics and political institutions.[51] In several of our cases, political leaders stand out, individually or collectively, for choices, initiatives, and strategies that crucially contributed to democratic development at a formative moment. We see in Valenzuela's chapter 4 that the early development of democracy in Chile cannot be understood without appreciating the role of General Manuel Bulnes, who, unlike the *caudillos* of his time, did not use his successful military command to impose a personalistic dictatorship. "Instead, like George Washington in the United States, he insisted on working within the framework of established political institutions and chose to leave office at the end of his term." By refusing to rule autocratically, emphasizing civilian over military authority (in part by reducing the regular army in size), and respecting the growing autonomy of the legislature and judiciary, Bulnes contributed in a formative way to the legitimacy and institutional strength of democracy in Chile.

The role of José Figueres in institutionalizing democracy in Costa Rica a century later presents some interesting parallels with the example of Bulnes. After his Army of National Liberation overthrew the fraud-ridden and communist-influenced electoral regime in 1948 during a six-week civil war, Figueres, at the command of a National Liberation junta and the only effective military force in the country, was in a position to do "anything he wanted, including setting up a personal dictatorship."[52] Instead, he followed through on his democratic pledges, administering honest Constituent Assembly elections in which his party lost badly, accepting the defeat of his proposed constitution while still achieving some important constitutional reforms (including abolition of the armed forces), and then transferring power in 1949 to the conservative victor in the 1948 elections, whose party had blocked Figueres's social democratic agenda. In so honoring the commitment to democratic procedures over substantive political goals, Figueres and his junta "established precedents of civility and accommodation between opponents which made the establishment of liberal democracy possible after 1949."[53] Four decades earlier, Booth notes, political leadership had also been instrumental in the democratization of Costa Rica's Liberal Republic, when González Víquez resisted precedent by tolerating vigorous opposition and then ensuring a free campaign for his successor in 1909.

In Colombia and Venezuela, the critical turns of democratic founding in the late 1950s were acts of collective leadership by contending party elites who managed—as a result of the political learning mentioned above—to transcend their rivalries and lay the foundation for stable democracy through the negotiation of elite pacts. In each case, these agreements produced a sharing of government power and patronage, limits on political competition and mobilization, and mechanisms emphasizing conciliation, consensus, and mutual guarantees over substantive political goals. The ability of opposing party leaders, so recently locked in bitter conflict, to negotiate creatively and flexibly and to win the consent of their followers to these difficult compromises was indispensable to the reconstruction of democracy in these two countries from 1957 to 1958, although inabilities to reform political rigidities subsequently had severe consequences for their democracies. These skillful acts of statecraft contrast significantly with the uncompromising attitudes of Colombian political leaders in the 1940s or with the brash style and militant, confrontational strategy of Acción Democrática when it ruled in the ill-fated democratic experiment known as the *trienio* (1945–1948).

Political adaptation and reform. As we suggested earlier, a common challenge facing the limited democracies of nineteenth- and early-twentieth-century Latin America was reform of the political system to make room for newly mobilized social groups demanding political participation and access to power. At times this was accompanied and even superseded by the challenge of social reform. Looking back now, the achievement of these reforms takes on an aura of inevitability that was in no way apparent at the time. Invariably—given not only the inertia of existing institutions but the conservatism of established interests—successful reform required shrewd and skillful leadership. Repeatedly, one finds behind reform able and even remarkable efforts of leadership, such as the interaction between the Radical Party leader Yrigoyen and opposing conservative leaders like Sáenz Peña that produced the historic Reform of 1912 in Argentina (which, in expanding the franchise to all male citizens, enabled the middle-class Radicals to win the subsequent presidential election); or the first dramatic expansion of Chile's electorate four decades earlier, championed by conservative leader José Manuel Irarrazával; or the sweeping political, social, and economic changes wrought in Uruguay by President José Batlle y Ordóñez, which laid the foundations of a modern democratic welfare state in the first decade of the twentieth century; or the political reforms of President Jiménez Oreamuno in Costa Rica (1909–1913), which extended to local peasant leaders access to the structures of municipal power.

That such reforms were not inevitable is suggested by the fact that in many Latin American countries they appeared only much later, after many cycles of political instability, regime breakdown, and crisis. In Peru— where the narrow and powerfully entrenched oligarchy admittedly present- ed a much stiffer obstacle to reform—the leaders of a briefer experiment in limited democracy concurrent with those above (the Aristocratic Republic of 1895 to 1919) repeatedly proved unwilling or unable to produce even modest political and social reforms. So did subsequent elected civilian presidents such as Manuel Prado and Fernando Belaúnde who promised but never delivered. The only significant socioeconomic reforms were pro- duced by authoritarian rulers—Leguía in the 1920s and Velasco in the 1970s, who laid (if unintentionally) a more promising foundation for democracy that unfortunately was not realized.

Today, we see again that manifest needs for political adaptation and socioeconomic reform call for courageous, creative, determined, and resourceful leadership that may simply not be forthcoming. Thus Hartlyn and Dugas find that Colombian statecraft responded tardily to changed social and political conditions by dismantling the consociational system negotiated in the late 1950s and opening up the political process. And Levine and Crisp also analyze the role of excessively cautious and consen- sus-minded leadership in the current Venezuelan crisis.

Response to economic crisis.   Political leadership assumes particular importance in periods of crisis, strain, vulnerability, and institutional challenge—when it may also face its most severe constraints. Economic crisis represents one of the most common threats to democratic stability. The policy choices and political capacities that democratically elected leaders bring to these crises can greatly affect the chances of the democratic regime to survive. Since severe or prolonged economic crisis may call the efficacy of democratic institutions into question, the ability of democratic leaders to implement effective solutions *democratically* is also crucial.

A classic example of effective democratic response to economic crisis was evidenced in Chile during the 1930s, when Arturo Alessandri brought the country out of the Great Depression with firm austerity measures and a strong commitment to democratic institutions, following a period of acute instability. More recently, the administration of César Gaviria in Colombia implemented an important array of economic (and political) reforms, although these were not capitalized upon successfully by the subsequent Samper administration. By contrast, the coalition government of Salvador

Allende aggravated inflation, destroyed business and middle-class confidence, and deepened the economic crisis by imposing "a host of ill-conceived redistributive and stimulative economic measures,"[54] while a succession of Uruguayan administrations deepened that country's economic stagnation by failing to choose and sustain any kind of coherent economic policies. These economic policy blunders contributed significantly to democratic breakdown in each case.

The mid-1980s were a difficult period for reformist presidents throughout the continent. Some presidents, such as Belisario Betancur in Colombia and Raúl Alfonsín in Argentina, responded with dignity and honesty (if not always with appropriate policies) to the difficult circumstances they confronted. Sadly, others such as Salvador Jorge Blanco in the Dominican Republic and especially Alan García in Peru responded with dubious practices and impulsive policies.

The response to economic crisis involved a wider element of elite choice with profound implications for the future in Argentina. Waisman traces the reversal of Argentina's democratic evolution and economic development to a series of fateful choices made during the 1930s and 1940s. During the same depression in which Chile reequilibrated its democracy, the Argentine agrarian upper class, fearing for its hegemony, abandoned democracy. Later, in the mid-1940s, an undemocratic leader, Juan Perón, imposed on the country the disastrous choice of radical protectionism cum state corporatism that led to decades of stalemate, decay, and praetorianism. A point of Waisman's we wish to emphasize is that this was not a structurally inevitable choice, politically or economically. A different path out of the country's economic morass was available by selective protection (within a continued long-term strategy of integration into the world economy) and the resumption of inclusionary strategies toward labor.

Response to generalized political crisis. Economic crisis is most dangerous for democracy when it is only one element in a generalized crisis of the democratic system, resulting from political polarization, stalemate, and widespread inefficacy. Such a generalized systemic crisis characterized both the Chilean and Uruguayan situations in the early 1970s. The times demanded extraordinary efforts of democratic statecraft to bridge yawning divisions and forge pragmatic, coherent policies. But as we have noted, leaders of political parties, groups, and factions insisted on pursuing their own rigid interests and agendas. From a precarious political position, Allende's Unidad Popular government tried to impose its radical program unilaterally, while conservative and business elements sought to sabotage it. Tragically, as Valenzuela notes in chapter 4, "center groups and moderate politicians on both sides of the political divide abdicated their responsibility [to forge a center consensus] in favor of narrower group stakes and short-term interests."

As the four-volume study of Linz and Stepan has demonstrated, mistakes and inadequacies of political leadership figure prominently in the breakdown of democracy.[55] Goulart's equivocal behavior with regard to adherence to constitutional rules played a crucial role in the democratic breakdown of Brazil in 1964. Nor can one ignore Quadros's resignation from the presidency in 1961 that suddenly thrust Goulart into the role while casting doubt on the viability of the democratic system. Historians of Brazil's New Republic will no doubt focus on the cruel twist of fate that thrust José Sarney, another vice-president with a weak political base, into the presidency in 1985—and this time at the start of a new regime, before the elected Tancredo Neves could ever take office. The mixture of acute political insecurity and weakness with grand political ambition that characterized President Sarney was no doubt a factor in his sometimes reckless economic policy choices, in pursuit of short-term political gains. Most recently, Colombia's drift into ever more serious violence, and its associated political and socioeconomic decline, were fostered by President Samper's desperate efforts to cling to office in the face of accusations that drug money had helped to finance his election campaign, and by the inability of the Colombian Congress to resolve the conflict in a sufficiently forthright manner to convince the Colombian public or international actors.

Political Culture

Few issues in the study of Latin American political development are more contentious than the role of political culture. Some scholars have insisted, as does Howard Wiarda in his chapter on the Dominican Republic in the first edition of this volume (and in a similar vein in other publications), that the "political culture, inherited from Spain, has been absolutist, elitist, hierarchical, corporatist and authoritarian," and that this enduring cultural legacy inevitably shapes and constrains the possibilities for democratic development. Wiarda does not rule out democratic development for countries like the Dominican Republic (partly because of various changes that have eroded and complicated the Iberian cultural legacy), but he does forcefully maintain that democracy, to be stable, must reconcile liberal, competitive political formulas (like those of Locke, Madison, and Jefferson) with an authoritarian "organic, integralist, and corporatist" tradition (Thomistic, Suarezian, and Rousseauian in conception) that emphasizes strong leadership over mass participation and group over individual interests.[56]

Most scholars of Latin American democracy reject this argument, partly because of its reductionist view of the nature and permanence of the Iberic heritage and partly because it implies that democratic systems in these countries can be stable only if they are less than fully democratic in assuring individual political rights and opportunities. Theoretically, the cultural thesis is rejected both by structural determinists who regard the very concept of political culture as epiphenomenal and superfluous (a position that will not be found in any of our chapters) and by those who find its sources more varied, its nature more plastic and malleable, and its effects less decisive than the cultural thesis allows.

Any assessment of these contending perspectives requires first some delineation of what we mean by the central concept. Political culture involves a number of different psychological orientations, including deeper elements of value and belief about how political authority should be structured and how the self should relate to it, and more temporary and mutable attitudes, sentiments, and evaluations concerning the political system.[57] Although scholars debate the necessary coherence of these dimensions, it is obvious that some dimensions adapt more readily to changes in political reality. It is also clear that different societal groups, such as the military, intellectuals, or the political elite in general, may have quite different political subcultures. At some historical junctures, elite values and beliefs may differ sharply from those of the public, and these differences may have crucial implications for democratic development, as we see in several of our chapters. Of particular concern to us here are the two obvious theoretical questions: What determines the political cultures (and subcultures) of Latin American countries? And how do these cultural phenomena affect democracy?

Sources of political culture. The cases in this volume strongly suggest a reciprocal relationship between the political culture and the political system. Democratic culture helps to maintain and also pressure for the return of democracy, but historically, the choice of democracy by political elites clearly preceded in many of our cases the presence of democratic values among the general public. This elite choice of democracy was no doubt influenced by values, including those induced by international diffusion and demonstration effects. Admiration for the political dynamism of the United States was reflected in the degree to which new democracies in Latin America modeled their constitutions after that of the United States. However, to a considerable degree, the option for a democratic regime was a matter of pragmatic, calculated strategy by conservative forces who, to quote Valenzuela on the case of Chile in chapter 4, "correctly perceived that representative institutions were in their best interest and the only real alternative once military solutions to domestic conflicts no longer seemed viable." Even at the elite level, deep normative commitments to democracy appear to have followed these rational choices. In Chile, Uruguay, and Costa Rica (and much later Venezuela), values of tolerance, participation, and commitment to democratic principles and procedures developed as a result of practice and experience with democratic institutions. This is what

Rustow refers to as the "habituation" phase, when "both politicians and citizens learn from the successful resolution of some issues to place their faith
in the new rules" and both groups come to internalize democratic norms.[58]

Intellectual and mass public commitment to democracy has been deepened by generally successful performance of democratic systems. The
growth in state capacity and effectiveness under democratic rule, the gradual expansion of democracy to incorporate newly mobilized social groups,
coupled with the steady expansion of the economy and of education, job
opportunities, and social welfare benefits to lower-class groups, produced
over time widespread belief in the legitimacy of democracy. Where
(proto)democratic regimes performed poorly, as in the Dominican
Republic, Peru, and Mexico, no deep cultural commitment to democracy
developed.

As suggested by the heavy borrowing from foreign constitutional
designs, elite and especially intellectual political thinking has often been
strongly influenced by foreign models and ideas. One characteristic of the
Latin American situation is that intellectuals play an important role in their
societies and are quite open to the world of ideas of the more advanced
Western countries. Understanding the crisis of democracy in the 1930s in a
number of Latin American countries requires, as Carlos Waisman shows,
some reference to the European intellectual, political, and social conflicts.
In contrast to the authoritarian regimes born in the 1960s, which lacked
intellectual and ideological legitimation, authoritarian ideas were important
in the late 1920s and 1930s. Space constraints have prevented an adequate
treatment of this aspect, particularly because in Latin America, with the
exception of the Brazilian *integralismo,* properly fascist movements and
organizations had limited success.[59] It is obviously much more difficult to
refer to the impact of ideas on other political actors, including the military
and political parties or movements, not openly identifying themselves as
fascist. However, right-wing, extremist nationalism in Argentina cannot be
understood without reference to developments in Europe, including the rise
of Italian fascism, the intellectual appeal of Charles Maurras and his disci-
ples, and the development of Catholic corporatist conservative thought. The
latter had a strong impact on elements of the Conservative Party in
Colombia in the 1940s and 1950s, helping to explain the breakdown of
democracy in 1949 and the failed attempt to institute a corporatist constitution in the early 1950s. Those antidemocratic ideologies of the 1930s had a
continued impact at a later date and were not fully irrelevant even for the
intellectuals supporting the Pinochet regime, although their loss of global
appeal led him to ignore their proposals in his constitutional designs. In this
post–Cold War era, the weakness of antidemocratic thought both on the
right and on the left represents an important transformation that bodes well
for democracy in countries where intellectual ideas are important to legitimize political activists.

Political events can also serve as a source of cultural change, as a result of political learning by Latin American elites and mass publics, though the permanence of the change may depend as well on subsequent events. In Colombia and Venezuela, democratic changes in political belief and practice may be attributed in part to learning from previous disastrous experiences with democracy in the late 1940s, which plunged Colombia into a decade of horrific interparty violence (*la violencia*) while unleashing a decade of repressive military dictatorship in Venezuela. Each of these painful experiences impressed upon party and group leaders the need for cooperation, compromise, accommodation, moderation, and consensus if democracy was to work. As Levine and Crisp write of Venezuela in chapter 7, "The experience of being overthrown, and the corrupt and capricious nature of military rule had a sobering effect on democratic leaders in many camps," demonstrating that "there is almost always something left to lose" and that "dictatorship has no virtues." This same lesson of the importance of democracy as an end in itself and the need for political prudence and accommodation was driven home to the publics and politicians of Brazil, Argentina, Chile, and Uruguay by the bitter experiences of economic and political stalemate, polarization, and violence, leading to democratic break-down and repressive, bureaucratic-authoritarian rule during the 1960s, 1970s, and early 1980s. The resulting "revalorization" of democracy and moderation of political behavior, however, is not necessarily fixed. We have also seen in Peru how antidemocratic leaders like Fujimori may nevertheless capitalize on discontent and how the mass public in Brazil maintains skeptical attitudes about democracy, as have growing proportions of the population in Venezuela.[60]

Political culture has also been shaped by social structure, and reshaped by socioeconomic change. Just as the highly undemocratic elements of political culture in Peru and the Dominican Republic, noted above, were fostered by extreme, cumulative, socioeconomic inequalities, rapid socioeconomic growth and change in these two countries have begun to shift political values and attitudes in a more democratic direction. The Dominican case highlights how new business and professional elites, and other educated middle-class groups, are more inclined to value democratic participation and to recognize the need for social and political accommodation. In Costa Rica, historically low levels of inequality and the absence of feudalistic social relations bred egalitarian social values that were highly conducive to political participation, tolerance, cooperation, and support for democratic liberties and procedures.

Effects. The case histories in this volume give strong support to theories (and to our own hypotheses) that the development and maintenance of democracy are greatly facilitated by values and behavioral dispositions (particularly at the elite level) of compromise, flexibility, tolerance, conciliation, moderation, and restraint. When contending elites, even initially for instrumental reasons, choose to wage their conflicts with restraint, and to bargain with and tolerate one another, recognizing the legitimacy of opposing interests, democracy is much more likely to emerge and to endure.[61] The early development of oligarchical democracy in Chile, Argentina, Uruguay, and Costa Rica clearly was advanced by the evolution of these behavioral patterns—and ultimately, if not initially, internalized values— among elites. Indeed, it was precisely when violent struggle began to be replaced at the elite level by conciliatory, accommodating behavioral norms that liberal competitive regimes began to develop and endure. As these democracies evolved, broad belief in the intrinsic desirability of democracy became an important underpinning of their stability. By the same token, where this belief in democratic legitimacy and in compromise and accommodation weakened or was highly contingent on continued elite hegemony, as in Argentina during the 1920s or in Venezuela in recent years, democracy was much more vulnerable to breakdown.

Just as democratic functioning promotes democratic values, we see in the case study of Costa Rica that democratic culture may contribute to democratic stability, even as the Venezuelan case underscores some of the limits of its contribution. In Costa Rica and initially in Venezuela, the two most stable of Latin America's democracies in the 1980s, popular and elite belief in democratic legitimacy remained high, despite prolonged severe economic crises. Indeed, John Booth argues it is precisely this high level of diffuse popular support for the democratic system that enabled Costa Rica to weather the crisis of regime performance in the 1980s. In Costa Rica, overall elite dispositions toward compromise, consensus building, inclusiveness, restraint, and respect for democratic procedures and principles reinforced legitimacy by avoiding political crisis and polarization, focusing political discontent on individual governments rather than the regime, and incorporating new groups into the political process. Democracy in Costa Rica is also culturally sustained at the mass level by broad and deep normative commitments to tolerance, moderation, and civil liberties, and by unusually high levels of citizen participation in associational life outside the state, motivated and structured by democratic norms.

Recent history also suggests that enduring democratic value commitments make it more difficult to consolidate and perpetuate authoritarian rule. In Uruguay, the military regime's lack of legitimacy hampered its effectiveness, while its need "to justify every action as necessary for the promotion of democracy" showed "the resilience of the democratic political culture permeating even the armed forces, and the inhospitable climate for authoritarian discourse."[62] No less striking was the concern of the Pinochet regime to construct a constitutional, legal basis for its authoritarian rule, and to seek periodic popular validation of its domination through electoral means. In both countries, the resort to plebiscite ultimately back-fired, leading to stunning electoral defeats for the Uruguayan regime in 1980 and the Chilean in 1988. Both the very fact of the plebiscites and the popular rejections of the military at the polls reflected the continuing vitali-ty of democratic culture and hastened the transition to democracy. Historically in Brazil, political elites have been less committed to democra-tic values than in Uruguay or Chile, but a similar kind of reverence for legal culture and electoral traditions attenuated the harshness and arbitrari-ness of authoritarian rule in Vargas's Estado Novo and again during mili-tary rule in the 1960s and 1970s.

A clear association is also apparent between the absence or disappear-ance of accommodating norms and democratic values, among elites in par-ticular, and the failure of attempts at democracy. Hierarchical, authoritarian elite norms and values, openly disdainful of lower-class aspirations and interests, along with low levels of political efficacy, knowledge, participa-tion, and social trust among the populace, presented an important cultural obstacle to democratic development in Peru and the Dominican Republic through the nineteenth and much of the twentieth centuries. Both McClintock for Peru and Espinal and Hartlyn for the Dominican Republic find recent changes in these value configurations to augur well for democ-racy. Perhaps the classic case of unraveling of democratic culture in our times occurred in Chile during the years preceding the 1973 military coup, when the commitment to the polarized options of radical change or the sta-tus quo came to exceed the commitment to democracy, and the breakdown of accommodative, tolerant norms and practices preceded and accelerated the breakdown of democracy.

More than in other sections, theoretical conclusions about political cul-ture must inevitably be qualified with many caveats. As we have just observed, the development of democratic values and norms is not irre-versible, but rather is always liable to erosion. The decay of democratic norms and practices—of communication, cooperation, moderation, and accommodation—in the face of rapid political polarization, escalating stakes, and declining commitment to democracy among key individual and group actors was central to the breakdowns of democracy in Chile and Uruguay in 1973. Similarly, what is learned politically may also be "unlearned" as a result of generational change or the overwhelming impact of structures and events, as highlighted by the descent into a spiral of vio-lence and political decay in Colombia, the Fujimori *autogolpe* in Peru, or the mass support for the failed military uprisings in Venezuela. Finally, a high level of popular commitment to democracy in the abstract does not, in itself, guarantee the maintenance of a democratic regime when, as in Uruguay in the late 1960s and early 1970s, the society is polarizing, the economy is collapsing, and politicians are seen as corrupt and ineffective.[63]

Socioeconomic Development and Economic Performance

One of the most robust statistical findings in the social sciences has been the positive relationship between levels of socioeconomic development and political democracy. At the same time, debates continue with regard to the precise connections between changing levels of development and various cultural, social-structural, or political-institutional changes these help unleash that are associated with democracy, as well as the relative importance of this connection and of the various factors affected. Furthermore, as one recent study has highlighted, several Latin American country cases (particularly Argentina and Uruguay) are statistical outliers given the military coups that took place at their relatively high levels of per capita income.[64] Intermediate levels of economic development—where a number of countries in the region are located—constitute what Huntington called a "zone of choice," which encompasses considerable variation in regime types and in the outcomes of regime transitions.[65] Variability in this zone underscores the importance of examining the other, more political factors discussed above.

Thus, we must reject the simplistic conclusion that the breakdown of democracy can always be attributed in some way to underdevelopment. Some of the Plata countries of South America achieved in the first decades of this century a high level of wealth, organization, education, social mobility, and, in the case of Uruguay, welfare state institutions. Argentina was ahead of a number of southern European countries and was among the most privileged in the world when its democratic system was overthrown in 1930. Chile also enjoyed a period of prosperity, although based on a more precarious export mining base, yet it began to develop democratic institutions in the first half of the nineteenth century, when it was overwhelmingly rural and preindustrial, with low levels of literacy. Certainly these three countries of the Southern Cone were not and are not like the typical economically and socially less developed countries of Africa and Asia, and are even fundamentally different from a number of Andean (not to mention Central American) republics.

We should be wary of aggregate economic explanations of the difficulties encountered in the process of democratization. Although latifundia have been an important factor in the agrarian structure of many Latin American countries, their different forms—labor-intensive plantations, large holdings rented to poor tenants, and large cattle-raising estates—represent different social structures with widely different political implications. Nor should we think that all Latin American countries have been lagging in economic development, if we consider absolute rates of economic growth over longer periods of time.

With this caution in mind, and with the assumption of a linear relationship between socioeconomic development and democracy quite obviously ruled out, what, if anything, can we conclude about the effect of socioeconomic development on democracy in Latin America? First, beyond a certain level of development, economic performance—in terms of steady, broadly distributed growth—is probably more important for democracy than higher and higher levels of socioeconomic development (measured either by per capita income or productive structure) achieved through more pendular, disruptive, and uneven means.[66] We have noted repeatedly how prolonged economic stagnation and widespread frustration of mobility expectations undermined democracy in Argentina and Uruguay and, through more sudden crisis, in Chile. On the other hand, democracy began taking shape at relatively modest levels of development in these and other countries, such as Costa Rica.

Second, the process of socioeconomic development generates social changes that can potentially facilitate democratization, but this depends on how political elites respond to them. Urbanization, industrialization, educational expansion, increasing literacy, communication, transportation linkages, and so forth alter the social structure and the configuration of political actors and expectations. As new classes and other functional groups arise, with more participatory values and skills, traditional (especially hierarchical, clientelist) political attachments erode, and new political interests demand expression and representation in the political system, partly as a means to pry rewards from it. These changes generate the basis, potentially, for a broader, more inclusive, legitimate and stable democracy, but only if the newly mobilized social groups are meaningfully included in the system. Such inclusion seems to involve two elements: access to political power, as a result of institutional expansion and adaptation, especially in the party system, and access to economic opportunity and rewards—more land, better jobs, health care, consumption goods, etc. These two generalizations buttress each other: over the long term, sustained economic development tends to undermine authoritarian rule, while in the short term, economic crisis affects all types of regimes, but well-established democracies are better able to withstand the strains. The interplay of long-term growth and short-term crisis has helped to generate recent pressures for democratization in Mexico, as it contributed to transition from the military regime in Brazil in the 1980s and from the Balaguer regime in the Dominican Republic in 1978.

Finally, socioeconomic development does promote other changes that are conducive to democratization. Most notable here may be the growth of all types of social organizations and of the middle class. But again, the real contribution to democracy depends on many other factors: the political autonomy, productive base, and economic security of new middle-class groups, and the autonomy and internal governance of new social organizations. Where democracy is already in place, as in Costa Rica, Venezuela, and Chile at different times, socioeconomic development may at once generate these new social forces and shape them democratically, while also increasing the legitimacy of the system. But one need only cite the case of Chile to appreciate that such gains are not irreversible.

In short, the contribution of socioeconomic development to democracy illustrates again the powerful and indeed inescapable mediating role of political leadership, choice, and institutionalization.

Economic performance. The varied experiences in Latin America show that democratic regimes are stable only to the extent that there is broad and resilient popular belief in their legitimacy. The salient question is what accounts for the presence of this system support, and for its erosion or disappearance. A primary factor, our authors repeatedly indicate, is the performance of the regime over time in delivering what people want and expect from government. One crucial dimension of this performance is economic.

Our cases suggest a strong correlation between the economic performance of democratic regimes in Latin America and their consolidation and persistence. As our chapters show, long-term economic expansions contributed significantly to the development and consolidation of democracy during the latter nineteenth and early twentieth centuries in Chile and Argentina. Sustained growth and high rates of social mobility helped to legitimate the emerging democratic order among a wide variety of social groups, including relatively disadvantaged ones. Steady and broad improvement in popular well-being made an important contribution to the consolidation of a secure and popular democracy from 1948 in Costa Rica (with particularly impressive gains in quality-of-life measures) and from 1958 in Venezuela, until the economic crises of the 1980s.

The recurrent economic crises in Latin America raise the question of how exactly economic performance is related to legitimacy over time. We find the bulk of our evidence in this volume to be consistent with the argument that a long record of successful performance tends to build a large reservoir of legitimacy that can be drawn on in times of temporary crisis.[67] The case of Argentina raises some question in this regard, however; the 1930 depression followed a long period of high economic growth, but as Waisman notes, it came when democratic norms were still being institutionalized, and the abandonment of democracy then was an elite rather than a mass phenomenon. The democratic breakdown in Chile was not solely the product of economic crises, but, perhaps even more preeminently, of political polarization and decay brought on by disastrous leadership and deeply flawed political institutions. A combination of prolonged economic stagnation, institutional decay, and political mismanagement also brought Venezuela to the brink of democratic breakdown in 1992, when the public failed to rally against military coup attempts and for democracy in the way it had in the early 1960s.

The 1980s and early 1990s marked one of the worst periods of economic crisis in this century for the countries of the region, including many new democracies considered here. At the same time, unlike what had occurred in some of these countries in an earlier era, these serious economic crises (associated as we shall see in the next section with sharply deteriorating levels of poverty and of income distribution) did not bring outright democratic breakdown (with the temporary exception of Peru).

Why have the new democracies of Latin America defied history and theory in this way? A few points bear emphasis. First, legitimacy is always assessed relative to available regime alternatives. Many Latin Americans appear disillusioned with their democracies, and save for Uruguay and Costa Rica, no more than a third of the public in any Latin American democracy expresses satisfaction with the way democracy is working.[68] However (with the partial exceptions of Brazil and Chile), most Latin American military regimes thoroughly discredited themselves by their gross human rights violations and economic mismanagement. Thus, whatever else may be wrong, people do not want to return to that alternative. Second, the international—and even more emphatically, the hemispheric—context is one in which democracy is hegemonic ideologically and politically, with no other regime form enjoying any broad legitimacy. With the socialist alternative also heavily discredited, and with military regimes now inviting automatic sanctions and isolation from the United States, the European Union, and collective actors such as the Organization of American States, there are strong external incentives to maintain a democratic form of government. But third, there is considerable room for slippage in what constitutes "democracy." As we note below, there has been significant erosion of civil liberties in some democracies of the region over the past decade. In others, the stresses that previously induced the breakdown of democracy may now be generating a more subtle and insidious erosion of the quality of democracy. A fourth possible factor that may augur well for the future is that Latin American publics appear to be more patient and sophisticated about the alternatives, or to have lowered their expectations. The experience of hyperinflation has undermined support for unfettered populism and generated new appreciation for the importance of macroeconomic stability and fiscal restraint. The economic success of Chile's opening to the market had important demonstration effects, and throughout the region market-oriented policy technocrats and institutes have become much more numerous and influential. Finally, during the 1990s, economic reforms did rekindle economic growth and attract large (if unstable) inflows of capital.

In the long run, four factors will shape the relationship between economic performance and democratic stability in Latin America. First, to what degree and in how undisruptive a fashion will the move to the market be completed and consolidated, laying the foundation for sustainable economic growth? Second, to what extent can Latin American democracies—

and all of the emerging markets of the world—find some way to shield themselves from wild instability in global capital flows that may be largely unrelated to their own policies and politics? Third, to what degree will economic peformance—good or bad—be accompanied (and if bad, compensated) by good political performance that provides not just regular and free electoral choice but the openness, responsiveness, accountability, freedom, and security and equality under the law that citizens expect of democracy? Finally, to what extent can economic growth in this new era attack the deeply entrenched inequalities that deny huge swaths of the region's populations a decent and dignified existence, while marginalizing them from political life? We turn next to this problem.

Inequality, Class, and Other Cleavages

Issues of socioeconomic inequality and class structure figure prominently in the experiences with democracy of many of our cases. This should come as no surprise given the levels of inequality in Latin America, which are, on average, the most extreme of any major region in the world.[69] The country chapters suggest there is a powerful tension, if not a negative correlation, between inequality and democracy in Latin America.

Historically, we have already seen that the countries with the most rigidly stratified and severely unequal class structures proved least successful in developing any kind of democratic polity in the nineteenth and early twentieth century. Quasi-feudalistic patterns of land tenure and labor exploitation, and enormous concentrations of land and other forms of wealth, were forbidding obstacles to democratic development in countries such as Mexico and Peru. The failure to implement even moderate redistributive reforms heightened political instability, giving rise to violent revolution in the former case and to polarized, politicized class cleavage in the latter. However, the impact of historic inequality on the possibility of democracy was mediated significantly, as we have argued, by political leadership and choice, both individually and collectively, at the level of ruling oligarchies. As Valenzuela notes, agrarian society in Chile during the nineteenth century was also rigidly stratified, with great concentrations of land ownership and semifeudalistic landlord-peasant relations. This extreme rural inequality persisted well into the twentieth century. What was most different in Chile was that economically privileged elites judged a gradual opening and democratization of the political system (and later, socioeconomic reform) to be in their interest. A similar judgment by the landed upper class in Argentina also led to gradual democratization, despite substantial inequality in land ownership. In Argentina, this political reform was made "cheaper," as Waisman notes, by the large numbers of recent immigrants lacking citizenship rights.

While substantial inequality was not necessarily incompatible with the development of democracy, it can certainly be argued that it was *less* conducive to democracy than a more egalitarian social structure. The historic absence of hacienda agriculture and large landholdings in Costa Rica, and the shortage of agricultural labor that kept rural wages high, bred an egalitarian social culture and what Booth terms an "interdependence among classes" that clearly helped to foster the development of democratic political institutions. As the political system continued to open in the late nineteenth and twentieth centuries, social reform attenuated the effects of newly increasing inequality and so enhanced democratic legitimacy. In sharp contrast, in the Dominican Republic the potential benefits of the "equalizing effects" of poverty were overshadowed by the concentration of power and the enhancement of the role of military prowess that the frequent civil wars provided to the victors. Although Colombia was also marked by the high costs of civil war, the absence there, as in Costa Rica, of a large class of landless laborers diminished the potential for radical class mobilization, just as the control of the major export crop (coffee) by an indigenous agrarian bourgeoisie reduced the potential for radical nationalist mobilization, both of which trends facilitated the emergence of oligarchical democracy.

The role of an emergent bourgeoisie in pressing for democratization and the limitation of state power in Latin America is an obvious and important issue for investigation. The case of Chile cautions against any simplistic analogies between the rise of democracy in Europe and its development in Latin America. In Chile, as elsewhere in the region, democratization preceded the emergence of a substantial urban bourgeoisie, and was spawned instead by landed elites. In some cases, however, the rural elites who pushed forward democratization were not really aristocrats but more properly an agrarian bourgeoisie, as were the coffee planters in Costa Rica.

An equally rich area for comparative analysis concerns the rise of middle-sector and working-class groups and the types of alliances they formed with each other as they became excluded from or incorporated into the political process. Middle-sector groups provided crucial leadership for political parties pushing for democracy in many of the country cases examined here; similarly, their sometimes ambivalent response to working-class mobilization helped to shape the nature and evolution of democracy in each of these cases. We have already cited the response to new social mobilization as a crucial factor in shaping the trajectory of political development in Latin America; the response to working-class mobilization was often the most fateful.[70] In Chile, open politics combined with repressive employment circumstances to produce class-based parties, the communists and the socialists, oriented to the electoral process. A similar development was probably aborted in Argentina by the coup of 1930, and subsequently by Perón's drastic reordering of the whole class structure through his dual strategy of state corporatism and radical protectionism. But the failure of his policies turned his strategy on its head, creating a highly mobilized and

organized labor movement with great political autonomy and an undemocratic character. With its political role crystallized in this way, labor
became a major player in the political and economic stalemate and instability that bedeviled Argentina during the 1950s, 1960s, and 1970s. By contrast, in Colombia and Uruguay, with their established two-party structures,
initial organization of the working class did not lead either to a corporatist
or an independent unified labor organization, facilitating the tendency of
the party system to cut across and diminish the salience of the class cleavage, though in ways that heightened clientelistic over autonomous political
expression. It was only later, as real wages declined precipitously during
the 1960s and radical ideology flourished, that labor militancy and government repression polarized into a crisis that contributed to democratic breakdown in Uruguay.[71]

It is notable that the major political parties in Costa Rica and in
Venezuela (until recently) also have tended to crosscut and soften class
cleavages. To the extent this provided for elite assurances while not resulting in the effective exclusion of strategic social forces from the political
process (as increasingly came to be the case in Venezuela), it would seem
to be conducive to democracy. It is not that more clearly class-based parties
(which were prevalent in Brazil, Chile, and Peru) are incompatible with
democracy, but rather that when class differences are as extreme as they are
in much of Latin America, they do have the potential to polarize party politics. The tendency of such party systems to fractionalization and polarization makes them better suited to a parliamentary system, with its greater
flexibility and capacity for coalition formation.

A review of our country cases in the more contemporary period underscores a tension between extreme inequality and/or class polarization on
the one hand, and stable democracy on the other. For most of the continent
and a majority of the country cases considered here, political democracy
today is being constructed in societies with extreme inequality, at a time
when the more gradualist type of process of building democracy which
took place in Europe, the United States, or selected countries in the region
is not possible.[72] The urgent need for "deconcentration" continues to constitute a crucial element in Lamounier's analysis of the democratic prospect
in Brazil, where inequality became especially severe and politically destabilizing during the country's rapid post–World War II transformation from
a predominantly rural and agricultural to a predominantly urban, industrial,
and service economy. The marked failure to reduce inequality, Lamounier
argues, was an important structural factor underlying the breakdown of
democracy in 1964, as it denied the established parties strong bases of popular support and eroded the overall legitimacy of the political system, while
at the same time subjecting that weakened system to a combination of pressures—tenacious rural clientelism and emerging urban radicalism and populism—that it could not manage. As Brazil has become even more urban-

ized and socially mobilized in the recent decades, while income inequality and by some accounts even absolute poverty further worsened, the imperative of deconcentration for democratic consolidation has been heightened. And yet policies to reduce inequality, such as land reform, carry serious political risks in the short run, while the reduction of absolute poverty requires a sustained policy commitment over the long term that may be equally difficult to achieve politically. This, Lamounier maintains, is the inescapable structural dilemma facing Brazil's New Republic in its quest for democratic consolidation. The strains surrounding it are visible in public opinion polls demonstrating widespread skepticism regarding democracy, in violent rural land conflicts, and in electoral support for clientelist, populist, and leftist parties and candidates.

In Peru, class, regional, and ethnic inequalities cumulate and overlap, even more so than in Brazil and to a degree that is unprecedented in Latin America. Although socioeconomic reform under the military regime did reduce inequality in general, it did little to penetrate the immense problems of land inequality, resource scarcity, and agonizing poverty in the remote southern highlands—the home of indigenous Indian peoples who do not share in the culture, language, or religion of white Peru, and the historic base of rebel movements, including Sendero Luminoso. Then, economic crisis and hyperinflation accelerated inequality and poverty in the 1980s, to the highest levels of the eight countries included in Table 1.1.

Although quantitative data on poverty levels and income distribution in developing countries are difficult to come by and still riskier to assess and compare, the data in Table 1.1 from the Economic Commission on Latin America and the Caribbean (ECLAC) for the 1980s and 1990s illustrate a rough correlation between overall poverty levels and problems with democracy (e.g., Brazil and Peru as negative examples and Costa Rica as a positive example), and between increased levels of poverty and inequality and democratic strains (e.g., Colombia and Venezuela over the past decade and a half). At the same time, going back one or more decades in time, there is a need to note that Uruguay and especially Argentina are outliers in terms of the timing of their democratic breakdowns in the mid to late 1900s, given their relatively high levels of socioeconomic development and low indices of inequality and poverty.

In terms of levels of poverty, the table shows that Brazil, Colombia, Mexico, and Peru have the highest proportion of their households under the poverty line (over 30 percent, which is also the Latin American average), joined by Venezuela beginning in 1990. Chile began with levels above 30 percent, but in the 1990s these declined to intermediate levels, where Costa Rica may also be categorized. Finally, Argentina has even lower numbers of households below the poverty line. The trend has been one of increasing poverty through the 1980s for all the countries, with some decline in the 1990s for Argentina, Costa Rica, Mexico, and especially Chile. Similarly,

Table 1.1   Latin America: Poverty and Income Distribution Indices

Country	Years	Household Under Poverty Line (%)	Households Under Extreme Poverty Line (%)	Income Distribution Ratio (10% top/40% bottom) Urban	Rural
Argentina	1980	9	2	6.7	
	1986	13	4	8.5	
	1994	12 (urban)	2 (urban)	9.8	
Brazil	1979	39	17	13.3	8.4
	1987	40	18	18.2	11.5
	1990	42	19	17.3	10.5
	1993	41	19	14.4	12.5
Chile	1987	39	14	12.6	7.7
	1990	33	11	11.7	11.6
	1992	28	7	11.9	9.0
	1994	23	6	11.7	8.8
	1996	20	5	11.8	8.5
Colombia	1980	39	16	15.0	
	1986	38	17	10.9	
	1993[a]	49	27	15.6	15.1
	1994[a]	47	25	14.5	13.8
Costa Rica	1981	22	6	4.9	6.0
	1988	25	8	6.4	6.2
	1990	24	10	5.5	5.6
	1992	25	10	6.4	5.8
	1994	21	8	6.3	6.6
Mexico	1984	34	11	5.1	5.2
	1989	39	14	9.1	5.9
	1992	36	12	8.4	6.0
	1994	36	12	8.2	5.4
Peru	1979	46	21	n.a.	
	1986	52	25		
Uruguay	1981	11	3	7.1	
	1986	15	3	7.8	
	1990	12 (urban)	2 (urban)	6.2	
	1992	8 (urban)	1 (urban)	4.7	
	1994	6 (urban)	1 (urban)	4.7	
Venezuela	1981	22	7	4.3	4.0
	1986	27	9	7.2	6.7
	1990	34	12	6.8	4.8
	1992	33	11	6.8	5.2
	1994	42	15	7.5	6.1
Latin America	1980	35	15		
(estimate for	1986	37	17		
19 countries)	1990	41	18		
	1994	39	17		

Source: UN/ECLAC, *Panorama Social de América Latina 1997,* Cuadro 16 for poverty and extreme poverty indices; Cuadro 23 for income distribution quotient (both tables as downloaded from website www.eclac.org). Based on special tabulations of household surveys in each country.
Note: a. Beginning in 1993, based on much broader sample base; prior to that, only around one-half of the country's urban population was included.

the most unequal income distribution ratios are found in Brazil and Colombia (there is no data reported for Peru), and Costa Rica reports the best. In fact, Brazil's index of income inequality (the gini coefficient) is the second highest in the world among ninety countries for which data is available, and several other Latin American countries, including Chile and Colombia, also have among the ten worst income distributions.[73] The high level of income inequality in Chile, despite the decline of poverty in that country to moderate levels, illustrates how economic globalization and liberalization may worsen income distribution even as growth reduces absolute poverty.[74]

The authors of our chapters on Brazil, Colombia, and Peru identify substantial, persistent, and even increasing inequalities of wealth and income as serious challenges to democracy, and the sharp growth in poverty and inequality is identified as a serious problem for democracy in Venezuela as well. For many of these countries, the neoliberal development model has yet to demonstrate its ability to correct the region's vast social inequities. While the relationship of inequality and democracy in the contemporary era remains to be clearly determined, we doubt that these countries can achieve or recover the broad and enduring legitimacy that is the hallmark of democratic consolidation unless progress is made in the coming years to reduce absolute poverty, and to improve education and employment opportunities for poor and marginal groups. Otherwise, these democracies seem likely to continue to suffer from high rates of crime, insurgency, and general lawlessness and anomie, and to be susceptible to the appeals of future populist demagogues who might (like Fujimori in Peru) seriously diminish the institutional foundations of democracy.

Ethnic and regional cleavage. Among the less developed and postcommunist regions of the world, Latin America stands out for its high degree of cultural and linguistic homogeneity. Although racial divisions are present in Brazil and the Dominican Republic, and correlate with socioeconomic inequality, they are not invested to the same extent with the feelings of enmity and exclusion that have polarized political and social life in so many other multiracial societies. Although Argentina and Uruguay both absorbed large immigrant populations in the nineteenth and early twentieth centuries, these ethnic differences did not crystallize into separate identities but rather softened over time. Generally in Latin America, the common bonds of Spanish language and Catholic faith provide a substantial degree of cultural homogeneity that is conducive to (at least in that it removes one potential obstacle to) democracy.

This generalization, however, must be qualified. First, as we observed earlier, regional cleavages have been historically important in many Latin American countries, and the balance of power and resources between cen-

ter and periphery remains a contentious and difficult issue. Particularly in
the Andean region, where the rugged topography has impeded integration,
regional cleavages remain important. The problem is especially serious in
countries such as Peru, where class, regional, and ethnic inequalities cumulate and overlap, and also Mexico. Second, current processes of economic
globalization are generating even more uneven patterns of regional development in much of the hemisphere (e.g., in terms of levels of foreign
investment between northern and southern Mexico). And third, growing
indigenous and black consciousness, in some cases facilitated by electoral
or constitutional changes and by groups better able to capitalize on domestic and international organizational links, are confronting countries such as
Brazil, Colombia, and especially Mexico with new demands for collective
rights and political inclusion.[75]

Civil Society and Associational Life

The cases in this volume give strong support to a corollary proposition
about the relationship between state and society: just as democracy requires
an effective but limited state, so it needs a pluralistic, autonomously organized civil society to check the power of the state and give expression
democratically to popular interests. Among our Latin American cases, there
is a strong correlation between the strength and autonomy of associational
life and the presence and vitality of democracy; there is also a correlation
between a more active and vibrant civil society and greater pressures for
democratization. The region's most stable and vibrant democracy, Costa
Rica, has a rich array of voluntary, independent organizations that elicit
high levels of citizen participation. In recent decades, greater activism from
civil society was important in democratic transitions in Brazil and Chile
and has been important in generating pressures for democratization in
countries such as the Dominican Republic and Mexico. This same activism
leads Levine and Crisp to characterize the current crisis of democracy in
Venezuela not simply as the decay of an established system but as a crisis
within democracy.

Yet the civic activism of recent years must also be counterposed to the
fragmentation and weakening of many previously organized groups, the
continuing high levels of distrust and low levels of formal organization in
most Latin American societies, and the complex implications of the often
antipolitical and antiparty perspective of popular organizations. Thus, the
view that popular organizations inevitably transform the consciousness of
their members in democratic directions and prepare them for vigorous participation in society increasingly must be considered as exaggerated.
Indeed, rather than challenging the state, in many cases popular organizations may be used to "fill the vacuum" created as states withdraw funding
for social services.[76]

The early development of active, independent popular organizations, especially trade unions, may benefit democracy by preempting the "political space" that could otherwise be occupied by authoritarian populist and state corporatist strategies of mobilization and inclusion, as Gillespie and González found for Uruguay in the first edition of this book. Such populist and corporatist mobilization and inclusion in Argentina and Mexico certainly figure prominently in those countries' failure to develop stable democracy in the past half century. Levy and Bruhn show how the early, forceful incorporation of popular groups from above, by the state, promoted the stability of the PRI's nondemocratic regime in Mexico by giving it a broad base while co-opting, preempting, constraining, or neutralizing the most serious sources of potential challenge to its domination. The hierarchical, authoritarian structures of governance inside Mexico's mass organizations discouraged autonomous political participation, depressed citizen efficacy, and buttressed the cultural and social foundation of authoritarianism. A less sophisticated and stable strategy has been simply to repress the development of trade unions and other popular and even middle-class organizations, a strategy typically found in countries with lower levels of socioeconomic development. As the histories of Peru and the Dominican Republic suggest, this may seriously weaken the prospect for democracy, but in the process it also inhibits the possibility of a stable, long-term authoritarian regime such as that of Mexico.

Almost by definition, autonomous voluntary associations should be freer to develop and to prosper in a democracy, although in reality their ability to do so may be constrained by socioeconomic factors, and crucial leadership energy may be drawn away by parties or other political organizations. Thus, under authoritarian regimes, there may well be a surprising explosion of groups in civil society, particularly as opposition to the regime grows. Booth shows that such groups began to develop very early in Costa Rica, to some extent preceding and certainly propelling forward the development and expansion of democracy. The effect of growth in the number, variety, and vitality of such organizations—trade unions, community groups, cooperatives, professional associations, school groups, etc.—was to mobilize ever increasing numbers of people into the political arena and to multiply political and socioeconomic demands in ways that could not be easily satisfied short of fundamental democratization. Levy and Bruhn also point to how, with continued socioeconomic modernization, middle-sector and business groups and more autonomous popular organizations have all continued to emerge in Mexico as part of a civil society self-consciously more independent from corporatist links with the state and the PRI.

The presence or growth of independent organizational life has also been a factor in frustrating authoritarian regimes and pressuring for regime termination or transition. Hartlyn and Dugas observe that strong and independent labor organization (along with established political parties) helped to frustrate General Rojas's effort to create a Peronist-style corporatist labor organization and a "Third Force" political movement. The growth or resurgence of independent associational activity—what Philippe Schmitter and Guillermo O'Donnell called "the resurrection of civil society"—was a key factor in the escalating pressure for democratization that culminated in the transition from authoritarianism of numerous Latin American countries in the 1980s.[77] In fact, recent analyses indicate that civil society mobilization has played an earlier and more central role in driving democratic transitions than many elite-centered theories acknowledge.[78]

As several of our chapters show, this growth of autonomous associational activity was partly the result of rapid socioeconomic modernization under both authoritarian and democratic regimes. In Brazil, Lamounier finds, the phenomenon gave rise to new, more autonomous types of entrepreneurial associations that pulled "out of the traditional corporatist framework," more authentic and independent trade union leadership, rural labor unions encouraged by the military to undermine traditional political bosses, and politicized urban middle-class groups such as white-collar unions and neighborhood and women's organizations. Economic growth and socioeconomic reform under General Velasco in Peru spawned a dramatic growth in both the number and memberships of autonomous popular organizations, which in turn (ironically) provided the basis for the popular mobilization against military rule under his successor, General Morales, in the late 1970s. And, in Venezuela, a dynamic society has spawned a more active civil society in the face of more stagnant political institutions. The risk, as Levine and Crisp underscore, is that civil society without the political mediation of viable parties to provide reasonable order and governability is unlikely to provide the basis for an enduring democracy.

The mass media. Both logic and theory should warn us against neglecting the role of the mass media in shaping the democratic prospect. As an important source of political values and information, and a potential check on the abuse of state power, we would expect the mass media to contribute to the emergence and maintenance of democracy to the extent they are autonomous, pluralistic, vigorous, and democratic in editorial orientation. Certainly, the obvious correlation seems to hold in Latin America: the press appears more vigorous, critical, pluralistic, and independent of state control in democratic countries (although the electronic media, especially television, tend to lag well behind in this regard). But our case studies tell us little about the historical process by which free and independent media emerge, and about the particular and sometimes more subtle components of journalistic ownership structure, editorializing, and reportage that contribute to the strength of democracy.

In the recent turn to democracy on the continent, the mass media has played a number of different roles. It has been crucial in investigating and airing corruption scandals that often would otherwise have been almost completely ignored in countries with weak judicial institutions. It has played an increasingly important role in election campaigns. For both these reasons, particular media outlets or journalists have sometimes been the targets of repression by antidemocratic state agents or actors from society, with notorious cases gaining attention in Argentina, Peru, and most especially Colombia. Of growing concern in a number of countries has been the concentration of ownership of mass media outlets, particularly given their increased importance in political mobilization.

Our understanding of the role of the press in democracy is sufficient to permit us to see some current of hope for democratization in the growing pluralism and autonomy of the press in Mexico, and to view with alarm the deepening intimidation and fear surrounding the exercise of independent and especially investigative and critical journalism in Colombia. But we need in the social sciences more studies of how a democratic press develops over time and articulates with other social and political institutions.[79]

International Factors

The historical analyses in this volume provide little support for the view that the source of Latin America's political turmoil and democratic failures is primarily external, in the form of U.S. intervention and manipulation or of economic dependence. Without exception, each of our authors attributes the course of political development and regime change primarily to internal structures and actions, while acknowledging the way these structures have been shaped historically by international influences. Thus, international factors have had an impact, and at times a crucial one, on the experience with different regimes in Latin America.

We have already mentioned the role of international demonstration and diffusion. Successful democratic models in Europe and the United States influenced the choice of regimes, and even constitutions, among many Latin American elites during the nineteenth and early twentieth centuries. Waisman sees the growth of democracy in Argentina during this time partly as a conscious strategy by elites to attract West European capital and immigrants and become integrated into a world economy dominated by democratic powers. Later, however, Argentine elites misunderstood and drew the wrong lessons from the experiences of the Spanish civil war and Italian fascism, exaggerating the danger of revolution and the need for state corporatist controls. In the contemporary period, there is reason to believe that these effects are especially potent, both at the level of state-to-state relations and through the increasingly important networks of nongovernmental organizations and other societal groups that are interacting across borders. At no point in the region's history has political democracy ideologically been more triumphant; the only current world competitors to the democratic model—Islamic fundamentalism and Asian authoritarian values (itself much weaker in mid-1998 due to that region's financial crisis)—have no echo in the Western Hemisphere.

Demonstration effects have perhaps been especially potent between Latin American countries. The Cuban Revolution reverberated powerfully throughout the entire region, inspiring other leftist revolutionary movements and heightening fear about revolutionary Marxist movements and parties within military and business circles. Similarly, the Brazilian military coup of 1964 and subsequent technocratic-repressive "economic miracle" may have helped to inspire other right-wing, technocratic military interventions, especially in Uruguay and Chile. Today, Latin American democracies are seeking to enhance international mechanisms (such as the Organization of American States [OAS] and the Mercado Común del Sur [Mercosur]) that foster "democratic contagion," and this favorable context has exerted at least some modest pro-democratic pressure in such unstable settings as Peru, Guatemala, and Paraguay, where in each case the OAS took action to reverse, sanction, or abort coups against democracy.

Our case studies do not reveal economic dependence to be a primary factor behind the lack of success with democracy in Latin America. To be sure, Latin American countries do have high levels of economic dependence that have rendered them acutely vulnerable to cycles in the global economy and particularly in relation to their largest trading partner, the United States. Moreover, several countries are highly dependent on the export earnings of one or two commodities whose prices on world markets are notoriously volatile: Colombia and Costa Rica (coffee), Chile (copper), and Venezuela and Mexico (oil). Concentration on mining commodities such as oil has particularly perverse effects on a country's economic and social structure, and hence on politics.[80] And the new export commodity boom in cocaine and marijuana, because of their illegality and the huge economic rents that are consequently captured by a criminal elite, has had no less perverse effects on the social and political structures of Colombia and Peru (and of Mexico, through which much of the drug trade passes), while seriously aggravating these countries' relations with the United States. These various factors do not make democracy impossible, but they certainly complicate the task of political leaders who seek to consolidate and maintain democratic rule.

Today, the steepest international challenge to democracy derives from the need for countries in the region to adapt to the demands of economic globalization while still recovering from the debt crisis of the 1980s, the attendant ongoing fiscal crisis, and the exhaustion of the model of import-substituting industrialization. Substantial changes in economic policies over this past decade, often associated in the 1980s with low or negative growth rates and high levels of inflation, have permitted most countries in the region to gain greater control over their levels of external debt even as international capital flows returned to the region (though with heightened volatility). Yet, as already noted, the economic and especially the social performance of most countries in the region in the 1990s has remained unsatisfactory.[81]

U.S. policy. Almost two centuries of conflict, tension, intervention, and even in some cases invasion and occupation have left Latin Americans extremely wary of their giant neighbor to the north, sometimes leading to a perception that behind major political and economic debacles in their countries was the hand of "Yankee imperialism." For the nine countries examined here, this suspicion is as exaggerated as it may be unavoidable. With the exception of direct military interventions—such as the 1965 invasion of the Dominican Republic to quash a democratic revolution (which sought to restore the elected reformer Juan Bosch to the presidency after a military coup)—the United States has typically been able to do no more than influence events, and sometimes not even that. Historically, U.S. influence and control have been greatest in Central America and the Caribbean.

In assessing the effect of deliberate U.S. policies on democracy in Latin America, one must consider their salience, their direction, and their effectiveness.[82] When national security concerns were paramount, policies of democracy promotion were tailored to these concerns, were superseded by them, or were actually scuttled. In this regard, it may be useful to recall Kennedy's dictum regarding the Dominican Republic, that in descending order of preferences the United States would prefer a democratic regime, continuation of a Trujillo regime, or a Castro regime, and that the United States should aim for the first, but not renounce the second until it was sure the third could be avoided. Thus, especially during the Cold War, most U.S. presidents were quite comfortable with and supportive of pro-U.S. dictators like Trujillo and Pérez Jiménez, and were even willing to conspire against or sabotage popularly elected regimes that seemed threatening. In the aftermath of the Cuban Revolution, there was renewed focus for a brief period on supporting reformist governments. However, the Kennedy administration failed to produce the moderate democratic regime it had sought in the Dominican Republic, although substantial U.S. assistance was instrumental in helping the vulnerable young democracy in Colombia stay afloat economically during the early 1960s, while in Venezuela, as Levine and Crisp find, strong U.S. political and diplomatic support "helped allay conservative fears and restrain potential military conspirators." Yet the United States quickly accepted the Brazilian military coup in 1964, as it did military governments elsewhere on the continent that followed. Until the late 1970s, U.S. policy did little to support democracy in Latin America, abiding and abetting military regimes in Brazil, Argentina, Uruguay, and Chile, and withholding needed economic assistance from the elected government of Belaúnde in Peru during the mid-1960s because of commercial disputes.

Under the Carter administration, as national security issues seemingly declined, U.S. policy seemed to tilt more decisively toward promotion of democracy and human rights. Human rights pressure from the Carter administration (as well as several European democracies) did not in itself bring down authoritarian rule in Argentina, but Waisman judges that it "saved many victims of indiscriminate repression in the late 1970s and was a factor in the international isolation of the regime." The Carter administration also played a forceful role in 1978 in preempting electoral fraud by the armed forces of the Dominican Republic—against the presidential candidate of the same democratic, populist party PRD (albeit now more moderate with the departure of Bosch) U.S. troops had stopped from coming to power in 1965. In the first term of the Reagan administration, democracy promotion was again subsumed to national security considerations and to an effort to gain a bipartisan consensus regarding U.S. policy toward Central America. Yet, as a consequence, during Reagan's second term and more clearly during the Bush and now the Clinton administrations, democracy promotion policies played important roles in U.S. support for the democratic opposition in Chile, and U.S. resistance to the attempted *autogolpes* in Peru and Guatemala and the veiled threats of a military coup in Paraguay.[83] With the end of the Cold War, support for democracy has become a much more clearly stated priority of the U.S. government, and considerable support for democratic institution building, civil society, and election monitoring has been offered by the U.S. Agency for International Development, the National Endowment for Democracy, and many other international actors, such as the German party foundations.[84]

The U.S. impact on democracy in Latin America has thus varied with the policy intentions and priorities of administrations. When it has wanted to, the United States has been able to assist the cause of democracy in the region, but only when there have been democratic forces and institutions able to make effective use of that assistance.

THE DEMOCRATIC PROSPECT

The broad regional trend from the 1980s to the present is often viewed simplistically as a "wave of democratization." However, the pattern is more complex. A review of the Freedom House annual ratings of political rights and civil liberties from 1980 to 1997 suggests that the trend in Latin America may be better characterized as regression toward a less-than-fully-democratic mean. Movement away from the harshest types of authoritarian rule (toward electoral democracy) has been accompanied by decline in progress toward unrestricted political democracies between 1987 and 1993, and a modest recovery from 1993 to 1997. Overall, Latin America has become more broadly democratic than in 1980 or even 1987, but it is not *deeply* democratic. Many of the region's electoral democracies are illiberal, and this is indicative of a more global undercurrent in the third wave of democratization (see Tables 1.2 and 1.3).[85]

Our nine country cases exemplify these three trends of retreat from open authoritarian rule from 1980 to the present, decline in political liberties and especially civil rights in many of them from 1987 to 1993, and a slight improvement in some of them from 1993 to 1997 (see Table 1.3). Costa Rica (and Uruguay) may be considered consolidated democracies, and Chile is in many respects a consolidated regime that can be considered fully democratic once certain elements are removed from its constitution. According to the Freedom House data, and as detailed by Waisman, under President Menem Argentina has experienced modest democratic decline, particularly in respect for freedom and the rule of law. Venezuela saw the unraveling of its consolidated democracy, and along with the Dominican Republic and especially with Peru, it experienced sharper declines and then either slight improvement or a trend in that direction. Brazil experienced a sharp deterioration with no improvement, while Colombia entered a spiral of state degeneration and political violence along with a steady weakening in respect for political liberties and civil rights. Mexico, in turn, saw progress toward a true electoral democracy.

These numbers provide a quick snapshot of the more complex picture presented by the authors of the country chapters. Deterioration in democratic quality in a number of these countries has reflected a combination of long-standing social, economic, and political problems in interaction with short-term crises provoked by the debt crisis and then more broadly by the crisis of the region's development model in the face of economic globalization. In spite of the fact that we expect that the worst economic horrors of this recent period are behind them—hyperinflation, sharp declines in growth rates, negative capital inflows—most Latin Americans are still not well off. Since the beginning of the 1990s, income distribution in the region overall has not improved, nor has the total number of poor people declined; furthermore, levels of unemployment were higher in the mid-1990s than they had been at the end of the 1980s.[86] Such levels of decline, distress, and suffering cannot persist indefinitely without gravely damaging democratic institutions and norms.

Given the current international realities, Latin American countries are expecting less and less in the form of international aid. However, even as they are being encouraged to open their economies to market forces domestically and internationally, they still confront protectionist challenges from the United States and other industrialized countries. At the same time, efforts by the United States to wage war on drug cultivation and trafficking run counter to a market-oriented logic and risk strengthening the autonomy

Table 1.2   Democratic Status of Latin American Countries, 1980–1997

Category	1980	1987	1993	1997
Liberal democracies (2–4)	4	8	4	5
Liberal democracies (5)	3	5	4	6
Electoral democracies and pseudodemocracies (6–9)	7	3	11	10
Authoritarian (10–14)	8	6	3	1
Total	22	22	22	22

Sources: Freedom in the World: Political Rights and Civil Liberties 1987–1988 and *1993–1994* (New York: Freedom House, 1988 and 1994) and *Freedom Review* (Jan.-Feb. 1998).

Note: Based on combined summary scores of Freedom House country scores for political rights (high of 1 to low of 7) and civil liberties (high of 1 to low of 7). Includes the 22 countries of Latin America and the Caribbean with over one million inhabitants. See Table 1.3 for references and additional discussion of these scores.

Table 1.3   Democratic Status of Nine Latin American Countries, 1987, 1993, and 1997

Regime Type and Combined Freedom Score	Countries and Freedom Scores (Political Rights, Civil Liberties)		
	1987	1993	1997
Liberal Democracies			
Freedom Score 2	Costa Rica (1,1)		
Freedom Score 3–4	Venezuela (1,2)	Costa Rica (1,2)[#]	Costa Rica (1,2)
	Argentina (2,1)	Chile (2,2)	Chile (2,2)
	Dom Republic (1,3)		
	Brazil (2,2)		
Freedom Score 5	Colombia (2,3)	Argentina (2,3)[↓]	Argentina (2,3)
	Peru (2,3)		Venezuela (2,3)
Electoral Democracies (and pseudodemocracies)			
Freedom Score 6–7		Colombia (2,4)[↓]	
		Dom Republic (3,3)[⇓]	Dom Republic (3,3)[↑]
		Venezuela (3,3)	Brazil (3,4)[⇓]
		Brazil (3,4)[⇓]	Mexico (3,4)[⇓↑]
Freedom Score 8–9	Mexico (4,4)	Mexico (4,4)[⇓]	Colombia (4,4)[↓]
			Peru (5,4)
Authoritarian			
Freedom Score 10–11	Chile (6,5)	Peru (5,5)[↑]	
Freedom score 12–14			

Sources: Freedom in the World: Political Rights and Civil Liberties 1987–1988 and 1993–1994 (New York: Freedom House, 1988 and 1994) and *Freedom Review* (Jan.-Feb. 1998).

Notes: Figures in parentheses are the Freedom House country scores (political rights and civil liberties, respectively). Each scale ranges from 1 to 7, with 1 being most free. # indicates rating was changed for purely methodological reasons. ⇓ signifies a shift downward and ⇑ a shift upward in the freedom score in the previous year. ↓ signifies a downward trend in the level of democracy, but not significant enough to have changed the freedom rating.

and distorting the missions of Latin American militaries. In this sense, U.S. pressure and military assistance may undermine democracy in a manner that reflects little learning from past mistakes.

None of this is to ignore, however, the large and predominant responsibility for the democratic prospect in the region that lies with Latin Americans themselves, at all levels. Throughout this introduction, we have noted numerous institutional deficiencies that threaten the stability of democracy. The rebuilding of efficient and, where appropriate, decentralized state structures, reassertion of state authority and the rule of law, subordination of the military to civilian democratic control, party building, and the invigoration of legislative and judicial institutions are essentially political challenges. Whether they are met effectively will depend on the capacity, courage, judgment, and values of domestic political actors. Even those sociopolitical challenges complicated by economic globalization—alleviation of poverty and inequality, incorporation of marginal groups, management of class conflict, reduction of still very high rates of population growth, termination of conflicts with insurgent groups—cannot be resolved without effective political leadership and action. Whatever international economic actors may do, sustaining economic growth in Latin America while implementing effective social policies will also heavily depend on domestic policy choices and implementation.

Although the return of outright military regimes in the region now seems unlikely, it is not difficult to conjure up a plausible pessimistic scenario for democracy in Latin America. Illiberal, unconsolidated democracies and hybrid regimes (along with a few more liberal democracies) could perdure in the absence of domestic threats to the established order and with the continued presence of a broad but not very demanding ideological hegemony in favor of democracy. In most of the region, more or less genuine electoral competition and alternation would be overshadowed by the failure of all major political parties, and of state institutions in all sectors and levels, to engage and respond to vast segments of the public, who in turn would become increasingly alienated from and distrustful (even disdainful) of formal democratic institutions. Delegative, populist, and neopatrimonial presidents would override the quest for horizontal accountability and a rule of law, and thereby eviscerate the vertical dimension of accountability as well. Unable to mobilize a policy consensus or any viable, coherent vision of a more just and dynamic country, parties and politicians would flounder in governing, failing to generate sustained economic growth, much less to relieve poverty and inequality. We do not think the current situation is this bad, but neither do we believe that such a "low-level equilibrium" of "democracy" in Latin America can be viable indefinitely. And even if it is viable, it is hardly desirable.

A more optimistic scenario would see the forces of globalization fostering effective regional integration throughout the continent, strengthening both vibrant market economies and political democracy while helping countries to put aside old enmities. Emerging from the painful processes of economic restructuring and second-stage reforms would be states that may be smaller in size and more modest in their goals and their reach, but more efficient and more capable in what they do: administering justice, implementing targeted programs of poverty alleviation, improving basic public education and health, and effectively regulating private economic actors to limit market abuse. Although many issues may no longer be channeled through the state or processed by political means, political parties and institutions would reemerge as important forums for mobilizing, articulating, aggregating, and compromising interests, and for responding to an invigorated civil society. Reform-minded forces in party politics and civil society would join together to rein in corruption, increase transparency, improve human rights protections, expand access to power, and subordinate the military—all by enhancing the political institutions of democracy.

The great challenge confronting most of Latin America today (including most of our cases) remains what it was ten years ago: to deepen and consolidate democracies that are real but still in too many respects superficial. At least at an intellectual level, we think there is better understanding today than ten years ago of what is required to achieve consolidation. If democracy is to become widely and unconditionally valued by the mass public and all significant social and political groups, it must at least deliver on its implicit political promise. It must become deeper, more liberal, more democratic, and thus more effective at articulating and aggregating diverse interests, and hopefully at governing. This is why the challenge of political institution building and reform is so important. However, the reform of stagnant, centralized, and corrupt state structures does not happen merely on initiative from above. Even with skilled and democratically enlightened leadership, democratic reform requires pressure from below and encouragement and support from outside, in the regional and international environment. One encouraging trend is the growing empowerment and democratic awareness of a plethora of social movements and civil society actors working on a host of reform issues, in a democratic spirit if not always through conventional political channels. The scope of this civil society efflorescence is without precedent in Latin America. However, to improve and help consolidate democracy, civil society actors must not only remain committed to democratic ends and means, protesting and criticizing where necessary; they must also learn to engage, cooperate, and even ally with political parties, with governmental institutions at all levels, and with one another.

Increasingly, as they become integrated into regional and global markets, and as the prospect of a hemispheric free trade zone draws nearer, Latin American democracies find themselves lodged in an external setting that discourages overt authoritarian regressions. For countries that need international trade and credit—and most of all, international investor confidence—to thrive economically, the costs of an old-fashioned military coup have risen exponentially. In this sense, and also because of the maturing from within, Latin America has entered a new era in which military coups may become the relics of history. However, there is a big difference between the persistence of a troubled and ineffective democracy and the consolidation of a well-functioning one. A military coup is not the only means by which democracy may be eroded, and democratic success encompasses much more than merely avoiding breakdown. For most of our cases and for the region as a whole, now nearly two decades (or more) after the return to democracy, much remains to be done to make democracy stable and secure. A long road of democratic reform and institutionalization still lies ahead.

NOTES

We would like to thank Jorge I. Domínguez and several of the authors in this volume for their comments on an earlier draft of this chapter.

1. Larry Diamond, Juan J. Linz, and Seymour Martin Lipset, eds., *Democracy in Developing Countries: Latin America* (Boulder, CO: Lynne Rienner Publishers, 1989). This chapter revises and updates the introduction to that first edition, coauthored by Larry Diamond and Juan J. Linz.

2. See Larry Diamond, Juan J. Linz, and Seymour Martin Lipset, eds., *Democracy in Developing Countries: Africa*, and *Democracy in Developing Countries: Asia* (Boulder, CO: Lynne Rienner Publishers, 1988 and 1989).

3. Uruguay was also included in our first edition. We regret that we were unable to include a new analysis of that important case in this revised edition, and we have retained several references to it in this introductory chapter.

4. Our conceptualization of democratic consolidation here follows that of Juan J. Linz and Alfred Stepan, *Problems of Democratic Transition and Consolidation: Southern Europe, South America and Post-Communist Europe* (Baltimore: Johns Hopkins University Press, 1997), chapter 2. See also Richard Gunther, Hans-Jürgen Puhle, and P. Nikiforos Diamandouros, "Introduction," in Gunther, Diamonandouros, and Puhle, eds., *The Politics of Democratic Consolidation: Southern Europe in Comparative Perspective* (Baltimore: Johns Hopkins University Press, 1995), pp. 7–10; and Larry Diamond, *Developing Democracy: Toward Consolidation* (Baltimore: Johns Hopkins University Press, 1999), chapter 3.

5. For comparative evidence on levels of democratic legitimacy and other public attitudes toward democracy, see Linz and Stepan, *Problems of Democratic Transition,* and Diamond, *Developing Democracy,* chapter 5.

6. Seymour Martin Lipset, *Political Man: The Social Bases of Politics,* expanded ed. (Baltimore: Johns Hopkins University Press, 1981), p. 64; Juan J. Linz, *The Breakdown of Democratic Regimes: Crisis, Breakdown and Reequilibration* (Baltimore: Johns Hopkins University Press, 1978), pp. 16–18; and Robert A. Dahl, *Polyarchy: Participation and Opposition* (New Haven: Yale University Press, 1971), pp. 129–131.

7. Linz and Stepan, *Problems of Democratic Transition;* Diamond, *Developing Democracy.*

8. Linz, *The Breakdown of Democratic Regimes,* pp. 28–38.

9. For a related statement about the need to steer a theoretical middle course between excessive cultural or socioeconomic determinism, on the one hand, and extreme political voluntarism, on the other, see Bolívar Lamounier, "Brazil: The Hyperactive Paralysis Syndrome," in Jorge I. Domínguez and Abraham F. Lowenthal, eds., *Constructing Democratic Governance: South America in the 1990s* (Baltimore: Johns Hopkins University Press, 1996), p. 167.

10. For supporting evidence, see Linz and Stepan, *Problems of Democratic Transition;* Diamond, *Developing Democracy;* Richard Rose, William Mishler, and Christian Haerpfer, *Democracy and Its Alternatives* (Oxford and Baltimore: Polity Press and Johns Hopkins University Press, 1998); Karen L. Remmer, "Democracy and Economic Crisis: The Latin American Experience," *World Politics* 42, no. 3 (April 1990): 315–335, "The Political Impact of Economic Crisis in Latin America," *American Political Science Review* 85 (1991), pp. 777–800, and "Democratization in Latin America," in Robert O. Slater, Barry M. Schutz, and Steven R. Dorr, eds., *Global Transformation and the Third World* (Boulder, CO: Lynne Rienner Publishers, 1993), pp. 91–111.

11. On the role of the monarchy in helping to avoid a "crisis of legitimacy" during periods of democratization in Europe, see Seymour Martin Lipset, *Political Man* (Baltimore: Johns Hopkins University Press, 1981), pp. 65–66.

12. Data are from Alejandro Bunge and Carlos Muta, quoted by M. Hernández Sánchez-Barba, "Los Estados de América en los Siglos XIX y XX," in Jaime Vicens Vivies, *Historia Social y Económica de España y América* (Barcelona: Teide, 1959), vol. IV, p. 532.

13. Andreas Schedler, Larry Diamond, and Marc F. Plattner, eds., *The Self-Restraining State* (Boulder, CO: Lynne Rienner Publishers, 1999); World Bank, *World Development Report 1997: The State in a Changing World* (New York: Oxford University Press, 1997).

14. Richard Morse put it very well: "In one case 'e pluribus unum' in the other 'ex uno plures'" in "The Heritage of Latin America," in Louis Hartz, ed., *The Founding of New Societies* (New York: Harcourt, Brace & World, 1964), p. 161.

15. In some countries, such as Brazil and Colombia, power was less concentrated in a single center or capital.

16. This is especially evident in the case of Argentina; see Carlos Escudé, *La Argentina vs. Las Grandes Potencias* (Buenos Aires: Editorial Belgrano, 1986), and "Argentine Territorial Nationalism," *Journal of Latin American Studies* 20: 139–165.

17. Peru did develop an elite democracy, the Aristocratic Republic, at the turn of the century (1895–1919) but failed to institutionalize it. Argentina, in turn, which did institutionalize a limited democracy in the nineteenth century, has had a very uneven history of democracy in the twentieth century.

18. See Michael Burton, Richard Gunther, and John Higley, "Introduction: Elite Transformations and Democratic Regimes," and Marcelo Cavarozzi, "Patterns of Elite Negotiation and Confrontation in Argentina and Chile," both in John Higley and Richard Gunther, eds., *Elites and Democratic Consolidation in Latin America and Southern Europe* (Cambridge: Cambridge University Press, 1992).

19. Robert Dahl, *Polyarchy: Participation and Opposition* (New Haven: Yale University Press, 1971), pp. 33–36.

20. See in particular Leonard Binder et al., *Crises and Sequences in Political Development* (Princeton: Princeton University Press, 1971). Our Latin American cases also fit substantially (though not perfectly) Rustow's model of the historical process of transition to democracy, which presumes a background condition of national unity, then "is set off by a prolonged and inconclusive political struggle," which in turn is concluded or resolved by "a deliberate decision on the part of political leaders . . . to institutionalize some crucial aspect of democratic procedure," marking the start of a democratization process that is consolidated in a "habituation" phase. The correspondence of the absence or presence of this sequence to the subsequent historical absence or development of aristocratic democracies in Latin America is especially striking given that Rustow developed his model with reference to the experiences of Europe, North America, and Turkey, not Latin America. See Dankwart Rustow, "Transitions to Democracy: Toward a Dynamic Model," *Comparative Politics* 2, no. 3 (April 1970): 337–363.

21. See, for example, Linz and Stepan, *Problems of Democratic Transition.* Today the problem is especially serious in the posttransition regimes of the former Soviet Union and Africa.

22. See Paulo Sérgio Pinheiro, "Democracies Without Citizenship," *NACLA—Report on the Americas,* vol. 30 (Sept.-Oct. 1996), pp. 17–23.

23. Charles Gillespie, "The Breakdown of Democracy in Uruguay: Alternative Political Models," Working Paper No. 143, Latin American Program, The Wilson Center, Washington, D.C., 1984, p. 25.

24. This builds on Joan Nelson, "Overview: How Market Reforms and Democratic Consolidation Affect Each Other," in Joan Nelson et al., *Intricate Links: Democratization and*

Market Reforms in Latin America and Eastern Europe (New Brunswick, NJ: Transaction Publishers, 1994), p. 21.

25. See, for example, World Bank, *World Development Report 1997*. An early forceful call for state strengthening and reform as a key to the third phase in Latin America's economic reform process was issued by Moisés Naím, "Latin America: The Second Stage of Reform," in Larry Diamond and Marc F. Plattner, eds., *Economic Reform and Democracy* (Baltimore: Johns Hopkins University Press, 1995), pp. 28–44, and in "Latin America's Journey to the Market: From Macroeconomic Shocks to Institutional Therapy," Occasional Paper No. 62, International Center for Economic Growth (San Francisco: Institute for Contemporary Studies, 1995).

26. For examples of contradictory effects of reforms in Mexico, see Jonathan Fox, "Latin America's Emerging Local Politics," *Journal of Democracy* 5, no. 2 (April 1994): 105–116; and on Colombia, see Pilar Gaitán Pavía and Carlos Moreno Ospina, *Poder Local: Realidad y utopía de la descentralización en Colombia* (Bogotá: IEPRI y Tercer Mundo, 1992), and Gustavo Bell Lemus, "The Decentralised State: An Administrative or Political Challenge?" in Eduardo Posada-Carbó, ed. *Colombia: The Politics of Reforming the State* (New York: St. Martin's Press, 1998), pp. 97–108.

27. Felipe Agüero, *Soldiers, Civilians, and Democracy: Post-Franco Spain in Comparative Perspective* (Baltimore: Johns Hopkins University Press, 1995), and "Toward Civilian Supremacy in South America," in Larry Diamond, Marc F. Plattner, Yun-han Chu, and Hung-mao Tien, eds., *Consolidating the Third Wave Democracies: Themes and Perspectives* (Baltimore: Johns Hopkins University Press, 1997), pp. 177–206.

28. On sultanism, see H. E. Chehabi and Juan J. Linz, "A Theory of Sultanism 1: A Type of Nondemocratic Rule," pp. 3–25, and "A Theory of Sultanism 2: Genesis and Demise of Sultanistic Regimes," pp. 26–48; and on Trujillo, see Jonathan Hartlyn, "The Trujillo Regime in the Dominican Republic," pp. 85–112, all in H. E. Chehabi and Juan J. Linz, eds., *Sultanistic Regimes* (Baltimore: Johns Hopkins University Press, 1998).

29. Manuel Antonio Garretón, "Human Rights in Democratization Processes," in Elizabeth Jelin and Eric Hershberg, eds., *Constructing Democracy: Human Rights, Citizenship, and Society in Latin America* (Boulder, CO: Westview Press, 1996), p. 41.

30. See A. James McAdams, ed., *Transitional Justice and the Rule of Law in New Democracies* (Notre Dame, IN: University of Notre Dame Press, 1997); and Alexandra Barahona de Brito, *Human Rights and Democratization in Latin America: Uruguay and Chile* (Oxford: Oxford University Press, 1997).

31. Consuelo Cruz and Rut Diamant, "The New Military Autonomy in Latin America," *Journal of Democracy* 9 (October 1998): 115–127.

32. See David Pion-Berlin, *Through Corridons of Power: Institutions and Civil-Military Relations in Argentina* (University Park: Pennsylvania State University Press, 1997), pp. 218–219; see also Wendy Hunter, "Civil-Military Relations in Argentina, Brazil, and Chile: Present Trends, Future Prospects," in Felipe Agüero and Jeffrey Stark, eds., *Fault Lines of Democracy in Post-Transition Latin America* (Miami: North-South Center Press, 1998), pp. 299–322.

33. In addition to the works by Agüero, see also Samuel P. Huntington, "Reforming Civil-Military Relations," in Larry Diamond and Marc F. Plattner, eds., *Civil-Military Relations and Democracy* (Baltimore: Johns Hopkins University Press, 1996), pp. 3–11; and Harold Crouch, "Civil-Military Relations in Southeast Asia," in Larry Diamond et al., eds., *Consolidating the Third Wave Democracies: Themes and Perspectives* (Baltimore: Johns Hopkins University, 1997), pp. 207–235.

34. Alfred Stepan, *Rethinking Military Politics: Brazil and the Southern Cone* (Princeton, NJ: Princeton University Press, 1988), pp. 138–139.

35. Wendy Hunter, "Contradictions of Civilian Control: Argentina, Brazil, and Chile in the 1990s," *Third World Quarterly* 15 (1994): 633–653.

36. Samuel P. Huntington, *The Third Wave: Democratization in the Late Twentieth Century* (Norman: University of Oklahoma Press, 1991), p. 231.

37. This paragraph and several others in this section are derived in part from Jonathan Hartlyn and Arturo Valenzuela, "Latin American Democracy Since 1930," in Leslie Bethell, ed., *Cambridge History of Latin America,* vol. VI, part II, pp. 119–129, 161. See also Scott Mainwaring and Timothy Scully, eds., *Building Democratic Institutions: Party Systems in Latin America* (Stanford: Stanford University Press, 1995); Scott P. Mainwaring, *Rethinking*

Party Systems in the Third Wave of Democratization: The Case of Brazil (Stanford: Stanford University Press, 1999); and Dieter Nohlen, *Sistemas electorales y partidos políticos,* 2nd ed. (Mexico: Fondo de Cultura Económica, 1994).

38. Argentina, with its strong and cohesive parties, has been an exception to the pattern, and within Peru, the Popular American Revolutionary Alliance (APRA) also resisted the tendency to weak and incoherent parties.

39. See also Michael Coppedge, *Strong Parties and Lame Ducks: Presidential Partyarchy and Factionalism in Venezuela* (Stanford: Stanford University Press, 1994).

40. Samuel P. Huntington, *Political Order in Changing Societies* (New Haven: Yale University Press, 1968), pp. 12–26.

41. Andreas Schedler, "Under- and Overinstitutionalization: Some Ideal Typical Propositions Concerning New and Old Party Systems," Working Paper No. 213, The Helen Kellogg Institute for International Studies, Notre Dame University, Notre Dame, Indiana (March 1995).

42. Kenneth Roberts, "The Politics of Informalization," oral presentation, Chapel Hill, North Carolina, February 1998. See also Andreas Schedler, ed., *The End of Politics? Explorations into Modern Antipolitics* (New York: St. Martin's Press, 1997).

43. For an eloquent defense of political parties and politicians, see Fernando Henrique Cardoso, "In Praise of the Art of Politics," *Journal of Democracy* 7, no. 3 (July 1996): 7–19.

44. Larry Diamond, "Three Paradoxes of Democracy," *Journal of Democracy* 1 (summer 1990): 48–61.

45. Among recent published works, see Juan J. Linz and Arturo Valenzuela, eds., *The Failure of Presidential Democracy* (Baltimore: Johns Hopkins University Press, 1994); and Scott Mainwaring and Matthew Shugart, eds., *Presidentialism and Democracy in Latin America* (Cambridge: Cambridge University Press, 1997).

46. See Linz, "Presidential or Parliamentary Democracy: Does It Make a Difference?" in Linz and Valenzuela, eds., *The Failure of Presidential Democracy* (Baltimore: Johns Hopkins University Press, 1994); see also Linz and Stepan, *Problems of Democratic Transition.*

47. Focusing especially on the cases of Argentina, Brazil, and Peru, Guillermo O'Donnell has labeled this a form of "delegative democracy," in contrast to more "representative-institutional" democracy apparent in countries like Chile and Uruguay; see his "Delegative Democracy," *Journal of Democracy* 5, no. 1 (January 1994): 55–69.

48. Although Latin American democracies have made some progress in eliminating discriminatory laws against women and in criminalizing violence against women, formal discrimination still remains in some constitutional texts, and in some civil and penal codes in the region. Moreover, weak implementation, problematic access, and prejudice on the part of judicial authorities often render existing laws ineffectual. See Mala N. Htun, "Women's Rights and Opportunities in Latin America: Problems and Prospects" (Washington, DC: Women's Leadership Conference of the Americas, Inter-American Dialogue and International Center for Research on Women, April 1998); and Mala N. Htun, "Women's Political Participation, Representation and Leadership in Latin America" (Washington, DC: Women's Leadership Conference of the Americas, Inter-American Dialogue and International Center for Research on Women, November 1998); also Merike Blofield, personal communication, March 1999.

49. For a valuable recent discussion of the weakness of these various forms of "horizontal accountability," and hence of republican and liberal practices, see Guillermo A. O'Donnell, "Horizontal Accountability in New Democracies," *Journal of Democracy* 9 (July 1998): 112–126, and the full version of this essay in Andreas Schedler, Larry Diamond, and Marc F. Plattner, eds., *The Self-Restraining State: Power and Accountability in New Democracies* (Boulder, CO: Lynne Rienner Publishers, 1999).

50. See Human Rights Watch/Americas, *Police Brutality in Urban Brazil* (New York: Human Rights Watch, 1977); and Robert Weiner, "War by Other Means: Colombia's Faceless Courts," *NACLA—Report on the Americas,* vol. 30, no. 2 (Sept.-Oct. 1996), pp. 31–36.

51. Seymour Martin Lipset, *The First New Nation: The United States in Comparative and Historical Perspective* (New York: W. W. Norton & Co., 1979), especially pp. 16–23.

52. John A. Peeler, *Latin American Democracies: Colombia, Costa Rica, Venezuela* (Chapel Hill: University of North Carolina Press, 1985), p. 73.

53. Ibid., p. 74.

54. Arturo Valenzuela, p. 219 in this volume.

55. Juan J. Linz and Alfred Stepan, eds., *The Breakdown of Democratic Regimes* (Baltimore: Johns Hopkins University Press, 1978). On the 1964 breakdown in Brazil, see Alfred Stepan, "Political Leadership and Regime Breakdown: Brazil," in Juan J. Linz and Alfred Stepan, eds., *The Breakdown of Democratic Regimes: Latin America* (Baltimore: Johns Hopkins University Press, 1978), pp. 110–137.

56. Howard J. Wiarda, "The Dominican Republic: Mirror Legacies of Democracy and Authoritarianism," in Larry Diamond, Juan J. Linz, and Seymour Martin Lipset, eds., *Democracy in Developing Countries: Latin America* (Boulder, CO: Lynne Rienner Publishers, 1989), pp. 423–458, quotes from p. 450, p. 453.

57. See, for example, Gabriel A. Almond and Sidney Verba, *The Civic Culture* (Princeton: Princeton University Press, 1963), p. 14.

58. Rustow, "Transitions to Democracy," p. 360.

59. Juan J. Linz, "O Integralismo e o fascismo internacional," *Revista do Instituto de Filosofia E Ciencias Humanas,* Universidad Federal de Rio Grande do Sul (1977), pp. 136–143.

60. For comparative evidence on belief in the legitimacy of democracy and related attitudes and values, see Marta Lagos, "Latin America's Smiling Mask," *Journal of Democracy* 8 (July 1997): 125–138; and Linz and Stepan, *Problems of Democratic Transition.* Consistent with many of our observations above, support for democracy is very high in Costa Rica and Uruguay (about 80 percent), and surprisingly high in Argentina, but significantly lower in Brazil and Central America, where there is also much less satisfaction with the way democracy works.

61. We refer the reader again to the seminal statements of this argument by Dahl, *Polyarchy,* and Rustow, "Transitions to Democracy."

62. Charles G. Gillespie and Luis Eduardo González, "Uruguay: The Survival of Old and Autonomous Institutions," in Larry Diamond, Juan J. Linz, and Seymour Martin Lipset, eds., *Democracy in Developing Countries: Latin America* (Boulder, CO: Lynne Rienner Publishers, 1989).

63. This phenomenon has been demonstrated in some detail by Gillespie in "The Breakdown of Democracy in Uruguay," especially pp. 27–28.

64. Adam Przeworski and Fernando Limongi, "Modernization: Theories and Facts," *World Politics* 49 (January 1997): 155–184.

65. Samuel P. Huntington, "Will More Countries Become Democratic?" *Political Science Quarterly* 99, no. 2 (1994): 193–218.

66. The absence of a relationship among our cases between stability of democracy and level of development may in part be an artifact of our excluding the poorest and least-democratic countries of the region from our selection of cases, although as we have noted it is also due to the existence of dramatic outliers such as Argentina and Uruguay and more modest ones such as Mexico.

67. Seymour Martin Lipset, *Political Man* (Baltimore: Johns Hopkins University Press, 1981), pp. 61–71.

68. Lagos, "Latin America's Smiling Mask," table 3, p. 133. Satisfaction is as low as 16 percent in Colombia and Guatemala, 20 percent in Brazil, and 28 percent in Peru, while it is slightly over 50 percent in Costa Rica and Uruguay. The figures are from the 1996 Latinobarómetro.

69. See Shahid Javed Burki and Guillermo E. Perry, *The Long March: A Reform Agenda for Latin America and the Caribbean in the Next Decade* (Washington, DC: The World Bank, 1997), pp. 87–90.

70. For two extraordinary systematic analyses of democracy and working-class incorporation in Latin America, see Ruth Berins Collier and David Collier, *Shaping the Political Arena: Critical Junctures, the Labor Movement, and Regime Dynamics in Latin America* (Princeton: Princeton University Press, 1991), and Dietrich Rueschemeyer, Evelyne Huber Stephens, and John D. Stephens, *Capitalist Development and Democracy* (Chicago: University of Chicago Press, 1992). In this introduction, like the Colliers', our starting point is more political-institutional, without eschewing the importance of other types of factors.

71. Gillespie, "The Breakdown of Democracy in Uruguay," p. 8.

72. See Jorge Castañeda, "Democracy and Inequality in Latin America," in Jorge I. Domínguez and Abraham F. Lowenthal, eds., *Constructing Democratic Governance: Latin America and the Caribbean in the 1990s—Themes and Issues* (Baltimore: Johns Hopkins University Press, 1996), p. 52. Anything but universal suffrage would now be unthinkable in Latin America, or indeed anywhere in the world. Of the nine countries considered here, literacy restrictions were lifted last in Peru (1979) and in Brazil (1985).

73. World Bank, *World Development Report 1998/1999* (New York: Oxford University Press, 1999), pp. 198–199, table 5. Brazil's "gini coefficient" was measured at 60.1 in 1995, Colombia's was 57.2, while the United States at 40.1 had one of the highest levels in the advanced industrial countries.

74. José Antonio Ocampo, "Income Distribution, Poverty and Social Expenditure in Latin America," prepared for a Conference of the Americas sponsored by the OAS, Washington D.C., March 1998, p. 2. He notes that it is not that the current wave of economic reforms are the cause of the region's current levels of inequality which respond to deep-rooted phenomena, but that the initial impact of these reforms has been to augment it (p. 4) (as downloaded from www.eclac.org, April 23, 1998).

75. See Rodolfo Stavenhagen, "Indigenous Rights: Some Conceptual Problems," in Jelin and Hershberg, eds., *Constructing Democracy;* and Deborah Yashar, "Indigenous Protest and Democracy in Latin America," in Domínguez and Lowenthal, eds., *Constructing Democratic Governance,* pp. 87–105.

76. See Judith Adler Hellman, "Social Movements: Revolution, Reform and Reaction," *NACLA—Report on the Americas* 30 (May-June 1997): 13–18, quote on p. 15.

77. Philippe Schmitter and Guillermo O'Donnell, *Transitions from Authoritarian Rule: Tentative Conclusions About Uncertain Democracies* (Baltimore: Johns Hopkins University Press, 1986).

78. Diamond, *Developing Democracy,* chapter 6. For useful analyses of the role of women's organizations in the struggle for democratic transition and their subsequent evolution, see Jane Jaquette, ed., *The Women's Movement in Latin America* (Boulder, CO: Westview Press, 1994).

79. Cf. Thomas Skidmore, ed., *Television, Politics, and the Transition to Democracy in Latin America* (Baltimore: Woodrow Wilson Center Press and Johns Hopkins University Press, 1993).

80. Terry Lynn Karl, *The Paradox of Plenty: Oil Booms and Petrostates* (Berkeley: University of California Press, 1997).

81. For a review, see Inter-American Development Bank, *Latin America After a Decade of Reforms: Economic and Social Progress 1997 Report* (Washington, DC: Inter-American Development Bank, 1997), pp. 31–96.

82. For a useful review, see Abraham F. Lowenthal, ed., *Exporting Democracy: The United States and Latin America* (Baltimore: Johns Hopkins University Press, 1991).

83. On the latter case, see Arturo Valenzuela, "Paraguay: The Coup That Didn't Happen," *Journal of Democracy* 8 (January 1997): 43–56.

84. Larry Diamond, *Promoting Democracy in the 1990s: Actors and Instruments, Issues and Imperatives* (New York: Carnegie Corporation of New York, 1996).

85. Larry Diamond, "Is the Third Wave Over?" *Journal of Democracy* 7 (July 1996): 20–37, and *Developing Democracy,* chapter 2; and Jonathan Hartlyn, "Democracies in Contemporary South America: Convergences and Diversities," in Joseph S. Tulchin with Allison M. Garland, eds., *Argentina: The Challenges of Modernization* (Wilmington, DE: Scholarly Resources Inc., 1998), pp. 83–116.

86. Inter-American Development Bank, *Latin America After a Decade of Reforms,* p. 31.

2

ARGENTINA:
Capitalism and Democracy

Carlos H. Waisman

The study of the causes of democracy in Argentina is interesting for two reasons. First, because the fate of democracy in this country has been highly correlated with the nature of its capitalist institutions. From the depression of the 1870s, which took place right after the organization of the national state and the full incorporation of the country into the world economy, to the present, the pattern is clear: a market economy has been coupled with expanding competitive politics, and the neomercantilist state has given rise to nondemocratic polities of different kinds. By the term *neomercantilism* I refer to the highly statist and semiclosed economic institutions the country had during the second half of the twentieth century. There were two economic and political turning points in this period: the 1930s and 1940s, when the economy turned inward and the state expanded downward, toward a greater control of the society, and the 1980s and 1990s, when liberal democracy was reestablished and the neomercantilist state was dismantled.

Second, Argentina could have been expected, from the point of view of a long but little-known tradition in social theory, to have a different pattern of political (and also economic) evolution. As I will show, the fact that democracy floundered and the economy weakened as the country became more industrialized is an issue that requires explanation.

The record of the new democracy established after the implosion of the authoritarian regime in the early 1980s is positive in important respects—for example, constitutional rule has been reestablished, and there is broad toleration of dissent and full participation—but the type of polity that is being institutionalized in the context of a society undergoing rapid economic liberalization departs from the liberal democratic model in substantial ways.

ARGENTINA

HISTORICAL ANALYSIS

I have argued that, for most of the twentieth century, there has been an "Argentine question": Why did this country fail to become an industrial democracy?[1] The pattern of political development of Argentina in this period is problematic for two reasons, theoretical and empirical. Argentina, rich in agrarian resources and with a population consisting mostly of Europeans who immigrated at the turn of the century, resembled the "new countries" or "lands of recent settlement," such as Australia, Canada, New Zealand, and, to some extent, the United States. There is a line of theoretical argument in the social sciences, which includes convergent theses by Adam Smith, Alexis de Tocqueville, Karl Marx, and others, predicting that agrarian countries with a high land-labor ratio and a labor shortage will develop dynamic capitalist economies and liberal democratic polities. These nations would differ from standard undeveloped ones, characterized by a low land-labor ratio and a labor surplus, whose evolution would couple nondynamic economies and undemocratic types of state.[2]

Argentina has not confirmed these propositions, for the country's social structure at the end of the nineteenth century fits the "new country" type. Export agriculture, based on the coastal and central regions—the littoral—was organized into large landholdings, as in Australia. As for importation of labor, Argentina was second only to the United States as a recipient of the "great migration" from Europe.

Five characteristics of this process are important for our analysis.[3] First, the ratio of immigrants to the preexisting population was, in 1914, 30 percent foreign-born, twice the ratio in the United States at the time of maximum foreign impact. Second, most newcomers settled in the littoral, deepening the social and cultural cleavage between it and the less populated interior. Third, unlike in the United States, land in Argentina was not available for ownership by settlers; it was monopolized by the agrarian upper class. Many immigrants became tenant farmers, but most went to the cities. Fourth, foreign impact on urban class structure was very strong. In 1914, immigrants accounted for about a third of the active population in agriculture, but they were two-thirds of the industrial proprietors, three-fourths of the merchants, and half of the industrial workers and employees. (The balance included native children of immigrants, for by that time mass immigration had been going on for four decades.) Fifth, unlike all lands of recent settlement (except the United States), most emigrants to Argentina originated in countries other than its original colonizer, Spain. A third were Spanish, and almost half were Italian.

The second, empirical reason for the problematic nature of the Argentine case is the fact I pointed out in the beginning: its curvilinear pattern of economic and political development. The century from the 1880s to the 1980s can be divided into halves, with radically different traits. Up to the Great Depression, Argentina combined a very dynamic economy and expanding and relatively stable competitive politics. Constitutional legality was interrupted by a military coup in 1930; from that year to 1983, Argentine politics was an unstable succession of military, populist-corporatist, and restrictive democratic regimes. The economy expanded until the end of the 1940s, then became sluggish for most of the subsequent period. There was a switch of developmental tracks: from behaving like a "new country," Argentina changed into a typical underdeveloped society, and this transformation calls for an explanation.

In the second half of the nineteenth century, Argentina was fully incorporated into the international division of labor as a supplier of grains, beef, and wool to Europe, especially to England. The period from the 1870s to the depression was one of rapid economic and social change. The population was 1.7 million in 1869, but from 1870 to 1930 it swelled by over 6 million immigrants. By the turn of the century, Argentina had attained a relatively high level of per capita income, comparable to Germany and Belgium and higher than southern Europe and Scandinavia.[4] Rapid growth of exports propelled Argentina to compete with Japan for the title of fastest growing country in the world between 1870 and 1913.[5] From the beginning of the century up to the Great Depression, gross domestic product (GDP) grew at a rate of 4.6 percent per annum.[6] The economy slowed after World War I from an annual growth rate of 6.3 during 1900–1914 to 3.5 percent during 1914–1929. However, Argentina's per capita GDP at the outbreak of World War I was higher than Sweden's or France's. When the depression hit, GDP was still much higher than that of Austria or Italy.[7]

The economy not only grew, it diversified. Manufacturing, which began in the late nineteenth century as a forward linkage of agriculture, expanded—in the 1920s as a result of foreign investment, and in the 1930s and 1940s as a consequence of the automatic protection that followed the depression and the war. In 1938, the contributions of manufacturing and agriculture to GDP were similar.[8] In the early 1940s, the labor force in the secondary sector was larger than that in the primary sector.[9] In the mid-1940s, Argentina was more highly urbanized than the United States and most of Europe.[10]

Economic growth and diversification allowed a relatively high standard of living. At the outbreak of the depression, indicators of nutrition, health, consumption, and access to higher education placed Argentina ahead of most of Europe, and it ranked ahead of Britain in per capita number of automotive vehicles.[11] At the beginning of World War II, Argentina had more physicians per capita than any country in Europe except Switzerland and Hungary.[12] Such facts are not easy to reconcile with the image of Argentina as a typical Latin American society.

Before the turning point of the 1930s and 1940s, the political system can be characterized as an expanding elite democracy. Competition and, more specifically, toleration of peaceful opposition existed, but participation was severely restricted by electoral practices and the large proportion of foreigners. Power was monopolized by the landed upper class, labeled "the oligarchy" by its opponents. Pressures for participation by the large middle class led to an electoral reform in 1912 that established secret and universal manhood suffrage—but only for the native-born. At the time of World War I, the Conservative Party peacefully transferred power to the opposition Radical Party.

Economic and political evolution after the depression and World War II has been a sharp reversal. Standards of living continued to be relatively high: life expectancy in the late 1970s was in the same range as in the United States and Europe.[13] Enrollment in higher education was higher in the mid-1960s than in any European nation except the Netherlands.[14] But well-being was deteriorating or stagnant in many areas, while European and other Latin American countries continued to improve. Steady economic growth came to a halt after a spectacular upsurge immediately after World War II. Per capita GDP grew at an annual rate of only 0.9 percent in the 1950s; it jumped to 2.8 percent in the 1960s; it fell to 0.3 percent in the 1970s; and it was negative (–2.8 percent) in the 1980s.[15] Argentina was not literally stagnant after World War II, but its economy was characterized by sharp fluctuations—stop/go cycles—so that good and bad years almost canceled out. The overall growth rate of per capita GDP during 1950–1983 was 1 percent. As a result of this sluggishness, Argentina is now closer to Latin American development levels than it is to those of the advanced countries of Europe or the lands of recent settlement. If, in 1913, Argentine per capita GDP was comparable to that of Switzerland, twice as large as Italy's, and almost half of Canada's, in the early 1980s the corresponding proportions were less than a sixth, a third, and a fifth. Further, the Argentine per capita gross national product (GNP) was then only slightly higher than those of Chile, Brazil, and Mexico.

The political transformation has been total following the depression. Argentina wavered among three types of polity: military dictatorship, populist-corporatist regime, and restrictive democracy. From 1930 to the reestablishment of liberal democracy in 1983, there were six major military coups (1930, 1943, 1955, 1962, 1966, and 1976) and countless minor ones. In that period, there were twenty-five presidents, though one administration (Juan D. Perón's) lasted for ten years (1946–1955). There were twenty-two years of military rule (1930–1931, 1943–1946, 1955–1958, 1966–1973, and 1976–1983); thirteen years of Peronism, a regime with a populist-corporatist ideology; and nineteen years of restrictive democracy (1932–1943 and 1958–1966), an intermediate type that preserved constitutional forms but banned the majority parties (the Radicals in the 1930s and the

Peronists in the 1960s). From 1955 to 1983, political instability reached critical levels. There were eighteen presidents, and all those elected were overthrown except one, Perón, who died less than a year after his election.

The second turning point corresponds to the 1980s, when democratic rule was reestablished, and the 1990s, when radical economic liberalization took place. As of this writing, there has been a decade and a half of constitutional rule, and economic growth has resumed since the dismantling of neomercantilism. In the mid-1990s, Argentine per capita GNP was similar to those of Greece and Portugal.

The Rise and Fall of Democracy

In the second half of the nineteenth century, Argentina seemed an unlikely place for the emergence of a stable liberal democracy. As in most of Europe and the whole of Latin America, social and cultural institutions such as the family, education, and religion were strongly authoritarian. Argentina, like the rest of the Hispanic world, lacked traditions of autonomous social organization, contestation, and toleration of dissent, in both the political and cultural spheres. Moreover, the country had just overcome decades of internal strife; the national state had begun to be reorganized in the middle of the nineteenth century. Also, Argentina was split between the littoral and the interior. Landed property—the central source of wealth, power, and prestige—was highly concentrated. Finally, large-scale immigration began soon after the national state was reconstituted, so that the new and fragile political institutions were in danger of being overwhelmed by the flow of new inhabitants, most of whom originated in countries with weak democratic traditions.

Three centuries of Spanish rule had left as a political legacy the norm of absolute authority, a centralized state, and the antiliberal ideology of the Counter-Reformation. The settler revolt known as the "revolution of independence" was the local repercussion of the Atlantic revolutionary wave initiated in the United States and France. The leaders of the independence movement were liberals seeking to transform the backward periphery of a backward empire into a modern nation with a capitalist economy, a democratic polity, and the culture of the Enlightenment. These plans foundered on the inhospitable reality of the new nation. Democratic schemes proved unfeasible; so did unified government. The state collapsed after independence in the early nineteenth century. Provincial chieftains, usually autocratic, who represented the local landed elites, grabbed power. For most of the fifty years following independence, Argentina lacked an effective central government. Several civil wars reflected economic, social, and cultural tensions among the provinces. Civil strife did not correspond precisely to the main line of regional cleavage, that between the littoral (centered in the city and province of Buenos Aires) and the interior (which in the nineteenth century meant the center and north). The littoral was the area that exported to Europe and through which European commodities, immigrants, and ideas entered Argentina, as well as where trade taxes were levied. The interior had mostly Native populations, traditional Hispanic culture, and subsistence or regional economies that were threatened by European imports and did not generate much revenue.

The national state was reestablished in the 1850s on the basis of a constitution adapted from that of the United States. The consolidation of democracy was facilitated by three factors—political, ideological, and economic—that overcame the weight of the legacy of Spanish rule. First, as a result of the long and inconclusive period of civil wars, the economic and political elites developed support for a political formula that sought reconciliation among the different provincial elites and political factions, and the sharing of power on the basis of consensus. Such a formula was more conducive to an elite democracy than to any alternative. Electoral laws (which established public voting and representation based on the "winner take all" principle) and tolerance for fraudulent practices guaranteed the provincial elites' continued control of their territories, while a federal constitution and the development of the norm of government by agreement allowed institutionalization of this political formula. Only in the second decade of the twentieth century did an electoral reform provide for the secret ballot, minority representation, and guarantees against electoral fraud. Second, the elite was determined to carry out the project that liberal Argentine intellectuals had conceived in previous decades: to transform the country into a modern nation by integrating it into the world economy and importing western European capital, immigrants, and institutions. They believed that Argentina could hope to attract English, French, and other European capital and population only if its institutions were similar, that is, based on economic and political liberalism. That the progress of the country owed in part to implementing this project sets Argentina apart from other Latin American nations.[16]

Third, there is no question that Argentine economic and political development was externally induced. European industrialization and urbanization created a large-scale demand for Argentine products and a large-scale supply of capital and immigrants. But Argentina's transformation into a major agrarian producer, recipient of immigrants, and democratic nation was more the result of the internal processes noted above than of the opportunity provided by European expansion. However, once the country was strongly integrated into international trade, the development of the export economy was a powerful factor encouraging the institutionalization of the democratic state. Sustained economic growth and the ensuing high rates of social mobility cushioned the effect of inequality and regional differences.

Urbanization, industrialization, and an expanding educational system facilitated both the legitimation of the new political order among all social classes and the absorption of the immigrant inflow.

When the country became a major exporter, the Argentine polity was similar in its basic traits to the elite or "Whig"[17] democracies in many agrarian societies in Europe and Latin America. First, the mass of the population was not mobilized; the upper class and some sectors of the middle classes were the only participants. Second, given that the various factions or parties represented different segments of the elite, competition embraced a relatively narrow range of contending interests.

What distinguishes evolving liberal democracies from preindustrial exclusionary regimes is not their level of participation, but their response to mobilization. The development of capitalism and the industrial and educational revolutions bring new political forces to the fore: the industrial bourgeoisie, other urban middle-class sectors, and the working class. Elite responses can be triggered by the mere formation of these new classes, or they can be a reaction to their mobilization. Elsewhere, I have classified these responses as three elite strategies: inclusion, which is the extension of the right to participate in the polity as an independent political force; exclusion, the denial of that right; and co-optation, an intermediate form consisting of participation controlled by the elite or the state apparatus, usually on the basis of corporatist mechanisms.[18]

In Argentina, the inclusionary response to the mobilization of the middle and working classes before 1930 is indicated by the tolerance for peaceful opposition from the Radical and Socialist Parties, which represented these new social forces; by the Reform of 1912, which enfranchised the Native middle classes; and by the transfer of political power to the Radicals in 1916. Exclusion existed as a secondary aspect, triggered by the violent activities of the anarchists and mainly directed against them.[19] Policies such as suspending constitutional guarantees through the state of siege and persecuting terrorists (but also labor militants and dissenters in general) were applied, but sparingly; only a few hundred foreigners, for instance, were deported under the "residence law."[20] In fact, it would be the Radicals rather than the administrations representing the Conservative oligarchy who responded to labor mobilization, in isolated instances, with large-scale repression.

Participation was restricted by the initially low level of mobilization among non-elite groups, but also by fraudulent electoral practices that covered the whole range from buying votes to falsifying results.[21] These practices disappeared or were minimized, however, with the Reform of 1912.

Mobilization of the middle and lower classes presented challenges that, for different reasons, could be met by the landed upper class without altering the existing distribution of wealth and power. The Radicals, with an elite leadership and a mass base including large segments of the middle classes, staged several armed revolts at the turn of the century. Their demands, however, were totally consistent with continued oligarchic rule. Their central goal was to extend electoral participation through the "universal" and secret manhood suffrage; nothing in their diffuse economic and social doctrine could be construed as antagonistic to the status quo.

Labor mobilization was intense in the first decade of the twentieth century and, because of the anarchist presence, was coupled with significant violence. However, mobilizing labor did not represent a high level of threat to elite rule for three reasons. First, the central themes of workers' protests were conventional bread-and-butter issues and opposition to repression. As such, they could be controlled by political reform and by institutionalizing the labor conflict, two measures that were feasible in the existing economic and political structure. Second, the distribution of forces in the labor movement—socialists and anarchists—presented an ideal combination for applying elite carrot-and-stick strategies. Including the socialists, who were convinced supporters of free trade and liberal democracy, could only strengthen existing institutions. Excluding the anarchists was facilitated by two traits of their ideology: their concentration on immediate demands and their rejection of participation in the existing state. Finally, most workers were foreign, a fact that facilitated elite strategies, as we shall see below. Thus, socialists and radicals were incorporated into the system, and government intervention in labor disputes grew during this period, especially after power was transferred to the Radical Party. The use of force by this party (there were two major incidents in the first postwar period) was more a reflection of panic and a lack of capability for riot control than a systematic policy of persecuting the labor movement.

This regime has to be evaluated in comparative perspective. Certainly, it did not rank very high on the democratic scale, but it does not make any sense to compare it with contemporary authoritarian polities such as Bismarckian Germany or the extreme case of czarist Russia. The crucial issue is that the Argentine elite did extend participation to the new classes generated by development and was willing to abide by the norms of the liberal democratic game—which included losing control of the government—as long as their basic economic interests were not endangered. Elites in many late industrializing nations were not so inclined.

The peculiarities of Argentine political evolution are related to two distinctive traits. Unlike other lands of recent settlement, it had a landed upper class that controlled the state apparatus, and unlike the modal Latin American setting, its population included a high proportion of immigrants. In the specific conditions of Argentina, the second trait was conducive to democracy, while the first one was not.

The immigrant presence contributed to democratic development not because of the culture they carried, but because their sheer weight and political marginality allowed the elite to reconcile its control of the state with the ideal norms of democracy. Two traits of this immigrant contingent in the beginning of the century indicate how "cheap" political reform was for the elite. In the littoral, where the bulk of the population was concentrated, 50 to 70 percent of males over twenty were foreign-born, and in the whole country, only 1.4 percent of immigrants had become Argentine citizens by 1914. These peculiarities of the immigrant contingent permitted the elite to legitimize the exclusionary aspects of its response to mobilization of the lower classes. Since most industrial workers were foreign-born, agitators and organizers could be deported. Also, the immigrant presence allowed the elite to live up to the ideal of universal manhood representation without enfranchising the lower classes. The Reform of 1912 established a universal, secret, and compulsory (male) ballot on the basis of new and complete rolls. However, in the 1916 election won by the opposition Radicals, voters were, in the most important districts, no more than 9 percent of the total population and only 30 percent of males over eighteen.[22]

This is not to imply that the reform was meaningless. It is true that the elite yielded to mobilization because it expected to win by the new rules. It is also true that in supporting the reform, some elite leaders had a hidden agenda: they expected, very reasonably, that participation would deflect labor militancy. Finally, there was some apprehension about Radical revolts, even though it would be an overstatement to claim that the 1912 law was a fearful reaction to the mobilized masses.[23] In spite of all these factors, the reform was a genuine, even if deferred, leap in the dark. The elite was aware that, in one or two decades, the children of immigrants would join the electorate; the whole male population would then be enfranchised.

The other Argentine peculiarity vis-à-vis lands of recent settlement was the existence of the landowning upper class itself. The local elites, both in the littoral and the interior, were constituted as political forces and had laboriously developed norms for their interaction before the constitution was adopted and applied. The half-century from independence to national organization is usually seen as "anarchic," but the counterpart of the protracted conflict among the provinces was the gradual development of consensus about the institutions of the new nation. In social terms, this meant the emergence of a relatively homogeneous national elite out of a fractious set of local ones.

The massive and swift transformation in all spheres of life following the establishment of democratic institutions had contradictory effects on legitimacy. The organization of the export economy, foreign investment, and mass immigration showed the effectiveness of the elite (enhancing the legitimacy of the social order) and rendered the upper class hegemonic. In the long run, however, the transformation undermined political legitimacy, in that it triggered mobilization before the new political institutions could attain a high level of legitimacy among the different social groups, the upper class in particular. A high level of legitimacy implies an acceptance that is automatic rather than deliberate, emotional rather than rational. Only then do social and political forces, and especially elites, develop a stable conception of the general interest as a product of impersonal institutions, binding on all social groups even when it contradicts particular interests. Attaining this sort of legitimacy presupposes at least two conditions: efficacy and time.[24] Time was missing in the Argentine case.

The Argentine elite was not deeply committed to democratic norms. Such commitment is not an intrinsic attribute of a social group, or the product of explicit socialization provided by the educational system. The lapse of time between the establishment of the new institutions and the appearance of fresh claimants to power was so brief that the outcome was natural. As long as it had no intense conflicts with these new forces, the agrarian upper class was willing to enfranchise the middle classes and even transfer power to the party representing them. It could also tolerate peaceful labor opposition. But, once its basic interests were in danger, the landed elite revoked its support for liberal democracy and seized control of the state.

Until 1930, all social and political forces, except the anarchist faction of the working class, coincided to support the basic characteristics of Argentine society and its position in the world economy. Conflicts involving interest groups and political parties were exclusively of a secondary or nonantagonistic nature. Since most manufacturing was a forward linkage of agriculture, there was no conflict between agriculture and industry. Foreign capital was combined or allied with domestic rural and urban capital, so there was no contradiction between them. Also, since the well-being of the middle and working classes depended on the export economy, vertical cleavages were moderate in content despite the occasional violent action. Thus, the oppositions between littoral and interior upper classes, domestic and foreign capital, landowners and tenant farmers, elite and urban middle class, capitalists and workers, and conservatives and radicals or socialists were all consistent with the hegemony of the dominant class. These were conflicts over participation in decisionmaking or distribution of surplus rather than over property or the nature of political institutions.

When the Radicals were in power from 1916 to 1930, their opposition to the Conservatives was exclusively political. As Peter Smith points out, the Radicals departed from the Conservative tradition of government by consensus and moved toward competitive decisionmaking. In addition, they aimed at weakening the Conservatives' local power base through the systematic intervention of the federal government in provincial administrations.[25] Nevertheless, as David Rock argues, the Radicals limited themselves to administering the existing economic and social order. They did not attempt to introduce any major changes in the structure of Argentine society or in its location in the international economy.[26] However, when the depression hit, the hegemony of the dominant classes was endangered. Not only did the position of the country in the international system have to be renegotiated, but the consent of subordinate classes could erode as domestic conflict took the appearance of a zero-sum game. The agrarian upper class turned away from democracy, more in order to face the critical situation than to restore the premobilization oligarchic state.

There is no question that the Great Depression was followed by the restoration of the rule of the agrarian elite, but this does not mean that the depression was the main cause of the 1930 coup that marked the end of democratization. This is still a debated issue. Smith has challenged the traditional interpretation, according to which there was a direct link between the economic crisis and the coup. He argued that the depression's important repercussions appeared only after the coup and explained the coup by the Radicals' refusal to abide by the Conservative tradition of power sharing. The ensuing separation between economic and political power led the agrarian elite to withdraw legitimacy from democratic institutions and seize power by force.[27] Opposing Smith, David Rock and Carl Solberg restated the conventional thesis, arguing that even before the overthrow of the Radical government, the economic situation had deteriorated significantly, and that the seriousness of the situation was already manifest to the economic and political elites.[28]

My own view is that regardless of the specific determinants of the coup, there was a causal connection between the depression and the establishment of nondemocratic regimes after the coup. The breakdown of democracy was not caused by the depression, but by its timing; the crisis took place when the norms of liberal democracy were being institutionalized. Power had been transferred from the Conservatives to the Radicals, but the different social and political forces were just beginning to develop norms for their interaction. These groups granted legitimacy to the social order and the political system, but it was still a pragmatic, tentative, contingent legitimacy. In such a situation, the depression, which affected the basic interests of all groups, ended democratization. Delegitimation did not begin at the bottom of the social structure, but at the top. Apprehensive about the effectiveness of democratic rules to protect its economic interests and its hegemony over other social forces, the agrarian upper class and its Conservative Party inaugurated a period of rule based on force, fraud, and proscription.

The Nondemocratic State

For almost all the period 1930–1983, the Argentine polity was organized on the basis of three types of nondemocratic regime.

The first was what I have called restrictive democracy. The president and other executive officials were elected; Congress and other representative assemblies functioned, but the largest party (Radicals in the 1940s,

Peronists in the late 1950s and early 1960s) was excluded from electoral participation and otherwise restricted in its activity. So, typically, was the extreme left. Usually there was significant toleration of dissent by other parties and groups, and considerable freedom of the press, assembly, and association.

In the corporatist-populist regime—the Peronist administrations of 1946–1955—there was an inclusive level of political participation and majority rule, but power was centralized by the leader. Congress and the judiciary became rubber stamps for the executive. Moreover, regard for political competition and for civil and political liberties was not systematic. Respect for liberal democracy by large sectors of Peronism, and probably by Perón himself, was purely pragmatic. Their ideal polity was hierarchical and corporatist, rather than representative and pluralistic.

Military regimes conformed to the authoritarian and bureaucratic-authoritarian models: the military ruled as an institution; representative assemblies were dissolved; political parties and political activity in general were restricted (occasionally banned altogether); and there was limited freedom of the press, assembly, and association.

The coup of 1930 did not lead to a stable authoritarian regime. The military faction that in Argentina's Orwellian political discourse was called "liberal" prevailed over the "nationalist" one, and proscriptive democracy was inaugurated. The organizations and procedures established by the constitution were reinstated, but the Radicals were excluded from elections. The means employed were not only conventional electoral fraud, but outright banning. Communists and other leftists were repressed. Nevertheless, the regime that existed until 1943 was a limited democracy, for there was a significant degree of pluralism and, in general, of political and ideological contestation.[29]

Given the contradiction between the ideal norms of democracy and the actual operation of the regime, political legitimacy foundered—this period is commonly called "the infamous decade"—but social legitimacy declined more slowly. Despite the cumulative impacts of the political and economic crises, and of the polarization in world politics, mass-based radicalism did not develop. The revolutionary left remained small; right-wing radicalism grew considerably but did not acquire a base among the subordinate classes. The social order preserved its legitimacy because it could still borrow from the "capital of trust," to use Jacques Blondel's expression, accumulated over two generations of satisfactory performance.[30] This capital was "well distributed," for it had reached precisely the potential mass base for radicalism: the immigrant working class. The anarchist rhetoric of a large segment of the labor movement up to World War I had reflected more the strains of transition into the industrial world and assimilation into the new society than an articulate opposition to the social order. Such opposition would have been surprising, given the intense social mobility in Argentina.

In fact, with the decline of anarchism and the growth of syndicalism, the labor movement became more moderate. With the new stage of industrialization after the depression, communism began to make some inroads into the industrial unions, a development that would be arrested by Peronism.

However, social legitimacy would eventually be undermined by the commitment, in the 1930s and 1940s, of a large proportion of the country's capital and labor to a noncompetitive form of manufacturing. Import substitution—begun in the 1930s in response to the depression and made permanent in the 1940s as a consequence of absolute protectionism—sapped legitimacy for two reasons. First, it generated two new social forces whose interests were incompatible with the hegemony of the agrarian upper class: a new industrial bourgeoisie, large but weak, and what would become (in the 1940s and 1950s) a powerful labor movement. Both were oriented to the internal market but needed the foreign exchange generated by agriculture. Second, absolute protectionism eroded legitimacy because it eventually led to lower growth rates and thus decreased the perceived efficacy of the social and political order. The new bourgeoisie was recruited from the middle and working classes, and the new proletariat from the rural lower class. The industrial sector was fragmented along economic and cultural lines. Old and new bourgeoisie were mostly of immigrant origin, but the old segment included a larger proportion of longtime residents in the country, it controlled larger and more efficient firms, and was tied to the agrarian upper class and foreign capital. In the working class, there was a cultural gulf between the older immigrant segment and the new Creole one.[31]

These new fractions constituted an available mass. The essence of Peronism was precisely the attempt and failure to incorporate these social forces through a corporatist state. The military coup of 1943, out of which Peronism sprang, was the first inflection point in Argentine economic and political development in this century. (As we will see, the second inflection point, which reversed the first, was, paradoxically, another Peronist regime, the Menem administration of the 1990s.) The military government that came to power in 1930 had modified the nature of the polity, and the economic policies followed by the agrarian elite after it regained control of the state had led to significant changes. But it was the authoritarian regime established in 1943, and its successor constitutional administration headed by Perón, that reoriented the economy inward and the state downward, that is, in a corporatist direction. These transformations led Argentina to switch developmental tracks and veer toward the Latin American type of society.

For the first time in its history, Argentina's polity in 1943–1946 fit the authoritarian model fully.[32] As in 1930, participation through elections and representative bodies was interrupted, but civil and political liberties were severely restricted as well. The dominant faction in the military was a coalition of new industrialists, right-wing nationalists, and fascists. The policies of the regime went beyond cultural fundamentalism and political exclusion. It banned all political parties, severely restricted freedom of the press, and harassed or persecuted leftist and pro-Allied organizations. It also initiated lasting changes in the economy and the society. The regime extended protection and credits to new industries and granted wage increases and favorable legislation to the working class. Perón, the labor secretary, mounted a massive organizational drive and established a system of labor organization and collective bargaining under government control. At the same time, leftists and other uncooperative unionists were repressed, and benefits, of course, were contingent on support for the regime.[33]

The initial social base of Peronism comprised not only the new urban sectors, but also segments of the old working and rural classes. Perón's central goal was to mobilize, from above, the working class and the bourgeoisie. This distinguished Peronism from European fascism, whose social base was the petty bourgeoisie and whose enemy was the labor movement, and also from the other instances of Latin American populism, whose blue-collar component was usually weaker.

Cleavage lines were clear: labor and the new bourgeoisie were Perón's initial social base, along with the armed forces, the church hierarchy, and the antiliberal right; against the regime were most of the agrarian upper class and the older bourgeoisie, and most of the middle classes, together with liberal and leftist parties and organizations.

The economic policies of the regime corresponded to this cleavage. Perón transferred surpluses from agriculture to manufacturing by nationalizing exports and controlling domestic terms of trade. He also nationalized railroads and utilities and further improved the working class's standard of living through protective legislation and wage increases. Agriculture was reoriented toward the domestic market; noncompetitive manufacturing was not only preserved, but expanded. The regime's central goal was employment; thus the long-term viability of industries geared toward captive markets and kept alive by impregnable tariff barriers was not a consideration. However, these policies had limits. There were no significant expropriations of land or industrial capital, and Perón shifted to a more moderate course when it became clear, after a few years, that his antiagrarian policies were leading to a reduction of output and exports.[34]

The failure of Peronism was the consequence of what I have called the intrinsic weakness of state corporatism.[35] It can be more properly considered its contradiction. In order to control them, Perón had to organize the new bourgeoisie and the working class. His expectation was, of course, that the new organizations would be a transmission belt for state power. But such a plan, to be workable, would have required continuous redistribution, that is, the steady transfer of surplus to these urban sectors. When stagnating tendencies appeared toward the end of the 1940s, the conflict between the powerful labor movement and the weak bourgeoisie surfaced; the latter distanced itself and finally left the coalition. Perón attempted to divert attention by provoking a conflict with the Catholic Church over the issues of divorce and the disestablishment of religion, but this maneuver expanded and strengthened agrarian and middle-class opposition to his rule. Eventually, he was overthrown by a military coup with substantial civilian support.

Workers accepted corporatist controls for as long as their incomes increased but became an autonomous political force after redistribution stopped. Thus, following the failure of the corporatist attempt, labor became a much stronger power contender than it would have been without initial state-sponsored and controlled organization.

How Argentina Became an Ungovernable Society

Conflict in the four decades following the Peronist regime was largely a contest for the distribution of surplus, the main players being labor, industrialists, agrarians, and the armed forces. The labor movement's power was a function of the trait that distinguished Argentina, up to the recent past, from the Latin American modal pattern: the absence of a large labor reserve. In countries such as Mexico or Brazil, corporatist-populist regimes did not have similar political consequences. There, import substitution has been as inefficient a lever for self-sustained economic growth as in Argentina, but its institutionalization did not produce a social stalemate. One central reason for this was a rural and urban labor reserve, which prevented the working class from becoming a central political actor.

In Argentina, no social force could replace the agrarian upper class as the hegemonic group. With strong interest organizations contending in an unstable and sluggish economy, the polity became highly polarized, the perfect embodiment of Samuel P. Huntington's praetorian society.[36] The prevailing interpretation of the post-Peronist period has seen political instability as the consequence of stalemate among the different social and political forces. Since no contender, or coalition of contenders, could accumulate enough power to overcome and dominate the others, illegitimacy and polarization resulted.

Agrarian interests and the fraction of the industrial bourgeoisie linked to them (such as international capital and the domestic capital less dependent on protection) made up one coalition. The opposing coalition consisted of the bulk of the domestic bourgeoisie—particularly its weaker segment, which was highly dependent on tariffs—and the labor movement. Besides this major line of cleavage, there were secondary conflicts within each bloc; there was also a latent cleavage between labor and the bourgeoisie as a whole. The interrelationship among the groups, interacting with the political parties representing some of them, was thus very complex: different alliances, with varying degrees of mobilization among their constituent members, were formed in particular circumstances or in relation to specific issues. The state, and especially the armed forces, intervened as a moderator or arbiter of the conflict, or as the political representative of the proagrarian coalition.

In this conflict, success could only be limited and temporary, and it was reversed quickly. Whenever one of the coalitions prevailed and seized control of the government, it carried out policies that protected or advanced the interests of its members. But it could not drastically alter the power position of the opposing bloc. Applying government programs led to economic or political outcomes that triggered mobilization of the other coalition, which eventually accumulated enough power to block policy implementation, force a retreat, or even capture the government.

Economic policies thus protected the basic or immediate interests of the two blocs in sequence, wavering, as Marcelo Diamand put it, like a pendulum between two poles: conservative or—in Argentine vocabulary—"liberal" policies (such as floating currency, incentives to agriculture, lower tariffs, wage controls, and reduced government spending) and "populist" policies (exchange controls, lower prices for agricultural commodities, higher tariffs and other incentives for manufacturing, higher wages, and increased government spending).

The pendulum's range of oscillation was determined by the power of the social forces. The barriers to conservative measures were mainly political. Mobilization of the labor movement, segments of the middle classes, and those of the bourgeoisie hurt by these policies raised the specter of popular revolt. In such a situation, the big bourgeoisie and the agrarians yielded power. The obstacles to populist strategies, on the other hand, were mainly economic. Their implementation led to disinvestment in agriculture, declines in agrarian output, and crises in the balance of payments. When that happened, labor and the less competitive segments of the bourgeoisie were paralyzed by the inefficacy of their program, and a segment of the middle class usually moved to the right, thus supporting the reinstatement of conservative policies, often as a consequence of military intervention and the establishment of an authoritarian regime.

I have argued that the cause of the peculiar economic and political dynamics in this period lies in the institutionalization of the industrial and labor policies followed by the Peronist regime in the postwar years.[37] The stalemate was the consequence of radical protectionism for manufacturing and a corporatist strategy toward labor. Their effects on the social structure were similar and cumulative: economic growth and legitimacy in the short run, a sluggish economy and political illegitimacy in the long run.

The internationally efficient agrarian sector coexisted with a manufacturing sector tied to a captive market and operating behind effective protection barriers that were among the highest in the world. Richard D. Mallon and Juan V. Sorrouille have aptly characterized this situation as a new form of dualism.[38] As in the old form, though, the connections between the sectors are more important than the differences; the survival of manufacturing depended on the surplus generated by agriculture. Manufacturers could import machinery and other necessary inputs only with the foreign exchange generated by the agrarian economy. This was the root of the stalemate described above: the conflict between the two sectors was coupled with a unilateral dependency of manufacturing on agriculture. Agrarians and their allies retained a veto power despite the fact that the majority of the country's capital and nonservice labor force was committed to manufacturing, and that foreign investment and the growth of finance capital in the decades following the 1960s increased the weight of the nonagrarian sector of the economic elite.

The economic consequences of hothouse capitalism are well known: high rates of growth until the captive market is saturated, and sluggishness thereafter. The size of the internal market limited the possibility of "deepening" industrialization, and the large-scale export of manufactured goods was not possible without subsidies. The political effects of radical protectionism have also varied with time. In the short run, expanding employment and income produced a satisfied working class, which consented to the state's control of the labor movement. In the long run, the working class generated by this type of industrialization became the foremost delegitimating force. Large-scale industrialization in an economy averse to adopting technological innovation and in a society then without a large labor reserve generated a highly mobilized and organized labor movement. The demands made by labor and by other social forces, including the large middle class, led at times to situations that contenders perceived as a zero-sum game. This was not necessarily due to actual stagnation, but to a large gap between the size of the surplus and the combined demands made by the different strata. This situation produced political instability.

Integrating the working class into the political system through a corporatist strategy (i.e., a strategy presupposing both participation and control by the state) had similar political effects: a positive relationship with legitimacy in the short run, and a negative one in the long run. It also had similar economic long-term consequences: it contributed to the low and unstable rate of growth. These results follow from the contradiction of corporatism: Perón's utilization of the working class as a political base required a powerful labor movement, albeit under state control.

Redistribution was a precondition for the stability of the corporatist arrangement. When radical protectionism led to an economic slowdown, and the regime collapsed, the labor movement became an autonomous political force, much more powerful than it would have been without organization from above. Thus, the Argentine crisis is the long-term result of Peronist policies that, on the one hand, allocated economic and human resources inefficiently and, on the other, increased the level of mobilization and organization of the labor movement.

I consider the 1943 coup the first turning point in twentieth-century Argentine history because, thereafter, both radical protectionism and corporatism began to be institutionalized. Despite antecedents for these industrial and labor policies, it is with Peronism that they began to be implemented systematically. In about a decade, they changed Argentina's social structure, economy, and polity.

Post-1943 industrial and labor policies were a sharp departure from the past. Up to that point, the industries Argentina was forced to develop in response to the depression and the war had usually been classified by the government into two categories: "emergency industries" (which would be dismantled when the world economy was reorganized) and "genuine industries" (which were compatible with reintegrating the country into the world economy and would continue being protected).[39] This distinction disappeared with Perón, who granted blanket protection to manufacturing. As for labor policy, inclusion and exclusion were practiced in different mixes until the early 1940s, but it was with the military coup of 1943 that the attempt to incorporate labor on the basis of a state corporatist mechanism became government policy.

It is important to understand the options available to the Argentine elites in the postwar years. The alternative to blanket protectionism would have been selective protection, in a few cases for welfare or defense considerations, but more generally on the basis of the "infant industry" argument. The alternative to state corporatism would have been the resumption of the inclusionary strategies toward the labor movement followed prior to the depression. This latter course would not have led to stalemate, and thus it would have allowed for different long-term economic and political outcomes.

Neither radical protectionism for manufacturing nor a corporatist strategy toward labor was carried out by the state as a response to demands made by the economic elite, for both policies were against elite interests. Agrarians could not support the perpetuation of noncompetitive manufacturing financed by taxes on agricultural exports; the older industrial bourgeoisie, linked to agriculture and foreign capital, could survive without radical protectionism, as it had done in the past. Further, corporatism entailed not only a strong state controlling the society, but also a setting in which the economic interests of the lower classes would loom larger than in the liberal inclusionary and authoritarian exclusionary arrangements the elites were familiar with.

The shift to radical protectionism and state corporatism was not determined by external constraints either. It is true that in the postwar period Europe could not buy Argentine products, and the United States boycotted Argentine trade as a consequence of the country's pro-Axis orientation during the war.[40] In those conditions, a partial closure of the economy may have appeared reasonable. These obstacles, however, were temporary, for by the end of the 1940s the European economies had regained their dynamism, and the U.S. boycott had ended. Resuming the open industrialization model would then have been entirely feasible. As for state corporatism, it is impossible to identify any postwar external economic or political process or constraint of which this form of corporatism in Argentina would have been a direct consequence. In fact, it is difficult to imagine a system of government-labor relations more at variance with the West's ideological climate at that time.

If the new industrial and labor policies were determined neither by the interests of the economic elites nor by external constraints, then their institutionalization was an instance of the state's autonomy. In fact, both radical protectionism and state corporatism were implemented by an administration whose main opponents were precisely the agrarian upper class and the big capitalists.

The economic and social stalemate that led Argentina to switch developmental tracks was the delayed effect of a process of differentiation between the state and the balance of social interests. This process began with the depression and intensified during the war. The depression triggered the period of military rule and restrictive democracy of 1930–1943, but these regimes still corresponded to the interests of the agrarian upper class, whose leaders and representatives remained in control of the state apparatus. The agrarians gradually lost their hegemony as a consequence of the crisis of the export economy brought about by the depression, and of the fact that in the 1930s they ruled by coercion and fraud. The decline of agrarian hegemony, however, was a precondition for state autonomy, not a cause in itself.

In my view, there were two determinants of state autonomy in the early 1940s. First, there were external constraints: British and U.S. pressures in relation to Argentine participation in the war, and military competition with Brazil, Argentina's traditional rival for regional power. Britain favored Argentine neutrality, for this would facilitate continuing trade. The United States pushed Argentina to enter the war and began to treat the country as a quasi-enemy when it refused. Regionally, the balance of power began to shift in Brazil's favor when Brazil joined the war and received large amounts of U.S. economic and military aid.[41]

The second factor was the fragmentation of economic elites. Capitalists were split in the early 1940s by several cleavages, some of which predated the depression but were intensified by it. Others emerged as a consequence of changes associated with the depression and the war: cattle breeders versus fatteners within the agrarian elite;[42] agrarians versus industrialists; the agrarian and the "older" bourgeoisie alliance versus the new manufacturing class generated by import substitution; pro-Allied versus neutralist factions. Factionalism, coupled with the decline of hegemony that had followed the depression, rendered the elite ineffective. It was at this point that the military captured the state and began implementing policies that were at variance with the interests of the dominant sectors.

State autonomy, however, does not determine the content of state policies: the fateful choice of radical protectionism and corporatism by the group controlling the state after 1943 does not follow from the state's relative independence from the dominant class. These industrial and labor policies were consistent with the right-wing nationalist and fascist ideologies then in circulation, but a regression from Peronist doctrines to nationalist or fascist ideology is not a satisfactory explanation.[43] The problem is to understand why all these related ideas were influential, why radical protectionism and corporatism made sense to the sectors of the state elite supporting Perón. A key to this question can be found in the response of different segments of the established elites to Peronism. The election of 1946, which brought Perón to power as a constitutional president, was a crucial juncture: Perón was supported by the military, the church hierarchy (to the dismay of liberal Catholics), and what could be called the "new right" (antiliberal conservatives and right-wing nationalists). He was opposed by the established economic elites, agrarian and industrial, and by most conservatives. The sector supporting Perón was obsessed by the fear of communism and revolution, and he focused on this issue in his discourse to the elites from the 1943 coup onward.

Perón was a Marxist in reverse, in the sense that he was a passionate anticommunist who nevertheless accepted the validity of basic Marxist propositions, for example, that the working class is intrinsically a revolutionary actor, and that the central content of our epoch is the spread of the revolutionary wave that began in Russia. More specifically, he argued that the immediate danger to Argentina was that the postwar reorganization of the international economy would produce mass unemployment, increasing the revolutionary menace. He proposed as remedies not only authoritarian corporatism, whereby the state would take control of labor, but also radical protectionism, for this was the only means by which mass unemployment could be prevented. Perón argued, then, that dismantling the emergency industries developed during the war, and the possible contraction of other industries as a consequence of reestablishing normal international trade, would produce a political cataclysm in the country.[44] It is irrelevant whether he was sincere when making such a forecast. A competent political entrepreneur, Perón told different audiences what he thought they wanted to hear. Eventually, he was rebuffed by the established economic elites, who considered Perón more a cause of the labor question than a solution to it. The sectors of the state elite accepting Perón's proposals, on the other hand, were guided by ideological considerations rather than by the protection or advancement of their interests, for the instrumental or organizational interests of the military or the church could have been safeguarded under the coalition opposing Perón.

The point here is that the postwar fear of communism was totally unrealistic: the level of class polarization was not very high, and the forecast that it would increase if Argentine manufacturing were reconverted was not reasonable. First, the Communist Party—the only substantial revolutionary organization—was small, and its influence limited by several factors: the repression it had suffered in the previous decades; the cultural cleavage between the party's European organizers and the "new" working class produced by import substitution since the depression (whose members were mostly recent rural migrants of non-European origin); and the wide gyrations of the party line (which, for instance, impelled the Communists to oppose strikes against firms owned by Allied corporations during the war). Second, not only were there no signs of increased radicalization in the labor movement, but the facts point to the growth of moderate and pragmatic trade unionism.

Finally, and most important, the fear of mass unemployment should emergency or "artificial" industries be dismantled after the war was unfounded. According to the best estimates, phasing out the exposed industries would have produced an unemployment rate of 2 percent, which was very manageable. The absolute number of unemployed would have been small (about 80,000) and concentrated in a small geographical area; the government had ample resources for public works or conversion programs, which would have been accepted by large segments of the labor movement.[45]

This inordinate fear of communism was grounded in distorted political knowledge: the sectors of the elite supporting Perón's diagnosis and remedies had an erroneous image of the working class, and they inaccurately understood and derived lessons from the Spanish civil war and Italian fascism, to whose demonstration effects Argentina was uniquely sensitive.

First, these sectors of the elite viewed the working class as intrinsically dangerous. This inaccurate evaluation of the current labor movement was the product of their recollection of experiences the Argentine elite had had with labor during the intense mobilization in the early 1900s and after World War I. That was a different working class and a different elite, but the image of the working class as an inherently menacing actor was ingrained in the right's collective memory and determined by the foreign and diverse origins of most workers.[46] In addition, while it is true that most immigrants' cultural background was close to that of the older Argentines, there were important dissimilarities. Only one-third came from Spain and thus spoke the same language as the Argentines. Moreover, all foreigners (Spaniards included) carried political traditions, experiences, and ideologies that differed from local ones. Nevertheless, the Argentine elite in the early 1900s had dealt with the lower classes pragmatically, and its strategy toward them was mainly inclusionary. It is paradoxical that this image of the dangerous lower classes was activated in the 1940s by bureaucratic elites such as the military, few of whose members were of upper-class origin, and most of whom were the children of immigrants. The large-scale rural-urban migration of the 1930s and 1940s contributed to the reappearance of this image: in the early 1940s, at least a third of the working class were recent immigrants and, as was the case earlier, they were imperfectly integrated into Argentine society.

Second, the sectors of the state elite supporting Perón were strongly affected, as was Argentine society generally, by the demonstration effects emanating from Italy and Spain, the countries from which the large majority of Argentines had emigrated in the previous two generations. The strength of personal and cultural networks tying Argentina with Italy and Spain meant that developments in these countries were lived as domestic ones by the mass of Argentines. The impact of Italian fascism and the Spanish civil war was much wider than in most of Latin America and the United States, where they affected mainly the political and intellectual elites and the relatively smaller immigrant communities. Demonstration effects were facilitated by the perceived generalizability of these examples. The Argentine antiliberal right interpreted the Spanish case as a model of democratic development, as if it showed that democracy and the ascent of labor necessarily lead to chaos and then to communism (a proposition that would be popular for several decades among supporters of military regimes in Latin America). Fascism, on the other hand, was understood as an equitable solution to the unrest brought about by industrialization and liberal democracy.

The Great Depression, the spread of communism, the Spanish civil war, and, later, World War II were interpreted as showing that liberalism—in both its economic and political senses—was no longer a viable institutional framework. Communism and fascism were seen as efficacious alternatives, for both Russia and Italy appeared to have developed stable and legitimate political institutions. For the Argentine counterrevolutionaries, it made sense to think that at least one mechanism of fascism, control of interest groups and arbitration of conflict by the state, was an effective response to the danger of revolution.[47]

The depression was therefore only an indirect determinant of the Argentine decline. In the final analysis, the switch of developmental tracks was the product of the interaction among the depression, the characteristics of the social structure of the country, and political choice. The depression led to the decline of the agrarian upper class's hegemony, to structural changes that resulted in fragmenting the economic elites in general, and ultimately to state autonomy. But it was the very "modernity" of the Argentine social structure, the fact that the country had land and labor endowments that corresponded to the lands of recent settlement, that produced an inordinate fear of revolution among sectors of the state elite and rendered Perón's success possible.

Finally, radical protectionism and corporatism had the consequences they did because Argentina was a "new country" rather than an underdeveloped one. Radical protectionism would have led to stagnation anyway, but the absence of a large labor reserve was a powerful determinant of the failure of state corporatism and of the subsequent economic and social stalemate.

From the Overthrow of Perón to the Reestablishment of Democracy

The overthrow of Perón by a broad military-civilian coalition in 1955 split Argentine society down the middle. In the following decades, the country gradually became ungovernable. The process of delegitimation ended in the 1970s, in large-scale terrorism and repression. Paradoxically, the prospect of chaos brought the different social and political forces to their senses and was eventually conducive to the reestablishment of constitutional rule and eventually of liberal economic institutions.

The coup that overthrew Perón was an attempt to restore the power of the agrarian upper class, but the structural changes that had taken place in the 1940s and 1950s rendered this unworkable. From 1958 to 1966, weak regimes of restrictive democracy tried vainly to govern in the face of continuous opposition by labor (which represented the excluded Peronist movement), and of military intervention whenever social unrest mounted or there was a possibility of reintegrating Peronism into the political system. A military regime came to power in 1966, with the explicit goal of ending the economic and political stalemate. The means to that end would be more orthodox economic policies, and the control of labor mobilization through coercion. The expectation was that resuming sustained economic growth would allow a subsequent "reopening" of the political system.[48]

The new economic policies, and the futile attempt to suppress political activity through banning parties and restricting trade unions, led to an erosion of whatever passive acceptance the regime had in its beginning. The consequence was the eruption of mass mobilization and riots, whose protagonists were labor and the middle classes. Mobilization of these two classes was a function of political exclusion, and of economic dissatisfaction derived from perceiving competition for surplus as a zero-sum game. There was significant economic growth in the 1960s, but the combined demands by intensely mobilized groups could not be satisfied in the context of the economic and social stalemate described above.

Mobilization of the middle classes was still anomic, due to their fragmentation. A crucial segment was the intelligentsia, which constituted the social base of the guerrilla organizations that were forming inside Peronism and the extreme left. The radicalization of part of the intelligentsia, which entailed an ideological shift in this traditionally anti-Peronist group, was not only the consequence of the disappointment with the economic and political performance of post-Peronist Argentina that affected all social strata. It was also due to its size, in the context of an unstable and sluggish economy. A large intelligentsia and social blockage makes up an explosive combination. Argentina had a mass higher-education system, and students expected rates of social mobility comparable to those experienced by their parents and grandparents in the first half of the century. Large segments of the intelligentsia reacted to social frustration in a typical manner, by wishing to change the society through identifying with "the people," that is, the working class, which was the backbone of Peronism.

As a consequence of this shift in a segment of the middle classes, a large left wing appeared in the movement, along with its traditional components, bread-and-butter unionism and centrist and rightist political factions. This heterogeneous coalition resembled original Peronism very little, and Perón's role as absolute leader eroded. Nevertheless, he came to be seen by all social forces, the economic elites and the military included, as the only one who could contain the mobilization of the lower and middle classes, and especially a new phenomenon in Argentine society: the guerrillas.[49]

The military regime recognized its defeat when it called for elections in which all parties could participate. This was tantamount to transferring power to the Peronists. In fact, elites were calling Perón's bluff: for thirty years, he had presented himself to them as the only effective bulwark against revolution. He was not believed in the 1940s, for there was no realistic revolutionary danger. The situation was different in the 1970s, and Perón was finally cast in the role he had defined for himself a generation before.

The Peronist administrations of 1973–1976 were spectacular failures: the old corporatist design was of no use with an autonomous working class and industrial bourgeoisie, and without a surplus available for redistribution. Moreover, Perón had no control over the radical leftists masquerading as Peronists, the guerrilla groups in particular. When he died in 1974, guerrilla action escalated, right-wing terrorism sponsored by the government developed, and praetorian mobilization intensified. The government, led by the ineffectual Isabel Perón and her corrupt circle, was paralyzed. The coup of 1976 was a foregone conclusion.

The military resumed rule as an institution, and political parties and political activity in general were banned. The new regime's central goal was military rather than political: the destruction of the guerrilla organizations and what the armed forces considered to be their social base, that is, the political left and considerable segments of the intelligentsia. Left-wing terrorism had triggered a new phenomenon on the Argentine political scene: state terrorism. Large-scale repression in the late 1970s, in which thousands disappeared, was directed not only against the actual terrorists and guerrillas, but also against left-wing political and trade union activists and a large segment of the intelligentsia. State violence was disproportionate and arbitrary, but guerrilla groups and their surface organizations were wiped out.[50]

Underlying this military conflict, the stalemate between industrial and nonindustrial coalitions was continuing. The coup replaced Isabel Perón's populist government, whose base of support was labor and the industrial bourgeoisie producing for the domestic market, and whose economic policies favored industrial expansion and higher wages, both at the expense of agrarian exporters. The new regime carried out the most systematic offensive against protected manufacturing since the establishment of autarkic capitalism. Overvaluation of the currency and lowering of tariffs led to massive bankruptcies, the fall of real wages, the growth of the informal sector of the economy, and open unemployment. From 1976 to 1981, the size of the industrial working class decreased by 26 percent.[51]

It has been argued that this was a deliberate policy aimed at weakening the social base of the populist coalition.[52] In any case, the combined effects of coercion and the reopening of the Argentine economy undermined the economic and social power of labor and the noncompetitive manufacturers. This does not mean, however, that these policies produced conditions favorable to the resumption of economic growth. First, few Argentine capitalists took advantage of the new conditions in order to develop competitive manufacturing. In a context of high uncertainty about the future of economic policy, and of national politics in general, most reacted to the inflow of imports and the contraction of domestic demand by reducing output or by transferring capital to unproductive activities or to foreign countries. Thus, deindustrialization ensued. Second, the military regime contracted a massive foreign debt, equal to over five years' worth of exports and the third largest in Latin America, which became a brake on the country's development.

Another long-lasting consequence of this regime was the delegitimation of the military, both as a professional organization and as a political actor. This was, paradoxically, a result of using force in both the domestic and the international arenas. Internally, indiscriminate repression of many sectors of the population not involved in terrorism or guerrilla activities undermined the legitimacy of the military as a player in the praetorian game, at least among labor and in the political center. Finally, the defeat in the Malvinas/Falklands War with Britain in 1982 was the most important blow to the legitimacy of the armed forces. It showed both recklessness— provoking a war with a more powerful nation over a minor territorial dispute in order to divert attention from the difficult economic situation and to redeem their image, tarnished by domestic repression—and limited competence (the air force excepted) when confronting professional opponents, rather than civilians and irregulars. The combined economic and political failure of the regime resulted in a collapse of whatever residual consent it had. In the face of the mass mobilization of the middle and lower classes that followed its defeat, the military called elections at the end of 1983. Military dictatorship, revolution, and Peronism had been tried, and all had failed. These experiences produced a new moderation in all political forces. The Radicals, the only mass party with a liberal democratic ideology, were the only possible beneficiaries of this cultural change.

The Second Turning Point:
Democratization and the Demise of Neomercantilism

The reestablishment of constitutional rule in 1983 took place in an inauspicious context: an economy characterized by stagnation, three-digit inflation, and a staggering debt, and a polity shaped by decades of mass praetorianism and authoritarian rule. There were, however, two favorable factors: the sincere commitment by the Alfonsín administration and the Radical Party to institutionalizing liberal democracy, and the shift toward moderation and tolerance that the recent traumatic experiences produced in most interest groups and political parties. But these democratic orientations in the polity and in civil society were so incompatible with the underlying economic and political structure that there was a clear danger that they might weaken as different social groups pursued their interests.[53]

First, mass praetorianism might reassert itself because its determinant, the coexistence of a large noncompetitive manufacturing sector and a society characterized by highly mobilized social forces, was still there. Such a combination could produce only a low-growth economy and a high propensity for social and political conflict. Stagnating tendencies were aggravated by a new factor: the large foreign debt. Instead of the sharp cyclical fluctuations that characterized it in the past, the prospect for the Argentine economy was now a protracted recession, as a large share of export income had to be allocated to debt service. Second, the institutional infrastructure of mass praetorianism and corporatism had not been broken. As long as the military operated as a semi-autonomous segment of the state, and the party system was relatively weak vis-à-vis interest groups, the mechanisms that destroyed elected governments in the past could still be activated.

Consolidating democracy would be facilitated by the resumption of economic growth and would require tearing down the institutional infrastructure of corporatism. These two changes amounted, in short, to the undoing of the wrong choices made in the 1940s. The first presupposed the abandonment of autarkic capitalism, and the most effective and radical way to accomplish this would be the dismantling of the neomercantilist state and the transition to an open-market economy.[54] The second entailed subordinating fully the armed forces to the government, and institutionalizing a party system completely committed to the liberal-democratic rules of the game. At that time, this implied the transformation of Peronism, still an

amorphous and ideologically heterogeneous movement, into a loyal opposition to the Radicals. These were complex processes, and the full realization
of the goal required minimally satisfactory outcomes in all. The three
issues were interrelated, and the results depended on many factors, but in
two instances—the resumption of economic growth and the subordination
of the military to civilian rule—responsibility rested primarily with the
government; the transformation of Peronism depended more on processes
that would take place within that movement.

As far as the first issue is concerned, the economic record of the
Alfonsín administration can only be considered a failure, even within the
Latin American context at that time. The slump that had begun under the
military continued, and toward the end of the 1980s the country's economy
was at the verge of collapse. The growth rate of the GDP was negative in
every year of the Alfonsín government, and at its end, in 1989, the per capita GDP was 10 percent lower than it had been in 1983.[55] Economic policy
was dominated by negotiations over the debt and the implementation of stabilization policies, but the new democratic government did not see the need
or the possibility of undertaking a structural transformation. Some officials
in charge of the economy understood the causes of the situation and its
realistic solutions, but Alfonsín himself and much of his immediate circle
were still wedded to the autarkic policies of the past, and refused to see that
these policies, and the institutions they had generated, were the ultimate
cause of the current catastrophe. The state faced the rigid requirements of a
bloated and deficit-ridden public sector and, in the new democratic climate,
the increasing sectoral claims for public funds. At the same time, there
were two obstacles to the growth of revenue: one was economic, the
shrinkage of the economy; the other was political, the resistance by the citizenry to continue financing the state (only a few tens of thousands of
Argentines paid any income tax).

The way out for the government (and the strategy institutionalized in
the country in the past decades) was an inflationary monetary policy: the
average rate of inflation in 1984–1988 was 344 percent.[56] The situation got
out of control at the end of the Alfonsín administration, when the country
sank into hyperinflation: the inflation rate was 4,924 percent in 1989, and it
was still 1,344 percent in 1990.[57] If "high inflation" could be managed, for
a while, on the basis of indexation and similar mechanisms, four-digit inflation could not. It became impossible to undertake the most basic business
and consumer calculations, and the economy appeared to be at the verge of
outright disintegration. Anxiety reached its climax, and Argentines tried to
control their desperation. Some could not do so, and the isolated instances
of looting of food stores in poor neighborhoods filled people in all social
classes with a mixture of perplexity and foreboding. It was hard for them to
understand the pillaging of food in a country that used to view itself as one

of the best-fed in the world, and many wondered which would be the next step in the descent into the abyss.

The government was more decisive in relation to the second issue, the military front, perhaps because Alfonsín had no choice in dealing with the armed forces: either he moved fast and tried to bring them back to their legal role within the state, or he soon would be at their mercy. Paradoxically, it is in relation to this issue, which was untouchable for two generations, that the constitutional administration had the best chance for success, because of the military's loss of legitimacy. Most leading officers were fired, the military budget was significantly reduced, and many of the agencies controlled by the military were removed from its jurisdiction. But the most important action was the trial of the leaders of the military regime and of various officers who ran the torture and illegal detention centers. Some of the defendants were found guilty of massive violations of human rights, and the two most important leaders were given life sentences. This was the first time since the breakdown of democracy in 1930 that authoritarian rulers had to answer for their actions before a court of law. This was immensely significant for institutionalizing democracy, even though it should be noted that these officers were prosecuted for kidnapping, torture, and murder, and not for having carried out a coup or for having usurped state power.

Initially, the armed forces absorbed this offensive, even though there was a great deal of discontent among them. However, when officers on active duty began to be summoned by the courts, localized rebellions broke out. Parties, labor, and other interest groups immediately mobilized to defend the constitutional order, but the government avoided a confrontation by granting an amnesty to officers who had violated the law while complying with orders, thus effectively blocking prosecution of all but a handful of leaders of the military regime. This policy obtained the support of the most moderate or professional segment of the armed forces, and extremist elements were isolated. However, mutinies still broke out, and the threat of military upheavals did not die out during the Alfonsín administration.

The third issue was the transformation of Peronism into a party committed to the rules of liberal democracy. This did happen, through a complex process of reorganization that took most of the 1980s. Once Perón left the stage, his followers learned the drawback of charisma. The leadership principle on which the movement was based had to be cast aside, and the different factions gradually institutionalized a conventional party organization. In addition, the Peronist mainstream shed its corporatist and antiliberal ideological legacy. The electoral defeat of 1983 reinvigorated the moderate social-democratic or social Christian segments of the movement, and right-wing circles and corporatist sectors linked to labor and the military were marginalized. As for the radical left, it had been destroyed by the military regime, and its surviving elements sensibly oriented themselves toward moderate positions.

This process of institutionalization reflected not only Peronist politicians' interest in the survival of their party, but also the new restraint, in relation to what had been the case in past democratic and semidemocratic experiences, shown by the key segment of Peronism's social base, the labor movement. Economic retrogression and the stabilization policies followed by the Alfonsín administration caused a significant drop in real wages, increasing unemployment, and the growth of the informal sector of the economy. There were important strikes, including several general ones, but on the whole the labor response was not destabilizing. This pragmatism was a consequence of the memory of repression under the military regime but, as we will see, its central cause was the structural weakening of labor after a period of protracted stagnation as well as, of course, the insecurity produced by growing impoverishment and hyperinflation.

The presidential election of 1989, a year in which the economy contracted by 3.2 percent and hyperinflation broke out, was won by the Peronist candidate, Carlos Menem. His presidential campaign was an exercise in populism, in the traditional Peronist mold: his avowed goals were a *salariazo,* slang for a large wage increase (in real terms, one would imagine), and a "productive revolution," that is, more jobs. He carefully avoided providing any details regarding how these goals would be achieved.

Once in power, though, Menem executed the most dramatic turnaround in Argentine politics in this century. He embarked on a policy of orthodox adjustment and gradually moved toward radical economic liberalization. Government firms, including the railroads and the oil monopoly, which were considered by the Peronists and many others as symbols of national sovereignty, were privatized. Much of the economy was deregulated and tariffs were slashed. Since 1991, the money supply has been linked to a currency board, and this mechanism—which would have been anathema to economic nationalists, because it implies no less than the abdication of monetary policy—brought an abrupt end to inflation.

This program amounted to a thorough dismantling of the neomercantilist state that had been instituted by the original Peronism, and consequently to a restructuring of the country's economy and polity. Growth picked up almost immediately, albeit from the low base of the 1980s: from 1990 to 1995, the GDP grew by over 40 percent, and exports increased by over 50 percent. Argentina also strengthened its integration with Brazil and other partners in Mercosur, the Southern Cone common market formed in the 1980s, and the participation of these countries in Argentine exports increased from 16 percent in 1991 to 33 percent in 1996. This has been a reorientation fraught with both opportunities and dangers, for Brazil represents both a huge market for the country's industry and agriculture, and a partner in which there is still considerable resistance to radical economic reform.

The distribution of the benefits of growth, as could be expected, was very uneven. The capitalist revolution split the society down the middle: there were "winners" and "losers" within and between social classes, sectors of the economy, and regions. Large-scale privatization and the opening up of the economy produced high rates of unemployment, this in a country, it should be remembered, whose economy had experienced a labor shortage for most of the period since the organization of the national state. The urban unemployment rate was hovering around the 5 percent figure at the time of the reestablishment of democracy, it increased to 9 percent in 1990, the first year of the Menem administration, and it climbed to about 19 percent in the mid-1990s. As of mid-1998, it was still about 13 percent. In addition, there is considerable underemployment: the estimate is that no less than one-third of the labor force experience employment problems. The economic stagnation, hyperinflation, and stabilization policies of the 1980s also provoked an increase of poverty, which reached its peak in 1989, when 38 percent of the households in Greater Buenos Aires lived under the poverty line. This proportion was reduced by the growth and stability of the 1990s, but at the end of 1996, 20 percent of the households were still in that situation.[58]

The process of subordinating the military to the government continued under Menem, and this is another area in which its success has been remarkable, even though it was attained at the price of compromising the principle of the rule of law. In the beginning of the new administration, there were still mutinies carried out by right-wing factions within the military, but they were forcefully put down, and their chieftains were sent to prison. In 1990, Menem pardoned the leaders of the military regime still in prison, even though he made it clear that this act did not imply an absolution for their crimes. This was part of a bargain: in exchange, the military relinquished their claims to autonomy, and forswore their self-proclaimed role of protectors of the nation and privileged interpreters of its interests. Eventually, the military leadership recognized, albeit less energetically than most Argentines would have wished, the crimes their organization had committed during the "dirty war." There were also drastic organizational changes: The draft, which was the symbolic basis for the military claim to represent the nation, was abolished, and the size and budget of the armed forces were sharply reduced. Military industries and the nuclear program were drastically curtailed, and a classified missile project carried out in cooperation with Arab countries was canceled. In the late 1990s, the military are under total government control, and remain outside politics.

The economic chaos of the late 1980s had been a traumatic experience. Monetary stability generated strong support for the government in all social classes, especially among the workers and the poor, and the overall institutional change turned the strongest segments of the economic elite into Menem's enthusiastic backers. The Peronist coalition consisted now basically of the lower classes and the economic establishment, while the Radicals and other small parties on the center and left represented the middle classes. Emboldened by his victories on the economic and military fronts, Menem pushed for a constitutional reform that would allow for his reelection. The Radicals, diminished by the new relation of forces, went along, but extracted from the government, in return, other constitutional changes that represent a very modest shift toward semipresidentialism: the most important are the institution of the position of the chief of cabinet, an official who is appointed by the president but who could be removed by congress, and the establishment of a Council of the Magistracy for the appointment of judges.

Menem was reelected by a landslide in 1995. The opposition was divided between the Radicals and the Frepaso, a new coalition formed by splinters of the two major parties and small organizations of the left and center. At that point, the Argentine polity seemed to be heading toward a hegemonic party model, along the lines of postwar Japan or, given Peronism's corporatist past, perhaps even postwar Mexico.

However, the relation of forces gradually changed during Menem's second period. Support for the government continued strong among the poor and the unskilled, a behavior that was not only the product of the memory of hyperinflation, but also of the concrete benefits economic stability brought to these groups. Unemployment was a central concern for them, of course, but they still felt that, in any case, a Peronist administration was more likely to defend their interests than one headed by the Radicals or the Frepasists. For the middle classes, on the contrary, the negative aspects of the overall social and political situation and the actual or imputed shortcomings of the government became paramount, as the memory of the economic crisis of the 1980s receded. Widespread poverty, which included the downwardly mobile "new poor," was a legacy of the stagnation of the 1980s, but its persistence could be linked to the Menem administration's fiscal discipline; and the high rate of unemployment appeared clearly to be a consequence of economic liberalization. Public opinion clamored for "active employment policies," with a fervor infrequently seen in mature market economies, whose average voters are more likely to connect government spending with government revenue, and revenue with their own pockets.

Beyond economic issues, the fact that the state was not fulfilling many of its basic functions with a minimum level of competence or even honesty became a central concern, especially among the middle classes. This had been the case for a long time, but the existence of democracy and economic stability allowed this question to move to the center of the political agenda;

thus, law and order issues turned into foci of intense dissatisfaction. There was a long history of judicial ineptitude, partiality, and venality, but now they were the cause of widespread indignation. Police brutality and association with criminals were known for decades, but the knowledge that the police had been involved in high-profile murders and even in mass killings associated with international terrorism shocked Argentine society.[59]

Corruption had been endemic, but allegations of improper or illegal acts involving high government officials and close associates of the president became commonplace during the Menem administration. Moreover, Menem could be depicted as a politician with autocratic tendencies, due to his frequent and questionable use of decree powers, and his proclivity to place the judiciary under his control and attempt to use it in order to protect his associates and punish his enemies. Finally, the constant teachers' strikes placed the severe underfinancing of the educational system at the center of public attention. This was, again, an old problem, and only one of the major deficiencies of Argentine education, but in a context of hurried state retrenchment and acceleration of both upward and downward social mobility, the predicament of education became, together with the growth of unemployment, crucial evidence in support of the arguments made by opponents of radical economic liberalization. Indeed, neoliberalism seemed to tear down community and society.

In 1997, the Radicals and the Frente por un País Solidario (FREPASO) formed a coalition, the Alliance for Work, Education, and Justice. The novelty was the fact that the Alliance, while opposing government policies in the areas invoked in its name, affirmed nevertheless its support for the economic liberalization carried out by the Menem administration. This consensus, surprising because the most important leaders of the two parties had been until the recent past supporters of neomercantilism, returned the party system to the kind of consensus that had existed before the depression: from then on, rotation in power would not imply a change of economic institutions. Important sectors of the economic elites, concerned about corruption and the shortcomings of the judiciary, made it clear that their alignment with Menem was not automatic, and that they shared the programmatic goals of the Alliance. Menem's coalition of the very rich and the poor is, then, under severe strain. The Alliance won the 1997 congressional election by a substantial margin, and surveys indicate that it may very well repeat this performance in the presidential contest of 1999. The transfer of power to the opposition for a second time would mark a further step in the consolidation of Argentine democracy.

The Causes of the Capitalist Revolution

The dismantling of neomercantilism was, as in the case of the first turning point, a revolution from above, an instance of state autonomy. It presup-

Table 2.1   Electoral Results in Argentina Since the Reestablishment of
Democracy

Party/Coalition	National Elections[a]							
	1983	1985	1987	1989	1991	1993	1995	1997
Unión Cívica Radical (Radicals)	52	44	37	32	29	30	17	
Partido Justicialista (Peronist)	40	35	43	47	40	43	50	36
FREPASO							30	
Alianza (Radicals and FREPASO)								46

Sources: For 1983–1993, Rosendo Fraga, *Argentina en las urnas, 1916–1994* (Buenos Aires: Editorial Centro de Estudios para la Nueva Mayoría, 1995). For 1995–1997, *Clarín* (Buenos Aires) and *Latin American Weekly Reports* (London).
Note: a. Presidential elections in 1983, 1989, and 1995; congressional elections in the other years. The table shows percentages obtained by the parties or coalitions getting more than 10 percent of the vote, and their allies.

posed not only the orientation of state leaders toward economic liberalization but also their capacity to produce this massive institutional transformation. For this to happen, the typical collective action problem of a closed economy had to be overcome.

This "problem" is as follows. With reconversion to a more open type of industrialization, capitalists, workers, and the state may prosper in the long run: their revenues (profits, wages, and taxes) could be greater than under hothouse capitalism. However, not all capitalists and workers would survive conversion, and the state would have to face a major social and political crisis. Inevitably, there would be losers in the short run (the least-competitive capitalists and their workers) and uncertainty regarding who they would be, even if the most elaborate industrial policy was applied. Thus, the fall or loss of incomes, for large segments of these groups and also for the state, would be definite and short-term, while the distribution of gains would be uncertain and, in any case, long-term. The result is collective paralysis. This was a central mechanism underlying the apparent inertia of autarkic capitalism once it had become obvious that the regime's costs for most groups far outweighed any benefits it might have had in the beginning.

Radical economic liberalization was an instance of state autonomy because it was not the result of pressures from domestic economic elites, which largely benefited with the old regime or, at least primarily, of external influences. In relation to the latter, international financial institutions had always advocated more orthodox economic policies. Further, international processes, including international demonstration effects, were influential, as I will argue. But the institutional transformation was not the direct or automatic consequence of these factors. Neither was it the necessary effect of the debt crisis: the debt did induce policies aimed at economic stabilization and fiscal responsibility, and it provided incentives for privatization via debt-equity swaps, but it did not determine by itself large-scale privatization, deregulation, and the opening-up of the economy, as shown by the foot-dragging policies of the Alfonsín administration, and even more so by the more radical strategies of the García administration in Peru at the same time. The agent of the transformation was the Argentine state. This said, two questions arise: Why did its leaders want to undertake the capitalist revolution, and why were they able to do so without provoking major economic or political upheavals?

The answer to these questions lies in two factors, one cognitive and the other structural. The cognitive factor was the awareness, among state managers and central segments of the elites in general, of the terminal nature of the crisis of autarkic capitalism. The structural factor was the changes in the balance of forces in Argentine society from the mid-1970s onward.

International demonstration effects—basically the spectacular crisis of communism, the failure of statist development formulae throughout Latin America, the prosperity and political stability of advanced capitalist nations, and the apparent success of economic liberalization in neighboring Chile—were a crucial cognitive-ideological mechanism that influenced both the government and key social groups in both the positive and the negative senses. On the one hand, these demonstration effects induced support for reconversion, or at least neutrality or resignation to it, among economic and political elites, especially among beneficiaries of autarky and statism who appeared to have good chances of surviving liberalization. On the other, they inhibited the action of the groups most oriented toward protection and rents, and of the left. The ideological formulae on whose basis nationalist, populist, and socialist policies were justified suddenly lost value: few would dare to appear as the advocates of failed, nonviable models; and even fewer would want to follow these advocates in any case.

But these international demonstration effects made sense not by reason of their abstract validity as confirmatory evidence for academic propositions, but because of their fit with the Argentine case, as experienced by both political elites and interest group leaders, capitalists and labor included. In this process of reinterpretation, the impact of hyperinflation and the food riots of 1989 were crucial. Gradually, large segments of these elites realized that existing economic institutions, whose most deficient aspect was defined by them more often as statism than as autarky, were just not viable. It was in this ideological context that they understood foreign experiences, most of which took place in structural contexts as different from Argentina as Western Europe and the Soviet Union, as object lessons relevant to the Argentine situation.

However, this exercise in collective reasoning could lead to the autonomization of the state and the switch to economic liberalization policies only because of the changes in the social structure and politics produced by autarkic industrialization itself.

The balance of power that I described in the post-Peronist period gradually changed from the mid-1970s to the early 1990s. In manufacturing, some sectors contracted and others expanded, but industrial capitalists increased their overall level of concentration. The sectors that declined were the ones most affected by foreign competition during the brief opening of the economy in the late 1970s, and the ones most dependent on mass consumption. The segment that strengthened included the one linked to foreign capital, the exporters of processed commodities, and the producers of manufactures with some competitive ability. As for the least-competitive hothouse capitalists, they had been wiped out or drastically enfeebled by the lowering of protection in the 1970s and 1980s, which allowed the entry of cheaper and better Asian and American goods; by the fiscal crisis of the state, which affected their financing and reduced their ability to win government contracts; and by hyperinflation, which affected small and independent firms with special severity. Agrarian exporters, finally, have not only retained but also bolstered their relative power, as a consequence of the introduction of technological innovations and the increase in agrarian productivity.

On the other hand, at the time democracy was reestablished, labor was weaker than in previous constitutional periods, as a consequence of three factors. The first was the reduction in the size of the blue-collar labor force employed by large firms. Contrary to a widespread perception, industrial employment as such did not decline as a consequence of the economic policies of the military regime. From 1973 to 1984, however, the number of employees, both blue- and white-collar, fell by 28 percent in firms with more than five hundred workers, and by 9 percent in those with more than a hundred workers. And surveys of medium-sized and large firms in urban areas show a decrease of 39 percent in the number of production workers between 1975 and 1982. The second factor was the expansion, during the military regime, of the "self-employed" sector of the economy, that is, of the individuals working on their own account in industry and services. In Greater Buenos Aires, this segment of the labor force grew by 25 percent from 1974 to 1980.

Third, labor had been weakened by the growth of poverty, a process I have described above. As for real wages, their trend was predominantly downward in the past two decades. There were substantial oscillations, but at the end of the military regime wages were 24 percent below their pre-coup level; they fell a further 11 percent under Alfonsín, and in the mid-1990s they were about 10 percent lower than in 1989, when Menem came to power.[60] Finally, as I also pointed out above, unemployment increased very substantially as a consequence of privatization and the opening-up of the economy.

The first of these processes, the reduction in the size of the blue-collar labor force employed by big firms, implied not only that unions had a smaller base, but also that the weight of blue-collars within the labor movement decreased (and also that the importance of white-collars and, especially, government employees increased correspondingly). Second, the expansion of the self-employed, many of whom had standards of living not very different from those of the working and lower classes, meant that the proportion of these classes controlled by the unions was smaller than in the past. Finally, the steady increase in the levels of unemployment and underemployment entailed the formation of a substantial labor reserve, a fact that by itself deflected labor militancy. These are the reasons for the fact that, even in the new conditions of democratic politics, labor was less able than in the past to block policies that hurt its basic interests.

This new correlation of forces is what allowed the state elite to carry out the capitalist revolution without unleashing the major social and political conflict that would have been inevitable in previous decades. Moreover, the weakness of the unions, plus the left's ideological disarmament and organizational disintegration, attenuated capitalists' disquiet about labor's capacity to extract surplus in distributional battles, and rendered absurd the fear of revolution that antiliberal segments of the state elites and other right-wing forces had harbored since the depression. If the deactivation of the military and the changes within Peronism are added to this picture, it becomes clear that what I have called the infrastructure of praetorianism and corporatism has been dissolved in Argentina. As we will see, this does not mean that the regime being institutionalized in the country fully fits the liberal democratic model.

Thus, the state was the main agent of the two turning points in Argentine development, and in both cases its autonomy resulted from the domestic balance of power and from international factors, in particular demonstration effects. In the two cases, state elites turned the society toward what they perceived as the dominant trends in the world system. But the characteristic of the domestic balance of power that allowed for state autonomy was different in the two cases: in the 1940s, it was intense elite fragmentation, and in the 1990s a combination of weakening of some sectors and programmatic paralysis and ideological resignation in others.

THEORETICAL ANALYSIS

Two relationships have general validity throughout Argentina's political development: there were (1) positive correlations between a competitive polity and the institutions of a market economy; and (2) a realistic evaluation, by elites in control of the state, of threats to their power, from below and from without.

The first proposition refers, of course, to the actual existence of a market economy, not to the presence of a government committed to the discourse of economic liberalism, as were the military regimes of the 1960s and 1970s when their so-called liberal factions controlled policy, and presided over a semiclosed, overregulated, and statized economy that they were willing to reform in some aspects (e.g., by lowering tariffs), but not to dismantle. The second proposition is linked to the first: the "realism" I am talking about existed in the beginning and at the end of the century, under conditions of pluralistic aggregation and articulation of interests and ideological pluralism, and was absent under the hierarchical, repressive, and praetorian conditions of most of the second half of the century.

I will now situate the Argentine case in relation to the theoretical framework of this project.

Political Culture

The Argentine experience supports hypotheses that link democratic government with two determinants: institutionalization of democratic beliefs and values in the society and, in particular, the depth of the elites' commitment to democratic values. Throughout Argentine history and until the reestablishment of democracy in 1983, acceptance of democratic institutions and practices by the most important social groups has been contingent and partial. Before 1930, the agrarian upper class and its Conservative Party were more committed to the toleration of peaceful opposition than to the extension of participation to non-elites, but they did eventually integrate the middle and lower classes into the political system, as well as transfer power to the Radical Party. Support for democracy in the elites, however, was a function of the fact that they were hegemonic. After 1930, economic elites and their political parties were the social base of restrictive democracy and of authoritarian regimes.

The middle classes and the Radical Party had a stronger commitment to constitutional rule up to World War II, but they participated, in the 1950s and 1960s, in restrictive democratic regimes that excluded labor and the largest political party, the Peronists. Peronism was also partially democratic: it espoused majority rule, but its commitment to the toleration of opposition was not systematic. There was, nevertheless, a difference between the Peronists and the Conservatives or the Radicals: the former never claimed to support, as an ideal, political liberalism, while the latter maintained a theoretical commitment to majority rule, the aspect of democracy they were in fact denying to their opponents.

This tension between theory and practice contributed, after World War II, to the collapse of the Conservative Party, and in the 1970s to the gradual acceptance of the legitimacy of Peronism by the Radicals, who wanted to avoid a similar fate. From the 1950s onward, the experience of economic and political stalemate, with its sequels of stagnation and violence, taught the different social and political forces the virtues of peaceful competition for power. Elites in the post-Peronist period thus replicated the experience of their nineteenth-century predecessors, among whom acceptance of the democratic formula had evolved slowly, as a product of their long, costly, and inconclusive conflict.

Historical Development

Hypotheses in the area of historical development relate democratic government to experience with democratic institutions prior to a country's independence, to the development of political competition prior to the extension of participation, and to the compatibility between democratic institutions and the country's conditions and traditions. Even though the Argentine case does not falsify these relationships, neither the development of democracy in the nineteenth century nor its demise in the twentieth century is entirely consistent with them.

First, Argentina did not have the opportunity to acquire experience with democratic institutions prior to independence, yet stable liberal democracy did develop, albeit after a half-century of internal conflict. Second, political competition began and competitive institutions developed before there was mass political participation, yet there was a correlation between mass participation since the second postwar period and the decline of democracy. This decline was not, however, due to a crisis of participation: the problem was not that new participants overwhelmed the system. Democracy foundered because a segment of the elite in control of the state turned the country's economy inward and its state downward, and changed the social structure in such a way that stable government became impossible.

Third, though it is obvious that the U.S.–style constitution superimposed on nineteenth-century Argentina was not very congruent with the nation's conditions or with its cultural and historical traditions, it worked quite well until the depression. Both classical Peronism and military rule appear a priori as much more compatible with the country's predominant traditions than does liberal democracy: the former because of its personalism, organic definition of the nation, and communitarian conception of economy and polity, and the latter because of its emphasis on hierarchy and intolerance for dissent. Yet these regimes emerged only after at least two generations of stable liberal democracy.

It is tempting to argue that Argentina's "Latin" or "Latin American" identity was latent throughout the constitutional period, but in any case this underlying culture does not seem to have been incompatible with liberal democratic institutions. At any rate, the relationship between institutions and culture is one of reciprocal causation: because institutions establish rules of the game that regulate behavior by establishing incentives and constraints, their stability is likely to alter culture, and render it, in the end, congruent with the institutional structure.

Class Structure

The relationship between the intensity of class polarization and democracy has not been consistent in Argentina: there were periods of relatively intense conflict between workers and capitalists both under liberal democracy (early in the century, before World War I, and in the first postwar period) and under nondemocratic regimes (in the restrictive democracies of the late 1930s, late 1950s, and early 1960s, and in the final stages of the military governments in the post-Peronist period).

Class polarization, however, was never high in absolute terms. Only in the beginning of the century was a large segment of the working class under revolutionary (anarchist) leadership, but the level of unionization was then low, and the predominant orientation among the rank and file was toward individual mobility. The Communist Party was an important force in the late 1930s, but its influence waned as a consequence of repression, state corporatism, cultural changes in the working class, and the incompetence of the party leadership. For the remainder of the century, labor was ideologically moderate and its demands, advanced sometimes in a very militant style, were either the standard economic ones or integration into the political system (in the post-Peronist period). Polarization after the slippage, then, was due more to the unsatisfactory rate of economic growth than to the radicalism of labor.

Argentina has both a substantial indigenous industrial bourgeoisie and a substantial middle class, but there is no positive correlation between the size or power of these classes and the stability of democratic institutions. In the case of the industrial bourgeoisie, the relationship was negative until the reestablishment of democracy. Throughout the twentieth century, there was a large stratum of small manufacturers, but before the depression the only economically and politically significant segment of the bourgeoisie was big business, which was allied to the agrarian upper class (e.g., in industries that were a forward linkage of agriculture), and foreign capital (mostly British and U.S.). After the depression and World War II, the bourgeoisie mushroomed as a consequence first of import substitution and later of radical protectionism. Since the new class of small and medium-sized manufacturers was exclusively oriented toward the internal market, non-competitive internationally, and dependent on the state for financing and tariff protection, it had a sharp conflict of interest with the old bourgeoisie. While the latter opposed Perón in 1946, as did the agrarian upper class, the former became, together with labor, the social base of the new movement. Over time, concentration and centralization of capital differentiated the new class in terms of size, competitiveness, and relation with foreign capital, but there is no evidence of a particular commitment to democracy by any fraction of the bourgeoisie in the post-Peronist period.

However, it is important to note that from the transformation of the Argentine social structure on the basis of radical protectionism and state corporatism until the very recent demise of the neomercantilist state, the bourgeoisie has hardly been autonomous. Most of it was, for all practical purposes, a creature of the state and continuously dependent on state economic and political support. For this reason, the fact that the bourgeoisie has not been inherently prone to democracy does not disprove the Marxist proposition that "bourgeoisie [equals] liberal democracy, except when there is a revolutionary situation." In any case, the general validity of the equation is still dubious. A typology of situations should be developed; the Argentine case points to the need to be especially sensitive to horizontal cleavages within the bourgeoisie, and to vertical coalitions involving segments of the bourgeoisie and labor or other "nonpossessing" classes.

We know that the parties representing the middle classes (mainly the Radicals) supported democracy before Peronism but opted for restrictive regimes in the post-Peronist period. There is, then, no consistent relationship between the middle classes and democracy. Like their counterparts in the cases of fascism in Europe and authoritarianism in Brazil or Chile, the Argentine middle classes supported antiliberal regimes of the right whenever they felt threatened by a mobilized working class.

National Structure

In terms of cultural integration, twentieth-century Argentina could be ranked "medium" or "medium high": its population is more diverse than that of homogeneous and relatively isolated nations, but the cultural differences among the main components have not led to enduring communal cleavages. The majority of the current population of Argentina descends from Italian and Spanish immigrants who arrived there between 1870 and 1930, but the Creole or pre-mass immigration segment is substantial. In the 1960s, Lambert estimated that 86 percent of the population was "white" and the remainder was "Mestizo or Indian,"[61] but there are no detailed analyses of the ethnic composition of the population. Half the immigrants were Italian, one-third were Spanish, and the remainder were mostly from other places in Europe (French, German, East European Jews, etc.) and the Ottoman Empire. Except for these latter groups, differences among the various components were significant but not major: cultural, religious, and linguistic congruity between Italians and Spaniards, and between them and the Native population, was considerable.

Non-whites had been acculturated during three centuries of Spanish rule. Unlike the English, the Spaniards practiced racial inclusion in their colonies. This led to the forced assimilation of Native populations into the dominant culture, widespread intermarriage, and the dampening of Native identities. This process went very far in Argentina, whose Indian population was small, fragmented, and economically and politically less advanced than those of Peru or Mexico. Moreover, nonintegrated communities were decimated in the Indian wars of the nineteenth century.

As a result, ethnic differences did not crystallize into separate identities, there was little segregation along nationality lines among the major groups, and Argentina never developed ethnic politics. The process of cultural integration among the different segments was relatively rapid. Given the size of the groups, however, this was not a process of assimilation into the majority culture, as in the United States, but one of amalgamation and development of a new, common culture, under the impact of interaction among Italians, Spaniards, and Creoles, continuous migration from the interior to the littoral, and the generalization of public elementary education in the early 1900s.

Over the past century, the correlation between variations in the level of cultural integration and the presence or stability of democracy was negative, but this does not mean, of course, that there was a causal link in this direction. Cultural integration was relatively low in the first half of the twentieth century, and this had different consequences for democracy according to whether the economic elite controlled the state, and whether the external environment was threatening and uncertain. Before World War I, in a state controlled by a hegemonic and secure economic elite, the foreign origin of much of the population actually facilitated extending the franchise by diluting its impact; during World War II, under an autonomous state insulated from economic elites and in a context of high uncertainty, the ethnic heterogeneity of the working class, and the networks that still tied much of the Argentine population to Latin Europe, facilitated a distorted image of the working class and demonstration effects not conducive to democracy.

The consolidation of democratic institutions up to the Great Depression and in the present supports the proposition that democracy will be more likely if a civil war or major conflict has been decisively resolved and followed by reconciliation. The establishment of the democratic state was part of a policy of compromise among provincial elites after decades of indecisive conflict. Thereafter, the gap between the littoral and the interior intensified, for the benefits of the export economy, immigration, urbanization, expansion of education, and growth of the state were concentrated in the former region, especially in its core, the city and province of Buenos Aires. By the turn of the century, there was no question that the civil wars had been decisively resolved. Thus, the cleavages between the regions were cumulative, but their impact was controlled initially through federal mechanisms and the norm of rule by agreement, and later through the growth of the national state. Most interior provinces were eliminated as significant power contenders because they were economically subordinate to the littoral.

Although there is a cumulation of class and ethnicity, in the sense that Creoles are overrepresented in the lower classes, this fact did not intensify social conflict in a lasting manner. However, there was an ethnic dimension in the antilabor and anti-Peronist attitude of the middle and upper classes during the large-scale migration of the 1940s and 1950s. Two factors mitigated the salience of ethnic cleavages: (1) the weakness of ethnic identities (and especially the eclipse of the mestizo and Indian ones); and (2) the fact that the correlation between class and ethnicity was specified by region of residence or origin (most poor Creoles lived either in interior provinces, where Creoles were represented in all social classes, or they were migrants into the big littoral cities, in which case their class status was attributed by them and others to their migrant origin rather than to their ethnicity).

State Structure and Strength

Democracy is more likely where state authority is effective, state power is not highly centralized, state control of the economy is limited, and autonomous intermediate groups limit state power.

The authority of the Argentine national state was effectively established in the nineteenth century, and this was without any doubt a precondition for democratization. The level of centralization was medium in the period of constitutional rule prior to the depression. Argentine presidents have had (and this is still the case) more power than their American counterparts: the ability to appoint ministers and other high officials without congressional approval, and considerable decree powers. This was tempered, to some extent, by the federal structure. The executive could still undermine power sharing among regional elites, as the Radicals did when they resorted extensively to the constitutional procedure of federal intervention (by which the central government was empowered to replace provincial authorities in loosely defined critical situations) in order to weaken the Conservatives' power bases. The central state departed quite early from the classical liberal model, in that it controlled public education and also, under the Radicals, began to develop government enterprises (the oil monopoly, in particular).

The level of centralization increased, as could be expected, in the nondemocratic period; this supports the above proposition. Under military rule, and also under Peronism, provincial and local administrations, Congress (when it existed), and the judiciary were, explicitly or in fact, subordinate to the national executive. State control of the economy grew with the anti-depression policies of the 1930s, but it leaped qualitatively after the turning point of 1943 with the new industrial and labor policies. Moreover, the Peronist government nationalized foreign trade, railroads, utilities, and a large share of banking. Eventually, a big and unwieldy public sector came into being. It included steel, military industries, and other activities ranging from meatpacking plants to hotels. In the 1960s and 1970s, many bankrupt firms in all areas were taken over by the state in order to prevent their liquidation and to save jobs (an original "Argentine road to socialism"). This triumphal march of the state over the society in the nondemocratic period is consistent with the propositions under discussion, but it is important to note that the expansion of the state was more a consequence than a cause of the breakdown of liberal democracy.

The Argentine state in the post-Peronist period has been large but weak. It turned autonomous at the end of the 1980s and became the agent of the capitalist revolution, as I have argued above, but this happened in an extreme situation in which the economy seemed to be at the verge of paralysis and signs of social despair could be discerned, a moment in which even the almost sure losers in the institutional transformation could not present alternatives to the Bonapartist solution.

In any case, what democracy does require is a state that may be small but must be strong, a state capable of performing with a minimum level of competence the functions left to it in the liberal model: at the very least, the protection of law and order, defense, the regulation of markets in order to promote competition and prevent monopolies, and the control and partial management of the educational, health, and social security systems. The Argentine state has a very limited capability to perform these basic functions in an adequate manner. In fact, I will argue below that the weakness of the state is precisely the main obstacle to the deepening of the new democracy. However, economic liberalization and the reestablishment of constitutional rule may contribute to enhancing state capacity: the first allows the state to concentrate its resources in the performance of the areas that remain in its purview, and the second presupposes that voters' behavior will be strongly influenced by politicians' accomplishment in these areas. Unfortunately, these incentives are likely to result in a selective enhancement of effectiveness: organized interest groups and voters in general are more likely to focus on macroeconomic management (growth, inflation, and unemployment) and on physical security (law and order) than on education, health, or welfare.[62]

Historical experience in the past two centuries confirms Tocqueville's proposition that a strong civil society is a necessary condition for a stable democracy. A civil society, that is, the network of private associations that represent different interests and values, is strong when the network in question is dense, the associations that make it up are autonomous vis-à-vis the state, and they have a high capacity for self-regulation, that is, for the management of intergroup conflict within institutional channels, and with little or no direct intervention by the state. Argentina in the twentieth century had a rich associational life, but the independence and self-regulation capacity of these associational units has been variable.

The power of the state was always restrained to some extent by organizations such as business groups, unions, the Catholic Church, universities, and professional associations. Even under military regimes, there was limited pluralism. The strength and autonomy of these organizations, however, has varied during the nondemocratic period that started in 1930. Probably the church has been the most immune to government control. It is, however, a semiestablished institution, anchored in both state and society. (The church is partially financed by the government and, until the early 1960s, the government participated in appointing bishops. This is why, in my analysis, I have included the church hierarchy within the state elite in the 1940s.)

Business organizations have also been autonomous, except for the Peronist period of 1946–1955, in which the government intervened in the manufacturers' association and created another organization under government control. Unions have been subject to positive state control during Peronism, and to negative controls of different types, including intervention, freezing of assets, and imprisonment of leaders and militants, during much of the post-Peronist period. Labor, however, retained a significant degree of autonomy until the 1970s because of a structural factor: in a society without a large labor reserve, unions had effective control of labor markets. In any case, the autonomy of business associations and unions since World War II was limited by governmental control of every aspect of economic activity, and by government participation in collective bargaining. Finally, there has been, since the University Reform movement at the time of World War I, a tradition of autonomy in public universities, but it was severely restricted or canceled under the first Peronist regime and most military governments.

Thus, the autonomy of intermediate groups has been generally lower under nondemocratic regimes, but in any case the consequences for democracy of the activity of large and politically involved intermediate groups have not always been positive. Most of these organizations have backed undemocratic options at different times, and all have been agents of mass praetorian conflict in the post-Peronist period. This includes the labor movement, a powerful contender in the 1960s and 1970s, with all due respect to the thesis advanced by Dietrich Rueschemeyer, Evelyne Stephens, and John Stephens.[63] These two decades, especially the 1970s, marked the lowest point in the self-regulatory capacity of civil society.

In the new democratic situation, civil society is weaker, but also more independent from the state, and more mature (i.e., with a greater capacity for self-regulation) than in previous constitutional or semiconstitutional periods. Its relative weakness is borne out by the fact that capitalists and worker's associations hurt by large-scale economic liberalization have been unable, in most cases, to prevent the massive attack on their interests. On the other hand, representative associations are now much more independent, due to the final demise of corporatism, and to privatization and deregulation. Finally, the relative moderation of social conflict since the reestablishment of democracy is not only a function of these groups' weakness, but also of the traumatic experience of the consequences of mass praetorianism for Argentine society: under the military regime of 1976–1983, not only did the workers experience repression, but the capitalists had to contend with a state that was imperious, arrogant, and even highly irresponsible (as shown by the launching of the Malvinas-Falklands War).

In the second half of the twentieth century, the armed forces have been the key sector of the state apparatus for analyzing the relationship between state and democracy. The hypotheses of this project postulate that democracy is more likely when the military is committed to democratic principles and civilian control, and where it is not dominated by any particular class (a reference, I assume, to economic elites). The Argentine case bears out both propositions, with some qualifications in regard to the latter. The Argentine military was subordinate to constitutional authorities up to the depression and during most of the Peronist regime of 1946–1955 and was the central component of the autonomous state in the authoritarian periods.

In the coup of 1930, the military clearly represented the interests of the dominant classes, and all the subsequent coups except that in 1943 shifted economic policies toward the interests of these classes. However, calling the military an instrument, or representative, of the dominant classes would be a gross simplification, except in the trivial sense that the military always had as its central objective containing revolution, and thus maintaining the status quo. This commitment, after the decline of the hegemony of the agrarian upper class, led the armed forces to develop doctrines that presented them as the central institution of society, not just as the core of the state but also of the nation, and consequently as the privileged definers and guardians of the national interest. This mentality guided the military bureaucracy from the 1940s to the 1990s, regardless of the ideological differences between "liberals" (supporters of a measure of economic laissez faire and of authoritarian rule, the latter because of pragmatic considerations rather than principle) and "nationalists" (committed to economic autarky, and to antiliberal political formulae).

This definition of their role led the armed forces, at different times, to support or to steer the state toward policies that were sometimes at variance with and even contradicted the interests of different segments of the economic elites. In fact, the military has shifted between two poles: the simple role of arbiter, which led to coups whenever elected governments were seen as ineffective or illegitimate (e.g., in 1955 and 1958), and an "activist" posture, in which it sought, beyond replacing a weak government and responding to real or alleged revolutionary threats, to restructure economy and society (in 1966 and 1976).

The counterrevolutionary orientation of the Argentine military is paradoxical for two reasons. First, I have already argued that their panic in the 1940s, which had fateful consequences for Argentine society, was unfounded, and the same was true in the post-Peronist period, until the late 1960s. The revolutionary threat was real enough in the 1970s, but the tradition of military intervention itself was one cause of guerrilla action: the choice of violence by a sector of the radicalized intelligentsia was determined by the system of mass praetorianism, one of whose central players was the military. They were the first ones to show that power grows out of the barrel of a gun. Second, this one time that the threat was realistic, the policy followed by the armed forces (the disproportionate and indiscriminate use of violence) was counterproductive from their point of view, for it led to the decline of their legitimacy, both as professionals and as players of the praetorian game.

Political Structure and Political Leadership

The Argentine case is generally consistent with hypotheses that expect democracy to be more likely where the major parties have been moderate and nonideological, extreme parties are not significant, the ideological and social distance between parties has been limited, and parties have not sponsored or condoned violence or coups.

Argentina has had, throughout the twentieth century, two major parties (Conservative and Radical up to the turning point in the 1940s, Radical and Peronist thereafter) and several smaller ones whose significance was a function of their regional weight, or their ability to enter coalitions with the major parties (Socialist and Progressive Democrat up to the 1940s, and several regionally based conservative or populist parties, the left-wing Intransigent, and small parties on the center and left in the post-Peronist period).[64] The recently formed FREPASO coalition has the potential to become a major party, the first such case after the reestablishment of democracy.

In the second half of the century, there have been major changes in the parties' ideology and levels of commitment to democracy. From the 1940s to the 1960s, the lines were clear. The Radicals represented the middle classes, and their ideology was liberal-democratic in politics and diffusely populist, with some nationalist overtones, on economic issues. The Peronists represented a coalition based on labor, small manufacturers, and antiliberal segments of the middle class and the intelligentsia. Their economic ideology was strongly populist and nationalist, and their political ideology combined majority rule with antiliberalism and state corporatism.

The two parties were moderate, but their divergent social bases and significant ideological differences, both aggravated by stagnating tendencies and sharp cyclical fluctuations in the economy, were in themselves factors of instability. Extreme parties were not important, but both Peronists and Radicals were antisystem, the former because of their ideology and the latter because of their willingness to condone restrictive democracy, and even to support military intervention (at least once, when Perón was overthrown in 1955; a courtesy returned by the Peronists in 1966, when they acquiesced to the coup that deposed a Radical president, Illía).

Both parties changed in the 1970s and 1980s, as I have indicated. The saga of Peronism in this period is especially dramatic: the entry into the party of a segment of the leftist intelligentsia and the rise of the left wing, the emergence of guerrillas and their military defeat, the weakening of labor because of repression and deindustrialization (both under the military regime and the reestablished constitutional rule), the leadership crisis after Perón's death, and the disastrous Peronist administration of 1973–1976. Peronism today is a moderate party that has accepted not only liberal democracy but also its old nemesis, economic liberalism (this in spite of a substantial nostalgia for populist and nationalist formulae among its ranks). Its social base retains much if not most of the working class, but Peronism's strongest sources of support are now the poor and the economic elites, a coalition that resembles more the one that backed conservatism before the turning point of the 1940s than the classical Peronist constituency.

Radicalism has also changed, albeit in less striking ways. The legacy of the past three decades rendered the Radicals more democratic, and the experience of governing the country at the time of the collapse of autarkic capitalism turned most of the party away from populist and nationalist economic formulae. In much of the leadership, however, support for economic liberalism is a matter of political expediency, rather than one of principle: it resonates positively with the large segment of the middle classes that have espoused the institutions of the market economy, and it allows the party to contend with the Peronists for the support of economic elites. FREPASO, finally, is based on the center-left segment of the middle classes and the intelligentsia (including sectors that had supported the small leftist parties in the past), but it is also making inroads in a traditional Peronist constituency, labor. FREPASO is strongly committed to liberal democracy, but its defense of economic liberalism is as pragmatic as that of the Radicals, if not more so.

Thus, social and ideological polarization among the parties has weakened, but paradoxically the Peronist leadership appears to stand up for economic liberalism more firmly than does the leadership of the Alliance for Work, Education, and Justice. Conversely, these parties are strong advocates of the strengthening of the rule of law, whereas the Peronists have

shown greater tolerance, during the Menem administration, for corruption
and the political manipulation of the judiciary.

There is a tradition of personalistic leadership in Argentine politics.
Since the organization of the modern state, strong leaders have been central
in the emergence of all the major parties: Julio A. Roca in what became the
Conservative Party, Hipólito Yrigoyen in the Radical Party, and Juan Perón
in Peronism. Personalistic leadership, however, did not become a permanent trait: all the parties eventually routinized their founders' charisma, and
developed as competitive political organizations. These and other leaders
have been, in many situations, very skillful practitioners of coalition, compromise, and the resolution of conflict on the basis of complex strategies.
Often in the twentieth century, leadership was a significant independent
variable in major political processes, but its effect on democracy varied
according to the nature of political institutions.

Before 1930, the Reform of 1912 stands out as an event in which skillful leadership was conducive to democracy. This reform was the product of
interaction between Yrigoyen and his Conservative opponents, especially
Roque Sáenz Peña (the intellectual author of the reform law). After the
breakdown, there were many instances in which leadership made a major
difference, but one that was not conducive to liberal democracy. Perón, for
example, was probably the most capable political leader in the century, as
shown by the disparate political coalition he wove in the 1940s and by his
comeback in the 1970s. But he was a political entrepreneur rather than a
statesman, and the consequences of his leadership exercises were always
destabilizing. In the 1940s, his industrial and labor policies led in the end to
stagnation and illegitimacy; in the 1970s, he condoned guerrilla activities
first and right-wing violence later; when reelected, he presided over a
chaotic administration; finally, his emphasis on the "leadership principle"
plunged his own movement into a major succession crisis after his death.
Toward the end of the century, another Peronist leader, Menem, had a
major impact; he refashioned his party's coalition by introducing the economic elites into it, and presided over a drastic reorganization of economic
institutions. Paradoxically, the effect of this reorganization was to reverse
Perón's autarkic choices and return the country to the pre-Peronist liberal
capitalist path. It follows from the central argument of this chapter that this
reorientation is in itself conducive to the strengthening of democracy, but
Menem has not been, as I have indicated, a firm and consistent advocate of
the rule of law.

International Factors

The Argentine case supports the hypothesis that democracy is more likely if
sources of potential diffusion have had democratic governments. I have discussed the consequences for democracy of international demonstration

effects that were salient at different times: positive influence of English and U.S. examples from the organization of the national state up to the depression, negative influence of Italian fascism and the Spanish civil war in the 1930s and 1940s, and the democratization wave of the 1980s.

In addition, other demonstration effects shaped the behavior of different social forces in the post-Peronist period. The Cuban Revolution had a powerful impact on both the left and the right: the local interpretation of its example led to guerrilla attempts and preemptive coups throughout Latin America, Argentina included. The case of Brazil, Argentina's traditional rival for regional hegemony, was also significant: the Brazilian coup of 1964 and the subsequent industrialization spurt were among the factors that prompted the coup in Argentina in 1966 and inspired the economic policies of the new regime. In the 1970s and 1980s, finally, the experience of the Allende government in Chile, its overthrow by the armed forces, and the apparently successful economic reconversion carried out by the Pinochet regime were also followed closely by Argentine political forces and state elites. In analyzing this experience, the left confirmed its belief that a peaceful revolution was impossible, the military and the right generalized the fact that an actual revolutionary threat could be effectively controlled by large-scale application of force, and a broad spectrum encompassing right and center concluded that only radical economic liberalization could unblock a closed economy and provide the basis for a stable democracy. The relevance of these demonstration effects was a function of three factors: (1) the existence of cultural networks between recipient and sender countries; (2) the degree of applicability of the foreign experiences as defined by locals; and (3) the perceived efficacy of foreign models as positive examples (to be copied) or negative ones (to be avoided).

Propositions that democracy is more likely if the nation has not undergone exogenous subversive activities, and if it has received assistance, in times of stress, from other democratic polities, have little relevance in relation to the Argentine experience up to the reestablishment of constitutional rule: I do not think that the development of guerrilla groups in the 1960s was a result of Soviet or Cuban intervention. Such was the claim made by the military regimes, under the so-called national security doctrine. Argentine guerrillas may have received, in addition to ideological inspiration, some training, arms, and funds from these and other foreign sources, but the emergence and activities of guerrilla organizations can be fully explained on the basis of domestic processes. The Soviet or Cuban governments may have taken some advantage of opportunities to spread their influence, but their participation in producing these opportunities was minor at best.

I am not aware of any specific action by other democratic nations that would have contributed directly to preserving or reestablishing democratic institutions in Argentina before 1983. However, there is no question that the human-rights policy of the Carter administration, as well as similar policies in France, Italy, and other European countries, saved many victims of indiscriminate repression in the late 1970s and was a factor in the international isolation of the military regime. On the other hand, the Argentine left saw U.S. intervention behind the coup of 1930, and behind every coup and military regime in the post-Peronist period. No adequate evidence has been produced, and in any case it is very difficult to support claims of this type. There is no reason to assume that destabilizing these elected regimes was in the United States' interest, but this is not an appropriate answer to these claims. Such an answer takes for granted what should be ascertained empirically, that is, the long-term rationality of U.S. foreign policy.

As with the symmetric allegations about Soviet involvement in the development of guerrillas in the 1960s and early 1970s, it is more productive to ask whether these coups can be fully explained on the basis of domestic factors, and this happens to be the case. This conclusion does not exempt the United States and some European nations from indirect responsibility in two typical situations. The first was the lack of sensitivity to the fact that the application of International Monetary Fund–style austerity plans in the face of balance-of-payment difficulties in Argentina in the post-Peronist period was one cause of labor unrest and the general social polarization that triggered military coups. Usually the Argentine government was fully responsible for its fiscal situation, but the moderation of conditionality terms would have contributed to the alleviation of social tension. Second, the United States supported, with economic assistance and political recognition, military governments once they were in place (in Argentina, I have noted the exception of the military regime in the late 1970s). In these two situations, narrow and even misguided considerations of short-term advantage were at work: concern for the interests of domestic creditors, even at the risk of provoking turmoil in countries of strategic significance for the United States; and the search for stability and for anticommunist allies, which prevented U.S. policymakers from realizing how illusory was the apparent legitimacy of authoritarian regimes, and the extent to which allegations about revolutionary danger could be more a justification for a military takeover than a reality.

Since the reestablishment of democracy, foreign actors have contributed moderately to the stability of the new regime. Creditor countries have extended favorable terms for the refinancing of the foreign debt, and international lending agencies have supported economic liberalization and introduced "good governance" or "second-generation reform" conditionality clauses in financial agreements. And Mercosur, to which the Argentine economy seems to be inexorably bound, has also established a democracy requirement for membership. At this point, therefore, the external environment is conducive to the maintenance of democracy, not only as a source of positive examples but also in terms of its institutional effects.

PROSPECTS

After a decade and a half of liberal democracy, the new regime appears to be consolidated, in terms of the criteria proposed by students of democratization. The Argentine record is stellar with reference to one of these criteria, rotation of power.[65] Radicals won the first presidential election and Peronists the second. Menem won reelection, but Peronism failed to become a hegemonic party and, as of mid-1998, the Alliance coalition appears poised to win the next presidential contest. As for congressional elections, thus far the party in government has won three, and the opposition two. Another criterion is the repudiation, by all the important social and political forces, of nondemocratic outcomes.[66] The state has shed its corporatist apparatus and, in general, the neomercantilist instruments with which it controlled much of economic and social life. The military have been placed under civilian command, and capitalist and trade-union elites' support for existing institutions does not seem to be contingent anymore. Liberal democracy is now "the only game in town."[67]

And yet, the political regime that is being institutionalized departs in important respects from the democratic model. The current Argentine democracy is fragile not because of the weakness of civil society, even though I will argue that this is likely to become a factor, but because of deficiencies of the state, its ineffectiveness being the most obvious. A vigorous democracy presupposes a state capable of performing competently its basic functions, and Argentines are painfully aware that such a state does not exist in a country in which tax evasion is rampant, corrupt judges and criminal policemen are commonplace, and in which public health, education, and welfare are well below the standards one would expect given Argentina's per capita income.

Shortcomings in performance are only the surface of the problem. The manner in which the Argentine state rules differs from the ideal-typical democratic pattern. Guillermo O'Donnell and Carlos Nino have pointed this out. The first of these scholars has shown the "delegative," as opposed to representative, nature of government, and the particularistic strand that runs through the state in Latin American countries, including Argentina,[68] and the second has highlighted the monarchic tendencies of Argentine presidents ("hyper-presidentialism"), as well as the fact that the respect for the rule of law is unstable and conditional.[69]

I have argued that a likely consequence of this situation is an articulation between state and society that also diverges from the pattern characteristic of established democracies.[70] The reason is that a state of this sort is particularly ill-equipped for facing the dualizing consequences of economic liberalization in a way conducive to the strengthening of democracy and the improvement of its quality. Argentina, like other "emerging markets" or societies undergoing simultaneously the "double transition," is institution-alizing liberal democracy in a society that is experiencing intense processes of segmentation. This is a paradoxical experience for a country that was an exception to the "structural dualism" characteristic of most of Latin America. A large proportion of those displaced by privatization, deregula-tion, and the opening-up of the economy is marginalized on a more or less long-term basis. The prospect is the development of cultural mechanisms that will lead to the crystallization of a segmented society. Such a society would be polarized into a "civic" pole, characterized by sturdy associations and a high capacity for self-regulation, that is, a strong civil society; and a "disorganized" or marginalized one, with a low level of autonomous group organization, and a low capacity for sustained mobilization, that is, a weak civil society. The predominant forms of political action would be citizen-ship in the first case, and either apathy, perhaps punctuated by short-lived mobilization, or subordinate participation, in the second.

Democracy facilitates the development of protest groups and move-ments, but its main effect in this regard is likely to be the reinforcement of dualization. A bifacial, Janus-like state may develop in correspondence with a segmented society. Marginalized strata and regions would have lower rates of political participation, and fewer resources that could be con-verted into political influence. For this reason, political parties and govern-ment agencies would be likely to interact with, and engage, the civic seg-ment in terms of the representation game: this pole would be, much more than the marginalized one, a vigorous source of demands and support and thus, in politicians' calculus, the determining factor of electoral outcomes. Democracy would then turn into a game whose strongest and most perma-nent players would be the organizations and groups within the civic pole.

Of course parties and governments would also relate to marginalized strata and regions, and build constituencies among them. These constituen-cies may even jump to the center of the political stage in some situations (especially when they display noninstitutionalized forms of behavior). However, the relationships between them and government and parties are likely to be clientelistic or even, in some cases, state-corporatist (e.g., in connection with the administration of welfare or antipoverty programs), and thus not conducive to the strengthening of civil society. Thus, the over-all outcome may be a state that is liberal-democratic and clientelist-corporatist at the same time.

Dualization tendencies exist also in advanced industrial societies, as a consequence of the spread of new technologies, globalization, and, in most Continental cases (and also in Argentina), the rigidity of labor markets. But the size of the marginalized segment is much larger in Argentina and other relatively industrialized "emerging markets." Moreover, the likelihood of the generation of bifacial states is lesser in established democracies, because they have stronger civil societies, more effective states, and larger resources for social policy, and in most cases lack state-corporatist traditions.

Of course, the institutionalization of this dual state is not ineluctable. A development of this sort would be the spontaneous product of the relationship between state and society, and such an outcome could be altered by agency. The key to the deepening of democracy in Argentina lies in the action of social coalitions and parties committed not only to the strengthening of the rule of law and the consolidation of the market economy, but also to the location of policies oriented toward the reduction of inequality and the strengthening of civil society at the center of the political agenda. This would involve greater spending in health, education, and welfare, and thus more effective taxation, that is, greater extraction of resources from the organized and autonomous groups in the "civic pole." But it would also imply a major effort of institutional design, especially in relation to labor markets, education, and health. In short, the future of democracy is linked to the construction of a welfare state compatible with the requirements of a market economy.

NOTES

1. Most of this section draws from chapters 1 and 3 of Carlos H. Waisman, *Reversal of Development in Argentina* (Princeton: Princeton University Press, 1987). For some historical interpretations of Argentina, see Juan E. Corradi, *The Fitful Republic: Economy, Society, and Politics in Argentina* (Boulder, CO: Westview Press, 1985); Pablo Gerchunoff and Lucas Llach, *El ciclo de la ilusión y el desencanto* (Buenos Aires: Ariel, 1998); David Rock, *Argentina 1516–1982: From Spanish Colonization to the Falklands War* (Berkeley: University of California Press, 1985); and Waisman, *Reversal of Development,* especially chapter 4.

2. For a summary of these arguments, see Waisman, *Reversal of Development,* chapter 2.

3. See Roberto Cortés Conde, *El progreso argentino, 1880–1914* (Buenos Aires: Sudamericana, 1979), chapter 4; Gino Germani, *Política y sociedad en una época de transición* (Buenos Aires: Paidós, 1962), chapter 7; Carl Solberg, *Immigration and Nationalism: Argentina and Chile, 1890–1914* (Austin: University of Texas Press, 1970), chapter 6; and Waisman, *Reversal of Development,* chapter 3.

4. Carlos F. Diaz Alejandro, *Essays on the Economic History of the Argentine Republic* (New Haven: Yale University Press, 1970), p. 1n.

5. W. Arthur Lewis, *Growth and Fluctuations, 1870–1914* (London: George Allen and Unwin, 1978), p. 197.

6. Naciones Unidas, *El Desarrollo económico de la Argentina,* vol. I (Mexico, D.F: Naciones Unidas, 1959), p. 15.

7. Alfred Maizels, *Industrial Growth and World Trade* (Cambridge: Cambridge University Press, 1963).

8. Estimates of the Central Bank of the Argentine Republic, in Diaz Alejandro, *Essays on the Economic History,* p. 406.

9. The secondary sector includes manufacturing, construction, transport, and utilities. Naciones Unidas, *Desarrollo económico,* vol. 1, p. 37.

10. W. S. Wyotinsky and E. S. Wyotinsky, *World Population and Production: Trends and Outlook* (New York: Twentieth Century Fund, 1953), p. 117.

11. Diaz Alejandro, *Essays on the Economic History,* p. 56.

12. Woytinsky and Woytinski, *World Population and Production.*

13. World Bank, *Poverty and Human Development* (New York: Oxford University Press, 1980), pp. 68–69.

14. Charles L. Taylor and Michael C. Hudson, *World Handbook of Political and Social Indicators,* 2d ed. (New Haven: Yale University Press, 1972), pp. 229–231.

15. United Nations, Economic Commission for Latin America, *Statistical Yearbook for Latin America 1984* (Santiago: United Nations, 1985), p. 146; República Argentina, Ministerio de Economía y Obras y Servicios Públicos, *Informe económico, año 1996* (Buenos Aires: Ministerio de Economía y Obras y Servicios Públicos, 1997), p. 157.

16. Tulio Halperin Donghi, "Prólogo," in *Proyecto y construcción de una nación (Argentina, 1846–1880)* (Caracas: Biblioteca Ayacucho,1980), p. xii. See also Natalio R. Botana, *La tradición republicana* (Buenos Aires: Sudamericana, 1984); and Nicolas Shumway, *The Invention of Argentina* (Berkeley: University of California Press, 1991).

17. This term refers to the classic case of England before the Reform Acts of the nineteenth century.

18. Carlos H. Waisman, *Modernization and the Working Class: The Politics of Legitimacy* (Austin: University of Texas Press, 1982), chapters 2 and 5.

19. For general discussions of the state in that period, see Natalio R. Botana, *El orden conservador* (Buenos Aires: Sudamericana, 1977); and two classical works: Jose N. Matienzo, *El gobierno representativo federal en la República Argentina* (Madrid: Editorial América, 1917); and Rodolfo Rivarola, *Del régimen federativo al unitario* (Buenos Aires, n.p., 1908).

20. David Rock, *Politics in Argentina 1890–1930: The Rise and Fall of Radicalism* (Cambridge: Cambridge University Press, 1975), p. 83.

21. See Botana, *El Orden conservador,* pp. 174–189; Dario Cantón, *Elecciones y partidos polítics en la Argentina* (Buenos Aires: Siglo XXI, 1973), chapter 1.

22. Botana, *El Orden conservador,* p. 328. See also Cantón, *Elecciones y partidos,* chapter 2.

23. On the Reform of 1912, see Botana, *El Orden conservador;* Cantón, *Elecciones y partidos;* Rock, *Politics in Argentina;* and Miguel Angel Cárcano, *Sáenz Peña: la Revolución por los comicios* (Buenos Aires: n.p., 1963).

24. See Samuel P. Huntington, *Political Order in Changing Societies* (New Haven: Yale University Press, 1968), chapter 1; Juan J. Linz, *Crisis, Breakdown, and Re-equilibration* (Baltimore: Johns Hopkins University Press, 1978), chapter 2; and Seymour M. Lipset, *Political Man: The Social Bases of Politics* (Garden City: Doubleday, 1960), chapter 3.

25. Peter H. Smith, "The Breakdown of Democracy in Argentina," in Juan J. Linz and Alfred Stepan, eds., *The Breakdown of Democratic Regimes: Latin America* (Baltimore: Johns Hopkins University Press, 1978), pp. 93–94. See also Anne L. Potter, *Political Institutions, Political Decay, and the Argentine Crisis of 1930,* Ph.D. diss., Stanford University, Stanford, CA, 1978.

26. Rock, *Politics in Argentina.*

27. Smith, "The Breakdown of Democracy."

28. Rock, *Politics in Argentina,* chapter 11; Carl E. Solberg, *Oil and Nationalism in Argentina* (Stanford: Stanford University Press, 1979), chapter 5; and Carlos A. Mayo et al., *Diplomacia, política y petróleo en la Argentina* (Buenos Aires: Rincón, 1976).

29. On this period, see Alberto Ciria, *Partidos y poder en la Argentina moderna, 1930–1946* (Buenos Aires: Jorge Alvarez, 1964); and Mark Falcoff and Ronald H. Dolkart, eds., *Prologue to Perón: Argentina in Depression and War, 1930–1943* (Berkeley: University of California Press, 1975).

30. Jacques Blondel, *Comparing Political Systems* (New York: Praeger, 1972), chapter 4. See also the discussion of legitimacy as capital in Waisman, *Modernization and the Working Class,* chapter 2.

31. See Miguel Murmis and Juan Carlos Portantiero, *Estudios sobre los orígenes del Peronismo* (Buenos Aires: Siglo XXI, 1971); Gino Germani, "El surgimiento del Peronismo: El rol de los obreros y de los migrantes internos" and Tulio Halperin Donghi, "Algunas observaciones sobre Germani, el surgimiento del Peronismo, y los migrantes internos," both in Manuel Mora and Araujo and Ignacio Llorente, eds., *El voto Peronista* (Buenos Aires:

Sudamericana, 1980); Hiroschi Matsushita, *Movimiento obrero argentino, 1930–1945* (Buenos Aires: Siglo Veinte, 1983); and David Tamarin, *The Argentine Labor Movement, 1930–1945* (Albuquerque: University of New Mexico Press, 1985).

32. For analyses of this regime, see Ciria, *Partidos y poder;* Enrique Diaz Araujo, *La conspiración del 43* (Buenos Aires: La Bastilla, 1971); Ruth and Leonard Greenup, *Revolution Before Breakfast: Argentina, 1941–1946* (Chapel Hill: University of North Carolina Press, 1947); Robert A. Potash, *The Army and Politics in Argentina, 1928–1945: Yrigoyen to Perón* (Stanford: Stanford University Press, 1969); and Alain Rouquie, *Pouvoir Militaire et société politique en Republique Argentine* (Paris: Presses de la Fondation Nationale des Sciences Politiques, 1978).

33. See Germani, "Surgimiento del Peronismo"; Felix Luna, *El 45: Crónica de un año decisivo* (Buenos Aires: Jorge Alvarez, 1969); Murmis and Portantiero, *Orígenes del Peronismo;* Waisman, *Modernization and the Working Class,* chapter 4.

34. For changes in the social structure in that period, see Susana Torrado, *Estructura social de la Argentina, 1945–1983* (Buenos Aires: Ediciones de la Flor, 1992).

35. Waisman, *Modernization and the Working Class,* pp. 22–23, 65–66; Waisman, *Reversal of Development,* pp. 121–124.

36. Samuel P. Huntington, *Political Order in Changing Societies* (New Haven: Yale University Press, 1968), chapter 1; Torcuato S. Di Tella, "Stalemate or Coexistence in Argentina," in James Petras and Maurice Zeitlin, eds., *Latin America: Reform or Revolution?* (Greenwich, CT: Fawcett, 1968); Guillermo A. O'Donnell, *Modernization and Bureaucratic Authoritarianism: Studies in South American Politics* (Berkeley: University of California, Institute of International Studies, 1973). The relation of forces underlying the conflict has been described by several authors. See Mario Brodersohn, "Conflicto entre los objetivos de política económica de corto plazo de la economía argentina." Occasional papers series (Buenos Aires: Instituto Torcuato Di Tella, 1977); Marcelo Diamand, *Doctrinas económicas, desarrollo, e independencia* (Buenos Aires: Paidós, 1973), "El péndulo argentino: empate politico o fracasos económicos?" Unpublished paper (Buenos Aires: mimeo, 1976); Aldo Ferrer, *Crisis y alternativas de la política económica argentina* (Buenos Aires: Fondo de Cultura Económica, 1980); Gilbert W. Mercx, "Sectoral Clashes and Political Change: The Argentine Experience," *Latin American Research Review* 4 (1969): 89–114; Guillermo A. O'Donnell, "Estado y alianzas en la Argentina, 1956–1976," *Desarrollo económico* 16, no. 64 (1977): 523–554; Lars Schoulz, *The Populist Challenge: Argentine Electoral Behavior in the Postwar Era* (Chapel Hill: University of North Carolina Press, 1983), pp. 85–95; and Gary W. Wynia, *Argentina in the Postwar Era* (Albuquerque: University of New Mexico Press, 1978).

37. Waisman, *Reversal of Development.*

38. Richard D. Mallon and Juan V. Sorrouille, *Economic Policy-Making in a Conflict Society: The Argentine Case* (Cambridge: Harvard University Press, 1975), p. 159. "Dualism," i.e., the existence of sharp social and economic discontinuities within the same society, has long been considered a central trait of most Latin American countries. The term usually refers to the contrast between more prosperous urban areas and more backward rural ones, or to the coexistence between capitalist and precapitalist regions (those whose social structure was based on subsistence agriculture or semifeudal property relations).

39. Javier Villanueva, "Aspectos de la estrategia de industrialización argentina," in Torcuato S. Di Tella and Tulio Halperin Donghi, eds., *Los fragmentos del poder* (Buenos Aires: Jorge Alvarez, 1969), pp. 339–350; and his "Economic Development," in Mark Falcoff and Roland H. Dolkart, eds., *Prologue to Perón: Argentina in Depression and War* (Berkeley: University of California Press, 1975), pp. 72–79; Eduardo F. Jorge, *Industria y concentración económica* (Buenos Aires: Siglo XXI, 1971), pp. 67, 131–132; Waisman, *Reversal of Development,* chapters 5, 6.

40. Jorge Fodor, "Perón's Policies for Agricultural Exports, 1946–1948: Dogmatism or Common Sense?" in David Rock, *ed., Argentina in the Twentieth Century* (Pittsburgh: University of Pittsburgh Press, 1975); Carlos Escudé, *Gran Bretaña, Estados Unidos y la declinación argentina* (Buenos Aires: Editorial de Belgrano, 1983).

41. See Michael J. Francis, *The Limits of Hegemony: United States Relations with Argentina and Chile during World War II* (Notre Dame: University of Notre Dame, 1977); R. A. Humphreys, *Latin America and the Second World War,* vol. 2 (London: Athlone, 1981–1982); and Mario Rapoport, *Gran Bretaña, Estados Unidos y las clases dirigentes argentinas, 1940–1945* (Buenos Aires: Editorial de Belgrano, 1981).

42. There was a conflict for the distribution of gains between these two groups. See Peter H. Smith, *Politics and Beef in Argentina* (New York: Columbia University Press, 1969).

43. On Argentine right-wing nationalism, see Cristian Buchrucker, *Nacionalismo y peronismo* (Buenos Aires: Sudamericana, 1987); Marysa Navarro Gerassi, *Los nacionalistas* (Buenos Aires: Jorge Alvarez, 1969); David Rock, *Authoritarian Argentina: The Nationalist Movement, Its History, and Its Impact* (Berkeley: University of California Press, 1993); and Enrique Zulueta Alvarez, *El nacionalismo argentino,* 2 vols. (Buenos Aires: Editorial La Bastilla, 1975).

44. Waisman, *Reversal of Development,* chapter 6; Perón's speeches 1943–1946 are collected in Juan Perón, *El pueblo quiere saber de qué se trata* (Buenos Aires: n.p., 1944), and *El pueblo ya sabe de qué se trata: Discursos* (Buenos Aires: n.p., n.d.).

45. See Banco Central de la República Argentina, Departmento de Investigaciones Económicas, *Informe preliminar sobre los efectos que tendría en las actividades industriales internas la libre reanudación de las importaciones* (Buenos Aires: Banco Central de la República Argentina, 1945); Waisman, *Reversal of Development,* chapter 6.

46. The image of the intrinsically dangerous working class recurs in the writings of right-wing nationalists and other antiliberals in the interwar period. For the labor movement in the beginning of the century, see Hobart Spalding, ed., *La clase trabajadora argentina: Documentos para su historia, 1880–1912* (Buenos Aires: Editorial Galerna, 1970); Samuel L. Baily, *Labor, Nationalism, and Politics in Argentina* (New Brunswick, NJ: Rutgers University Press, 1967), chapter 1; Julio Godio, *Historia del movimiento obrero argentino: Inmigrantes, asalariados y lucha de clases, 1880–1910* (Buenos Aires: Editorial Tiempo Contemporáneo, 1973); Rubén Iscaro, *Origen y desarrollo del movimiento sindical argentino* (Buenos Aires: Editorial Anteo, 1958), chapter 5; Alfredo López, *Historia del movimiento social y la clase obrera argentina* (Buenos Aires: Editorial Programa, n.d.), chapters 20–27; Sebastián Marotta, *El movimiento sindical argentino,* vol. 2 (Buenos Aires: Ediciones Lacio, 1961); Jacinto Oddone, *Gremialismo proletario argentino* (Buenos Aires: Editorial La Vanguardia, 1949), chapters 16–36; Jose Panettieri, *Los trabajadores* (Buenos Aires: Jorge Alvarez, 1967), chapters 6, 7; and Rubén Rotondaro, *Realidad y cambio en el sindicalismo* (Buenos Aires: Editorial Pleamar, 1971), chapter 2.

On the socialists, see Oddone, *Gremialismo proletario;* Nicolás Repetto, *Mi paso por la política: De Roca a Yrigoyen* (Buenos Aires: Santiago Rveda, 1957); Jose Vazeilles, *Los socialistas* (Buenos Aires: Jorge Alvarez, 1967); and Richard J. Walter, *The Socialist Party of Argentina, 1890–1930* (Austin: University of Texas Press, 1977).

On the anarchists, see Diego Abad de Santillán, *El movimiento anarquista en la Argentina* (Buenos Aires: Argonauta, 1930), and *La FORA: Ideología y trayectoria,* 2d ed. (Buenos Aires: Editorial Proyección, 1971); and Iaacov Oved, *El anarquismo y el movimiento obrero en Argentina* (Mexico: Siglo XXI, 1978).

On labor conflicts after World War I, see Julio Godio, *La semana trágica de enero de 1919* (Buenos Aires: Granica Editor, 1972); Marotta, *El movimiento sindical argentino,* chapter 16; David Rock, "Lucha civil en la Argentina: La semana trágica de enero de 1919," *Desarrollo económico* 42 (1972): 165–215, and *Politics in Argentina,* chapter 7; and Osvaldo Bayer, *La Patagonia rebelde* (Mexico: Editorial Nueva Imagen, 1980).

47. The strength of the Spanish and Italian demonstration effects is obvious in the political writings of the antiliberal right. For a representative example of the impact of fascism on the work of a prominent mainstream intellectual, see Leopoldo Lugones, *El estado equitativo* (Buenos Aires: La Editora Argentina, 1932). See also Carlos Ibarguren, *La historia que he vivido* (Buenos Aires: Editorial Peuser, 1955), and Mario Amadeo, *Ayer, hoy, y mañana* (Buenos Aires: Editorial Gure, 1956). For general discussions, see Ciria, *Partidos y poder;* John J. Kennedy, *Catholicism, Nationalism, and Democracy in Argentina* (Notre Dame, IN: University of Notre Dame Press, 1958); Mark Falcoff, "Argentina," in Mark Falcoff and Frederick B. Pike, eds., *The Spanish Civil War, 1936–1939: American Hemispheric Perspectives* (Lincoln: University of Nebraska Press, 1982); and Waisman, *Reversal of Development,* chapter 7.

48. On this regime, see Guillermo A. O'Donnell, *Bureaucratic Authoritarianism: Argentina 1966–1973 in Comparative Perspective* (Berkeley: University of California Press, 1988); and William C. Smith, *Authoritarianism and the Crisis of the Argentine Political Economy* (Stanford: Stanford University Press, 1989).

49. See Donald C. Hodges, *Argentina, 1943–1976: The National Revolution and*

Resistance (Albuquerque: University of New Mexico Press, 1976); Richard Gillespie, *Soldiers of Perón: Argentina's Montoneros* (New York: Oxford University Press, 1982); Pablo Giussani, *Montoneros: La soberbia armada* (Buenos Aires: Sudamericana-Planeta, 1984); Maria M. Moyano, *Argentina's Last Patrol: Armed Struggle, 1969–1979* (New Haven: Yale University Press, 1995); and María M. Ollier, *La creencia y la pasión* (Buenos Aires: Ariel, 1998).

50. See the report by the official commission of inquiry on the disappearance of persons: Comision Nacional Sobre la Desaparición de Personas, *Nunca más* (Buenos Aires: EUDEBA, 1984). See also Marguerite Fetlowicz, *A Lexicon of Terror: Argentina and the Legacy of Torture* (New York: Oxford University Press, 1998), and Gerardo L. Munck, *Authoritarianism and Democratization: Soldiers and Workers in Argentina, 1976–1983* (University Park: Pennsylvania State University Press, 1998).

51. Adolfo Canitrot, "Teoria y práctica del liberalismo: Política anti-inflacionaria y apertura económica en la Argentina, 1976–1981," *Estudios CEDES* 3, no. 10 (1981); on the economic policies of the regime, see also Gerchunoff and Llach, *El ciclo de la ilusión;* and Alejandro Foxley, *Latin American Experiments in Neoconservative Economics* (Berkeley: University of California Press, 1983). For an overall view of changes in the social structure in the period, see Torrado, *Estructura social.*

52. Canitrot, "Teoria y práctica del liberalismo"; Juan M. Villarreal, "Changes in Argentine Society: The Heritage of the Dictatorship," in Carlos H. Waisman and Mónica Peralta Ramos, eds., *From Military Rule to Liberal Democracy in Argentina* (Boulder, CO: Westview Press, 1987).

53. On the Alfonsín administration, see the essays in Edward C. Epstein, ed., *The New Argentine Democracy* (Westport, CT: Praeger, 1992); and Colin M. Lewis and Nissa Torrents, eds., *Argentina in the Crisis Years, 1983–1990: From Alfonsín to Menem* (London: Institute of Latin American Studies, 1993).

54. The alternative would have been to follow an East Asian strategy: maintain neomercantilism but turn its orientation outward, by maintaining the closure of the internal market and promoting export industries at the same time. It is obvious that such a strategy was beyond the reach of a weak and incompetent state like the Argentine one.

55. Inter American Development Bank, *Economic and Social Progress in Latin America: 1992 Report* (Washington, DC: Inter-American Development Bank, 1992), p. 286.

56. United Nations, Economic Commission for Latin America and the Caribbean, *Preliminary Overview of the Economy of Latin America and the Caribbean 1992* (Santiago: United Nations, 1992), p. 43.

57. Ibid.

58. República Argentina, Ministerio de Economía y Obras y Servicios Públicos, *Informe económico: Año 1996* (Buenos Aires: Ministerio de Economía y Obras y Servicios Públicos, 1997), p. 62. See Laura Golbert and Emilio Tenti Fanfani, *Poverty and Social Structure in Argentina: Outlook for the 1990s* (Notre Dame, IN: Kellogg Institute for International Studies, 1994); and Alberto Minujin et al., *Cuesta abajo, los nuevos pobres: Efectos de la crisis en la sociedad argentina* (Buenos Aires: UNICEF-Losada, 1992).

59. High police officials have been implicated in the "local connection" of the bombings of the Israeli Embassy and of a Jewish community center, which left over a hundred dead and a large number of wounded.

60. República Argentina, Ministerio de Trabajo y Seguridad Social, *Boletín de Estadísticas Laborales* (Buenos Aires: Ministerio de Trabajo y Seguridad Social, 1996), pp. 146–153.

61. Jacques Lambert, *Latin America: Social Structures and Political Institutions* (Berkeley: University of California Press, 1967), p. 29.

62. See Carlos H. Waisman, "Civil Society, State Capacity, and the Conflicting Logics of Economic and Political Change," in Philip Oxhorn and Pamela Starr, eds., *Market or Democracy?* (Boulder, CO: Lynne Rienner Publishers, 1998).

63. Dietrich Rueschemeyer, Evelyne H. Stephens, and John D. Stephens, *Capitalist Development and Democracy* (Chicago: University of Chicago Press, 1992).

64. On conservative parties, see Edward L. Gibson, *Class and Conservative Parties: Argentina in a Comparative Perspective* (Baltimore: Johns Hopkins University Press, 1996).

65. See Samuel P. Huntington, *The Third Wave: Democratization in the Late Twentieth Century* (Norman: University of Oklahoma Press, 1991), pp. 266–267.

66. See Juan J. Linz and Albert Stepan, *Problems of Democratic Transition and Consolidation* (Baltimore: Johns Hopkins University Press, 1996), pp. 5–6.

67. Ibid.

68. Guillermo O'Donnell, "Delegative Democracy," *Journal of Democracy* 5, no. 1 (1994): 56–69, "Illusions About Consolidation," *Journal of Democracy* 7, no. 2 (1996): 34–51, and "Horizontal Accountability in New Democracies," *Journal of Democracy* 9, no. 3 (1998): 112–126.

69. Carlos S. Nino, "Hyper-Presidentialism and Constitutional Reform in Argentina," in Arend Lijphart and Carlos H. Waisman, eds., *Institutional Design in New Democracies* (Boulder, CO: Westview Press, 1996), and *Un país al margen de la ley* (Buenos Aires: Emece, 1992).

70. Waisman, "Civil Society, State Capacity."

BRAZIL

3

BRAZIL:
Inequality Against Democracy

Bolívar Lamounier

Political scientists have repeatedly emphasized the advantages of viewing democracy as a political subsystem rather than as a total pattern of society. The study of democratic breakdowns has given them every reason to insist on that view, since it has shown that in many cases dictatorship could have been avoided through institutional change and conscious political effort. Observing processes of "opening" (*abertura*) or "decompression" in authoritarian regimes has certainly reinforced that preference, not least because the importance of prior institution building came clearly to light during some of these processes. Democracy, then, is a political subsystem, not a total pattern of social organization. But how sharply can we draw the line between the development of political institutions and the substantive democratization of society? How should we approach the fact that enormous tensions develop between these processes, especially when we move from the dilemmas of democratic opening to those of democratic consolidation?

The Brazilian case is certainly worth examining in this connection. Recall that on March 31, 1964, a military coup overthrew President Goulart and inaugurated the longest period of ostensible authoritarian rule in Brazil's history. It was more than two decades later, on January 15, 1985, that the electoral college instituted by the military to ratify their presidential nominations elected Tancredo Neves, a civilian and a moderate oppositionist since 1964, to the presidency of the republic. The Brazilian authoritarian regime was ending by peaceful means. Seven years later, in 1992, Fernando Collor de Mello, elected president in 1989, was impeached on charges of corruption and replaced by Vice President Itamar Franco—again in an orderly way. Yet, after the inauguration of Franco, two-digit inflation persisted, keeping the country under high risk of instability until the remarkable reequilibration achieved with the emergence of Fernando Henrique Cardoso at center stage as finance minister, and then by his election to the presidency in October 1994. Obviously, these are not the kinds of changes that take place in countries without a fair degree of institutional development. Protest and popular resistance played an important role from 1984 until 1992, but with these and subsequent events, there was also an element of flexibility among power-holders and a weight of their own among traditional representative institutions.

Can we then say that the Brazilian political system is fully democratic and fully consolidated? The answer to this question transcends the Brazilian case. It depends on our evaluation of the historical record, but also on our conceptualization of democracy and on our models of consolidation. Our first step here should be an attempt to determine Brazil's position on the scale of democracy employed in this book. Few would have major doubts about Brazil's position; it is clearly not a case of high success or of extreme failure. The optimist would think of Brazil as a "mixed success," noting that we have some democratic tradition, despite many interruptions, and that civilian rule is again in place after twenty years of ostensible military domination. The pessimist will prefer to speak of "partial development," rejecting the view that democracy has been the dominant pattern. Mixed or partial, both will agree that we are a case of unstable democracy, since the democratic system cannot be said to be fully institutionalized in Brazil.

Facing sharp inequality and major social strains, a political system—democratic or authoritarian—can hardly be said to be institutionalized completely. In some cases, democracy succeeds in becoming accepted as the institutional structure under which the promotion of substantive changes should be made. Not every contender accepts democracy as an end in itself, but all or at least the key ones trust that its continuing practice will make substantive improvement in the well-being of the majority of people more feasible at some future date.

Moreover, the distinction between state and democratic institutions properly so called is not as simple as it seems when one is still close to the historical process of state building. Brazilian history can be told as a series of steps toward state formation or toward democracy, depending on one's viewpoint. This has an important bearing on the evaluation of democratic development and seems to demand some conceptual refinement.

FROM GEISEL TO TANCREDO: OPENING THROUGH ELECTIONS

The Brazilian *abertura* begun under General Ernesto Geisel (1974–1979), which lasted through the 1970s into the early 1980s, seems unique by virtue of a third characteristic: it was essentially an opening through elections. It was not the result of sharp mass mobilization and was not precipitated by dramatic or external events, as in Portugal, Greece, and Argentina. In this sense, Brazil must be distinguished even from Spain, if we consider that the death of Franco brought the Spanish political system to an inevitable moment of restructuring. The Brazilian process had no such moment. Here, a gradual accumulation of pressures was channeled through the electoral process. Election results functioned as indicators of the degree to which the authoritarian regime was losing legitimacy and, in turn, helped to aggregate further pressures against it.[1]

Taking the 1964–1984 period as a whole and ignoring for a while certain moments of authoritarian exacerbation, three important democratic formalisms seem to have been at work, channeling the opening process in the direction just described: (1) an element of self-restraint on the part of military institutions; (2) electoral rules and practices kept at an acceptable level of credibility, despite some manipulations; and (3) a clear (and after 1974 virtually unanimous) preference on the part of the opposition to play the electoral game and to avoid violent confrontation. The Brazilian *abertura* has a strong element of deliberate decompression, starting with the Geisel administration. It amounted, from this point of view, to recognition among the regime's power-holders that an indefinite monopoly of power, or control by means of a Mexican-style hegemonic party, would not be viable. The opposition seems on the whole to have evaluated the situation correctly and to have sought to explore the political spaces that appeared at each moment. Its formidable success in the 1974 elections helped it to organize under the label of the Movimento Democrático Brasileiro (MDB) while at the same time establishing bridges among a variety of social movements and associations then increasingly (re)politicizing.

It would be naive to gloss over the tensions inherent in these changes, as if the actors were simply following a previously conceived blueprint. The point is rather that both sides, government and opposition, found enough space to redefine their respective roles through several stages, since each perceived what it stood to gain from the continuity of the process. The opposition was capable of extracting important concessions while at the same time organizing itself as a powerful electoral force. The government also benefited in many ways. Most important, it saw a gradual reduction in the costs of coercion. Decompression helped it to contain the growing autonomy of the repressive apparatus, which had led to violations of human rights and seriously compromised the country's image abroad. In short, the government could capitalize on the political benefits of an atmosphere of progressive "normalcy" as if exchanging losses of legitimacy arising from discontent with its past for gains based on the increasing credibility of its intentions as to the future. Paradoxically, the erosion of authoritarian legiti-

macy since 1974 amounted to a revitalization of governmental authority—
because such authority was thus invested in the role of conductor of the
decompression (later rebaptized normalization and eventually redemocratization).

I have said that the electoral game was the institutional expression of
an implicit negotiation between the parliamentary opposition and the liberal sectors of the military—or of the regime as a whole. Three examples will
make these arguments more concrete. All three refer to the legitimation, in
practice, of a congressional majority that the government would hardly
have been capable of putting together if it had not had semidictatorial powers. The first is the so-called Pacote de Abril (April Package) of 1977.
Using the "revolutionary" powers of Institutional Act 5, President Geisel
decreed several measures designed to preserve a majority for the Aliança
Renovadora Nacional (ARENA, the government party) in the Senate, to
make an opposition victory in the lower chamber unlikely, and to postpone
the return to direct state gubernatorial elections from 1978 to 1982.[2]
Despite the incredibly massive and arbitrary nature of this intervention, the
opposition chose not to reject the electoral process and went confidently to
the polls. In so doing it legitimized the new authoritarian parameters; the
actual election results confirmed ARENA's majority, though by a small
margin. This meant that the government, with an absolute majority in both
houses and controlling all but one of the twenty-three states, kept a complete monopoly of the presidential succession and of the political initiative.
On the other hand, because it had such a monopoly, the government agreed
to relinquish the supraconstitutional powers of Act 5 in December 1978,
and negotiated a fairly comprehensive amnesty law, finally approved the
following August.

The second example is the party reform of 1979, which ended the compulsory two-party structure established by the first "revolutionary" government in 1965. Knowing that the continuity of the electoral disputes within
the two-party framework would inevitably lead to a major defeat, perhaps
forcing the regime to violate its own rules, the government of João Baptista
Figueiredo (1979–1985) resorted to its majority in both houses and
changed the party legislation, precipitating the return to a multiparty system. The ambiguity of the process of democratic opening was again
brought to the surface. On one hand, the procedure was formally impecca-
ble, since the government did have the majority, and the reform was
demanded even by some sectors of the opposition; on the other, the evident
intention was to break up the opposition party, the MDB, in order to keep
the agenda under control for a more extended period of time and to set the
conditions under which the new party structure would be formed.

The third example is the imposition, in November 1981, of a new set of
electoral rules, requiring a straight party vote at all levels (councilman,

mayor, state and federal deputy, governor, and senator). This effectively prohibited any kind of alliance among the opposition parties in the 1982 elections. Care was thus taken to avoid a serious defeat for the government, since that election would affect the composition of the electoral college that would choose the next president in January 1985. Again, though the straight ticket helped the government's party in the overall count, many thought that it would (and certainly did) help the opposition in some key states. Also, despite its manipulative intent, this new set of rules was approved by a congressional majority that had, just a month before, broken up over two bills deemed essential to the government's interests.[3]

Although my focus in this chapter is mainly political and institutional, I must note as well the economic legitimation of the authoritarian governments up to 1984. With the exception of the first three years (1964–1966), the post-1964 governments gave an enormous impetus to modernization and economic growth. The rapid internationalization of the economy and the heavily regressive effect of government policies on income distribution eventually alienated many sectors initially favorable to the authoritarian experiment. However, during most of the post-1964 period, growth rates were high enough to grant the regime an important claim to legitimacy. Under the administration of Emílio Garrastazu Médici (1969–1974), which was the most repressive and culturally stagnant, such rates were extremely high (the Brazilian "economic miracle").

Geisel, chosen for the presidency in 1973, started the decompression project exactly when the international environment began to become severely adverse. However, his economic policies were designed not only to sustain high rates of growth but, through an ambitious strategy of import substitution in basic sectors, to reduce Brazil's external dependency significantly. With the help of hindsight, it is not difficult to question some of these measures, which aggravated Brazil's external debt intolerably. However, this was not an authoritarian government lost in its internal contradictions and without any semblance of a project. On the contrary: in addition to engaging the opposition in gradual political decompression, Geisel's administration was sometimes praised by representatives of the opposition, who perceived his economic policies as nationalistic and anti-recessionist.[4]

The first two years of Figueiredo's administration (1979–1980) can be regarded as a continuation of Geisel's strategy, but 1981 was a clear dividing line. On the economic side, sustaining high rates of growth became clearly impossible after the second oil and interest-rate shocks of 1979. Politically, Figueiredo's unwillingness to support a thorough investigation of a terrorist attempt against a May 1 artistic show in Rio de Janeiro struck a heavy blow to the credibility of the *abertura*. The attempt was seemingly planned by the information and security agencies. The lack of a thorough investigation thus brought to the surface with stunning clarity the suspicion that the whole process was subject to a military veto, regardless of electoral results or of public opinion trends.

The election of 1982 inaugurated a fundamentally different situation. Together, the opposition parties constituted a majority (albeit small) in the lower chamber. Even more important, gaining control of a large number of local governments and of ten of the twenty-three state governments, including São Paulo and Rio de Janeiro, the opposition now had significant bases of power. The only secure institutional instruments of containment at the disposal of the regime were now the Senate and the electoral college, both severely questioned in their legitimacy.[5] This strange "diarchy," pitting the military-bureaucratic system against state governments and a lower chamber enjoying stronger popular legitimacy, was bound to affect the presidential succession, and thereby the fate of the regime. A proposed amendment to the constitution, determining that Figueiredo's successor would be chosen by direct election, set the stage for a major popular campaign led by the opposition parties and supported by the opposition state governors. This was the *diretas já* (direct elections now), marked by a series of impressive popular rallies in early 1984, which not only revealed the further loss of regime legitimacy but also paved the way for a formal dissidence, the Frente Liberal within the government party, the Partido Democrático Social (PDS), the successor of the extinct ARENA. The proposed amendment failed to get the two-thirds majority in the chamber, but after the vote the process of democratic opening was close to irreversible. Combined, the Frente Liberal and the largest of the opposition parties, the Partido do Movimento Democrático Brasileiro (PMDB), established the Democratic Alliance and led Tancredo Neves to victory in the electoral college in January 1985. Tancredo died without taking office and was succeeded in the presidency by José Sarney, a PDS dissident who had been nominated for vice-president.

It can thus be said that the outcome of the opening process became clear only when the parameter that guided it during ten years—an implicit negotiation between the regime and the opposition with the former setting the political agenda—was annulled. Deep recession and the succession crisis combined to make this negotiation virtually impossible after 1982, or rather, to make it possible only insofar as it was embodied in the already existing institutional rules, without further manipulation. The presidency, as an expression of military tutelage over the political system, was forced to stay neutral in the succession struggle.

This rather peculiar process of decompression was made possible because, in the initial stages, the opposition party was fighting for institutional positions almost totally emptied of real power. Up to 1982, the state governments were chosen indirectly, in effect appointed by the federal government. Congress had completely lost its main functions and prerogatives. The docility of the government party (ARENA) and of the (indirectly elected) "bionic" senators, one-third of the upper house, made it hopelessly weak. Hence, the return to civilian rule did not amount to a clear-cut return to a preexisting order. Congress, political parties, the state governments: all of these regained some prestige and strength but did not automatically invest themselves in their traditional roles—first because the traditions themselves were modest, and second because the country had changed immensely under authoritarian rule. To understand how the postauthoritarian regime evolved and the prospects for democratic consolidation in Brazil, one must appreciate these historical traditions and legacies.

INSTITUTIONAL HISTORY: AN OVERVIEW

Our interpretation of the Brazilian *abertura* stressed that the electoral process and conventional representative institutions had preserved their potential as vehicles for an orderly and peaceful transition. This element seems to have been missed by some academic theories and pieces of journalistic analysis that depicted a far more petrified authoritarian regime. Linz, one of the few scholars who did pay attention to this problem, correctly observed that the Brazilian authoritarian rulers would have had a hard time if they had seriously decided to search for an alternative and durable legitimacy formula.[6]

Our reconstruction of Brazilian institutional history starts with a view of the nineteenth-century empire as an extremely difficult and slow process of state building. In fact, that process is best seen as a Hobbesian construction seeking a centralized order, not in the vulgar sense of violent or tyrannical domination, but rather in the terms that certain legal fictions had to be established lest naked force become imperative—which even then might not be available in the requisite amount. Stretching further, the empire can be regarded as a political system that developed in order to build a state, not the other way around.[7]

The concept of representation will help us bring the process of state building into the analysis.[8] In fact, the original or Hobbesian meaning of representation is simply formal authorization: it is the fiction that creates the state as an institution. It is prior to Dahl's legitimate contestation, since it corresponds to establishing the state framework within which contestation may later take place.[9] The democratic components of the concept appear at a more advanced stage. Social conflict and participation demands give rise to the descriptive image of representation, that is, the notion that representative bodies should be like a sample or miniature, reflecting society's diversity. Increasing conflict and cultural strains may at the same time give rise to a demand for symbolic representation, that is, institutions or charismatic leaders embodying a collective self-image of the nation. A fourth concept eventually emerges, focusing on the behavior of representatives. It expresses itself in the demand for faithfulness and relevance, for greater coherence in the party system, greater independence for unions and other associations, and the like. It corresponds, in short, to a more watchful state of public opinion. Let us now see what these ideas of representation look like in historical perspective.[10]

The Empire: Hobbesian State Building

The only Portuguese colony in the New World, Brazil took a political path after independence that was completely different from that followed by her Spanish-speaking neighbors. Independence, obtained in 1822, was already marked by a unique feature: it came without a war against the Portuguese metropolis. A proclamation by the regent prince effected the separation and turned Brazil into an independent monarchy. After some years of instability, the monarchical form of government succeeded in establishing a stable political order and in keeping the integrity of the national territory.

The key factor accounting for stability during most of the nineteenth century was the existence of a cohesive political elite entrusted with the legal control of the country. The political system, considered more broadly, was a coalition of the rural aristocracy with the bureaucratic elite, but at the top these two sectors became strongly integrated. Recruited among landowners, urban merchants, and miners, this political elite was trained in the spirit of Roman law, Portuguese absolutism, and mercantilism.[11] The ideological unity of the elite helped it cope with threats to territorial integrity, despite the centrifugal tendencies inherent in continental size, inadequate means of communication and transportation, the thinness of the economic linkages among provinces and regions, and the absence of a strong sense of national identity. Another important factor, in contrast with the old Spanish colonies, lies in the field of civil-military relations. During the empire, there was no threat to civil hegemony in Brazil. A parliamentary monarchy thus developed. The whole arrangement was elitist, no doubt, but cabinets were elected and governed, liberals and conservatives rotated in office, and representative practices thus developed to some extent.

The "artificial" character of this political system has been frequently pointed out. Constitutional arrangements gave the emperor the so-called moderating power, which placed him above parties and factions, in fact allowing him to make and unmake majorities when he decided to dissolve parliament and call new elections. The two parties hardly differed, it is said, and had no significant roots in society. Elections not only tended to return the same people but were frequently fraudulent. This account is as correct as it is anachronistic; it completely misses the fact that here we are not talking about descriptive representation in a highly differentiated society, but rather about Hobbesian authorization in the course of state building. In order to understand this, we must take a broader look at the function of elections and at the way in which they were regulated up to 1930.[12]

The endless series of electoral reforms and the constant accusations of fraud were primarily a result of the absence of any independent judicial organization to manage elections. The whole process, from voter registration (or rather, recognition) to counting ballots and proclaiming results, was, in one way or another, subject to the interference of those involved and especially of police authorities subject to the provincial governors. To this extent, the importance of elections was indeed reduced. But local councils did affect the choice of state and national deputies. The government was thus constantly concerned with elections at all levels; in fact, it is said that the main function of the provincial governor, under the empire, was to win elections. From our Hobbesian standpoint, it may be deduced that losing them too frequently would force the central government to resort to its *ultima ratio* (i.e., to open intervention).

Not a few observers have gone as far as to say that in Brazil, elections were totally farcical, and that more "authentic" results would have been achieved through a plain recognition of whoever held power in a given region or locality, or, on the other extreme, through complete centralization. The argument seems persuasive simply because it ignores the difficult issues of governability and state building. If recognition in this sense means granting a legal title to rule (as elections do), at that time it would have been tantamount to unleashing an endless series of small civil wars, since in each case public authority would be bestowed on a specifically named individual or faction, to the exclusion of others. The central government would thus be multiplying the conflicts it was seeking to avoid.

It is equally evident that the imperial government did not possess material capabilities to intervene everywhere and "centralize" power, as the recipe goes. Centralization did occur, but in a different sense. The representative mechanism of the empire operated by means of a highly aristocratic two-party system. Rotation between the two was partly a matter of elections, but it also had a lot to do with imperial inducement. The whole point of this courtly and apparently alien system was actually to control the processes of party formation. Monarchical government meant that, contrary to the United States, Brazil did not have the formative impact of presidential elections. Formation through class conflict was out of the question, given the rudimentary state of the productive structure and the low level of social mobilization. But two other alternatives can still be imagined, and the empire carefully controlled both. One was parties of principle, in

Burkean language, that is, parties based on religious or otherwise doctrinal views. Some initiatives of this kind appeared toward the end of the century and were adequately controlled or repressed. The other, certainly more significant, was a gradual evolution from kinship groups (with their private armies) toward nationally organized parties. Something of this sort happened in Uruguay, for example. Brazil's territorial extension made it far less likely, but, in any case, it was prevented exactly by the flexible rotation allowed at the top of the pyramid and managed by the emperor.

The nineteenth-century constitutional monarchy was clearly not a democratic system. Its equilibrium rested largely on the bureaucracy, but this arrangement worked well only as long as it was attractive to a few key actors. When it ceased to be attractive to landowners and slave owners, and when new interests, most notably the military, became more differentiated, it fell without anyone to defend it and without violence.

The First Republic: Hobbes II

When Marshall Deodoro da Fonseca marched before the troops in Rio de Janeiro on November 15, 1889, signaling the change of the regime, military discontent with the monarchy had already reached its peak. During most of the nineteenth century, the military had played virtually no role in Brazilian politics. The Paraguayan war (1865–1870), however, led to the development of a strong professional army. Victorious, the military decided to claim a share in power and greater respect from society. This was also the time when Comtean positivism and republican ideas began to penetrate military circles, starting a long tradition of military politicization.[13]

Another major source of opposition to the political system of the empire was the São Paulo coffee growers. One of the links between the bureaucratic elite and the landowners under the empire was the underlying agreement to preserve slavery. But the coffee plantations of São Paulo, which developed rapidly during the last decades of the century, depended on wage labor, and indeed on the free labor of European migrants. Republican ideas thus became clearly linked to economic modernization. But the republic was, at the beginning, just as bad for the coffee growers, first because an inexperienced military exerted decisive influence and made the system potentially very unstable, and second because the unitary monarchy gave way to a federal system that promoted extreme decentralization. The republican Constitution of 1891, closely inspired by the U.S. model, gave a great deal of autonomy to the states, including extensive fiscal rights. The country thus faced a precocious "ungovernability" syndrome. The weakness of the central government affected the interests of the more dynamic sectors of the economy very adversely, which were exactly those located in São Paulo. For the *paulista* coffee growers, the fiscal and exchange policies were vital.

These elements do not exhaust the picture but go a long way toward explaining the changes that took place in the political system of the First Republic, producing a generalized feeling that the "real" Brazil had little to do with its liberal constitution. First, the political leaders of the two major states, São Paulo and Minas Gerais, decided to establish between themselves the backbone of a functioning polity. A key aspect of the pact was that they would alternate controlling the federal executive. From this vantage point, they went on to develop a new "doctrine," called politics of the governors: they would support whichever oligarchy was dominant in each of the other states, in exchange for support for their arrangement at the federal level. The central government thus refrained from passing judgment on the quality of the political practices of each state.[14] This was the new guise of the Hobbesian construction. Needless to say, it went rather far toward making liberal "formalities" indeed a farce. The legislative and judicial branches were decisively reduced to a secondary role; Congress became increasingly docile and lost its potential as a locus of party formation; and opposition was curbed in most of the states, so much so that statewide single parties became the rule.

The end of slavery and the extension of voting rights to large numbers of town dwellers and rural workers made it imperative for the federal government to be sure it would gain these votes. The governor's role thus became one of disciplining an extended electoral base, which he did by granting extensive extralegal authority to local bosses in exchange for electoral support. This is the root of the phenomenon of *coronelismo,* which did so much to demoralize the electoral process in the eyes of the urban middle class up to 1930 and to generalize the notion that electoral institutions were somehow "alien" to Brazilian soil. Another result of this process of state building was to make the strong relationship between political and private power—the latter based on land ownership—extremely transparent and resistant to change.

In exchange for the votes they garnered, the *coronéis* (backland bosses) received support from the oligarchy in control of the state machinery, thus reproducing further down the scale the arrangement between the states and the federal government. Control of the state machinery thus became rather literally a matter of life and death, since in addition to hiring and firing it could easily arrest or release.

Getúlio Vargas: Hobbes III

It is in many ways astounding that the political system of the First Republic lasted forty-one years. In addition to the modest development of the urban middle strata and to the very incipient advances toward forming an industrial working class, that longevity was facilitated by the hierarchical character of nonurban politics, which was the real center of gravity of the whole construction. The votes of the peasants and other lower strata were controlled by rival factions of *coronéis,* who tended to be unified in a single pyramid because of the single-party structures in the states.

In October 1930, the First Republic was terminated by a revolutionary movement led by Getúlio Vargas, who until then was a rather conventional politician from the southernmost state, Rio Grande do Sul. The Revolution of 1930 cannot be explained by a single set of causes. It was a reflection of regional cleavages as well as of urban middle-class and military discontent. It was made possible by the obsolescence of the political pact between the two major states, Minas Gerais and São Paulo. The rapid development of the latter toward modern capitalist agriculture and even toward industrialization gradually unbalanced the initial arrangements. However, São Paulo was hit hardest by the international crisis of 1929; other important states, Minas Gerais included, thus made a bid for greater power and influence.[15]

The main institutional result of the movement headed by Getúlio Vargas was an irreversible increase in central authority: the federative excesses of the First Republic were curtailed; government intervention in the economy was legitimized to a far greater degree; and, last but not least, important changes in representation concepts and practices were quickly introduced. Descriptive and symbolic meanings of representation finally made headway into the legal and political culture.

Descriptive representation is based on the notion that representative bodies ought somehow to look like a sample of society. It is therefore a demand that the Hobbesian process of formal authorization be enriched, in order to bring the diversity of social cleavages into those bodies. Perhaps we should stress the word *enriched,* since, for the 1930s, it is not always possible to speak of an articulate demand on the part of autonomous and identifiable social groups. A great deal of the legislation adopted must be understood as having a preemptive character (as was clearly the case with corporatism in the field of labor organization). In the electoral field, the introduction of a scheme of proportional representation (through the Electoral Code of 1932) was intimately linked to other changes that together were designed to enhance governmental authority. Indeed, the revolution rapidly moved to lower the voting age to eighteen, to extend the right to vote to women, to introduce the secret ballot, and to create an Electoral Court in charge of the whole process, from voter registration to certifying the victor.

These advances beg the question of how efficacious voting rights could be at that moment. But the point is that the First Republic had seriously degraded parliamentary and electoral institutions. To recover them would, of course, have a democratizing impact in the long run; but there was a pressing problem of reorganizing and reasserting authority in the short run. The revolution, after all, had decisively strengthened the federal executive vis-à-vis states and regions; signs of left/right polarization and especially resistance to a quick return to institutional normalcy were quite visible.

The provisional government was thus obliged to meet, and drew a great deal of legitimacy from meeting, the prior demand for "moralization of electoral practices." What most attracted Assis Brasil (the main author of the Electoral Code of 1932) to proportional representation (PR) was the enhancement he thought it would give to government legitimacy and stability, rather than the faithful representation of social diversity. Because it represented the (electoral) minority, PR strengthened its involvement with the state system and its acceptance of the majority. Also, PR was based on larger geographical divisions (actually, the states), thus making the mandate of elected representatives more independent, in the Burkean sense, instead of the almost imperative mandate that might result from small districts under the direct influence of landowners and local potentates. It should also be noted that Assis Brasil's model prevails even today insofar as the representation of the different states in the federal chamber is concerned. The latter is based on the overrepresentation of the smaller and on the underrepresentation of the very large states (especially São Paulo), thus introducing considerations of federative equilibrium, and not simply of electoral justice, in the composition of the lower chamber. In recent years this has been much criticized, but at the time it was established the logic was clearly the same that underlies Assis Brasil's reference to minority support.

It was also thought that PR on a broad geographical basis would practically force the consolidation of the other elements of the electoral reform, such as the secret ballot and administration of the electoral process by an independent Electoral Court. It is noteworthy that one of the most capable analysts of Brazilian institutional history, Nunes Leal, hardly emphasizes the element of proportionality when he discusses the reform of the early 1930s. The important aspect for him is the advance toward "moralization," that is, the Electoral Court. This is also remarkable in that Nunes Leal was deeply skeptical about the development of representative democracy in Brazil without a major change in the agrarian structure. Even so, he wrote, in 1948,

> Despite the excesses and frauds that may have occurred here and there, most testimonies have been favorable to the electoral laws of the early thirties. The gravest accusations against our system of political representation ended simply as a consequence of the fact that those laws withdrew the prerogative of certifying who was elected from the chambers themselves. The *ins* ended up defeated in some states and a numerous opposition, later reinforced by contestation in the presidential election, found its way even to the Federal Chamber.[16]

One irony of modern Brazil is that these initial and decisive advances toward Dahlsian democratization were in part instrumental to the new Hobbesian/Getúlian thrust.[17] Moreover, they were in part effected under the auspices of protofascist thinking.[18] The forty-one-year experience of the first republican constitution had given rise to a deep strain in political culture: liberal forms had come to be regarded as an alien factor, distorting or corrupting the "true" nature of Brazilian society. There arose a demand for "authentic" representation, for an institutional structure truly adapted to Brazilian reality. For some, this meant an improvement, but for others it meant the suppression of electoral, party, and parliamentary institutions. The Constitutional Congress of 1934 included a section of "corporatist" deputies, an experiment that did not take root and would never be repeated. But corporatist views of representation were widely propagated and became in fact the framework within which so-called social rights were extended to the urban working class.[19] Such views were part and parcel of the Getúlian thrust toward an authoritarian (as distinguished from totalitarian) integration of the political order. Under Getúlio Vargas's guidance, protofascist thinking quickly became antifascist, that is, an edge against the further development of mobilizational fascism. More than that, it became an ideological framework helping him effectively to repress the two extremes, *integralistas* and communists, starting in 1935 and leading to the formal announcement of the dictatorial Estado Novo (1937–1945).

The two pillars of this move toward a far more centralized state structure must be considered, since they embodied the presence, apparently for the first time in Brazilian history, of a comprehensive experiment in symbolic representation. One was the increasingly charismatic nature of the presidential office, with Getúlio Vargas in the role of founding father. At the time, however, this was a limited and cautious change, compared with the more portentous events that would soon take place in Argentina with Perón. In Brazil, the charismatic presidency developed without a confrontation with the system's element of limited pluralism (in Linz's sense): a de facto federation continued to exist, with strongly oligarchical features within each state; the church's traditional legitimacy went on receiving a great deal of deference; and the elite (strange as this may sound) did not give up its reverence for legal culture and for the Brazilian legal tradition.

Another pillar in the emergence of Getúlian representation was the reinforcement, and, indeed, a considered invention of certain symbols of national identity. It is surely possible to assert that at this time we witness the emergence of culture policy, that such policy was closely associated with a process of nation (as opposed to state) building, and finally that both would have long-range effects in crystallizing a whole new notion of representation in Brazilian political culture. This cultural construction vigorously asserted that zero-sum conflict could not reasonably emerge in Brazilian society. This view became truly encompassing and persuasive in part because it was espoused by leading intellectuals and artists, but also because it reflected important historical and social traits. It was, first, a celebration of past success in keeping together such a vast territory, in turn always associated with the notion of unlimited opportunity. Second, it suggested that Brazilian social structure had indeed evolved in the direction of increased equality and mobility, not least in the field of race relations.[20] Third, it was a view of Brazilian politics that effectively retrieved the experience of the early empire, especially conciliation, when elite restraint and skill put an end to regional and factional struggles. But in the 1930s, a subtle turn seems to have occurred: instead of reinforcing its nascent negative image as oligarchical, intra-elite behavior, this cultural construction came to regard political flexibility and realism as an emanation of similar traits in the social system, implying that Brazilian politics at its best would always be flexible. Finally, it was a reassertion, on a grand scale, of the conservative (patriarchal) view of conflict as childish behavior, an image that could only be persuasive in a country that had virtually no experience with principled politics and that felt threatened by its emergence in the guise of communism and mobilizational fascism.

The Failure to Consolidate: 1945–1964

Getúlio Vargas was forced to resign on October 29, 1945. His fall and the subsequent developments had a lot to do with the changed international environment. The defeat of the Axis powers in World War II had discredited the Estado Novo internally and externally, despite the fact that it did not belong to the family of mobilizational fascism. At least at first sight, the democratic "experiment" that followed the fall of the Estado Novo had very favorable conditions to prosper and succeed. The international environment was certainly favorable; the domestic economy was not under unusual strain; the armed forces had developed a high degree of organization and an antipersonalistic outlook as a result of their close attention to the weakness of Italian fascism; and the Getúlian dictatorship had led to the emergence of a vigorous liberal opposition, with outstanding parliamentary leadership: the União Democrática Nacional (UDN). The deepest of all Brazilian evils, in the eyes of Nunes Leal, the sin of *governismo*—pragmatic support for the government of the day by all relevant political forces—seemed to have ended.[21] The transition had once again been peaceful: if the lack of a clear break with the Estado Novo made further democratization more difficult later on, the absence of bloody cleavages could have made it easier.

Why did the democratic system then fail to consolidate itself in the next twenty years? The first difficulty was the important institutional contradiction that had developed after 1930 and as a consequence of the Estado Novo. Authority now seemed to bifurcate between a truly charismatic image of the presidency on one side, and an enormous assertion of the par- liamentary institution—not least because of the formation of the UDN in the struggle against Vargas—on the other. This was not an immediate threat, since Vargas withdrew to a silent role after his downfall, but became extremely serious when he came back, riding the tide of a direct presiden- tial election in 1950. The political system was now torn between an execu- tive with strong Caesarist overtones and a parliamentary center of gravity that pulled toward some sort of congressional or party government. Needless to say, Vargas's second presidency was extremely tense, and the contradiction was aggravated instead of diluted by his suicide in August 1954.[22]

Second, this newly assertive and formally powerful Congress was essentially made up of notables. It understandably had not developed a technical substructure to speak of and was not supported by a modern party system. In order to appreciate this difficulty, it is necessary to recall that the scope of government intervention had been enormously enlarged since 1930. The bureaucracy, traditionally large by virtue of the patrimonial ori- gins of the Brazilian state, had again been expanded and modernized under Vargas. The legislature had constitutional powers but lacked everything else it needed to supervise and check this massive amount of policy- making.[23]

Interpretations of the 1964 breakdown have diverged a great deal. Stating his preference for those that stress the "internal sociopolitical situa- tion" rather than "causes exogenous to the polity," Merquior aptly summa- rizes the former literature:

> Government instability, the disintegration of the party system, virtual paralysis of legislative decision-making, equivocal attitudes on the part of President Goulart, not least with regard to his own succession; the threat of an ill-defined agrarian reform; military concern with government- blessed sergeants' mutinies; and mounting radicalism on both the right and the left . . . all of this compounded by soaring inflation and, of course, by the haunting ghost of the Cuban revolution.[24]

The fate of the party system should be specifically noted. I have suggested that from 1945 onward Brazil had for the first time some basic conditions to develop a competitive party structure. Most observers seem to agree that the start was promising, but that the new party system underwent a sharp deinstitutionalization from the second half of the 1950s up to 1964. Some impute this to sheer erosion, that is, rapid social mobilization in the wake of industrialization and urbanization, decreasing efficacy of traditional con- trol mechanisms of the patron-client type, and so forth. Others place greater emphasis on institutional regulations, especially the electoral system based on PR and the preferential vote (open party lists). The fact, however, is that from Jânio Quadros's presidential resignation (August 1961) to the military takeover (March 1964), the party system was overpowered by the worst of all worlds. It became highly fractionalized and subject to increasing radicalization at the same time that each of the major parties was internally divided; the tide of antiparty populism became truly exponential (the election of Jânio Quadros to the presidency in 1960 being an example); and the party traditionally identified with moderation and equilibrium, the Partido Social Democrático (PSD), became fragmented.[25]

However, we must guard against an overly political interpretation. On a broader canvas, the fragmentation of the party system was itself associated with the overall process of economic and social change. This relationship operated in two ways. On one hand, urbanization and social mobilization eroded traditional attachments and social-control mechanisms. On the other, the lack of substantial advance toward deconcentration (reduction of social inequality) left the parties, individually and as a system, without strong bases of popular support. This was the structural framework within which older ideological and institutional conflicts were acted out, setting the stage for the military takeover. On March 31, 1964, the incumbent president, João Goulart, Getúlio Vargas's political heir, was ousted from office and sent to exile.

Thus, over this period Brazil moved rapidly toward instituting the form of democracy—political contestation and participation—but failed to consolidate democracy by reducing socioeconomic inequality. Unable to channel social conflict toward concrete policies, the party system entered a cycle of deinstitutionalization, rather than of consolidation in the new democratic mold. Had there been substantial advances toward reducing inequality, there might have been major conflict among the parties and along class lines, but not the combination of radicalism and populism that took place in big cities, plus survival or even reassertion of basically clientelistic structures in the less developed areas of the country. The crisis of the party system was thus rather telling and cannot be understood simply in terms of the traditional view of those parties as being premodern, preideological, or otherwise not ripe for serious representative democracy. It was more in the nature of an induced suicide, by means of which the society seems to have expelled an extraneous body: a trend toward seeking stronger political representation in the absence of any substantial deconcentration.

An Overview of the Overview

Brazilian institutional development was, so to speak, preeminently state-centered. It must be understood in terms of the prolonged process of state building and the cautious strategies on which it was based, since a small central elite and state structure were confronted with the challenge of preserving territorial unity in a country of continental dimensions. Today's heavy bureaucratic machinery, the ponderous legalistic ethos (despite the fact that legal norms are frequently bypassed), the continuing weight of clientelism and of conservative interests based on land ownership, not to speak of the increasingly tutelary role of the military since the Estado Novo—all these can be traced to or partly explained by that fundamental thrust of our state formation. These aspects of state building have also been held responsible for what is felt to be an absence of public authority, or a lack of differentiation of the political system vis-à-vis societal structures. This is often phrased as an absence of political institutions properly so called. This chapter has argued, to the contrary, that there has been significant institution building, though not necessarily of a formally democratic character. Certain aspects of the post-1964 regime, relevant for understanding the *abertura*, are clearly related to that prior institutional development.

The literature on the authoritarian experiment rightly stresses that its economic project was one of capitalist modernization and greater integration in the world capitalist system, and further, that this led, from 1967 on, to a strategy of accelerated industrial growth rather than of income redistribution or of reduction of absolute poverty. It is also correctly said that the initial perceptions led policymakers to curb labor unions and "progressive" organizations; and finally, that this overall thrust, combined with the need to repress guerrilla activities, ended up engaging the regime, from 1968 to 1974, in a highly repressive phase, with very high costs in terms of human rights. Yet, two features of the post-1964 regime helped preserve institutional continuity, which in this context meant a chance for a peaceful resumption of democracy. The first was the impersonal concept of government, which materialized in tighter rules to contain politicization among the military, conservation of the presidency as an elective office, at least through an electoral college, and keeping the traditional limit on the presidential term and the norm against reelection.[26]

The second feature was the preservation of the representative system. Needless to say, representation here meant formal authorization, in the Hobbesian sense, but it now took place within institutional parameters that not even the military could afford to ignore or distort completely. Interestingly, the pre-1964 party structure was not immediately suppressed. The decision to terminate the old parties was made only in October 1965, eighteen months after the coup, and was immediately followed by the creation of at least a "provisional" party structure, that is, the two-party system that was to remain until 1979. The military governments obviously manipulated the conditions under which elections were held in the ensuing twenty years but did not try to do away with the electoral mechanism as such or to replace it by a totally different doctrine of representation.

THEORETICAL REVIEW

State building in Brazil left a highly contradictory legacy for contemporary democratic development. As a skillful extension of central regulatory capabilities, it was constantly oriented toward keeping intra-elite conflict at a low level and preventing the eruption of large-scale political violence. But this preemptive pattern of growth undoubtedly made Brazilian society too "backward" from the standpoint of autonomous associational participation. This, in turn, gave the elites and the bureaucracy an excessive latitude to define policy priorities, sustained unjustifiable income differentials, and left the political system constantly exposed to a dangerous legitimacy gap.

Overall Historical Pattern

Brazil was a part of the Portuguese empire from 1500 to 1822. During those three centuries, it was in essence a commercial (as opposed to a settlement) colony, featuring mining and large-scale plantations based on slave labor. Even the colonizers were few, since the Portuguese population was pathetically small compared to the vast world empire it tried to build. These are some of the reasons that the colonial system left neither a powerful central authority nor an integrated national community in its wake.

From a comparative perspective, then, the failure of Brazil's colonial past to provide a democratic tradition, whether imported or indigenous, is not the issue at stake.[27] Rather, the key question concerns the relatively smooth transition to a process of political development that we see as consciously oriented toward long-range goals. Political competition and the appropriate institutions began to develop under the empire, at a time when mass political participation was totally absent. From then on, political changes became comparatively nonviolent, allowing enough room for the contending groups to accommodate their differences afterward. Since the nineteenth century, large-scale violence has been increasingly controlled, and bitter memories have not accumulated, at least not among the political elite.

Robert Dahl's theoretical judgment that democracy is better off when peaceful contestation among elites precedes mass participation may be accepted, but requires some qualifications in the Brazilian case. First, there is a matter of degree, since that process ultimately led in Brazil to a state structure that seems excessively strong vis-à-vis civil society: too large and clientelistic to be effectively controlled by the citizenry and constantly reinforced by the constraints of so-called late industrialization. Second, the Dahlian sequence seems to have left serious strains in terms of legitimacy and political culture, as indicated by the alleged excess of conciliation and elitist character of the political system.

State Structure and Strength

Historians who see a strong state in Brazil in the nineteenth century normally stress that the empire kept the country's territorial integrity, though compelled to use force against important separatist movements. Other analyses attempt to trace the bureaucratic organization of the Brazilian government directly back to the Portuguese absolutist state. But these arguments overstate the case, since they overlook the fact that state structures never became entirely distinguished qua public authority. Symbiotic arrangements with private power (e.g., landed wealth) were part and parcel of a gradual extension of regulatory capabilities. The effectiveness of the central authority in keeping public order and eventually in undertaking social changes is, then, recent in Brazilian history. It is difficult to see how it could exist at a time when the national army hardly existed, or even before it developed organizational responses to its own internal divisions.[28]

The organizational "maturity" of the army would appear only after the Revolution of 1930. From the 1930s onward, the armed forces developed an increasingly tutelary conception of their role vis-à-vis civilian institutions and society as a whole. Thus, in 1945 they pressured Getúlio Vargas out of office, on the understanding that the days of the Estado Novo were gone. Friction with elected presidents or with their ministers was evident throughout the 1950s and early 1960s. In 1961, following Jânio Quadros's resignation from the presidency, the military ministers actually vetoed the transfer of power to the elected vice-president, João Goulart. This move brought the country to the brink of civil war and was defeated only because the military ministers failed to achieve unitary backing for their position among the regional commanders. In 1964, with substantial popular support, the military overthrew Goulart and took power.

However, this tutelary role should not be taken to mean that the Brazilian military is quintessentially opposed to democratic principles and institutions. The tutelary self-conception clearly belongs to the broader authoritarian ideology that presided over the last phase of state building, that is, the Getúlian thrust of the 1930s. That ideology includes elements that, paradoxically, help sustain some of the institutional mechanisms of representative democracy. Being, at root, antipopulist and nonmobilizational, it stresses the distinction between private and public roles—hence the limits on the duration of mandates, the electoral calendar, and, more generally, the importance of keeping the legislature, at least as an institution capable of being reactivated—all of these clearly practiced by the post-1964 regime.

Brazil's political development has also benefited from the paucity of direct armed challenges to the state in this century and the effective repression since the 1930s of those few that did occur. Ethnic separatism has been virtually nonexistent in modern Brazil. In this regard, too, state building was brought to a conclusion that certainly favors democracy.

On the other hand, the procedures and justifications used to repress armed challenges, in the 1930s and again after 1964, led to threatening precedents. In both cases, those challenges were treated in terms of "internal war," far more than as unlawful behavior that perhaps could be dealt with by judicial or political means. The legislature, political parties, and the judiciary came out clearly weakened vis-à-vis the executive (which in fact meant the military). With the military directly in power after 1964, this trend became far more serious. First there came the arrests, proscriptions, and similar measures designed to curb opposition and promote societal demobilization. From 1968 to 1974, confronting armed underground movements, the regime adopted widespread censorship and all sorts of cover-up of repressive practices. The cost of this phase in terms of human rights was not as high as that endured by Argentina shortly afterward, but it cannot be underestimated as a negative effect for democratic prospects. As argued in my first section, some of the military seem to have recognized that they had gone too far, when they opted (circa 1973) for a gradual "opening from above."

The description of the Brazilian military as exerting a tutelary role and as having directly established an authoritarian regime that would last for twenty-one years obviously does not square well with the image presented by some analysts of an emerging, vigorous civil society. In fact, there have been exaggerations in applying the latter concept to the Brazilian case. It is true, of course, that Brazilian society has become highly differentiated and complex. Combined with resistance to the military regime, this has led to a rapid increase in associational politicization. But a more appropriate reading of this trend would update the picture of a society marked by unusually low participation and predominantly organized along corporatist lines. Corporatist political organization (i.e., based essentially on occupational criteria) traditionally facilitated control by the state (as in the case of labor unions) and the petrification of differential privileges among professions, the gradient of such differences being guaranteed by the state.

After twenty-one years of military-authoritarian rule (1964–1985), the Brazilian state was highly centralized in practice, since the "majority-constraining" effects of the federation could not work fully through the National Congress, whose power had been substantially reduced. The predominant concern with state building from the nineteenth through the first half of the twentieth century, and the high degree of cohesion of the political elite in those early days, contrasting with the dispersion and abysmal poverty of the populace, not to mention the recent authoritarian period, meant that the central authorities enjoyed a wide margin of discretion, especially in economic policymaking. But some recent developments are now significantly altering that picture. The 1988 Constitution promoted an unprecedented decentralization of tax receipts, strengthening local and, to a lesser extent, state governments, at the expense of the federal government. Moreover, the privatization of some of the largest state enterprises (e.g., steel mills like CSN and USIMINAS, CVRD, the mining giant, and Telebrás, the telecommunication company), a process started in the early 1990s, has reduced the share of the nation's productive sector directly controlled by the state.

Development Performance

Disregarding redistributive issues for a moment, there can be no question that Brazilian governments have been consistently seeking to promote economic growth for a long time, and that their record is fairly impressive. The Brazilian economy is now among the ten or twelve largest in the world, bigger than Australia's. This rank is the result of continuously high rates of growth since the early 1930s, and especially of steady advances toward industrialization. The average growth rate of GDP during this whole period has been about 6 percent a year, with a peak of 10 percent a year from 1968 to 1974. Industrial growth rates have been twice or thrice that of agriculture, and in 1968, ten times higher. This growth pattern accounts for the vast scale of the structural changes the country has undergone (see Table 3.1, p. 155), which Santos finds at least as impressive as that promoted by the Meiji restoration in Japan or by the Soviet government in its initial two decades.[29]

Some structural aspects of Brazil's "late-developer" pattern of growth must be underlined if we are to understand its political implications. Far from deconcentrating state power, the growth record mentioned above has greatly reinforced it. Reacting to the constraints brought by World War I and by the economic crisis of 1929, subsequent governments assumed an increasingly direct role in the economic sphere. Starting with the Volta Redonda steel complex, in 1942, state and mixed enterprises were created to foster industrial infrastructure. Foreign trade was regulated not only through fiscal and exchange policies, but also through government entities specifically designed to supervise the commercialization of coffee, sugar, and other commodities. Four decades later, Hewlett could aptly describe the Brazilian state as "a significant producer of basic industrial goods and infra-structural items, an important agent of protection and subsidy, a powerful regulator of economic activity, and the determiner of the direction of national economic development."[30]

Needless to say, this record of growth underlies the proven ability of the Brazilian political system to avoid the generalization of zero-sum perceptions and expectations. But these successes have not been sufficient to dilute a syndrome of illegitimacy that permanently surrounds the political system, if not authorities in general. In fact, the Brazilian state, having relied heavily on economic growth for legitimacy, has been reasonably successful in promoting growth but seems rather far from overcoming its legitimacy deficit. In theory, the state can manipulate the supply of key inputs and thus start altering the many perverse aspects of the growth pattern, but it cannot readily do that in practice, as Hewlett points out, since interfering with the market conditions toward which major enterprises are oriented would often mean reducing the rate of growth—hence, losing legitimacy. Moreover, insufficient domestic savings, technological dependence, and other imbalances have increasingly led the country, since the 1950s, to a strategy of growth-cum-debt and inflationary financing. In the 1970s and early 1980s, as is well known, foreign debt skyrocketed to over $100 billion and inflation rapidly moved to the three-digit altitude. Only after successive failures in the attempt to control inflation by means of heterodox shocks between 1986 and 1990 did policymakers, academic economists, and the business community become convinced that a thorough revision of this state-centered growth model had become imperative.

In conclusion, Brazilian development from the 1930s through the late 1970s can thus be said to have had very positive and very negative aspects. High rates of growth (hence variable-sum perceptions among different strata of society) coexist with dramatic imbalances: regionally, against the northeast; sectorally, against small-scale agriculture and rural labor; and by class, against the poor in general. But there is no persuasive evidence that those positive or negative aspects are predominantly associated by the mass public with either democratic or authoritarian governments. Memories of high growth flash back on democratic (e.g., Kubitschek, 1955–1960) as well as on extreme authoritarian (e.g., Médici, 1969–1973) administrations.

A significant distinction emerged in the 1970s and early 1980s among the educated, urban middle class. In this segment, there undoubtedly was an increase in the proportion of those thinking that the military-authoritarian regime achieved growth at an unacceptable social cost: income concentration, neglect of welfare investments, denationalization of economy and culture, damage to the environment, and corruption. This change was crucially important for the Brazilian political *abertura,* expressing itself in electoral mobilization as well as in the political activation of professional and civic associations of numerous types.

Concerning corruption, very important changes have taken place. Up to 1964, corruption was perceived in a patrimonial rather than in a capitalist framework. The widespread feeling that politicians were corrupt was primarily focused on clientelistic (patronage) practices. Undue use of public funds for private enrichment was not unknown, of course, but it was perceived as being associated with only a few practices (e.g., dubious credits to landowners and co-optation of union leaders). Under the post-1964 military governments, the context and, therefore, the whole perception of corruption underwent an enormous change—perhaps we should say that both moved to an exponential scale. Accelerated industrialization, increasing internationalization of the economy, the whole strategy of growth-cum-debt—all of these took place, we must recall, without any effective parliamentary oversight and often under the protection of pervasive press censorship. No wonder, then, that the idea of corruption became associated with financial scandals, alleged "commissions" in foreign dealings, and so on—the number of known cases being sufficient, needless to say, to lend credence to the most extravagant generalizations.

Since the transition, the growth of investigative journalism, the impeachment of President Collor in 1992, and a scandal involving members of the congressional Budget Commission in 1993 have substantially changed this long-standing picture of governmental corruption and public complacency. It is not far-fetched to say that Brazilian political culture has gained an important ethical dimension in recent years, which is bound to have practical and institutional consequences during the turn of the century. If this assumption proves correct, democracy will come out stronger. In a country historically marked by poverty and inequality, insufficient governability, and a political culture strongly affected by corrupt practices, it comes as no surprise that even as remarkable a record of economic growth as Brazil's should for so long have fallen short of full legitimation as a democratic regime.

Class Structure, Income Distribution, and Social Organization

No matter how one measures them, levels of income inequality and mass poverty in Brazil are among the worst in the world. The main determinants of present income differentials and class structure undoubtedly have their roots in the pattern of land appropriation inherited from the colonial past. Concentration of landed wealth and use of the best land to produce export commodities have always been the major "push" factors behind the enormous supply of cheap labor constantly flocking to the cities.[31] Rapid industrial growth oriented toward a predominantly middle-class market, high rates of population growth, and the insufficiency of investment in basic welfare services have combined to maintain extreme inequalities and indeed to make a mockery of the "trickle-down" theory of indirect redistribution.[32] Needless to say, the full implications of Brazilian-size poverty and inequality for democratic prospects must also take into account that the country has now become highly urbanized and "mobilized" (in Deutsch's sense).

Throughout the empire and the First Republic, both working-class and urban middle strata were numerically unimportant. The vast majority of the population lived in rural areas or in very small villages and towns, where society was steeply stratified. Here, there was no middle class worth speaking of. At the bottom were the peasants, a sprinkling of very poor independent farmers, and similar strata in the towns. At that time, a crisis in the coffee business was tantamount to economic recession, but it did not necessarily mean that a large number of laborers lost their jobs. From World War II onward, the picture started changing dramatically. Total population grew from 41 million in 1940 to 146 million in 1990; during this same half-century, urban population grew from 13 to 119 million, the population living in the nine largest cities from 6 to 48 million, and voters from 6 to over 80 million. These changes were accompanied by major shifts in the labor force out of agriculture and into industry and services (see Table 3.1).

Table 3.1   Socioeconomic Change in Brazil, 1940–1990

Socioeconomic Factors	1940	1950	1960	1970	1980	1990
Population (in millions)	41.2	51.9	70.1	93.1	119.1	145.6
% of population in urban areas	31.2	35.1	45.1	55.9	67.6	75.0
% of population in metropolitan areas						
(nine largest cities)	15.2	17.9	21.5	25.5	29.0	33.0
% of the labor force in						
Agriculture	67.4	60.2	54.5	44.6	30.5	22.8
Industry	12.6	13.3	12.4	18.1	24.9	22.7
Services	19.9	26.4	33.1	37.8	44.6	54.5
Per capita gross national product (GNP)						
(in U.S.$)	391[a]	444	640	960	1,708	2,680

Sources: For population data: Fundação IBGE (Censos Demográficos e Tabulações Avançadas de 1980). For GNP: Conjuntura Econômica 26, no. 11 (1972), and Gazeta Mercantil (1970–1985).
    Note: a. Data for 1947.

Despite the impressive overall rates of economic growth during the "economic miracle" period of the military regime (the late 1960s and early 1970s), there is ample evidence that income differentials and some telling indicators of basic welfare (such as infant mortality) continued to decline. By the early 1970s, several studies were showing that income inequality had increased relative to the early 1960s. Writing in 1976, Graham offered the following summary of the evidence:

(a) income concentration (as measured by the standard Gini index) increased overall, and in all regions, during the sixties; (b) the rates of concentration were more pronounced in the more developed (and most rapidly growing) areas like São Paulo and the south than in the lesser developed regions; (c) real income increased in all areas; (d) average monthly real income per urban worker increased much more rapidly (43 percent) than income per agricultural worker (14 percent), thereby increasing the intersectoral income differentials during the decade; (e) these intersectoral income differentials stood out much more dramatically in the northeast than in São Paulo and the center and south.[33]

Using data from 1960 to 1980, Serra reported continuing income concentration through the 1970s. The lowest 20 percent of the economically active population had gone from 3.9 percent of total income in 1960 to 3.4 percent in 1970, to 2.8 percent in 1980; the top 10 percent, from 39.6 percent to 46.7 percent, to 50.9 percent.[34] This means that the governmental policies practiced throughout this period, at best, did not counteract structural forces making for greater inequality; at worst, they aggravated their effect. Slow growth, soaring inflation, and a sharp deterioration of social services throughout the 1980s and early 1990s further worsened this picture. By the end of the 1990s, the top tenth of the population was earning 51.3 percent of all income, the top fifth more than two-thirds (67.5 percent), and the bottom fifth, 2.1 percent. These figures represent the single worst income distribution of the sixty-five countries for which the World Bank had data (forty-five of them in the developing and postcommunist worlds). Significantly, the successful introduction of the Real Plan in 1994 reduced the income share of the top fifth of the population to 62.7 percent.[35] Combined with the appalling extent of absolute poverty that prevails in the northeast and in the outskirts of all major cities, this degree of income concentration is undoubtedly one of the steepest challenges to democratic consolidation.

In terms of class structure, the starting point must be the corporatist order imposed from above in the 1930s.[36] This system can be seen as a highly successful attempt to control, not to say petrify, the process of class formation, by which we mean development of differentiated collective identities and autonomous political organization. The lowest extremity of the class structure, made up of landless peasants and very poor small farmers, was not regulated in a strict sense, since they lacked the occupational differentiation that formed the basis of the whole system; rather, they were excluded from it. The upper extremity, made up of large landowners, provided another parameter—untouchable property rights. But this should not be confounded with total political autonomy, much less with monolithic control of the state: the political sphere (embodied in the military, the bureaucracy, and the political "class") retained considerable decisional discretion.

Between these two extremes, a corporatist gradient was imposed on the rest of society, that is, on urban wage labor and middle-class independent occupations in general. The privilege of "representing" a given sector was thoroughly subjected to state (legal) control, as well as to effective means to circumscribe each sector's agenda building and other overt political moves. This pattern applied even to industrial and commercial entrepreneurs, through corporatist pyramids exactly paralleling those of urban labor. As Santos points out, this whole structure remained virtually unchanged through the "democratic experiment" based on the Constitution of 1946. Attempts at self-organization on the part of rural labor in the early 1960s were quickly repressed by the post-1964 regime, obviously with full applause and cooperation from the landowners, who saw such attempts as outright subversion.

Ironically enough, serious and lasting "subversion" of the regulated order would occur—first as the result of the scale of the economic changes induced by the military governments, second, as an unintended by-product of some of their "modernizing" reforms, and finally, in that context of large-scale structural change, from the reactivation of civil society during the political opening. Development of large-scale industry led entrepreneurs, especially in the heaviest and most dynamic sectors, to organize in new types of associations, pulling themselves out of the traditional corporatist framework. Ousted, as it were, from the administration of social security funds, labor leaders found themselves with nothing to offer their constituencies, nothing but more authentic leadership. This was the origin of so-called new unionism, which thrived in the most dynamic sectors of the economy and struck a blow against the old corporatist structure.

Trying to sidestep political clientelism in their attempt to extend social security to the rural areas, the military governments stimulated the formation of rural labor unions. From 1976 to 1983, unionized rural labor increased from slightly over 3 to more than 8 million, accounting now for more than half of total union membership in the country, even though rural labor accounts for only 30 percent of the economically active population. Needless to say, rural unions did not conform to the passive blueprint that the government probably conceived for them. In less than two decades they organized the Movimento dos Sem Terra (MST, or the Landless Movement), a social movement born in the early 1980s, which gained worldwide fame for its aggressive tactics and the violence many of its members have been subject to. As for its tactics, the MST often threatens to invade large privately owned lands, and sometimes it actually loots food stores and supermarkets, as was seen in Brazil's northeast in 1998. By doing so the MST has successfully managed to place agrarian reform at a higher position on the public agenda.[37]

The politicization of the urban middle strata has not lagged behind. White-collar unions, neighborhood organizations, and associations of numerous types quickly emerged, undoubtedly reflecting the increasing complexity and, in many ways, the increasing technical and professional sophistication of Brazilian urban life.

The conclusion, then, is that, in Brazil, medieval economic inequalities exist side by side with a dynamic and increasingly sophisticated society. So-called external dependency does not mean that an indigenous bourgeoisie failed to develop. There is, in fact, a modern entrepreneurial class, in industry as well as agriculture. This class has become much more affirmative in the last decade, profiting from the process of political opening. Perceiving that it could not unconditionally count on the military or on elected politicians, it became highly and autonomously organized. This process in fact underwent a remarkable acceleration during the 1980s, first in view of the Constitutional Congress (1987–1988) and also because successive attempts to control inflation by means of heterodox plans (such as the introduction of generalized price controls) politicized the economy to a very great extent.

I have so far emphasized the economic bases and the organizational aspects of class formation. Needless to say, the picture becomes much less politicized when we look at the rank and file and especially at class consciousness. A very large proportion of the urban working class is young, politically inexperienced, and made up of recent migrants. Wage strikes can be mobilized without much difficulty, but both unions and political parties must reckon with a great deal of instability, even volatility, when it comes to broader electoral or ideological disputes.

Although the stagnation and inflation of the 1980s worsened this picture, Brazilian development, as I have repeatedly stressed, has been able to create a basically non-zero-sum perception of social conflict. Overall, spatial mobility has been extremely high and has, in fact, meant better life chances for poor migrants. The belief in upward social mobility is probably not as deep today as it was in the 1950s, but access to education and to consumption has increased considerably with increases in total income. Some fashionable descriptions of Brazilian society as being rigidly hierarchical must, then, be taken with a grain of salt. The concentration of property, twenty-one years of authoritarian rule, and huge income inequalities have not meant petrification of status inequality.

On the other hand, socioeconomic inequalities do tend to cumulate to some extent. Although extremely high correlation among education, occupation, income, and, say, "honor" certainly does not exist, the overall structure of inequalities has an evident regional component. The southeast (where São Paulo is located) and the extreme south are "rich" regions, whereas the northeast, with 35 million inhabitants, is one of the major examples of mass poverty in the world. This regional disparity has an important overlap with the country's ethnic differentiation. Blacks and *pardoes* (mulattos) account for well over two-thirds of the northern and northeastern states, while the reverse proportion obtains in the southeast and the south. These definitions are known to be very imprecise in Brazilian population statistics, but the difference is large enough to merit attention.

Nationality and Ethnic Cleavages

Political conflict among language or religious groups is virtually nonexistent in Brazil. On these two dimensions, let alone nationality, the country is comparatively very homogeneous. The picture is much more complex in the field of race relations. Interpretations range from the belief in a genuinely "peaceful" evolution to the notion that underprivileged minorities (especially blacks) lack collective identity and organization as a consequence of white economic and political domination. The extremes do seem to agree that overt ethnic strife is not prevalent. There can be no doubt, however, that poverty and color are significantly correlated.[38] Blacks, and especially black women, are disproportionately locked in low-status and low-income occupations.

But the country does have an overarching national identity. Living generations have virtually no memory of separatist movements or politically relevant subcultures, whether based on language, race, or religion. It can, of course, be said that this high degree of cultural uniformity reflects a process of authoritarian state building under colonial and then imperial government. The fact, however, is that Brazil is not presently confronted with serious ethnic or cultural strife. Given the immense burden that socioeconomic cleavages place on the political agenda, this relative homogeneity is clearly a positive factor for democratic development.

Political Structure

The formal structure of the Brazilian state has varied a great deal since independence (see Table 3.2), but the concentration of power in the national executive has been a constant. Accepted as a hallmark of state building and, more recently, as necessary for the sake of economic development and national security, that concentration was often carried out at the expense of state and local governments, of legislative and judicial powers, and even more clearly of the party system.[39]

The First Republic (1889–1930) tried to adapt the U.S. model, providing for a popularly elected president and granting extensive autonomy to the provinces, now called states, of the old unitary empire. The result was full of perverse effects, as the "politics of the governors" decisively weakened the national legislature and judiciary and seriously compromised elections and party competition. In practice, the republican government became as oligarchical and probably less legitimate than the empire, in the eyes of the relevant strata. This process of political decay eventually led to the Revolution of 1930 (and, in 1937, to Vargas's Estado Novo), which again concentrated federal power, but now within a framework of nonmobilizational and partyless authoritarian rule.

Table 3.2   Brazilian Political Structure Since Independence

Regimes	Form of Government	Party System	Civil/Military Relations	Social Mobilization	Demise
Empire (1822–1889)	Unitary state; parliamentary monarchy cum "moderating power"	Two parties (Liberal and Conservative) since the 1830s; district voting (very unstable)	Civil hegemony through National Guard; weak army	Extremely low	Republican military coup; no resistance
First Republic (1889–1930)	Directly elected president; highly decentralized federation	One-pary systems at state level; multi-member district voting; unstable rules	Increasing tension between military (especially young officers) and politicians	Very low	Revolutionary movement headed by Getúlio Vargas; three weeks fighting
Revolution of 1930 (1930–1937)	Provisional government headed by Vargas; in 1934, Weimar-inspired constitution with strong corporatist leanings	Numerous, unstable party groupings; growing fascist/ communist polarization	Army becoming dominant national institution	Growing significantly in urban areas	Vargas's coup, with military backing, leads to Estado Novo
Estado Novo (1937–1945)	Authoritarian non-mobilizational regime; Vargas dictator	None; all parties and elections suppressed	Army identified with regime through national security ideology	Growing rapidly; population 31% urban in 1940	Senior army officers force Vargas to resign; 1945: controlled redemocratization

(continues)

Table 3.2 (continued)

Regimes	Form of Government	Party System	Civil/Military Relations	Social Mobilization	Demise
Democratic Regime (1946–1964)	Directly elected president; weak federation and powerful national legislature	Multiparty system with 13 parties; increasing polarization at end of period; PR electoral system	Frequent friction between military factions and civilian governments; threats of military intervention	Fairly high; increasing even in rural areas; population 45% urban in 1960	Military coup with substantial popular backing in middle strata ousts President Goulart
Military Regime (1964–1985)	Republican form; presidency de facto monopoly of the military; nominations ratified by electoral college only up to 1985; federation severely weakened	Compulsory two-party system from 1965 on; partial return to pluralism in 1979, still barring communist parties; PR electoral system	Unmistakable hegemony of military as institution, guaranteeing "technocratic" governments	Very high; population 67% urban in 1980	Very gradual, negotiated transition culminating in election of Tancredo Neves (civilian, oppositionist) through electoral college
New Democratic Regime (1985–)	Direct election of president reestablished as constitutional principle; growing influence of states and legislature; new constitution promulgated in October 1988; right to one consecutive reelection for executive posts established in 1997 for the first time in Brazil's republican history	Multiparty system; no legal restrictions on Marxist parties; dominance by center-right coalitions in both chambers of Congress; permissive PR electoral system	Civilian control formally guaranteed; military influence has been declining	Very high	

The Revolution of 1930 is undoubtedly the founding mark of the modern Brazilian political system, but again with contradictory effects in terms of democratic prospects. In the short run, advances in stateness (bureaucratic reach, military complexity, greater regulation of economy) were certainly favorable, since they reduced the scope of private power and made an involution to a purely oligarchic rule thenceforth unlikely. In the long run, however, some of those advances seem to have outlived their function. The corporatist system of labor relations has certainly been detrimental to the political organization of the working class. The conventional PR electoral system then established has clearly not contributed to developing a stable party system. Worse still, the presidential office became overloaded with contradictory expectations. For professional politicians, it became the ultimate distributor of patronage, credits, and public investments, and the arbiter among regional interests. For the newly mobilized urban masses after 1945, it was the focal point of demands for better wages and improvements in living conditions. From the viewpoint of the military establishment, it came to be the very embodiment of national security, implying containment of both oligarchic and "mob" rule.

These cross-pressures and institutional deficiencies were clearly operative in the 1964 breakdown. The democratic experiment initiated in 1945 was based, in comparison with the earlier periods, on a far stronger representative system. The national legislature and the main political parties started as fundamental political actors. However, growing social mobilization and persistent inflation made it impossible for the two major parties (UDN and PSD) to retain their initially safe electoral advantage. As a typical "institutional" party, the PSD became increasingly vulnerable to a bipolar (left and right) opposition, roughly as suggested by Sartori's "polarized pluralism" model.[40]

The erosion of party and congressional support meant that Goulart (1961–1964) had to carry the full burden of maintaining institutional equilibrium exactly when the Caesarist ghost that so often surrounds Latin American presidentialism came, full-bodied, to the fore. The Caesarist dilemma stems from the need to cope with stringent and clearly defined contradictory situational constraints. Frustrating mass demands in the name of austerity or economic rationality alienates diffuse support and thus deprives the president of the one resource that makes him strong vis-à-vis elected politicians. If, on the contrary, he chooses to court those demands too closely, the specter of a mob-based dictatorship is immediately raised by the propertied classes and, often, by the military organization. The middle course is often unavailable because of the very weakness and inconsistency of the party system. When the difficulties inherent in these situational constraints are compounded by ambiguous personal behavior, as was evidently the case in the Goulart presidency, the breaking point is near.

Leadership

From 1961 to 1964, President Goulart proved unable to escape the Caesarist trap. He in fact made it more inexorable by allowing too much room for doubt as to his intention to abide by the constitutional rules that would govern his succession. Few analysts would dispute that Goulart's equivocal behavior was a crucial precipitating factor in the democratic breakdown.[41] The important question, then, is how does it come about that a country with an important institutional history and a fairly impersonal conception of governing falls prey to that sort of populistic retrogression and thence to breakdown?

Part of the answer may indeed be an oversupply of leaders willing to violate the rules of the game. The pattern was set by Getúlio Vargas in 1930 and especially with the Estado Novo coup of 1937. Liberal opposition to the Varguista tradition, after 1945, often displayed the same ambiguous behavior of which Goulart was later accused. Prominent UDN leaders, like Carlos Lacerda, were not only *golpistas* but, in fact, strongly inclined to (and skillful at) impassioned demagogic rhetoric.

Yet, personalistic leadership has not been as successful as implied in the common lore. Vargas did not establish a personality cult comparable to that of Perón in Argentina. Former president Kubitschek (1955–1960) is remembered as a modernizer and a "nice guy," not as a power-seeking *caudillo.* Quadros ascended to the presidency in 1960, riding a protest vote that he cleverly mobilized by means of a rancorous, theatrical style. In August 1961, he resigned, claiming that the country was ungovernable (in his terms, of course). His decision was fateful in the ensuing years, but is it not a blessing for our hypothesis that the Brazilian political system has developed antibodies against wild personalism? His successful comeback as the elected mayor of São Paulo in 1985 would seem to deny our view, but it is noteworthy that Quadros has carefully confined his protofascist appeal to the electoral arena, never daring to establish some sort of paramilitary apparatus.

The leadership problem cannot therefore be considered simply as a lack of men with the appropriate skills and civic virtues, and not even as an absence of antibodies against irresponsible demagogues. It is rather the inherent instability of democracy amid rapid social mobilization and extreme inequality, trying to escape the Scylla of Caesarist *caudillismo* and the Charybdis of uninspiring clientelistic politics. A proper understanding of the leadership problem must then consider, in addition to the already cited situational constraints, some underlying cultural elements that contribute to shaping them.

Political Culture

Brazilian political culture is sometimes said to embody an unchanging Iberian propensity toward monolithism, and thus to be irreducibly inimical to democratic development. We argue that, on balance, the effects of political culture may indeed be negative, but hardly for that reason. The views that do operate in the political system (i.e., those put forward by influential writers, journalists, and the like) show a pervasive and persistent concern, indeed an obsession, with the alleged incongruence between elite and mass culture. Since the early decades of this century, outstanding writers of different persuasions have insisted that powerful cultural strains tend to undermine the idea of a Western-style democracy in Brazil. Alberto Torres was only one among hundreds who emphasized the discrepancy between the "legal" Brazil, expressed in political institutions, and the "real" one, embodied in actual social behavior.

Somehow, popular culture came to be seen as the only real thing, while political institutions became irremediably artificial. What is certainly disturbing in this dichotomous approach is that, through it, we may be unconsciously demanding a degree of congruence among different spheres of society, and especially between "center" and "periphery," that does not in fact exist anywhere among advanced democracies. The starting point is the Aristotelian ideal that social institutions (familial, educational, religious) must buttress and reinforce the overarching principle of legitimacy. But that ideal is then used to imply that democratic political principles are irrelevant or illegitimate when they fail to mold each and every subsystem. Even in the advanced democracies, we find, as in Brazil, that knowledge of and support for democratic rules of the game are undoubtedly correlated with education and other indicators of social status. In Brazil, this is hardly surprising, if we consider that elite political socialization has been closely associated, since the nineteenth century, with the law schools (hence with a reverence for legal culture) as well as with a free press and more recently with a sizable and reasonably cosmopolitan academic community.[42]

The dichotomous view just described derives historically from the state-centered pattern of political development and from the fact that elite contestation preceded, by far, the expansion of participation. In fact, elite culture became political at a time when the bulk of the populace, poor and widely dispersed over a large territory, was totally excluded from the system. In 1900, the illiteracy rate among the population over fifteen was 75 percent. There thus arose an excessive predominance of state over societal development and hence a deep anxiety, among opinionators, that liberal-democratic development would not be viable under such conditions.

However, this picture has changed in surprising ways during the decompression process of the 1970s and especially since the transition to civilian rule in 1985. The Aristotelian craving for congruence remains, but its contents and ideas to correct incongruence have become more complex. Under the impact of high social mobilization (see Table 3.1), of repoliticization, and, of course, of protest against income inequality, there appeared an Augustinian strand, according to which the people are good and the state is evil. Stimulated by religious movements and by abundant leadership coming from the now much larger wage-earning middle sectors, the implied correction is no longer to replace liberal by authoritarian politics, as in the 1920s, but rather to substitute some sort of Rousseaunean "participatory politics" for representative democracy.

The historical sequence of institutional development, combined with persistently wide income differentials and other factors, thus seemed to have produced very negative cultural conditions for representative democracy. These negative effects do not derive from a would-be unitary worldview, but rather from a pervasive utopian standard against which democratic development is constantly measured by the leadership of some popular movements and by influential opinionators. The political impact of these trends on parliamentary politics has increased noticeably as the Partido dos Trabalhadores (PT) became stronger in Congress, and these views spread among the clergy and academics, and especially among grassroots reform movements.

The usual pessimistic account of Brazilian political culture must be qualified in many ways. Consideration of some positive developments that took place despite allegedly authoritarian Iberian origins and recent authoritarian experiences may be useful as an antidote. First, since the establishment of the Electoral Court in 1932, there has been unmistakable progress toward orderliness and fairness in administering the electoral process. On the side of the voters, sheer size (95 million registered voters in 1994) allied to social mobilization has made the assumption of individual autonomy increasingly realistic. Despite abysmal poverty and the prevalence of patron-client relationships in many regions, there can be no doubt that the electoral process now operates with the requisite quantum of aggregate uncertainty.

Second, there is no monolithic domination, not even at the local level. This is in part a consequence of the overall changes in the electoral process and in part the result of local rivalries, even among landowners. A monolithic image has been frequently maintained by students of Brazilian social structure, but they tend to underestimate the impact of political and electoral competition when it is not linked to ideological or class cleavages.

Third, as I noted earlier, even the authoritarian ideology of the 1920s and 1930s (and hence the idea of military tutelage) has been tempered by antipopulist elements that help sustain some democratic institutions and practices. Hence, the limits on the duration of executive and legislative terms of office, the electoral calendar, and, more generally, the importance of keeping the legislature as an institution capable of being reactivated were all practiced by the post-1964 regime.

Fourth, as noted above, a significant degree of social mobility exists, despite severe income inequality. Here, the cultural process of modernization does seem to have an impact of its own, judging from the increasingly informal character of social relationships. Urban living and mass communications work massively in the direction of an egalitarian culture.

Finally, the development of representative institutions, in a general way, clearly implies that primitive *caudillismo* and unitary blueprints are not deemed desirable or realistic by the political elite. Three features seem to characterize the Brazilian "doctrine" of representation. One is the recognition of diversity among the elite. This should not be understood primarily in ideological terms and even less in terms of cultural or ethnic segmentation. It is rather an acceptance of the fact that politics involves constant division and disagreement, making monolithic rule inconceivable. This recognition is deeply rooted in the country's cultural and legal system because, if for no other reason, it was historically a sine qua non for holding the provinces and local governments together.

The second feature is the electoral process. Countless writers have seen a puzzle, or worse, a mimetic disease, in the Brazilian tendency to import such profoundly "alien" liberal institutions. But the fact is that electoral mechanisms, with many of the classical provisions for fair competition, have strong roots in Brazil. Despite the equally countless instances of violence, fraud, and manipulation that can be cited, it is perfectly legitimate to speak of a Brazilian electoral tradition, and even more to recognize that the recent struggle against authoritarian rule has reinforced it.

The third feature, which has the military institution as its main guardian, is the notion that the government must be an impersonal entity. Hence the military's fundamental dislike for any kind of plebiscitarian *caudillismo* and their (reluctant, no doubt) understanding that elections are the ultimate safeguard against some sort of personalistic appropriation of the state.

Do these three features of Brazilian political culture amount to an unambiguous concept of democratic representation? Not quite: one indication that they do not is the powerful cultural strains that constantly delegitimize the representative process. Public debate is full of references to the "elitist" character of such institutions. The image of politicians is incessantly associated with clientelism, co-optation, and conciliation—the last being a reference to the early nineteenth century, but also a way of saying that our pluralism is still oligarchical, without substantive meaning for the average citizen. Indeed, what we can assume, in the Brazilian case, is that substantial institutional development was achieved in the past, but some authoritarian traits of the state-building process and of the social structure are still reflected in the democratic system.

International Factors

The international environment is a positive factor for representative democracy—especially now that the Cold War is over—but it was negative on the economic dimension during the 1980s, especially in view of the tremendous internal impact of the debt crisis. Brazil is a fully Western nation in cultural terms, and a dependent (if you will) part of the world capitalist system. One oft-neglected consequence of this is that Brazilian elites, including the military, do not ignore the risks involved in toying with fundamentally different principles of political organization. Brazil's territory acquired its present shape a long time ago. Nature provided most of the solution to Brazil's frontier problem. Diplomatic efforts polished it up early in this century. Participation in foreign wars and military readiness are unknown to the vast majority of Brazilians. Were it otherwise, the weight of the military vis-à-vis civilian institutions would undoubtedly be much greater than it has been. Proper understanding of the negative effects of the economic dimension requires a broad historical perspective. Dependency on export commodities, with its attendant instability, was extremely high until the 1950s at least. Import-substituting industrialization began during World War I but was insufficient to alter that basic link to the external world until roughly the mid-1970s.

An important change took place in the 1950s. Under President Kubitschek, the Brazilian government gave up its formerly cautious strategy and started emphasizing durable consumer goods as a means to accelerate industrial growth. The automobile industry was the driving force of that new phase. The impact of industrialization on the overall social structure became thenceforth much greater. A rapidly expanding population, large cities, and the demonstration effect of foreign consumption patterns now made for permanent tension, leaving no option but constantly high rates of growth. Major inflationary pressures and the need to increase exports at any price and, of course, to attract investments and credits now became permanent features of the economic system. Internationalization had come to stay.

This, in a rough sketch, is the background of Brazil's deep involvement in the international debt crisis. Having again accelerated growth in the late 1960s and early 1970s, the military governments, especially under President Geisel (1974–1978), undertook major new steps toward import substitution, this time in basic or "difficult" sectors.[43] The premise of that effort, needless to say, was the easy credit situation of that decade. The oil and interest-rate shocks of the late 1970s and early 1980s thus caught Brazil in an extremely vulnerable position.

PROSPECTS FOR DEMOCRATIC CONSOLIDATION

Reconceptualizing Democratic Consolidation

Liberalization and participation are described by Dahl as distinct theoretical dimensions of democratization. However, when we think about consolidating democracies recently reinstated as a consequence of authoritarian demise, socioeconomic conditions must be incorporated more effectively into our models. It is a trivial observation that a large amount of genuine political democracy tends to be incompatible with a rigid or unequal society, or even with a low rate of change toward greater mobility and equality. Thus, when we think about consolidation, social and economic conditions cannot remain in the category of purely external correlates or prerequisites. They must be "politicized," that is, brought into the model, and this for two important reasons. The first is that, like liberalization and participation, those conditions will necessarily appear to political actors as objects of decision, and therefore as so many choices they will be forced to make. Land reform is the obvious example in Third World countries. Whether and how such choices are faced may make the difference between keeping and losing support; the loss may transcend individual leaders and parties and extend to the newly constituted democratic system as a whole. The second reason has to do with the change from procedural to substantive demands in the course of redemocratization. Cast in a different theoretical language, this means that, once achieved, formal democracy becomes an Olsonian collective good. Since it already exists and benefits everyone, the incentive to defend and protect it decreases sharply.[44] In Third World countries, the implications of this fact are obviously more dramatic because elites have not completely consolidated pluralism among themselves, frequently perceive conflicts as zero-sum, and are vastly more threatened by the substantive demands of the masses.

It thus seems clear that we need not two but three dimensions. The graphic representation of democratic consolidation would thus be a cube made up of Dahl's liberalization and participation plus another dimension referring to policy advances toward structural deconcentration, which means greater equality, social mobility, and the like. Taking all three dimensions at once, the dilemmas of democratic consolidation will, I believe, appear in a more realistic light. If our questions about the democratic character of the present Brazilian political system were to deal only with Dahl's two-dimensional scheme, the answer would be unequivocally positive. Looking at the "liberalization" axis, we would find that all legal restrictions on political competition have been lifted and that the franchise is now among the broadest in the world. If difficulties remain, they are somehow produced by hidden veto points (e.g., the military), by the sheer weight of certain resources (e.g., bureaucratic power), and by other, "nonpolitical" determinants (e.g., those determining the concentration of power in the societal environment of the political system).

Probing somewhat further, it seems possible to combine Dahl's liberalization and participation into a single dimension, which would be representation, that is, strength of the representative system. Where contestation becomes the normal way of doing things among political elites and where such elites are regarded as adequate foci for support or as spokespeople for demands arising from participation, what we have is a strong representative system. We can thus come back to a two-dimensional space, with strength of the representative system on one axis and advances toward social change, or deconcentration, on the other (see Figure 3.1).

The New Republic period (1985–1990) and the extreme political isolation in which President Collor (1990–1992) found himself, quite aside from the corruption charges that finally brought him down, have shown that the reinstatement of formal democracy may be a far cry from true consolidation. On the horizontal axis of Figure 3.1, the new civilian government was faced with what might be called the vicious circle of transition. The prior authoritarian suppression of politics and the prolonged struggle for rede-

Figure 3.1   Representation, Deconcentration, and Democratization

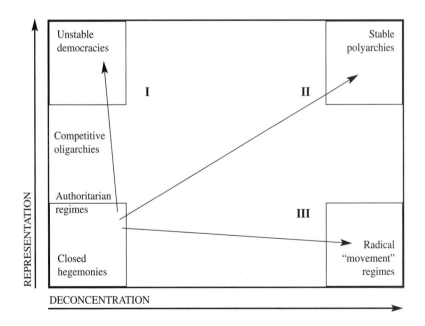

mocratization dammed up enormous (substantive) expectations, which could not (in fact cannot) be met in the short run. Not meeting them at an adequate rate, the government quickly loses the support it needs in order to undertake more forceful policies, the lack of which reinforces the circle. The "moving horizon" that worked so well during the decompression process at the institutional level (i.e., on the vertical axis) thus seems far more difficult to sustain when it comes to our horizontal axis.

Toward Deconcentration?

The proposition that greater equality helps sustain democracy is certainly correct in the long run, but the concrete steps and policies that will reduce inequality may also undermine support for the democratic system in the short run. This is evident enough when we speak of deconcentrating income and wealth, and especially land ownership. Virtually any policy intended to achieve deconcentration produces visible and immediate losses and thus tends to change the basis of political support, often in the direction of undemocratic forces. But there is, in addition, the worst face of inequality, so-called absolute poverty. The problem here is that a truly substantial effort would have to be sustained over many years; this presupposes a degree of consistency in political support and implementation that is not easily forthcoming in fragile, underdeveloped democracies. In order to consolidate itself, a functioning democratic system should be capable not only of undertaking substantial measures to reduce inequality but, also, of conveying to the deprived majority that such measures are serious efforts undertaken on their behalf and, at the same time, that underdevelopment and the pattern of inequalities traditionally associated with it cannot be overcome on short notice.

Up to 1994 the New Republic clearly did not find a consistent answer to these problems and made them worse, as it failed to control soaring inflation. The initial idea was to launch an emergency program of assistance (while at the same time designing alternative economic policies and starting a moderate, long-range land-reform project). There would be, for example, a milk program directed toward groups known to have a desperate nutritional deficit. The results of this phase could not have been more disastrous. Insufficient production, inadequate implementation networks, and political disputes all combined to paralyze such initiatives. Toward the end of 1985, these difficulties were compounded by the ghosts of hyperinflation and an unprecedented strike wave in the subsequent few months. The "illegitimate" origins of Sarney's presidency (i.e., the fact that he was the conservative side of the ticket, as Tancredo Neves's running mate, and that both had been elected indirectly) began to be recalled. Support for the government rapidly dwindled.

It is therefore probably correct to infer that the so-called Cruzado Plan had political as well as economic objectives. The stabilization plan and monetary reform introduced by President Sarney on February 28, 1986, were decisive in stopping a dangerous erosion of authority. Popular acquiescence to the plan immediately reinforced presidential leadership. But, clearly, such acquiescence was entirely due to the price freeze, the difficulties of which began to appear rather soon. In a country with tremendous income inequalities, the redistribution of money income implicit in the price freeze quickly led to an explosive demand for consumer goods of all kinds. Entrepreneurs responded to the price freeze by reducing supply and enhancing their political organization. To make things worse, a decisive election was scheduled to take place in November (state deputies and governors, and federal deputies and senators, the latter two making up the Constitutional Congress). Sarney's enormous popularity after the economic reforms of February was the one big asset of the governing Democratic Alliance, hence the enormous pressures to go on with the price freeze, despite the evident distortions to which it was giving rise. Confronted with an enlarged demand and a reduced internal supply, the government resorted to massive imports of food products. The result was that reserves fell sharply. By early 1987, readjustment measures had proved insufficient and the country had no alternative but to declare a partial default on foreign interest payments.

The irony, or tragedy, is that the Cruzado Plan was the closest thing to actual income redistribution in several decades; it was also the one moment in which the government seemed capable of gaining widespread support. But short-run euphoria should not obscure the dark contours of the broader picture. To begin with, bold measures like the Cruzado Plan reflect the institutional weakness of the political system, not its sources of institutional strength. Presidential authority was reinforced by the populist, indeed Caesarist components of the situation, not by the denser substrata of the country's power structure. It is perhaps unnecessary to point out that not every government faces such an opportunity, that the gains were short-lived, and indeed that such a sweeping reform was introduced through a decree-law, and not by means of a prior amalgamation of party and congressional support. In stark contrast, the Real Plan's success nearly a decade later was partly due to a hard-won agreement struck by then finance minister Fernando Henrique Cardoso with Congress in February 1994. After two months of negotiations, Congress adopted a constitutional amendment (the so-called Emergency Social Fund) substantially reducing the amount of constitutionally earmarked receipts, thus allowing the executive to exert greater discretion in spending and improving fiscal management. This was essential for the launching of the stabilization program under what seemed to be very unfavorable conditions.

BRAZILIAN DEMOCRACY FROM THE 1980s TO THE 1990s

Sharp social inequality poses a constant challenge to democratic institutions, but the Brazilian case can also be read as a showcase of the relevance of institutional formalisms for the growth of democracy. A fair degree of self-restraint among the military during the authoritarian period (1964–1985), the transition from authoritarian rule through a gradual expansion of the electoral arena (and not as a consequence of some abrupt event—for example, the Falklands/Malvinas War in Argentina), and the intense search for institutional reorganization during the late 1980s and early 1990s come readily to mind as illustrations of that assertion. With thirteen years of hindsight, it seems clear that the depth of the economic crisis and the resilience of democracy have both been greater than what one would have expected in 1985, when the transition to civilian rule was formally completed.

In addition to its protracted (1974–1985) character, Brazilian redemocratization was completed under a very adverse set of circumstances. During the last military administration (that of General Figueiredo, 1978–1985), the overheated Brazilian economy was hit hard by the oil and interest-rate shocks and by the Mexican default in 1982, which led to a sudden interruption of the flow of foreign lending to Brazil as well. Policies oriented toward high growth underwent a sharp reversal in the 1981–1984 period, as the country plunged into its worst recession ever, and the government cut its social expenditures sharply.

These almost unbearable economic constraints and the protracted nature of the decompression process thus led to a sharp fall of aggregate authority in the political system from 1981 to 1985: on one hand, the military could veto but not really make policy; on the other, the emerging civilian leadership was already liable to erosion of its authority, since it controlled key state governments but could not yet make policy at the national level. Highly symbolic events like the *diretas já* (direct elections now) mobilization of 1984, the campaign to elect opposition candidate Tancredo Neves through the electoral college in January 1985, and the shock caused by his untimely death without taking office in April of that year misled many analysts into thinking that the new democratic leadership had gained the people's hearts and minds—some even to the extreme view that a compact elite had somehow engineered an *arreglo* (compromise) to keep the levers of power under tight control. My view is, on the contrary, that both military and civilian leaders were sharply weakened by the crisis of the early 1980s, sowing the seeds of a crisis that lasted for the next ten years.

In his well-known book *Polyarchy,* Robert Dahl included the "centralized control of the economy," regardless of the form of ownership, among the conditions he considered negative for democracy.[45] In Brazil, the implications of state intervention in the economy have gone far beyond the issue of bureaucratic-military power. Unlike the Chilean dictatorship, the Brazilian military did not prepare the transition to a more market-oriented economy. On the contrary, the military greatly expanded the public entrepreneurial sector, leaving the tasks of reforming this sector and finding a solution for the underlying fiscal imbalances to the emerging civilian leadership. To make things worse, neither the policymaking and business communities nor the academic community was convinced of the need for such reforms in the mid-1980s. Although disastrous with regard to social equity and monetary order, the Brazilian state-centered model was highly successful as a growth engine, and this record of past success made its ideological legacy accordingly much heavier than that in either Argentina or Chile, for example. However, the end of the constitutionally guaranteed state monopolies in the oil industry and telecommunications and the privatization program under way since the early 1990s are compelling evidence that the statist ideology is gradually losing its grip.

Throughout the 1980s, as economic and political difficulties grew worse, the phrase "the crisis is more political than economic" became standard jargon, but few analysts explained exactly what it meant. My view is that it reflected this very adverse set of circumstances: a sharp fall in the aggregate amount of political authority as a result of the mutual weakening of both military and civilian leaders; economic structures and ideologies still strongly skewed toward state interventionism, despite domestic and worldwide trends indicating the need to open up the economy and enhance market forces; and the formidable pressure of accumulated substantive demands. Add to this the highly fragmented nature of the Brazilian party system and one can readily understand why Brazilian politicians quickly overloaded the reform agenda and engaged in piecemeal and often cumbersome procedures.

Given that the issue of party-system fragmentation is in the forefront of public debate, a brief comment about its consequences for governance is in order. According to a survey of fifty-four democracies, Brazil had one of the world's most fragmented lower chambers in the late 1980s.[46] Moreover, Brazil's legislature has been governed by loosely disciplined parties. Although the legislative behavior of Brazilian parties is not unpredictable,[47] the fact that there is approximately a 10–15 percent minority voting against the majority within the governing parties (the opposition parties on the left, on the other hand, are highly disciplined, particularly the PT) further worsens the problems caused by high fragmentation. Dealing with loosely disciplined parties is thus a major problem for presidents because it makes the formation of stable congressional majorities much harder to achieve due to the excessive number of

Table 3.3   Percentage of Seat Shares per Party in the Chamber of Deputies After Five Elections (1983–1999)

Party	1983	1987	1991	1995	1999
PDS/PPR/PPB	49.1	6.8	8.3	10.1	11.7
PMDB	41.8	53.4	21.5	20.9	16.0
PDT	4.8	4.9	9.1	6.6	4.9
PTB	2.7	3.5	6.8	6.0	6.0
PT	1.7	3.3	7.0	9.6	11.3
PFL		24.2	16.5	17.3	20.7
PDC		1.0	4.4		
PSB		0.2	2.2	2.9	3.7
PC do B		0.6	1.0	1.9	1.4
PCB/PPS		0.6	0.6	0.4	0.6
PL		1.2	3.0	2.5	2.3
PSC		0.2	1.0	0.6	0.4
PSDB			7.4	12.1	19.3
PRN			8.2	0.2	
PMN			0.2	0.8	0.4
PRP			0.2	0.2	
PTR			1.0		
PSD			0.2	0.6	0.6
PRS			0.8		
PRT			0.2		
PST			0.4		0.2
PP[a]				7.0	
PRONA					0.2
PV				0.2	0.2
PSL					0.2
Total seats (= 100%)	(479)	(487)	(503)	(513)	(513)

Sources: Jairo Marconi Nicolau, *Multipartidarismo e Democracia* (Rio de Janeiro: Fundação Getúlio Vargas, 1996), p. 78; and "Brazil—Tribunal Superior Eleitoral," available at http://www.tse.gov.br/divulgacao/.
Note: a. The PP merged with the PPR to form the PPB.

party factions whose demands need to be met before each floor or committee action.

Lacking interlocutors capable of efficiently aggregating issues for negotiation, the Brazilian political system succumbed to what I have elsewhere dubbed the "hyper-active paralysis syndrome": a tendency to believe in the miraculous power of institutional reforms while paying no heed to the fact that excessive inter- and intraparty fragmentation made such reforms either politically unviable or too costly.[48]

A full-fledged constitution-making Congress was elected in November 1986. This Congress insisted on working from scratch, accepting no previous draft and not wanting even an internal grand commission to set guidelines. The task of providing the new democracy with a new constitution was thus entrusted to a Congress with no internal coherence. As a sovereign

Table 3.4   Vote Shares per Candidate in Presidential Elections in Brazil
(1989–1998)

1989 (first round)		1989 (second round)		1994 (first round)		1998 (first round)	
Candidate and Party or Coalition	% of Vote	Candidate and Party or Coalition	% of Vote	Candidate and Party or Coalition	% of Vote	Candidate and Party or Coalition	% of Vote
Collor (PRN-PST PSL)	30.5	Collor (PRN-PST-PSL)	53.0	Cardoso (PSDB-PFL -PTB)	54.3	Cardoso (PSDB-PFL -PPB-PTB-PSD)	53.1
Lula (PT-PSB-PCdoB)	17.2	Lula (PT-PSB-PCdoB)	47.0	Lula (PT-PSB-PCdoB-PPS -PV-PSTU)	27.0	Lula (PT-PDT-PSB-PCdoB -PCB)	31.7
Brizola (PDT)	16.5			Enéas (PRONA)	7.4	Gomes (PPS-PL)	11.0
Covas (PSDB)	11.5			Quércia (PMDB-PSD)	4.4	Enéas (PRONA)	2.1
Maluf (PDS)	8.9			Brizola (PDT)	3.2	Other Candi-dates (=8)	2.1
Affif (PL-PDC)	4.8			Amim (PPR)	2.7		
Guimarães (PMDB)	4.7			Other Candi-dates (=2)	1.0		
Freire (PCB)	1.1						
Other Candidates (=13)	4.8						
Total no. of Valid Votes (= 100%)	67,613,337		66,156,191		63,305,971		67,723,027

Sources: Jairo Marconi Nicolau, *Dados Eleitorais do Brasil (1982–1996)* (Rio de Janeiro: IUPERJ-UCAM, 1998); and "Brazil—Tribunal Superior Eleitoral," available at http://www.tse.gov.br/divulgacao/.

constitution-making body, this Congress theoretically had the power and seemed inclined to shorten the term of office of President Sarney (who had taken office upon the death of Tancredo Neves and had ambiguous democratic credentials at this time because of his prior association with the military regime). The crisis potential imbedded in this situation ended up being diluted, but after the collapse of the Cruzado Plan in late 1986, Sarney never recovered the popularity and authority he briefly enjoyed.

Lacking constructive leadership from the executive, the constitution-making Congress finally adopted a text on October 5, 1988. This constitution was not only wildly detailed but was also disastrous for governability since it greatly aggravated existing fiscal imbalances, maintained and in some cases expanded state economic interventionism and nationalism, and took no steps to attenuate the unparalleled battery of incentives to party fragmentation generated by Brazil's electoral system and party legislation. In fact, it ratified the questionable combination of a presidential system with multipartyism and a highly permissive proportional electoral system, gave a lease on life to old-fashioned nationalist rhetoric and paternalistic welfare provisions, and, last but not least, confirmed in a democratic way, with strong support from the labor unions, the corporatist system established by Vargas's dictatorship (1937–1945)—which had been branded as fascist throughout the preceding forty years.

Needless to say, the newly revised constitution did little to allay apprehensions about the fragility of Brazilian democracy under the Sarney administration. Perhaps because they were conscious of such difficulties, the constitution makers added two highly controversial clauses, one requiring a plebiscite on presidential versus parliamentary government (as well the possible return to a monarchical system) to be held after five years, and another providing for a full revision of the constitution by unicameral vote and absolute majority (instead of 60 percent separately in the House and Senate). The plebiscite was held in April 1993 and the attempt to revise the constitution was made in October of that year. Both were fiascos because of the inability of the party system to engender consistent support for any change.[49]

Eighty-two million voters went to the polls in November 1989 to elect Sarney's successor—the first direct and totally free presidential election in twenty-nine years. By that time the inflation rate had soared to 50 percent a month, and the proportion of voters willing to rate Sarney's administration as "excellent" or "good" had plummeted to 8 percent in the electorate as a whole and to about half that figure among the highly schooled. The stage was thus set for a difficult and, as it turned out, extremely radicalized election. The two largest parties—PMDB and Partido da Frente Liberal (PFL)—that made up the governing Democratic Alliance were discredited to the point of receiving only 4 percent and 1 percent of the vote, respectively, for their presidential candidates. The front-runners were Fernando Collor de Mello of the Partido da Reconstrução Nacional (PRN) and Luís "Lula" Inácio da Silva of the PT.

Despite his determination to curb inflation and to tackle the intractable problem of public-sector reform, President Collor was bound to fail in view of not only his lack of parliamentary support but also, as it turned out, the corrupt practices and entourage he tolerated and allowed to grow around the presidential palace. In May 1992, a congressional committee started the dramatic and, for Brazil, unprecedented investigations that led to an overwhelming impeachment vote in late September. Forced to step down, Collor was succeeded by Vice President Itamar Franco, a former senator known for his strongly nationalist and statist views. In other words, Brazil seemed to be exchanging one terrible problem (a president the country came to reject as corrupt) for another. The new president seemed not to assign a high priority to curbing inflation and appeared even less to understand that in order to achieve this goal, tough structural reforms, even constitutional reforms and a thorough reshuffling of the public sector, would be needed. In fact, from his inauguration in September 1992 until March 1993, President Franco did little to prove that such apprehensions were unfounded. By that time he had already fired three finance ministers and submitted economic agents to a continuous flow of contradictory signals. The press devoted substantial space to what it defined as a crisis climate and did not shun speculations about the dangers posed to democratic stability. Proposals to shorten Franco's term of office and to move up the elections scheduled to take place in October 1994 began to proliferate.

The stage was again set for another radicalized election, with Lula (Workers' Party) possibly facing Paulo Maluf (mayor of São Paulo) as his right-wing opponent. Under such conditions, Lula's victory, perhaps even on the first ballot, looked like a foregone conclusion. With Congress highly divided, as usual, and now facing a serious corruption scandal, important legislation continued to be made by decree-law (or "provisional measures" in Brazil's constitutional language). Considerable apprehension thus began to mount among investors, both domestic and foreign, and not without reason since it seemed unlikely that a serious effort at fiscal balance and market-oriented reform could be made under a party strongly influenced by Marxist and religious reform groups of every description.

It was at this juncture that Franco took an audacious step, appointing Fernando Henrique Cardoso as finance minister and making him virtually prime minister of a de facto parliamentary government. A world-renowned sociologist and respected senator, Cardoso had been in charge of the foreign ministry since the beginning of Franco's term. His appointment to the Finance Ministry and the first-rate team of economic advisers he immediately mobilized quickly renewed hopes that a serious effort to control inflation would be made and dissipated apprehensions of a serious political crisis.

Mustering support both to his monetary stabilization plan and election bid proved easier than most observers thought when Cardoso was appointed finance minister in May 1993. In fact, he not only won over Lula but won on the first ballot, with 54 percent of the vote compared to Lula's 27 percent. The expectation that Brazil was headed toward intense left-right polarization, which might harden resistance to economic reform and perhaps even increase the chance of political instability, simply did not materialize. Cardoso's performance as finance minister and the initiation of the stabilization process quickly allayed such fears.

Cardoso's victory over six opponents, including three former state governors and the most important labor leader in Brazil's history, was an enormous political accomplishment. First, it was a very important step toward the consolidation of representative democracy in Brazil, party fragility and the excessively "consociational" character of the underlying institutional system notwithstanding.[50] Second, it was an exceptionally clear mandate for the continuation of the economic policies Cardoso came to personify—monetary stability and market-oriented reforms—provided such policies are combined with a serious effort to ameliorate social conditions over the next few years.

CONCLUSION

Despite sharp social inequalities and the extremely adverse circumstances under which the transition from military rule was completed, Brazilian democracy survived rather well the polarization of the 1989 presidential elections and the crisis that led to the impeachment of president Collor in 1992. In 1994 the country escaped the prospect of a dangerously radicalized right-left election scenario.

Contrary to most predictions, the 1994 campaign was rather mild. As indicated, the election can be said to have been polarized only in statistical terms and only because of the provision for a runoff election in the context of a multiparty system. In a two-party system, the outcome would clearly have been a landslide for Cardoso. This conjecture is borne out by the low intensity of the campaign at the grassroots, despite the well-known dedication of the PT faithful. This convergent pattern is clearly more conducive to political stability and government effectiveness than a highly antagonistic one would have been.

Although Cardoso's standing as a public figure has long been formidable, his growth as a presidential candidate was clearly a consequence of his role as initiator of the stabilization plan and, *contrario sensu,* of the voters' perception that Lula and the PT stood against the plan. Indeed, support for Cardoso grew spectacularly in the two weeks following the currency change of July 1, 1994—before an actual improvement in purchasing power could be felt among the lowest-income groups. Thus, his success is best understood as a consequence of a "receptive predisposition"—that is, a preexisting demand for monetary stability: a positive attitude born of the discomfort associated with an unstable monetary environment and of at least a dim understanding that stabilization was the necessary first step toward economic recovery. There is substantial evidence that among middle- and high-schooled voters, economic attitudes have changed markedly over the past decade, with a greater value placed on monetary stability and public-sector reform. Old statist beliefs have grown weaker even among left-of-center voters, who now demand concentration of resources and managerial talent on social policies rather than on steel mills and other large industrial projects, as used to be the case in the heyday of state-centered, import-substituting industrialization.

Another important feature of the 1994 election was that Cardoso and the group of economists who designed the Real Plan repeatedly emphasized that complementary reforms, some requiring constitutional amendments, were needed to ensure fiscal balance and consolidate monetary stability. They also forcefully advocated reducing the entrepreneurial role of the public sector through privatization and "flexibilization"—an awkward term I reproduce here only to be faithful to their campaign terminology—of the existing constitutional monopolies in oil and telecommunications in order to allow for public-private partnerships.

At the time of Cardoso's inauguration in January 1995, the question of course was whether his administration would have the necessary backing in Congress and among state governors to undertake such changes. The 1994 gubernatorial elections were very favorable to Cardoso: his Partido do Social-Democracia Brasileira (PSDB) elected the governors of the three largest states (São Paulo, Minas Gerais, and Rio de Janeiro) and altogether six of the twenty-seven governors. Despite the proverbial fragmentation of the Brazilian party system, which makes it virtually impossible for a president to have a stable majority in Congress, even weaker presidents (even Collor) have been able to win passage of needed legislation. *Contrario sensu,* in 1986 the PMDB-PFL alliance, which backed Sarney, came out with an absolute majority in both the House and the Senate and all of the then twenty-three state governorships—and the result could not have been worse.

The Brazilian "problem" of the 1980s and early 1990s was, therefore, more complex. Party weakness and congressional fragmentation were among the key ingredients of that protracted crisis, but at least two other contributing factors must be taken into account. One was the still dense statist ideological legacy: the state-centered industrialization model continued to be perceived as successful, and, hence, most of Brazilian society was still sending contradictory signals as to which route Congress should take. The other factor was insufficient presidential leadership—in part a result of the protracted nature of the Brazilian transition from military to civilian rule from the mid-1970s to the mid-1980s, which weakened the presidential office as such, and in part a result of the fact that each president, from General Figueiredo to Itamar Franco, for different reasons failed to provide constructive leadership.

By the end of his fourth year in office Cardoso was probably the most powerful president Brazil has ever had under democratic rule. In fact, the political system as a whole seems to have become more stable due to: (1) the new worldwide economic agenda, narrowing the country's perceived room for choice and hence the ideological antagonisms that used to be rampant on issues like trade and financial opening, inflation, and privatization; (2) more stable support among the mass public resulting chiefly from the administration's success in keeping inflation at bay (by Brazilian standards) for a long period of time; and hence, (3) the dilution of the presidency's plebiscitarian character, that is, its traditionally close dependence on volatile popular support.

The traditional close watch on popular support has been largely replaced by continuous congressional maneuvering. The extremely rigid and detailed Brazilian Constitution poses serious obstacles to economic and public-sector reform. Constitutional amendments must be approved by 60 percent of all legislators, twice and separately in both chambers of Congress. As Brazil's largest party commands about 20 percent of the votes at best, the consequence is that continuous interparty negotiation becomes absolutely imperative. In 1994 a previously unthinkable coalition between the PSDB and the PFL was formed to endorse Cardoso's nomination. This coalition was later expanded to include four other parties, a nominal majority totaling 80 percent of the congressional seats. Observers of the Brazilian political scene have seen this as a relative parliamentarization of the political system—a trend not belied by Cardoso's frequent use of provisional measures and his occasional resort to "silent majority" rhetoric. On constitutional issues, we might even speak of a perverse kind of parliamentarization, as the executive is heavily dependent on that precarious 80 percent coalition to muster 60 percent of the votes and of course does not possess the countervailing prerogative of threatening to dissolve the legislature and call new elections in case of an executive-legislative deadlock, which is typical of parliamentary heads of state. On ordinary matters, it is the legislature that remains virtually hostage to the executive, given the latter's prerogative of issuing provisional measures.[51]

Despite the downturn in the economy begun in early 1998 as a consequence of the financial collapse of Southeast Asian countries in 1997, subsequently reinforced by the collapse of Russia in August 1998, it seems likely that current market-oriented economic policies will continue and that the executive will keep on being supported by a broad multiparty coalition.

This raises the question of the impact of the 1998 presidential succession on the political system, particularly on the party system.

The October 1998 presidential election was easily won by Cardoso due to the compounded effects of four factors: (1) Cardoso's own merits as a caliber candidate and his performance in office; (2) Lula's failure to convince the voters that he was a viable alternative to the incumbent; (3) massive strategic voting; and (4) the relatively low percentage of protest votes.

The last three factors need some explanation. As for Lula, it is plausible to surmise that the PT is accepted by voters as a valid alternative only at the state and local levels, not at the national level. With regard to the third factor, the point is that many voters who would rather have voted for hopeless candidates decided not to waste their ballots on the latter, and opted instead for Cardoso, who was closer than Lula to their preferences. If we were to add the vote shares that small-party candidates could have possibly obtained had voters decided to vote sincerely (as opposed to strategically) to the shares of Lula and Ciro Gomes, a runoff might have occurred. Finally, it seems that protest votes loom large only when the country's political atmosphere is one of complete cynicism, which has not been the case since the launching of the Real Plan in July 1994 and the inauguration of the Cardoso presidency in January 1995. Before these events cynicism was rampant as a result above all of hyperinflation—which hampered any possibility of individual planning—and frequent corruption scandals. Under Cardoso, Brazil's atmosphere has been marked by a moderate optimism with regard to the economy and the absence of corruption scandals. Without cynicism, antisystem candidates like the protofascist Enéas were not able to prosper. The role of such candidates in the 1998 campaign was reduced to that of blurring the communication lines between the relevant parties and the voters, thus rendering the electoral contest less intelligible to the latter. This was a problem particularly to Lula, who needed a more intense and clearer public debate to grow in the electorate.

In addition, there is the related question of the institutional reforms that Brazilians debated throughout the 1980s (notably during the 1987–1988 Constitutional Congress) and early 1990s (a plebiscite on presidential versus parliamentary government was held in 1993). One issue in this debate was the perceived need to make Brazil's multiparty presidentialism more functional by reducing the number of parties and creating more efficient mechanisms to coordinate executive-legislative relations.

The fact of the matter seems to be that progress already achieved in economic and public-sector reform and the approval of the constitutional amendment allowing presidents to run for a second term (more on that below) may well turn the political reform debate into a dead letter. Political reform has begun to take place in real terms, though only partially in constitutional terms. The issue now is increasingly the direction rather than the scope or the pace of change. If economic reform continues and the presidency retains the strength it gained under Cardoso, it is quite plausible to hypothesize that the party system will be simplified over the next decade or so in practice, if not in terms of nominal labels. Many of the existing party labels are only legal vehicles for personal or otherwise narrow political interests, and even some of the more consistent ones are clearly losing importance as the political process becomes structured as a bipolar competition between Cardoso's center-right coalition and a left-to-center one headed by the PT. This trend is likely to be reinforced if the de facto single-member district pattern of electoral competition that already prevails in many regions becomes more widespread.[52] Under this broad hypothesis, Brazil's party system may formally continue to look like a European one some years from now, with a number of labels striving to enact nineteenth-century ideological roles; but the system's actual dynamics may well become simpler, and perhaps even take on the contours of a two-block competition like that of France or even a two-party one as in the United States. Needless to say, this trend may be stalled or delayed by the electoral law, which in Brazil tends to make life easier for small parties. The news, however, is that economic reform and presidential reelection are now working powerfully on the contrary direction.

Finally, a note on Brazil's first experience with reelection is in order. The constitutional amendment that granted, for the first time in Brazil's republican history, the right to one consecutive reelection for executive posts was approved in June 1997. There are sensible arguments in favor of and against the consecutive reelection of presidents in Latin America. In Brazil the right to run for one consecutive reelection had always been considered unacceptable out of fear that incumbents would use the governmental machine to stay in power. So under the Old Republic (1889–1930) the constitution established a nonrenewable four-year term. In the 1946–1964 period the term was five years, also without the right to one consecutive term. The military regime (1964–1985) initially provided for a president with a nonrenewable five-year term. However, the last military president (João Figueiredo, 1979–1985) served a six-year term. The 1988 Constitution reenacted the five-year term, and, as always, without the right to one consecutive reelection. Yet by this time many thought that the country would adopt a parliamentary regime in the upcoming constitutionally mandated 1993 plebiscite on the system of government. Had parliamentarism won the plebiscite, the main institutional issue would have been how to appoint a prime minister (chief of government), and not so much the duration of the president's term of office, which might have been extended as a sort of compensation for the reduction of his or her powers as chief of state. With the defeat of parliamentarism and, what's even worse, the reduction of the president's term from five to four years as a result of the 1994 constitutional reforms, the country was left with the worst of all worlds, namely, pure presidentialism with a nonrenewable four-year term.

Yet with the election of Cardoso and the launching of long-term structural reforms, reelection became more acceptable, and a constitutional amendment was finally approved in 1997. In fact, support for reelection had become stronger as constitutional reforms—particularly those of the civil service and of the pension system, essential to the country's search for fiscal balance and, therefore, to safeguard the Real Plan—lagged in Congress. The approval of the reelection amendment was not the result of manipulation; on the contrary, it was achieved within the very stringent rules that the 1988 Constitution established for the acceptance of constitutional amendments; but it is certainly true that the circumstantial factors referred to above were relevant for Cardoso's and the Congress's decision to abandon the time-honored principle of no immediate reelection. Rather than taking place as a likely corollary of the Real Plan's and its attendant structural reforms' success, reelection became a necessary cnndition for Cardoso to continue to pursue that success.

It is also true that the 1998 electoral campaign was characterized by sharp asymmetry of forces between the government and the opposition. Such asymmetry was due to three factors: (1) the Cardoso government's high job approval rate; (2) the strong social rejection of Lula and the PT as alternatives to the current governing coalition, as already mentioned above; and (3) the undeniable weight of the governmental machine, not so much in the age-old sense of abusing patronage powers, but rather in the sense that the incumbent was able to make electorally relevant policy decisions and was constantly in the media center stage. One could argue that the last factor is a strong indictment of reelection. However, one should bear in mind that Cardoso's tenure in office would not have been so beneficial to his reelection bid had his performance been poor in the eyes of the majority of voters. What's more, the alternative to reelection in a presidential regime can be even worse; a longer term of five or six years, for example, involves the danger of eventually leaving the country in the hands of a failed or deadlocked president who cannot be unseated by means of regular constitutional procedures.

Another important aspect of Brazil's first experience with the right to reelection is that governors and mayors were also entitled to it. This part of the 1997 constitutional decision is more controversial; not a few politicians and analysts think that, at these lower levels, patronage and abuse of power are still real dangers, and would therefore have preferred to see reelection approved only for presidents and governors, or see it be gradually extended, first to presidents, then to governors, and, finally, after a long period of practice, to mayors.

NOTES

This chapter (except for the last section) was initially drafted in 1986. Luís Aureliano Gama Andrade, Wanderley G. Santos, Amaury de Souza, and my colleagues at the Instituto de Estudos Econômicos, Sociais e Políticos de São Paulo (IDESP), all made valuable suggestions to improve the initial version. I am grateful to Octavio Amorim Neto's substantial and substantive help in this second revision.

1. The opposition Movimento Democrático Brasileiro elected sixteen of the twenty-two senators in 1974 (renovating one-third of the Senate), with a strong showing in the more urban and modernized states. An extended discussion of the structure of electoral competition as a factor capable of preventing authoritarian consolidation in Brazil can be found in Bolívar Lamounier, "Authoritarian Brasil Revisited," in Alfred Stepan, ed., *Democratizing Brazil* (Oxford and New York: Oxford University Press, 1988).

2. The Institutional Act 5 was decreed by the military regime in December 1968. It granted the president extensive and unchecked powers to adjourn the Congress, to intervene in the states and in municipalities, to cancel the term of elected officials, to suspend political rights of any citizen for ten years, and to suspend the right to habeas corpus. Based on the Act 5, President Geisel introduced indirect elections for one-third of the senators. These senators were quickly nicknamed "bionic" and were never accepted as legitimate by public opinion. Another measure was the severe curtailing of electoral propaganda through radio and television, generalizing restrictions previously applied only in the municipal election of 1976.

3. One of these bills aimed at increasing contributions to finance the social security system; the other attempted to extend the *sublegendas* (triple candidacies in each party) to the gubernatorial elections.

4. Cardoso was probably the first scholar to stress that the Brazilian authoritarian regime did not pursue stagnant economic policies; that it was, on the contrary, decidedly modernizing. See Fernando H. Cardoso, "Dependent-Associated Development: Theoretical and Practical Implications," in Alfred Stepan, ed., *Authoritarian Brazil: Origins, Outputs, Future* (New Haven: Yale University Press, 1973). On economic policy in the 1970s, see Bolívar Lamounier and Alkimar R. Moura, "Economic Policy and Political Opening in Brazil," in Jonathan Hartlyn and Samuel A. Morley, eds., *Latin American Political Economy: Financial Crisis and Political Change* (Boulder, CO: Westview Press, 1986). For a comprehensive overview of economic and political developments since the 1930s, see Bolívar Lamounier and Edmar Bacha, "Democracy and Economic Reforms in Brazil," in Joan Nelson, ed., *Precarious Balance: Democracy and Economic Reforms in Eastern Europe and Latin America* (San Francisco: ICS Press, 1994).

5. In addition to the "bionic" senators, created in 1977, the government majority increased the weight of the smaller states in the electoral college through Constitutional Amendment 22 of 1982. The traditional but now controversial overrepresentation that those states enjoy in the federal chamber was thus unacceptably extended to the presidential succession. It is worth noting that the opposition assimilated even this change when it decided to present Tancredo Neves to the electoral college as a presidential candidate.

6. See Juan J. Linz, "The Future of an Authoritarian Situation or the Institutionalization of an Authoritarian Regime," in Alfred Stepan, ed., *Authoritarian Brazil: Origins, Outputs, and Future* (New Haven: Yale University Press, 1973).

7. Bureaucratic continuity has led many historians to accept the naive idea that Brazil inherited a ready-made state from the Portuguese at the time of independence in 1822. The more cautious view that Brazilian state building was "completed" by 1860 or 1870 may be accepted, but even this with important qualifications. See J. G. Merquior, "Patterns of State-Building in Brazil and Argentina," in John A. Hall, ed., *States in History* (London: Blackwell, 1986).

8. My treatment of these questions is evidently inspired by Hannah Pitkin's now-classic work. However, searching for different images of representation in the Brazilian case, we placed them in a historical sequence she may not have intended, at least not as a general rule. See Hannah Pitkin, *The Concept of Representation* (Berkeley and Los Angeles: University of California Press, 1972).

9. See Robert Dahl, *Polyarchy: Participation and Opposition* (New Haven: Yale University Press, 1971). On the formation of a central power as a prebondition for peaceful competition, see the excellent treatment of the English case in Harvey Mansfield Jr., "Party Government and the Settlement of 1688," *American Political Science Review* 63, no. 4 (1964): 933–950; on the U.S. case, see Richard Hofstadter, *The Idea of a Party System* (Berkeley and Los Angeles: University of California Press, 1972).

10. To place the notion of Hobbesian state building in proper perspective, we must distinguish among states founded through negotiation among previously existing and autonomous units (e.g., the United States) and states whose foundation was a progressive result of a center's striving to control a larger "periphery" (e.g., the Prussian-led foundation of Germany, or Brazil). In the case of states founded through negotiation, if a representative system is instituted to regulate the political order, elected officials will act as agents of the regional forces brought together in the state formation process, who thus serve as the "principal" to whom the agents tend to be most responsive. Authority is delegated to these agents so they can perform the tasks of mirroring and furthering the interests of their constituencies vis-à-vis the newly established (or reinforced) central government. Representation, thus, is a bottom-up delegation, consistent with the Lockean paradigm.

The second case is rather different. Here, assuming that the center's effort to control a larger territory cannot be achieved either by sheer force or entirely by negotiation, the institution of a nominally representative system is likely to function as a top-down delegation. The central elite striving to impose a new (or keep a) territorial order will tend to use elections as a mechanism for choosing loyal political agents in the regions and/or to avoid costly involvement in local or regional factional struggles. In this arrangement, the central elite is the "principal" and the co-opted local factions are its agents. Due to the key role performed by local factions in enforcing the domination of the center, the latter is prone to stack the electoral rules in favor of its loyalists, but there is a limit to this, since elections also have the function of reducing the political costs of the center's involvement. The reverse side of the co-optation mechanism is therefore the progressive emergence of neutral rules of representation, and here lies the Hobbesian nature of the whole arrangement. Despite its fundamentally top-down accountability model, Hobbesian state building is flexible enough to accommodate the demands at least of the more powerful and/or complex regions, where some degree of pluralism is likely to have developed, and whose political conflicts cannot be solved by the sheer imposition of the center's will.

11. See José Murilo de Carvalho, *A construção da ordem* (Rio de Janeiro: Editora Campus, 1980).

12. The classic here is Victor Nunes Leal, *Coronelismo, enxada e voto: O município e a regime representativo no Brasil* (Rio de Janeiro: Editora Forense, 1948).

13. On the evolution of military institutions, see Edmundo Campos Coelho, *Em busca da identidade: O exército e a política na sociedade brasileira* (Rio de Janeiro: Editora Forense, 1976); José Murilo de Carvalho, "As Forças Armadas na Primeira República: O poder Desestabilizador" (Belo Horizonte: UFMG, Cadernos do Departamento de Ciência Política no. 1, March 1974). On the nineteenth-century National Guard, see Fernando Uricoechea, *O minotauro imperial* (São Paulo: Difel, 1978).

14. Control of the credentials commission (Comissão de Verificação de Poderes) of the federal chamber was the key to the system, since through it undesirable deputies eventually elected in the states would not be allowed to take up their position. This became popularly known as *degola* ("beheading"). Souza provides an excellent treatment of this question: "If the sedimentation of the [state] oligarchies was essential to consolidate the federation, it was also the reason for its future weakness. Contrary to the imperial framework, rotation in power among state oligarchies now became impossible." See Maria do Carmo Campello de Souza, "O processo político-partidário na velha república," in Carlos Guilherme Mota, ed., *Brasil em Perspectiva* (São Paulo: Difel, 1971), p. 203.

15. There is an extensive literature on the Revolution of 1930. Especially useful for our purposes is Campello de Souza, "Processo político-partidário." See also Boris Fausto, ed., *O Brasil republicano,* 3 vols. (São Paulo: Difel, 1978, 1982, and 1983); and Paulo Brandi, *Getulio Vargas: Da vida para a história* (Rio de Janeiro: Zahar Editores, 1985).

16. Nunes Leal, *Coronelismo,* pp. 170–171.

17. Dahlsian democratization, as already referred to above, means the establishment of legitimate contestation. See Dahl, *Polyarchy,* pp. 1–47.

18. Protofascism is used here in the same sense given to it by James Gregor, *The Ideology of Fascism* (New York: Free Press, 1969), chapter 2. He deals with important theoretical precursors, such as Gumplowicz, Pareto, and Mosca, stressing their antiparliamentarianism, their view on the relation between elite and mass, on the function of political myths, and the like.

19. On the corporatist "regulation" of citizenship, see Wanderley Guilherme dos Santos, *Cidadania e justiça* (Rio de Janeiro: Editora Campus, 1979). Comprehensive accounts of the corporatist features of the labor relations system can be found in P. Schmitter, *Interest Conflict and Political Change in Brazil* (Stanford: Stanford University Press, 1971); Amaury de Souza, *The Nature of Corporatist Representation: Leaders and Members of Organized Labor in Brazil* (Ph.D. diss., Massachusetts Institute of Technology, 1978); and Youssef Cohen, *The Manipulation of Consent: The State and Working Class in Brazil* (Pittsburgh: University of Pittsburgh Press, 1991).

20. The name of Gilberto Freyre comes readily to mind in connection with race relations and nationality in Brazil. On these themes, see T. Skidmore, *Black into White* (New York: Oxford University Press, 1974). The impact of these developments in Brazilian political culture was of course enormous in the 1930s and as a support to the Estado Novo. The factual importance of these core beliefs has been recognized quite broadly in the ideological spectrum since then. On intellectuals and culture policy in that period, see Simon Schwartzman et al., *Tempos de capanema* (Rio de Janeiro: Paz e Terra, 1984); Sérgio Miceli, *Intelectuais e classe dirigente no Brasil (1920–1945)* (São Paulo: Difel, 1979); Lúcia Lippi de Oliveira, *Estado Novo: Ideologia e poder* (Rio de Janeiro: Zahar Editores, 1982).

21. On the downfall of the Estado Novo, see Maria do Carmo Campello de Souza, *Estado e Partidos Políticos no Brasil* (São Paulo: Editora Alfa-Omega, 1976); T. Skidmore, *Politics in Brazil: An Experiment in Democracy* (New York: Oxford University Press, 1968); Peter Flynn, *Brazil: A Political Analysis* (Boulder, CO: Westview Press, 1975). On the UDN, see Maria Vitória Benevides, *UDN e udenismo* (Rio de Janeiro: Paz e Terra, 1981).

22. The literature on Vargas's second government is surprisingly small. In addition to the works of Flynn and Skidmore, already cited, see Maria Celina Soares D'Araujo, *O segundo governo Vargas, 1951–1954* (Rio de Janeiro: Zahar Editores, 1982); and Edgard Carone, *A república liberal II* (São Paulo: Difel, 1985).

23. Useful data on bureaucratic growth under the Estado Novo can be found in Maria do Carmo Campello de Souza, *Estado e Partidos Políticos no Brasil.* On economic policymaking from the 1930s to the mid-1950s, see John Wirth, *The Politics of Brazilian Development 1930–1954* (Stanford: Stanford University Press, 1970); and Luciano Martins, *Pouvoir et développement économique au Brésil* (Paris: Editions Anthropos, 1976).

24. J. G. Merquior, "Patterns of State-Building," p. 284.

25. An overview of these hypotheses and of the relevant literature can be found in Bolívar Lamounier and Rachel Meneguello, *Partidos políticos e consolidação democrática: O caso brasileiro* (São Paulo: Editora Brasiliense, 1986), chapter 4. Rigorous analysis of the crisis leading to 1964 was pioneered by Wanderley Guilherme dos Santos, *The Calculus of Conflict: Impasse in Brazilian Politics* (Ph.D. diss., Stanford University, 1974). Important works for the understanding of executive-legislative relations in the 1950s and early 1960s include Celso Lafer, *The Planning Process and the Political System in Brazil* (Ph.D. diss., Cornell University, 1970); Maria Vitória Benevides, *O governo Kubitschek* (Rio de Janeiro: Paz e Terra, 1976); Lúcia Hippolito, *De raposas e reformistas: o PSD e a experiência democrática brasileira (1945–64)* (Rio de Janeiro: Paz e Terra, 1985); Scott Mainwaring, "Brazil: Weak Parties, Feckless Democracy," in Scott Mainwaring and Timothy Scully, eds., *Building Democratic Institutions: Party Systems in Latin America* (Stanford: Stanford University Press, 1995); Scott Mainwaring, "Multipartism, Robust Federalism, and Presidentialism in Brazil," in Scott Mainwaring and Matthew S. Shugart, eds., *Presidentialism and Democracy in Latin America* (New York: Cambridge University Press, 1997); and Octavio Amorim Neto and Fabiano Santos, "The Executive Connection: Explaining the Puzzles of Party Cohesion in Brazil," paper presented at 20th meeting of the Latin American Studies Association (Guadalajara, Mexico, 1997).

26. On the ambiguities of military-directed institution building after 1964, see Juan Linz, "The Future of an Authoritarian Situation"; Bolívar Lamounier, "Authoritarian Brazil Revisited"; Wanderley Guilherme dos Santos, *Poder e política: Crônica do autoritarismo brasileiro* (Rio de Janeiro: Forense, 1978). Roett synthesized those ambiguities as follows: "In Brazil, although the latitude given to the civilian political process is severely compromised, it does exist. The commitment to political participation—limited, elitist, and manipulable as it is—is strongly rooted in Brazilian constitutional history. Geisel's efforts at decompression were part of that historical belief that there should be a more open system." See Riordan Roett, "The Political Future of Brazil," in William Overholt, ed., *The Future of Brazil* (Boulder, CO: Westview Press, 1978).

27. Before independence and especially before the intensification of mining, in the early eighteenth century, the local chambers (*câmaras municipais*) were almost exclusively made up of landowners and had virtually unlimited authority, concentrating executive, legislative, and judiciary functions. Their members were chosen by means of a crude electoral system set forth in the *ordenações* of the Portuguese crown. During the nineteenth century, detailed regulations were established to control local and statewide elections. Needless to say, the franchise was limited and voting was not secret. In addition, the empire kept the tradition of not allowing a clear distinction between legislative and executive functions at the local level; an elected local executive would appear only under the republic, and especially after 1930.

28. On bureaucratic continuity, see Raimundo Faoro, *Os donos do poder* (Porto Alegre: Editora Globo, 1958); for a comparative analysis, see Merquior, "Patterns of State-Building"; on the military organization, see Coelho, *Em busca da identidade.*

29. See Wanderley Guilherme dos Santos, "A Pós-'revolução' brasileira," in Hélio Jaguaribe, ed., *Brasil: Sociedade democrática* (Rio de Janeiro: José Olympio Editora, 1985).

30. Sylvia A. Hewlett, "The State and Brazilian Economic Development," in William Overholt, ed., *The Future of Brazil* (Boulder, CO: Westview Press, 1978), p. 150.

31. Russett calculated Gini coefficients for inequality in land tenure circa 1960 in forty-seven countries and found Brazil to be the thirty-sixth from low to high concentration. See Bruce M. Russett, "Inequality and Instability: The Relation of Land Tenure to Politics," in Robert A. Dahl and Deanne E. Neubauer, eds., *Readings in Modern Political Analysis* (Englewood Cliffs, NJ: Prentice-Hall, 1968), pp. 150–162. There is no reason to assume that landed property is less concentrated today than in the 1960s. What did happen was that agrarian social relations became thoroughly capitalist. Landed property in Brazil was never "feudal" in a technical sense. Land was essentially used for capitalist purposes, i.e., to produce for a market or to function as a reserve of value in a highly inflationary economy. True, social relations were often paternalistic and exploitative, but this, too, is now undergoing rapid change.

32. The literature on growth and income distribution in this period is, of course, voluminous. A convenient starting point is Ricardo Tolipan and Artur Carlos Tinelli, eds, *A controvérsia sobre distribuição de renda e desenvolvimento* (Rio de Janeiro: Zahar Editores, 1975); see also Edmar Bacha, *Os mitos de uma década* (Rio de Janeiro: Editora Paz e Terra, 1976); and World Bank, *World Development Report 1983* and *World Development Report 1986* (New York: Oxford University Press, 1986).

33. Douglas H. Graham, "The Brazilian Economy: Structural Legacies and Future Prospects," in William Overholt, ed., *The Future of Brazil* (Boulder, CO: Westview Press, 1978), p. 122.

34. See José Serra, "Ciclos e mudanças estruturais na economia brasileira do pós-guerra," in L. G. Belluzzo and Renata Coutinho, eds., *Desenvolvimento capitalista no Brasil: Ensaios sobre a crise,* no. 2 (São Paulo: Editora Brasiliense, 1983), p. 64.

35. World Bank, *World Development Report 1994* (New York: Oxford University Press, 1994); Instituto de Pesquisa Econômica Aplicada (IPEA), "Três anos de plano real" (Brasília: IPEA, Carta de Conjuntura 73, June 1997), available at http://www.ipea.gov.br/pub/.

36. The following account of class structure in relation to the corporatist system draws heavily on dos Santos's important essay, "A pós-'revoluçao' brasileira."

37. Despite its partly revolutionary, partly messianic rhetoric, the MST does not represent a danger to institutional stability in the near future. This is because, first, the MST's demands are being increasingly met by the government. For example, between 1964 and 1994,

218,033 families received land property titles from the government's agrarian reform program, an average of 7,033 families per year. Significantly, 104,956 families were benefited with land property titles in 1995–1996, an average of 52,478 families per year (see Brazil—Presidência da República, *Reforma agrária—Compromisso de todos* [Brasília: Presidência da República, Secretaria de Comunicação Social, 1997]). Second, there is a strong social rejection to its revolutionary rhetoric. And finally, agrarian problems in Brazil are becoming residual given that most of the country's agricultural sector is organized in large-scale capitalist enterprises, a trend that will certainly be reinforced in the years to come.

38. See dos Santos, "A pós-'revolução' brasileira," p. 258; see also Carlos A. Hasenbalg, *Discriminação e desigualdades raciais no Brasil* (Rio de Janeiro: Ediçoes Graal, 1979).

39. On Brazilian party history, see Lamounier and Meneguello, *Partidos políticos.*

40. See the works cited in note 25, above.

41. Alfred Stepan, "Political Leadership and Regime Breakdown: Brazil," in Juan Linz and Alfred Stepan, eds., *The Breakdown of Democracies* (Baltimore: Johns Hopkins University Press, 1978); Argelina C. Figueiredo, *Democracia ou reformas? Alternativas democráticas à crise política: 1961–1964* (Rio de Janeiro: Paz e Terra, 1993).

42. The importance of law schools throughout the nineteenth century and up to 1945 is beyond dispute. Resistance to Vargas's Estado Novo and again to the post-1964 military governments gave them a new lease on life. The Brazilian Lawyers Association was a basic reference point for the opposition during the decompression period.

43. A detailed analysis of Geisel's economic and political strategies can be found in Lamounier and Moura, "Economic Policy and Political Opening"; see also, Lamounier and Bacha, "Democracy and Economic Reforms."

44. Perhaps we can interpret in this light the familiar finding that support for the democratic "rules of the game" is often more a matter of elite ethos than of mass attitudes. On "collective goods" as a tool in political analysis, see Mancur Olson Jr., *The Logic of Collective Action* (New York: Schocken Books, 1968).

45. Dahl, *Polyarchy,* pp. 57–61.

46. Octavio Amorim Neto and Gary W. Cox, "Electoral Institutions, Cleavage Structures, and the Number of Parties," *American Journal of Political Science* 41, no. 1 (January 1997): 149–174. For detailed information on fragmentation and an analysis of its causes in Brazil, see Jairo Marconi Nicolau, *Multipartidarismo e democracia* (Rio de Janeiro: Fundação Getúlio Vargas, 1996).

47. Fernando Limongi and Argelina C. Figueiredo, "Partidos políticos na câmara dos deputados: 1989–1994," *Dados* 38, no. 3 (1995): 497–525. See also Bolívar Lamounier and Amaury de Souza, "O congresso nacional frente aos desafios da reforma do estado: Relatório de pesquisa" (São Paulo: IDESP, 1996). This research report analyzes a survey on congressmembers' preferences over economic reforms conducted by IDESP in 1995. The survey shows that Brazilian legislators are divided along well-defined ideological cleavages, which provide a basis for predictability in congressional behavior.

48. Bolívar Lamounier, "Impasse in Brazil," *Journal of Democracy* 5, no. 3 (July 1994): 72–87.

49. For an analysis of the presidential-parliamentary debate, see my chapter "Brazil: Towards Parliamentarism?" in Juan J. Linz and Arturo Valenzuela, eds. *The Failure of Presidential Democracy* (Baltimore: Johns Hopkins University Press, 1994); plebiscite results and a brief analysis of the reasons parliamentarism was defeated can be found in pp. 289–290.

50. On the "consociational" nature of Brazilian institutional arrangements, see my chapter "Institutional Structure and Governability in the 1990s," in Maria D'Alva G. Kinzo, ed., *Brazil: Economic, Social and Political Challenges of the 1990s* (London: British Academic Press, 1992); also Lamounier and Bacha, "Democracy and Economic Reforms."

51. On the politics of provisional measures in Brazil, see Argelina Cheibub Figueiredo and Fernando Limongi, "O congresso e as medidas provisórias: Abdicação ou delegação?" *Novos estudos cebrap* 47 (March 1997): 127–154; and Timothy J. Power, "The Pen Is Mightier Than the Congress: Presidential Decree in Brazil," in John M. Carey and Matthew S. Shugart, eds., *Executive Decree Authority* (New York: Cambridge University Press, 1998).

52. For an analysis of spatial patterns of electoral competition in Brazil, see Barry Ames, "Electoral Strategy Under Open-List Proportional Representation," *American Journal of Political Science* 39, no. 2 (May 1995): 406–433.

PERU

Arica

Iquique

BOLIVIA

Antofagasta CHILE

PARAGUAY

BRAZIL

Pacific

Ocean

ARGENTINA

URUGUAY

Valparaiso

★ Santiago

Concepcion

Valdivia

Puerto Montt

Atlantic

Ocean

FALKLAND/MALVINAS ISLANDS

CHILE

4

CHILE:
Origins and Consolidation of a
Latin American Democracy

Arturo Valenzuela

With the inauguration of President Eduardo Frei Ruiz-Tagle on March 11, 1994, the Chilean people witnessed the installation of the second democratic administration since the sixteen-year dictatorship of General Augusto Pinochet. Frei's predecessor, Patricio Aylwin Azócar, who gained the presidency when the general lost a plebiscite on his continued rule, successfully steered the country back to civilian rule, reestablishing the democratic traditions that had set Chile apart from most of its neighbors on the South American continent.

Before the 1973 breakdown of democracy, which led to the longest and most brutal authoritarian interlude in the nation's history, Chile would have been classified, following the criteria used by the editors of this book, as a high success, a stable and uninterrupted case of democratic rule. For most of the preceding one hundred years, Chilean politics had been characterized by a high level of party competition and popular participation, open and fair elections, and strong respect for democratic freedoms. Indeed, Kenneth A. Bollen, in one of the most comprehensive cross-national efforts to rank countries on a scale of political democracy, placed Chile in the top 15 percent in 1965, a score higher than that of the United States, France, Italy, or West Germany. For 1960, Chile's score was higher than that of Britain.[1]

However, synchronic studies such as Bollen's fail to account for the fact that Chile's democratic tradition was not a recent phenomenon, but goes back several generations. In the nineteenth century, Chile developed democratic institutions and procedures, setting the country apart from many of its European counterparts, as well as its Latin American neighbors. As Leon Epstein has noted, in Europe "political power was not often effectively transferred from hereditary rulers to representative assemblies no matter how narrow their electorates until late in the nineteenth century."[2] By contrast, Chile had, by the turn of the century, experienced several decades in which political authority was vested in elected presidents, and Congress wielded substantial influence over the formulation of public policy.[3] Indeed, from 1830 until 1973, nearly all Chilean presidents were followed in office by their duly elected successors. Deviations to this pattern occurred only in 1891, in the aftermath of a brief civil war, and in the turbulent period between 1924 and 1932, when four chief executives felt pressured to resign in an atmosphere of political and social unrest and military involvement in politics. In 143 years, Chile experienced only thirteen months of unconstitutional rule under some form of junta, and only four months under a junta dominated exclusively by the military; and, though the executive was preeminent in the decades after independence, Congress gradually increased its prerogatives, becoming an important arena for national debate and one of the most powerful legislatures in the world.

Robert Dahl has noted that the development of democracy entails not only establishing institutions for public contestation and leadership renewal, but also popular sovereignty.[4] In nineteenth-century Chile, citizenship was sharply restricted, first to men who owned property and later to those who were literate. Thus, Chile was only a partial democracy, according to the definition used here, until well into the twentieth century, when women's suffrage was established, the literacy requirement was abolished, and eighteen-year-olds were given the right to vote.[5] It must be stressed, however, that Chile did not deviate substantially from other nascent democracies in extending citizenship. In 1846, only 2 percent of the Chilean population voted, but this figure was comparable to that in Britain in 1830, Luxembourg in 1848, the Netherlands in 1851, and Italy in 1871. In 1876, two years after it had abolished the property requirement, Chile had 106,000 registered voters, compared to 84,000 in Norway for a comparable adult male population. Secret voting was established in Chile in 1874, shortly after its adoption in Britain, Sweden, and Germany, and before its adoption in Belgium, Denmark, France, Prussia, and Norway.[6]

Reflecting the profound social changes brought about by urbanization, incipient industrialization, and a booming export economy, Chile's middle- and then working-class groups were incorporated into the democratic political game by the second decade of the twentieth century. With the rise of an organized left, Chilean politics became sharply polarized between vastly different conceptions of what the country's future should be. This division, articulated by powerful and institutionalized parties functioning within the framework of Chile's presidential system, placed increasing strains on democracy. In the 1970s, these strains contributed to the breakdown of democracy soon after the first leftist candidate in Chilean history had been elected to the nation's highest office.

The years of military rule had a profound effect on the life of the nation. Chile, one of the most politicized and participatory countries in the world, became one of the most depoliticized. Political parties were banned or dismantled, their leaders killed, exiled, or persecuted. Representative institutions, including the national Congress and local governments, were closed down, with all authority devolving on a four-person military junta dominated increasingly by army commander Pinochet.

The junta sought to change the underlying physiognomy of national politics, convinced that the leaders, parties, and ideologies of the past could be rendered obsolete by a combination of harsh discipline and revolutionary economic and social policies. Blaming Chile's woes not only on the Marxist regime of Salvador Allende but also on Chile's statist and protectionist policies forged over several administrations, the junta slashed state subsidies and government spending, dramatically lowering tariff barriers to encourage export-led economic growth.

Although the social costs were extremely high, by the mid-1980s Chile's military rulers succeeded in setting the country on a course of dynamic development. Pinochet failed, however, to eliminate the parties and politicians he held responsible for the nation's shortcomings. They were far more rooted in society than the military leaders had believed; they gradually rebuilt their ties to militants and followers and stunned Pinochet by defeating him decisively in his own prearranged plebiscite on September 11, 1988.

To accomplish this historic event, however, party leaders were forced to moderate their ideological disputes and forge a new consensus aimed at making democracy work. The hard lessons of the hyperpolarization of the 1960s and the repressive years of military rule contributed to the development of a strong and cohesive multiparty coalition that formed the base of support for the government of Patricio Aylwin, inaugurated on March 11, 1990.

This chapter begins with a historical overview of the major trends in Chilean politics. It is not intended to cover all periods in equal depth; rather, it gives disproportionate attention to those historical developments that are especially important in formulating analytical arguments about the development and breakdown of Chilean democracy. Following this is a theoretical assessment of the applicability to the Chilean case of several leading hypotheses generated by social scientists to account for the emergence of democratic politics. The third part analyzes the breakdown of democracy, highlighting those variables that best explain the complex process resulting in the 1973 military coup. The fourth gives an overview of military rule in Chile, explaining how authoritarian politics was first institutionalized and why the transition back to democracy was so slow and painful. It ends with a brief review of the first civilian administration after the end of military rule and an assessment of the future course of Chilean democracy.

HISTORICAL OVERVIEW

Origins and Consolidation of Chilean Democracy, 1830–1960

As in the rest of Latin America, attempts in Chile to inaugurate republican institutions based on democratic principles inspired by the framers of the U.S. Constitution met with resounding failure.[7] For a quarter-century after Chile's declaration of independence from Spain in 1810, the new nation alternated between dictatorship and anarchy. The war of independence was a prolonged and bloody civil war "to the death," as much as a war to end colonial rule, as many Chileans supported the royalist cause. The final defeat of Spanish forces left the territory's administrative and governing institutions in shambles, and local elites bitterly divided by regional, family, ideological, and personal disputes. Gone were the complex, far-flung patrimonial bureaucracy and the mediating power of the crown, which for centuries had imposed a traditional style of political authority over a distant colony. In 1830, the clear military victory of one coalition of forces permitted the inauguration of a concerted effort to institute political order and encourage economic progress. However, despite the able leadership of Cabinet Minister Diego Portales and military President Joaquín Prieto, and the establishment of a new constitution in 1833, coup attempts and conspiracies continued to plague Chile; Portales himself was assassinated in 1837 by troops he had thought loyal.

Portales's death was widely, though probably erroneously, blamed on interference in Chilean affairs by General Andrés Santa Cruz, the ruler of the Peru-Bolivia Confederation and a powerful rival for hegemony in Pacific commerce. The Bolivian dictator, after gaining control over Peru, had made no secret of his ambition to extend his empire southward. In response, Portales engineered, in 1836, a declaration of war, an unpopular move widely condemned in political circles. Ironically, Portales's death helped galvanize support for the war among disparate Chilean political factions; incensed at foreign intervention, several groups agreed to back an expeditionary force to Peru.

The war effort and the resounding victory achieved by the Chilean military had a profound impact. Individuals of all stations enthusiastically welcomed home the returning expeditionary force. The victory ball at the presidential palace was attended by rival families who had not spoken to each other in years, helping to heal long-standing wounds and forge a sense of common purpose. In the wake of triumph, authorities decreed a broad amnesty and the restitution of military ranks and pensions for those defeated in the civil war of 1830. As historian Francisco Antonio Encina notes, defeat of the Chilean forces would have magnified political divisions and seriously imperiled the already tenuous governmental stability. Military success gave the Prieto government and Chile's fledgling institutions a new lease on life.[8]

The 1837–1838 war had another, equally important consequence for Chile's political development. It created a national hero, the first Chilean leader to rise unambiguously above factional disputes. General Manuel Bulnes, the embodiment of national unity, was easily able to succeed Prieto in the presidential elections of 1840, a transition facilitated by Prieto's willingness to leave office in favor of his nephew. In his two terms, Bulnes took two important steps to implement the principles set forth in the nation's republican constitution, principles that were nothing less than revolutionary at the time.[9]

First, Bulnes refused to rule autocratically, giving substantial authority to a designated cabinet carefully balanced to represent some of the most important factions of the loose governing coalition. Though executive power was paramount, Bulnes permitted growing autonomy of the courts and the legislature. In time, Congress became increasingly more assertive, delaying approval of budget laws in exchange for modifications in cabinet policy. The cabinet's response to growing congressional activism was not to silence the institution but to capture it by manipulating the electoral process. Ironically, while this practice was condemned by opponents as a perversion of suffrage, it contributed to reinforcing the legitimacy of the legislature as a full-fledged branch of government. Eventually, as presidents changed ministers or as political coalitions shifted, even legislatures originally elected through fraud became centers for the expression of opposition sentiments, reinforcing presidential accountability to legislative majorities.

Second, Bulnes firmly exchanged his role as commander-in-chief of the armed forces for that of civilian president. Under his guidance, the professional military was sharply cut back, its personnel was thinned out, and many of its assets were sold. Instead, and to the dismay of his former military colleagues, Bulnes poured resources into the National Guard, a force of citizen soldiers closely tied to the government patronage network, who served as a ready pool of voters for government-sponsored candidates. In his last presidential address to the nation, Bulnes proudly described the reduction of the regular army and the expansion of the militia as the most convincing evidence of his administration's fidelity to republican institutions.[10]

The transition to a new president, however, was not easy. Many of the country's elites rejected the candidacy of Manuel Montt, a civil servant and cabinet minister of middle-class extraction, to succeed Bulnes. His candidacy was also rejected by elements in the professional army, who believed Bulnes would support a revolt to prevent Montt's accession to power and thus ensure the continuity of leadership from his native area of Concepción. When a revolt was attempted, however, Bulnes personally led the National Guard to defeat the rebel forces.

With the mid-nineteenth-century development of a new class of government functionaries and political leaders who espoused the liberal creed, the state gained substantial autonomy from the traditional landed elite, the pillar of social and economic power. State autonomy was reinforced by the government's success in promoting economic progress, particularly the booming export trade in wheat and minerals, which encouraged economic elites to give the authorities substantial leeway in policy formulation and implementation. Just as important, however, the export-import trade gave the authorities a ready and expanding source of income from customs duties, without their having to make the politically risky decision to tax property or income. Ironically, had the Chilean economy been more balanced and less dependent on foreign trade, the state would have been much more vulnerable to the immediate and direct pressures of economic elites. In Chile, economic "dependency" contributed to strengthening, not weakening, the state.[11] From 1830 to 1860, customs revenues, which represented 60 percent of all revenues, increased sevenfold, enabling the Chilean state to undertake extensive public-works projects, including constructing Latin America's second railroad, and to invest large sums of money in education, which officials believed to be the key to prosperity and national greatness.

In time, however, the state, rapidly extending its administrative jurisdiction and public-works projects throughout the national territory and actively promoting domestic programs in education and civil registries, clashed sharply with landowners, the church, and regional interests. Discontent in the ranks of the conservative landed elite was such that it led to the formation of the country's first real party, the Conservative Party, in direct opposition to Montt's administration. The Conservatives were committed to preserving the traditional order, and defending the values and interests of the church. At the same time, and also in opposition to the state, a group of ideological liberals, influenced by the Revolution of 1848 in France, pressed to accelerate secularization and decentralization and to expand suffrage and democratization. The secular-religious issue, with state elites taking a middle ground, would become the most salient political cleavage in nineteenth-century Chile, and the basis for crystallizing partisan alignments.

By 1859, discontent with the government from various quarters was such that a disparate coalition, composed of aristocratic Conservatives, regional groups, and the newly formed Radical Party representing the anticlerical and mining interests, challenged the government by force. In particular, the dissidents objected to the widespread state intervention in the 1858 congressional election, in which the government obtained a large majority in the Chamber of Deputies. Once again, however, state officials, with strong support from provincial interests and urban groups, were able to make use of the National Guard to put down the revolt. In the process, they put to rest the lingering center-periphery cleavages that had challenged central authority from the days of independence. The new president, following earlier precedents, granted a national amnesty and incorporated many dissidents into policymaking positions. Even the Radical Party obtained congressional representation in the next election.

The monopoly that the government had obtained over the country's most effective fighting forces made it difficult for Conservatives and other opposition elements to contemplate victory through armed challenge. Because of official intervention in the electoral process, moreover, opponents were unable to wrest control of the state from incumbents. Ironically, Conservatives soon realized that they had no choice but to push for expanded suffrage if they were to succeed in capturing the state. Even more oddly, in opposing the government they structured alliances of convenience in Congress with their nemeses, the staunchly ideological liberals, who were worried about electoral intervention and the authorities' refusal to press for increased democratization. This strategic adoption of a "liberal" creed by conservative forces in a traditional society explains one of the most extraordinary paradoxes of Chilean history: the legislative alliance of ultramontane Catholics and radical liberals, both seeking for different reasons the fulfillment of democratic ideals.

Clearly, the Conservatives did not become democrats because of an ideological conversion, though many with close ties to England had come to believe that parliamentary government was a requirement for any civilized nation-state. But they correctly perceived that representative institutions were in their best interest, and the only real alternative once military solutions to domestic conflicts no longer seemed viable. Conservatives were forced to make the liberal creed their own precisely because they had lost ground to a new political class, which had gained strength by dominating the state. In turn, the pragmatic "liberals" (known as the Montt-Varistas) were not acting irrationally when they resisted attempts to expand suffrage and bar official manipulation of the electoral process. They fully realized that in an overwhelmingly rural society, with traditional landlord-peasant relationships, the Conservatives would beat them at the polls and challenge their monopoly of power.[12]

Under the leadership of Conservative José Manuel Irarrazaval, who became a champion of electoral reform, the right sought to advance its interests through the democratic electoral process, rather than through military conspiracies or direct ties with elements of the central bureaucracy, as was the case in many other countries at the time. As a result, the church, hostile to electoral democracy in much of Latin Europe, also came to accept the legitimacy of suffrage in generating public officials. From a position of strength in Congress, the Conservatives, together with Radicals and ideological liberals and over the objections of the executive, successfully pressed for a series of reforms that restricted presidential power. The president was limited to a single five-year term, and his veto power was restricted. The adoption of the Electoral Reform Act in 1874 tripled the electorate from 50,000 to 150,000 voters over the 1872 total.[13]

Nevertheless, official intervention in the electoral process did not end with this electoral reform, and the stakes in controlling the state continued to increase. With its victory in the War of the Pacific (1879–1883), Chile gained vast new territory and rich nitrate deposits. Customs duties climbed to over 70 percent of government income, eliminating the need for property taxes and swelling state coffers. President José Manuel Balmaceda (1886–1891) refused to give in to congressional demands that ministers serve with congressional approval. He also balked at proposals that local governments be given substantial autonomy from the central administration, and that local notables be given control of the electoral process. When his cabinet was censured, Balmaceda sought to govern without congressional approval, adopting the national budget by decree. Finally, a civil war broke out between Congress, backed by the navy, and the president, backed by the army; Balmaceda was defeated in August 1891 and committed suicide.

With the country in disarray and the president dead, a junta headed by a navy captain, the vice-president of the Senate, and the president of the Chamber of Deputies assumed control of the government for three months. This marked the first time since 1830 that political power had been exercised in a manner not prescribed by the constitution. But the brief period of unconstitutional rule did not involve imposing an authoritarian regime, nor did the military as an institution involve itself in politics except to take orders from civilian leaders. The cabinet continued to be a civilian cabinet, and Congress remained in session with virtually no interruption.

The victory of the congressional forces ushered in almost four decades of parliamentary government (1891–1927), in which the center of gravity of the political system shifted from the executive to the legislature, from the capital to local areas, and from state officials and their agents to local party leaders and political brokers. Politics became an elaborate log-rolling game centered in Congress, in which national resources were divided for the benefit of local constituents. Democratization, implied by these changes, had important effects on the political system. With the expansion of suffrage and local control of elections, parliamentary parties expanded beyond the confines of congressional corridors and became national networks with grassroots organizations.

Just as significant, however, was the emergence of parties outside the congressional arena (in Maurice Duverger's terms) in response to increased democratization and to other dramatic changes taking place in Chilean society.[14] While the Conservatives initially gained from electoral reform and were able to dominate the politics of the Parliamentary Republic, they did not foresee that the country's social structure would change so quickly in a quarter-century, and that electoral reform would soon benefit a new group of parties with far different agendas. The urban population, which accounted for 26 percent of the total in 1875, had soared to 45 percent by

1900. Nitrate production, employing between 10 and 15 percent of the population, spawned a host of ancillary industries and created a new working class, which soon found expression in new political parties when the traditional parties, particularly the modern Radicals, failed to provide the leadership required to address its grievances.

Both the state and private employers were slow to recognize the legitimacy of working-class demands and often brutally repressed the infant labor movement. But, as Samuel Valenzuela so brilliantly noted, the openness of the political system, and the sharp competition among traditional parties searching for alliances to maximize electoral gain, permitted the development of electorally oriented class-based parties.[15] By 1921, the year the Chilean Communist Party was officially founded, it had elected two members to Congress; four years later, it achieved representation in the Senate. Thus, to the secular-religious cleavage of the nineteenth century was added the worker-employer cleavage of the early twentieth century—generative cleavages that would shape the basic physiognomy of Chile's contemporary party system.

The 1920s were years of considerable political upheaval. The invention of synthetic nitrates during World War 1 led to the collapse of the Chilean nitrate industry, with far-reaching ramifications for the whole economy. The cumbersome and venal Parliamentary Republic fell increasingly into disrepute, criticized by the right for allowing politics to become corrupt and overly democratic, denounced by the center and left for its inability to address national problems. President Arturo Alessandri (1920–1924) violated political norms by becoming an activist president and pressing for change in the face of congressional inaction and opposition. In September 1924, a group of young military officers unsheathed their swords in the congressional galleries, demanding reforms and the defeat of a congressional pay increase. Bowing to the unprecedented pressure, Alessandri resigned his post and left the country in the hands of a military junta—the first time in over a hundred years that military men had played a direct role in governing the nation.

Senior officers, however, objected to the reform agenda of their younger colleagues; uncomfortable with the responsibility of governing, they soon began to defer to civilian leaders of the right. This prompted a national movement to have Alessandri return, backed by younger officers who identified with the September *pronunciamiento*. In January 1925, the president resumed his position, marking the end of the first extraconstitutional government since 1891. During Alessandri's term, the 1925 Constitution was adopted with the expectation that it would increase the power of the president. It was the first full reform of the basic document since the Constitution of 1833, but it also embodied many elements of continuity.

Alessandri's elected successor, Emiliano Figueroa, proved unable to stand up to political pressures and the growing influence of Minister of War Colonel Carlos Ibañez, a military officer who had participated in the 1924 movement. In 1927 Figueroa resigned, and Ibañez was elected with broad support from all major parties, who sensed the country's and the military's demand for a "nonpolitical" and forceful chief executive. During his administration, Ibañez sought to alter fundamentally Chilean politics by introducing "efficient and modern" administrative practices, disdaining the role of Congress in cabinet appointments, and resorting to emergency and executive measures, such as forced exile, in attempting to crush labor and opposition political parties. It is important to stress, however, that Ibañez's government was not a military dictatorship. While his authority derived in large measure from support in the barracks, army officers did not govern. The vast majority of cabinet officials were civilians, though most were newcomers to politics who criticized the intrigues of the traditional political class.

Ibañez soon discovered that he, too, could run out of political capital. His inability to curb the influence of parties, and his growing isolation, combined with the catastrophic effects of the Great Depression (in which Chilean exports dropped to a fifth of their former value) and mounting street unrest, finally led the demoralized president to submit his resignation in July 1931. After a period of political instability, which included the resignation of yet another president and the ninety-day "Socialist Republic" proclaimed by a civil-military junta that attempted to press for social change, elections were scheduled in 1932. Once again, Arturo Alessandri was elected to a full constitutional term, thereby restoring the continuity of Chile's institutional system. During his second administration, Alessandri was far more cautious than during his first, successfully bringing the country out of the depression with firm austerity measures and reaffirming the value of institutions based on democratic values and procedures at a time when they were under profound attack in Europe.

The 1938 presidential election represented another major turning point in Chilean politics and a vivid confirmation of the extent to which ordinary citizens had become the fundamental source of political authority. In an extremely close election, the center, in a Popular Front alliance with the Marxist left, captured the presidency, and Radical Pedro Aguirre Cerda was elected. Despite the often bitter opposition of the right, the government for a decade expanded social-welfare policies, encouraged the rise of legal unionism, and actively pursued import-substituting industrialization through a new Corporación de Fomento de la Producción (Corporation for the Development of Production). The trend toward urbanization continued: in 1940, 53 percent of the population lived in cities; by 1970, that figure had increased to 76 percent.

By 1948, the new Cold War climate abroad and the increased local electoral successes of the Communist Party were making both Socialists and Radicals increasingly uneasy. Encouraged by Radical leaders, President Gabriel González Videla dissolved the Popular Front, outlawed the Communist Party, and sent many of its members to detention camps. These actions, combined with the wear of incumbency and general dissatisfaction with the opportunistic Radicals, contributed to the election of Carlos Ibañez as president in 1952 on an antiparty platform. But Ibañez, unable to govern without party support, was forced to shift his initial populist programs to a severe austerity plan that contributed to wage and salary declines. He was succeeded in 1958 by conservative businessman Jorge Alessandri, the former president's son, who edged out Socialist Salvador Allende by only 2.7 percent of the vote. Alessandri applied more austerity measures, provoking cries for profound reform from a populace tired of spiraling inflation and economic stagnation. In the 1964 presidential elections, fear of the growing strength of the left led Chile's traditional rightist parties to reluctantly support Eduardo Frei, the candidate of the new Christian Democratic Party, which had replaced the Radicals as the largest party in Chile and the most powerful party of the center. With massive financial assistance from the United States, the Frei government attempted to implement far-reaching reforms, but after dissolving their tacit alliance with the right, the Christian Democrats were unable to increase their share of the vote. In 1970, claiming to have been betrayed by Frei's reformist policies, the right refused to support Christian Democratic candidate Radomiro Tomic, making possible the election of leftist candidate Salvador Allende and his Popular Unity coalition, with only 36.2 percent of the vote. The Christian Democratic and Popular Unity governments are treated in more detail in the discussion of the breakdown of Chilean democracy below.

Characteristics of Chilean Politics at Mid-Century

By the 1930s, with the rise of Marxist parties at a time of electoral expansion, the Chilean party system, in Seymour Lipset and Stein Rokkan's terms, had become complete.[16] In addition to the traditional conservative and liberal parties that had emerged from church-state cleavages in the early nineteenth century, and the Radical Party that had developed later in that century out of similar divisions, communist and socialist parties had now developed in response to a growing class cleavage. The only new party to emerge after the 1930s, the Christian Democratic Party, was an offshoot of the Conservative Party and sought to address social and economic issues from the vantage point of reform Catholicism.

Yet this "complete" system was characterized by sharp social polarization in which the organized electorate was divided almost equally among the three political tendencies. Although numerous small parties appeared after 1932, the six major parties continued to dominate politics, commanding over 80 percent of the vote by the 1960s. Elections and politics became a national "sport," as parties became so deeply ingrained in the nation's social fabric that Chileans would refer to a Radical or a Communist or a Christian Democratic "subculture." Parties helped to structure people's friendships and social life. Partisan affiliation continued to be reinforced by both class and religion, so that Christian Democratic elites were more likely to go to Catholic schools and universities and come from upper-middle-class backgrounds, while Socialist elites went to public schools and state universities and came from lower-middle-class backgrounds. Communist strength was heavily concentrated in mining communities and industrial areas, Christian Democrats appealed to middle-class and women voters, while the right retained substantial support in rural Chile.

The major parties framed political options not only in municipal and congressional elections but also in private and secondary associations. The penetration of parties into Chilean society was such that even high school student associations, community groups, universities, and professional societies selected leaders on party slates. Political democracy helped democratize social groups and erode historic patterns of authoritarian social relations.

It is crucial to stress that there were no giants in the Chilean political system. Table 4.1, which reports the percentage of the vote received by the parties of the right, center, and left in congressional elections from 1937 to 1997, shows that no coalition, let alone party, received over 50 percent of the vote, with the exception of the 1965 congressional race when the Christian Democrats benefited from defections from the right. This pattern

Table 4.1   Percentage of the Vote Received by Major Chilean Parties Grouped into Right, Center, and Left Tendencies, 1937–1997

Political Preference	1932	1937	1941	1945	1949	1953	1957	1961	1965	1969	1973	1989	1993	1997
Right	35	42	31	44	42	28	39	39	13	20	21	34	34	36
Center	32	28	31	31	47	49	49	44	60	43	32	33	31	26
Left		15	34	23	9	14	11	22	23	28	35	24	32	34

Sources: Data from the Dirección del Registro Electoral for 1932 to 1973 and drawn from Arturo Valenzuela, "Party Politics and the Crisis of Presidentialism in Chile: A Proposal for a Parliamentary Form of Government," in Juan J. Linz and Arturo Valenzuela, eds., *The Failure of Presidential Democracy* (Baltimore: Johns Hopkins University Press, 1994), pp. 174–175. Data for 1989–1997 from Peter Siavelis, "Party System Continuity and Transformation in a 'Model' Transition," paper delivered at the conference "Chile: The Model Country for Democracy and Development, 1990–99?" December 10–12, 1998, University of California at San Diego, La Jolla, Table IV.

of support had clear implications for the functioning of Chile's presidential system.

Since majorities were impossible to achieve, Chilean presidents were invariably elected by coalitions or were forced to build governing coalitions with opposing parties in Congress after the election. However, because preelection coalitions were constituted primarily for electoral reasons, in an atmosphere of considerable political uncertainty, they tended to disintegrate after a few months of the new administration.

Ideological disputes were often at the root of coalition changes, as partisans of one formula would resist the proposals of opponents. But narrow political considerations were also important. Since a president could not succeed himself, leaders of other parties in his coalition often realized they could best improve their fortunes in succeeding municipal and congressional elections by disassociating themselves from the difficulties of incumbency in a society fraught with economic problems. In the final analysis, only by proving their independent electoral strength in nonpresidential elections could parties demonstrate their value to future presidential coalitions.

Because Chilean presidents could not dissolve Congress in case of an impasse or loss of congressional support, they needed to build alternative alliances in order to govern. Parties assured their influence by requiring that candidates nominated for cabinet posts seek their party's permission (*pase*) to serve in office. Presidents, required continually to forge working coalitions, were repeatedly frustrated by the sense of instability and permanent crisis that this bargaining process gave Chilean politics.

An image of Chile's party system as excessively competitive and polarized, however, is incomplete and inaccurate. The collapse of party agreements, the censure of ministers, and the sharp disagreement over major policy issues captured the headlines and inflamed people's passions. But the vast majority of political transactions were characterized by compromise, flexibility, and respect for the institutions and procedures of constitutional democracy. Over the years, working agreements among political rivals led to implementing far-reaching policies, including state-sponsored industrialization; comprehensive national health, welfare, and educational systems; agrarian reform; and copper nationalization. Agreements were also structured around the more mundane aspects of politics. Congressmen and party leaders of different stripes would join in efforts to promote a particular region or to provide special benefits to constituency groups and individuals.[17]

This pattern of give-and-take can be attributed to three mutually reinforcing factors: a pragmatic center, the viability of representative arenas of decisionmaking and neutrality of public institutions, and the imperatives of electoral politics. Compromise would have been difficult without the flexibility provided by center parties, notably the Radical Party, which inherited the role of the nineteenth-century liberals as the fulcrum of coalition politics. The Radicals supported, at one time or another, the rightist presidencies of the two Alessandris in the 1930s and 1960s and governed with support of the right in the late 1940s. In the late 1930s and through most of the 1940s, however, they allied with the left to form Popular Front governments under a Radical president, and in the 1970s, a substantial portion of the party supported Salvador Allende, though by then the party's strength had been severely eroded.

Accommodation and compromise were also the hallmarks of democratic institutions such as the Chilean Congress, whose lawmaking, budgetary, and investigatory powers provided incentives for party leaders to set aside disagreements in matters of mutual benefit. Indeed, the folkways of the legislative institution, stemming from years of close working relationships in committees and on the floor, contributed to the development of legendary private friendships among leaders who were strong public antagonists. Just as significant, however, were such prestigious institutions as the armed forces, the judiciary, and the comptroller general, respected for their "neutrality" and remoteness from the clamor of everyday politics. These institutions provided an important safety valve from the hyperpoliticization of most of public life.

The legitimacy of public institutions was further reinforced by a strong commitment to public service, which extended from the presidential palace to the rural police station. Although electoral fraud and vote buying by political party machines were common, financial corruption did not flourish in Chilean public life. The vigilance of the Congress and the courts, kept accountable by strong political oppositions, helped prevent wrongdoing for personal gain by public officeholders. The Chilean experience suggests that highly competitive politics over time strengthens democratic institutions and contributes to the consolidation of state practices devoid of blatant corruption.

Finally, the press of continuous elections forced political leaders to turn away from ideological pursuits and attend to the more mundane side of politics, such as personal favors and other particularistic tasks inherent in a representative system. Congressmen and senators had to look after their party brokers in municipalities and neighborhoods, being sure to provide public funds for a local bridge or jobs for constituents. Often political leaders from different parties joined in advancing the common interests of their constituencies, setting aside acrimonious, abstract debates over the role of the state in the economy or Soviet policy in Asia. In Chile, the politics of ideology, rooted in strong social inequalities, was counterbalanced by the clientelistic politics of electoral accountability reinforced by that same inequality. As will be noted below, many of these elements disappeared during the later 1960s and early 1970s, putting the democratic system under great strain and ultimately contributing to its total collapse.

ORIGINS OF CHILEAN DEMOCRACY:
A THEORETICAL ASSESSMENT

Because it is one of the few cases in which a democratic government was successfully established in the mid-1900s, and an especially dramatic example of democratic failure, Chile constitutes a valuable paradigmatic case in the effort to construct theoretical propositions explaining the origins, consolidation, breakdown, and reconsolidation of democratic regimes. Its theoretical utility is enhanced by the fact that there are no comparable cases of democratic development outside the Western European–North American context, or among primarily Catholic or export-oriented countries. As a deviant case, which has been largely neglected in scholarly literature, Chile can serve as a useful test for the validity of theoretical propositions generated by observing the experience of other countries, primarily European.[18]

The most prominent theses aimed at explaining the development of democracy assume that political practices and institutions can be understood by reference to a series of historical, cultural, or economic determinants. It is the central argument of this chapter that such approaches fall short in accounting for Chilean exceptionality, and that the Chilean case can be best explained by considering political factors as independent variables in their own right. This section will review the determinants of democracy embodied in what can be called the colonial-continuity thesis, the political-culture thesis, and the economic-class-structure thesis.[19] It will then turn to an analysis of those political variables that are most helpful in understanding Chile's political evolution, variables that can add to the development of theoretical propositions to be tested in other contexts.

The Colonial-Continuity Thesis

According to the colonial-continuity thesis, democratic practices will flourish in postcolonial regimes if institutions for self-rule, even if limited, were in place for several generations during colonial times, and if the transition from colony to independent state was accomplished without too much violence and destruction of those institutions. Both these conditions figure prominently in accounts of the outcome of the British decolonization experiences of the eighteenth and twentieth centuries.[20] It is clear that this thesis cannot account for the Chilean case. Although Chile was a more isolated colony than the major centers of Spanish rule in the New World, there is no evidence that the colony was able to gain the necessary autonomy to develop institutions of self-rule that would carry it into the postindependence period. Chile was subject to the same patrimonial administration and mercantilistic policies that discouraged expressions of political or economic independence and frowned on participatory institutions as contrary to the

fundamental conception of monarchical rule. The colonies were the personal property of the king, subject to his direct control. Moreover, the Chilean
wars of independence were profoundly disruptive of the previous political
order, plunging the nation into a fratricidal conflict that tore asunder institutions and political practices that had been in place for generations.
Although Chileans later established democratic rule, this accomplishment
had little to do with the political experiences gained in colonial times.[21]

There is, however, a variant of the continuity thesis that must be
addressed because it constitutes the principal explanation found in the his-
toriographical literature dealing with Chilean exceptionality. According to
this thesis, Chile deviated from the pattern that held sway in nineteenth-
century Latin America not because its colonial institutions were more liberal, but because its postindependence institutions were more conservative.
This argument holds that Diego Portales, the cabinet minister who dominated the government of President Prieto during the 1830s, helped to establish
firm and authoritarian rule equivalent to that of the Spanish crown during
the colonial era, thus rescuing Chile from misguided liberals enamored
with unrealistic federal formulae and excessive freedoms.[22] Chile succeeded not because it broke from the colonial past, this argument holds, but
because it reimposed that past. Richard Morse articulates the point:

> Chile was an example perhaps unparalleled of a Spanish American coun-
> try which managed, after a twelve-year transitional period, to avoid the
> extremes of tyranny and anarchy with a political system unencumbered by
> the mechanisms and party rhetoric of exotic liberalism. . . . The structure
> of the Spanish patrimonial state was recreated with only those minimum
> concessions to Anglo-French constitutionalism that were necessary for a
> nineteenth century republic which had just rejected monarchical rule.[23]

It is disingenuous to argue, as most Chilean historians do, that Portales
forged Chile's institutions single-handedly. The minister was in office for
only a total of three years, had little to do with drafting the 1833
Constitution, and died in office at a time when his government was under
serious challenge.[24] Regardless of Portales's role, it is also profoundly mistaken to argue that Chile's concessions to Anglo-French constitutionalism
were minimal. The political system established by the Constitution of 1833
was qualitatively different from the colonial system of the past, bearing far
greater resemblance to the institutions and practices followed in the North
American colonies, and the compromises struck at the Constitutional
Convention in Philadelphia, than to the institutions set up by the Castilian
rulers.

In Weberian terms, Chile's new constitutional formula substituted
rational-legal authority for traditional authority; that is, it replaced the
authority of a hereditary monarch, whose power was inherent in his person
by virtue of divinely ordained practices going back generations, with the

authority of an elected president whose power derived from the office as defined by law. Moreover, rather than re-creating colonial patterns of political domination, nineteenth-century Chilean politics from the outset expanded the concept of citizenship (a radical notion at the time) and affirmed the legitimacy of elected assemblies to claim political sovereignty equally with the chief executive.

When viewed in this light, the achievements of the forgers of Chilean institutionality are very significant in contrast to those of their North American counterparts, who fashioned their institutions and practices by drawing on generations of experience with self-rule within the political framework of Tudor England.[25]

The Political-Culture Thesis

Perhaps the most influential set of propositions associated with the development of democratic institutions are those that hold that democracy requires a country's citizens, or at the very least its politically active elites, to share the liberal beliefs and values that are the hallmark of the Enlightenment. These include values conducive to accepting the equality of all people and their fundamental worth, values tolerating opposition and the free expression of ideas, and values celebrating the legitimacy of moderation and compromise. In short, they are the values associated with participatory politics as opposed to authoritarian patterns of governance. These political-culture variables have figured prominently in efforts to explain the general failure of democracy in Latin America and in Latin Europe, and the success of democracy in Protestant Europe and the United States. Democracy succeeded in the United States, this argument holds, because the British colonies were populated by settlers already imbued with more egalitarian values stemming from the Enlightenment and the Protestant Reformation. By contrast, the colonizers of Latin America brought aristocratic and feudal values reinforced by a Catholic faith stressing the importance of hierarchy, authority, corporativism, and the immutability of the traditional social order.[26]

But if the absence of democracy in Latin America is explained by the lack of appropriate beliefs, how can we account for the Chilean case? Were Chileans, located in one of the most remote colonies of the empire and dominated by an aristocracy of Basque descent, less tied to royal institutions? Or was the Chilean church more liberal or less influential in the social and political life of the colony? None of the historical evidence supports these contentions. To the contrary, Chile's isolation had made the colony one of the most traditional on the continent. Royalist sentiment was as strong in Chile as anywhere else, and troops who fought with the Spaniards to suppress the insurrection were recruited locally. Similarly, the church was as conservative as in other countries and retained the strong backing of the local aristocracy despite its close ties with the colonial power. Chilean elites were no less Catholic than the political elites of other former colonies.[27]

A variant of the political-culture thesis holds that it is not so much the religious traditions or political practices of the past that condition political beliefs and attitudes, but the authority relations found in secondary spheres of society: the workplace, the family, or the educational system.[28] Of particular importance in a predominantly agricultural society are the social relations of production resulting from the country's land-tenure system. Where land is concentrated in a small number of estates with traditional patron-client authority relations, this thesis argues, political values will be hierarchical and authoritarian. Where land is divided more equally and exploited by family farmers and contract labor, political values will be more egalitarian and democratic, facilitating the development of democratic politics. This is the argument that John Booth makes in attempting to account for democratic development in Costa Rica.[29] Dahl echoes this approach when he suggests that the Chilean case can be explained by "considerable equality in distribution of land and instruments of coercion, reinforced by norms favoring social and political equality."[30]

However, Dahl's argument also fails to stand up to historical scrutiny. Chile's system of social relations and stratification was one of the most rigid and traditional on the continent, based on large landed estates and semifeudal relationships of authority between landlord and peasant. Authority relations in the family and in the educational system, still under church tutelage, were also authoritarian and hierarchical.[31] The wars of independence disrupted the country's social structure less than they did elsewhere. As Jorge Dominguez notes,

> Chile lagged behind the other colonies, although it had experienced economic growth and mobilization. Its society had been transformed the least. The social bonds within it remained strong. Centralization had not been advanced nor had society been pluralized. Traditional elites remained strong, and traditional orientations prevailed.[32]

Throughout the nineteenth and well into the twentieth century, the traditional nature of social relations in the countryside remained one of the most striking features of the Chilean social structure. Despite the rise of an urban working class and the democratization of other spheres of social life, rural social relations were not significantly altered until the 1960s, when agrarian reform was finally undertaken as national policy.[33]

There is no reason to assume that the evolution of democratic politics in Chile in the nineteenth century was due to more "favorable" political-culture variables. The failure of cultural explanations to account for the Chilean case raises serious questions about the underlying assumption that there is a direct fit between societal values and political institutions. It is very unlikely that Chile had societal values comparable to those of Norway, Australia, or the United States (though they may not have been too dissimilar to those found in class-conscious Britain), yet the political outcomes were not dissimilar. Several students of democracy have argued that "stable" democracy is the product not only of liberal and participatory values, but of a mixture of participatory and deferential ones. However, in the absence of a clearly defined set of values that relate to democracy, it is difficult to ascertain which mix is appropriate. As a result, there is a real temptation to engage in circular reasoning: if a particular regime was stable or had the requisite democratic characteristics, it was assumed it had ipso facto the appropriate value structure.

Although egalitarian and democratic values were not necessary to structure democratic institutions and procedures, the Chilean case suggests that the exercise of democratic practices over a period of time encourages the development of certain norms of political conduct and reinforces belief in the legitimacy of the rules of the game. As early as the 1850s, Chilean political elites of different ideological persuasions worked together in Congress to advance common objectives, thus developing habits of flexibility and compromise. The Radicals, who were excluded from decision-making roles in Argentina until after the 1912 Saenz Peña Law, were invited to serve in cabinets fifty years earlier in Chile.

As an industrial working class developed, moreover, Chilean elites, despite serious objections to accepting the principle of collective bargaining at the workplace and brutal repression of the incipient labor movement, accepted the legitimate role of working-class parties in the arena of electoral competition and eventually in the corridors of power. Democratic institutions came to be accepted by most Chileans as the best way to resolve disagreements and set national policy. By the mid–twentieth century, ordinary Chileans took great pride in their civic duties, participating enthusiastically in an electoral process that made Chile distinctive among Third World nations. In sum, Chilean democracy emerged without strongly held democratic values. But the practice of democracy itself instilled norms of give-and-take, tolerance, and respect for fundamental liberties that were widely shared by the population as a whole.[34]

This does not mean that democratic politics in Chile were centrist-oriented and devoid of sharp conflict. In 1891, after thirty years of domestic tranquility, the strongly felt political antagonisms generated by the executive-congressional impasse spilled onto the battlefield, a conflict that nonetheless pales by comparison with the U.S. Civil War, which also took place eighty years after the Declaration of Independence. The deep ideological disagreements of twentieth-century Chile continuously challenged the country's institutions and practices. The Chilean case and those of other highly polarized political systems, such as Italy, France, and Finland, show that consensus on the fundamentals of public policy can be relatively low, while consensus on the rules and procedures for arriving at policy decisions can be high.

It was not moderation that made Chilean democracy function; it was Chilean democracy that helped moderate political passions and manage deep-seated divisions. A democratic political culture is not an abstract set of beliefs or psychological predispositions governing interpersonal relations in the body politic, but practical and ingrained traditions and working relations based on regularized patterns of political interaction in the context of representative institutions. As will be noted below, with the breakdown of democracy, Chile lost not only representative rule, but the institutional fabric that helped define many of the values of democratic human conduct.

The Economic-Class-Structure Thesis

While there is broad variation in studies emphasizing the economic determinants of democracy, they can be divided into two categories: those relating democracy to overall levels of economic development, and those focusing on the contribution to the creation of democratic institutions of particular groups or classes that emerge as a result of economic transformations in society.

The first group draws on the insights of "modernization" theory, arguing that economic development leads to more complex, differentiated, secularized, and educated societies, opening the way for the rise of new groups and institutions that find expression in democratic practices.[35] In addition, economic growth is said to provide channels for upward mobility and for ameliorating the sharp social disparities found in poor societies, disparities that undermine democratic performance. Empirical evidence for these propositions was advanced in a host of cross-national studies conducted in the late 1960s, inspired by Lipset's classic article on the "economic correlates of democracy."[36] The main difficulty with these studies in explaining the Chilean case is that they are ahistorical. Chile in the nineteenth century, like most incipient democracies of the time, was a rural, preindustrial society with very low levels of personal wealth and literacy, yet it met many of the criteria for democratic performance. In the twentieth century, as several authors have noted, Chile was clearly an outlier, exhibiting many of the characteristics of economic underdevelopment while boasting high scores on democratic performance.[37] As Juan Linz has argued, explanations that draw on levels of economic development do not contribute much to our understanding of the origins and development of democratic politics.[38]

Scholars writing in a Marxist tradition have argued that the most important variable is not overall economic development, but the rise of rural and urban middle classes capable of challenging the monopoly of landed elites and breaking their political power. Based on his reflections on the European case, Goran Therborn attributes the rise of democracy to the emergence of agrarian bourgeois groups, giving particular emphasis to "the strength of these agrarian classes and the degree of their independence from the landowning aristocracy and urban big capital."[39] Barrington Moore goes further, presenting a more complex argument. For Moore, as for Therborn, the development of a bourgeoisie was central to the development of democracy. However, whether a country actually followed a democratic path depended on how agriculture was commercialized, whether or not it became "labor repressive" or "market commercial."[40]

As with the political-culture thesis, it is difficult to accept the applicability of the economic-class-structure thesis to the Chilean case. As noted earlier, Chilean agriculture remained labor-repressive well into the twentieth century, retaining a high concentration of land ownership. Though, as Dominguez notes, Chilean agriculture was geared by the eighteenth century to the export of wheat, wheat production was never commercialized as in North America. As in czarist Russia, it was expanded with only minimal modifications to the traditional manorial system.[41] By the same token, and despite some interpretations of Chilean history that stress the rise of an urban bourgeoisie as the key liberalizing force, Chile did not develop a strong and independent urban-based bourgeoisie before the development of democratic rules and procedures. Although mining interests became powerful and some of the most prominent mine owners were identified with the Radical Party, it is mistaken to identify Chilean mining interests as representatives of a new and differentiated bourgeois class. Other, equally prominent mine owners had close ties to the Conservative Party, and many members of the Chilean elite had both mining and agricultural interests.[42]

However, the most telling argument against the economic-class-structure thesis has already been anticipated in the historical discussion at the beginning of this chapter. The rise of democracy in Chile—including the limitations on presidential authority, the expansion of legislative prerogatives, and the extension of suffrage—took place not over the objections of the conservative landed elites but, as in Britain, at their instigation. If the traditional landowning class, which championed the Roman Catholic Church, decided to support suffrage expansion and the development of democratic institutions, then theoretical explanations that hold that democracy emerges only with the destruction of that class are less than adequate. This is a central point, to which we will return.

The Political-Determinants Thesis

An examination of various theses dealing with the historical, cultural, and economic "determinants" of democracy suggests that they are not particularly useful in explaining the Chilean case. What is more, the Chilean case, as one of successful democratic development that does not conform to the principal arguments of those theses, raises serious questions about their

overall validity. However, from this evidence alone it would be clearly mistaken to argue that these factors play no substantial role in democratic
development. A "liberal" colonial tradition, egalitarian values, economic
development, and a variegated social structure are undoubtedly conducive
to the implementation and acceptance of institutions of self-governance.
Indeed, a perspective such as the one advocated here—the political-
determinants thesis, which stresses the importance of discrete political variables and even historical accidents as independent variables—need not
eschew the economic and cultural constants or shy away from developing
generalizations that relate socioeconomic to political variables. The point is
that these cultural and economic variables are hardly determinants of
democratic practices. They may very well be powerful contributory conditions, but they are not necessary or sufficient ones.

A historical review of the development of Chilean political institutions
immediately suggests the utility of the "political-crisis" literature developed by political scientists. According to this literature, all countries face
severe challenges in developing democratic institutions and, depending on
the timing and sequence of those challenges, have greater or lesser success
in achieving democratic stability.[43] Although the challenges vary in kind
and number, most authors view the crises of national identity (creating a
sense of national community over parochial loyalties), authority (establishing viable state structures), and participation (incorporating the citizenry
into the political system) as crucial.

In addition, the sequence and timing of the appearance of these problems on the historical scene can seriously affect the political outcome. As
Eric Nordlinger puts it, "the probabilities of a political system developing
in a nonviolent, nonauthoritarian, and eventually democratically viable
manner are maximized when a national identity emerges first, followed by
the institutionalization of the central government, and then the emergence
of mass parties and mass electorate."[44] It can be argued that Chile followed
this "optimal" sequence and that the timing was also favorable, particularly
with respect to the emergence of the participation crisis, which did not
become a critical issue until after central authority structures had been consolidated.[45]

National identity. It is doubtful that Chileans considered themselves a nation
before independence, because there were far fewer mechanisms of social
communication and exchange than in North America and a far more ubiquitous set of colonial authority structures.[46] However, the clear-cut military
victory in the war against the Peru-Bolivia Confederation, a victory without
parallel in Latin America, gave the small, divided nation a powerful new
sense of confidence and purpose, creating tangible symbols of patriotism
and nationality. These feelings were reinforced with the victory of Chilean

forces in the War of the Pacific, which led to the incorporation of large portions of Peruvian and Bolivian territory into national boundaries.

Political authority. Rustow has noted the importance of distinguishing between establishing and consolidating institutions of democracy. Consolidation involves a lengthy process of "habituation," which is not necessarily unilinear: there can be reversals and even breakdown.[47] In consolidating political authority in Chile, five factors were critically important: leadership, state autonomy, government efficacy, civilian control of the armed forces, and conservative support for democratic rules.

The first important element was leadership. General Bulnes, drawing on his command of the most powerful armed forces in the country and his widespread popularity, could have easily used his position to establish personal rule, following the pattern of notable Latin American *caudillos* such as Paez in Venezuela, Rosas in Argentina, or Santa Ana in Mexico. Instead, like Washington in the United States, he insisted on working within the framework of established political institutions and chose to leave office at the end of his term, making way for his successor. His willingness while in office to underscore the autonomy of the courts, accept the role of Congress in policy, and allow ministerial cabinets to formulate the government's program set a precedent for his successor and future administrations, and helped to establish the legitimacy of democratic institutions.[48]

The second important factor was state autonomy. A crucial legacy of Bulnes's and, later, Montt's respect for constitutionally mandated institutions was the development of politics and government service as a vocation. An impressive group of functionaries and legislators emerged who were committed to strengthening and expanding the secular state. By 1860, more than 2,500 people worked for the state, not including local officials, construction workers, and members of the armed forces. All of Chile's nineteenth-century presidents save one had extensive congressional experience before being elected to office, and five who took office before 1886 began their careers in the Bulnes administration. Between Bulnes and Pinochet, only two of Chile's twenty-two presidents were career military officers, and both of those were freely elected with political-party support in moments of political crisis.[49]

The third element was governmental efficacy. Under the leadership of the first three presidents to serve after 1830, the Chilean economy performed relatively well. This not only brought credit to the new institutions and leaders of the independent nation, but more important, it gave the government elites time and autonomy to begin state consolidation. By the time important interests sought to stop the expansion of the secular state, it had garnered significant political, financial, and military strength.[50]

The fourth factor was control of the armed forces by civilian governmental leaders. By deliberately refusing until after the War of the Pacific to create a professional military establishment, while retaining close political control over an effective national militia, Chilean officials were able to establish a monopoly over the control of force and a tradition of civilian supremacy over the military. The military challenges of 1851 and 1859 were defeated, discouraging dissident elites from gathering their own military force to challenge national authority structures.

The fifth factor was conservative support for democratic rules. This factor is directly related to the development of state autonomy and control of the military. Control of the military prevented aggrieved sectors of the elites from resorting to insurrectionary movements in order to prevent state action or to capture the state by force. Thus such elites, including conservative landholders, were forced to turn to democratic procedures already in place, and indeed to seek their expansion, in order to preserve and advance their interests. Far from being a minor footnote in history, this support of the Chilean conservatives for liberal rules was of central importance. It led to the creation of a Conservative Party, committed to representative institutions, which had no exact parallel in Latin America or Latin Europe.

This leads to a basic proposition: that the origins and evolution of democratic institutions and procedures are determined more by the choices made by key elites seeking to maximize their interests within the framework of specific structural and political parameters, than they are by abstract cultural or economic factors. Chilean elites, initially hostile to democracy, came to embrace democratic rules as a conscious choice for political survival, in the process contributing to the strengthening of those institutions over the years.[51] Where political elites have fewer incentives to support democratic institutions, and, in particular, where resorting to force to prevent the distribution of power through the expansion of citizenship is a viable option for those elites, the consolidation of democratic authority structures is seriously jeopardized.

Participation. Perhaps the greatest challenge to the consolidation of stable democracy is the expansion of citizenship rights to non-elite elements, and the incorporation into the political process of new groups and classes. Like Britain and Norway, but unlike Latin Europe, the consolidation of democratic institutions in Chile benefited from a gradual extension of suffrage, less in response to pressures from below than as a consequence of inter-elite rivalries and strategies to maximize electoral gain. Like Britain, but unlike Latin Europe, Chile found in the elites of the Conservative Party the driving force in the first pivotal extension of suffrage in 1874. This took place a dozen years before the French Third Republic teetered on the brink of collapse with Boulangisme, and twenty-five years before the French right, still resisting republicanism and democracy, became embroiled in the

Dreyfus Affair. It also took place forty years before the pope lifted the *non-expedit* that barred Catholics from participating in Italian elections.

The extension of suffrage in Chile clearly benefited the Conservatives who controlled the countryside, but it also benefited middle-class sectors who identified with the growing urban-based Radical Party. Forty-two years before the adoption of the Saenz Peña Law in Argentina, which forced reluctant Conservatives to suddenly expand the electoral system to permit the Radical Party's eruption on the political stage, Chile had initiated the gradual expansion of suffrage, permitting middle-class sectors to become full participants in ministerial and congressional politics.

In a classic case of what R. K. Merton calls the unanticipated consequences of purposive social action, the expansion of suffrage in Chile also soon benefited the growing working class.[52] But the entry of the working class into politics in Chile was also gradual, coming both after the consolidation of parliamentary institutions and after middle-class parties had become full actors in the political process. Indeed, in the 1910s, initial suffrage expansion was actually limited by complex electoral rules and Byzantine electoral pacts in which the working-class parties became full participants.

The gradual expansion of suffrage and incorporation of new groups in Chile had some clear implications for the country's democratic development. Had the pressure for full participation coincided with attempts to set up democratic institutions, it is difficult to see how these could have survived. At the same time, however, it is important to stress that in Chile, suffrage expansion and party development occurred prior to the growth of a powerful and centralized state bureaucracy. The growth of the public sector was consequently shaped by organizations whose primary goals were electoral success and accountability. This reinforced the viability of representative institutions. Where strong bureaucracies emerged before strong parties or legislatures, as in Brazil or Argentina, informal or officially sponsored linkage networks without popular representation were much more likely to develop, encouraging corporatist and authoritarian patterns of interest representation.[53]

In sum, the political-determinants thesis suggests that the development of democracy must be understood as a complex process that owes much to fortuitous events and variables, such as leadership, that defy quantification and precise definition. It is a long and difficult course, subject to challenges and reversals as societal conditions and the correlations of political forces change. Its chances of success are better in some contexts than in others and may depend on the timing and sequence of fundamental societal challenges.

In the final analysis, however, democracy involves human choice by competing groups and leaders who must determine whether peaceful mech-

anisms for the resolution of conflict, based on the concept of popular sovereignty, provide them with the best possible guarantees under the circumstances. More often than not, this choice may stem from an inconclusive
struggle for power, a situation of stalemate where there are no clear winners. That being so, democracy can be understood as resulting from a set of
compromises—second-preference choices—in which the concurrence of
nondemocrats may be as important as the support of democrats. Once
democracy is structured, it provides the key rules of the game, defining the
parameters for action and the strategies to be pursued by relevant actors. In
time, democratic rules may be accepted as the only proper norms for political conduct, but only if democracy continues to provide guarantees to all
politically relevant players, even if it is not the preferred system of all.

THE BREAKDOWN OF CHILEAN DEMOCRACY

Chilean Politics and the Dialectic of Regime Breakdown

The breakdown of Chilean democracy did not occur overnight. Several
developments contributed to the erosion of the country's system of political
compromise and accommodation, even before the 1970 election of
President Salvador Allende. These included the adoption of a series of
reforms aimed at making Chilean politics more "efficient," and the rise of a
new and more ideological center, less willing to play the game of political
give-and-take.[54]

In 1958, a coalition of the center and left joined in enacting a series of
electoral reforms aimed at abolishing what were considered corrupt electoral practices. Among the measures was the abolition of joint lists, a long-
established tradition of political pacts that permitted parties of opposing
ideological persuasions to structure agreements for mutual electoral benefit. While this reform succeeded in making preelection arrangements less
"political," it also eliminated an important tool for cross-party bargaining.
More important were reforms aimed at curbing congressional authority,
promulgated in the guise of strengthening the executive's ability to deal
with Chile's chronic economic troubles. Congressional politics were
viewed by chief executives and party elites of various political persuasions
as excessively incremental and old-fashioned—the antithesis of modern
administrative practices. In the name of modernity, the executive was given
control of the budgetary process in 1959, and Congress was restricted in its
ability to allocate fiscal resources. Indeed, under the Christian Democratic
administration (1964–1970), government technocrats pushed strongly to
restrict entirely congressional allocations of funds for small patronage projects, even though these represented an infinitesimal portion of the total
budget.

The most serious blow to congressional authority came with the constitutional reforms enacted in 1970, this time through a coalition of the right and center. Among other provisions, the reforms prohibited amendments not germane to a given piece of legislation and sanctioned the use of executive decrees to implement programs approved by the legislature in very broad terms. More significantly, it barred Congress from matters dealing with social security, salary adjustments, and pensions in the private and public sectors—the heart of legislative bargaining in an inflation-ridden society.[55]

These reforms went a long way toward cutting back on many of the traditional sources of patronage and log-rolling, reducing the most important political arena for compromise in Chilean politics. Again, the principal motivation was to strengthen executive efficiency. It is clear, however, that the reformers were also convinced they would be able to win the 1970 presidential election and did not want to have to deal with a difficult Congress in which the left had a strong presence. Ironically, it was the left that won the presidency, leaving a legislature with reduced powers in the hands of the right and center.

Although these changes were significant, they were symptomatic of other far-reaching changes in Chilean politics, the most notable of which was the rise in the 1960s of a new center party with a markedly different political style. Unlike their predecessor, the pragmatic Radicals, the Chilean Christian Democrats conceived of themselves as a new and vital ideological force in Chilean politics, a middle road between Marxist transformation and preservation of the status quo. The Christian Democrats believed they would be capable of capturing the allegiance of large portions of the electorate from both sides of the political divide, and become a new majority force. In the early 1960s, they began an unprecedented effort at popular mobilization, appealing to women and middle-class voters, as well as factory workers and especially shantytown dwellers. Their determination to transform the physiognomy of Chilean politics was strengthened by their success in capturing the presidency under the leadership of Eduardo Frei in 1964, in an electoral coalition with the right, and by their impressive victory in the 1965 congressional race, the best showing by a single party in Chile's modern history. Their success presented a serious challenge to the parties of both the right and left. The right was practically obliterated in the 1965 election, while the left redoubled its efforts to maintain its constituents and to appeal with a more militant cry to Chile's most destitute citizens.

Once in office and heartened by their electoral success, the Christian Democrats sought to implement their "revolution in liberty" by disdaining the traditional coalition politics of the past. They were particularly hard on the now-diminished Radicals, refusing any overtures for collaboration. Unlike the Radicals, they were unwilling to tolerate clientelistic and log-rolling politics or to serve as an effective bridge across parties and groups. Although they enacted critical copper "Chileanization" legislation in concert with the right, and agrarian reform in coalition with the left, the Christian Democrats went out of their way to govern as a single party and refused to deal with opponents unless they had to. At the same time, they expended large amounts of state resources and vast amounts of U.S. foreign-aid funds on programs that were clearly designed to enhance their electoral superiority at the expense of both right and left.[56]

The Christian Democrats' rigid posture added to the growing radicalization of elites on the left (particularly the Socialist Party), who feared the electoral challenge of the center party, and to profound resentment among elites on the right, who felt betrayed by the reforms, especially in land redistribution, enacted by their erstwhile coalition partners. Radicalization of the left was also profoundly affected by international events, notably the Cuban Revolution, which set a new standard for the Latin American left to emulate.

Had the Christian Democrats succeeded in becoming a genuine center majority, the increased ideological tension would not have had such serious institutional repercussions. But despite vast organizational efforts and extraordinary levels of foreign aid from the Johnson administration in Washington, which was anxious to promote Chile as a showcase of democracy on a continent fascinated by Cuba, they did not succeed in breaking the tripartite deadlock of Chilean politics.

As a result, even when it became apparent that the Christian Democrats would not be able to win the 1970 presidential election in their own right, they were unable to structure preelection coalitions with either the right or the left. The bulk of the Radical Party joined in supporting Salvador Allende, who stunned most observers by edging out rightist Jorge Alessandri by a plurality of 36.2 percent to 34.9 percent of the vote. Christian Democratic candidate Radomiro Tomic received only 27.8 percent of the votes. The election of Allende was not the result of growing radicalization or political mobilization. Nor was it due, in Huntington's terms, to the inability of Chile's political institutions to channel societal demands. Allende won even though he received a smaller percentage of the vote than he had received in his loss to Frei in the two-way race of 1964. Electoral analysis suggests that a greater percentage of newly mobilized voters voted for the right than for the left. The election results simply underscored the repercussions of the failure of the right and center to structure a preelection coalition.[57]

Because no candidate received an absolute majority, the election had to be decided in Congress, forcing the creation of a postelection coalition. Christian Democrats joined legislators of the left in confirming Allende's accession to the highest office in the nation. But the president's minority status, and his lack of majority support in Congress, meant that like other presidents before him, he would have to tailor his program to the realities of coalition politics in order to succeed, even though the very reforms that the right and the Christian Democrats had enacted made such compromises more difficult. But compromise was easier said than done. Important elements in the Unidad Popular (UP) coalition, including Allende's own Socialist Party, were openly committed to a revolutionary transformation in the socioeconomic order and the institutional framework of Chilean politics. Furthermore, the coalition was unwieldy and fractious, with parties and groups competing as much with one another for spoils and popular support as with the opposition.

At the same time, Allende's election touched off an extraordinary reaction from other sectors of Chilean society who feared a pro-Moscow, Marxist-Leninist system might be established in Chile, to their detriment. They encouraged sabotage, subversion, and foreign intrigue. On both sides of Chile's divided party system, the commitment to change or preservation of the status quo now exceeded the commitment to the principles and practices of Chile's historic democracy.

Under these circumstances, structuring a center coalition committed to social change within the framework of traditional liberties and democratic guarantees was crucial to the system's survival. However, like the Christian Democrats before them, many leaders of the UP coalition became convinced that bold use of state power could break the political deadlock and swing the balance to the left. This misconception led them to enact a host of ill-conceived redistributive and stimulative economic measures that aggravated inflation and generated serious economic difficulties. When combined with measures of questionable legality to bring private business under state control, these policies alienated not only Chile's corporate elite, but also small-business people and much of Chile's middle class.

In an atmosphere of growing suspicion and violence, the lines of communication between leaders and followers of opposing parties eroded, accentuating the polarization of Chilean politics. At several key junctures, and despite pressures from both sides, attempts were made to forge a center consensus and structure the necessary compromises that would have saved the regime. But center groups and moderate politicians on both sides of the political divide abdicated their responsibility in favor of narrower group stakes and short-term interests. The involvement of "neutral" powers, such as the courts and the military, only served to politicize those institutions and pave the way for the military coup, a coup that undermined the very institutions of compromise and accommodation moderate leaders had professed to defend.

With the failure of Congress, parties, the courts, and other state institutions to serve as viable arenas to resolve conflict, politics became more and more confrontational; contending groups resorted to mobilizing ever greater numbers of their followers to "prove" their power capabilities.

Politics spilled out of the chambers of government onto the streets, exacerbating an atmosphere of fear and confrontation.[58]

Adding to this atmosphere of confrontation was the effort of U.S. policymakers to undermine the Allende government and support, through overt and covert means, some of the government's most determined opponents. Although it would be mistaken to conclude that Allende's overthrow would not have happened without U.S. intervention, U.S. policy aimed at crippling the Chilean economy and bolstering Chile's antidemocratic opposition contributed to the erosion of spaces of potential accommodation and compromise.

The Chilean breakdown was a complex and dialectical process, in which time-tested patterns of accommodation were eroded by the rise of a center unwilling to bridge the gap between extremes, by the decline of institutional arenas of accommodation in the name of technical efficiency, and by the hardening of ideological distance between leaders with radically different conceptions of a good society. It was also the product of gross miscalculations, extremism, narrow group stakes, and the lack of courage in key circumstances. Breakdown was not inevitable. Although human action was severely circumscribed by the structural characteristics of Chilean politics and by the course of events, there was still room for choice, for a leadership willing to prevent the final denouement. Nor did most Chileans want a military solution to the country's problems. Surveys taken in the weeks before the coup indicated an overwhelming support for democracy and a peaceful outcome of the political crisis.[59]

Political Structures and Regime Breakdown:
A Critique of Presidentialism

Although it was not inevitable, the breakdown of Chilean democracy raises serious questions about the viability of particular institutional forms of governance in democratic regimes. It is a premise of this chapter that in Chile there was an inadequate fit between the country's highly polarized and competitive party system, which was incapable of generating majorities, and a presidential system of centralized authority.[60]

The starting point for this argument must be a recognition that through much of the twentieth century, presidentialism in Chile was in crisis. By definition, a presidential election is a zero-sum game that freezes the outcome for a fixed period of time. In Chile, the winner invariably represented only a third of the electorate, and yet, as the head of government and head of state, he felt responsible for the national destiny as the embodiment of popular sovereignty. As minority presidents, however, Chilean chief executives received weak legislative support or outright congressional opposition. Because he could not seek reelection, there was little incentive for parties, including the president's, to support him beyond midterm. The fixed terms for both president and Congress contributed to an atmosphere of ungovernability and a feeling of permanent crisis, alleviated only by the willingness of centrist parties or politicians to provide last-minute reprieves to beleaguered presidents in exchange for ambassadorial appointments or concessions on policy.

Paradoxically, the response to this problem of governance was to seek an increase in presidential power. The resolution of the country's pressing social and economic problems required strong leadership, it was argued, and such leadership should not be thwarted by ideological wrangling and the narrow partisan interest of the parties and the legislature. However, increased presidential power only aggravated the problem by further reducing arenas for accommodation and by making executive-legislative relations more bitter. Indeed, the stronger the power of the presidency as a separate constitutional actor, the greater were the disincentives for structuring presidential support among parties and groups jealous of their autonomy and future electoral prospects.

In Chile, there was an inverse correlation between the power of the presidency and the success of presidential government. The stronger the president, the weaker the presidential system—a perverse logic that came to a tragic head in the Allende years. A parliamentary system of government would have defused the enormous pressures for structuring high-stakes coalitions around a winner-take-all presidential option, which only reinforced political polarization. At the same time, it would have eliminated the stalemate and confrontation in executive-legislative relations. Had Chile had a parliamentary regime in the early 1970s, Allende's government might have fallen, but democracy would have survived. The working majority in Congress that elected Allende to the presidential post would have had to continue for him to have retained his position. This was not out of the question. The Christian Democrats were close to the UP government on many key points of substance, as attested by the near-agreements at several key junctures of the unfolding drama of the UP years. Had the coalition collapsed, it is quite likely that a Christian Democrat, or perhaps a member of the small leftist Radical Party, would have formed a new government with support from elements on the right.

It is important to stress that parliamentary politics would have had the opposite effect of presidential politics on party distance. It would have contributed to moderating Chilean politics by reinforcing the time-honored traditions of compromise honed by generations of politicians. Moderate leaders on both sides of the congressional aisle would have gained strength, encouraging centripetal drives toward coalition and compromise, rather than being outclassed by maximalist leaders who thrived in the public arenas of high-stakes electoral battles. Moreover, legislators of all parties would have thought twice about abandoning hard-fought coalition arrangements if they had faced the prospect of immediate reelection, and the greater accountability of having been part of an agreement to structure executive authority.

MILITARY RULE IN CHILE

With the collapse of democracy, Chile was abruptly transformed from an open and participatory political system into a repressive and authoritarian one. Few Chileans could have imagined in September 1973 that military intervention would lead to a government so alien to institutions and traditions dating from the nation's founding. Fewer still would have believed that Chile would produce an authoritarian regime capable of outlasting other contemporary military governments on the continent, or that General Pinochet, the obedient commander who assured President Allende of his undivided loyalty, would achieve a degree of personal power rare in the annals of modern dictatorship.

Soon after the coup, it became clear that Chile's military commanders, with no experience of direct involvement in politics, were not about to turn power back to civilian leaders after a brief interregnum. From the outset, they articulated two basic aims.[61] The first was to destroy the parties of the left and their collaborators. The Chilean military did not interpret its intervention as a simple intervention aimed at replacing a government, but as an all-out war to crush an enemy that it believed had infiltrated close to half the population. Moreover, military leaders were convinced that it was not only foreign "doctrines" that were to blame for Chile's predicament. They believed the left had been able to make inroads precisely because of the inherent weaknesses of liberal democracy, which they believed encouraged corruption, radicalism, and demagoguery.

Thus, their second objective was to engineer a fundamental restructuring of Chilean political institutions and political life, aimed at "cleansing" impurities from the body politic while creating a new political order of committed and patriotic citizens, dedicated to modernizing the country without the bickering confrontation and partisanship of the past.

The junta had a clear idea of how to pursue its first objective: it relied on the years of training, awesome firepower, and the many contingency plans that had been developed to protect the constitutional order, and applied them with a vengeance to the task of finding and neutralizing the enemy. Military units moved in to "clean up" neighborhoods that were strongholds of the left as if they were securing enemy territory during wartime.[62] Thousands of party leaders, trade-union officials, and community activists associated with the parties of the left were "neutralized" through arrests, exile, torture, and extrajudicial killings. Close to 3,000 people may have died as a result of officially sanctioned repression. The

National Commission for Truth and Reconciliation appointed after the end of military rule was able to document 2,279 cases of human rights victims who died as a result of official action, 957 of whom were made to "disappear."[63]

At the same time, labor unions were sharply circumscribed, parties were banned or declared in "recess," and internal elections were prohibited or closely monitored in all private organizations, including professional associations and nonprofit agencies. Citizens who during the Allende years and before had been repeatedly enlisted for one cause or another now turned inward and avoided public affairs entirely, either out of fear of reprisals or outright support for military rule. Politics, which for generations had revolved around parties and interest groups that penetrated all levels of society, was now confined to small groups of individuals and cabals in the inner corridors of power.

In the immediate aftermath of the coup, the commanders of the army, navy, and air force and the director general of the Carabineros (Chile's paramilitary police) constituted themselves as a governmental junta that would exercise executive, legislative, and constitutional authority through unanimous agreement of its members. General Pinochet was selected to be junta president by virtue of his position as leader of the oldest military branch. They agreed that the junta presidency would rotate on a periodic basis among the commanders and that they would divide up policy areas so that each of the services would handle the affairs of different ministries. Even the appointments of university presidents were parceled out, so that Pinochet, as commander of the army, named the president of the University of Chile, while Admiral Merino appointed one of his fellow officers to the top post at the private Catholic University.

Pinochet, however, moved swiftly to break the principle of collegiality and assert his own power. Although Air Force General Gustavo Leigh was the most articulate, visible, and hard-line member of the junta, Pinochet proved more politically skillful, ruthless, and ambitious than his colleague.[64] He proceeded firmly to consolidate his power within the army, by far the most powerful service, by retiring those members of his cohort group who had planned the coup and were suspicious of Pinochet, a latecomer to the plotting, and then promoting officers who were loyal to him and the institutional chain of command. All colonels promoted to the rank of general were required to provide the army commander with a signed letter of resignation, which Pinochet could use at any moment to end the officer's career.

Loyalty was assured with more than the threat of sanctions. Under military rule, officers enjoyed privileges that they had never dreamed of. In addition to increases in pay and fringe benefits, officers could look forward to attractive rewards such as ambassadorships or membership on boards of public and semipublic corporations. Government service provided military men with responsibility and status they had never before enjoyed in the nation's history.[65]

By serving both as president and commander in chief of the army with direct responsibility over the institution, and by strictly observing the separation of the military as government from the military as institution, Pinochet avoided the inherent tensions that develop in military regimes between officers occupying government positions and those serving in the institution itself.[66]

Aiding the general's ascendancy was the growing power of the secret police. The DINA (Dirección de Inteligencia Nacional—National Intelligence Bureau), under the direction of Colonel Manuel Contreras, a close associate of Pinochet's family, soon became a law unto itself. It eliminated with efficient brutality the clandestine leadership of leftist parties and carried out with impunity a series of high-risk political assassinations abroad, aimed at silencing prominent critics of the regime. But DINA's power extended beyond its role in fighting the resistance movement. The secret organization came to be feared in military and governmental circles. It soon developed its own cadres of experts in fields including economic policy, as it sought to establish control over sectors of the Chilean state, particularly the nationalized industries. Pinochet made use of Contreras's services to counter other advisory groups and to strengthen his own hand vis-à-vis the junta and the military.[67]

The consolidation of Pinochet's authority was also spurred by key conservative civilian and military collaborators of the junta who became increasingly uncomfortable with the chaos and inefficiency of collegial rule and feared that divided authority would undermine the regime's viability. They were profoundly influenced by Chilean constitutional precepts and could not conceive of a system of authority that did not reproduce the structure of Chile's presidential constitution. Working directly with Pinochet, they proposed to the junta, overwhelmed with legislative and policy complexities, the adoption of several measures aimed at "rationalizing" military rule in conformity with traditional constitutional doctrine. This led to Pinochet's being named "Supreme Chief of the Nation," granting him executive powers while the junta (with Pinochet still serving as one of its four members) retained "legislative" authority. Although the other commanders had qualms about Pinochet's new title, they went along with the effort to improve governmental efficiency. It was only a matter of time before he would insist on the title of "President of the Republic."

As Pinochet asserted his control, he repeatedly clashed with his fellow commanders. General Leigh, in particular, bitterly opposed Pinochet's ambitions as well as the growing influence over public and economic policy of a group of free-market economists protected by Pinochet. In retaliation, Leigh blocked, in mid-1977, Pinochet's proposal to have junta laws approved by a majority rather than by unanimity. He also blocked Pinochet's request for junta approval of a referendum endorsing "President Pinochet in his defense of the dignity of Chile" in the face of widespread international criticisms of human rights abuses in Chile. Leigh correctly perceived this as a move on the president's part to gain popular legitimacy for his own mandate and increase his supremacy over the junta. Pinochet, in the face of junta objections, called the referendum anyway.

Finally, on July 28, 1978, with the support of the other two junta members, Pinochet forcibly and illegally removed General Leigh from office, overcoming a bitter and tense showdown with the air force in order to accomplish his objective.[68] With this coup within the coup, Pinochet was able to consolidate his dictatorial rule.

Leigh's departure allowed Pinochet to concentrate on the task of designing a new constitutional order for the country, one that would fundamentally modify Chile's historic institutions while guaranteeing his permanence in power. He unceremoniously discarded the constitutional draft proposed by a commission of conservative leaders that called for elections as early as 1985 and insisted on a document that would keep him in power for at least a quarter of a century, until 1998. Pinochet eventually relented when his advisers told him that he would have difficulty winning a plebiscite on those terms and agreed to a formulation whereby the commanders would pick, in 1988 or 1989, a candidate to be ratified in a plebiscite for an eight-year term in office. The general was explicitly exempted from any prohibition on serving, making it clear that he had every intention of being the candidate. The provisional articles of the constitution gave the military regime broad powers to restrict political rights and curtail due process of law with no right of appeal.[69]

The permanent articles of the Constitution, ratified in a highly questionable plebiscite in 1980, aimed to create a "modern and protected democracy," one that stressed the value of national security over popular sovereignty. As such it established a permanent role for the armed forces as "guarantors" of the nation's institutions, imposed a permanent ban on certain political groups and ideologies, and sharply limited institutional expressions of popular sovereignty.

The tutelary role for the armed forces was expressed through the National Security Council, a body whose voting members consisted of the "President of the Republic," the president of the Senate, the chief justice of the Supreme Court, and the four commanders of the armed services, giving the latter a majority. The council was empowered to admonish (*representar*) any governmental authority (including the president and the Congress) if it believed the institutional order or national security were threatened. Although the text did not make clear what would transpire should the council's views be ignored, its authors clearly intended to give the armed forces constitutional license to take matters into their own hands should they deem fit.

The National Security Council was also empowered to name a majority of the Constitutional Tribunal, a body with final authority to interpret the constitutionality of acts of Congress, and a majority of the nine designated senators that would constitute a third of the Senate. Only the council could remove a commander of the armed forces, a prerogative the president would no longer enjoy.

The 1980 Constitution, through Article 8, sought to ban the parties of the left by holding that "any act by a person or group intended to propagate doctrines that are antagonistic to the family or that advocate violence or a totalitarian concept of society, the state, or the juridical order or class struggle is illicit and contrary to the institutional order of the Republic." Through Articles 19, 23, and 57 it barred all parties from intervening in activities that were "foreign to them" and prohibited union, community, and association leaders from exercising leadership roles in parties.

Finally, the 1980 Constitution sought to severely limit popular sovereignty by abolishing all local and provincial elected governments, establishing a Senate with almost one-third of its members "designated" by other authorities including the commanders of the armed forces, and granting the president the power to dissolve the lower house of Congress once during his term. Constitutional amendments could only be approved with the concurrence of the president and two succeeding legislatures with three-fifths of the members voting in favor. The Constitution created a hyperpresidential regime with sharply reduced prerogatives for the Congress, which was to be transferred out of town to the city of Valparaiso.

With Leigh's departure Pinochet also further empowered the free-market economists who were revolutionizing the Chilean economy by lowering tariffs, privatizing state corporations and pension systems, and reducing the size of the state.[70] Although business groups were profoundly affected by these measures, they were reticent to criticize the regime for fear of undermining its strength. For Chile's business leaders, democracy had meant the electoral triumph of political forces bent on destroying them. No matter how objectionable the government's free-market policies, the military government was a far preferable alternative to the uncertainties of democratic politics.

Many people in Chile's middle classes, despite economic hardship, shared these views. Pinochet's success and the durability of Chile's military regime cannot be understood without underscoring the latitude the military government enjoyed in pursuing its policies. The Chilean military enjoyed a degree of autonomy not shared by its counterparts in countries such as Argentina and Brazil, allowing it to pursue policies unencumbered by the potentially damaging opposition of powerful economic groups.

Opposition to Dictatorship and the Defeat of Pinochet

The coup that ended Chile's long trajectory of democratic politics was applauded by many sectors of society, while condemned by others. Chile's rightist parties welcomed the new authorities and soon agreed to disband, confident that the military would represent their interests.[71]

The Christian Democrats, Chile's largest party, reluctantly accepted the coup as the inevitable result of the Popular Unity government's policies. However, Christian Democrats were not prepared to accept the diagnosis of the country's new rulers that democracy was also at fault and that military rule should be maintained for an indefinite period of time. Soon, the Christian Democrats began to join the parties of the left in strong criticism of the regime's human rights abuses and its redrafting of the nation's institutional structures. By the late 1970s, Christian Democrats were able to begin a dialogue with elements on the left, as both groups attempted to come to terms with their collective responsibility in the failure of Chile's political order.

It was not until 1983, with the collapse of Chile's much-vaunted economy (a downturn of 14.3 percent of GDP in 1982 alone pushing unemployment rates up to close to 30 percent), that Chile's political parties began to reassert themselves, demonstrating that the regime had failed to fully obliterate them from national life. The spontaneous protest movement, spurred by labor leaders, surprised the parties as much as it did the regime. The government's repressive measures against labor, rendered vulnerable by high levels of unemployment, opened the door for the parties to take over the leadership of the opposition movement.

In the moderate opposition, the Christian Democrats sought to forge an alliance with smaller parties on both the right and left in order to structure a proposal for an alternative government and force the military to negotiate. On the left, the Communist Party, which was supporting an armed strategy against the regime, sought to mobilize popular discontent through militant protests in the expectation that the regime would simply capitulate as in Nicaragua or the Philippines. Even on the right some influential voices warned that if Pinochet did not alter his chronology and seek negotiations, the regime could become ungovernable.

Despite high hopes and the weakness of the regime, the opposition failed to seriously challenge Pinochet. This failure was due largely to the deep split in opposition forces between those who sought peaceful mobilization to engage in negotiations with the authorities, and those that sought confrontation through mobilization to force the authorities out of office.[72] The 1985 initiative sponsored by moderates on both sides of Chile's divide and supported by the church, known as the National Accord for Transition to Democracy, failed precisely because of fear of increased mobilization and confrontation. The attempted assassination of Pinochet in September of

1986 by a group close to the Communist Party brought to a standstill efforts to build a broad antigovernment coalition.

At the root of this division was the continued polarization of Chilean politics between a strong Marxist left, which advocated far-reaching socioeconomic reforms, and a rejuvenated right, which preferred authoritarianism and feared changes in the new economic model. While significant political learning took place in broad quarters of Chilean party life, with Socialists embracing democratic practices as important ends in their own right, and Christian Democrats vowing not to pursue single-party strategies for their own gain, mistrust remained high as elements on both extremes pressed for radically divergent solutions.

The same logic of polarization that made it difficult to maintain a center consensus and finally helped bring Chilean democracy crashing down in 1973 conspired against structuring a broad and coherent opposition movement to force the military from power. Widespread rejection of the authoritarian government as illegitimate could not translate into an early return to democracy for lack of a clear alternative.[73]

Paradoxically, it was the regime that provided the opposition with a rationale for unity and a means to define the transition process in its favor. Although no opposition leader accepted the legitimacy of the plebiscite formula spelled out in the 1980 Constitution, calling instead for open and fair presidential elections as soon as possible, by 1987 most democratic opponents seemed resigned to accepting the plebiscite as a fact of political life.[74]

The Communist Party and sectors of the socialist left continued to object to any "participation in the legality of the regime." They were convinced that registering and voting would simply serve to further legitimize the regime, since they felt that the authorities would not permit a negative result and would resort to fraud if necessary to impose their candidate.

Moderate opposition leaders, on the other hand, argued that the Yes/No plebiscite represented a valuable tool for popular mobilization and an important opportunity to try to defeat the regime at its own game—the only viable alternative for an opposition that had not succeeded in overthrowing the dictatorship through other means. Their hand was strengthened as leaders of the Socialist Party distanced themselves from the Communists in the wake of the Pinochet assassination attempt.

With great trepidation, the democratic opposition proceeded to officially register their parties, which limited their autonomy and forced them to collect signatures to gain legal standing, engendering fear among potential signatories concerned about possible reprisals. And yet, party registration was essential to permit opposition groups to name poll watchers and monitor the fairness of the election. The Christian Democratic Party and a loose coalition of left-of-center groups spearheaded by moderate socialists calling itself the Party for Democracy both registered in time to play a role in the plebiscite.

In governmental circles there was considerable speculation that the four commanders (including Pinochet as commander of the army) would select someone other than Pinochet to stand for office. Key leaders on the right felt that the government needed to project its institutions into the future without tying them to the figure of one man. They also feared that Pinochet was too controversial a leader, one around whom the opposition could unite in a simple zero-sum decision. Two of the four commanders shared this view.

In late August 1988, however, Pinochet once again used the force of his personality and his political and institutional clout to gain the nomination. Without strong vocal support from the right, the dissenting commanders were not able to press for an alternative. The sharp economic downturn of 1982–1983, resulting in state takeover of the banking system, had left the business sector more vulnerable than ever to state decisions—not a very propitious moment for the politically cautious economic right to abandon Pinochet. The army in particular took on the challenge of the plebiscite as if it were a military campaign. Government and military leaders were confident that the revolutionary changes in the Chilean economy that had finally begun to bear fruit, combined with massive housing and public-works programs and an extensive television campaign aimed at instilling fear of a return to the chaos and divisions of the past, would strongly favor ratification of Pinochet's right to continue to rule Chile.

Chilean authorities came under considerable pressure internally and internationally to stage a fair contest, even though the plebiscite was widely criticized as a profoundly undemocratic exercise. Chile's tradition of fair and free elections, combined with the military regime's own desire to assert its legitimacy, contributed to the structuring of virtually fraud-proof voting procedures.

To the surprise of most people, particularly in the government, Chile's fractious opposition put aside its divisions and mounted an extraordinarily successful media and door-to-door campaign in the last few weeks before the elections. With limited resources and relying on volunteer workers, they successfully countered the fear campaign of the government by stressing a positive and upbeat message. To vote "No" in the plebiseite came to denote happiness and the future, while the "Yes" campaign remained mired in the past. The drive to produce advertisements, to recruit poll watchers, to set up an effective parallel vote count, and to conduct door-to-door campaigns cemented the unity of the sixteen parties that formed the No command. International support, particularly through the National Democratic Institute for International Affairs, contributed critical resources for the media campaign and for the computer system designed to monitor the electoral count.

The victory of opposition forces by a 12 percent margin was a stunning achievement. Ninety-seven percent of the registered voters (representing 92 percent of the eligible population) went to the polls, and the opposition won in all but two of the country's twelve regions. Pinochet lost among most categories of voters.

Two elements were critical in making it possible for the No vote to win and derail plans by some elements close to Pinochet to create a climate of violence that they hoped would lead to canceling the plebiscite. First, the military and the civilian political right expected a fair contest and would not have tolerated any disruption of the process. Even in the army, institutional loyalties and respect for "legality" were more important factors than allegiance to the ambitions of the commander in chief. Second, opposition leaders were successful in persuading voters to stay home, waiting calmly for results on election night, and to celebrate peacefully the next day. The violence that some elements in the regime had expected, and hoped to manipulate to their advantage in case of an electoral loss, simply did not materialize. The Communist Party played an important role by insisting that its own militants refrain from organizing street demonstrations.

The plebiscite showed how easy it is for an authoritarian regime to engage in collective self-delusion. Countless polls and newspaper accounts suggested that if voters overcame their skepticism about the election's fairness, the No vote stood a good chance of winning. Yet Pinochet and his supporters in the military and the business community were absolutely convinced that the government could not lose. A generalized contempt for politics and politicians, even those supporting the regime, made it difficult for them to sense the mood of the country, one that strongly supported a return to Chile's democratic traditions.

The Communist Party and far left also lost ground as many longtime supporters rejected its hard line and joined the movement to defeat Pinochet at the ballot box. In the aftermath of the election the party would see its influence and support wane dramatically as the Socialists, its weaker ally during the authoritarian interlude, gained in strength and electoral following. While the Communists may have been more effective in maintaining their organizational discipline during dictatorship, their inability to understand the demand of Chile's population for a peaceful transition contributed to their loss of credibility.

REDEMOCRATIZATION AND
COALITION POLITICS OF COMPROMISE

The dramatic defeat of General Pinochet in the 1988 plebiscite derailed his carefully orchestrated chronology for regime transition. Yet the victorious opposition faced a serious dilemma. It had campaigned on a platform calling for the dismantling of the "itinerary" and "institutionality" of the outgoing regime, one they viewed as fundamentally undemocratic. But the electoral defeat of Pinochet did not mean the defeat of the armed forces, and opposition leaders feared that they might renege on the promise of holding free and open presidential elections if they felt overly threatened. The fact that Pinochet had received over 40 percent of the vote reinforced their view that they had to proceed with extreme caution.

Moderates within the military government also feared the aftermath of the plebiscite. They were worried that the country faced a period of increasingly violent confrontations unless the government acknowledged its defeat and the legitimacy of the opposition's demand for key changes in the institutional order. They reasoned that it was in the interest of the government to seek some kind of common ground in order to lock in the fundamental features of the junta's constitutional framework. Unless reforms were adopted before open and competitive elections were held, the military authorities might not be able to control the outcome. Their position vis-à-vis the hard-liners of the regime was bolstered by the support for reforms on the part of key leaders in Renovacion Nacional, the largest party on the right, who were critical of many of the undemocratic features of the military constitution.

The negotiations that ensued between opposition party leaders, the military government, and party leaders of the right set the stage for a new style of politics in Chile that would profoundly mark the Chilean transition.[75] They led to the opposition's acceptance of the fundamental legitimacy of the 1980 Constitution, in return for fifty-four amendments that would substantially temper some of the more undemocratic features of the document.

The tutelary role of the military was substantially reduced by enlarging the composition of the National Security Council and giving civilians parity with its military members. More significantly, the council's power to admonish the authorities with an implicit enforcement function was reduced to an advisory role.

Restrictions on the right to organize political parties were fundamentally changed by noting that parties could be sanctioned only for actions against the democratic order and not simply for their doctrines or beliefs. Restrictions on party membership or leadership in other secondary associations were eliminated.

The reforms also reduced the weight of the designated senators from one-third to one-fourth by enlarging that body. It eliminated the president's ability to dissolve the lower house, reduced the qualified majorities required to amend the constitutions, and increased the oversight functions of the Senate. Although opposition leaders publicly argued that they would seek further constitutional reforms after the return of democracy, they were pleased that the most objectionable features of the Pinochet Constitution had been eliminated.

On July 30, 1989, and by an 85.7 percent majority, Chileans ratified the constitution as amended, paving the way for reestablishment of democratic rule with the election, on December 14, 1989, of Christian Democratic Party president Patricio Aylwin, as president of Chile. Supported by the parties that backed the No campaign, he handily defeated the architect of Pinochet's economic recovery, former minister of finance Hernán Büchi, by 55.2 percent of the vote to 29.4 percent, with independent businessman Javier Errázuriz obtaining 15.4 percent. The opposition coalition also won a majority of the contests for seats in both chambers of the legislature, although the electoral system inherited from the military government favored the parties of the right. The alliance, known as the Concertación de Partidos por la Democracia, however, did not gain control of the Senate because of the presence of eight designated senators appointed by the outgoing regime.

Despite considerable initial uncertainty, including fears of economic instability and authoritarian reversal, the four-year Aylwin administration succeeded in setting the country on a solid course of redemocratization, while presiding over notable economic progress. The most important factor accounting for the success of Chile's transition was the ability of Chile's opposition parties to put aside historic rivalries and constitute a disciplined and coherent coalition, fashioning the most constructive and enduring multiparty alliance in the nation's twentieth-century history, the Concertación de Partidos por La Democracia.

Although sixteen different parties originally constituted the Concertación, the dominant parties were the Christian Democrats, the Socialists, the Radicals, and the newly formed Partido por la Democracia (PPD). In the opposition, Renovación Nacional (RN), which traced its roots to Chile's historic Liberal and Conservative parties, and the Unión Democrática Independiente (UDI), a party closely tied to the Pinochet regime and its reform technocrats, divided the bulk of the electorate on the right. The largest party in Chile remained the Christian Democratic Party with 37.5 percent of the preferences of the electorate in December 1990. The runner-up was Renovación Nacional with 8.1 percent. The Socialists and the PPD combined enjoyed the support of 13.4 percent of the electorate.

With the cohesive support of the Concertación, the Aylwin government moved resolutely to address three challenges: maintain economic growth while improving social conditions, confront the issue of human rights, and seek further democratization.

The close ties between coalition parties and labor and popular groups, coupled with the weakness of the Communist Party in the postauthoritarian period, gave the authorities the necessary political space to deepen the free-market economic reforms of the military government without engendering significant social unrest. Thus, the government significantly expanded social spending (20 percent by 1991 compared with the last year of the Pinochet government) without incurring deficit spending, making a significant dent in poverty and inequality, although income distribution remained heavily skewed in favor of upper-income groups. By the end of Aylwin's administration, the country had been set on a course of unprecedented economic progress, making Chile the fastest-growing economy in Latin America. From 1991 to 1997 Chile enjoyed average growth rates of over 7 percent, raising per capita income by close to 50 percent. During the same period, the percentage of the population in poverty dropped from 39 percent in 1990 to 23 percent in 1996.

President Aylwin was also able to draw on his considerable popular support and the cohesiveness of his coalition to address the demand for an accounting of human rights violations by appointing the Commission on Truth and Reconciliation. After an exhaustive review, the commission documented 2,279 cases of human rights abuses resulting in death.[76] President Aylwin officially acknowledged the complicity of the Chilean state in these crimes, while admitting that the strength of the right and the military made it impossible to repeal earlier amnesty laws that protected the perpetrators from being brought to trial. The only notable exception was the successful sentencing of General Manuel Contreras, the former head of DINA, for ordering the assassination of former foreign minister Orlando Letelier in Washington, D.C., in 1976. Chile's democrats hoped that by seeking the truth, albeit without real justice, they would help to heal the wounds of the past and forge the necessary consensus to rebuild democracy.

Finally, the civilian government sought additional constitutional reforms to strengthen representative institutions. The most notable achievement was the constitutional reform that reestablished elected local government, paving the way for the June 1992 municipal elections. In that race, the Concertación gained 53.3 percent of the vote, to 29.7 percent for the parties of the right. The reforms, however, did not provide for elected state governments, contemplated in the 1925 Constitution although never implemented. Chile, thus, remained a highly centralized unitary state with appointed regional intendants serving as agents for the national government.

Despite repeated efforts, the Concertación was not able to engineer additional changes in the constitutional legacy of the military regime. The eight designated senators appointed by the outgoing government deprived the Concertación of a senatorial majority and contributed to placing constitutional amendments out of reach, unless supported by at least a sector of the right. Thus changes in the composition of the Constitutional Tribunal, the electoral law, or the institution of the designated senators itself were not attained.

Most dramatically for its symbolic importance, President Aylwin failed to change the provisions of the 1980 Constitution that restricted the president's ability to retire the commanders of the armed forces. Although he asked Pinochet to step down as commander in chief of the army, the general refused, leading to an uncomfortable situation of having the former dictator ensconced in the powerful post of army head.

Aylwin, however, skillfully asserted his presidential authority, and Pinochet's influence in all matters except those related directly to the military as an institution waned dramatically. Ironically, his presence as a visible symbol of the authoritarian regime may have initially helped the Concertación by discouraging irrational outbursts in an institution that still believed it had a historic mission to guard the nation from the irresponsible actions of politicians.

The opposition's acquiescence to a transition following the rules established by the authoritarian regime was also critical in providing the military and its supporters, in a country still traumatized by the divisions of the past, with institutional guarantees that they would not be overwhelmed by the "threat" of majority rule.

Chile's growing stability and prosperity and the success of the Aylwin government propelled the governing coalition to a stunning victory in the December 1993 presidential race to replace Aylwin, who could not succeed himself. The Concertación candidate was another Christian Democrat, Eduardo Frei Ruiz Tagle, son of the former president, who defeated Ricardo Lagos, the titular leader of the moderate left, in a primary contest. Frei improved over his predecessors' electoral tally, garnering an impressive 58.1 percent of the vote, the highest percentage obtained by any president since the 1920s. If the vote of several minor candidates is added to his total, the center-left obtained 69.4 percent of the vote to only 30.2 percent for those forces identified with the right and the military regime. Indeed, the right lost ground in the presidential race with respect to 1989.[77]

In the congressional races the Concertación garnered 55.4 percent of the vote, retaining 70 out of the 120 seats in the Chamber of Deputies. The governing coalition also won a majority of the seats in the forty-six member Senate, but because of the continuing presence of the eight senators designated during Pinochet's last year in office, it failed to gain a majority in that chamber, forcing the government to continue to negotiate with parties of the right to enact legislation. The election was notable because the parties of the Concertación's left gained ground, obtaining 23.8 percent of the vote to the Christian Democratic Party's 27.2 percent.

The second democratic election after the restoration of democracy illustrates the degree of continuity in Chilean politics despite the fact that the country remained divided into three strongly identifiable blocks on the right, center, and left. Including the smaller parties outside of the two main coalitions, the right obtained 28.3 percent, the center 30.3 percent, and the left 33.7 percent of the vote cast for the Chamber of Deputies.[78] These figures are consistent with historical trends in Chile, as reported above in Table 4.1, although the degree of ideological polarization and the meaning of the terms *right, left,* and *center* have changed in Chile, as elsewhere, in the post–Cold War era.[79]

Electoral results are paralleled by those reported in public-opinion surveys. Table 4.2 shows the ideological self-placement of the Chilean electorate from June 1990 to March 1993, and compares it with the results of an earlier survey conducted in 1958. Although the right had greater support in the earlier survey, the overall trends are remarkably consistent almost forty years later. As in 1958, a substantial portion of the electorate (between 19 percent and 39 percent) prefers to call itself independent or is unwilling to label itself in any given survey. This self-professed independence does not, however, translate into support for independent candidates at the polls as Chileans continue to support the traditional parties.

Table 4.2 Ideological Orientation of the Electorate, June 1990, March 1993, June 1995, and June 1998 (percentage)

Ideological Orientation	June 1990	March 1993	June 1995	June 1998
Right or Center-Right	14.3	22.8	26	22
Center	25.3	24.6	15	10
Left or Center-Left	28.5	33.7	25	25
Independent, none, or don't know	32.0	19.0	30	43

Source: Centro de Estudios Públicos, "Estudio Nacional de opinión pública," for respective years.

The Frei administration followed the broad policy outlines of its predecessor, while seeking to strengthen the country's public-works infrastructure and educational systems. Chile continued to maintain high growth spurred by record levels of direct foreign investment, while inflation levels declined even further as the country maintained a positive macroeconomic balance sheet.

Not until the Asian crisis of 1998 did the economy experience a serious downturn, one directly linked to Chile's success in diversifying its markets. But that crisis underscored the fact that Chile's rapid growth was based primarily on the export of raw materials, with their significant price volatility. Chilean policymakers are keenly aware that continued growth will depend on producing more manufactured products with greater "added value," but that innovation and productivity require a more educated work force.

In the political sphere, Frei faced the same dilemma his predecessor had. Although important reforms were adopted, particularly regarding the judiciary, the opposition majority in the Senate barred any significant constitutional changes that would eliminate the designated senators, redesign the Constitutional Tribunal, bring the military under closer presidential control, and change the electoral system that favored the minority rightist coalition.

Partly because he took the helm of the government in less "heroic" times, and partly because he projected the image of a more workmanlike governor without strong charismatic appeal, Frei's job approval fell considerably by comparison with his predecessor, although the public continued to regard him highly as a person. Where Aylwin's job approval ratings remained consistently above 49 percent, by 1996 Frei's had dropped into the mid-30s. Low job approval levels were related to heightened concerns on the part of the citizenry with the problems of delinquency and crime, health care, poverty, education, and drugs. Issues such as corruption, the functioning of the judicial system, human rights, or constitutional reforms were far lower on the people's priority list.

In this climate of lower expectations, the 1997 congressional elections proved to be a rude awakening for the Concertación and Chile's political class. Whereas in the 1989 election 18 percent of the electorate had abstained or cast blank or null votes, in 1997 that figure surged to 40.1 percent. While the rightist coalition declined only slightly from 36.6 percent to 36.2 percent by comparison with the 1993 race, the Concertación's total went down from 55.5 percent to 50.5%. More telling was the drop in the absolute number of voters: 800,000 fewer citizens voted for the Concertación in 1997 than in 1993. Although the right also lost voters, the proportional loss was less.

Particularly hurt was the Christian Democratic Party, which lost 60 percent of the Concertación's vote while reducing its overall percentage of the vote from 27.2 percent to 23 percent. The combined vote of the PPD and the Socialists, by contrast, was 23.6 percent. In a sharp blow to Chile's largest party, for the first time its partners on the left of the Concertación had obtained a larger share of the electorate than it had. On the right, the moderate Renovación Nacional maintained its 16.3 percent of the total vote while the Unión Democrática Independiente increased its share from 12.1 to 14.4 percent, bringing both parties closer to parity.

Commentators on both sides of the political spectrum decried the results, arguing that they revealed a deep alienation with the political system and politics in general on the part of a substantial portion of the population, one that did not bode well particularly for the Concertación or the Christian Democrats. Survey research, however, does not support the view that nonvoters are a particularly alienated substrata of the Chilean voting public.[80] As Table 4.3 shows, nonvoters were no different than voters in their attitudes and partisan preferences or in their degree of support of the Frei administration. They were also similar with regard to demographic characteristics, with one exception: nonvoters tended to be younger.

Table 4.3   Responses of Voters and Nonvoters to Selected Questions, April
            1998 (percentage)

Questions	Did Vote (75% of sample)	Did Not Vote (25% of sample)
Problems the government should solve		
Poverty	44.2	51.0
Health	40.2	32.0
Delinquency	38.4	32.8
Employment	30.1	30.9
Economic situation of the country		
Bad–Very Bad	39.2	38.2
Neither Bad nor Good	46.6	46.4
Good–Very Good	13.1	15.4
The country is		
Progressing	37.4	43.9
Stagnating	42.8	38.7
Declining	15.4	12.5
Approval of Frei's leadership of the country		
Approves	33.1	33.9
Disapproves	36.9	38.0
Does Not Approve or Disapprove	21.4	18.0

Source: Carla Lehmann, "La voz de los que no votaron," Centro de Estudios Públicos, *Puntos de Referencia,* No. 197 (April 1998), p. 6.

In explaining their failure to vote, most respondents argued that politics did not interest them, that politicians don't concern themselves with real problems, or that voting would not make much difference. These results, which are comparable to findings in other countries, suggest that political apathy rather than political alienation may underlie greater levels of absenteeism. Nor is it certain that this trend toward greater political apathy is negative for Chile's body politic. A good case can be made for the proposition that Chile had been overly politicized in the past, with politics overshadowing other societal values and pursuits.

Because the left surpassed the vote of the Christian Democrats, the 1997 elections provided an important defining moment for Chile's process of democratic consolidation, one that could lead to the breakup of the governing coalition. With these results, the leaders of the Socialist Party and the Party for Democracy could legitimately argue that one of their own should be the Concertación's presidential candidate in the year 1999 to succeed Frei. Adding fuel to their arguments is the fact that Ricardo Lagos, their standard-bearer, is by far the most popular political figure in Chile.[81]

The Christian Democrats are extremely reluctant to cede the top spot to

Lagos. Some party leaders argue simply that, as the largest and most visible party in Chile, they have the right to nominate a third party member to lead the Concertación and the country. Others go further, expressing fears that a Lagos candidacy could seriously undermine the party's already waning strength. Like center parties in Europe, the Christian Democrats find themselves uncomfortably wedged in by a highly ideological right and a moderate "Third Wave" left that have encroached on its more centrist positions. Unable to differentiate itself from the left on economic issues, and divided on key issues such as divorce that have driven the church away from the party and toward the right, the Christian Democrats have yet to articulate a coherent position in this postdictatorial era, while absorbing the inevitable erosion of support of any incumbent party.

The left in the Concertación, however, is equally adamant in insisting that they should field the presidential candidate next time. They voice concern that a failure to do so could significantly weaken their appeal and organizational support. With Lagos as their helmsman, they hope to recapture the imagination of Chileans and revitalize their parties by articulating a new agenda stressing a commitment to social justice, equal opportunity, environmental health, and a continued role for government action.

The divisions between the left and the Christian Democrats raise the specter of the demise of Chile's successful governing coalition. Although it is unlikely, if the Concertación cannot agree on a joint candidate and runs two separate candidates, it runs the risk of laying the groundwork for a successful candidate of the right. More significantly, however, it could signal a return to the politics of minority governments with shifting short-term coalitions that contributed to policy incoherence in the past.

Aggravating the political climate as Frei enters his last two years in office is Chile's as yet unfinished transition. The departure, mandated by the constitution, of General Pinochet from the post of commander of the army in March 1997 rekindled the earlier divisions when the general insisted on being sworn in as a senator for life, a prerogative spelled out in the constitution. Efforts to block him from being seated failed when the Concertación split on the issue. Subsequently, the general's arrest in London, where he traveled for medical treatment, by order of a Spanish court seeking his extradition to stand trial for human rights abuses, opened further the wounds of the past.

These controversies reveal that the divisions that led to the breakdown of democracy and authoritarian rule have not been fully put to rest. Chileans still have not come to terms with their past. Despite President Aylwin's Truth and Reconciliation Commission, Chile may have acknowledged the truth, but it has not found reconciliation.

This is in part due to the fact that amnesty for human rights abuses was not accompanied by recognition or acknowledgment on the part of the military and its supporters that unspeakable abuses did take place in Chile, let alone expression of regrets or apologies for them. The left in Chile has largely done its self-criticism by recognizing the folly of many of the actions of the Allende government and its responsibility for the chaos and polarization of the country. They have come to accept the value and importance of democracy and as an end in itself and not simply a means toward another end, thereby valuing moderation and compromise. The right, by contrast, has continued to believe that the military government saved Chile, doing no wrong in the process, and that its own leaders are immune from responsibility for the excesses of state repression.

The lack of full acknowledgment of responsibility for the past is a far more serious obstacle to Chile's democratic consolidation than some of the institutional features of the military regime that have defied reform. Chile's parties have shown that they are sufficiently disciplined and cohesive to work around the binomial electoral law that was instituted to fragment the old parties and create new party structures. The law remains dangerous because it might contribute to disenfranchising important sectors of public opinion if Chile moves to a tripartite division of the electorate.[82] But it is not any less democratic than first-past-the-post systems used in other democracies.

At the same time, the institution of the designated senators, so roundly criticized by the democratic opposition in the Aylwin years, has lost some of its sting as the Frei government moved following the 1997 congressional races to designate institutional senators whose terms had expired. Chile's Senate remains no less democratic than the United States Senate, with its cloture rule permitting a minority of forty-one senators to block legislation, or the Brazilian and Argentine Senates with their extreme overrepresentation of sparsely populated provincial units. Finally, the retirement of Pinochet and the promotion of a new generation of officers have rendered provisions in the constitution barring presidents from removing military commanders less objectionable. Although these matters remain on the agenda for future reform, their cumulative weight is no longer significant enough to argue that Chile's democratic transition continues to be hampered by "authoritarian enclaves."

What is of far greater concern is the exaggerated powers of the presidency enshrined in the 1980 Constitution, powers that are likely to generate serious institutional and political controversies in the future. For example, the president, and not the Congress, has sole authority to introduce bills involving spending, change the duties and characteristics of public-sector administrative units, modify the political or administrative configuration of the state, and change the rules for collective bargaining. The president may insist on the priority of some legislation and require Congress to act on it in as little as three days. The chief executive can also call the legislature into special session to consider only legislation proposed by the president. Thus the president alone sets the legislative and political agenda and Congress is reduced to being a reactive body.

In the transition governments, congressional leaders, working closely with party leaders in the executive, were willing to accept strong presidential prerogatives to avoid weakening the transitional government. Hyperpresidentialism, however, created strong resentment among legislative elites, including those of the Concertación, while undermining the critical role of the legislature as an arena for accommodation, compromise, and oversight of executive authority. An exaggerated presidentialism is particularly serious in Chile given the survival of the country's strong multiparty system and the continuing division of the country into thirds. Almost seventeen years of military rule and a host of institutional arrangements failed to create a party system with fewer than five major party organizations, none of which can expect to command a majority of the vote on its own.

In the absence of a strong coalition arrangement, it is unlikely that any president will command a majority of the vote or obtain majority support from his or her party in the legislature. Although the Aylwin and Frei governments enjoyed notable success precisely because of the formation of such a coalition, its unity was based on a common struggle against authoritarianism and a strong fear of democratic reversal. As Chilean politics moves from the heroic politics of the transition period to "normal" politics revolving around policy differences and competition for power, the unity of the governing coalition is bound to fray.

Exaggerated presidentialism is likely to exacerbate conflict by centering too much power in one person, thus risking the transformation of the legislature into an arena of negative opposition. Although competition and conflict are normal in democratic contexts, Chilean political elites should attempt to ensure that the country's institutions are able to channel them without straining the democratic order.

Despite these misgivings, there is considerable room for optimism as Chile enters the first years of the twenty-first century. The sharp and bitter conflicts of the past have been attenuated by a painful learning experience and the end of the Cold War, although Chile still has a way to go in healing the wounds of the past and acknowledging shared responsibilities. The dramatic success of Chile's economic reforms promises to help the country emerge from the ranks of the underdeveloped world within a generation. In overcoming the wrenching crisis of the recent past by turning to their country's historical democratic traditions, Chileans have set the foundation for a promising future as a democratic nation.

NOTES

1. Kenneth A. Bollen, "Comparative Measurement of Political Democracy," *American Sociological Review* 45, no. 3 (June 1980): 370–390. See also Robert W. Jackman, "On the Relations of Economic Development to Democratic Performance," *American Journal of Political Science* 17, no. 3 (August 1973): 611–621, and his "Political Democracy and Social Equality: A Comparative Analysis," *American Sociological Review* 39, no. 1 (February 1974): 29–44.

2. Leon Epstein, *Political Parties in Western Democracies* (New York: Praeger, 1967), p. 192. For a discussion of the rise of parliamentary opposition in Western Europe, see the excellent collection in Robert Dahl, ed., *Political Oppositions in Western Democracies* (New Haven: Yale University Press, 1966). See also Dahl's *Polyarchy: Participation and Opposition* (New Haven: Yale University Press, 1971).

3. Some countries, including Britain and Norway, developed political contestation with parliamentary responsibility before Chile did. Others, such as Belgium and the Netherlands, began to develop parliamentary influence at around the same time. The Swedish king was able to choose ministers without regard to parliamentary majorities until 1917, though the parliament's views were taken into consideration earlier. Italy was not unified until the 1860s and did not establish a system of parliamentary rule until the 1880s. Republican France dates from 1871, and many observers, noting the importance of the Napoleonic bureaucracy, question the degree of authority wielded by the French parliament. Because of the importance of the monarchies in Europe, Chile comes closer to the United States in the origins and evolution of its political institutions. For historical discussions of these issues, see Dahl, *Political Oppositions;* and Stein Rokkan, *Citizens, Elections, Parties* (Oslo: Universitetsforlaget, 1970).

4. See Dahl, *Polyarchy,* chapter 1. Dahl's definition informs the discussion of democracy in chapter 1 of this volume.

5. Women were able to vote in national elections for the first time in 1952. The voting age was reduced from twenty-one to eighteen and illiterates were given the right to vote with the constitutional reforms of 1970. The best discussion of Chilean electoral practices can be found in Federico Gil, *The Political System of Chile* (Boston: Houghton Mifflin, 1966). The 1970 reforms are discussed in Guillermo Piedrabuena Richards, *La reforma constitucional* (Santiago: Ediciones Encina, 1970). The intricacies of the electoral system are described in Mario Bernaschina G., *Cartilla electoral* (Santiago: Editorial Jurídica de Chile, 1958). For an overview of electoral participation, see Atilio Borón, "La evolución del régimen electoral y sus efectos en la representación de los intereses populares: El caso de Chile," estudio no. 24 (Santiago: Escuela Latinoamericana de Ciencia Política y Administración Pública, FLACSO, April 1971).

6. Voting data for Europe can be found in Stein Rokkan, *Citizens.* Voting data on Chile are found in J. Samuel Valenzuela, *Democratización vía reforma: La expansión del sufragio en Chile* (Buenos Aires: Ediciones del IDES, 1985). This is the best study of the critical decisions that led to suffrage expansion in Chile in the nineteenth century, underscoring the important role of the Conservatives in that process. As such, it is an important revisionary study in Chilean historiography.

7. This section draws extensively from J. Samuel Valenzuela and Arturo Valenzuela, "Chile and the Breakdown of Democracy," in Howard J. Wiarda and Harvey F. Kline, eds., *Latin American Politics and Development* (Boston: Houghton Mifflin, 1979), pp. 234–249. The author is grateful to J. Samuel Valenzuela for his contribution to this work and to much of the thinking that is reflected in this chapter. See also Arturo Valenzuela, *Political Brokers in Chile: Local Government in a Centralized Polity* (Durham, NC: Duke University Press, 1977), chapter 8.

8. Francisco Antonio Encina, *Historia de Chile,* vol. 9 (Santiago: Editorial Nacimiento, 1941–1942), p. 493, cited in Arturo Valenzuela, *Political Brokers,* p. 175.

9. This thesis is at variance with standard interpretations that attribute to Diego Portales a pivotal role in forming the Chilean institutional system. See Arturo Valenzuela, *Political Brokers,* chapter 8, and his "El mito de Portales: La institucionalización del régimen político chileno en el siglo XIX," unpublished manuscript.

10. Chile, *Documentos parlamentarios correspondientes al segundo quinquenio de la administración Bulnes, 1846–1850,* vol. 3 (Santiago: Imprenta del Ferrocarril, 1858), p. 795.

11. Some of the generalizations from the "world-system" and "dependency" literature to the effect that dependent capitalist development leads to weak states do not fully apply to the Chilean case.

12. This section draws heavily on Arturo Valenzuela and J. Samuel Valenzuela, "Los orígenes de la democracia: Reflexiones teóricas sobre el caso de Chile," *Estudios públicos* 12 (spring 1983): 3–39; and J. S. Valenzuela, *Democratización.*

13. In 1863, the total electorate was about 22,000. By 1878, the electorate had expanded sevenfold. See J. S. Valenzuela, *Democratización,* pp. 118–119.

14. Maurice Duverger, *Political Parties* (New York: John Wiley, 1965), pp. xxiii–xxxvii.

15. For this argument, see J. Samuel Valenzuela, "Labor Movement Formation and Politics: The Chilean and French Cases in Comparative Perspective, 1850–1950," Ph.D. diss., Columbia University, 1979.

16. This section draws heavily on Arturo Valenzuela, *The Breakdown of Democratic Regimes: Chile* (Baltimore: Johns Hopkins University Press, 1978), chapter 1. On complete party systems, see Seymour Martin Lipset and Stein Rokkan, *Party Systems and Voter Alignments* (New York: Free Press, 1967), pp. 50, 56.

17. For a further discussion of this, see Arturo Valenzuela, *Political Brokers*.

18. An exception to this generalization is Dahl's *Polyarchy*. Not only has Chile been neglected in the broader literature, Latin America in general has been left out. The volumes of the Committee on Comparative Politics of the Social Science Research Council had only a few studies dealing with Latin America, and Latin America did not figure prominently in the theoretical efforts of the 1960s. In his excellent study of parties in Western democracies, Epstein acknowledges that a few Latin American countries meet his criteria for inclusion but leaves them out "mainly because the whole of Latin America is customarily treated along with developing nations." See Epstein, *Political Parties*, p. 4. For a discussion of the place of Latin America in the literature on comparative politics, see Arturo Valenzuela, "Political Science and Latin America: A Discipline in Search of Political Reality," in Christopher Mitchell, ed., *Changing Perspectives in Latin American Studies* (Stanford: Stanford University Press, 1988), pp. 63–86.

19. These terms are designed to group in analytically similar categories propositions that are sometimes advanced in more discrete fashion. They are drawn from previous work of the author on the subject, some of which has been done in collaboration with J. Samuel Valenzuela. I have attempted to address within each category the relevant variables advanced in this book. I do not treat what can be called the national-cohesiveness thesis because it is not as relevant to the Chilean case. Ethnic, regional, and center-periphery cleavages were defused in the early half of the nineteenth century.

20. The importance of gradual evolution without significant upheaval is stressed by Dahl in *Polyarchy*, pp. 40–47. The continuity of institutions from the colonial period is one of the points advanced by Seymour Martin Lipset in his provocative study of the United States, *The First New Nation* (New York: Doubleday, 1967), pp. 106–107. For a discussion of differences in the colonial experience, see Rupert Emerson's classic *From Empire to Nation* (Boston: Beacon Press, 1960).

21. Chile inaugurated a polyarchy through a struggle for independence that led to the collapse of the remnants of the old colonial regime and not, as Dahl holds, through an evolutionary process comparable to that of England or Sweden. In this sense, the Chilean case is closer to that of France than England. See Dahl, *Polyarchy*, p. 42.

22. See Frederick Pike, *Chile and the United States, 1880–1962* (Notre Dame, IN: University of Notre Dame Press, 1963), p. 11. The literature on Portales is voluminous. An influential work that argues this thesis is Alberto Edwards Vives, *La fronda aristocrática* (Santiago: Ediciones Ercilla, 1936), pp. 50–51. For a sampling of views, see B. Vicuña Mackenna, J. Victorino Lastarria, and R. Sotomayor Valdés, *Portales: Juicio histórico* (Santiago: Editorial del Pacífico, 1973).

23. Richard Morse, "The Heritage of Latin America," in Louis Hartz, ed., *The Founding of New Societies* (New York: Harcourt, Brace and World, 1964), pp. 163–164. See also Hartz's comments on the Chilean case on p. 88 of that work.

24. For an elaboration of this argument see Arturo Valenzuela, *Political Brokers,* chapter 8.

25. See Samuel P. Huntington, *Political Order in Changing Societies* (New Haven: Yale University Press, 1968), chapter 2.

26. David Martin argues that "the incidence of pluralism and democracy is related to the incidence of those religious bodies which are themselves inherently pluralistic and democratic. . . . Such bodies . . . are much more prevalent in the Anglo-American situation than elsewhere. . . . In Russia and Latin America democratic and individualistic Protestantism arrived late in the process and could not have an important effect." See his *A General Theory of Secularization* (New York: Harper and Row, 1978), p. 25. For an influential essay dealing with Latin America along these same lines, see Seymour Martin Lipset, "Values, Education and Entrepreneurship," in Seymour Martin Lipset and Aldo Solari, eds., *Elites in Latin America*

(New York: Oxford University Press, 1963), pp. 3–60. See also Howard Wiarda, "Toward a Framework for the Study of Political Change in the Iberic-Latin Tradition: The Corporative Model," *World Politics* 25, no. 2 (January 1973): 206–235. For a classic work that links liberal values stemming from the Protestant tradition with the growth of democracy in the United States, see Louis Hartz, *The Liberal Tradition in America* (New York: Harcourt, Brace and World, 1955).

27. See Jorge I. Dominguez, *Insurrection or Loyalty* (Cambridge: Harvard University Press, 1979) for a discussion of some of these points.

28. Harry Eckstein, *Division and Cohesion in a Democracy: A Study of Norway* (Princeton: Princeton University Press, 1966).

29. See John A. Booth, "Costa Rica: The Roots of Democratic Stability," in Larry Diamond, Juan J. Linz, and Seymour Martin Lipset, eds., *Democracy in Developing Countries: Vol. 4, Latin America* (Boulder, CO: Lynne Rienner, 1989), pp. 387–422.

30. Dahl, *Polyarchy,* p. 140.

31. For a description of Chile's hacienda system, see George M. McBride, *Chile: Land and Society* (New York: American Geographical Society, 1936). For the origins, the classic study is Mario Góngora, *Origen de los inquilinos del Valle Central* (Santiago: Editorial Universitaria, 1960). See also Arnold J. Bauer, *Chilean Rural Society from the Spanish Conquest to 1930* (New York: Cambridge University Press, 1975).

32. Dominguez, *Insurrection,* p. 141.

33. See Robert Kaufman, *The Politics of Land Reform in Chile, 1950–1970* (Cambridge, MA: Harvard University Press, 1972); and Brian Loveman, *Struggle in the Countryside: Politics and Rural Labor in Chile, 1919–1973* (Bloomington: Indiana University Press, 1976).

34. Chile is a good illustration of Dankwart Rustow's argument that democracies must go through a "habituation" phase before they are consolidated. See his "Transitions to Democracy: Toward a Dynamic Model," *Comparative Politics* 2, no. 3 (April 1970): 337–363. I am indebted to J. Samuel Valenzuela for the insights on the acceptance of the legitimacy of the electoral process in Chile at the same time that labor organization was viewed as a threat to Chile's elites. See his "Labor Movement Formation and Politics: The Chilean and French Cases in Comparative Perspective, 1850–1950" (Ph.D. diss., Columbia University, 1979).

35. See Daniel Lerner, *The Passing of Traditional Society* (New York: Free Press, 1958). See also S. N. Eisenstadt, "Social Change, Differentiation and Evolution," *American Sociological Review* 29 (June 1964): 375–387.

36. Seymour Martin Lipset, "Some Social Requisites of Democracy: Economic Development and Political Legitimacy," *American Political Science Review* 53, no. 1 (March 1959): 69–105. For collections of articles on "empirical democratic theory," see J. V. Gillespie and B. A. Nesvold, eds., *Macroquantitative Analysis: Conflict, Development and Democratization* (Beverly Hills: Sage Publications, 1971); and Charles Cnudde and Deane Neubauer, eds., *Empirical Democratic Theory* (Chicago: Markham, 1969). For an excellent review of this literature, see Leonardo Morlino, "Misure di democrazia e di libertá: Discusione di alcune analisi empiriche," *Rivista Italiana di scienza política* 5, no. 1 (April 1975): 131–166.

37. See, for example, Phillips Cutright, "National Political Development: Measurement and Analysis," *American Sociological Review* 28, no. 2 (April 1963): 253–264; and Bollen, "Comparative Measurement."

38. Juan Linz, "Totalitarian and Authoritarian Regimes," in Fred I. Greenstein and Nelson W. Polsby, eds., *Handbook of Political Science,* vol. 3 (Reading, MA: Addison Wesley, 1975), p. 182. As Dahl notes, the United States in the nineteenth century did not meet the development criteria but met the political criteria. See Dahl, *Polyarchy,* p. 72.

39. Goran Therborn, "The Rule of Capital and the Rise of Democracy," *New Left Review* 103 (May–June 1977): 3–41. Therborn adds that the rarity of bourgeois democracy in capitalist Third World countries is a result of the vulnerability of commodity-oriented economies, which give the "indigenous bourgeoisie little room for maneuver vis-à-vis the exploited classes." In such contexts there is an "intertwining of capitalist with feudal, slave or other precapitalist modes of exploitations . . . impeding the development of impersonal rule of capital and free labor market, thereby seriously limiting the growth of both the labor movement and an agrarian petty bourgeoisie." Ibid., pp. 1, 32. Although he is not dealing with the development of democracy per se, Immanuel Wallerstein argues that peripheral states in the world sys-

tem were much weaker in part because the social structure of export economies did not permit the development of bourgeois sectors. See his *The Modern World System*, 2 vols. (New York: Academic Press, 1974, 1980).

40. Barrington Moore, *Social Origins of Dictatorship and Democracy: Lord and Peasant in the Making of the Modern World* (Boston: Beacon Press, 1966). As he notes, for democracy to emerge,

> the political hegemony of the landed upper class had to be broken or transformed. The peasant had to be turned into a farmer producing for the market instead of for his own consumption and that of the overlord. In this process the landed upper class either became an important part of the capitalist and democratic tide, as in England, or, if they came to oppose it, they were swept aside in the convulsions of revolutions (France) or civil war (U.S.). In a word the landed upper classes either helped to make the bourgeois revolution or were destroyed by it. (Ibid., pp. 429–430)

Moore's analysis, though brilliant in scope, leaves much to be desired in terms of clarity. For a valuable critique, see Theda Skocpol, "A Critical Review of Barrington Moore's Social Origins of Dictatorship and Democracy, " *Politics and Society* 4 (fall 1973): 1–34. See also Joseph V. Femia, "Barrington Moore and the Preconditions for Democracy," *British Journal of Political Science* 2 (January 1972): 21–26; and Ronald Dore, "Making Sense of History," *Archive européenes de sociology* 10 (1969): 295–305.

41. See Dominguez, *Insurrection,* p. 131.

42. Influential works of Chilean historians in this vein include Julio César Jobet, *Ensayo crítico del desarrollo económico-social de Chile* (Santiago: Editorial Latinoamericana, 1965); and Hernán Ramirez Necochea, *Historia del movimiento obrero en Chile, antecedentes siglo XIX* (Santiago: Editorial Austral, 1956). The most fully developed version of this thesis is in Luis Vitale, *Interpretación marxista de la historia de Chile* (Frankfurt: Verlag Jugend und Politik, 1975). Maurice Zeitlin's *The Civil Wars in Chile: 1851 and 1859* (Princeton: Princeton University Press, 1984) draws uncritically from the work of Vitale and others.

43. See Leonard Binder et al., *Crises and Sequences in Political Development* (Princeton: Princeton University Press, 1971). For a volume of essays applying the framework to particular cases, see Raymond Grew, ed., *Crises of Political Development in Europe and the United States* (Princeton: Princeton University Press, 1978). Influential earlier studies that anticipate the arguments in these books include Dankwart Rustow, *A World of Nations* (Washington, DC: Brookings Institution, 1967); Seymour Martin Lipset and Stein Rokkan, eds., *Party Systems and Voter Alignments* (New York: Free Press, 1967); and Gabriel Almond, Scott Flanigan, and Roger Mundt, eds., *Crisis, Choice and Change: Historical Studies of Political Development* (Boston: Little, Brown, 1973). Although some of these works focus on political development more generally, and not on the development of democracy as such, their framework is oriented toward democratic regimes rather than other regime types.

44. Eric Nordlinger, "Political Development, Time Sequences and Rates of Change," in Jason L. Finkle and Robert W. Gable, eds., *Political Development and Social Change*, 2d ed. (New York: John Wiley, 1971), p. 458. This argument is made in Rustow, *World of Nations*, pp. 120–123.

45. Of the three crises, the most difficult to deal with is that of national identity. Its definition is imprecise, and in the absence of survey-research data it is virtually impossible to find empirical evidence to document its relative strength. Much of this analysis has to be speculative and informed by general historical accounts. Particularly useful in capturing the mood of Chile in the early period is the work of Diego Barros Arana, which is also an eyewitness account. In particular, see his *Un decenio de la historia de Chile,* 2 vols. (Santiago: Imprenta Universitaria, 1906).

46. See Richard Merritt, "Nation-Building in America: The Colonial Years," in Karl W. Deutsch and William J. Foltz, eds., *Nation Building* (New York: Atherton Press, 1966); and Karl Deutch, *Nationalism and Social Communication: An Inquiry into the Foundations of Nationality,* 2d ed. (Cambridge, MA: MIT Press, 1966). Lipset discusses the question of national identity in the United States in his *First New Nation,* chapter 2.

47. See Rustow, "Transitions to Democracy."

48. For a discussion of Washington's impact, see Lipset, *The First New Nation,* pp. 18–23.

49. For lists of all Chilean presidents, cabinet officials, and members of Congress from independence until the 1940s, see Luis Valencia Avaria, *Anales de la república,* 2 vols. (Santiago: Imprenta Universitana, 1951). Most presidents had extensive parliamentary experience.

50. On the question of efficacy, see the arguments of Juan J. Linz in *The Breakdown of Democratic Regimes: Crisis, Breakdown and Reequilibration* (Baltimore: Johns Hopkins University Press, 1978), pp. 20–21.

51. For an elaboration of this argument, see Valenzuela and Valenzuela, "Orígenes de la democracia."

52. R. K. Merton, "The Unanticipated Consequences of Purposive Social Action," *American Sociological Review* 1 (1936): 894–904.

53. This point is made in Arturo Valenzuela and Alexander Wilde, "Presidentialist Politics and the Decline of the Chilean Congress," in Joel Smith and Lloyd Musolf, eds., *Legislatures in Development: Dynamics of Change in New and Old States* (Durham, NC: Duke University Press, 1979), p. 194.

54. The material in this section is taken from the author's *Breakdown.* For other books on the Chilean breakdown, see Paul Sigmund, *The Overthrow of Allende and the Politics of Chile* (Pittsburgh: Pittsburgh University Press, 1977); Ian Roxborough, Phil O'Brien, and Jackie Roddick, *Chile: The State and Revolution* (New York: Holmes and Meier, 1977); and Manuel A. Garretón and Tomás Moulian, *Análisis coyuntural y proceso político: Las fases del conflicto en Chile (1970–73)* (San José, Costa Rica: Editorial Universitaria Centro-Americana, 1978). The last-named is drawn from the comprehensive and detailed daily account of the most important events of the Allende administration, published in Manuel Antonio Garretón et al., *Cronología del período 1970–73,* 9 vols. (Santiago: Facultad Latinoamericana de Ciencias Sociales, 1978), an invaluable publication including extensive indices to parties, individuals, and events. In the immediate aftermath of the coup, a host of primarily more polemical works were published. For a review essay of thirty-one books, see Arturo Valenzuela and J. Samuel Valenzuela, "Visions of Chile," *Latin American Research Review* 10 (fall 1975): 155–176.

55. See Valenzuela and Wilde, "Presidentialism and Decline of Congress," pp. 204–210.

56. The most comprehensive study of U.S. involvement was conducted by the U.S. Select Committee to Study Governmental Operations with respect to Intelligence Activities (Church Committee) of the 94th Congress, 1st Session. See its *Covert Action in Chile 1963–1973* (Washington, DC: Government Printing Office, 1975).

57. The fact that Allende received a lower percentage of the votes votes in 1970 than in 1964 suggests that his victory was not the result of an increase in popular discontent and mobilization fueled by a worsening socioeconomic crisis. An examination of socioeconomic indicators in the late 1960s does not support the argument that the lot of the average Chilean was becoming worse or that political mobilization was exceeding historic levels. Survey data also support the view that a majority of voters would have preferred a center-right to a center-left coalition. Huntington's thesis, in *Political Order,* that political order collapses when political institutions are too weak is not supported by the Chilean case. Chile's parties prior to the election of Allende were very strong (perhaps too dominant), and political mobilization was the product of deliberate strategies on the part of the parties and the government to bring people into the political process, rather than the product of widespread discontent or anomic behavior. In Chile, the election of Allende and the economic and social crisis of the Allende years was more the product of the sharp political crisis than vice-versa. For a full elaboration of this argument, see my *Breakdown,* chapter 3. An article that argues that mobilization in Chile became excessive is Henry Landberger and Tim McDaniel, "Hypermobilization in Chile, 1970–73," *World Politics* 28, no. 4 (July 1976): 502–543.

58. For the concept of neutral powers, see Linz, *The Breakdown of Democratic Regimes,* pp. 76–80. For a discussion of the growing confrontation, suggesting that mobilization was more the result of political crisis than its cause, see Valenzuela, *Breakdown,* p. 34.

59. Seventy-two percent of those polled thought Chile was living through extraordinary times, but only 27 percent of the respondents felt the military should be involved in the political process. See Valenzuela, *Breakdown,* p. 65. The Chilean case suggests that even where

democratic norms are widespread and deeply rooted in a society, political crisis resulting from institutional struggles and competing claims can seriously erode democratic practices. A democratic political culture is no guarantee for the maintenance of democratic institutions.

60. This argument is elaborated in Arturo Valenzuela, "Orígenes y características del sistema de partidos políticos en Chile: Una proposición para un gobierno parlamentario," *Estudios públicos* 18 (fall 1985): 87–154, and "Party Politics and the Failure of Presidentialism in Chile," in Juan J. Linz and Arturo Valenzuela, eds., *The Failure of Presidential Democracy* (Baltimore: Johns Hopkins University Press, 1994), pp. 91–150. The author is grateful to Juan Linz for his reflections on this subject. See the suggestive discussion in Linz, *The Breakdown of Democratic Regimes,* pp. 71–74, and his "Democracy, Presidential or Parliamentary: Does It Make a Difference?" in Linz and Valenzuela, eds., *The Failure of Presidential Democracy,* pp. 3–87.

61. This section draws on Pamela Constable and Arturo Valenzuela, *A Nation of Enemies: Chile Under Pinochet* (New York: W. W. Norton, 1994).

62. This section is based on interviews, conducted in August 1987, with high-ranking military officers who commanded troops during the coup and were responsible for "cleaning up" or "neutralizing" Santiago neighborhoods.

63. See *Informe Rettig: Informe de la Comisión Nacional de Verdad y Reconciliación,* vol. 2 (Santiago: Talleres la Nación), pp. 883–886.

64. This section is based on extensive interviews with advisers close to the junta and General Pinochet in 1973–1978. See Arturo Valenzuela, "The Military in Power: The Consolidation of One-Man Rule," in Paul Drake and Ivan Jaksic, eds., *The Struggle for Democracy in Chile: 1982–1990* (Lincoln: University of Nebraska Press, 1991), pp. 21–72.

65. For an excellent study that gives a picture of rising military expenditures for personnel, see Jorge Marshall, "Gasto público en Chile 1969–1979," *Colección estudios cieplan* 5 (July 1981): 53–84. For an article detailing the service of military men in government positions, see Carlos Huneeus and Jorge Olave, "La partecipazione dei militari nei nuovi: Autoritatismi in una prospettive comparata," *Rivista italiana di scienza politica* [Rome] 17, no. 1 (April 1987): 65–78.

66. See Alfred Stepan's now classic elaboration of this problem in *The Military in Politics: Changing Patterns in Brazil* (Princeton: Princeton University Press, 1971). The Chilean military regime was *of* the military but not *by* the military. I am indebted to the excellent work of Genaro Arriagada for this insight. See his *La política militar de Pinochet* (Santiago: Salesianos, 1985).

67. Senior officers such as General Oscar Bonilla, perhaps the most powerful general at the time of the coup, were not successful in their attempts to control Contreras. Bonilla died in an accident of suspicious nature. Many civilian advisers came to fear that Contreras could come to threaten Pinochet, though the general succeeded in playing various groups off against each other. Contreras was finally fired and the DINA restructured as relations between the United States and Chile deteriorated following U.S. demands for extradition of Contreras to the United States for his alleged involvement in the assassination of Orlando Letelier, Allende's foreign minister, in the streets of Washington. For studies that deal with the Letelier case and provide insights into the DINA, see John Dinges and Saul Landau, *Assassination on Embassy Row* (New York: Pantheon, 1980); and Taylor Branch and Eugene M. Propper, *Labyrinth* (New York: Viking, 1982).

68. These observations are based on interviews conducted with General Leigh in Santiago, Chile, during November 1985. An excellent published interview is in Florencia Varas, *Gustavo Leigh: El general disidente* (Santiago: Editorial Aconcagua, 1979). Pinochet retired eighteen air force generals before finding one who would accept his action and replace Leigh on the junta. Had Leigh had better intelligence, the conflict might have been much more dramatic.

69. For decree laws that shaped the constitutional underpinnings of the military regime before the adoption of a new constitution, see Eduardo Soto Kloss, *Ordenamiento constitucional* (Santiago: Editorial Jurídica de Chile, 1980). For the Constitution, see Chile, *Constitución de la República de Chile 1980* (Santiago: Editorial Jurídica, 1981).

70. A valuable discussion of the economic policies applied by the Chilean military regime from a critical perspective is Pilar Vergara, *Auge y caída del neoliberalismo en Chile* (Santiago: FLACSO, 1985). For a favorable perspective see Alvaro Bardón, Camilo Carrasco

M., and Alvaro Vial G., *Una decada de cambios económicos: La experiencia chilena, 1973–1983* (Santiago: Editorial Andrés Bello, 1985) and Sebastian Edwards and Alejandra Cox Edwards, *Monetarism and Liberalism in Chile* (Chicago: University of Chicago Press, 1991).

71. For a discussion of political parties under authoritarianism, see Arturo Valenzuela and J. Samuel Valenzuela, "Party Oppositions Under the Chilean Authoritarian Regime," in J. Samuel Valenzuela and Arturo Valenzuela, eds., *Military Rule in Chile: Dictatorship and Oppositions* (Baltimore: Johns Hopkins University Press, 1986).

72. See Pamela Constable and Arturo Valenzuela, "Is Chile Next?" *Foreign Policy* 63 (summer 1986): 58–75.

73. See Adam Przeworski's persuasive critique of the notion that the lack of legitimacy is a sufficient condition for the breakdown of a regime in "Some Problems in the Study of the Transition to Democracy," in Guillermo O'Donnell, Philippe C. Schmitter, and Laurence Whitehead, eds., *Transitions from Authoritarian Rule* (Baltimore: Johns Hopkins University Press, 1986), pp. 184–229.

74. This section is based on field research conducted by the author in Chile in 1987 and 1988. For a more detailed description of the events leading up to the plebiscite, see Pamela Constable and Arturo Valenzuela, "Plebiscite in Chile: End of the Pinochet Era?" *Current History* 87 (January 1988): 29–33, 41; and Pamela Constable and Arturo Valenzuela, "Chile's Return to Democracy," *Foreign Affairs* (winter 1989/1990): 169–186. See also Arturo Valenzuela, "Government and Politics," in Rex A. Hudson, ed., *Chile: A Country Study* (Washington, DC: Government Printing Office, 1994), pp. 199–273.

75. This section draws on Arturo Valenzuela, "Government and Politics."

76. *Informe Rettig*, p. 883.

77. Óscar Godoy Arcaya, "Las elecciones de 1993," *Estudios públicos*, no. 54 (fall 1994): 301–338.

78. See Samuel Valenzuela and Timothy Scully, "Electoral Choices and the Party System in Chile: Continuities and Changes in the Recovery of Democracy," *Comparative Politics* (July 1997): 511–527.

79. Manuel Mora y Araujo and Paula Montoya, "Las actitudes de la población ante el cambio político y económico en la Argentina y Chile," *Estudios públicos*, no. 67 (winter 1997): 299–328.

80. Carla Lehmann, "La voz de los que no votaron," *Centro de estudios públicos— Puntos de referencia*, no. 197 (April 1998).

81. See Centro de Estudios Públicos, Estudio Nacional de Opinión Pública, various surveys.

82. See Arturo Valenzuela and Peter Siavelis, "Ley electoral y estabilidad democrática: Un ejercicio de simulación para el caso de Chile," *Estudios públicos*, no. 43 (winter 1997): 27–87.

COLOMBIA

5

COLOMBIA:
The Politics of Violence and Democratic Transformation

Jonathan Hartlyn & John Dugas

From the perspective of democratic politics, the Colombian case is not easy to categorize. Colombia has experienced tremendous political violence, yet also extensive periods of constitutional civilian rule. In recent decades, it has had moderate patterns of socioeconomic growth and has suffered less of a decline due to the debt crisis of the 1980s than most other Latin American countries. Colombia delayed undertaking significant economic liberalization until the early 1990s, and its immediate effects were less harsh than those experienced by many other countries in the hemisphere. Yet it continues to have sharp socioeconomic disparities. Since 1958, the country has had a civilian political regime and has consistently held elections for all major political offices, though for much of this time under a restrictive political arrangement.

Currently, Colombia remains far from consolidating a democratic political regime, despite the introduction of a number of significant political reforms, including a notably democratic constitution in 1991. Indeed, basic state coherence and civil rights continue to be challenged by multifaceted violence from left-wing guerrillas, drug traffickers, state security forces, right-wing paramilitary groups, and common delinquency. Since the mid-1980s, Colombia has found itself caught in a horrendous spiral of political violence, including armed combat, massacres of defenseless citizens, bombings, assassinations, and "disappearances," even as the country's overall rates of criminal violence also remain among the highest on the continent. The term "crisis" may appear overused when it refers to a prolonged contemporary period such as that of Colombia from the early to mid-1980s to the present; from a normative perspective, though, it is appropriate in its rejection of the country's current circumstances as "normal," even if it occasionally forces analysts to refer to particular subperiods as ones of "supercrisis."[1] If political democracy is often analyzed as a type of political regime, this is because a state that is coherent and able to impose a democratic rule of law has been assumed; this assumption, always at least somewhat problematic in Latin America, is especially so in Colombia today.[2] Political violence and human rights violations carried out by non-state actors (some in collaboration with state agents), on the one hand, and widespread criminal violence carried out with near total impunity, on the other, both reflect dramatic state weaknesses.

Colombia has experienced many of the same historical, economic, and cultural conditions as other Latin American countries: Spanish colonial domination followed by economic dependency on major capitalist powers; a dominant role for the Catholic Church; and vastly unequal land-tenure patterns. Yet, given the significant differences in the democratic experiences of various Latin American countries, these factors would appear less significant in explaining the fate of attempts at democracy than others that relate more explicitly to the political process. The latter include the interaction, timing, and sequence of various social, economic, and political variables and the role of key political elites in certain periods.

In the study of Latin American politics, interest has shifted increasingly to regime-level and more explicitly "political" variables, in part as a reaction to the failure of economically or culturally deterministic theories to explain changes in political-regime type.[3] Arguments for democratic success or failure based on the restricting impact of levels of economic development, international economic dependency, or (especially) cultural traditions of authoritarianism have often been too broad to distinguish across Latin American cases or to explain changes in countries over time. This is not to deny their (at times overwhelming) importance, but to caution against treating them as necessary conditions in most instances.[4]

This chapter stresses the importance of political factors—parties, electoral dynamics, leaders, statecraft—to the success or failure of Colombia's regimes.[5] At the same time, it indicates how different structural economic and social factors have facilitated or constrained political processes. Several elements of Colombia's historical development have been crucial in explaining the country's political trajectory in different historical periods; particularly the consolidation of its two traditional parties in the context of a relatively weak state, the interaction between its political party system and its evolving economy and class structure, and the successes and failures of political leadership and statecraft have been crucial in explaining the country's evolution in different historical moments. The inability or unwillingness of the traditional parties (and of economically dominant interests) to respond adequately to the dramatic socioeconomic changes of the past several decades and the incredible erosion of the state are major causes of the country's current critical period.

Unlike many of its continental neighbors, Colombia has avoided both military rule and chronic economic instability since 1958, when the leaders of the two major parties came together to form the consociational National Front. Intense violence between adherents of the two parties in the late 1940s and 1950s, known as *la violencia* (the violence), left 200,000 casualties and led to regime breakdown and military rule. Civilian rule was facilitated by mutual interparty guarantees and the coalition government resulting from party negotiations. As it finally emerged, their National Front agreement established presidential alternation between the two parties until 1974, and bipartisan parity in executive, legislative, and judicial posts. It also required a two-thirds majority for most measures to be approved in Congress. A 1968 constitutional reform led to the partial dismantling of the National Front. It imposed a simple majority vote for most measures in Congress and called for competitive elections at the local level in 1970, and at the national level in 1974. Parity in the judicial branch was maintained; in the executive branch, it was extended until 1978, after which the party receiving the second-highest number of votes was to be offered "adequate and equitable" representation by the winning party.

From 1958 to 1986, all governments in Colombia consisted of bipartisan coalitions. In a context of intensifying political and criminal violence, efforts to dismantle coalition rule more fully continued to fail in the late 1970s and early 1980s. Finally, following the enactment of a number of decentralizing reforms, including the popular election of mayors (previously appointed by departmental governors, themselves appointed by the central authority), and a landslide Liberal Party victory in 1986, the Conservative Party refused participation in the administration of President Virgilio Barco (1986–1990). The Barco administration attempted unsuccessfully to enact a far-reaching constitutional reform with the explicit intent of democratizing the political regime. Despite its failure, a harrowing combination of drug terrorism, guerrilla violence, and a growing crisis of political legitimacy in the late 1980s and early 1990s opened the way for a specially elected National Constituent Assembly to draft a new constitution in 1991. The new constitution eliminated all vestiges of parity, restructured the judicial system, provided an extensive bill of citizen rights, and instituted new mechanisms of democratic participation. Despite the democratic advances contained in the 1991 Constitution, the administrations of César Gaviria (1990–1994), Ernesto Samper (1994–1998), and Andrés Pastrana (1998–) have continued to confront problems of eroded state authority, marked by chronic political violence, corruption, and difficulties in governance.

Because of the sharp restrictions on majoritarian democracy imposed by the National Front and because the country has been governed for most of the time since the late 1940s under a state of siege,[6] most analysts have viewed Colombia since 1958 as a qualified democracy, using adjectives such as "controlled,"[7] "oligarchical,"[8] "traditional bipartisan elitist,"[9] "near polyarchy,"[10] or "restricted" (*democracia restringida*).[11] Others have characterized the country from the other side of the democracy-authoritarianism continuum, as "inclusionary authoritarian,"[12] or as simply "authoritarian" because of its National Front electoral restrictions.[13] There have also been characterizations of the country that fall in between these two, which see it as in a lengthy "transition" from dictatorship to democratic government,[14] or as in an extended period of "consolidation" of democracy that began with the National Front agreement.[15]

In our view, the best characterization of the contemporary Colombian government is that it was a limited democratic consociational regime until the late 1980s, and it is currently in an uncertain process of transformation that combines elements of democratization at the regime level with declining state capacity, which inevitably constrains the former. Colombia was consociational because a return to civilian rule in 1958 was inconceivable without mutual guarantees between the major parties, assured by the National Front agreement. Colombia's two major parties represented functional alternatives, though not exact equivalents, to the segmental divisions along religious, ethnic, or linguistic lines, identified in other consociational cases.[16]

At the same time, the rigid consociational practices (relaxed in the post-1974 period), combined with other restrictions, sharply limited the regime's democratic nature. However, the importance of elections for leadership succession, the overall—if clearly uneven—respect for political and civil liberties, and the existence of a judiciary independent of the executive all indicate it was more appropriately considered democratic rather than authoritarian. The 1991 Constitution reinforced the democratic nature of the regime. Yet, it did so in a context not only of severe structural inequalities, but of continued political violence and high levels of general violence, in which impunity reigned and the state was incapable of imposing sovereign control, order, and a rule of law over vast sectors of the country's territory in even a minimal sense.[17]

Analyzing the dynamics of the regime's coalition rule and continuing relations between the two traditional parties is central to understanding the moderate political and economic successes of the country in the decades since 1958, as well as the growing spiral of violence and efforts toward democratic transformation. Contemporary Colombia illustrates the challenges confronted by a consociational regime when the political bases of its initial arrangement erode and it must seek a new political accommodation. The sources of this erosion were the political regime structure itself and socioeconomic changes that produced a younger, more urban, better-educated population. By the 1970s, these factors generated both a decline in party segmentation (which had initially led to the creation of the National Front) and an expansion of organized societal interests demanding that their voices be heard within the regime. Over the next decade, the continuing exclusionary tactics of traditional politicians and regional landowners in the countryside were to be dramatically supplemented by the changes induced in the countryside by drug traffickers and drug cultivation, which helped lead in some areas to a significant reconcentration of land through purchases, extortion, and expulsion, and in others to new zones of colonization devoted to coca cultivation. All of these factors commingled with the growing presence of guerrilla forces within an increasing number of rural municipalities, leading to complex, regionally differentiated situations largely outside of state control.

The political realities that led to establishing consociationalism had been superseded, and regime arrangements required transformation. As a consequence of this alone, the country would almost certainly have experienced political turmoil in the late 1970s and in the 1980s as efforts to move the country toward a more competitive, more participatory, and more responsive type of politics continued to be resisted. We must also consider the impact of drug trafficking, which has provided extensive resources to major violent nonstate actors within both the guerrilla and paramilitary groups, generating violence and corruption with severe consequences for state structures, political institutions, and societal groups that have been extremely corrosive for democracy and for state coherence.

Colombia is not easily categorized on the summary scale of this volume's editors. Should the country be placed low in the "democratic" category or somewhere in the "semidemocratic" category"? In recent years, has movement been more in the democratic direction, as a consequence of the end of coalition rule and the drafting of the 1991 Constitution, or more toward authoritarianism, indicated by increased political and criminal violence, including targeted killings of left-wing politicians and activists? Was the National Front ever "stable," and should the regime now be considered "unstable"? We would place Colombia low in the "democratic" category, characterizing it as "mixed success—democratic but unstable" on the six-point scale of the initial project. This placement highlights the fact that although civilian rule has been in place in Colombia since 1958 and the democratic nature of the regime was reinforced by the 1991 Constitution, democracy in Colombia remains unconsolidated; this will remain so at least as long as basic questions about state capacity and control over territory and issues of uncontrolled political violence remain, and perhaps longer as resolution of these issues alone is not sufficient to ensure democratic success.

HISTORICAL REVIEW AND ANALYSIS

Political Parties, Civil Wars, and National Integration

The essential feature of the National Front and post–National Front political regime has been the political dominance of the country's two traditional parties, formed in the nineteenth century. The current political turmoil reflects the difficulty of moving beyond traditional bipartisanism and its constraining features. Other key aspects that emerged in the nineteenth century and have had a sustained impact on the country's historical evolution include strong regionalism and a weak state and military. Subsequently, as a result of the nature of Colombia's primary export crop (coffee) and initial industrialization, there was little of the sectoral conflict between the agro-export sector and early industrialists that occurred in some other Latin American countries. Combined with the process of early labor organization, and in conjunction with the established party structure and very limited foreign investment, this meant that Colombia's experience with populism was attenuated. Both political parties became multiclass parties, though the urbanization that accelerated in the 1930s led to a substantial Liberal electoral majority still evident to this day (see Tables 5.1 and 5.2, pp. 258 and 263). In addition, these various factors acted to limit the role and autonomy of the state, though there was a strongly centralized presidential system and state ownership of utilities.

Colombia shares with most of the rest of Latin America a common cultural heritage of Spanish colonial rule. Although not as important a colonial center as Lima or Mexico City, Bogotá (officially Santafé de Bogotá), the capital, became the center of the viceroyalty of Nueva Granada, which included what are today Colombia, Ecuador, Venezuela, and Panama. The colonial period also bequeathed to the country one of the continent's most powerful and conservative church hierarchies. The struggle for independence was drawn out (1810–1821), and questions of national unity plagued the country as the efforts of Simón Bolívar to keep Gran Colombia (the old viceroyalty) together failed. Venezuela and Ecuador finally broke away in 1830, and Panama gained its independence in 1903.

Colombia's record of civilian, republican rule in the nineteenth and twentieth centuries cannot be explained entirely by theories linking postindependence political patterns to a single colonial heritage, though initial problems of integration and legitimacy are certainly associated with its colonial past. Although their origins remain controversial, by the 1850s the Conservative and Liberal Parties had established themselves, dividing the country politically while promoting a degree of national unity. The parties were capable of generating extensive electoral turnouts as well as mobilizing for violence.[18] They were loose confederations of large landowners and merchants, who possessed considerable autonomy in their region, rather than tight-knit organizations. The country's rugged topography impeded effective national integration and aided the development of a number of regional centers significant to this day.[19]

Ideological differences between the two parties were more significant in the nineteenth century than in the twentieth. In general, the Conservatives were wedded to a view that approximated the previous colonial order, emphasizing close cooperation between church and state, a strong central administration, and protectionism. The Liberals, more influenced by the industrial, liberal-democratic powers of the nineteenth century, generally argued for federalism, separation of church and state, and free-trade economic policies.[20] These ideological differences blended with, and at times were superseded by, more purely personalistic and regional disputes.

That the military establishment was relatively weak and insignificant, in sharp contrast to other Latin American countries at this time, aided the establishment of the political parties as primary actors. The Colombian elite distrusted Bolívar's predominantly Venezuelan liberation army, and after the breakup of the Gran Colombia federation in 1830, the army was further reduced in size and influence. In subsequent decades, the civilian bands the parties were able to mobilize were often larger than the national army. The army's inability to sustain its overthrow of a civilian government during the 1850s in the face of an armed coalition of Liberals and Conservatives led to further reductions in its size. Thus, as the political parties began to consolidate in the 1850s, the military institution was practically nonexistent. Not until the beginning of the twentieth century did a professional corps of specialized military personnel develop.[21]

In approximate quarter-century cycles beginning in the 1880s, political parties and the state established new institutional arrangements in the face of economic and societal challenges. These arrangements were preceded or surrounded by sometimes intense violence, channeled through the two parties. At the same time, the two-party system helped limit the development of more class-based organizations within the peasantry, the working class, or the middle sectors. Bipartisan coalitions were significant in facilitating major transition points that led to important institutional and constitutional changes in the 1880s, 1910s, 1930s, and 1950s. In the 1970s and 1980s—in spite of some important efforts—Colombia was incapable of achieving such a transition point, and in the 1990s, even after the promulgation of the 1991 Constitution, the question is whether agreement among a much broader set of political and social actors can ultimately be achieved, reducing violence and enhancing democracy.

The initial postindependence decades of consolidation of the two major political parties were followed first by Liberal dominance (1863–1885) and then by Conservative hegemony (1886–1930). The civil wars of the nineteenth century played a central role in generating population-wide identification with either party. Following the major postindependence conflicts of 1827–1832 and 1839–1842, seven major civil confrontations were fought in the second half of the century: 1851, 1854, 1861–1863, 1876–1877, 1885, 1895, and 1899–1902. Numerous other smaller-scale regional conflicts were also fought during this period. Some 24,600 lives were lost in the civil conflicts between 1830 and 1876, and 100,000 were killed in the turn-of-the-century War of the Thousand Days.[22]

The Liberals emerged victorious at midcentury. Their 1863 Constitution was extremely federalist, secularist, and politically liberal. At least nominal observance of constitutional procedures became more important. Although fraud on the part of incumbents and abstention on the part of opposition groups was common, of the eleven men who occupied the federal presidency between 1863 and 1886, only one attained his post by irregular means. The constitution's recognition of some regional autonomy, given the central government's inability to extend its control over the entire country, made a virtue of necessity. Federalism and free trade brought the country to the brink of economic ruin, destroyed its incipient industrial base, and impeded national integration, submerging the country in crisis.[23]

A centralizing reaction with considerable bipartisan support, known as La Regeneración, followed. This movement, spearheaded by Rafael Núñez, sought to reestablish the authority of the central state and the church. The 1886 Constitution strengthened considerably the powers of the central state and of the presidency. The role of the church was further consolidated by a concordat with the Vatican in 1887. In addition, by the 1890s, the parties had established more formal structures, with party directorates and conventions.[24] By then, though, the Liberals were almost completely excluded from political power. Conflicts regarding Núñez's political and economic reforms, and political exclusion, eventually led to one of the longest and by far the bloodiest of the country's civil confrontations, the War of the Thousand Days. It essentially ended in a draw, though the Conservatives retained power.

Oligarchical Democracy

The early 1900s were marked by the emergence from civil war and the loss of Panama. This was followed by the dictatorial government of the Conservative Rafael Reyes, who eventually closed Congress and called for a National Assembly. Reyes reached out to Liberals by including a small number in his cabinet, permitting them representation in the National Assembly, and promoting passage of a measure that would guarantee them representation in future sessions of Congress. Following the civil war, many Liberal leaders rejected violence as a means of promoting their aims or of seeking political office. They sought the adoption of electoral reforms to guarantee proportional representation of the parties and associated economic reforms, such as increased regional autonomy.[25] Violent conflict was followed by consociational practices in an attempt to prevent renewed violence.

Eventually, a bipartisan opposition movement, which flirted with the idea of creating a new party, the Partido Republicano, emerged and led a political struggle to depose Reyes. Supported particularly by merchants and industrialists, the movement never developed a popular power base.[26]

However, because it came after a period of extensive violence and sought bipartisan consensus and political demobilization, it foreshadowed the National Front. A Constituent Assembly, established by the Republicanos in 1910, confirmed minority representation in Congress, and in a reform that obviated some of the problems faced by other Latin American democratic (and undemocratic) regimes, it also decreed direct presidential elections for a four-year term with no immediate reelection.

In contrast to the end-of-the-century years, the period following 1910 was an era of remarkable political stability. Between 1910 and 1949, Colombia had, as Alexander Wilde has argued, an oligarchical democracy "of notable stability, openness, and competitiveness."[27] These decades also brought Colombia into far more extensive contact with the outside world. A sustained coffee boom in the late 1800s and early 1900s set the stage for industrialization. Significantly, it incorporated groups from both the Liberal and Conservative Parties into the export trade, even as its characteristics helped block development of a more radical nationalist politics. Throughout this period, coffee production in the *latifundia* of primarily Liberal landowners eventually came to be challenged by production in small family-owned farms established in the western highlands by coloniz- ers from the predominantly Conservative department of Antioquia. Many of these landowning small growers were less receptive to the radical ideolo- gies that had made inroads in other countries where agrarian wage earners were more prevalent, or where the major landowners were foreigners.[28] That the country's major export product was largely in local hands further inhibited the development of nationalist radical political movements built around opposition to foreign penetration (in contrast, for example, with the Alianza Popular Revolucionaria Americana [APRA] in Peru).

Economic growth and social differentiation picked up tempo in the 1920s, led by the coffee boom, an installment of the U.S. indemnification to Colombia for the loss of Panama in 1923, and a rapid increase in foreign loans.[29] However, the dramatic economic decline of the late 1920s caught the Conservative government unprepared, as it did most governments in Latin America. This paved the way for an unprecedented constitutional transfer of power between political parties, as the badly divided Conservatives presented two candidates and the Liberals presented a mod- erate figure who had some Conservative support. Once inaugurated, the Liberal president formed a bipartisan government but confronted a Conservative majority in Congress. Partisan violence, particularly in rural areas, marked the 1930 elections and intensified during the 1931 elections. It ended as the country mobilized for a brief border conflict with Peru in 1932.

By 1934, a "Liberal Republic" party had emerged. Mindful of past Conservative fraud and exclusivism, Liberals employed highly fraudulent elections to place Alfonso López Pumarejo, who was in fact the only candidate, in the presidency. Conservatives practiced opposition as the Liberals had in earlier years. Electorally, this included a refusal to participate in elections (*retraimiento*) in 1934 and 1938, supporting a dissident figure from the other party in 1942, and, ultimately and successfully, presenting their own candidate in 1946 (see Table 5.1).

López's presidency was a period of tumultuous reform and institutional change, known as the Revolution on the March (Revolución en Marcha). Under López, constitutional and legal reforms were enacted to increase the electorate (universal male suffrage) and to modernize and expand the state in the face of the economic challenges of the worldwide depression and growing urbanization. López also encouraged legislation to deal with peasant unrest, supported labor organization, co-opted or neutralized dissident political movements from the radical and progressive left, and struggled against those of the fascist right. López's reforms were a pragmatic response to "an incipient crisis of the old order." Yet they also served more narrow partisan purposes, consolidating the position of the Liberal Party by limiting the influence of the church, expanding the electorate in urban areas, and increasing the party's support base within labor.[30]

Significant industrial growth and organization and incorporation of the working class came during this period. Bipartisan participation in the coffee trade also came to be reflected in industry. In contrast to other Latin American countries, there was no rupture between industrialists and export-oriented landowners during the 1930s, and none of the Liberal presidents developed a conscious statist industrial policy.[31] In addition, in the early years of unionization, labor was not a very important center for radical activity. This was due in part to low rates of immigration (a focus for anarcho-syndicalist movements in many other Latin American countries) and to low levels of foreign investment in these years of initial industrialization.

Table 5.1   Electoral Results for the Presidency, 1930–1998

Year	Liberal		Conservative		Total Votes	Participation Rate
	A	B	A	B		
1930–1949						
1930	44.9% Olaya	—	29.1% Valencia	25.9% Vásquez	824,530	n.a.
1934	97.6% López	—	—	—	942,309	n.a
1938	100.0% Santos	—	—	—	513,520	30.2%
1942	48.5% López	41.3% Arango	—	—	1,147,806	55.8%
1946	32.3% Turbay	26.3% Gaitán	41.4% Ospina	—	1,336,005	55.7%
1949	—	—	100.0% Gómez	—	1,140,646	39.9%

(continues)

Table 5.1 (continued)

Year	Official National Front	ANAPO	Other A	Other B	Total Votes	Participation
1958–1970						
1958	79.9% Lleras C.	—	19.8% Leyva	—	3,108,567	57.7%
1962	62.1% Valencia	—	11.7% Leyva	25.9% López M.	2,634,840	48.7%
1966	71.4% Lleras R.	28.0% Jaramillo	—	—	2,649,258	40.1%
1970	40.3% Pastrana	38.7% Rojas	11.7% Betancur	8.3% Sourdís	4,036,458	52.6%

Year	Liberal	Conservative	ANAPO	Left	Other	Total Votes	Participation
1974–1990							
1974	56.2% López	31.4% Gómez	9.4% María Rojas	2.6% Echeverri	0.1% Duarte	5,212,133	59.1%
1978	49.3% Turbay	46.4% Betancur	—	2.6% 3 candidates	1.3% Valencia	5,075,719	40.3%
1982	40.9% López	46.6% Betancur	—	1.2% Molina	10.9% Galán	6,840,392	49.8%
1986	58.3% Barco	35.8% Gómez	—	4.5% Pardo	0.6% Liska	7,229,937	44.8%
1990	47.8% Gaviria	23.7% Gómez 12.2% Lloreda	—	12.5% Navarro	1.8% 6 candidates	6,047,576	43.5%

Year	Liberal	Conservative	Left	Other	Total Votes	Participation Rate
1994–1998						
1994						
First round	45.1% Samper	44.7% Pastrana	3.8% Navarro	4.8% 15 candidates	5,821,331	33.9%
Runoff	50.3% Samper	48.2% Pastrana	—	—	7,427,742	43.6%
1998						
First round	34.4% Serpa	34.0% Pastrana		26.5% Sanín 2.9% Others	10,751,465	51.8%
Runoff	46.0% Serpa	49.7% Pastrana	—	—	12,310,107	59.3%

Source: For 1930–1986, Jonathan Hartlyn, *The Politics of Coalition Rule in Colombia* (Cambridge: Cambridge University Press, 1988), pp. 152–153, corrected and standardized; for 1990, Rubén Sánchez David, ed., *Los Nuevos Retos Electorales* (Bogotá: CEREC-Universidad do los Andes, 1991), pp. 127, 131, 212; for 1994, *Elecciones de Presidente y Vicepresidente May 29 y Junio 19 de 1994* (Bogotá: Registraduría Nacional del Estado Civil, 1994); for 1998, Registraduría Nacional del Estado Civil website at www.registraduria.gov.co, and personal communication with Gary Hoskin.

The country's first major labor federation, the Confederación de Trabajadores de Colombia (CTC), was founded in 1936 with critical political support from President López.

López, though, met intense opposition from landowners, merchants, industrialists, and leaders from both parties. Opposition from Conservatives, expressed in strongly ideological language, intensified particularly because of the massive dismissals of Conservatives from government. Yet even within his own party, López experienced such intense opposition that late in his term he agreed the country required a "pause" in reformism. López regained the presidency in 1942, in elections pitting him against another Liberal supported by the Conservatives (see Table 5.1). But he now confronted a hostile Congress and an economy buffeted by inflation and lacking, because of the war, needed inputs. After surviving a coup attempt by Conservative military sympathizers in 1944, and in spite of continued labor support, López resigned in August 1945. Besieged by attacks from both Conservatives, led by Laureano Gómez, and Liberals, particularly the populist Jorge Eliécer Gaitán, he hoped his resignation would pave the way for interparty accord.

The parties had managed one peaceful constitutional transfer of power in 1930, though regionalized partisan violence then had only ended with the border war with Peru. They would not be capable of managing a second such transfer.

From La Violencia to the National Front

The period 1946–1958 is one of tragic violence and intense drama in Colombian history. The causes of regime breakdown and of *la violencia* remain complex and controversial. We share the perspective that emphasizes the importance of political factors over purely class or economic factors in explaining the breakdown and the initiation of violence, and, ultimately, the establishment of the National Front.[32] At the same time, as argued below, political factors alone cannot explain the evolution of *la violencia* or the successful establishment of the National Front.

The 1946 elections represented the second transfer of power between the two parties in this century and occurred in a mirror image of events in 1930. The Liberal Party was irreparably split, with regional figures, moderate national leaders, and most Liberal CTC labor leaders (as well as communist leaders pursuing a "Popular Front" strategy) supporting a traditional Liberal candidate. In contrast, many rank-and-file CTC members and communist sympathizers backed the Liberal populist Gaitán. Just six weeks before the elections, the Conservatives nominated Mariano Ospina Pérez, a far less acerbic and more compromising figure than Gómez, whose candidacy would almost certainly have unified the Liberals.[33] Ospina won, his plurality of votes resulting from the Liberal split (see Table 5.1), and entered office with a bipartisan National Union government (as he pledged he would during the campaign, in spite of Gómez's opposition).

Politicization, polarization, and violence accelerated following the 1946 elections. Although it resembled the violence that followed the 1930 elections, the stakes were higher. Liberals feared that Conservatives, as a minority party, would attempt to consolidate a permanent grip on power by force. Conservatives, mindful of the recent exclusivism by the Liberals in power, feared that if they were to lose the presidency, they would be able to regain it only with great difficulty.[34] With the social and economic changes of the 1920s and 1930s, there were more economically integrated and polit-ically mobilized groups. Party control of the state was more and more cru-cial, not only for patronage and contracts but also for favorable administra-tive and judicial decisions. Economic interests and political sectarianism began to reinforce each other, polarizing the country in the opposing fig-ures of Gómez for the Conservatives and Gaitán for the Liberals.

Government-labor relations were reshaped. The CTC, its largest union broken by the interim Liberal government of Alberto Lleras in 1945, attempted a nationwide strike against the Ospina government in May 1947; it failed dismally. Interpreted as part of a Liberal plot to overthrow Ospina's government, it led to further repression and decline of the Liberal labor confederation, and to the encouragement of a new confederation being formed under Jesuit auspices, the Unión de Trabajadores de Colombia (UTC).[35] The UTC was committed to collective bargaining at the firm level, had a much more centralized organization, and firmly rejected state syndicalism. Given these characteristics, the UTC prospered under Ospina, who saw it as an alternative to the Liberal- and communist-linked CTC. The result, in contrast to the corporatist experience of other Latin American countries, was a labor movement relatively independent from the state, though linked to different political parties and thus divided and neither par-ticularly powerful nor autonomous.

Liberal divisions remained severe. As a result of the 1947 congression-al elections, Gaitán emerged as the leader of the party and almost certainly its sole candidate for the 1950 presidential elections. He opposed Liberal participation in Ospina's government, which ended in March 1948. Then, on April 9, the assassination of Gaitán on the streets of Bogotá led to the *bogotazo*—mobs burned commercial buildings, destroyed churches, and attacked government buildings in the capital city; riots spread to other cities.[36] The regime survived, barely. Moderate Liberals, confronted with Ospina's refusal to resign, agreed to reenter the government, which implanted a state of siege. But moderates in each party were finding it diffi-cult to disassociate themselves from the statements and actions of party extremists without endangering their own position and influence.

The conflict between Conservatives and Liberals became a struggle between the executive and the legislature. In May 1949, the Liberals once again left the government. The following month's congressional elections confirmed their control of Congress, even as high turnout demonstrated the country's growing polarization (Table 5.2). Gómez called for Ospina to close Congress, while moderates in both parties established a Pro-Peace Committee with industrial, commercial, and financial representation. Ospina proposed postponement of presidential elections by four years and interim bipartisan rule by a four-man government council, with major organs of the state under equal control and a two-thirds majority requirement for legislation. Yet, even as this proposal was being transmitted to the Liberals (by Gómez, who personally opposed it), hard-liners were replacing moderate Conservatives in government. Official repression against Liberals continued. Following Gómez's nomination as the Conservative's presidential candidate and the failure to reach an accord, the Liberals decided to withdraw entirely from the elections they had moved up to November 1949 and began impeachment proceedings against Ospina.[37]

The result was regime breakdown. On November 9, 1949, the president responded to the Liberal actions by declaring a state of siege, closing Congress, banning public meetings, and censoring the press. Unopposed, Gómez was elected president. The intensified violence and conflict, though fueled by social and economic changes that had generated significant regional variations, were essentially the result of partisan polarization. What led regional conflicts to spiral into the breakdown of the regime, a "partial collapse" of state authority,[38] and one of the "greatest armed mobilization[s] of peasants . . . in the recent history of the western hemisphere,"[39] was the inability of some and the unwillingness of other elements of the top leadership in both parties to negotiate in good faith. With their direct or ambivalent support for the violent activities of their regional party subordinates, given all the other social and economic dislocations and the country's ideologized condition, they soon found they had helped unleash a wave of violence they were unable to control.[40]

The worst casualties were suffered in the earlier years, when the partisan motivation was strongest: an estimated 145,000 deaths are attributable to *la violencia* between 1948 and 1953. Another 25,000 are believed to have been killed between 1954 and 1960.[41] Remarkably, the country experienced healthy economic growth during most of this period, as export crops reached the ports and urban industrial areas were little affected. This may help to explain why reaction against the continued violence grew so slowly under the Gómez presidency.

Under Gómez, censorship tightened, repression against labor increased, and violence against Liberals and Protestants, sometimes with the cooperation of the local clergy, intensified. Additional efforts to establish interparty accords failed. Gómez's government (headed by another figure after his 1951 heart attack) convened a constituent assembly in order to impose a new falangist-corporatist constitution, inspired by Franco's Spain,

Table 5.2   Electoral Results for the Legislature (Chamber of Representatives),
             1935–1998

Year	Liberal (%)	Conservative (%)	Other[a] (%)	Total Votes	Participation Rate (%)
1935	100.0	—[b]	—	430,728	33.4
1937	100.0	—[b]	—	550,726	32.5
1939	64.4	35.1	—	919,569	—
1941	63.8	35.7	—	885,525	—
1943	64.4	33.8	—	882,647	—
1945	63.0	33.6	3.2	875,856	38.4
1947	54.7	44.4	0.8	1,472,689	56.3
1949	53.5	46.1	0.4	1,751,804	63.1
1951	0.6	98.6	0.5	934,580	—
1953	—[b]	99.7	—	1,028,323	—
1958	57.7	42.1	—	3,693,939	68.9
1960	44.0	41.7	12.0	2,542,651	57.8
1962	35.0	41.7	23.2	3,090,203	57.9
1964	46.2	35.5	18.0	2,261,190	36.9
1966	52.1	29.8	17.8	2,939,222	44.5
1968	49.9	33.7	16.1	2,496,455	37.3
1970	37.0	27.2	35.5	3,980,201	51.9
1974	55.6	32.0	12.6	5,100,099	57.1
1978	55.1	39.4	4.3	4,180,121	33.4
1982	56.3	40.3	2.5	5,584,037	40.7
1986	54.2	37.2	4.4	6,909,851	42.9
1990	59.0	33.2	7.5	7,631,694	55.4
1991	50.6	25.6	23.8	5,486,636	35.9
1994	47.0	23.2	29.8	5,576,174	32.7
1998	48.4	24.5	27.1	8,480,893	n.a.

Sources: For 1935–1986, Jonathan Hartlyn, The Politics of Coalition Rule in Colombia (Cambridge: Cambridge University Press, 1988), pp. 150–151; for 1990, John Dugas et al., "La Asamblea Nacional Constituyente: Expresión de una voluntad general," in Rubén Sánchez David, ed., Los Nuevos Retos Electorales (Bogotá: CEREC-Universidad de los Andes, 1991), pp. 211, 215; for 1991 and 1994, Gary Hoskin, "The Consequences of Constitutional Reform on the Colombian Party System," paper presented at the 17th International Congress of Latin American Studies Association, 1994, p. 28, and Gary Hoskin, "The State and Political Parties in Colombia," in Eduardo Posada-Carbó, ed., Colombia: The Politics of Reforming the State (New York: St. Martin's Press, 1998), p. 57, and Juan Fernando Jaramillo, "Cinco elecciones sin partidos," in Luis Alberto Restrepo Moreno, ed., Síntesis '95 Colombia (Bogotá: IEPRI-Fundación Social-Tercer Mundo Editores, 1995), p. 77; for 1998, statistics calculated from data at the website of the Registraduría Nacional del Estado Civil at www.registraduria.gov.co. The percentages for 1991, 1994, and 1998 do not take into account blank and null ballots.

Notes: a. Other Parties: In 1945, 1949, and 1951, the Communist Party; in 1947, the Socialist Party; in 1960, the Movimiento Revolucionario Liberal (MRL); in 1962, the MRL and the Alianza Nacional Popular (ANAPO); in 1964, ANAPO and the MRL linea dura; in 1966, 1968, and 1970, ANAPO; in 1974, ANAPO and the Unión Nacional de Oposición (UNO); in 1978, UNO, the Frente Unido del Pueblo (FUP), and Unidad Obrera y Socialista (UNIOS); in 1982, FUP, Frente Democrático (FD), Unidad Democrática, Liberal-FD, and Movimiento Izquierda Democrática; in 1986, the Unión Patriótica (UP) and joint Liberal-UP lists; in 1990, the UP, the Movimiento Unitario Metapolítico (MUM), coalition lists, and other minor movements; in 1991, the UP, the Alianza Democrática M-19 (AD M-19), and other movements; in 1994, the UP, the AD M-19, coalitions, and other minority parties; and in 1998, a variety of coalitions and minority parties/movements, many of which were probably the personal political vehicles for a traditional Liberal or Conservative candidate.
b. Abstained from election.

that would free the presidency of most congressional constraints, further centralize power, and convert the Senate into a corporatist body.[42] Yet this constitutional counterreform divided Gómez's own party. Some feared it was a means of perpetuating his followers in office, and others thought it unnecessary or irrelevant in the face of more crucial national issues, including *la violencia*.

Military government and failed populism. Although dictatorial rule (such as by Gómez or by Reyes at the turn of the century) was not unknown in Colombia, direct military rule was uncommon. The country's historical tradition had been largely civilian and republican, if violent and not fully democratic, built around two dominant multiclass parties.

Yet party leaders now welcomed military intervention. Gómez was overthrown by General Gustavo Rojas Pinilla in June 1953, with the active support of many Conservative leaders, particularly former president Ospina, and with the encouragement of the Liberals, many of whose top leaders had fled into exile. Neither Rojas nor the Colombian military, though, had the capability or the inclination to govern the country without civilian assistance. Most of the officer corps, including Rojas, strongly identified with the Conservative Party and sought church support and approval. Initially, Rojas's goal appeared to have been to stem the violence and broaden and improve the Conservative Party.[43] Rojas's government was staffed heavily with Conservatives, particularly *ospinistas,* and his major economic and political advisers were civilian.

As it became clearer that Rojas was not intending a rapid return to civilian rule but was instead seeking to consolidate and probably prolong his stay in office, opposition began to intensify. The opposition to Rojas crystallized in the bipartisan movement that led to the National Front. The inability of his government to end the violence, as well as the fact that groups of insurgents were taking on a more radical revolutionary purpose, helped generate opposition to Rojas among important civilian sectors. His Peronist leanings and economic policies gained him U.S. and World Bank opposition. By the second half of 1956, this opposition intensified as the country's economic situation suffered from a sharp drop in world coffee prices.[44]

Rojas's most significant failure was his inability to establish a political movement outside the two political parties. The organizational space already occupied by the political parties and existing labor organizations, as well as domestic implications of the international environment, weighed against his succeeding in creating a corporatist labor organization and a "Third Force" (Tercera Fuerza) political movement. In addition, the church began to reconsider the partisan role it had played following Gómez's bitter attacks against it after his fall from power and in reaction to the horror of *la violencia;* the church also increasingly distrusted Rojas's government because of its Peronist trappings.[45]

Consociation and transition. Generating a political alternative to Rojas and moving to civilian rule was almost inconceivable without extensive mutual guarantees between the two parties. These were provided through a series of political pacts, eventually enshrined as part of the constitution by means of a national plebiscite. The Liberal Alberto Lleras sought out Laureano Gómez in his Spanish exile in July 1956. The resulting Declaration of Benidorm and subsequent Pact of March, signed in Bogotá, called for a return to civilian rule by means of coalition governments. Party opposition to Rojas coalesced around Conservative Guillermo León Valencia as their joint candidate for the 1958 elections.

The growing crisis came to its resolution during the "days of May." Following business strikes and middle-sector and student protest, rather than mass mobilization, Rojas finally flew into exile on May 10, 1957. The junta that replaced him formed a bipartisan cabinet, closed Rojas's Constituent Assembly, reestablished freedom of the press, and called for elections to replace itself at the end of Rojas's presidential term in August 1958. While the junta implemented an economic austerity program, party leaders sought to provide assurances to the armed forces that they would be delinked from the attacks on Rojas and his close collaborators. They also continued to work on the mechanisms by which they would provide guarantees to each other in order to ensure a transition of power from the military. The major problem, apparent before the fall of Rojas, was a serious split within the Conservative Party: Gómez bitterly opposed the Valencia candidacy.

Tumultuous and complex negotiations ensued. Alberto Lleras traveled again to Spain, and in the Pact of Sitges, he and Gómez agreed to most of the measures of political parity and other mutual guarantees that were eventually approved by the national plebiscite later that year. Every element eventually incorporated into the agreement had been suggested or tried in the late 1940s. However, on his return to Colombia, Gómez threatened to withdraw support from the plebiscite vote. A Pact of San Carlos, agreed to only days before the plebiscite vote (in which 95 percent of those voting approved the National Front agreement), specified that congressional elections would precede presidential ones, and that Valencia would be the candidate only if congressional lists supporting him gained a victory over Gómez's lists. Gómez's gamble succeeded, but the parties could not agree on a different Conservative candidate. Finally, with Gómez's urging, Alberto Lleras became the presidential candidate only nine days before the elections. The parties agreed to approve a constitutional reform calling for presidential alternation until 1974. The transition effort was marred by several failed coup attempts, including one just two days before the presidential elections. Lleras won an overwhelming victory against Jorge Leyva, a sectarian Conservative candidate (see Table 5.1).

The transition to civilian rule in Colombia can be viewed as consociational in a descriptive sense, because of the particular political arrangement of the National Front, with its extensive mutual guarantees between the Conservative and Liberal Parties. But it is also consociational in a theoretical sense. These arrangements appear necessary for the transition to occur, and for the regime to persist in its initial years given the nature of the country's two hierarchical, multiclass, historically rooted, and deeply entrenched parties, and the ferocity of the violence in the 1950s. It was difficult to conceive of extinguishing this violence if one party sought to govern over another. Yet Colombia also illustrates the difficulties of moving to more open and democratic practices from such a rigid, constitutionally enshrined agreement.[46]

Coalition Rule and Uncertain Transformation

The National Front was a pragmatic, though conservative, response to the country's deep crisis. It promised something for all major party groups and economic actors. Yet, different and sometimes contradictory aspects of the agreement and the regime it established generated support among these actors. Liberals regained a share of political power; Conservative *ospinistas* retained a position of influence without the burden of their untrustworthy military allies; and Conservative *laureanistas* (followers of Gómez) regained their position within the party and a chance at political power. The consociational arrangement of parity and alternation soon came to serve the bureaucratic and pork-barrel interests of national and regional party leaders so effectively that few could imagine doing away with coalition rule. The church could view itself as a force of conciliation for all Colombians as both parties now recognized its privileged position; the military was promised autonomy and respect; and producer groups saw economic policies they favored and the promise of greater access to policy circles. The absence of bitterly contested, ideologized elections and of opposition politics meshed well with the development strategies of foreign-aid advisers and international financial agencies, which encouraged the emergence of a state sector protected from partisan politics. Lacking was any effective, organized presence of different popular groups. They had played no direct role in the regime's creation, and party elites had seen how their mobilization had gotten out of their control. For these groups, the agreement heralded peace and the promise—largely unrealized—of social reform.

Constrained by these contradictory forces and a restrictive set of political rules, the regime sustained a precarious balance. It generated a set of informal "rules of the game"—increased presidential authority, ad hoc decision forums and summit negotiations, secrecy, increased state capacity combined with selective privatization, patron-client and brokerage ties, and government-sponsored mass organizations—that allowed it to operate in a context of continual short-term crises. The regime appeared more contingent than consolidated, and its balance became more precarious in the post–National Front period (1978 on), as levels of protest and violence increased and state capacity declined. The political parties were seeking to maintain essentially the same political mechanisms they had established in 1958 in a societal structure that had been changed not only by massive population growth, rural-to-urban migration, and industrialization, but also by the very experience of the National Front.[47]

The immobilism generated by the consociational agreement (parity in all branches of government and a required two-thirds majority vote in Congress), and the party factionalization that it further encouraged, initially weakened the political parties (one of which had begun the National Front already divided) and led to numerous executive-legislative deadlocks. Combined with a technocratic emphasis of certain national leaders, reinforced by international lending agencies, the agreement also increasingly marginalized Congress from many key decisions, leading to increased presidential authority. Congress ceded extraordinary powers to presidents to legislate on specific issues; presidents also legislated after declaring a state of siege or, following the 1968 Constitutional Reform, by declaring a state of national economic emergency. Nominal but only rarely substantive bipartisan participation was assured by the fact that the signatures of the entire cabinet were required on all such presidential decrees. The use of special powers by the president has been common to Latin American presidentialist systems. In Colombia, it took on added importance because of the consociational arrangement, an ironic situation since Colombia was unique among consociational regimes in having a presidential system.[48]

No single institutional forum emerged in lieu of Congress to serve as the locus for bipartisan discussion. Because party factions were sometimes not represented in a cabinet or because ministers identified with a particular faction sometimes were more "technical" than "political," the cabinet—which logically might have served such a function—did so only occasionally. Thus, on specific issues such as agrarian reform or during periods of acute economic or political crisis such as 1965, ad hoc decision forums and summit negotiations among top party leaders, many times ex-presidents, were often employed in seeking to break apparent deadlocks. Attempts to create institutionalized decisionmaking structures in Colombia essentially failed at both the congressional level and at a corporatist state-society level.

Structural pressures from the economy, the influence of international agencies, and the drive to satisfy minimum levels of efficiency led to increasing state capacity in terms of planning, regulating, and investing, though there were important variations from one presidential administration to another. At the same time, in order to avoid potential immobilism or politicization and to seek greater efficiency, or because of concerted efforts by particular producer groups, the regime continued with the historical pattern of selective privatization of certain economic areas and functions (such as with the legally private Coffee Federation, which was extensively involved in key pricing and marketing decisions and even in managing state revenues).

Politicians relied extensively on patron-client and brokerage ties to consolidate their electoral position and felt threatened by increased state capacity, which increased the programs and investments channeled through various state agencies and weakened politicians' regional bases of strength. The parties made no serious attempts to institutionalize or to develop auxiliary organizations, even as their ties to the traditional labor confederations weakened. Some popular-sector groups were able to influence policy or attain limited goals by various means, including political ties (through government bureaucrats or through clientelist or brokerage connections with politicians), mass occupations, civic and labor strikes, demonstrations, and appeals to the press. Nevertheless, the regime at times employed or condoned the use of undemocratic practices.

There were also ambivalent and only partially successful efforts at government-sponsored organizations of the lower classes. In the end, the National Front did not create loyal popular-sector organizations by corporatist mechanisms, in part because presidential alternation and partisan fears worked against it. The regime sought to pursue more a policy of demobilization and of "divide and conquer" toward the popular sector than one of corporatist mobilization, centralization, and control. The example of the Asociación Nacional de Usurios Campesinos (ANUC) is telling. ANUC was created by the reformist Liberal president Carlos Lleras (1966–1970) to serve as a "pressure group" in favor of land reform and as a potential mass base for a future reelection bid. With the change to a Conservative administration and retrenchment on agrarian reform, ANUC became radicalized and sponsored numerous land invasions. The government responded by withdrawing financial support, dividing the organization, and repressing its more radical leaders.[49]

"Moderate" economic policies and growth.   One factor that was facilitated by, and also facilitated, Colombia's consociational regime was its economic policies. These policies were largely "moderate" and relatively continuous, similar to those of countries such as Mexico and Venezuela until their oil

boom-and-bust cycles began in the 1970s, in contrast to the more "pendu-lar" policies of countries such as Argentina, Chile, and Peru. These differences of degree (rather than of kind) meant that Colombia, while not eluding economic problems and shifts in policy, generally avoided sharp swings from extreme populist policies—with high inflation, extreme protectionism, dramatic wage increases, and extensive fiscal deficits—to radical neoliberal ones, such as brusquely eliminating state subsidies and fiscal deficits, imposing massive devaluations, sharply curtailing wage increases, clamping down on the money supply, and slashing tariffs.

Colombia's economic policies in recent decades have entailed continued attention to variables such as fiscal deficits and growth; its inflation rate never spun out of control, typically ranging between 20 percent and 30 percent per year. Facilitated by the nature of its regime, these policies also kept dissenting conservative economic interests within the regime rather than seeking to overthrow it. These policies had some important successes, as the country maintained one of the steadiest growth rates in the region in the period from 1957 to the present. Even in the difficult years of the 1980s, Colombia's record of growth, inflation, and fiscal deficits was comparatively favorable.[50]

From the 1950s to the 1990s, the country underwent massive economic, social, and demographic changes. It more than doubled its population and became a substantially younger and more urban country. Significant changes in its labor force resulted from shifts from agriculture toward services and, to a lesser extent, industry. The economy became more diversified and complex, and larger middle-sector groups emerged (see Table 5.3).

Improvements in health and education (e.g., life expectancy and literacy rates), however, were not paralleled by improvements of similar scale in the country's vastly unequal income distribution. This was in part because distributionist policies were rarely formulated and, if formulated, were largely thwarted in implementation. (For data on Colombia and other Latin American countries, see Table 1.1.)

The regime pursued economic policies akin to those of its continental neighbors in the late 1950s and early 1960s. Thus, it also suffered some of the same kinds of economic and political problems associated with seeking to move beyond initial import-substituting industrialization in a period of poor export performance. Over the 1957–1968 period, it sought to forge ahead with import-substituting industrialization in a context of low world prices for coffee. Confronted with recurring balance-of-payments problems, the regime applied stabilization programs of differing effectiveness in 1957–1958, 1962, and 1965.

International aid (and especially generous U.S. support under the Alliance for Progress) was critical in keeping the economy afloat. The economic problems and growing social discontent that marked the administra-

Table 5.3   Colombia: Demographic and Social Indicators, 1960, 1980, and
             1995

Indicators	1960	1980	1995
Total population (millions)	14.5	28	37
Gross domestic product			
(per capita, U.S.$)	479	1,380[a]	1,910
Urban population (%)	48	64[a]	73
Labor force (%)			
Agriculture	52	39[b]	25[c]
Industry	19	20	22
Services	29	41	53
Life expectancy	53	63[a]	70
Number enrolled in primary			
schools as % of age group	77	128	119
Literacy rate	63	81	91
Average annual growth of			
population (%)[d]			
1960–1980	2.6		
1980–1995		1.9	

Sources: Data for 1960 from the *Statistical Abstract for Latin America,* vol. 21 (Los Angeles: University of California, Latin American Center, 1981), and the Inter-American Development Bank, *Economic and Social Progress in Latin America* (Washington, DC: IDB, 1982). Data for 1980, World Bank, *World Development Report 1983* (Oxford University Press, 1983). Data for 1995, World Bank, *World Development Report 1997* (Oxford University Press, 1997).

Notes: a. Data for GDP, urban population, and life expectancy is for 1981.

b. Labor force distribution for 1980 is from World Bank, *World Development Report 1997.*

c. In 1995, data is for labor force ratio.

d. Information compiled is from all three data sources and is collapsed into categories.

tion of Conservative Guillermo León Valencia (1962–1966) brought the regime to the brink of collapse. In early 1965, a national strike was only narrowly averted; talk of a military coup gradually subsided.

Yet a partial economic shift occurred during the administration of the reformist Liberal president Carlos Lleras Restrepo (1966–1970). A nationalist reaction against International Monetary Fund (IMF) demands was followed by pragmatic negotiations leading to the establishment, in 1967, of a new framework for trade and a "crawling peg" exchange rate. The latter sharply reduced political conflicts over devaluation and provided the means for a partial reorientation of the economy from an import-substitution model to one of export promotion.[51] In this way, Colombia avoided some (not all) disastrous experiences in import substitution and did not implement sharply pendular policies with their devastating political consequences, as occurred in Argentina, Chile, Peru, and Uruguay.

Lleras sought unsuccessfully to create a new reformist coalition of industrialists, workers, and peasant beneficiaries against traditional landowners, while establishing the basis for an active interventionist state.

However, his aggressive actions generated opposition from politicians concerned about the trimming of pork-barrel funds, numerous producer groups fearful of a more interventionist state, and especially landowners threatened by the encouragement of land reform and peasant associations. The backlash was felt both at election time, when General Rojas's populist Alianza Nacional Popular (ANAPO) movement nearly won, and in the orientation of the subsequent Pastrana administration.

Conservative president Misael Pastrana (1970–1974), after two years of general economic policy continuity, combined with retrenchment on agrarian reform and co-optive urban policies to prevent further successes for ANAPO, enacted a new development program oriented toward urban construction and further expansion of commercial agriculture and agro-exports. These policies were perceived as having helped to foster higher inflation and were partially abandoned by the incoming administration of Liberal Alfonso López Michelsen (1974–1978). Elected by an overwhelming margin in the first competitive national elections since 1946, López began with a strong reformist orientation, though he also emphasized more conventional strategies focusing on agricultural and manufactured exports. However, his administration was unprepared for the foreign-exchange bonanza that resulted from a boom in coffee prices and the rapid expansion of illegal drug exports. Prudently, though, it borrowed little on international capital markets, permitting the country to postpone and partially mitigate the effects of the debt crisis that its continental neighbors faced a few years later as the world went into recession and interest rates climbed.

Colombia's coffee bonanza ended in 1980, and the administration of Liberal Julio César Turbay (1978–1982) borrowed more extensively both internally and abroad to finance its development program. Yet, affected by the international recession and the economic crises of its neighbors, the country's growth rates flattened, budget deficits mushroomed, industry went into recession, and unemployment grew. These trends continued during the government of Conservative Belisario Betancur (1982–1986). By mid-1984, confronting balance-of-payments problems, Colombia moved to implement an economic austerity program, though one more moderate than those adopted by its neighbors. The country's economic difficulties came at a particularly unfortunate period, as the government was seeking a new political reaccommodation and a negotiated peace with the country's major guerrilla groups, even as it confronted increased violence from drug traffickers. By the time the Liberal Virgilio Barco (1986–1990) was inaugurated, the country's economy had partially recovered, assisted by an increase in coffee prices, major investments in coal and oil, and continuing dollar inflows from narcotics traffic. Yet, as political violence continued to escalate in the mid-1980s, it began to affect investor confidence and augment capital flight.

In early 1990, the Barco administration began a process of opening up the Colombian economy to greater international competition by reducing the protective barriers that shielded national industries. Barco sought to stimulate domestic productivity through a process of economic liberalization that would be implemented gradually over a five-year period.[52] The administration of Liberal César Gaviria (1990–1994), more clearly neoliberal in orientation, accelerated liberalization with the result that the average nominal tariff on imports dropped from 38.6 percent in 1989 to 11.4 percent in 1991.[53] Gaviria complemented the economic opening with an array of liberalizing reforms in the labor, exchange, and financial markets.

Despite the relative rapidity of the changes, the Colombian economy continued to perform fairly well, avoiding much of the social devastation associated with the introduction of neoliberal market-oriented reforms in several other countries of the hemisphere. Although the rate of economic growth fell to 2 percent in 1991, it rapidly recovered and exceeded 5 percent in the final two years of the Gaviria administration. Moreover, inflation fell from 32.4 percent in 1990 to 22.6 percent in 1994, while unemployment in the principal metropolitan areas dropped from 10.6 percent in 1990 to 7.9 percent in 1994.[54]

Gaviria's economic reforms were not directly associated with the concurrent constitutional reform. The 1991 Constitution, in fact, has an abundance of articles on the economy, not all from the same philosophical tradition, resulting in a hybrid document that embraced a market economy while simultaneously subjecting it to certain limitations.[55] Taken as a whole, the 1991 Constitution supports economically liberal views that economic activity is to be free, though this activity can and must be constrained when so required by the broader interests of society.[56] Two economic measures in the new constitution did produce controversy. First, the constitution allows for expropriation to occur by means of an administrative decision, subject to subsequent challenge in the judicial system. Although the rationale behind this measure was to expedite the extraordinarily slow-moving process of expropriation that had limited progress toward agrarian and urban reform, critics of the measure argued that it established uncertainty in property rights that would discourage foreign direct investment.[57] Second, the constitution mandates an increasing transfer of financial resources from the central government to the departments and municipalities in order to strengthen the decentralization begun during the 1980s. Indeed, by the late 1990s these transfers began to place severe strain on a central government budget already in deficit.

The administration of Liberal Ernesto Samper (1994–1998) was markedly less neoliberal in orientation than its predecessor and sought to moderate the negative effects of the economic opening by means of greater social spending. Samper's four-year economic development plan, labeled the "Social Leap" (Salto Social), endeavored to maintain relatively high rates of economic growth while investing significant resources in social services. Nonetheless, the socioeconomic improvement sought by Samper was frustrated by a decline in economic growth, heightened unemployment, and a growing fiscal deficit. These were affected by declining investor confidence and by growing government expenditures in pork-barrel projects for congressional support, stemming in part from the drug corruption scandal and ultimately failed impeachment hearings in which the Samper administration found itself engulfed.[58]

The political regime, controlled by the two factionalized multiclass elitist political parties, had largely inhibited radical policy shifts (in any direction). However, this also meant that even though some elements of the coalition governments had been interested in reformist-redistributive goals, their achievements were quite limited. Presidential alternation (until 1974) and coalition rule (until 1986), as well as the opposition of producer groups represented in both parties, inhibited socioeconomic reform. The formal end of consociationalism in the early 1990s failed to change this logic of moderate economic policymaking, given the continued dominance of the factionalized traditional parties and the relative influence of producer groups, even as the country increasingly adopted market-oriented reforms like its continental neighbors.

Political tensions. As a result both of the National Front agreement and of the country's massive social changes, many of the factors that helped shape the political regime's establishment and evolution declined in importance. Most important, the centrality of the parties in the country's political life declined, even as they maintained their near-monopoly in the electoral arena (see Table 5.2). The result was the emergence or the strengthening of nonelectoral opposition—labor confederations independent of the two parties, and civic protest movements. Rather than perceive them as a healthy part of the democratic process, regime leaders viewed them with suspicion.

Even more problematic for the state and the regime was the growing strength of violent nonstate actors. These included several guerrilla organizations, some with roots in the 1950s, and others in the 1960s and 1970s. By the 1980s, still another obstacle was posed by the expanding influence of drug cartels, who challenged the regime both directly by means of violence, and indirectly through bribery and corruption, and who were among the major promoters of right-wing paramilitary groups. At the same time, the military gradually disassociated itself from the two parties to become a more coherent institutional force. However, the credibility of the military was undermined by persistent accusations of acquiescence in, and in some cases clandestine support for, the growing violence perpetrated by these right-wing paramilitary groups.[59]

Whether the growing political problems of the 1970s and 1980s stemmed from a regime "birth defect" or from the fact that regime leaders were unwilling to respond in time to the country's changing conditions by dismantling the remnants of consociationalism and opening up the political process remains a topic of scholarly debate. A consociational National Front type of agreement had been necessary to reestablish civilian rule, and *la violencia* had led party leaders to fear popular mobilization. At the same time, in retrospect it is not obvious that one as rigid and as difficult to modify was truly necessary, as the attraction of continued coalition rule, for differing reasons, remained high for regional party leaders, major economic groups, and international actors. Under these circumstances, the country would almost certainly have experienced considerable political turmoil in the 1980s, and the transformation of the regime would almost certainly have been traumatic, uneven, and perhaps even sporadically violent. However, drug trafficking, by its deinstitutionalizing impact on the state, its demoralizing effects on the regime, its diverse temporary alliances, and its impact on a wide variety of other social processes, combined with the consequences of the attempted responses to it, helped provoke a more generalized crisis of state authority and a horrific wave of violence.[60]

Through time, the parties' continued dominance of the electoral arena came to mask significant regime and growing state weaknesses. As a result of the National Front agreement, party leaders sought to pursue three principal goals in the electoral process: to generate popular support for the National Front agreement, to defuse continued interparty conflict, and to prevent alternative populist and revolutionary movements from gaining support. These three goals were partially contradictory. Parity and alternation effectively eliminated interparty competition and, thus, a major reason to vote. Yet, mobilizing the vote continued to be important for National Front party leaders: the presence of party factions opposed to the National Front turned each election in effect into a new plebiscite on the National Front. Drops in voter turnout could be (and were) interpreted as a result of the declining legitimacy of the National Front.[61] As the National Front continued, nonsectarianism in government increasingly made attempts to revive the party faithful at election time untenable. The initial high participation rates, further facilitated by relaxing registration procedures, were unsustainable. Especially low participation rates were evident in mid-term elections.

Population growth, massive rural-to-urban migration, and the very experience of the National Front—in which competition at election time was followed invariably by coalition rule and which twice asked Liberals and Conservatives to support presidential candidates of the opposing party—led to declines in party identification. In Bogotá, Liberal Party identifiers declined from 50 percent of those sampled in 1970 to 36 percent in 1982, and Conservatives from 21 percent to 19 percent, while those stating no party preference climbed from 5 percent to 38 percent. The last tended to be younger, from lower socioeconomic strata, less politically informed, and less willing to express opinions on political issues. Indeed, by the late

1980s less than 50 percent of Colombians under the age of thirty-five expressed identification with either of the traditional parties. This data and other studies suggest that abstention did not reflect a coherent ideological position of regime rejection.[62] Yet, the inability of the traditional parties to motivate the growing urban population to vote did reflect their institutional weakness, even as they only weakly penetrated rural areas through traditional clientelist means.

Yet, opposition parties and movements have largely been unable to take advantage of this weakness. Perhaps the strongest rejection of the traditional parties took place in the 1970 elections, in which the ANAPO movement of General Gustavo Rojas nearly won (many feel fraud kept the victory from him). In 1970, because of the National Front structure, Rojas could maintain the ambiguous stature of populist opposition figure and of candidate within the Conservative Party; similarly, the ANAPO lists for Congress were also listed under either party rubric: dissident traditional figures could run under the ANAPO banner, yet remain within their party. Another advantage for Rojas was that voters in predominantly Liberal cities had no Liberal presidential candidate for whom to vote. Yet, after its 1970 defeat, the movement quickly faded due to the paucity of resources at the departmental and municipal level, obstructionism from other parts of government, and internal divisions.[63]

With the return to competitive elections, the electoral record of opposition movements further deteriorated. In 1974, some Rojas supporters and many Liberal sympathizers who traditionally abstained from voting turned out in large numbers to give Liberal Alfonso López an overwhelming victory. His disappointing administration, though, led to a sharp decline in voter turnout in the 1978 elections. The narrow victory in those elections of the traditional Liberal machine politician Julio César Turbay, as well as of the party factions that had been participating in government, strengthened the perception that parties or factions could not survive as a "loyal opposition," making regime modification away from coalition rule more difficult.

The political model was stagnating, its legitimacy increasingly in question. The inexorable logic of mobilizing small numbers of voters by distributing public resources in the context of high-abstention elections made politicians reluctant to change the model of coalition rule. If patronage and machine politics is a "glue" that can help keep otherwise ideologically polarized party systems together (as in Chile), in countries such as Colombia where parties are not strongly ideological, the dominance of particularistic, short-term stakes in the political arena with few effective restraints can ultimately impair party coherence and regime legitimacy.

Over the 1970s, important nonelectoral opposition made its presence felt. Although only a small percentage of the country's labor force was organized, key sectors responded to newer organizations independent from the regime or the traditional parties. Both in and out of the public sector, these labor organizations gained adherents at the expense of the traditional labor confederations (the UTC and the CTC), which also distanced themselves from the regime. In 1977, this led to an unprecedented joint national strike by all major confederations, and by the mid-1980s to the merging of numerous labor groups into a single predominant labor confederation. Further reflecting the economic frustration of urban groups, particularly in smaller cities, and the declining intermediary role of the traditional parties was the sharp rise in civic movements and protests in the 1970s.[64]

By the late 1970s, the regime confronted a growing challenge from various guerrilla movements. The largest and most important was the peasant-based Fuerzas Armadas Revolucionarias de Colombia (FARC), with strong links to the Communist Party. Officially formed in 1964, FARC and many of its leaders were spawned by *la violencia*. Another major group was the Movimiento del 19 de Abril (M-19), initially a largely urban movement that took its name from the date of the 1970 elections it felt had fraudulently denied Rojas his victory. It found considerable support among disenchanted middle- and lower-sector groups and professionals who found themselves increasingly squeezed economically in an era of presumed bonanza and apparent large-scale corruption. A third group was the Ejército de Liberación Nacional (ELN), founded in the 1960s initially under the influence of the Cuban Revolution, and which had been nearly decimated in the early 1970s.[65]

President Turbay responded in hard-line fashion to the guerrilla challenge. Shortly after he came to office, he enacted a tough Statute on Security using state-of-siege powers. During his administration, accusations of human rights violations by the armed forces increased, right-wing death squads (some with military ties) appeared, and in some rural areas large landowners unleashed land-grabbing violence against peasants. However, in late 1981, Turbay moved haltingly toward negotiating a "peace" with remaining guerrillas, even as the theme of peace became a major campaign topic in the 1982 elections because of escalating violence of all kinds. Unfortunately, reflecting a continuing spiral of violence, "peace" has remained a central campaign theme in all the subsequent presidential campaigns, including the 1998 campaign.

Escalating violence, declining state capacity, and the crisis of political legitimacy. Conservative president Belisario Betancur seized the issues of "peace" with the guerrillas (amnesty and political incorporation) and of political reforms (democratization) with an intensity and doggedness that surprised everyone. He had been the surprising but convincing victor in the 1982 elections, as his strategy of reaching out to the independent urban vote while also gaining the traditional Conservative "machine" vote succeeded. In some respects, the period was propitious for a peace effort. In addition to a degree of consensus among national political leaders, the M-19 was militarily decimated, other guerrilla groups were weak, and the FARC had let it be known that after decades of rural struggle it was ready to talk.

The peace process achieved some early successes, most notably in the passage of an amnesty law in 1982 and the signing of peace accords with the FARC, M-19, and the Ejército Popular de Liberación (EPL) in 1984.[66] The accords, while important, were essentially armed truces as they did not require the guerrilla movements to lay down their arms. Rather, the goal was to establish a period of cease-fire to prepare for the eventual incorporation of the guerrillas into civilian life. Nonetheless, the possibility of a successful outcome for the peace process was seriously hampered by negative short-term economic circumstances, an ambiguous negotiating strategy by the Betancur administration, the opposition of key members of the armed forces, and the military strengthening of the guerrilla movements. Under these circumstances, it is not surprising that the accords were violated by both sides.

In June 1985, the M-19 broke the truce, and in November, seeking to regain the political offensive, it took over the country's Palace of Justice (where the Supreme Court and the Council of State were housed). The ensuing military assault resulted in the death of half the country's Supreme Court judges, all of the M-19 participants, and scores of others. The president was left assuming responsibility for a military action many asserted he did not fully control.[67]

By the end of the Betancur administration, the EPL had joined the M-19 in declaring the peace accords broken and were again engaged in open conflict with the state. In this they were joined by the ELN, which had never participated in the peace negotiations. Only the FARC maintained a tenuous cease-fire with the state, but this rapidly deteriorated into open and intermittent fighting during the Barco administration.

Yet, limited political reforms were enacted under Betancur. The most significant step was a constitutional amendment calling for the popular election of mayors beginning in 1988. It was given added meaning because it was coupled with various fiscal measures to increase the flow of resources at the departmental and municipal levels. However, other far-reaching political changes, such as multilevel implementation of civil service reform, effective campaign financing controls, or electoral reforms to provide minority parties more access to legislative posts, were not approved. Once again, politicians from the traditional parties proved unwilling to enact democratic reforms that might undercut their hold on power.

One positive political step that occurred during the Betancur administration was the formation of the left-wing political movement, the Unión Patriótica (UP). Comprising former members of the FARC, the Communist Party, and other leftist activists, the UP held promise as a left-wing party that would seek radical social change through peaceful constitutional means. Nonetheless, the UP was accused by critics of serving as the political arm of the FARC. The result was an atrocious campaign of extermination carried out against the UP, with more than 1,000 of its members assassinated between 1985 and 1991.[68] The decimation of the UP illustrated yet again the difficulty of achieving meaningful democratization in Colombia.

In the 1986 presidential elections, the Liberal Virgilio Barco won an overwhelming victory over his Conservative opponent, Alvaro Gómez (son of former Conservative patriarch Laureano Gómez). Although Barco had close ties with the top party leadership, he was not a natural politician; indeed, his low-key, technocratic, and uncommunicative style of governance came to trouble many Colombians who sought more vigorous leadership in a time of growing crisis. During the Barco administration (1986–1990), the political crisis continued to deepen as the country experienced a combination of growing guerrilla activity, paramilitary violence, and the terrorist actions of the drug cartels. In the first half of his administration, Barco confronted the political crisis with a mixed strategy that combined a transformed peace process with limited socioeconomic and political initiatives. The failure of these initiatives, in conjunction with renewed violence on the part of the drug cartels, pushed Barco to embrace the idea of a profoundly democratizing constitutional reform.

Barco substantially modified the peace process that he had inherited from the Betancur administration.[69] In particular, he insisted that negotiations could only proceed if the clear goal of the talks was the disarmament and reincorporation of the guerrilla movements into civilian life. However, the elimination of the discussion of political and socioeconomic reforms from any potential peace talks robbed the guerrilla movements of incentive to negotiate. The impasse was broken in May 1988 with the M-19's kidnapping of Conservative politician Alvaro Gómez. The M-19 utilized this gambit as a means of reopening a dialogue with sectors of civil society and to pressure the government into opening broad-gauged negotiations. After a lengthy period of negotiations with the Barco administration, the M-19 signed a peace accord and turned in its arms in March 1990.

The principal political reform of Barco during his first year and a half in office was the introduction of the "government-opposition" scheme, a change intended to end coalition rule and revitalize the political party system. Barco had emphasized in the 1986 electoral campaign his desire to end the tradition of coalition government, and to provide instead a single-party government of the Liberal Party (which he correctly assumed would garner the majority of seats in Congress), with the Conservative Party and the UP serving as opposition parties.[70] The government-opposition scheme did, in fact, hold some potential for transforming the Colombian political regime. With a single majority party in power, a party program could conceivably be enacted without delay and clear partisan responsibility for governmental actions could be established.

In practice, however, the government-opposition scheme did not work well. Barco never developed close ties with the Liberal congressional leaders, an obstacle that prevented him from successfully advancing a partisan government program. Moreover, many Conservatives chafed at being the "loyal opposition," particularly since this translated into a reduction of state patronage. At the same time, the UP found it exceedingly difficult to exercise effective opposition given the widespread assassination of its militants. Finally, there simply were no significant ideological or political differences separating the Liberal and Conservative Parties—both parties were depoliticized, fragmented entities that sought power by means of broker clientelism. In the absence of more disciplined, hierarchically organized political parties with distinct programs, as well as of guarantees for the physical integrity of opposition politicians, the government-opposition system was doomed to failure.[71]

Even as the government-opposition scheme was failing to revitalize Colombian democracy, the country's political crisis was exacerbated by the growing power of drug traffickers. The powerful drug cartels of the late 1980s developed from modest and disperse drug-trafficking activities in Colombia in the 1960s and early 1970s. Originally focused on the production and transportation of limited amounts of marijuana, by the late 1980s the drug trade had largely shifted to cocaine and had come under the control of the Medellín and Cali cartels. Between them, the cartels were estimated to control between 75 and 80 percent of the Andean cocaine traffic, employ nearly 100,000 Colombians, and derive annual incomes of between 2 and 4 billion dollars.[72]

The effects of the drug trade on the Colombian economy were decidedly mixed.[73] However, the more lasting consequences for Colombia derived from the challenge the drug cartels posed to the state. The illegal nature of the drug trade meant that the cartels came to rely increasingly upon violence against the state and bribery of government officials, both of which were carried out with the end of protecting their trafficking activities.[74] Furthermore, revenues generated by the drug trade increasingly supported an array of violent nonstate actors, ranging from guerrilla groups such as the FARC (because of their control over coca growing regions of the country) to paramilitary groups with links to trafficking cartels who were their bitter enemies. In turn, another guerrilla group, the ELN, profited from the discovery of oil in the remote eastern areas of Arauca, as it reportedly extorted millions of dollars through terrorism and kidnapings from the foreign companies that constructed the oil pipeline from Arauca to the Atlantic coast.[75]

During the Barco administration, the violence perpetuated by the cartels and the repression of the drug trade on the part of the state escalated in an increasingly vicious cycle. In 1989, the violent activities of the drug traffickers, particularly the Medellín cartel, reached a critical threshold with the assassination of several prominent Colombian political figures. Most significantly, in August 1989 the cartel was charged with the murder of Luis Carlos Galán, a popular Liberal senator and the clear favorite to become president of Colombia in the 1990 elections. Galán was unique among the presidential candidates in his strong support for the extradition of drug traffickers to the United States, a stance that had earned him the enmity of the drug cartels. In the aftermath of Galán's death, President Barco implemented a series of state-of-siege decrees intended to break the back of the drug cartels.[76]

In the face of a massive state crackdown, the Medellín cartel issued its own declaration of war, backed by a campaign of terror designed to destabilize the state and intimidate Colombian society. Its principal weapons were dynamite attacks, car bombs, kidnappings, and assassinations. By the end of September 1989, the drug traffickers had carried out more than 140 dynamite attacks against government offices, banks, businesses, hotels, and schools. They destroyed the main offices of the Bogotá newspaper *El Espectador* and made a similar attack against the offices of a regional newspaper, *Vanguardia Liberal,* in Bucaramanga. On November 27, 1989, a cartel bomb destroyed an Avianca passenger plane in midflight, resulting in the deaths of over a hundred passengers. One week later, a massive car bomb destroyed the headquarters of the Departamento Administrativo de Seguridad (DAS) in Bogotá, killing sixty-four people and injuring over seven hundred. This unrelenting violence took its toll on public support for the Barco administration's battle with the drug cartels.

Paradoxically, though, the Medellín cartel's vicious war against the state during 1989–1990 became key to the transformation of the Colombian political regime. Since 1988, the Barco administration had pushed to introduce significant constitutional reform to democratize the regime. In December 1989, at the peak of the state-cartel violence, Congress failed to pass the Barco reform.[77] For many observers, the failure to pass constitutional reform during this heightened crisis of political legitimacy proved that the traditional parties were profoundly unwilling to transform the political regime. A broad-based student movement began to mobilize in favor of reforming the constitution by means of a popularly elected National Constituent Assembly. The student proposal was to establish a forum that could democratize the political regime outside the bounds of Congress. Through a combination of hard work, publicity provided by major news media, and the support of key presidential aspirants (who sought to portray themselves as democrats), the students were able to convince the Barco administration to hold a plebiscite on the National Constituent Assembly alongside the May 1990 presidential elections. In the plebiscite, 86.6 percent of the voters cast their ballot in favor of the National Constituent Assembly, demonstrating the evident popularity of introducing democratic reforms through a mechanism that circumvented Congress.

Regime transformation and further state weakening. The winner of the 1990 presidential elections was Liberal César Gaviria. In previous years, Gaviria had served as minister of government during the Barco administration and then as campaign manager for Luis Carlos Galán. When Galán was assassinated in August 1989, Gaviria took over the campaign at the behest of Galán's son. Benefiting from the positive image of the deceased reformist leader, Gaviria secured a respectable victory against three major contenders (two Conservatives and the candidate of the recently reincorporated M-19). The campaign, however, was marred by the assassinations early in 1990 of Bernardo Jaramillo Ossa, presidential candidate of the UP, and then of Carlos Pizarro Leongómez, presidential candidate of the M-19.

Gaviria pursued the option of a National Constituent Assembly in a determined fashion, and the negotiations were reminiscent of previous political accords in Colombian history.[78] Although they were more inclusive than the bipartisan conversations that produced the National Front, they excluded key political actors (including the UP and the student movement) and were criticized for limiting constitutional debate to specified areas. Notably, the Supreme Court in a landmark decision subsequently ruled that the National Constituent Assembly had complete autonomy.

Elections for the Assembly were held in December 1990. Turnout was surprisingly low, even by Colombian standards (see Tables 5.1 and 5.2), with 73.9 percent of registered voters failing to cast their ballots.[79] The low voter turnout is explained in part by the fact that many legislators chose not to run for a seat in the Assembly and thus did not activate their broker clientele networks. This decision had an important effect: it enabled nontraditional parties and movements to do extraordinarily well at the polls. As a consequence, the Liberal Party and the Conservative Party controlled less than half of the seats in the Assembly, and there was a notable presence of groups representing nontraditional options, such as the Alianza Democrática M-19 (AD M-19) and the Movimiento de Salvación Nacional (MSN).[80] These were joined by a number of minority forces such as indigenous groups, evangelical Christians, the UP, and ex-guerrillas from the EPL, the Partido Revolucionario de los Trabajadores (PRT), and the Quintín Lame.

The political composition of the Assembly had one consequence of overriding importance: politicians from the traditional parties were unable to impose the agenda, control the debate, or determine the final outcome of the Assembly. However, while the predominance of nontraditional politicians favored the emergence of a more democratic constitution, their own lack of cohesiveness meant that they were unable to impose a coherent project of political reform. The coalition that came to dominate within the Assembly was composed Liberals close to Gaviria, the MSN of Alvaro Gómez, and representatives of the AD M-19.

The 1991 Constitution marked the formal transformation of the consociational political regime into a more democratic and fully competitive regime. It removed all remnants of coalition government, such as parity provisions, while instituting a variety of electoral, participatory, and institutional reforms.[81] In electoral matters, the constitution established the popular election of both departmental governors and the vice-president; provided a runoff system for presidential elections; mandated official distribution of all electoral ballots; prohibited nonresident voting in municipal elections; and eliminated the election of alternate delegates (*suplentes*) to public office. It also provided for special seats for the election of representatives from indigenous and black communities, as well as other extensive ethnic rights for Indians, Pacific Coast blacks, and Raizals (English-speaking blacks found in San Andrés, Santa Catalina, and Providencia).[82] In terms of participatory reforms, the constitution instituted a recall vote for governors and mayors; established a mechanism for "popular consultation" at all levels of government; provided for referendums to repeal national laws or to amend the constitution; introduced the legislative initiative at all levels of government; and explicitly confirmed the right to organize and participate in political parties and movements.

With regard to institutional reform, the 1991 Constitution reduced presidential power by decreasing the president's nominating power, weakening his veto power, placing limits on his "extraordinary powers" to issue legal norms, and curtailing his state-of-siege emergency powers. At the same time, the constitution strengthened the political and legislative powers of Congress and attempted to correct its traditional vices. Specifically, it established strict eligibility requirements for candidates to Congress, abolished the congressional discretionary funds (*auxilios*) that had been a mainstay of broker clientelism, expanded the period of congressional sessions, prohibited the election of legislators to other public offices, and established a legislative motion of censure against cabinet members. Of particular note, the constitution established a single national electoral district for the election of the Senate with the aim of giving greater proportional representation to minority political and social movements. The 1991 Constitution also significantly transformed the judicial branch in an attempt to counter chronic problems of weakness, corruption, and lack of resources.[83] Not least, the 1991 Constitution introduced an extensive bill of citizen rights, along with a number of judicial mechanisms that citizens can employ to help protect these rights.

Despite the democratic character of the 1991 Constitution, a few notable lacunae are present. First, the National Constituent Assembly failed to undertake any significant reform of the country's armed forces. This failure reflected the unwillingness of the government or the Assembly delegates to provoke the military, as well as concern on the part of the M-19 delegates who feared for their future safety.[84] The new constitution thus maintains intact the existing system of military justice (*fuero militar*) that had encouraged human rights abuses in the past.

Second, the Assembly failed to enact a serious reform of the political party system. Most notably, the 1991 Constitution maintains the existing electoral procedure by which seats in representative bodies are allocated by *factional* lists, rather than by official *party* lists. This electoral procedure has helped to foster the extreme factionalism and clientelism characteristic of the political party system. Because parties do not control the use of the party label, any number of candidates can launch their own list for office in a given electoral district under the same party label. The result has been elections that are as much intraparty disputes as interparty contests. In order to maintain sufficient votes in this atmosphere of intense inter- and intraparty competition, each candidate attempts to construct a clientelistic network of supporters who will deliver votes in exchange for services, jobs, or cash. By failing to give political parties control over the formation of electoral lists, the National Constituent Assembly missed one of its best opportunities for squelching clientelism and fostering democratic reform.[85]

Following the enactment of the constitution, Congress was dissolved and new legislative elections were held in October 1991. However, Assembly delegates were prohibited from running as candidates in these elections, thus limiting the possibility of broad electoral gains by the non-traditional parties and movements. The October 1991 elections produced relatively limited renovation in the partisan composition of the legislature (see Table 5.1).

In spite of the dramatic changes promised (and in some respects realized) by the 1991 Constitution, democracy continued to deteriorate in Colombia over the 1990s. This was fundamentally due to the state's inability to bring an end to political violence and to control criminal violence. With regard to the guerrillas, Gaviria initially benefited from the fruits of the Barco administration's peace process with the M-19. In the aftermath of M-19's return to civilian life, the EPL and two smaller guerrilla movements, the PRT and Quintín Lame, entered into negotiations aimed at their demobilization. The possibility of participating in the National Constituent Assembly served as a concrete incentive for the reincorporation of these guerrilla movements. All three movements signed definitive peace accords with the Gaviria administration in 1991, turned in their arms, and were rewarded with seats in the National Constituent Assembly.

Negotiations with the remaining guerrilla movements (the significantly larger FARC and ELN, and a small dissident faction of the EPL) ultimately failed, in spite of a lengthy process of negotiations in Caracas, Venezuela (1991), and Tlaxcala, Mexico (1992). State-guerrilla conflict was as prevalent at the end of the Gaviria administration as at its beginning.[86]

Gaviria fared slightly better in his effort to resolve the problem of drug-related violence that had engulfed the Barco administration, although his policies were controversial and drug trafficking continued largely unabated. Soon after assuming office, Gaviria issued a series of decrees that guaranteed a reduced sentence and nonextradition to drug traffickers who turned themselves in and confessed to at least one crime. Although a handful of top drug traffickers took advantage of this policy, most key members of the Medellín cartel, including its leader, Pablo Escobar, refused to surrender to judicial authorities. Instead, the cartel carried out a number of kidnappings of prominent journalists in 1990 and 1991 to pressure the Gaviria administration to enact even more favorable policies.[87] With the passage of an article by the National Constituent Assembly that expressly prohibited extradition and the establishment of a special prison that accorded with his own specified security needs, Escobar and his top henchmen finally surrendered to Colombian authorities in June 1991.

The surrender proved to be an ephemeral victory for the Gaviria administration, since Escobar and his accomplices continued to engage in criminal activity from prison. Then it became an acute embarrassment, when, following the decision to transfer them to a more secure prison in July 1992, Escobar and nine of his men escaped. This reinitiated a period of drug-related violence that lasted until Escobar was finally killed by state security forces in December 1993. The Cali cartel, however, quickly took over the Medellín cartel's business and no appreciable reduction in drug trafficking occurred. Moreover, because of corruption, the infiltration of state security forces, and a relative lack of interest, the Gaviria administration made little headway toward dismantling the Cali cartel.[88]

The difficulties of the Gaviria administration in consolidating the democratic transformation contained in the 1991 Constitution and in regaining state coherence were compounded during the administration of his successor, Ernesto Samper. Samper was also from the Liberal Party, but he distanced himself from Gaviria's neoliberal policies, portraying himself instead as a social democrat. Samper entered the May 1994 presidential elections with the institutional support of a united Liberal Party, yet he found himself in an unexpectedly tight race with the Conservative candidate, Andrés Pastrana. The son of former president Misael Pastrana, Andrés Pastrana benefited from the positive image he had established as the first elected mayor of Bogotá. In a campaign largely devoid of ideological debates, Samper won a narrow victory over Pastrana in the first electoral round. However, because Samper did not garner an absolute majority of the votes, a runoff election was held one month later in which Samper defeated Pastrana by a paper-thin margin, winning 50.3 percent of the votes cast (see Table 5.1).

Soon after the elections, Samper became mired in a serious drug scandal that was to vex him for his entire presidential term, complicating efforts to consolidate the country's democratic transformation.[89] In the days following the runoff election, Pastrana charged the Samper campaign with accepting several million dollars from the Cali cartel. Although Samper rejected the accusation, mounting evidence led the Office of the General

Prosecutor to arrest his campaign treasurer in July 1995, who subsequently testified that the campaign had, in fact, received significant sums of money from the cartel, and that Samper had known of this arrangement. This testimony was later corroborated by Guillermo Pallomari, the Cali cartel's treasurer, who turned himself in to the U.S. Drug Enforcement Agency (DEA) in September 1995.

Samper strenuously denied all charges, declaring that if drug money *had* entered the campaign, it had done so without his knowledge. Despite the growing crisis, Samper was bolstered temporarily by the success of state security forces in dismantling the top leadership of the Cali cartel in mid-1995. The Accusations Committee of the Chamber of Representatives declared in December 1995 that it had not encountered sufficient evidence to open a formal criminal investigation against the president. The committee's finding was harshly criticized by Samper's domestic opponents as well as by the U.S. State Department. The scandal erupted again in January 1996, when Samper's former campaign manager testified that Samper did indeed have knowledge of the cartel funding. This revelation led to new criminal charges against Samper. After a second highly criticized congressional investigation, efforts to impeach Samper again failed in June 1996 by an exonerating vote of 111 to 43 in the Chamber of Representatives.

Although Samper ultimately retained his hold on the presidency, the drug scandal had numerous negative political repercussions. Several of Samper's cabinet ministers and ambassadors resigned, as did his vice-president, Humberto de la Calle. Moreover, the criminal investigation of illegal campaign funding was quickly expanded to include some seventeen members of Congress, as well as the procurator general and the comptroller. At the same time, there were credible charges that Samper had distributed generous state resources among legislators to ensure their support for him in the criminal investigations. Indeed, by the end of the Samper administration, it was clear that, despite the 1991 Constitution, the Colombian political regime was mired in a severe crisis of political legitimacy.

Throughout the drug scandal, the United States maintained constant pressure on the Samper administration to crack down on drug trafficking.[90] This was revealed most clearly in the 1996 and 1997 decisions by the Clinton administration to "decertify" Colombia in the annual review of international cooperation with the United States in its war on drugs. A more personal rebuke was contained in the State Department's 1996 cancellation of Samper's visa to the United States. However, this approach had contradictory effects: although it encouraged the Samper administration to act more decisively against drug trafficking, it also provoked angry charges of U.S. intervention in Colombian internal affairs and encouraged some Colombians to rally to the defense of Samper. From the Clinton administration's perspective, significant gains were achieved as the result of such pressure. In addition to the dismantling of the top leadership of the Cali cartel, the Colombian Congress eventually passed legislation strengthening penalties for drug trafficking and allowing the retroactive confiscation of drug traffickers' properties, as well as a 1997 constitutional amendment that reinstated the extradition of Colombian citizens. In 1998, concerned that a new decertification would further erode U.S.-Colombian relations and help Horacio Serpa, the Liberal candidate in the presidential election and a close ally of Samper, the United States proceeded to waive decertification on national-security grounds.

Even as the Samper administration was crippled by the drug scandal, it failed to show significant progress in dealing with the country's guerrilla movements.[91] Instead, the guerrilla movements continued to profit from their control over coca-growing or oil-rich parts of the country and to further expand their territorial presence in the country, as many Colombians despaired as to whether the guerrillas saw peace negotiations to be in their interests. Indeed, the expansion of the guerrilla movements in the preceding decade had been significant: whereas in 1985 guerrillas were present in 173 municipalities, by 1995 they were in 622 municipalities (of approximately 1,050 municipalities).[92] The military capacity of the guerrillas was demonstrated in August 1996 when they successfully attacked the army base of Las Delicias in Putumayo, killing several dozen military personnel, taking sixty soldiers hostage, and capturing all of the base's weaponry. The soldiers were only released in June 1997 after the Samper administration agreed to withdraw the armed forces temporarily from a 13,000-square-kilometer region in the department of Caquetá, thus assuring safety to the guerrillas during the handover.

In the face of the continued militancy of the guerrilla movements, the strategy of the Samper administration evolved away from its early emphasis on dialogue toward an effort to strengthen the armed forces, declare special zones of public order under military rule, and establish rural security cooperatives meant to function as local self-defense groups. Critics soon charged these local cooperatives, known as Convivir, with paramilitary violence. Whatever the participation of the Convivir, there is no question that paramilitary violence increased significantly during the Samper administration, often with the acquiescence of the armed forces, who failed to take decisive action against paramilitary groups. Between October 1995 and September 1996, paramilitary groups were responsible for 655 deaths, 96 disappearances, and the torture of 108 individuals. Moreover, the percentage of the country's political homicides committed by paramilitary groups (in cases for which authorship has been determined) increased from 17.9% in 1993 to 62.7% in 1996.[93] This was occurring in a country whose overall homicide rate had roughly quadrupled from the early 1970s to the early 1990s (from some 4,000 homicides and a rate of around 20 per 100,000 to some 25,000 homicides and a rate of around 80 per 100,000), making it one of the highest in the region and the world.[94]

The decline in the country's economy, the continued violence, and the sense of paralysis and drift that characterized the Samper administration ultimately had an effect in the electoral arena and on the Liberal Party. In the first round of the presidential elections in 1998, Liberal candidate Horacio Serpa received the lowest-percentage vote (34.4 percent) a candidate of his party had received since the 1946 election, when the poor record was due to the presence of two Liberal candidates; this time, however, the Conservative Andrés Pastrana (not officially a candidate of the party) obtained almost the same vote, and Noemí Sanín, a former Conservative running as an independent, captured a surprising 26.5 percent of the vote; in the second round, Pastrana edged out Serpa (Table 5.1). Although historical trends of Liberal dominance continued to be reflected in the congressional results (Table 5.2), these disguised the continued organizational decay of the party, even as the Conservative Party further declined as a variety of independent movements and candidates continued to score greater success; all of these trends promise to complicate Pastrana's relationship with Congress.

Pastrana immediately embarked upon an ambitious plan of negotiations with the guerrillas, with strong support from elements within Colombian civil society and from multiple international actors, even as he sought to repair the country's relations with the United States. Whether this would mark only another parenthesis in the deadly spiral of violence and decline the country had been experiencing or, at last, the beginning of a process that would enable the state to regain coherence and lead the country toward a more democratic and more peaceful future remained to be seen.

THEORETICAL ANALYSIS

Colombia combines a long history of civilian, republican rule with tremendous violence and continuing inequalities. This chapter has argued that the relative success or failure of democratic politics at different junctures has depended particularly on the ability of political structures to adapt or democratize in the face of changing social realities. Thus, particular emphasis has been placed on the party system, the political structure, and state structures associated with the construction and maintenance of a coherent state and a democratic rule of law. These structures, in turn, have interacted in crucial ways with major social actors, including producer groups, drug traffickers, and guerrilla movements. Especially in times of crisis, political leadership can play a critical role, and in some instances it appears to have aided the country and in others to have had the opposite consequence. Issues related to the country's development performance and international factors, and features of political culture, have also affected the country's experience with democratic politics.

Party System and Political Structure

Colombia's single most dominant political feature has been its two-party system. As a consequence of how they evolved following independence and a series of bloody civil wars, the two traditional parties from the nineteenth century became "subcultures" in Colombian society. They divided the population but facilitated national integration, impeded the emergence of a strong military institution, and were able to incorporate new social groups and movements into the twentieth century, inhibiting class polarization. When they accommodated each other, democracy of an oligarchical or limited consociational sort prospered; when they did not, political tensions escalated, and bloody conflict often resulted.

As argued above, the consociational elements of the National Front agreement appeared necessary for a return to civilian rule in 1958, following *la violencia*. The rigid National Front agreement, though, reflected not only concerns over rekindling party violence but a more general fear of mass mobilization. At the same time, its complex mutual guarantees practically assured governmental immobilism, forcing crisis decisionmaking and limiting the possibilities for political change and social reform.

Both the regime structure and societal change blurred party divisions and conflicts. Although the National Front rested on the country's two traditional parties, it had features of both a one-party and a multiparty system. Through the 1970 election, presidential alternation required both parties to agree on an official National Front candidate, which made the regime appear to be based upon a single party with hegemonic aspirations. There was no way to express interparty dissent by "voting the rascals out," and each election became in effect a new plebiscite on the National Front. At the same time, party factionalism forced each president to create and re-create an effective governing coalition, making the National Front period resemble a multiparty system. Thus, in these years most of the remaining distinctions between the parties became blurred.

The country's massive urbanization, dramatic improvements in levels of education, and changes in the workforce also decreased the centrality of the two traditional parties. In spite of the continued electoral dominance of the two parties, population-wide identification with either of them began to decline; an independent electorate began to emerge. Most important, frustrated by the strictures of coalition politics, opposition increasingly came to express itself outside of electoral channels. The apparent electoral successes of the two traditional parties masked their organizational and leadership weaknesses, and they were reluctant to move beyond coalition rule even though the social realities that initially required it had changed.

Although the 1991 Constitution formally terminated consociational rule in Colombia, the traditional parties maintained their electoral dominance. Yet, though the 1998 election continued a trend of decline in this dominance in the face of emerging independent movements and parties, many of which also showed tendencies toward organizational weakness and factionalism. The strength of the traditional parties has rested on the increasingly more tenuous logic of broker clientelism in contexts of high abstention. The new constitution did not adequately counter broker clientelism, particularly because it continued to permit parties to present multiple lists and also failed to give party leaders control over the formation of these lists.

Presidentialism, Centralization, and Broker Clientelism

The 1886 Constitution provided for a strongly presidentialist and centralized system of governance. Presidential powers increased even more during the National Front years as a way of circumventing the immobilism generated by the requirements of parity and two-thirds majority vote, and as a consequence of the growing importance of the state in the economy. Presidents were also strong as a consequence of the centralized nature of government. The process of decentralization begun in the 1980s, together with reforms contained in the 1991 Constitution, have placed important limits on the centralized powers of the presidency. Significant state resources have been channeled to the departments and municipalities. Moreover, departmental governors, once appointed by the president, are now popularly elected, as are municipal mayors, who were previously appointed by the governors. The constitution also reduced the president's nominating powers, weakened some of the president's traditional legislative powers, introduced a legislative check on the executive through a "motion of censure" against cabinet officers, and placed strictures on the president's emergency powers.

Nonetheless, the executive retains control over the central budget, with Congress having only the ability to reduce or eliminate budget appropriations proposed by the president. The central budget continues to be significant, even with the process of decentralization, thus giving the president the power to utilize state resources to build coalitions in support of executive policies. For example, although the 1991 Constitution eliminated congressional discretionary funds that were often used for clientelistic purposes, these have been resurrected in a new form.[95]

The state resources controlled by the executive have thus provided added incentive for broker clientelism, particularly given the characteristics of Colombia's current two-party system. The traditional parties have increasingly lost ideological or programmatic content and are dominated by regional politicians with almost exclusively brokerage and clientelist motivations. For these politicians, access to patronage, which has meant positive relations with the executive, is viewed as critical, particularly in the context of high-abstention elections in which small numbers of voters could spell the difference between victory and defeat. At the same time, in this context decentralization has frequently enhanced clientelism, corruption, and inefficiency.[96]

Although the 1991 Constitution formally ended the period of consociational rule in Colombia, broker clientelism has ensured the dominance of the traditional parties in the executive and legislative branches. Opposition parties and movements have found it difficult to make inroads, given the quantity of state resources monopolized by the traditional parties. Informal bipartisan rule is thus likely to continue unless more vigorous efforts are made to assure alternative political forces access to power at the local level and adequate representation at the national level. Complicating any such effort, though, has been a dramatic decline in state coherence and state capacity.

State Structure

Historically, the Colombian state has been relatively weak. In the nineteenth century, this was partially a consequence of the early consolidation and power of the two traditional parties. In the twentieth century, the role of the Colombian state in industrialization was limited, as was also true in other Latin American countries where initial export-led growth and incorporation into the world market occurred by means of a product that was nationally controlled.[97] This limited state role, combined with the low level of agricultural-industrial conflict, facilitated the initial incorporation of the working class through party rather than state ties, attenuating the country's experience with populism.[98] At the same time, the traditional parties continued to rely heavily on clientelist ties to secure support, especially in rural areas.

However, the role of the state changed partially during the National Front period. With the assistance of international agencies and the U.S. government, the state's economic and technical capacities increased substantially. At the same time, though, a complex labyrinth of legal requirements on state action evolved, and state employees came to be organized by labor associations hostile to the regime. In addition, the armed forces became more professionalized and developed a corporate identity distinct from the two traditional parties. The military has been strongly anti-communist and has opposed many successive peace initiatives as excessively generous. Although decades of direct conflict with guerrilla groups have led some in the armed forces to believe that a purely military solution to the guerrilla problem is probably not viable, such officers are in the minority, particularly given the increased belligerence of the guerrilla movements in the 1990s and the concomitant growth in the size of the armed forces. The institution of a civilian minister of defense during the Gaviria administration does not appear to have weakened notably the relative autonomy of the armed forces within the state. At the same time, during the early 1990s the struggle against the guerrillas was being carried out increasingly by paramilitary forces that the armed forces do not control.[99]

The institutional capacities of the judiciary, local governments, the electoral system, and Congress have lagged tremendously behind the state's technical, economic, and repressive agencies; impunity has been increasingly the norm in the country as the rule of law has further suffered. The combination of their deterioration and the excessively long retention of coalition rule, along with deleterious effects of international drug trafficking, guerrilla activities, and criminal violence, dramatically reduced state coherence in the 1980s and early 1990s, exacerbating the crisis of political legitimacy and opening the way for the 1991 National Constituent Assembly. Despite the efforts of the Assembly delegates to introduce needed institutional reforms, subsequent years have shown that the new constitution alone has proven inadequate to revive state capacity. Indeed, certain efforts to strengthen the state, such as the establishment of special courts (Justicia Regional) with anonymous "faceless" judges (*jueces sin rostro*) or the enhanced scope for military justice, have weakened efforts to build democratic institutions.[100]

In particular, the judicial system remains extremely inefficient and congested, with criminal investigations and convictions largely paralyzed. Although the Medellín and Cali cartels have been dismantled, drug trafficking continues unabated as new organizations have stepped in to fill the void. The corruption engendered by drug trafficking has been felt throughout all parts of the Colombian state and society. In the 1990s, drug-related corruption had clearly reached the upper echelons of politics as evidenced by the Samper drug scandal and the investigation and arrest of several legislators on charges of drug-financed political activity. The extensiveness of this corruption weakened still further the precarious political legitimacy of Congress, thus undermining the proposed legislative renewal of the 1991 Constitution.

Consolidating the democratic transformation of the political regime will only be possible if state coherence is regained and state capacity augmented. Yet, this will require, at the very least, not only reductions in the levels of political violence and the activities of guerrilla organizations, but also subordination of the military to civilian rule, a more effective judiciary, the consolidation of the fragmented political party system, firmer electoral oversight, and the exercise of effective and visionary presidential leadership.

Producer Groups and the Media

If the Colombian state has been weak, organized societal interests have also tended to be weak, though the capabilities of producer associations have extended far beyond those of working-class or peasant associations.

Reflecting the country's relatively late integration into the world market, and its somewhat delayed industrialization compared to other major Latin American countries, most producer associations in Colombia have been formed fairly recently, since the 1940s. In the 1990s the major producer associations joined together to form a single peak association, the Consejo Gremial, to represent private-sector interests. However, the relative weakness of this association became apparent during the Samper administration, when the Consejo was unable to establish a cohesive and consistent position with regard to the drug scandal. Moreover, the relative power of the producer associations appears to have been challenged in recent years by the influence of large economic conglomerates owned by national capitalists such as Julio Mario Santo Domingo, Carlos Ardilla Lulle, and Luis Carlos Sarmiento Angulo.

Producer associations have generally supported civilian rule. As a consequence of the heterogeneity of the two traditional parties, all major producer associations have been bipartisan in makeup, often carefully balancing partisan and regional representation on their boards of directors. The establishment of the National Front was facilitated by the support of industrialists, bankers, and merchants. They perceived that return to civilian rule would assure them greater access and policy influence than had been the case with the military regime, and their interest associations continued to play a supportive role in moments of crisis. In fact, because of its bipartisan nature, coalition rule increased channels of access for producer groups even as it fragmented power across party factions, particularly in periods of a weak presidency. Both Gaviria's economic opening and Samper's drug scandal revealed significant divisions among the producer groups, as well as differential access to key policymakers. Nonetheless, given their overall access to policy circles and the regime's general policy orientation, producer associations have remained supportive of civilian rule.

Historically, the country's major newspapers have also supported civilian rule, in part because they have had a clear partisan and sometimes factional identification. Because of interfactional disputes, the newspapers have sometimes provided a glimpse of the country's "invisible politics," but by and large, they have remained supportive of the National Front system, indulged in very little serious investigative reporting, and largely ignored the activities of opposition figures. The directors of the major dailies have also provided discreet behind-the-scenes communications links within their own parties or sometimes between the parties in efforts to settle political crises. This began to change in the past several decades, and, on occasion, the newspapers have taken more risky positions. For example, *El Espectador*'s valiant campaign against the drug cartels in the 1980s resulted in both the assassination of its director and the destruction of its headquarters by a car bomb. Additionally, in 1990 the major Bogotá dailies gave critical support and publicity to the student movement's call for a

National Constituent Assembly. Moreover, in recent years, journalists have reported more widely on the activities and views of guerrilla and other opposition figures, though often in the face of government hostility. Those who have reported on drug trafficking have been primary targets of intimidation and assassination. This has severely impaired press freedom and integrity.

Class Structure and the Popular Sector

Colombia has sharp disparities of wealth and income across population groups and regions. These especially affect its relatively small black and Indian populations, and as in other less developed countries, the most serious poverty is found in rural areas. Despite various land-reform laws, the concentration of land ownership remains extremely high in Colombia, a problem that was further exacerbated in the 1980s as the country's drug traffickers purchased huge tracts of land. As reported in Table 1.1, of the countries discussed in this volume, Colombia had the highest percentage of its population living in conditions of extreme poverty (around 25 percent in 1994) and (with Brazil) the most unequal income distribution ratios.[101]

Class differences, as already noted, have not been reflected in the party system because of the historic capability of the traditional parties to incorporate new social groups. From the beginning, the National Front agreement was viewed as a means of mass demobilization, even as the parties sought partial mobilization of their electorate at election time. The avoidance of extreme populist or neoliberal economic policies may also have mitigated mobilization around class divisions. There were ambivalent and only partially successful efforts at state-sponsored organization of the lower classes (corporatism). Attempts at autonomy and greater coordination by popular-sector organizations were met with "divide and conquer" strategies (as noted above in the case of the peasant association, ANUC). This appeared to reflect concern about the potential autonomous capabilities of mass organizations.

From the late 1970s to the present, the parties have lacked substantial links to mass organizations in contrast to the close ties they had had in the early days of the labor organizations. In these more recent years, a sense of political blockage has led many popular-sector groups to seek nonelectoral channels to express their views. Although still only a small percentage of the country's total workforce, organized labor is now somewhat more unified, and civic movements and neighborhood associations are also somewhat stronger than in previous years. Over the past decade, a more conscious set of movements within a self-identified "civil society" has also begun to emerge. All these groups represent the potential for contributing to a lasting peace process, to the strengthening of a more coherent and democratic state, and to the democratic transformation of the regime; however, to a certain extent they also reflect and could give further impulse to tendencies to fragment and weaken effective movements for change. Whether they will be met by accommodation or by repression by the various actors who perceive they have more to gain from continued violence is far from clear. What does seem clear is that democratic consolidation is highly implausible without some reduction in class disparities.

Political Culture

The impact of political culture on regime type has probably not been very large, and its legacy is ambiguous. Both violence and accommodation have strong historical antecedents in the country, and thus both have significant "cultural carriers" and are available as "options" for core groups at critical moments. There may well be guerrillas whose parents fought in the days of *la violencia,* and whose grandparents, in turn, were active in the turn-of-the-century War of the Thousand Days.[102] This "culture of violence" is certainly inimical to democratic politics, though it also means that since violence has been employed so indiscriminately for such differing objectives, it has been difficult for revolutionary movements to link their use of it to their particular political objectives. In the recent past, the drug trade has almost certainly heightened levels of cynicism, corruption, resentment, loss of trust in public institutions, and declines in social solidarity. At the same time, many individuals with bloody family legacies have not turned to violence, and over the past decade more and more groups have organized in society to promote peace.

Elitist class distinctions and family background continue to play a role in society and in politics, albeit a declining one. The 1974 presidential election, for example, was between the sons of two former presidents (López and Gómez) and the daughter of General Rojas. In 1998, Andrés Pastrana, the son of the Conservative president who oversaw those 1974 elections, gained the presidency. Upward mobility, though, is not unknown (President Betancur is a recent example). One consequence of drug trafficking has been to create a new power group, though its violent tactics and the concentration of wealth in such a small number of people sets it apart from the emergence of coffee, industrial, or other influential groups earlier in the country's history.

If societal culture is elitist, it has also been civilian, republican, and *machista.* Political parties and elections gained early legitimacy, and military governments have been few and disappointing. Party appeals rested strongly on clientelist ties that built upon unequal social structures and weak popular-sector organizations. Major producer groups have not been predisposed to jettison democratic rights, which they recognize have given them considerable access to policymaking circles. Yet, as the conspiratorial activities of some regional economic groups in conjunction with paramilitary squads, and the advocacy by others of "military" solutions to guerrilla and popular-sector mobilization indicate, support for democracy is still more instrumental than entrenched across all elements of this crucial group. Among many intellectual groups, influenced both by the country's horrible history of violence without radical social change and by the experience with bureaucratic-authoritarian regimes of the Southern Cone countries, there is strong advocacy of democratic rights as well as of socioeconomic reforms.[103] In many ways, the National Constituent Assembly ratified these democratic aspirations in the 1991 Constitution.

Ultimately more important than an ambiguous cultural legacy in determining the evolution of democracy in the country have been the concrete actions of political leaders and other major actors in society in specific structural contexts.

Leadership and Statecraft

The role of political leadership and statecraft in putting together the original National Front agreement in 1957 and 1958 was critical to its success. One could argue there had been "political learning" from the earlier failures to compromise that had led to *la violencia*. The change in behavior and in attitude of major political leaders and church officials was significant. At the same time, the structure of incentives for compromise was much stronger in the 1950s than it had been some ten years earlier, and this undoubtedly facilitated agreement. Furthermore, fear of uncontrollable popular mobilization (stemming initially from the experience of *la violencia*), the extremely limited role of popular groups in the transition to civilian rule, and the rigid nature of the National Front agreement all discouraged greater political incorporation of the population.

In recent years, statecraft has played a key role in crafting the agreements that led to the election of the National Constituent Assembly and the successful drafting of the 1991 Constitution. President Gaviria skillfully negotiated with the leadership of the major parties and political movements to ensure agreement on the structure and functioning of the Assembly, as well as on such controversial decisions as the dissolution of Congress and the calling of new legislative elections. Although these political negotiations were far more inclusive than the bipartisan pact-making that established the National Front, they were still criticized for not including all interested parties.

More recently, though, the political leadership required to consolidate the country's democratic transformation has been lacking. The Samper administration dedicated most of its energies to preventing the president's removal from office. Although Samper exhibited a rare degree of wiliness, his political maneuvering did nothing to further the democratic transformation of Colombian politics. Indeed, what has been clear to date is the continuing ability of traditional politicians to rely on existing political institutions—and at times targeted violence—to delay political reform, or if enacted, to thwart or obstruct its effective implementation.

Development Performance and International Factors

Not graced by the natural wealth of neighboring Venezuela, Colombia has traditionally pursued an eclectic mix of import substitution and export-promotion strategies, facilitated by a diversified natural resource base. This strategy was superseded somewhat by a significant economic opening in the early years of the 1990s. Overall, however, its prudent, "moderate," relatively consistent economic policies, controlling inflation and fiscal deficits, have permitted the country to achieve steady economic growth rates, maintained support for the regime among principal economic actors, and helped preclude political cycles of democratic populism followed by military repression. Nevertheless, the country's satisfactory growth record did not generate the kind of economic surpluses for the state that could have facilitated agrarian reform or economic benefits for amnestied guerrillas, as occurred, for example, in Venezuela. In fact, Colombia still suffers from widespread poverty and wealth disparities.

In the early 1980s, Colombia was affected by the international recession, climbing world interest rates, and sharp retrenchment of commercial-bank lending that sunk Latin America into deep financial crisis. The impact of the debt crisis was felt in Colombia somewhat later and to a lesser extent, in part because the country was prudent in its borrowing in the late 1970s. Yet, the country was forced to introduce an economic stabilization program in the mid-1980s, which placed unfortunate limitations on President Betancur's peace process. By the latter half of the 1980s, the Colombian economy began to recover, fueled by a coffee bonanza and the increased sales of coal and oil.

In the 1990s the Barco and Gaviria administrations opened the Colombian economy to greater international competition by reducing the protective barriers that shielded national producers. The Barco administration intended the economic opening to be a gradual process, but it was accelerated significantly by Gaviria in 1990 and 1991. The opening required significant adjustments by Colombian producers; however, the immediate economic effects were not nearly as traumatic as those experienced by other Latin American countries.

The Samper administration, clearly less neoliberal in orientation than the Gaviria administration, instituted a pause in the process of economic liberalization. Although rhetorically Samper acknowledged the need for an economic opening, he was partisan to a more gradual process that would be cushioned by greater social spending. Whatever the merits of such a position, economic growth declined during the Samper administration and the economy entered into recession in late 1996. Economic recovery was complicated by a high fiscal deficit and the weakening of investor confidence that stemmed from concerns over the ongoing drug scandal.

Colombia's boom in the export of cocaine and then increasingly heroin to the U.S. market would appear, on balance, not to have been beneficial. Initially accepted for its generation of foreign exchange (and to a lesser extent employment), the narcotics traffic has dramatically weakened the state as it brought violence, corruption, confrontations with the United States, and a growing drug-consumption problem in Colombia. U.S. agencies combating the drug problem, constrained domestically by civil liberties and environmental considerations, have "exported" their efforts to producing countries, which often have neither the state capacity nor the resources to address the problem effectively (notwithstanding U.S. pressure).

Particularly during the Samper administration, U.S.-Colombian relations became almost completely "narcotized" as the United States demanded ever more stringent measures from a government that it clearly distrusted. The successive decertifications of Colombia for its perceived laxity in the drug war, combined with the revocation of President Samper's visa, brought relations to their lowest level in the second half of the twentieth century. U.S. concern was not without merit, given the penetration of drug-related corruption into the highest levels of the political system. Nevertheless, the single-minded U.S. policy of supply reduction generated intense resentment in the country, not only because Colombians felt that they were unjustly shedding blood for a struggle that stemmed from U.S. drug abuse and addiction, but also because of the evident failure of repressive policies to stop drug production and shipment. In late 1998, many Colombians feared that a single-minded U.S. focus on narcotics could potentially derail the Pastrana administration's efforts to launch a new peace process.

FUTURE PROSPECTS

The Colombian state is currently under challenge and the country's political regime is in the midst of an uncertain democratic transformation. The 1991 Constitution marked the formal end to consociational rule, but the consolidation of a more open, democratic regime has yet to take place. Early hopes that the new constitution would be a panacea for the country's myriad problems have proven unfounded. Although the constitution contains significant democratic measures, its effects have been limited by the continued violence and impunity from criminal prosecution; by electoral dominance of the traditional parties; by the lack of an effective political opposition; by widespread political corruption, often linked to drug money;

and by the weakness and inefficiency of state institutions, particularly the judiciary. These factors have meant that the crisis of political legitimacy that gave rise to the 1991 Constitution has not been resolved. Indeed, it took on a new form, exacerbated by the Samper drug scandal, which further undermined public trust in the executive and legislative branches while encouraging the guerrilla movements in their pursuit of power through armed struggle. Whether President Pastrana, whose term began in August 1998, can break this vicious cycle remains to be seen.

The consolidation of Colombian democracy requires greater state cohesion and capacity, channeled by a democratic regime. Thus, it depends to a significant degree on political factors. Among the most important of these is the strengthening and reconfiguration of the political party system. The current system of fragmented political parties encourages broker clientelism, which in turns hinders the ability of opposition parties and movements to achieve elected office. Although consociational rule has formally ended, in practice Liberal and Conservative politicians continue to dominate the electoral realm and to control state resources.

Of the crucial state reforms required, probably none is more important than improvement in the efficacy of the judicial system to ensure that the perpetrators of political violence do not continue to enjoy impunity. Likewise, there must be firm civilian control over the armed forces and an end to any type of military aid for, or acquiescence in, the activities of paramilitary groups.

The possibility of democratic consolidation is weakened by the presence of drug trafficking. Even if drug traffickers do not engage in the type of political violence employed by the Medellín cartel in the late 1980s and early 1990s, the immense profits generated by the drug trade can give traffickers powerful influence over cash-strapped regional and national politicians. The negative political, economic, and international effects of a political system permeated by drug money were only too well illustrated during the Samper administration.

Likewise, democratic consolidation will remain uncertain as long as guerrilla and paramilitary violence continues. It may appear paradoxical that a country that has become increasingly urban has had such a sustained, and even growing, guerrilla movement predominantly in rural areas. This is a reflection of the poor reach of the state, the growing inefficacy of clientelist ties, the severity of social inequities, and, probably most important in recent years given this context, the extensive resources (coca and oil) found in these rural areas. Given the longevity of the Colombian guerrilla movements and their organic support in certain regions of the country, it is questionable whether they will be willing to negotiate a transition to civilian political opposition anytime in the near future unless they receive considerable concessions. For their part, the paramilitary groups, with or without the military's support and acquiescence, are likely to continue to operate as long as the guerrilla movements are involved in armed struggle. A lasting resolution of the political violence must thus be comprehensive in nature.

On the brink of the twenty-first century, the democratic future of the Colombian political regime remains unclear. Beset by corruption and violence, the prospects for democratic consolidation appear limited. For the longer term, however, there are grounds to hope that the foundations of a consolidated democracy are being laid. The 1991 Constitution is a significant step toward a more democratic polity. The democratic mechanisms contained in the new constitution have yet to be fully utilized by political movements and organizations in civil society that are seeking change. Growing international awareness of the extreme human rights situation in the country may also help to pressure all of the involved actors toward a negotiated political solution. The economic underpinnings of the country appear solid. There is recognition within the country that state strengthening must enhance democratic controls rather than weaken them. Skillful political leadership, which Colombian elites have often demonstrated in the past, in combination with a favorable structural context, may allow for democratic consolidation to occur in a generation. Whether, and how, such a scenario plays itself out is currently being decided.

NOTES

1. See "La supercrisis," *Análisis político,* no. 8 (Sept.-Dec., 1989): 67–88.

2. For a discussion of the state and of the rule of law as crucial components for democratic consolidation, see Juan J. Linz and Alfred Stepan, *Problems of Democratic Transition and Consolidation: Southern Europe, South America and Post-Communist Europe* (Baltimore: Johns Hopkins University Press, 1997); and Guillermo O'Donnell, "Polyarchies and the (Un)rule of Law in Latin America," in Juan Méndez, Guillermo O'Donnell, and Paulo Sérgio Pinheiro, eds., *The (Un)Rule of Law and the Underprivileged in Latin America* (Notre Dame, IN: University of Notre Dame Press, 1999).

3. See, for example, the concluding work and many of the articles in Guillermo O'Donnell, Philippe C. Schmitter, and Laurence Whitehead, eds., *Transitions from Authoritarian Rule* (Baltimore: Johns Hopkins University Press, 1986).

4. This is not to deny that one of the more robust statistical findings remains the positive relationship between level of economic development and political democracy. It is only to suggest that, though the social conditions associated with a certain minimum level of economic development may be necessary for political democracy, they are hardly sufficient. We are required to consider more interactive and political processes.

Because there appear to be a number of possible routes to democracy and so many various factors that may impinge on the possibilities of its emergence and consolidation, the absence of one or more of these factors may in part be overcome or "compensated" for by the presence of others. Thus, the search for a *single* rank-ordering of variables or factors is probably wrongheaded. In addition, if enough cases emerge with successful or relatively successful democratic experiences, even though they have the "wrong" cultural, socioeconomic, or class-structure profiles, then the nature of those arguments must be qualified and additional or other factors considered. Colombia would appear to be one such case.

5. In its central approach and for many of its specific arguments, this chapter borrows liberally from Jonathan Hartlyn, *The Politics of Coalition Rule in Colombia* (Cambridge: Cambridge University Press, 1988). Other more recent book-length analyses of Colombia in English include John D. Martz, *The Politics of Clientelism: Democracy and the State in*

Colombia (New Brunswick, NJ: Transaction Publishers, 1997); Harvey F. Kline, Colombia: Democracy Under Assault, 2d ed. (Boulder, CO: Westview, 1995); and David Bushnell, The Making of Modern Colombia (Berkeley: University of California Press, 1993).

6. The state of siege was usually invoked during the National Front and post–National Front years to address student protests, labor demonstrations, or guerrilla violence. However, especially in the 1960s, it was often retained not so much to restrict civil liberties but to provide the president with special decree powers to circumvent congressional immobilism.

7. Miles Williams, "El Frente Nacional: Colombia's Experiment in Controlled Democracy" (Ph.D. diss., Vanderbilt University, 1976); and Bruce M. Bagley, "Political Power, Public Policy and the State in Colombia: Case Studies of the Urban and Agrarian Reforms During the National Front, 1958–1974" (Ph.D. diss., University of California at Los Angeles, 1979).

8. Alexander W. Wilde, "Conversations Among Gentlemen: Oligarchical Democracy in Colombia," in Juan Linz and Alfred Stepan, eds., The Breakdown of Democratic Regimes: Latin America (Baltimore: Johns Hopkins University Press, 1978), pp. 28–81.

9. Fernando Henrique Cardoso and Enzo Faletto, Dependency and Development in Latin America (Berkeley: University of California Press, 1979), p. 179.

10. Robert A. Dahl, Polyarchy: Participation and Opposition (New Haven: Yale University Press, 1971), p. 84.

11. Francisco Leal Buitrago, Estado y política en Colombia (Bogotá: Siglo XXI, 1984).

12. Bruce M. Bagley, "National Front and Economic Development," in Robert Wesson, ed., Politics, Policies and Economic Development in Latin America (Stanford, CA: Hoover Institution, 1984), pp. 124–160.

13. Samuel P. Huntington and Clement H. Moore, eds., Authoritarian Politics in Modern Society (New York: Basic Books, 1970).

14. See Marc W. Chernick, "Negotiations and Armed Conflict: A Study of the Colombian Peace Process (1982–1987)," paper presented to the 13th International Congress of the Latin American Studies Association, 1988.

15. Andrés Dávila Ladrón de Guevara, "Democracia pactada: El Frente Nacional y el Proceso Constituyente de 1991 en Colombia" (Ph.D. diss., FLACSO, Mexico, D.F., 1997).

16. Arend Lijphart coined the term "consociational democracy" to describe the politics of countries such as the Netherlands in which actual or potential violence between major societal segments was avoided within an open political regime by means of overarching elite cooperation. See Arend Lijphart, "Consociational Democracy," World Politics 21 (January 1969): 207–225; Arend Lijphart, Democracy in Plural Societies: A Comparative Exploration (New Haven: Yale University Press, 1977); and Eric Nordlinger, Conflict Regulation in Divided Societies, Occasional Papers in International Affairs no. 29 (Cambridge, MA: Center for International Affairs, Harvard University, January 1972). See also Robert H. Dix, "Consociational Democracy: The Case of Colombia," Comparative Politics 12 (April 1980): 303–321.

17. Issues of conceptualization of the "state" and the "political regime" are complex and cannot be resolved here. In one sense, a political regime may be viewed as a concrete manifestation of a state. It refers to the structures of governmental rules and processes, including such issues as the basis for legitimacy of rule, patterns of leadership recruitment, mechanisms of representation, and forms and scope of domination and control; see David Collier, ed., The New Authoritarianism in Latin America (Princeton: Princeton University Press, 1979), pp. 402–403. The state is a more general and abstract concept involving a compulsory association that claims control over territory and the people within it; see Theda Skocpol, "Bringing the State Back In: Strategies of Analysis in Current Research," in Peter B. Evans, Dietrich Rueschemeyer, and Theda Skocpol, eds., Bringing the State Back In (Cambridge: Cambridge University Press, 1985), pp. 3–37. For additional conceptual discussions of the state and articulation of the argument—relevant to contemporary Colombia—that "[d]emocracy requires statehood" (p. 19), see Linz and Stepan, Problems of Democratic Transition, pp. 7–37.

18. See David Bushnell, "Bolivarismo y Santanderismo," in David Bushnell, ed., Política y sociedad en el siglo XX, Lecturas de Historia no. 3 (Tunja: Ediciones Pato Marino, 1975); for electoral statistics of this early period, see David Bushnell, "Elecciones presidenciales colombianas 1825–1856," in Miguel Urrutia and Mario Arrubla, eds., Compendio de estadísticas históricas de Colombia (Bogotá: Universidad Nacional de Colombia, Dirección de Divulgación Cultural, 1970).

19. The western half of Colombia is traversed by three Andean mountain ranges, but the country's highest peaks are located off the Caribbean coast in the Sierra Nevada. South and east from the eastern highlands (*llanos orientales*) are the relatively unpopulated Amazon territories.

20. See Alvaro Tirado Mejía, "Colombia: Siglo y medio de bipartidismo," in *Colombia: Hoy* (Bogotá: Siglo XXI, 1978), pp. 102–130; and Robert H. Dix, *Colombia: The Political Dimensions of Change* (New Haven: Yale University Press, 1967), pp. 231–255.

21. See J. Mark Ruhl, "The Military," in Albert Berry, Ronald Hellman, and Mauricio Solaún, eds., *Politics of Compromise: Coalition Government in Colombia* (New Brunswick, NJ: Transaction Books, 1980), pp. 181–206, especially p. 182; James L. Payne, *Patterns of Conflict in Colombia* (New Haven: Yale University Press), pp. 111–133; and Leal, *Estado y política*.

22. Paul Oquist, *Violence, Conflict and Politics in Colombia* (New York: Academic Press, 1980), pp. 21–88; certain dates have been modified in accordance with more customary Colombian historiography, discussed in Helen Delpar, *Red Against Blue: The Liberal Party in Colombian Politics 1863–1899* (University: University of Alabama Press, 1981). Casualty figures are from Payne, *Patterns of Conflict*, p. 4.

23. For a complete compilation and analysis of nineteenth-century Colombian constitutions, including the 1863 Constitution, see Diego Uribe Vargas, *Las Constituciones de Colombia*, vols. 1 and 2 (Madrid: Ediciones Cultura Hispánica, 1977). English translations of earlier ones may be found in William Marion Gibson, *The Constitutions of Colombia* (Durham, NC: Duke University Press, 1948). On constitutional procedures and elections, see Delpar, *Red Against Blue*, pp. 15, 96; on the economy, see William P. McGreevey, *An Economic History of Colombia 1845–1930* (New York: Cambridge University Press, 1971).

24. See Delpar, *Red Against Blue*, p. xi.

25. Ibid., pp. 188–189.

26. Christopher Abel, "Conservative Party in Colombia, 1930–1953" (Ph.D. diss., University of Oxford, 1974).

27. Wilde, "Conversations Among Gentlemen," p. 29.

28. See Marco Palacios, *Coffee in Colombia, 1850–1970: An Economic, Social and Political History* (Cambridge: Cambridge University Press, 1980); F. Rojas Ruiz, "El Frente Nacional: Solución política a un problema de desarrollo?" In Rodrigo Parra Sandoval, ed., *La dependencia externa y el desarrollo político de Colombia* (Bogotá: Universidad Nacional de Colombia, Dirección de Divulgación Cultural, 1970), especially p. 109; and Charles W. Bergquist, *Labor in Latin America: Comparative Essays on Chile, Argentina, Venezuela, and Colombia* (Stanford: Stanford University Press, 1986).

29. During this period, Colombia adopted a pragmatic foreign policy of *respice polum*—following the "north star" of the United States—as first stated by Conservative president Marco Fidel Suárez (1918–1922). Colombia essentially maintained a low-profile foreign policy, with close ties to the United States, until the presidency of Belisario Betancur (1982–1986). See Bruce M. Bagley and Juan Tokatlian, "Colombian Foreign Policy in the 1980s: The Search for Leverage," *Journal of Interamerican Studies and World Affairs* 27 (fall 1985): 27–61. For a valuable analysis of U.S.–Colombian relations in the crisis years of the Samper administration, see "Colombia: Una nueva sociedad en un mundo nuevo. Informe de la Comisión de Análisis y Recomendaciones sobre las Relaciones entre Colombia y Estados Unidos," *Análisis político*, edición especial (July 1997): 1–95.

30. Dix, *Colombia*, p. 85.

31. See Palacios, *Coffee in Colombia*; and Gabriel Poveda Ramos, *Políticas económicas, desarrollo industrial y tecnología en Colombia 1925–1975* (Bogotá: Editora Guadalupe, Colciencias, 1976).

32. For a more detailed analysis of the 1957–1958 period and the establishment of the National Front, from which some of the paragraphs below have been taken, see Hartlyn, *The Politics of Coalition Rule*, pp. 42–74. A valuable study of the breakdown, which also borrows from the consociational literature, is Wilde, "Conversations Among Gentlemen."

33. See Carlos Lleras Restrepo, *Borradores para una historica de la República Liberal*, vol. 1 (Bogotá: Editora Nueva Frontera, 1975); and John D. Martz, *Colombia: A Contemporary Political Survey* (Chapel Hill: University of North Carolina Press, 1962), pp. 44–46.

34. See Payne, *Patterns of Conflict*, pp. 159–182.

35. Miguel Urrutia Montoya, *The Development of the Colombian Labor Movement* (New Haven: Yale University Press, 1969); and Kenneth N. Medhurst, *The Church and Labour in Colombia* (Manchester, England: Manchester University Press, 1984).

36. See Herbert Braun, *The Assassination of Gaitán: Public Life and Urban Violence in Colombia* (Madison: University of Wisconsin Press, 1985).

37. Wilde, "Conversations Among Gentlemen," pp. 51–58.

38. Oquist, *Violence.*

39. Eric Hobsbawm, "The Anatomy of Violence," *New Society* (April 11, 1963): 16–18.

40. Other analysts who share this emphasis on the central role of party leadership include Wilde, "Conversations Among Gentlemen"; Gerardo Molina, *Las ideas liberales en Colombia de 1935 a la iniciación del Frente Nacional,* vol. 3 (Bogotá: Ediciones Tercer Mundo, 1977), pp. 251–253; and John C. Pollock, "Violence, Politics and Elite Performance: The Political Sociology of La Violencia in Colombia," *Studies in Comparative International Development* 10 (summer 1975): 22–50. Oquist, *Violence,* is an excellent study and useful regionalization of *la violencia,* presented under an overall interpretation of the "partial collapse of the state," but it may somewhat exaggerate the extension and coherence of the Colombian state in the 1940s (see Hartlyn, *Politics of Coalition Rule,* pp. 42–48). Useful regional studies of this period include James D. Henderson, *When Colombia Bled: A History of the Violencia in Tolima* (University: University of Albama Press, 1985) and Carlos Miguel Ortiz Sarmiento, *Estado y subversión en Colombia: La violencia en el Quindío años 50* (Bogotá: Fondo Editorial CEREC, 1985). An excellent study of the latter period of violence is Gonzalo Sánchez and Donny Meertens, *Bandoleros, gamonales y campesinos: El caso de la violencia en Colombia* (Bogotá: El Ancora Editores, 1983).

41. Oquist, *Violence,* pp. 17–18.

42. Martz, *Colombia,* pp. 147–154; Vernon Lee Fluharty, *Dance of the Millions: Military Rule and the Social Revolution in Colombia, 1930–1956* (Pittsburgh: University of Pittsburgh Press, 1957), pp. 127–135.

43. Dix, *Colombia,* p. 116.

44. For descriptions of this period, see Martz, *Colombia;* Dix, *Colombia;* and Tirado, "Colombia."

45. Daniel H. Levine and Alexander Wilde, "The Catholic Church, 'Politics,' and Violence: The Colombian Case," *Review of Politics* 39 (April 1977): 220–249.

46. For a lengthier discussion of these issues, with contrasts to the cases of Venezuela, Uruguay, and Chile, see Hartlyn, *Politics of Coalition Rule,* pp. 237–243.

47. In Hartlyn, *Politics of Coalition Rule,* pp. 75–78, he discusses how the various "rules of the game" emerged in response to three predicaments inherent to the political formula of consociationalism: threatened immobilism, lack of popular responsiveness, and policy incoherence.

The political regime's essential continuity and the only partial constitutional dismantling of the National Front requirements makes it difficult to specify when the National Front "ended" and a post–National Front period "began." National-level competitive elections were first held in 1974, but parity in the executive branch was mandated until 1978. Even after 1978, by constitutional mandate the party receiving the second highest number of votes had to be offered participation in government. In 1986, for the first time, the losing party refused to form part of the incoming Liberal administration. In 1991, the National Constituent Assembly formally eliminated all vestiges of power sharing between the Liberal and Conservative Parties, although these parties have continued to dominate the electoral realm and to engage in informal power sharing in subsequent years.

48. See Fernando Cepeda and Christopher Mitchell, "The Trend Toward Technocracy," in Albert Berry, Ronald Hellman, and Mauricio Solaún, eds., *Politics of Compromise* (New Brunswick, NJ: Transaction Books, 1980), 237–255. For further discussion of the increase in presidential power, see Ronald P. Archer and Marc W. Chernick, "El presidente frente a las instituciones nacionales," in Patricia Vásquez de Urrutia, ed., *La Democracia en Blanco y Negro: Colombia en los Años Ochenta* (Bogotá: Ediciones Uniandes, Departamento de Ciencia Política—CEREC, 1989), pp. 31–79, especially pp. 33–44; and Jonathan Hartlyn, "Presidentialism and Colombian Politics," in Juan Linz and Arturo Valenzuela, eds., *The Failure of Presidential Democracy* (Baltimore: Johns Hopkins University Press, 1994), pp. 294–327. For an analysis of a similar phenomenon in the case of Chile, see Arturo Valenzuela

and Alexander Wilde, """Presidential Politics and the Decline of the Chilean Congress," in Joel Smith and Lloyd D. Musolf, eds., *Legislatures in Development* (Durham, NC: Duke University Press, 1979), pp. 189–215.

49. See Bruce M. Bagley and Fernando Botero, "Organizaciones campesinas contemporáneas en Colombia: Un estudio de la Asociación Nacional de Usuarios Campesinos (ANUC)," *Estudios rurales latinoamericanos* 1 (January-April 1978): 59–96; and Leon Zamosc, *The Agrarian Question and the Peasant Movement in Colombia* (Cambridge: Cambridge University Press, 1986).

50. See Jonathan Hartlyn and Samuel A. Morley, eds., *Latin American Political Economy: Financial Crisis and Political Change* (Boulder, CO: Westview, 1986). See also Inter-American Development Bank, *Economic and Social Progress in Latin America 1997 Report: Overcoming Volatility* (Washington, DC: IADB 1995), p. 194, which reports Colombia to have the lowest standard deviation of GDP growth over the 1970–1992 period of twenty-six Latin American and Caribbean countries (with 1.96); of the countries included in this volume, Chile (with 6.34) and Peru (with 6.16) had the highest.

51. See Richard L. Maullin, "The Colombia-IMF Disagreement of November-December 1966: An Interpretation of Its Place in Colombian Politics," Memorandum RM-5314-RC (Santa Monica: The RAND Corporation, 1967); and Carlos Díaz Alejandro, *Foreign Trade Regimes and Economic Development: Colombia* (New York: Columbia University Press, 1976).

52. For an overview of the Barco program of economic liberalization, see María Mercedes de Martínez, "Elementos generales de la política económica," in Malcolm Deas and Carlos Ossa, eds., *El Gobierno Barco: Política, Economía, y Desarrollo Social en Colombia 1986–1990* (Santafé de Bogotá: Fedesarrollo—Fondo Cultural Cafetero, 1994), pp. 211–217. See also José Antonio Ocampo, "La internacionalización de la economía colombiana," in Miguel Urrutia, ed., *Colombia ante la Economía Mundial* (Santafé de Bogotá: Tercer Mundo Editores—Fedesarrollo, 1993), pp. 17–65.

53. Rudolf Hommes, Armando Montenegro, and Pablo Roda, *Una apertura hacia el futuro* (Santafé de Bogotá: Ministerio de Hacienda y Crédito Público—Departamento Nacional de Planeación—Fondo Nacional de Desarrollo Económico, 1994), pp. 35–37. This volume provides an overview of (and justification for) the entire range of neoliberal economic reforms carried out by the Gaviria administration. For a somewhat more critical perspective, see José Antonio Ocampo, "Economía y economía política de la reforma comercial colombiana" (Santiago: Comisión Económica para América Latina y el Caribe, Serie Reformas de Política Pública, 1993).

54. Luis Alberto Restrepo, ed., *Síntesis '97 Colombia* (Santafé de Bogotá: IEPRI-Fundación Social, 1997), pp. 254, 259.

55. For an overall discussion of the economic aspects of the 1991 Constitution, see Caroline Hartzell, "Las reformas económicas en la Constitución de 1991," in John Dugas, ed., *La Constitución de 1991: ¿Un pacto político viable?* (Bogotá: Universidad de los Andes, 1993), pp. 77–96. More detailed examination of specific issues may be found in *Constitución económica colombiana* (Santafé de Bogotá: El Navegante Editores, 1996).

56. The balance between economic liberty and state restrictions seeking to favor the common good is ubiquitous in the constitutional articles on the economy. Thus, Article 333 mandates that "economic activity and private initiative are free, *within the limits of the common good*" (emphasis added). Furthermore, "free economic competition is a right of everyone *which supposes responsibilities*" (Article 333, emphasis added). In addition, "the state will impede the obstruction or restriction of economic liberty *and will prevent or control any abuse that persons or businesses bring about with their dominant position in the market*" (Article 333, emphasis added). This language, which embraces both economic liberty and potential restrictions in the same breath, is the result of compromise in an assembly characterized by a broad spectrum of ideological views.

57. For an explanation of the process of expropriation in Colombia and the reasons for the new method of administrative expropriation, see Guillermo Perry Rubio, "Propiedad y expropiación," in Néstor Hernando Parra, ed., *Los Cambios Constitucionales* (Santafé de Bogotá: Sociedad Económica de Amigos del País, 1992), pp. 209–219.

58. Initial evaluations of Samper's program of economic development may be found in Libardo Sarmiento Anzola, "La cuestión social: Una transición aplazada," in Luis Alberto

Restrepo, ed., *Síntesis '96 Colombia* (Santafé de Bogotá: IEPRI—Fundación Social—Tercer Mundo Editores, 1996), pp. 95–104; and Ricardo Bonilla G., "El pacto social descertificó al gobierno," in Restrepo, ed., *Síntesis '97 Colombia,* pp. 107–117.

59. See Human Rights Watch, *War Without Quarter: Colombia and International Humanitarian Law* (New York: 1998).

60. Jonathan Hartlyn, "Drug Trafficking and Democracy in Colombia in the 1980s" (Barcelona: Institut de Ciències Polítiques i Socials, Working Paper No. 70, 1993, pp. 16–17).

61. Elections for Congress, departmental assemblies, and municipal councils are determined by proportional representation, and there is no limitation on the number of lists that can be presented under a party name. In the years that parity was in effect, each party label automatically received one-half of the legislative seats; within each party, factional apportionment was determined by the percentage of the vote received.

62. The data on 1970 is from Miles Williams and Rodrigo Losada Lora, "Análisis de la votación presidencial: 1970," in DANE, *Colombia política* (Bogotá: 1972); on 1982 from Elsa Gómez Gómez, *La elección presidencial de 1982 en Bogotá: Dinámica de la opinión electoral* (Bogotá: ANIF Fondo Editorial, 1982); and on the late 1980s from Ronald Archer, "Party Strength and Weakness in Colombia's Besieged Democracy," in Scott Mainwaring and Timothy R. Scully, eds., *Building Democratic Institutions: Party Systems in Latin America* (Stanford: Stanford University Press, 1995), pp. 164–199. See also Gabriel Murillo and Miles Williams, "Análisis de las elecciones presidenciales en 1974 en Bogotá" (Bogotá: Universidad de los Andes, Departamento de Ciencia Política, 1975); Rubén Sánchez et al., "El comportamiento electoral de los bogotanos en las elecciones de 1978" (Bogotá: Universidad de los Andes, Departamento de Ciencia Política, 1981); and Oscar Delgado and Miguel A. Cárdenas, "Franja electoral y opinión crítica en Colombia," *Revista Foro* (September 1994), pp. 76–89.

63. See Robert H. Dix, "Political Oppositions Under the National Front," in Albert Berry, Ronald Hellman, and Mauricio Solaún, *Politics of Compromise* (New Brunswick, NJ: Transaction Books, 1980), pp. 131–179.

64. On labor and civic movements during this period, see Luz Amparo Fonseca, "Huelgas y paros cívicos en Colombia," tésis de post-grado, Universidad de los Andes, Facultad de Economía, 1982; see also Victor Manuel Moncayo and Fernando Rojas, *Luchas obreras y política laboral en Colombia* (Bogotá: Editorial La Carreta, 1978), and Guillermo Perry Rubio, Hernando Gómez Buendía, and Rocío Londoño Botero, "Sindicalismo y política económica," *Coyuntura económica* 12 (December 1982): 176–200.

65. See Eduardo Pizarro Leongómez, "La insurgencia armada: Raíces y perspectivas," in Francisco Leal Buitrago and Leon Zamosc, eds., *Al filo del caos: Crisis política en la Colombia de los años 80* (Bogotá: Tercer Mundo and Universidad Nacional, 1990), pp. 411–443.

66. Due to its novelty and ultimately tragic failure, the Betancur peace process received a significant degree of attention from journalists and social scientists. For good overviews of the peace process, see Ana María Bejarano, "Estrategias de paz y apertura democrática: Un balance de las administraciones Betancur y Barco," in Francisco Leal Buitrago and Leon Zamosc, eds., *Al filo del caos* (Bogotá: Tercer Mundo and Universidad Nacional, 1990), pp. 57–124; Marc W. Chernick, "Negotiated Settlement to Armed Conflict: Lessons from the Colombian Peace Process," *Journal of Interamerican Studies and World Affairs* 30, no. 4 (1988–1989): 53–88; and Socorro Ramírez and Luis Alberto Restrepo, *Actores en conflicto por la paz: El proceso de paz durante el gobierno de Belisario Betancur (1982–1986)* (Bogotá: Siglo Veintiuno Editores—CINEP, 1988). Fascinating interviews with, and opinion pieces by, some of the principal protagonists may be found in Arturo Alape, *La paz, la violencia: Testigos de excepción,* 3d ed. (Bogotá: Planeta Editorial Colombiana, 1985); Jacobo Arenas, *Correspondencia secreta del proceso de paz* (Bogotá: Editorial La Abeja Negra, 1989); Olga Behar, *Las guerras de la paz* (Bogotá: Planeta Colombiana Editorial, 1985); and Alvaro Leyva Durán, ed., *¿Paz? ¡Paz! Testimonios y reflexiones sobre un proceso* (Bogotá: Leyva Durán Editores—Editorial La Oveja Negra, 1987). Critical views of the peace process from opposite ends of the political spectrum are presented in Fernando Landazábal Reyes, *El precio de la paz* (Bogotá: Planeta Colombiana Editorial, 1985), and Laura Restrepo, *Historia de una traición* (Bogotá: Plaza & Janes, 1986).

67. For the Palace of Justice tragedy, see Juan Manuel López Caballero, *El Palacio de Justicia: ¿Defensa de nuestras instituciones?* (Bogotá: Editorial Retina, 1987); Olga Behar,

Noches de humo (Bogotá: Planeta Colombiana Editorial, 1988); Ramón Jimeno, *Noche de lobos* (Bogotá: Siglo Vientiuno Editores, 1989); and Ana Carrigan, *The Palace of Justice: A Colombian Tragedy* (New York: Four Walls, Eight Windows, 1993).

68. Gustavo Gallón Giraldo, ed. *Derechos humanos y conflicto armado en Colombia* (Bogotá: Comisión Andina de Juristas, Seccional Colombiana, 1991), p. 18.

69. The Barco peace process is discussed in Bejarano, "Estrategias de paz"; and Mauricio García Durán, *Procesos de paz: De la Uribe a Tlaxcala* (Santafé de Bogotá: CINEP, 1992).

70. Barco technically complied with the constitutional requirement that "adequate and equitable" participation in government be offered to the party receiving the second-highest number of votes by naming three Conservatives to cabinet posts. The Conservatives rejected the positions and entered into what they called "reflexive opposition."

71. A defense of the government-opposition scheme may be found in Fernando Cepeda, "Una Colombia nueva: La visión política de Barco," in Malcolm Deas and Carlos Ossa, *El Gobierno Barco* (Santafé de Bogotá: Fedesarrollo—Fondo Cultural Cafetero, 1994), pp. 49–78. For a more critical appraisal see Archer and Chernick, "El presidente frente," pp. 69–77.

72. Bruce Bagley, "Narcotráfico: Colombia asediada," in Francisco Leal Buitrago and Leon Zamosc, eds., *Al filo del caos* (Bogotá: Tercer Mundo and Universidad Nacional, 1990), pp. 445–446.

73. For the repercussions of the drug trade on the Colombian economy, see Richard B. Craig, "Illicit Drug Traffic: Implications for South American Source Countries," *Journal of Interamerican Studies and World Affairs* 29, no. 2 (summer 1987): 1–34; and Francisco E. Thoumi, "Some Implications of the Growth of the Underground Economy in Colombia," *Journal of Interamerican Studies and World Affairs* 29, no. 2 (summer 1987): 35–53.

74. See Ciro Krauthausen and Luis Fernando Sarmiento, *Cocaína & Co.: Un mercado ilegal por dentro* (Bogotá: Tercer Mundo Editores—Universidad Nacional, Instituto de Estudios Políticos y Relaciones Internacionales, 1991).

75. See Rafael Pardo Rueda, *De primera mano: Colombia 1986–1994: Entre conflictos y esperanzas* (Santafé de Bogotá: Grupo Editorial Norma y CEREC, 1996), pp. 495–500.

76. Virgilio Barco, "Intervención por televisión para explicar las últimas medidas de Estado de Sitio, Agosto 18 de 1989," in *Discursos 1986–1990*, vol. 2, *Paz, lucha contra el narcotráfico y orden público* (Bogotá: Presidencia de la República, 1990), pp. 471–475.

77. The Barco administration had attempted for two years to introduce significant democratizing reform to the Colombian constitution. For a description of these attempts and their ultimate failure, see John Dugas, "Explaining Democratic Reform in Colombia: The Origins of the 1991 Constitution" (Ph.D. diss., Indiana University, 1997), pp. 290–305.

78. The political accord negotiated by the Gaviria administration provided for a National Constituent Assembly consisting of seventy members elected in a single nationwide voting district, a formula that was perceived to give greater opportunity to minority parties and movements. The assembly was to meet for a period of five months in 1991 to reform the existing constitution, with deliberations to be limited to ten specific constitutional areas.

79. John Dugas, Rubén Sánchez, and Elizabeth Ungar, "La Asamblea Nacional Constituyente: Expresión de una voluntad general," in Rubén Sánchez David, ed., *Los nuevos retos electorales* (Bogotá: Universidad de los Andes, Departamento de Ciencia Política, 1991), pp. 187–215.

80. This is true only if the Movimiento de Salvación Nacional (MSN) is counted as separate from the Conservative Party. The MSN began in March 1990 when Alvaro Gómez broke with the Conservative Party to launch his own campaign for the presidency.

81. For a detailed discussion of the democratic reforms contained in the 1991 Constitution, see Dugas, "Explaining Democratic Reform in Colombia," chapter 2. See also Manuel José Cepeda, *Introducción a la Constitución de 1991: Hacia un nuevo constitucionalismo* (Santafé de Bogotá: Presidencia de la República—Consejería para el Desarrollo de la Constitución, 1992); Manuel José Cepeda, *La Constituyente por dentro: Mitos y realidades* (Santafé de Bogotá: Presidencia de la República—Consejería para el Desarrollo de la Constitución, 1993); Dugas, ed., *La Constitución de 1991;* and Carlos Lleras de la Fuente and Marcel Tangarife Torres, *Constitución política de Colombia: Origen, evolución y vigencia,* 3 vols. (Medellín: Biblioteca Jurídica Diké, 1996).

82. See Donna Lee Van Cott, "The Impact of the 1991 Colombian Constitution: Ethnic Rights," paper delivered to the XXI Congress of the Latin American Studies Association, September 1998.

83. Specifically, the 1991 Constitution established the Office of the General Prosecutor (Fiscalía General), a separate body charged with investigating crimes and prosecuting accused criminals; created the Superior Council of Judicial Affairs (Consejo Superior de la Judicatura), meant to ensure the administrative and budgetary independence of the judiciary; established the Constitutional Court, which is to determine the constitutionality of all laws, bills, referenda, and treaties; and created the People's Defender (Defensor del Pueblo), whose specific task is to promote and protect human rights in Colombia.

84. Francisco Leal Buitrago, *El Oficio de la Guerra* (Santafé de Bogotá: Tercer Mundo Editores—IEPRI, 1994), p. 129 and appendix 1, pp. 255–267; see also Eduardo Pizarro Leongómez, "La reforma militar en un contexto de democratización política," in *En busca de la estabilidad perdida* (Santafé de Bogotá: Tercer Mundo Editores—IEPRI—Colciencias, 1995), pp. 159–208.

85. Matthew Soberg Shugart, "Leaders, Rank and File, and Constituents: Electoral Reform in Colombia and Venezuela," *Electoral Studies* 11, no. 1 (1992): 21–45; and Ronald P. Archer and Matthew Soberg Shugart, "The Unrealized Potential of Presidential Dominance in Colombia," in Scott Mainwaring and Matthew Soberg Shugart, eds., *Presidentialism and Democracy in Latin America* (Cambridge: Cambridge University Press, 1997), pp. 110–159.

86. The Gaviria administration did successfully conclude a peace accord in April 1994 with the Corriente de Renovación Socialista (CRS), a dissident faction of the ELN. For descriptions and analyses of the peace process during the Gaviria administration, see García Durán, *Procesos de paz,* pp. 205–243; William Ramírez Tobón, "Las nuevas ceremonias de la paz," *Análisis político,* no. 14 (1991): 8–33; William Ramírez Tobón, "¿Alguien quiere volver a Tlaxcala?" *Análisis político,* no. 16 (1992): 55–68; Alejandro Reyes Posada, "Violencia," in Luis Alberto Restrepo, ed., *Síntesis '93 Colombia* (Santafé de Bogotá: Tercer Mundo Editores—IEPRI, 1993), pp. 117–127; Alejandro Reyes Posada, "La violencia política: La evolución de las guerrillas," in Luis Alberto Restrepo, ed., *Síntesis '94 Colombia* (Santafé de Bogotá: Tercer Mundo Editores—IEPRI, 1994), pp. 33–38; and Jaime Zuluaga Nieto, "Entre la guerra y la paz," in Luis Alberto Restrepo, ed., *Síntesis '95 Colombia* (Santafé de Bogotá: Tercer Mundo Editores—IEPRI—Fundación Social, 1995), pp. 105–110.

87. See Gabriel García Márquez, *News of a Kidnapping* (New York: Alfred A. Knopf, 1997). As García Márquez notes in the acknowledgments, the "gruesome drama" that his book details of these ten kidnappings (in which two of the victims were killed, including Diana Turbay, daughter of former president Turbay) is "only one episode in the biblical holocaust that has been consuming Colombia for more than twenty years."

88. Inside accounts of the Gaviria administration's policies toward the drug cartels may be found in Pardo Rueda, *De primera mano,* chapters 10, 13, and 14; and Mauricio Vargas, *Memorias secretas del revolcón* (Santafé de Bogotá: Tercer Mundo Editores, 1996), chapters 6 and 11. See also Alvaro Camacho Guizado and Gonzálo Sánchez Gómez, "Narcotráfico," in Restrepo, ed., *Síntesis '93 Colombia,* pp. 103–116; and Luis Alberto Restrepo, "El tráfico de drogas: Muerto el narcoterrorismo, continúa el narcotráfico," in Restrepo, ed., *Síntesis '94 Colombia,* pp. 27–32.

89. A useful overview of the Samper drug scandal and its associated political effects is Francisco Leal Buitrago, ed., *Tras las huellas de la crisis política* (Santafé de Bogotá: Tercer Mundo Editores—Fescol—IEPRI, 1996). See also Alejandro Reyes Posada, "Narcotráfico y política: La drogadicción política," in Restrepo, ed., *Síntesis '96 Colombia,* pp. 55–61; and Luis Alberto Restrepo, "Un elefante en palacio: La crisis del ejecutivo nacional," in Restrepo, ed., *Síntesis '97 Colombia,* pp. 67–73. For the journalistic uncovering of the scandal, see Mauricio Vargas, Jorge Lesmes, and Edgar Téllez, *El Presidente que se iba a caer* (Santafé de Bogotá: Planeta Editorial, 1996). The insider account of Samper's campaign treasurer is presented in Santiago Medina Serna, *La verdad sobre las mentiras* (Santafé de Bogotá: Planeta Colombia Editorial, 1997), while Samper's attorney defends the president's position in Luis Guillermo Nieto Roa, *La verdad para la historia* (Colombia: Planeta Colombiana Editorial—Ediciones Monte Verde, 1996).

90. On the role of the United States during the Samper administration, see Juan Gabriel Tokatlian, "Relaciones con los Estados Unidos: Los efectos de una narcodiplomacia adictiva,"

in Restrepo, ed., *Síntesis '96 Colombia*, pp. 143–151; and Juan Gabriel Tokatlian, "Colombia–Estados Unidos: Una relación hipernarcotizada," in Restrepo, ed., *Síntesis '97 Colombia*, pp. 159–166.

91. The Samper policy toward the guerrilla movements is discussed in Zuluaga Nieto, "Entre la guerra"; Jaime Zuluaga Nieto, "Política de paz: Entre las negociaciones y la conmoción interior," in Restrepo, ed., *Síntesis '96 Colombia*, pp. 69–74; and Jaime Zuluaga Neito "¿Hacia la paz por medio de la guerra?" in Restrepo, ed., *Síntesis '97 Colombia*, pp. 97–104.

92. Zuluaga Nieto, "¿Hacia la paz?" p. 97.

93. All statistics on paramilitary violence are taken from Comisión Colombiana de Juristas, *Colombia, derechos humanos y derechos humanitario: 1996* (Santafé de Bogotá: Comisión Colombiana de Juristas, 1997), pp. 7, 13.

94. See the data reported in Pardo Rueda, *De primera mano*, pp. 326–328.

95. The Fondos de Cofinanciación (Co-Financing Funds) have been used by the executive to channel state resources to the departments of legislators whose support is needed for a particular piece of legislation.

96. See Gustavo Bell Lemus, "The Decentralised State: An Administrative or Political Challenge?" in Eduardo Posada-Carbó, ed., *Colombia: The Politics of Reforming the State* (New York: St. Martin's Press, 1998), pp. 97–108.

97. See Fernando Henrique Cardoso and Enzo Faletto, *Dependency and Development* (Berkeley: University of California Press, 1979).

98. See Bergquist, *Labor in Latin America;* and Ruth Berins Collier and David Collier, *Shaping the Political Arena: Critical Junctures, the Labor Movement, and Regime Dynamics in Latin America* (Princeton: Princeton University Press, 1991).

99. Marc W. Chernick, "The Paramilitarization of the War in Colombia," *NACLA—Report on the Americas*, vol. 31, no. 5 (March-April 1998), pp. 2–33.

100. See Lawyer's Committee for Human Rights, "Colombia: Public Order, Private Injustice" (New York: February 1994); Gabriel Ricardo Nemogá et. al., *Justicia sin rostro: Estudio sobre la justicia regional* (Santafé de Bogotá: Universidad Nacional de Colombia, 1996); and Juan Gabriel Gómez, "Fueros y desafueros: Justicia y contrarreforma en Colombia," *Análisis Político*, no. 25 (May-August 1995): 71–79.

101. Using different data, the World Bank found that "extreme" poverty levels in the country in the early 1990s were approximately 17 percent, though it acknowledged that severe problems remained in terms of health care, adequate housing, and access to potable water and sewerage services. See World Bank, *Poverty in Colombia* (Washington, DC: The World Bank, 1994), pp. 2, 6.

102. See Gonzalo Sánchez et al., *Colombia: Violencia y democracia, informe presentado al Ministerio de Gobierno* (Bogotá: Universidad Nacional de Colombia, 1987), p. 22.

103. Ibid.

COSTA
RICA
PANAMA

VENEZUELA   GUYANA

COLOMBIA

ECUADOR

BRAZIL

Talara   ·Iquitos
Sullana
PERU
Chiclayo   ·Orellana
Trujillo
Huaraz
·Huánuco   Cocama·
Cerro De Pasco
Huancayo
Lima
Ayacucho·   ·Cuzco
·Ica

Puno   BOLIVIA
·Arequipa
·Tacna

Pacific

Ocean   PARAGUAY

CHILE

ARGENTINA

PERU

6

PERU:
Precarious Regimes,
Authoritarian and Democratic

Cynthia McClintock

Among the Latin American nations examined in this volume, Peru stands out as a country where both democratic and authoritarian regimes have been precarious.[1] Since 1919, no Peruvian political regime—neither constitutional nor de facto—has endured more than twelve years. Repeatedly, democratic government has been attempted but not sustained. Repeatedly as well, authoritarian governments have worn out their welcomes.

Between 1930 and 1968, elections were held and the country's president was inaugurated under constitutional auspices five times—in 1930, 1939, 1945, 1956, and 1963. Clearly, Peru is a nation where there has been experience with democratic norms and practices. Constitutions were written, political parties were established, legislatures played a role, and considerable interest in political competition was evident among citizens. It should also be pointed out, however, that Peru's elected governments between 1930 and 1968 were not sufficiently inclusive to meet the criteria for the "democratic" label used in this book. The franchise was severely restricted; even during the 1960s, illiterates were not allowed to vote.[2] The democratic label was also inappropriate because the mass political party Alianza Popular Revolucionaria Americana (APRA) was excluded from executive power for most of this period.

Peru's history of failure with democracy is not surprising. While in the 1960s many social scientists expected democratic consolidation in Latin America's Southern Cone, they did not in Peru or most other Andean nations. In the theoretical analysis in this chapter, considerable blame is placed on Peru's historical legacy: the traumatic Spanish conquest and abusive colonial rule. For several centuries, a small coterie of Caucasian elites based in Lima dominated vast numbers of impoverished indigenous peasants in the Andean mountains. In other words, ethnic, class, and geographic

309

cleavages were unusually sharp and overlapping in Peru, provoking a mixture of scorn and fear among elites, resignation and rebellion among the peasants, and mistrust on all sides. Also, most of Peru's political leaders did not make choices that might have narrowed these gaps. Peru's elected governments maintained restrictive electoral clauses and eschewed the construction of sustainable political parties. They failed to summon the capacity to dramatically redress Peru's poverty and inequality, which were extreme even by Latin American standards. For their part, non-elites' demands for economic and political change were intense; through the APRA—the only Peruvian political party to date that had appeared to achieve institutionalization—their challenge to the entrenched order was aggressive.

When elections were held in 1980 and the country's president was inaugurated under constitutional auspices, hopes were high that this time the new regime would be sustained. In the wake of the military government's social and economic reforms, Peru's traditional elites had lost much of their political power. It was the first time that the franchise had been extended to all adults and competition opened to all political groups, and accordingly the first time that the regime fully deserved the democratic label. Citizens who had previously been politically excluded and economically disadvantaged had become much more politically active, and it appeared likely that they would both feel represented and in fact be represented by the country's active leftist political parties. Between 1980 and 1992, Peru clearly met the criteria for "electoral democracy."[3]

The hopes for sustained democratic rule were not realized, however. On April 5, 1992, President Alberto Fujimori suspended the 1979 Constitution, arrested several opposition leaders, padlocked the Congress, and moved quickly to dismantle the judiciary. These decisions were dubbed the *autogolpe* (coup by the president's own hand). Peru became the sole Latin American nation that returned to democracy during the 1980s only to undergo a democratic breakdown in the 1990s.[4]

While there was scholarly consensus that Fujimori had ruptured Peru's electoral democracy, there was no consensus about why the rupture had occurred. President Fujimori and some analysts contended that the rupture was necessary in order to correct fatal flaws in the 1980–1992 regime; they emphasized in particular the legislature's capacity to obstruct the executive and corrupt leaders' power over political parties. Other analysts, including this author, believe that the rupture was primarily a result of the political will and strategic calculation of President Fujimori, with the encouragement of the military. It is also true, however, that the rupture was possible because of the poor democratic performance in 1980–1992, a poor performance that reflected not only the enduring problems of social mistrust and weak civilian political institutions but also the preponderance of leftist attitudes among Peru's citizens and leaders at the time of the Latin American debt crisis and shift toward free-market economic policies.

In 1993 a new constitution was promulgated and in 1995 Fujimori was reelected president by a wide margin. Could Peru again be classified as an electoral democracy? Or was the regime only a "pseudodemocracy," in which the executive permits only contestation that does not threaten his power?[5] Or was even the concept "pseudodemocratic" too lax, and was the blunt label "authoritarian" in fact most appropriate?[6] The answer to this question is controversial.[7] Indeed, the answer may become clear only at a later date when Fujimori's power is more directly threatened by contestation, or when the thresholds for free and fair contestation in the scholarly definition of electoral democracy are established. However, for this author the Fujimori government is more appropriately classified as a pseudodemocracy or authoritarian regime than as an electoral democracy—primarily because Fujimori was trying to permit only contestation that did not threaten his own power, although it was not clear if he would achieve his goal.

More unusual among Latin American nations in the twentieth century than the breakdown of Peru's democratic governments was that Peru's de facto governments were short-lived, too. While several earned considerable support for a time as a result of their populist or reformist measures, no authoritarian government achieved political institutionalization or long-standing legitimacy. All three governments of the twentieth century that were patently authoritarian (Augusto Leguía, 1919–1930; Manuel Odría, 1948–1956; and Juan Velasco Alvarado and Francisco Morales Bermúdez, 1968–1980) failed to build progovernment political parties and apparently also failed to satisfy citizens' desires for open political competition and debate, desires that became stronger when economic prosperity ended. Fujimori's government appears to be following a similar trajectory.

HISTORICAL OVERVIEW

Governments in Peru have been more unstable than in any other South American country except perhaps Bolivia. The country's longest period of uninterrupted rule (constitutional or de facto), the Aristocratic Republic, lasted for only nineteen years (1895–1914). During the twentieth century, the common pattern has been alternation between constitutional and de facto rule every five to twelve years. Overall, between independence in the early 1820s and 1995, approximately 60 percent of Peru's presidents have been military, ruling for about 100 of those 170 years. Between 1945 and 1992, Peru's government was civilian and constitutional almost 60 percent of the time, and a military regime 40 percent of the time.

The Colonial Era

Peru's colonial experience was harsh. The Inca Empire was rich and very large; its territory extended some 3,000 miles from present-day Chile to Ecuador and embraced 7 to 12 million people.[8] Developing sophisticated irrigation, storage, and distribution facilities throughout their lands, the Inca eradicated hunger among their peoples—a feat rarely achieved subsequently. In 1532, however, Francisco Pizarro led a force of about 62 horsemen and 106 foot soldiers to victory against some 10,000 Incan warriors.[9] Pizarro arrived just after a bitter struggle for the Incan throne between the victorious new emperor Atahualpa and his half-brother Huascar, and the Spaniards had horses, gunpowder, and swords. Furthermore, the Incas believed that the Spaniards might be gods. Incan illusions about the nature of the Spaniards ended rapidly. After the Spaniards captured Atahualpa, they held him for a huge ransom; but after its payment, the Spaniards strangled the Incan emperor anyway.

Peru became one of Spain's two viceroyalties in Spanish America (the other was Mexico). Richly endowed with gold, silver, and mercury mines, Peru became a source of tremendous treasure for Spain. Needing the indigenous Indians to work in the mines, the Spanish did not massacre the Indians as they did elsewhere, but they did force them to labor under harsh conditions, which, by 1600, in combination with new European diseases, decimated the Indian population. The Spanish also forced the Indians to pay tribute and dispossessed them of much of the best agricultural land.

Confronting these brutal conditions, the Indians rebelled, often proclaiming that they would restore the Incan regime. The largest Indian rebellion against Spanish rule was led by Túpac Amaru II in 1780, and gathered substantial peasant support in the central and southern highlands. The crown repressed the rebellion harshly, killing thousands of Indians. Túpac Amaru II was publicly drawn and quartered in the main square of Cuzco. Still, sporadic rebellions continued.

When the movement for independence grew in Latin America in the early nineteenth century, Peru's *criollos* (descendants of the Spanish born in the colonies) were wary. With Lima as the administrative center of Spain's South American colonies, Peru's *criollos* had received greater political and economic benefits from the crown than their counterparts elsewhere, and they also worried that independence would promote liberal and egalitarian ideas among the Indian population. Lima became the center of the Spanish counterattack against the independence movement. Ultimately, it was predominantly foreign forces—Argentine, Venezuelan, Chilean, and Colombian, led by José de San Martín and Simón Bolívar—that brought independence to Peru in 1824.

Independence to 1930

The period between independence and the late 1800s was turbulent. As the country's colonial aristocrats were not at the forefront in the wars of independence, they were displaced from political power by the military leaders of the struggle. For about fifteen years after independence, these military leaders (*caudillos*) continued to fight over national boundaries in the Andean region, as well as over executive power from different regional bases. In Peru's first fifty years of independence, there were thirty-three different presidents, twenty-seven of whom were military officers.[10] Constitutions were written, national congresses were held, and a few civilians became president through indirect congressional selection, but the civilian institutions were all short-lived.[11]

A major effort to establish a liberal state was not made until 1872, a late date for Latin American countries. The initiative followed Peru's first export-led economic boom: the guano boom (1845–1870). In 1840, guano (dung that had been deposited on Peru's off-shore islands by millions of sea-birds) was discovered to be an excellent fertilizer. The Peruvian state, which owned the rights to the guano and chose the recipients of licenses to collect and export the guano, did not prudently manage its guano resources.[12] Rather, unscrupulous relationships emerged between the state authorities and the guano consignees (many of whom were to use their profits to establish coastal haciendas and become members of the Peruvian oligarchy). Also, rather than saving some of its new funds, the government borrowed against anticipated guano earnings; by the late 1860s, as the guano resources were depleted, a severe fiscal crisis emerged.

The mismanagement was of serious concern to Nicolás de Piérola, the finance minister during the administration of Colonel José Balta (1868–1872). Despite his own aristocratic origins, the fiery Piérola rebuked the Peruvian families who had become wealthy through the guano trade by transferring the consignment contract to a French firm. Enraged, the Peruvian families joined with other elites to form Peru's first political party, the Civilista Party, under the leadership of Manuel Pardo. In the 1872 "elections," in which 3,778 voters participated, Pardo triumphed.[13]

This liberal experiment under the Civilistas was brief. The guano boom was nearing its end and economic problems were soon severe. Then, in 1879, the War of the Pacific broke out among Peru, Chile, and Bolivia. The Civilistas did not really want to fight the war; they feared that if the indigenous peasants were mobilized against the Chileans, the peasants would subsequently turn against them. Ultimately, Piérola declared himself president and organized military efforts against the Chileans, which ultimately failed as Lima was occupied in January 1881 by the Chilean military. Outside Lima, different leaders emerged, and armed peasant groups attacked both the Chileans and large landowners, often gaining considerable local autonomy. Finally, in 1883, Peru ceded to Chile southern territories rich in nitrates (a valuable fertilizer), and peace was achieved.

In the first election after the war, in 1885, General Andrés Cáceres, who had earned prestige as a leader of Peruvian peasants against Chileans in the highlands, emerged triumphant—but the country was economically devastated and socially and politically demoralized. During the next decade, General Cáceres and his successor, General Remigio Morales Bermúdez, sought to reestablish the authority of the state in most of the national territory and to restore Peru's international creditworthiness. The government negotiated the Grace Contract, which gave the British the right to operate Peru's railroad system for sixty-six years in return for the cancellation of Peru's foreign debt, a contract that provoked widespread nationalist opposition.

The opposition was led by Piérola, whose previous political roles had earned him considerable popularity. In 1895, he came to power in a popular uprising, supported by his own Partido Demócrata as well as by his previous rivals, the Civilistas (who opposed Cáceres's military rule). Piérola's government was the first in Peru's longest constitutional era to date, and was called the Aristocratic Republic; it endured from 1895 to 1914 and, after a coup in 1914, was restored in 1915 to survive until 1919. The relative longevity of the Aristocratic Republic is attributed primarily to robust export-oriented growth and to reforms that enhanced the professionalism of civilian and military bureaucracies.

The Aristocratic Republic cannot be deemed democratic by our definition. Suffrage was restricted to adult males and subject to strict property and literacy qualifications. Although the electorate increased approximately tenfold between 1894 and the early 1900s, by 1912 only about 10 percent of adult males were registered voters.[14]

During the Aristocratic Republic, Peru's oligarchy was consolidated—an oligarchy of some thirty families that was to control a large share of Peru's wealth and vast political power until 1968.[15] Oligarchical families based their wealth almost exclusively upon exports: first upon guano and then upon sugar and cotton from coastal haciendas, and to a lesser degree minerals and wool in the highlands. Between 1898 and 1918, the value of total exports—primarily sugar, cotton, copper, and oil—multiplied eight times. Some of these families had come to Peru during the colonial era but did not become rich until the late nineteenth century; but about two-thirds were immigrants from Italy, Germany, or other Latin American countries who arrived after independence. Peru's new oligarchical families joined their predecessors in the Civilista Party, which became the dominant party in Peru at the end of Piérola's administration in 1899 until the end of the Aristocratic Republic in 1919. Two Civilista sugar magnates became presidents.[16]

The export-oriented growth that occurred during the Aristocratic Republic entailed advantages and disadvantages for Peru's majorities. On the one hand, both in the Peruvian-owned sugar and cotton haciendas and in the predominantly U.S.-owned mines in the highlands, the demand not only for labor but also for at least some relatively skilled labor increased sharply. A working class emerged for the first time; and, in some enterprises during some periods, wage levels were sufficient to enhance living standards considerably.[17] Educational opportunities expanded.

However, the export-oriented growth entailed disadvantages as well. On Peru's coast, the haciendas expanded at the expense of smaller farmers.[18] In the highlands, haciendas encroached not only on smaller farmers but also on the lands of indigenous peasant communities.[19] Also in the highlands, copper mines such as the immense U.S.-owned Cerro de Pasco Corporation used production processes that devastated the ecology of peasant communities for miles around. Many indigenous peasants went to work through *enganche,* a system of luring highlands peasants to the new enterprises by cash and extravagant promises, and then using debt peonage to retain them under harsh and frequently dangerous conditions.

These disadvantageous effects of export-oriented growth were not addressed by the administrations of the Aristocratic Republic. For example, in 1912 Guillermo Billinghurst became president and proposed an eight-hour day, a minimum wage, and more open and honest electoral procedures—proposals that were adamantly opposed by the Civilista-dominated Congress. When Billinghurst appealed directly to Peru's workers to provide armed support for the dissolution of the Congress and new elections, the Civilistas succeeded in encouraging a military coup against Billinghurst.

New elections were held in 1915, and José de Pardo y Barreda, a sugar magnate, became president. Amidst the global economic dislocations of World War I, social tensions became severe toward the end of Pardo's term. When elections were held in 1919, the winner was Augusto Leguía, a former Civilista president (1908–1912) who had broken with the party, been exiled for several years, and campaigned as a populist reformer against a status-quo Civilista candidate. Fearing that the Civilista-dominated electoral board would try to nullify his election and that the Civilista-dominated legislature would block his initiatives as it had Billinghurst's, Leguía carried out what might now be called Peru's first *autogolpe:* he secured military support for an end to the Aristocratic Republic and its constitution.

Leguía governed Peru between 1919 and 1930, an eleven-year period called the *oncenio*—the longest government to date in Peru's history and one that enjoyed considerable popular support in its initial years. Fortunately for Leguía, the post–World War I recession was brief, and economic growth resumed. However, growth was fueled not primarily by the expansion of the export sector or by the initiation of manufacturing, but rather first and foremost by substantial foreign investment and loans.[20] Leguía established close ties to the United States, and large loans from U.S. banks were important to the doubling of government revenues during the *oncenio* and the financing of water, road, and other large public works.[21] Leguía gained popular support by these expenditures and also by various reforms: for workers, the eight-hour day and the minimum wage; for peasants, the legal standing of peasant communities and an Indian affairs bureau.

However, Leguía was authoritarian. He amended the constitution so that he could run for reelection in 1924 and again in 1929; periodically detaining journalists and repressing labor and student militants, he was not opposed in either election. Leguía was disinterested in political institutions and did not seek to build a political party. Corruption among the president's family members and other presidential cronies was rampant.

In 1929, the Great Depression hit. Most Latin American governments collapsed; for a regime such as Leguía's that was intimately tied to international capital, the depression was a death knell. U.S. bank loans to Peru ceased. Between 1929 and 1932, Peru's export earnings plummeted by more than two-thirds and many export enterprises fired half their workers.[22] Leguía was overthrown by a mestizo army commander, Luis Sánchez Cerro.

The APRA Challenge: 1930–1968[23]

The period 1930–1968 in Peru spans the years between the depression and the military coup by General Juan Velasco Alvarado. During this period, Peru became a more socially and politically mobilized country, and many more citizens participated in elections than had previously.[24] Table 6.1 summarizes electoral outcomes during this period. But citizens' hopes for social reform through the electoral process were consistently dashed. The most important reason for the political frustration of this era was what might be called the "APRA dilemma." APRA, Peru's first reformist, mass political party, developed before any conservative political parties had been institutionalized and quickly frightened Peru's oligarchy. Soon there was a vicious political circle: Peru's oligarchy refused to accept APRA as a legitimate political party; barred from electoral participation, APRA's behavior was often intransigent and at times even violent; and APRA's antidemocratic actions stiffened the elites' resolve to repress the party.

In the early 1920s, a group of students, intellectuals, and journalists called the *indigenistas* gained attention with their writings about the plight of Peru's Indians. In 1924, Haya de la Torre, a former student leader from Trujillo on Peru's sugar-growing north coast, founded APRA. Inspired by the Mexican Revolution, Haya advocated anti-imperialism and reform, but not Marxism. At about the same time, José Carlos Mariátegui, a Marxist,

Table 6.1   Results for Presidential Elections, 1930–1963[a]

Year	Winner	Winner's Party	Winner's % of Vote	Runner-Up	Runner-Up's % of Vote
1931	Luis Sánchez Cerro	Unión Revolucionaria	51	APRA	35
1939	Manuel Prado	No name[b]	77.5	Frente Patriótico	22.5
1945	José Luis Bustamante	Frente Democrático Nacional	67	Unión Revolucionaria	33
1956	Manuel Prado	Movimiento Democrático Pradista	45	Frente de Juventudes Democráticas[c]	37
1962	Haya de la Torre	APRA	33	Acción Popular	32
1963	Fernando Belaúnde	Acción Popular-Democracia Cristiana	39	APRA	34

Source: Fernando Tuesta Soldevilla, *Perú político en cifras* (Lima: Fundación Friedrich Ebert, 1994), pp. 218–234.
Notes: a. All percentages are percentages of valid votes.
b. Coalition supported by APRA, a faction of the Unión Revolucionaria, and the Coalición Conservadora.
c. Presidential candidate was Fernando Belaúnde Terry.

founded the Peruvian Socialist Party. Mariátegui was among the first Marxists to emphasize peasant support as essential to revolutionary victory in the Latin American context, but he died at a relatively young age without having built a strong Marxist movement in Peru.

As the world depression worsened in the early 1930s, Peru's social tensions increased. In part because of APRA's stands and in part because of a leadership cult around the charismatic figure of Haya, the party attracted support from Peru's workers, the lower middle class, and students, and it built a permanent base among the sugar workers on the haciendas of the north coast. Labor protests became more intense.

In 1931, the most open and probably the most honest election heretofore in Peru's history was held, pitting the mestizo army commander who had ousted Leguía, Sánchez Cerro, against Haya de la Torre.[25] The election was to be the only one in which APRA was allowed to compete for executive power until 1962. During the campaign, APRA spokespeople crudely vilified Sánchez Cerro, and one of the party's key slogans was: "Only APRA will save Peru."[26] The election was won handily by Sánchez Cerro, in good part due to the respect he had gained through his coup against Leguía as well as to his modest, provincial background and mestizo appearance.

After the election, APRA continued to alienate both the Sánchez Cerro group and the oligarchy, especially by its factually unsupported charge that the electoral outcome had been fraudulent. The Sánchez Cerro government quickly allied with oligarchical groups and repressed APRA.[27] APRA's entire congressional representation and many other top leaders were arrested and deported, and the party's publications were closed down. Soon thereafter, in July 1932, *aprista* activists rebelled in Trujillo, holding the city for two days. About sixty army officers died in the struggle. In retaliation, when the army regained control of the city, it rounded up and shot between 1,000 and 2,000 suspected *apristas*. Finally, in 1933, Sánchez Cerro was assassinated by an *aprista*.

After the assassination of Sánchez Cerro, General Oscar Benavides was named president by Congress and ruled for six years, until 1939. Under considerable oligarchical pressure, Benavides resumed Sánchez Cerro's hard line against APRA. Most *aprista* leaders were either imprisoned or forced into exile. By one estimate, several thousand *apristas* and one hundred non-*apristas* were killed.[28] For their part, *aprista* militants continued to resort to political violence. In 1935, they assassinated the editor of Lima's preeminent newspaper, *El Comercio;* the oligarchical family owning the paper reinforced hostility toward APRA in its features and editorials for decades. Also, although Haya de la Torre rejected mass violence as a means to power, he hoped to infiltrate the army and identify an officer who would lead a coup and then turn power over to APRA.[29]

The electoral cause did not fare well in the 1930s. General Benavides called elections in 1936 but annulled them when the APRA-backed candidate appeared to be winning. Benavides called elections again in 1939, and this time was more careful to put the resources and power of the state behind his favored candidate, Manuel Prado, who was from one of Peru's wealthiest families.

Prado won the 1939 election and became the only civilian president to complete his elected term between 1919 and 1980. His success was due in good measure to propitious circumstances. As a result of the onset of World War II, not only was there strong support for democratic governments from the United States, but the global depression finally ended, and the Peruvian economy recovered. In 1941, Peru won a border war with Ecuador. Prado himself was also an astute politician.

In 1945, a three-year period began that was to be Peru's most reformist until 1968. Amid the strongly pro-democratic climate at the end of World War II, the 1945 election was unusually free. APRA was not allowed to run a presidential candidate, but it was permitted to ally with reform-oriented elements in the National Democratic Front, led by José Luis Bustamante. Bustamante was a scholarly lawyer with little political experience and no political base of his own. The National Democratic Front won in a landslide, and APRA gained a majority of congressional seats.

Whereas many Latin American nations adopted import-substitution industrialization policies during the 1930s after the global depression, Peru adopted them for the first time during the Bustamante government. With strong support from the *aprista* majority in the legislature, tariffs were raised to protect nascent domestic industries, import and exchange controls were introduced, numerous public works were planned, and wages and benefits were increased. APRA initiated new mobilization efforts on the coastal haciendas and orchestrated strikes. Not surprisingly, these new policies were vigorously opposed by oligarchical families, in particular in the country's second-most important newspaper at the time, *La Prensa,* published by a cotton magnate.

When one of *La Prensa*'s managers was assassinated in January 1947, APRA was blamed. The Bustamante government began to marginalize APRA. In retaliation, Haya de la Torre explored the possibility of military support for a pro-*aprista* coup; meanwhile, perceiving Haya as too cautious, *aprista* cadres in the lower ranks of the navy mutinied at Lima's port in October 1948. The mutiny was rapidly repressed; the Bustamante government declared APRA illegal once again. Yet, to the oligarchs and many sectors of the military, Bustamante's stance toward APRA was still irresolute, and a few weeks later his civilian regime was ended by a military coup.

The military coup of 1948 was led by General Manuel Odría, with the strong support of the oligarchy. Under Odría, the government reverted to extremely harsh persecution of APRA; Haya remained for five years in the

Colombian Embassy as a political refugee. Odría also reestablished orthodox liberal economic policies and assiduously courted U.S. investors. Amid
the Korean War, not only did Peru's agricultural exports flourish, but new
copper mines were developed by the U.S.-based Southern Peru Copper
Corporation and new iron mines by the U.S.-based Marcona Mining
Company, and fish meal (used primarily for pet food) became an important
new export. In this context, Odría was able to launch a large-scale public-
works program, and was not an unpopular president. He was able to engineer his own election in 1950; but, just like Peru's other authoritarian executives, Odría sought a personalist, populist relationship with Peru's poor at
the same time that he restricted civil liberties, and did not build a political
party that could withstand subsequent economic pressures. When the export
boom ended with the Korean War in 1953, Odría refused to cut public
spending. Disaffected, agricultural exporters began to fear that Odría
intended to perpetuate his rule indefinitely. Political conflict between Odría
and various oligarchs erupted, and Odría resorted to gangsterish tactics
against them, including the imprisonment of the editor of *La Prensa*.
Ultimately, however, with scant elite or military support, Odría saw little
choice but to hold the elections scheduled for 1956. Odría hand-picked a
candidate for these elections, Hernando de Lavalle, whose candidacy fared
poorly.

In the 1956 election, the franchise was given to women, and the size of
the electorate jumped. Still, only about 1.6 million Peruvians, or approximately 40 percent of the adult population, were registered to vote, of whom
84 percent cast ballots.[30] Former president Manuel Prado won with 45 percent of the vote. Remarkably, Prado came within days of completing his
term once again. As in his first administration, his economic and social
policies were orthodox, and no reforms were launched. Yet Prado ameliorated social and political tensions by reaching out further to APRA than
most oligarchs wanted, in what was termed La Convivencia: legalization of
APRA and freedom for the party to organize, in exchange for *aprista* electoral support and moderation of APRA's ideological stands.

As in 1945, the real test of the constitutional regime was over APRA's
political power in the upcoming (1962) election. Apparently, APRA won by
the barest of margins over Fernando Belaúnde's Acción Popular (AP), but
its 32.9 percent plurality was a shade under the one-third legally required
for election. According to the constitution, Congress would choose among
the top three candidates: in this case Haya, Belaúnde, and former dictator
Odría. For about five weeks after the elections, the top three candidates
debated and negotiated. Then, in July 1962, the military intervened.
Officers ruled for about a year; new elections were held in June 1963 and
won by Belaúnde.

Why did the military intervene in 1962? Probably the most important factor was its continuing anti-*aprismo*. About three weeks after the election, Haya was informed by the armed forces that he was unacceptable to them as president. The military preferred Belaúnde, who offered social reform without *aprismo*.

A second factor was the military's doubt that any of the governments to emerge from the election would be legitimate or viable. The vote tallies had been close and, while fraud was not massive, the voting rolls were also in disarray. These problems might have shifted electoral outcomes. Further, denied the presidency himself, Haya could not negotiate an agreement with the only ideologically compatible alternative, Belaúnde; expecting victory in a new election, Belaúnde rejected Haya's overture and called for an annulment of the elections. Haya's only remaining alternative was to negotiate with his archrival Odría. The specter of a government led by the presidential candidate who had finished third, in an ideologically disparate coalition of two parties that had been enemies for decades, may have been the last straw for the military.

As the military hoped, Belaúnde won the 1963 election. The Christian Democrat, Socialist, and Marxist candidates withdrew from the race, and the bulk of their votes (about 6 to 7 percent of the total) went to Acción Popular rather than to APRA. Whereas APRA called for social reform but was often perceived as sectarian and out-of-date, Acción Popular called for social reform along with development; Belaúnde seemed "modern" and a model leader for the Alliance for Progress era. The perception—which was valid (see the sections "Political Culture," "Socioeconomic Cleavages," and "Development Performance")—was that poverty and inequality were severe in Peru by regional standards, and that reform was overdue.[31]

Belaúnde attracted important political constituencies that were newly influential in Peruvian politics. During the 1950s and early 1960s, the Peruvian economy had done very well (see "Development Performance"). With a boom in fish-meal exports and the initiation of manufacturing, new entrepreneurs had gained economic and political power. A professional class had also emerged; white-collar employment (in education in particular) had doubled during the 1950s to 15 percent of the workforce.[32] Also, for the first time in Peru's history, the peasantry played a role in the election, despite the literacy clause in the voting law. Belaúnde had campaigned more extensively in the rural highlands than any previous presidential candidate, and his promise of agrarian reform, also a major component of the U.S. Alliance for Progress, was salient. Although the percentage of the adult population voting in the highlands was still extremely low (under 10 percent in 1963), voters went strongly for Belaúnde.[33]

The Belaúnde government delivered on some of its reform promises. Public expenditure for education and for infrastructure increased dramatically. The government increased tariffs and implemented a 1959 law that provided lavish incentives for investment in manufacturing—explicitly ending Peru's traditional export-led open economy and adopting import-substitution industrialization.[34]

However, Belaúnde had promised more social reform than he was able to deliver. From an aristocratic, political family in Arequipa, he was an architect who had traveled extensively throughout Peru and whose policy priority was the development of Peru's roads and other infrastructure. He did not vigorously pursue the modest agrarian reform bill that was passed by the Congress. Nor did he take rapid action against the International Petroleum Company (IPC, a subsidiary of Standard Oil), a company against which Peruvians' nationalistic sentiments were strong. The potential for reform during this period was also limited by the unseemly alliance in the legislature between two parties that had been archrivals—APRA and Odría's party. To many Peruvians' dismay, APRA apparently feared that Acción Popular would steal APRA's thunder as Peru's true reformist party if major reforms were implemented, and through this alliance was able to stymie the government.

The Velasco Government: 1968–1975[35]

The year 1968 was a watershed in Peruvian politics. Whereas traditionally Peruvian military officers had collaborated with the country's oligarchy, in 1968 General Juan Velasco Alvarado took power determined to end its power. The social and economic changes implemented during the Velasco government were the most dramatic changes in a leftist direction made by a Latin American military in the twentieth century.

The Peruvian military developed much more reformist inclinations than other Latin American militaries for various reasons. First, in contrast to some Latin American militaries, the Peruvian was not closely allied to landowning elites, and its primary concern was not internal repression but external war. Deeply affected by its loss to the Chileans in the War of the Pacific, the Peruvian military envied the level of national integration achieved by Chile and doubted that Peru could win a second war against Chile if the Peruvian peasantry did not develop a sense of national identity. Especially after the counterinsurgency struggle of the mid–1960s, the military was aware of the poverty and political marginalization of most peasants. The military came to believe that, without agrarian reform, defeat in a war with Chile was likely, and renewed insurgencies inevitable.

Such beliefs became conventional wisdom in the Peruvian military in part as a result of officers' socioeconomic background and education. To an unusual degree among Latin American nations, Peru's officers were drawn from lower-middle-class, mestizo, and provincial backgrounds; also to an unusual degree, they became well-educated.[36] At the pinnacle of Peru's military educational system was the Centro de Altos Estudios Militares

(CAEM), where a full-year course was devoted to the critical analysis of Peru's social and political problems.

While the Velasco coup was thus a response to the military's interpretation of long-standing Peruvian problems, it was also a specific reaction to what the military perceived as the failure of Peru's "last, best democratic hope"—the Belaúnde government. As noted above, the Belaúnde government failed to implement agrarian reform and failed to nationalize the IPC—both initiatives that the military considered important and overdue. Significant sectors in the military also remained wary of APRA, which had become the likely winner of the upcoming 1969 elections. Officers had also become critical of the U.S. government, which had not only vigorously backed IPC in its negotiations with the Belaúnde government, but had also held up a sale of Northrop F-5 jets to Peru and rejected Peru's claim to a 200-mile sovereign offshore zone for fishing.

In any case, on October 3, 1968, President Belaúnde was put on an airplane and, with considerable popular support, General Velasco proclaimed the Revolutionary Government of the Armed Forces. Velasco (whose personal background was provincial lower-middle-class and whose appearance prompted the nickname "El Chino") was one of the most progressive officers in the coup coalition. His proclaimed goal was a "fully participatory social democracy"; the previous Peruvian political order was not judged democratic, but a "sellout of the national interest" by "bad politicians" who "acted only to defend the interests of the powerful," and who "kowtowed to the United States."[37]

The Velasco government's highest priorities were to eclipse the power of the Peruvian oligarchy and of the U.S. government, primarily by means of property reform. The military government's agrarian reform was more devastating to large landowners than any other in Latin America, except for the Cuban. The reform expropriated almost all landholdings over fifty hectares and transformed them into various kinds of cooperatives—providing major benefits to the roughly 10 percent of all Peruvian agricultural families who became members of reasonably well-endowed cooperatives (most of which were on the country's coast) and some benefit to an additional 15 percent of farm families.[38] The Velasco government expropriated nonagricultural oligarchical bastions as well, ranging from fishing, mining, and banking companies to the daily newspapers. Overall, between 1968 and 1975 the share of Peru's GDP owned by the state catapulted from 13 to 23 percent; the share of GDP in workers' cooperatives rose from 1 to 10 percent; and income was transferred from the top 1 percent and top 5 percent of Peru's households to the next 20 percent in the income distribution.[39]

The government distanced Peru from the United States in various ways. Not only was IPC nationalized within a matter of days, but subsequently other U.S. companies as well. Most previous collaborative activities with the U.S. military were ended and major arms purchases were made from the Soviet Union. At the same time, the government championed the interests of "the nonaligned nations" and "the South." For example, the principle of a two-hundred-mile territorial sea limit was emphasized in numerous forums. Peru became an active proponent of the Andean Pact, an effort at collaborative trade and development among the Andean nations and control of foreign investment.

In a continuation of the Belaúnde government's policy, the Velasco government dramatically expanded educational opportunities. Literacy increased from approximately 61 percent of the fifteen-years-and-over age group around 1960 to 73 percent around 1970.[40] Although Peru's gross domestic product was below average for the Latin American region, the percentages of Peruvian young people enrolled in secondary schools and universities were well above average.[41]

As an anomalous kind of regime—a leftist military regime—it is perhaps not surprising that the Velasco government's political agenda was ambiguous and often contradictory. Officers were undecided whether their government was to last a few years, a decade, or longer; no electoral calendar was specified and no progovernment political party was established. While they claimed to seek a "fully participatory social democracy," their own government was hierarchical and at the highest levels closed to input from most civilian groups. The government was not repressive by Latin American standards, although several intellectuals were deported and political-party activities (especially by APRA) were severely restricted. After the government's 1974 expropriation of the country's major newspapers, they gradually became mouthpieces for the regime.

The government did, however, establish various new political institutions and provide political space for others. In particular, drawing upon the Yugoslav experience as well as from Allende's Chile, the government established various programs for peasants' and workers' participation in the management and profits of both agrarian cooperatives and "industrial communities."[42] Velasco said that he aspired to a political economy "in which the means of production are predominantly social property, under the direct control of those whose work generates the wealth; and . . . social, economic, and political institutions [are] directed . . . by the men and women who form them."[43]

The government also created a political agency, the Sistema Nacional por Mobilización Social (SINAMOS, an acronym that meant "Without Masters"). Top officials' goals for this agency were contradictory; some officials hoped that it would control and co-opt citizens' political activities, whereas others hoped that the agency would in fact promote a "fully participatory social democracy." In any case, the leftist rhetoric that was concurrent with SINAMOS and the activities of many of its officials at the grassroots level did foster organization that was increasingly autonomous of the military regime. Between 1968 and 1975, the number of recognized trade unions almost doubled; by the early 1980s, about 12 percent of the Peruvian labor force belonged to officially recognized unions, and another 3 percent to unrecognized unions.[44] The largest and most important labor federation, the Confederación General de Trabajadores del Perú (CGTP), and the largest and most important peasant federation, the Confederación de Campesinos del Perú (CCP), were both Marxist.

The Morales Bermúdez Government and the Transition to Electoral Democracy, 1975–1980[45]

After 1973, the Velasco government faltered. At this time, the reforms that had relatively widespread support had been implemented, Velasco fell ill and factionalism within the military institution became more intense, and the contradictions in the reform program became more blatant. Also, for various reasons, the economy weakened. In the wake of rioting in February 1975, almost no group stood up to support the regime. In September 1975, Velasco was ousted in a palace coup by General Francisco Morales Bermúdez, who was considered a political moderate.

The economic clouds of the early and mid-1970s gathered into a devastating storm by the late 1970s. Payments on Peru's debt jumped; when Morales Bermúdez reluctantly sought to refinance the debt, the International Monetary Fund (IMF) designed a stabilization program that seemed draconian to most Peruvians. Popular protest mounted. Calling for economic change and for democratic freedoms, the protesters organized a general strike on July 19, 1977, which virtually shut the entire nation down; the general strike was Peru's first since 1919 and the most massive in the country's history.

Less than two weeks after the 1977 general strike, Morales Bermúdez announced a transition to democracy in his annual address to the nation. The transition from military rule to elected government had a number of elements that boded well for democracy. During this period, the military governed, but a Constituent Assembly wrote a new and much more democratic constitution for the country, approved in July 1979. The most important new features were the enfranchisement of illiterates and a second-round balloting system. The new constitution also reduced the presidential term from six to five years.

Also promising for the subsequent democratic process was the end of the hostilities between the military and APRA. In the 1978 elections for the Constituent Assembly, APRA won a 35 percent plurality of the valid vote, and Haya de la Torre was elected president of the Assembly.[46] President Morales Bermúdez and Haya de la Torre worked closely together during the drafting of the new constitution and sought to assure mutual tolerance between officers and *apristas* in the future.

More complex in its implications for Peruvian democracy was the rise of the Marxist left. In the 1978 elections for the Constituent Assembly, four leftist parties that were later to become the Izquierda Unida (IU) won a dramatic 29 percent of the vote; in previous elections, the Marxist left had never won as much as 5 percent.[47] The rise of the left was a result of the longer-term implications of many of the Velasco government's reforms mentioned above, as well as of continuing economic crisis and the desire for a more rapid return to civilian government.

In principle, there were advantages to the drafting of a new constitution by a popularly elected assembly. Not only should such a constitution be more legitimate than one developed in any other way, but working together in the Constituent Assembly should have given Peru's key political parties opportunities for the establishment of more constructive relationships within each party, and among them. This latter hope was only partially realized. First, Acción Popular was not present in the Assembly; it had abstained from the 1978 elections, arguing for a more rapid return to democracy. Second, with the death of Haya in 1979, APRA's attention was soon to focus on leadership succession within the party. Third, on most issues in the Constituent Assembly, APRA allied with the relatively rightist Partido Popular Cristiano (PPC), which had won 24 percent of the 1978 vote;[48] leftist leaders were often isolated and, in continuing to emphasize grassroots protest and the need for radical socioeconomic change, did not seek to work with the other parties. Ultimately, leftist leaders did not sign the new constitution.

The 1980–1992 Electoral Democracy

The 1980 elections were the first in Peru that met the criteria for democracy in this volume: neither APRA nor the Marxist left nor any other party was excluded, and illiterates could vote. In 1980, Peruvians elected Acción Popular's Belaúnde, the very president whom the military had deposed in 1968 (see Table 6.2). Angry at what they saw as the brutal and unsophisticated behavior of the military, citizens valued the statesmanlike character of the former president. The former president campaigned as a center-leftist; one of his most salient campaign promises was a million new jobs, and he attracted votes from across the political spectrum. Furthermore, Armando Villanueva (the *aprista* candidate who had succeeded the late Haya de la Torre as the party's leader) reminded citizens of the party's aggressive past, and the Marxist left divided into more than five factions.

Belaúnde's administration was beset by two formidable problems: the region-wide debt crisis and the Sendero Luminoso (Shining Path) guerrillas. Tragically, Belaúnde appeared at a loss to resolve either problem. Once in the presidency, Belaúnde spoke as a neoliberal, but continued to act as a populist. The large state role in the economy was retained and, after securing significant international loans, the government increased public

Table 6.2   Results for Presidential Elections, 1980–1995[a]

	1980	1985	1990	1995
Winning party	Acción Popular	APRA	Cambio 90	Cambio 90[b]
President-elect	Fernando Belaúnde	Alan García	Alberto Fujimori	Alberto Fujimori
Winning party's tally (%)	45	53	29	64
Party in second place	APRA	Izquierda Unida[c]	FREDEMO[d]	Unión por el Perú[e]
Second-place party's tally (%)	27	25	33	24

Sources: For pre-1995 contests, Richard Webb and Graciela Fernández Baca, *Perú en números 1991* (Lima: Cuánto, 1991), pp. 1028–1030. For 1995, Richard Webb and Graciela Fernández Baca, *Perú en números 1996*, pp. 399–400.

Notes: a. All percentages are percentages of valid votes in the first round. Please note that information about the number of seats in the legislature held by all major political parties 1980–1995 is indicated in Tables 6.3 and 6.4.

b. Officially named Cambio 90–Nueva Mayoría in 1995.

c. Coalition of leftists parties led in 1985 by Alfonso Barrantes.

d. Coalition of parties led by Mario Vargas Llosa.

e. Coalition of parties led by Javier Pérez de Cuéllar.

expenditure, especially in super-scale projects that facilitated financial gain for government officials and their business cronies, but failed to alleviate poverty (see the section "Development Performance"). In 1981 and 1982, Peru was hurt by the same international economic trends that affected most of the region—a marked increase in external interest rates and falling international prices for its main exports; and, just as in most of the region, Peru's trade balance turned negative. Still, the Belaúnde government continued to spend: the budget deficit soared to 9.7 percent of GDP.[49] The country's economic problems were exacerbated by a severe 1982–1983 El Niño. Facing payments on the foreign debt that exceeded 37 percent of export earnings, President Belaúnde began negotiations with the International Monetary Fund.[50] Under a 1984 agreement, Peru reduced its fiscal deficit, but the adjustment was insufficient to comply with the IMF's targets. Quietly, the government stopped servicing its foreign debt.

At the same time, Peru was threatened by the most serious guerrilla challenge in its history. The Shining Path was perhaps the most sectarian revolutionary movement ever to expand in Latin America; virulently Maoist, it assassinated political leaders from other Marxist groups as readily as those from the right, and repudiated the Soviet Union as well as the United States. The Sendero Luminoso was also unusually savage, brutally killing not only political leaders and security personnel but also development engineers, church people, and peasants whom it deemed traitors. The Belaúnde government's response was ineffective. For almost two years, the government did nothing; then, in 1983 and 1984, Belaúnde endorsed

wholesale repressive action by the Peruvian military, failing to urge respect
for human rights and failing to consider social or economic problems. By
the end of Belaúnde's term, the Shining Path controlled broad swaths of
Peru's southern highlands and was extending its reach into the country's
coca-producing departments. By 1985, more than 55 percent of the respondents in one survey judged his administration "one of the worst Peru has
ever had" or "a bad government."[51] In cartoons, Belaúnde was portrayed as
sitting in the clouds, impervious to the suffering of the Peruvian people
below. The major achievements of his second government were considered
to be the restoration of media freedoms and the constitutional transfer of
power in 1985.

In the 1985 elections Peruvians were looking for a president who
would be very different. In a groundswell, they turned to the charismatic
aprista candidate, Alan García. Although García was Haya de la Torre's
principal protégé, and he maintained the themes of spiritualist regeneration
that had been salient under Haya, García worked to soften the image of
APRA as a sectarian party.[52] García's message was for hope and change
under an energetic, innovative leader who sympathized with the plight of
the poor. García won an astounding 53 percent of the valid votes in a contest among four major parties (see Table 6.2).

Relative to Belaúnde, Alan García raised hopes much higher and
dashed them more completely. At a time when the debt crisis was the most
salient issue for the region and many nations were turning toward accommodation with the international financial community, García staked out a
position well to the left of his South American counterparts. In his inaugural address, García indicated his desire to assume a leadership position in the
Third World against "imperialism"; he blamed the Third World's debt crisis
in large part upon the United States; and he said that Peru would not pay
more than 10 percent of its export earnings to service its debt.[53] García's
militant rhetoric pleased Peruvians (almost 80 percent of whom had voted
either for García or for the candidate to his left, Izquierda Unida's Alfonso
Barrantes); during his first year in office, García's approval rating exceeded
80 percent.[54] Needless to say, however, García's position deeply alienated
the Reagan administration.[55]

For two years, García's expansionary fiscal policies appeared to succeed: in 1986 GDP per capita grew by almost 6 percent, real wages
increased by more than 40 percent, employment rose, and inflation
slowed.[56] However, these achievements were based on an unsustainable
increase in public spending and the depletion of international reserves.
García had hoped that Peru's wealthy business groups would invest in Peru,
but this investment was not forthcoming and an angry García retaliated by
proposing to nationalize private banks, a proposal that was ultimately with-
drawn but that enraged Peru's elites. By the end of 1987, Peru's reserves
ran out, and the government had little choice but to abandon its expansion-

ary policies. For the second half of García's term, the government was ambivalent, wanting new international loans but ultimately unwilling to implement as drastic and thorough a program as the international financial community required. The result was "one of the worst economic performances in modern history."[57] By the end of the García administration, real per capita GDP was estimated to be less than in 1960, and accumulated inflation over the five years was more than 2 million percent.[58]

At the same time, the Shining Path expanded—seemingly inexorably on the path to taking over the Peruvian state. In contrast to Belaúnde, García interpreted Sendero as a serious problem that was the result of the destitution and marginalization of Peru's southern highlands. Especially during the first two years of his term, President García sought to provide economic aid to the southern highlands and to raise respect for human rights standards by the military. However, the government's economic-aid effort failed amidst Sendero's attacks on development officials, the paucity of state resources after 1987, and corruption; further, the government's human rights initiative infuriated the military. By 1989, the Shining Path numbered approximately 10,000 combatants, had the support of roughly 15 percent of Peru's citizens, and controlled about 28 percent of the country's municipalities.[59]

At the start of 1990, APRA was seriously discredited and Peru's left was demoralized as a result of Alfonso Barrantes's split from Izquierda Unida to form his own Izquierda Socialista. Accordingly, the odds-on favorite to win the 1990 presidential contest was Mario Vargas Llosa, the renowned novelist who had spearheaded opposition to García's attempt to nationalize commercial banks and had subsequently assumed leadership of the rightist coalition FREDEMO (Frente Democrático), which included Acción Popular, the Partido Popular Cristiano, and SODE (Solidaridad y Democracia) as well as his own Movimiento Libertad. But the FREDEMO coalition was fractious, and during the campaign Vargas Llosa's arrogance and disconnection with the Peruvian people were evident. Moreover, even after the economic catastrophe of the García adminstration, Vargas Llosa's emphasis upon the need for drastic neoliberal adjustment policies—a "shock"—frightened Peruvians, and they were looking for an alternative candidate.

This alternative appeared in the person of Alberto Fujimori, who emerged as the surprise second-place finisher of the first round and the easy winner of the second round.[60] Fujimori was the son of humble Japanese immigrants whose physical appearance was much more similar to most Peruvians' than other political leaders', and he was able to persuade citizens that he was indeed, in the words of his slogan, "Un presidente como tú" ("A president like you"). Fujimori also clearly opposed Vargas Llosa's "shock" program, and his most salient campaign promise was that he could restore economic prosperity through "gradual" changes. He also appealed broadly to citizens and political leaders whose primary concern was the defeat of Vargas Llosa; as an "independent" candidate who hailed from neither the APRA nor the Marxist left, he was likely to secure both these political groups' support in the second round.

During his first fifteen months, President Fujimori enjoyed tremendous policymaking power. In contrast to his presidential predecessors who were at least somewhat constrained by their political parties (for example, filling most cabinet offices with their partisans), Fujimori disregarded his vehicle, Cambio 90, which included primarily politically inexperienced representatives of small-business groups and the evangelical Protestant community. After Fujimori's first six months in office, almost all of his cabinet members were political independents appointed by the president himself. At the same time that Fujimori distanced himself from Cambio 90, he allied with men whose social and political networks were in the security forces.

Almost immediately after his inauguration, Fujimori reversed his populist campaign promises.[61] In order to receive the International Monetary Fund's stamp of approval, Fujimori implemented a shock program that many analysts considered even more drastic than Vargas Llosa's proposal. Fujimori committed his government to servicing the country's debt (at the same time that he sought renegotiation of the terms of payment) as well as to stabilizing and liberalizing the economy. Amid what was dubbed the "Fujishock," state expenditure was slashed, foreign investment laws were eased, privatization was initiated, and tariffs were cut. Also, a new institution was diligently built: the SUNAT (National Superintendency of Tax Administration), to provide Peru an effective tax capability. These policies were successful in restoring Peru to the good graces of the international financial community as well as in taming hyperinflation (which had raged to over 7,000 percent in 1990), but poverty predictably worsened.

Fujimori also promoted counterinsurgency and antinarcotics policies that were at odds with his campaign promises. Whereas during the campaign Fujimori's counterinsurgency proposals were not particularly clear but tended to focus upon economic development, once in office Fujimori vigorously promoted civilian self-defense patrols (*rondas*). In May 1991, Fujimori signed a crucial antinarcotics agreement with the United States that was much more to the right than Fujimori's campaign position on the issue.

Why was Fujimori able to implement his preferred policies when Cambio 90 held only about a quarter of the seats in the legislature? First and most obviously, the largest political coalition in the legislature, FREDEMO, supported most of Fujimori's initiatives, in particular his economic initiatives. Second, the political parties that would have been expected to oppose his policies were in disarray. APRA was maligned for its governing record during the previous five years: for much of 1990 and 1991, the party and García were mired in charges of corruption. For its part, the Marxist coalition IU had fragmented and declined. Third, provisions in the 1979 Constitution allowed the executive to wield vast unilateral power over economic policy, and also to issue decrees in any policy area if authority were delegated to it by the legislature. In the Belaúnde and García administrations, this authority had frequently been delegated, especially at the start of the new presidency, and it was to Fujimori as well.

However, as 1991 ended, tensions between the executive and the legislature increased. In November, just as the legislative power granted to Fujimori was about to expire, Fujimori issued an avalanche of 126 decrees; more than three-quarters were approved, but 28—most of which were draconian decrees about counterinsurgency—were modified or repealed by the legislature.[62] Disagreement about the 1992 budget was intense, and Fujimori's minister of agriculture was censured by the Chamber of Deputies. Also, García was exonerated from charges of illicit enrichment by the Supreme Court and reelected secretary general of APRA.

Although for some scholars these new actions by Peru's legislature constituted legislative obstruction of the executive sufficient to constitute the primary explanation for the April 1992 *autogolpe,* for most scholars they were not.[63] Scholars who did not deem the legislature obstructionist point out that whereas the legislature under Fujimori censured one minister in twenty months, the legislature during Belaúnde's first term had censured more than fifty; they also emphasize that right up to the *autogolpe,* FREDEMO legislators were pursuing an agreement with Fujimori. For these scholars, the primary reason for the *autogolpe* was the political will of President Fujimori and of the military. Fujimori was an authoritarian personality who did not want to spend his time negotiating with opposition political leaders and who wanted his presidential term to extend beyond five years (prohibited in the 1979 Constitution).[64] And many military and intelligence officers believed that an authoritarian regime was necessary for the defeat of Sendero.[65]

In any case, on April 5, 1992, Fujimori suspended the 1979 Constitution, arrested several opposition leaders, dissolved the Congress, and dismantled the judiciary. While the *autogolpe* was condemned by the vast majority of intellectuals and political leaders, it was supported by almost 80 percent of the Peruvian population.[66] Their support was not a reflection of their belief that Fujimori's policies were working. To the contrary, economic and security conditions were worse than ever before. Although hyperinflation had ended, poverty had increased and the Shining Path had expanded dramatically in Peru's cities, especially Lima.[67] These ills were consistently blamed on Peru's political regime by Fujimori; for almost two years, he vilified Peru's party leaders, legislators, and judges as corrupt, inefficient, and antidemocratic.[68] There was, of course, an element of truth in Fujimori's charges; but perhaps even more important, his charges inspired hope that a "simple" change of political regime would end their country's nightmare.

The Fujimori Government After the 1992 Autogolpe

As indicated in the introduction to this chapter, scholars agree that from April 5, 1992, until at least the promulgation of a new constitution in November 1993, the Fujimori government could not be classified as democratic, no matter what adjective qualified the label. However, when new presidential and congressional elections were held in April 1995 and Fujimori was reelected in a landslide, classification of the regime became more controversial and more difficult. On the one hand, there was no doubt that in 1995 Fujimori was reelected in a context that was as free and fair as most in Latin America. On the other hand, from 1992 until August 1998, Fujimori's government was a triumvirate in which the president shared power with a cashiered army captain and de facto head of the Servicio Intelligencia Nacional (SIN), Vladimiro Montesinos, and the commander of the armed forces, General Nicolás Hermoza; based institutionally upon the SIN and the military, this triumvirate rode roughshod over Peru's civilian institutions.[69]

The first six months after the *autogolpe* were rocky and the political outcome uncertain. While the *autogolpe* was supported by most Peruvians, the move was opposed by many international groups (see the section "International Factors," p. 353). In a compromise reached at a May 18 meeting of the Organization of American States in the Bahamas, President Fujimori agreed to hold elections for a constituent assembly within five months. For its part, the international community agreed that Peru's reentry into the international financial community would proceed smoothly.

Still, obstacles remained on the road to Fujimori's consolidation of power under a new constitution of his own design. The government's politicization of the military institution was opposed by a significant sector of the military; a countercoup plot was put down in November. At the same time, attacks by the Shining Path were escalating rather than diminishing; in one of the worst incidents of the war, on July 16 a car bomb killed 21 people and injured 250 in Miraflores (a posh area of the capital). Also, in part because of the uncertainties provoked by the *autogolpe*, GDP declined by 2.9 percent in 1992; poverty levels, which had worsened dramatically in the wake of the August 1990 "Fujishock," were not abating.[70]

Another question was whether or not the Fujimori government would keep its promise to hold elections meeting the international community's and the domestic opposition's standards for freedom and fairness. In the two most important popular votes in the wake of the *autogolpe*, government machinations were numerous. For the November 1992 elections of

Table 6.3 Parties' Seats in the Peruvian Legislature, 1980, 1985, and 1990[a]

Party	1980 Senate (n = 60)	1980 Chamber (n = 180)	1985 Senate (n = 61)	1985 Chamber (n = 180)	1990 Senate (n = 62)	1990 Chamber (n = 180)
Acción Popular	26	98	6*	10	8*	27
Partido Popular Cristiano (PPC)[b]	6	10	3	9	5	25
APRA	18	58	32	107	17*	53
Izquierda Unida[c]	9	10	15	48	6	16
Izquierda Socialista	n.a.	n.a.	n.a.	n.a.	4	3
Frenetraca	1	4	1	1	1	3
Cambio 90	n.a.	n.a.	n.a.	n.a.	14	32
Independents	0	0	0	2	0	3

Sources: Richard Webb and Graciela Fernández Baca, *Perú en números 1996* (Lima: Cuánto, 1996), p. 393, and Fernando Tuesta Soldevilla, *Perú político en cifras* (Lima: Fundación Friedrich Ebert, 1994), p. 65.

Notes: a. Numbers do not add to the totals in the two houses because of the omission of small, transient parties or coalitions: in 1985, Convergencia Democrática (4 seats besides PPC's in the Senate and 3 seats besides PPC's in the Chamber) and, in 1990, Libertad and SODE in FREDEMO, and the Frente Independiente Moralizador.

b. In 1985, ran with dissident *apristas* in Convergencia Democrática and in 1990 in FREDEMO.

c. The parties widely perceived as the Marxist left ran united under this name only in 1985. In 1980, the parties with legislative seats that had run within Izquierda Unida in 1978 and ran within it in 1985 included the Partido Revolucionario de los Trabajadores, Alianza Unidad de Izquierda, Unión de Izquierda Revolucionaria, and Frente Obrero Campesino Estudiantil. In 1990, these groups divided between Izquierda Unida and Izquierda Socialista.

*Numbers include the parties' former presidents, who became "senators for life."

the Congreso Constituyente Democrático (CCD) that was to write Peru's new constitution, Fujimori delayed the establishment of procedural guidelines and said that members of the CCD would be ineligible to run for elective office for at least one term. Although this prohibition was subsequently rescinded, it of course discouraged participation by established political leaders. Most of Peru's better-known parties (APRA, AP, and the largest leftist party) abstained. Still, Fujimori won only a bare majority of the seats in the CCD: forty-four out of eighty (see Table 6.4).

Even more doubts were raised about the fairness of the referendum on the CCD's constitution held in October 1993.[71] The results of the referendum were unexpectedly close—52.2 percent for the "yes" to 47.5 percent for the "no" in the official tally—but, especially after reports of election-day irregularities in remote areas began to reach Lima, the actual result was believed to have been a victory for the "no" by political-opposition analysts. The opposition parties' primary objection was that, in remote emergency zones where military commanders were the top authorities, they distorted voting procedures and vote counts. Yet the Fujimori government's

Table 6.4   Parties' Seats in the Peruvian Legislature, 1990, 1992, and 1995

Party/Coalition	1990[a]		1992	1995
	Senate (n = 62)	Chamber (n = 180)	Democratic Constituent (n = 80)[b]	Congress (n = 120)[c]
FREDEMO	21	63	n.a.	n.a.
Acción Popular	8	27	n.a.	4
PPC	5	25	8	3
Libertad	6	9	n.a.	n.a.
SODE	1	2	1	n.a.
Cambio 90[d]	14	32	44	67
APRA	17	53	n.a.	8
Unión por el Perú	n.a.	n.a.	n.a.	17
Izquierda Unida	6	16	n.a.	2
Izquierda Socialista	4	3	n.a.	n.a.
Frenetraca	1	3	3	1
Frente Independiente Moralizador	0	7	7	6
Renovación	n.a.	n.a.	6	3

Sources: Richard Webb and Graciela Fernández Baca, *Perú en números 1996* (Lima: Cuánto, 1996), p. 393, and Fernando Tuesta Soldevilla, *Perú político en cifras* (Lima: Fundación Friedrich Ebert, 1994), pp. 64–65.

Notes: a. Additional seats were held by one nonpartisan FREDEMO member in Senate; 3 independents in the Chamber.

b. Additional seats were held by Movimiento Democrático de Izquierda, 4; Coordinadora Democrática, 4; Frepap, 2; Movimiento Independiente Agrario, 1.

c. Additional seats were held by CODE (País Posible), 5; Obras, 2; Frepap, 1; Movimiento Independiente Agrario, 1.

d. After 1990, this party became the coalition Cambio 90/Nueva Mayoría.

machinations were tolerated; if the voting outcomes were to have been repudiated, more vigorous coordination would have been necessary between the domestic opposition and the international community.

Ultimately, however, the path toward Fujimori's consolidation of power under a constitution of his own design was smoothed first by triumphs against the Shining Path and then by economic recovery. In September 1992, the Grupo Especial de Inteligencia (GEIN), a small, elite squad within Peru's antiterrorist police that had been established under President García, captured the leader of the Shining Path, Abimael Guzmán. Within the next few weeks, using information found in Guzmán's hideout, police arrested more than 1,000 suspected Senderistas. The Shining Path's previous psychological advantage—their image of omniscience, omnipresence, and invincibility against a corrupt and inefficient state—was reversed. During the next few years, the Shining Path was decimated.[72]

As relative political peace returned at the same time that the government achieved macroeconomic stabilization, the economy grew. The government's privatization program was successful and foreign direct investment increased dramatically.[73] Real GDP rose at an average annual rate of 6.4 percent in 1993 and 13.1 percent in 1994—the highest rate in the region.[74] Growth was especially robust in those rural areas where conventional economic activities were resuming after many years of violence. Still, for the majority of Peruvians the primary benefit of the new economic policies was the low inflation rate (24 percent in 1994).[75]

The Fujimori government's surmounting of both guerrilla violence and economic crisis paved the way to the president's reelection in April 1995. In contrast to the 1992 and 1993 contests, the April 1995 election was a landslide. Fujimori won an impressive 64 percent of the valid votes in a field of fourteen candidates—more than twice as many votes as the runner-up and more than enough to avoid a runoff (see Table 6.2). The strong support for Fujimori was attributable not only to his first-term achievements, but also, as Kenneth Roberts first pointed out, to an increasingly populist strategy.[76] From Fujimori's entry into politics in 1990, the property of populism as political mobilization by a personalist leader who subordinated institutions was clearly applicable to Fujimori's approach. But salient also in definitions of populism has been the leader's capacity to forge a multi-class alliance and, in particular, to build support among the poor. Although this alliance had traditionally been forged through import-substitution industrialization policies and economic expansionism, it became clear that the alliance could also be established in a neoliberal economic context. As the government gained several billion dollars from privatization, it allocated at least $875 million—approximately half the privatization dividend—for social and investment programs.[77] The pattern of expenditure was quintessentially populist: the vast bulk of this money was allocated by the Ministry of the Presidency, with Fujimori himself traveling frequently to lower-class communities to inaugurate projects and, dressed in a poncho and Andean-style hat, even helicoptering to remote peasant communities.[78] Responding to a question about the principal achievements of the Fujimori government, citizens ranked its counterinsurgency effort first, but school construction second and road improvement fourth.[79]

The runner-up in the 1995 presidential election was Javier Pérez de Cuéllar, who headed the new "independent" political party Unión por el Perú (UPP). It had been hoped that, as the distinguished former secretary-general of the United Nations, Pérez de Cuéllar would be a presidential candidate around whom ideologically diverse opposition groups would unite. Yet, at 75, Caucasian, and having resided abroad most of his life, Pérez de Cuéllar was not "a president like you," and did not interact easily with most Peruvians. Also, the hope that he would be a unifying candidate for the opposition was not realized, as the only long-standing party that fully backed Pérez de Cuéllar in the presidential race was the PPC.

While it was clear that voters chose Fujimori as their president in 1995, it was not clear that they chose Cambio 90/Nueva Mayoría as the majority party in the legislature. Whereas 39 percent of Peru's registered voters cast their ballots for Cambio 90/Nueva Mayoria's presidential candidate, only 18 percent cast their ballots for its legislative candidates.[80] A whopping 41 percent of the ballots were "null" in the legislative race (more than triple the percentages in the previous 1990 and 1985 legislative races).[81] Moreover, 6.8 percent of the voters were "missing."[82] In addition, whereas the result for the presidential race was similar to the opinion-poll prediction, the result for the legislative race was not; the opinion-poll prediction for the congressional contest had been that Cambio 90/Nueva Mayoría would win 25 percent to 35 percent of the valid vote and 28 of the 120 seats (versus the official result of 52 percent of the votes and 67 of the seats).[83]

Not long after the 1995 elections, support for the Fujimori government began to erode, falling in polls from above 50 percent over the period from September 1992 until October 1996 to around 30 percent through September 1998.[84] The reasons were economic and political. The economy slowed; GDP growth decelerated from an annual average of almost 9 percent in 1993–1995 to an annual average of approximately 4 percent in 1996–1998 and a scant 1 percent in 1998; and the slight improvements in the unemployment and poverty rates that had occurred in 1993–1995 did not continue.[85] As of 1998, the current account deficit was deeper into red ink as a result of El Niño and the Asian financial crisis. High tax and interest rates posed serious obstacles for many businesses, especially new ones, which in turn reduced employment opportunities.

The government lost support as it was increasingly perceived as authoritarian.[86] Citizens were concerned that the shadowy, Rasputin-like Montesinos—who had no official appointment and was accordingly not accountable to any democratic institution—was becoming ever more powerful, perhaps more powerful than Fujimori himself.[87] It became apparent that President Fujimori sought the possibility of a third presidential term and that his Cambio 90/Nueva Mayoría would block any judicial interpretation or other initiative (such as a referendum) that would prevent Fuijimori's candidacy in 2000. Evidence also mounted that, primarily through Montesinos's SIN, the government had resorted to dirty tricks against opposition candidates during the 1995 election and that it was doing all that it could to skew the electoral playing field in its favor for the year-2000 elections. In particular, the government tried to assure the representation of as many pro-Fujimori judges as possible in Peru's three key electoral institutions.[88] Accordingly, whereas in 1996 46 percent of Peruvians—above the regional average—believed that, in general, the country's elections were clean rather than fraudulent, by 1998 the figure had fallen to 26 percent, below the regional average.[89]

What are the possible scenarios for Peru's political future? For this author, it appeared likely that, as has been the historical pattern in Peru, citizens' concerns about both their executive's economic policies and his authoritarian proclivities would coalesce to end his regime before it lasted fifteen years, and that Peru would return to the set of Latin American nations that are noncontroversially classified as electoral democracies.

The return to an electoral democracy would be smoothed by the victory of an independent or opposition candidate in the year-2000 elections, whether or not Fujimori ultimately decides to run. As of the writing of this chapter in early 1999, the strongest candidate appeared likely to be a political independent whose political party was a personal electoral vehicle, such as Luis Cantañeda Lossio, a former head of the state health service, or Alberto Andrade, the mayor of Lima. Due both to the government's capacity to harass and intimidate opposition candidates from Peru's longer-standing political parties as well as their own disunity and ineffectiveness, a winning candidate did not appear likely to emerge from their ranks.

It was also possible, however, that Fujimori would opt to run for a third term and would claim to win, and that the return to electoral democracy would be turbulent. For obvious reasons, the possibility of Fujimori competing and faring well enough to claim victory depended a great deal on economic trends within the country, and the president's capacity to use state resources for partisan purposes as well as to skew electoral procedures in his favor. However, as the public-opinion polls cited above suggest, a clear majority of Peruvians do not favor a third term for Fujimori and would question the legitimacy of his second reelection. As political unrest has increased even during the final years of Fujimori's second term, it seemed unlikely that he would survive until the end of a third term in 2005. In this scenario, the international community would be called upon to help put Peru back on the road toward electoral democracy, and its stance would be important.

THEORETICAL ANALYSIS

Peru's history of failure with democracy is not surprising; virtually every independent variable predicted in this book to enhance the potential for democratic consolidation was absent in the Peruvian case at least until the 1970s. Because every variable was negative, and real democracy was not even attempted until 1980, one variable cannot be rigorously demonstrated to have been more important than any other. Rather, there was a vicious political circle in which each negative variable exacerbated others. The character of the circle that I believe to have been most significant is as follows: (1) the fissures and tensions of the nation's political culture weakened democratic political institutions; (2) weak democratic institutions led to failures of democratic governance and of development performance; and (3) completing the circle, amid these failures the historical wounds in the nation's political culture were not healed.

The variables in this circle highlighted below include historical legacies, socioeconomic cleavages, and civil society (or more briefly, political culture); constitutional structure; political parties; the state; development performance; and international factors. In these paragraphs introducing this theoretical section, I suggest some of the interactions among these variables.

In the aftermath of Peru's harsh colonial experience, the class, ethnic, and geographic cleavages in the country—primarily between Peru's elite, Caucasian descendants of the Spanish and the indigenous population—were overlapping and extremely sharp. Amid these cleavages, Peruvians did not trust one another and were ambivalent toward authority—at times humble before a leader and at times rebellious. The willingness to compromise and put the interests of political parties or other institutions above personal interests was rare; the relationships among political leaders were often conflictual and the relationship between leaders and citizens at the grassroots level were troubled (if the latter existed at all). In this political culture, the institutionalization of political parties was extremely difficult; rather, there was a widespread perception that a "strong leader" was necessary: a *caudillo* who could whip fractious, egotistical politicians into line and, ideally also, a populist whose message could somehow appeal to disparate social groups.

The dearth of institutionalized political parties and the apparent desire for a "stronger leader" prompted the framers of Peru's constitutions to grant large powers to the president. Presidentialism—defined as the direct election of the president for a fixed term—has been a constant feature of Peru's thirteen constitutions; the parliamentary alternative has never been attempted. Presidentialism was unlikely to enhance the development of Peru's political parties or other democratic institutions, and it has not.

Without institutionalized political parties, Peru's state was not autonomous but penetrated by elite and personalistic interests. Political elites set policies to advance the economic and political interests of their own circles, not of the nation as a whole. A logical result was a development performance that for centuries failed to redress the country's unequal income distribution. Peru's cleavages endured—and the vicious political circle was complete. Only in the 1970s and the 1980s did Peru's income distribution become more equal; unfortunately, however, while the figures for income equality were improving, the record for economic growth was dismal.

Although international influences were not decisive in the rise or fall of any Peruvian government, the influence of the United States was yet a variable interacting with others not only in the emergence of various democratic governments, but also in their demise. Overall, the U.S. record in support of democracy in Peru was not highly positive. Except perhaps at the time of the 1992 *autogolpe,* the United States appeared to place economic and other policy priorities above concern for democracy. While domestic forces within the United States are of course most important to the establishment of U.S. foreign policy priorities, it is also the case that various Peruvian democratic governments did not effectively manage their relations with the United States.

Do Peru's vicious political circles endure today? On the one hand, the most significant positive change has been the post-1960s attenuation of Peru's cleavages and the increased political sophistication of Peru's majorities. On the other hand, in the wake of Fujimori's *autogolpe,* a new constitution was written that strengthened presidential power even more than in the past, and the political parties were further weakened. The deinstitutionalization of Peru's political parties became one of the most serious obstacles to redemocratization.

Historical Legacies, Socioeconomic Cleavages, and Civil Society

This section examines in greater depth the problematical political attitudes that emerged in Peru in the wake of the Spanish conquest and colonial rule and the subsequent severe socioeconomic cleavages in the country. It also explores more recent changes in the country's political culture.

The Spanish conquest (see Historical Overview in this chapter) provoked one complex set of attitudes among the Spanish *conquistadores* and a very different set among the Incas and other conquered indigenous peoples. For the small group of Spanish *conquistadores,* there was the knowledge that they had easily overwhelmed a population perhaps 100,000 times larger—but that they had done so through deceit and murder, and that Peru's indigenous peoples might seek revenge. For Peru's indigenous peoples, there was indeed the anger and thirst for revenge that the Spaniards feared, especially given the brutality of the Spaniards' colonial rule, and these indigenous peoples did rebel. At the same time, though, their anger and mistrust were tempered with humiliation and a view that perhaps the most rational option for each individual was to maximize his or her own opportunities with the nation's powerful elites.

The clash during the Conquest and pursuant colonial era established two ethnic, class, and geographic poles in Peru. At one pole was the small (now approximately 8 percent) of the population who were Caucasian, whose religion was Catholic, whose first language was Spanish, and who were relatively wealthy.[90] Especially after the early nineteenth century and the expansion of sugar and cotton production, most of these families' landholdings were on the coast, and most of their primary residences were in Lima. At the other pole was the approximate half of Peru's population (until 1940) that lived in the Andean mountains who were called "Indians": they were relatively dark-skinned with other specific facial characteristics, they maintained various Incan beliefs, their first language was Quechua, their attire and grooming were distinctive, and they were peasants who struggled merely to subsist.[91] Their numbers were especially large in the departments of the southern highlands (Cuzco, Puno, Ayacucho, Huancavelica, and Apurímac).

The economic gap between these two poles was vast—vaster than in most other Latin American nations. Although the precise figures varied somewhat, virtually every analysis of Peru's income distribution showed it to be one of the most skewed in Latin America; in probably the most careful study, in 1961, the wealthiest 1 percent of Peru's economically active population received a staggering 30 percent of the national income.[92] At approximately the same time, a mere 280 families—less than 0.1 percent of all farm families—owned approximately 30 percent of the land in Peru and well over half of Peru's best arable soil (most of which was coastal land dedicated to export crops).[93] By contrast, Peru's Natives eked out a living on tiny plots that were usually rocky, precipitous, and at extremely high altitudes.[94]

The economic gap was exacerbated by Peru's topography. Access between the coast and the Andean highlands—which are steeper and higher in Peru than in any other Andean country except Bolivia—is difficult. Unlike the other Andean countries, the capital of Peru is on the coast, rather than in the mountains. Thus, whereas the elites in other Andean countries were likely to at least visit the highlands occasionally, in Peru they often did not.

At the same time, it is important to emphasize that although these ethnic, class, and geographic poles were salient in Peru, they were poles on a continuum; as the decades and centuries passed, there were many Peruvians at numerous points on the continuum as well as at the poles.[95] First, although the Spanish conquerors may have perceived the Natives as a homogeneous ethnic group, Peru's pre-Columbian civilizations were diverse. Second, given the small number of Spanish women in Peru after the Conquest, Spanish men consorted with Native women, and miscegenation was considerable. At the same time, many Natives sought to escape their ethnic status by adopting Spanish speech and dress and leaving their communities, and it was often difficult to distinguish "Indians" from mestizos. After 1940, migration from the highlands to the coast skyrocketed, and primary education dramatically reduced the number of monolingual Quechua speakers.[96] Also, considerable numbers of Chinese and Japanese immigrated to Peru, working first in guano extraction and then in hacienda agriculture.

Still, however, Peru's socioeconomic disparities reinforced the dimensions of Peruvian political culture that were unconducive to democracy. As

Seymour Lipset has emphasized, in a nation where class polarization is intense, the upper classes' attitudes tend to be arrogant and aloof, and the lower classes' resentful and envious.[97] This was certainly the case in Peru; in the mid–1950s, a leading intellectual of aristocratic origins described his fellow oligarchs' attitudes contemptuously: "How slack and feeble was the patriotism of the creole bourgeoisie! In the souls of these newly-rich merchants, what ignorance of ancient Peruvian traditions, what stupid and suicidal contempt for the nation, what sordid Levantine egotism!"[98] As noted above, elites' arrogance was also mixed with fear at what might happen if the lower classes mobilized, and both arrogance and fear were factors in their decisions (even during nominally democratic governments) to severely restrict peasants' educational opportunities as well as peasants' rights to vote or join political organizations.[99]

For their part, most poor, darker-skinned individuals understood that "to get along, you have to go along"; but, among some, there was at the same time resentment and even hate. In the classical clientelist pattern, a peasant sought to get ahead by establishing a relationship with a "patron," who would reward the peasant for his hard work and obedience, and also for his understanding that he was not to conspire with other peasants against the traditional order.[100] Amidst the struggle for ingratiation with a patron who discouraged peasant solidarity, it is not surprising that peasants were wary and mistrustful of each other.[101] As the country's political history indicates, poor Peruvians tolerated the hierarchical, clientelist order most of the time—but not always. For example, in a survey among the urban poor in 1965, only 45 percent strongly agreed that "violence should never be the way to resolve political problems."[102]

Peru's ethnic, class, and geographical cleavages were not only a real set of problems for the country, but a perceived set of problems. Many of Peru's best-known authors have emphasized the disparities among the nation's key social groups and the difficulties in the construction of a sense of citizenship and national identity. In turn, this perception provoked further atttitudes that were not conducive to democracy—in particular the idea that Peru was such a troubled nation that a "messiah" was necessary to "save" it. Accordingly, periodically Peruvians have pinned their hopes for the country upon one leader; perhaps inevitably, given the size of their expectations, they are disappointed and turn against the leader. Not surprisingly but unfortunately for Peru, none of these leaders was an institution builder.

The Velasco government's reforms (1968–1975) spearheaded various positive changes in Peru's political culture. Most important, of course, the oligarchy was eclipsed. New elites gained their wealth more as a result of their achievement and less as a result of their social background, and their political attitudes were not overtly antidemocratic.[103] But, amidst Peru's

recent anomalous political regimes—a leftist military government and ineffective elected governments in the 1980s—elites' political attitudes were
not consistent, and perhaps best characterized as opportunistic.[104]

Among Peru's middle and lower strata, political attitudes became more
democratic, more participatory, and at times also confrontational and
leftist.[105] By 1980, when Peruvians had been hearing the military government's calls for a "fully participatory social democracy" for more than a
decade and had observed the contradiction between political participation
in their localities and rule-by-fiat in the nation, they repudiated Peru's military regime and were enthusiastic about Peru's return to electoral democracy.[106] Table 6.5 shows that, as of 1982, majorities of Limeños preferred
democracy to other regime types, and that by 1986—when popular enthusiasm for Alan García was fervent—an overwhelming 88 percent preferred
democracy, a larger percentage than in Venezuela, a nation where democracy appeared strongly institutionalized at the time.[107] Moreover, democratic
principles were not only endorsed by Peruvians, but acted upon: high percentages of citizens followed the political news and voted.[108]

Table 6.5 also shows that leftist attitudes were prevalent during the
1980s. The reasons were various. First, the military government's own
rhetoric had raised expectations that were subsequently dashed, prompting
confrontational attitudes that had previously been repressed. Also important, many of the NGOs established during the 1970s, namely, the industrial

Table 6.5   Preferred Type of Government, 1982–1994 (percentage)

	Lima				Nationwide	
Type of Government	February 1982	June 1986	September 1990	March 1993	March 1988	August 1994
Democratic (elected)	66	88	70	83	75	83
Socialist (by revolution)	16	6	6	2	13	3
Military (by coup)	11	3	17	7	7	n.o.
Other, don't know	7	4	7	8	6	n.a.

Sources: Datum polls for the 1980s and Apoyo polls for the 1990s. The question was:
"Which of these types of governments do you consider to be the most adequate for a country
such as ours?" "N" is in the 400 to 800 range for each sample. The 1982 data were reported in
Caretas, December 13, 1982, p. 22; the Datum data for other years were provided directly by
Manuel Torrado, the director of Datum. The Apoyo data for Lima are reported in Julio F.
Carrión, "La brecha de apoyo a la democracia en el Perú: Reacciones ciudadanas al
Fujigolpe," unpublished paper, FLACSO-Ecuador (1995), p. 6; the nationwide Apoyo data are
reported in Apoyo, "Documento de información base para el Proyecto Democracia
Participativa (PARDY)," Lima (September 1994), p. 15.

Note: n.o. = Not an option in the item in the poll.

communities, agrarian cooperatives, and trade unions, as well as neighborhood organizations established during the 1980s, such as the Comedores
Populares (Communal Kitchens) and the Vaso de Leche (Glass of Milk)
programs, were linked to leftist political parties, and leftist leaders recruited effectively among the members of these NGOs. In any case, the table
shows that 16 percent of a 1982 Lima sample endorsed the "socialist by
revolution" alternative, as did 13 percent of a March 1988 nationwide sample.[109] The Marxist left parties fared better at the polls in Peru than in any
other democratic Latin American nation during the 1980s.[110] The strong
support for the Marxist left and center-left in Peru during the 1980s is vital
to understanding the policy choices made by Presidents Belaúnde and
García, described above.

During the 1990s, there was continuity and change in Peruvians' political attitudes. On the one hand, democratic ideals remained prevalent (see
Table 6.5). At the same time, it was evident that Peruvians' definitions of
democracy varied considerably, and were usually not the liberal,
Madisonian definition common in the United States; otherwise, of course,
their support for democracy would not have jibed with their support for the
1992 *autogolpe*.[111] Interest in politics also remained strong during the
1990s.[112] This interest sustained news media that courageously criticized
the Fujimori government despite its reprisals.

By contrast, Table 6.5 indicates a dramatic decline in leftist political
attitudes in Peru during the 1990s. Amidst the economic debacle and
intense political violence of the 1980–1992 period, leftist NGOs dissipated
and leftist aspirations were abandoned.[113] As in much of Latin America,
political attitutes became more pragmatic.

More uncertain for Peru's democratic future was the evolution of other
forms of civil society and concomitant attitudes. With considerable international support, the rate of Peruvians' participation in NGOs (54 percent)
and the kinds of NGOs in which they participated (predominantly neighborhood organizations, sports clubs, and church organizations) were very
similar to regional norms.[114] However, whereas during the 1970s the trends
within Peruvian NGOs were toward greater social trust, by the 1990s these
trends had apparently been reversed. In a 1996 survey, only 27 percent of
Peruvians said that their fellow citizens were supportive of one another,
versus a 57 percent regional Latin American average.[115]

Peru's Constitutional Structure

Whereas it might be expected that, as Peru or other Latin American nations
gain democratic experience, their constitutions would shift gradually from
the ratification of personalist norms to the encouragement of democratic
institutions, the trend in Peru has actually been the reverse. Of Peru's four
twentieth-century constitutions (1920, 1933, 1979, and 1993), the 1933 doc-

ument gave the most power to the legislature and the political parties com-
posing it. By contrast, the 1979 Constitution shifted power toward the executive, primarily because the framers of the 1979 document blamed the 1968
democratic breakdown in part upon executive-legislative conflict and political parties that were not "parliamentary fit." The 1993 Constitution not only
intensified this shift but removed the provisions in the 1979 Constitution
that provided a greater impetus to decentralization out of Lima.

Under both the 1979 and 1993 Constitutions, a predominant concern
has been that their presidentialist principles relegate political parties to
irrelevance and, accordingly, doom them to weakness.[116] This concern
intensified when in three out of the four national elections since 1980 the
victorious presidential candidate's party achieved a majority or near-
majority in the legislature (see Tables 6.3 and 6.4), which of course greatly
enhanced the power of the president relative to the legislature. Important to
the capacity of the governing party to gain and hold a majority in the legislature was that the election of the president and the legislature was simultaneous and also that midterm elections were not held.

The 1979 Constitution gave numerous powers to the executive that the
1933 document had not. The most important were (1) a provision about the
president's power in economic and financial policy that was vaguely stated
and accordingly enabled presidential abuse, (2) permission to the legislature to delegate lawmaking to the executive, and (3) restrictions upon the
previous privileges of the legislature to interrogate and censure ministers.
These provisions were retained or tipped even further in the president's
favor in the 1993 Constitution. By far the most controversial innovation of
the 1993 document, however, was to allow the immediate reelection of the
president, a provision that of course strengthens his hand in numerous critical respects. In sum, under the 1979 Constitution and to an even greater
degree under the 1993 version, a president enjoying a legislative majority
could govern largely as he wanted, and political parties had scant opportunity for effective democratic opposition or political learning.

Especially under the 1993 Constitution, the procedures for the election
of the legislature have not encouraged the development of large parties
with strong social bases. Provisions that facilitate the establishment of new
parties or small parties exacerbate the problem of collaboration among
Peru's party leaders and leadership succession within a party; if the long-
standing head of a party does not easily yield to a viable successor, that
successor is likely to withdraw and begin a new party rather than to try to
rally the party's militants and forge a new consensus. One of these electoral
procedures is the use, since 1950, of proportional representation rather than
the first-past-the-post system. A second is the introduction in 1963 of the
D'Hondt formula for proportional representation without thresholds for the
percentage that a party had to win to achieve representation. Primarily as a
result of these electoral procedures, a party with less than 0.8 percent of the
valid vote won a seat in the 1995–2000 legislature.

Further, whereas an objective of the 1979 Constitution was that political power be devolved to the local and regional levels, the 1993 Constitution was overwhelmingly centralist. Specifically, the 1979 document established a bicameral legislature including a Chamber of Deputies and a Senate in which seats in the Chamber of Deputies were apportioned on the basis of votes in Peru's departments, but the 1993 Constitution set up a unicameral legislature (Distrito Unico) apportioned on the basis of votes in the nation as a whole. Under the new procedure, a political party could win large numbers of seats as a result of a media campaign targeted at large cities; neither grassroots networks nor accountability to these networks was necessary. Another significant shift away from regional political power in the 1993 Constitution was the end of independent regional government, which had been established only a few years before in the final years of the García administration.

Political Parties Prior to 1992

Political parties prior to 1992 were predominantly personalist parties that failed to achieve institutionalization. Both of Peru's twice-elected presidents during this period, Manuel Prado and Fernando Belaúnde, were personalist leaders; their Movimiento Democrático Pradista and Acción Popular, respectively, were first and foremost their leaders' political vehicles. Both apparently believed that "strong leadership" was necessary to the continuation of the party, and both were loath to transfer the reins of the party to a new leader. Also, amidst Peru's sharp social and economic cleavages, neither seemed to believe that the articulation of a clear ideology or the establishment of grassroots networks around ideological principles would be advantageous; rather, they preferred that their ideologies and social bases be flexible and that they be free to build bridges to *apristas* (in Prado's case) and leftists and center-leftists (in Belaúnde's case).

The likely validity of Prado's and Belaúnde's strategy was indicated by the fates of Peru's openly rightist political parties during this period. The rightist Partido Popular Cristiano failed to build electoral support beyond Lima's middle and upper classes.[117] About a year before the 1990 presidential election, facing a discredited APRA and a demoralized Izquierda Unida, the rightist FREDEMO appeared likely to win easily. Unfortunately for Peru's right, however, Vargas Llosa was not only a brilliant novelist but, arrogant and living abroad most of his life, in many respects a caricature of what most Peruvians thought was wrong about their country's political elites. After Vargas Llosa lost to Fujimori, he left Peru; FREDEMO, which had already been weakened by blatantly self-interested politicking by individual party members during the 1990 campaign, gradually dissolved.

In contrast to Peru's rightist political groups or might-have-been rightist groups, Izquierda Unida (IU) secured a grassroots base—but it also failed to achieve institutionalization. As pointed out above, for most of the 1980s Izquierda Unida was the strongest electoral leftist party in South America. In the 1980, 1983, and 1986 municipal elections and the 1985 congressional elections, its electoral tally was the second largest, and it was especially strong in Peru's southern highlands as well as in Lima. However, the relationships among the coalition's various leaders were tense; in both the 1980 and 1990 elections, the coalition splintered, and was punished by voters (see Tables 6.3 and 6.4). Alfonso Barrantes, who was elected mayor of Lima in 1983, was the coalition's most popular leader; but, as personal and ideological tensions among coalition members worsened, in 1990 Barrantes withdrew to form his own Izquierda Socialista and fared poorly in the election (see Table 6.3). Also, during the late 1980s Izquierda Unida was battered directly by the effects of the country's economic crisis and political violence and also indirectly as numerous IU leaders worked closely with the incumbent APRA party. Next, the coalition of Marxist parties was damaged by the demise of the Soviet bloc, and then further by the weakening of labor and other nongovernmental organizations under the Fujimori government's free-market economic policies.[118]

The APRA was the only party throughout Peru's history that appeared to achieve institutionalization. Haya de la Torre stood out among Peru's political leaders because he was not only a charismatic speaker and a brilliant intellectual, conveying a message of salvation and redemption for a suffering people that resonated in the deepest parts of many Peruvians' psyches, but also the architect of a cohesive, disciplined political organization.[119] In the early 1980s, after the death of Haya de la Torre, Alan García became APRA's leader, and the party became Peru's first to pass this crucial test of institutionalization.

In 1985, Alan García ran a brilliant campaign that swept him to the presidency in a landslide and his party to a majority in both houses of the legislature. However, once in power, tensions between "strong leadership" and the institutionalization of the party became apparent. Apparently, at least in the first few years of his administration, García was convinced that he could fulfill the decades-old *aprista* promise to "save Peru." He dominated his party's legislators and other militants; in 1990, elite Peruvians identified "authoritarianism," "demagoguery," and "arrogance" as García's three worst defects.[120] Still, the conflict between President García and his party should not be exaggerated; throughout García's five-year term, APRA retained a disciplined majority in the legislature, and the party won 23 percent of the valid vote in the first round of the 1990 presidential elections.[121]

Political Parties After the Autogolpe

During the 1990s Peru's "traditional" political parties collapsed.[122] None of the political coalitions or parties that composed large majorities of the

Peruvian legislature during the 1980s—APRA, Izquierda Unida, Acción Popular, or the Partido Popular Cristiano—secured as much as 5 percent of the valid vote in the presidential race in 1995.[123] Between 1980 and 1995, the shift away from "traditional" political parties to "independent" candidates was arguably sharper in Peru than in any other country in the region.[124] In the 1995 municipal contest, the overwhelming majority of candidates described themselves as "independents" and the number of candidates was so large that electoral tallies for the nation as a whole were essentially meaningless and were rarely printed.[125]

To a certain extent, however, the distinction between traditional and independent was a mere rhetorical device, based upon leaders' desires to distance themselves from the political debacle of the late 1980s. Both of the two major forces in the 1995 presidential election, Cambio 90/Nueva Mayoría and Unión por el Perú, described themselves as independent, but it was not precisely clear how their structure or principles were different from a party such as Acción Popular, which had a strong leader and a flexible ideology. Unión por el Perú included former rightist, centrist, and leftist leaders from the traditional political parties as well as independents. Unfortunately for the development of Unión por el Perú, after his 1995 electoral loss Pérez de Cuéllar followed the footsteps of Mario Vargas Llosa out of the country, and UPP was in disarray.

There were various reasons for the collapse of Peru's political parties. First, of course, were the problems in Peru's political culture and the catastrophic policy results of the 1980s, for which many Peruvian citizens blamed the traditional governing parties and their allies—Acción Popular, the Partido Popular Cristiano, APRA, and Izquierda Unida. Also very important, however, was that during the 1990s Fujimori derided not only Peru's traditional political parties but also the basic concept of the political party. Fujimori contrasted vigorous leadership on the nation's behalf to what he contended was endless, compromised debate among political-party members seeking their own political or material advantage.

Accordingly, of course, Fujimori was not inclined to build his own political vehicle, originally dubbed Cambio 90 and then renamed Cambio 90/Nueva Mayoría, into an effective political party. As we have seen, Fujimori's closest advisers were not from his political party but from the intelligence or military services. Fujimori was not eager to recruit capable leaders into Cambio 90/Nueva Mayoría or, indeed, at times to recruit any leaders at all; for example, candidates were fielded for only a handful of contests in the 1993 and 1996 municipal elections. Cambio 90/Nueva Mayoría legislators were perceived to bow consistently to the president's will.

In the context of Peru's numerous and fragmented political parties that are for the most part without significant ties to grassroots organizations, the recruitment of a viable opposition candidate to Fujimori was much more difficult. In other words, deinstitutionalization implies woefully deficient political contestation—and, without political contestation, many scholars would argue that there is no democracy.

The State

Although rigorous comparisons and contrasts of the capabilities and professionalism of Latin American states are rare, it is clear that the Peruvian state has been deficient. For the most part, the rules that should provide for an efficient, professional state have been bent in Peru; the goal has been to favor either the country's economic and political elites—sometimes broadly construed, sometimes construed as a small governing circle. Cronyism and corruption have been common. These various problems are highlighted in this section for the development and judicial agencies of Peru's state.

Tragically, in the decades after independence prior to 1968, Peru's resources were not managed so as to benefit disadvantaged majorities (see the historical overview). The bias against the poor continued when the state grew dramatically after 1968. To an extraordinary degree, public investment was skewed toward grandiose, supertechnology projects that were cost-ineffective and were of greatest benefit to the engineers and the upper and middle strata who were able to buy into the projects.[126] The common perception was that state officials opted for large projects because these projects entailed collaboration with major international and domestic companies from which officials could secure kickbacks.[127] Peruvian public expenditure was also highly skewed toward the military.[128]

In the 1970s and 1980s, Peru's newly large state failed not only to redirect resources toward the poor, but also to stimulate economic growth. In part because of policies of subsidized prices and in part because of cronyism and corruption, most of Peru's 200-plus state corporations operated at a loss; between 1980 and 1988, the annual deficit of these enterprises averaged 2.5 percent of GDP.[129] Red tape became voluminous. For example, it was estimated that in the early 1980s the legal registration of a small clothing factory with two sewing machines required 289 workdays by professionals, plus more than $1,000 (including several bribes to government officials).[130]

Under Fujimori, problems of professionalism in the allocation of state resources continued, but they were of a different variety. On the one hand, the state shrank and problems of bureaucratic red tape receded. Also, one of the Fujimori government's most important achievements was its use of the "privatization dividend" for schools, roads, and other similar projects in disadvantaged communities. However, decisions about the allocation of these resources were highly concentrated in the hands of the president and very often made largely on political grounds.[131]

Another key component of the state is the judiciary. Again, just as cronyism and corruption were prevalent problems in Peru's development agencies, they were also in the country's judiciary. In surveys in both the 1970s and the 1980s, overwhelming majorities of Peruvians believed that judicial decisions were based on contacts and money rather than on the law.[132]

Probably to a greater degree than ever before, the Fujimori government added politics to the mix of factors bending judicial decisions away from sheer right and wrong. The *autogolpe* enabled Fujimori to purge many corrupt judges, especially *aprista* judges appointed under García. But the majority of new judicial appointments were "provisional" rather than permanent; in other words, these judges' appointments were subject to renewal. The common perception was that the government had the power to remove any judge whose decisions were not to its liking; a salient example was the emasculation of the Constitutional Tribunal in 1997.

Development Performance

Peru's development performance has been inferior to the Latin American norm in key respects. First, between 1900 and 1987 Peru's real GDP growth averaged approximately 3.6 percent, versus 3.8 percent for the region.[133] Second, growth in Peru remained based almost exclusively on exports for a longer period of time than in most Latin American nations; the open-economy model had some positive results but also various negative dimensions, in particular the failure to redress Peru's historical economic inequalities. Finally, but of particular importance for this study, there has not been a positive correlation between democratic government and economic growth or redistribution.

Whereas in many Latin American nations one or two exports have remained the most important ones for more than a century, the composition of Peru's exports has fluctuated. During the colonial era, the key exports were gold and silver; next, in the mid–nineteenth century, guano; then, for the first fifty years of the twentieth century, sugar, cotton, copper, and oil; and finally, between 1950 and the early 1960s, not only further expansion of copper but also new mineral exports and fish products, in particular fish meal.[134]

Peru's pattern of export-based growth had numerous implications. The most important positive result was economic growth that, while below the regional average, was not insignificant. However, in good part because the composition of Peru's exports was unusually volatile, economic instability in Peru was more extreme than in most of the region and the export busts that followed export booms were longer and deeper.[135] It also seems likely that the volatility in the composition of Peru's exports increased turnover in the composition of Peru's elite families—in many respects a positive result, enhancing social mobility, but also perhaps diminishing the sense of com-

mon purpose among elite families that might have facilitated their construction of a viable political party.

As previously mentioned, whereas many Latin American nations
adopted import-substitution industrialization policies after the global
depression, except for three years in the 1940s Peru retained an open,
export-led economy into the early 1960s. There were rewards to Peru for
this economic model: economic growth between 1950 and 1965 was one of
the most robust in the region.[136] However, the various trends that had
prompted many Latin American nations to shift from export-led policies
toward import-substitution industrialization were at work in Peru. Most
important, income distribution was worsening.[137] In the early 1960s,
income distribution was more unequal in Peru than in Brazil, Colombia,
Mexico, or a forty-four-developing-country average.[138] The Peruvian economy was described as "dualistic," including on the one hand a "modern"
sector based on the export of primary commodities that registered economic growth, but on the other a "traditional" sector based on subsistence agriculture that did not grow.[139]

The worsening of income distribution was in good part a result of
increasing concentration of land ownership as well as land scarcity, both of
which trends exacerbated landlessness. First, as mentioned previously, during the expansion of cotton, sugar, copper, and wool exports between 1890
and 1930, peasants were displaced from their lands; as of 1961 the Gini
index of land distribution in Peru was the most unequal among fifty-four
nations for which data were reported.[140] Second, the amount of new land
brought under cultivation was scant relative to many Latin American
nations, while the rural population grew at average rates; as of 1979, only
one-fifth of an arable hectare of land was available per capita in Peru, a
smaller amount than in any of the twelve Latin American nations for which
data were reported (with the exception of El Salvador).[141]

The perception that Peru's worsening income distribution was the
result of its open, export-oriented economic policies sparked first the shift
toward import-substitution industrialization under Belaúnde and then the
dramatic property reform under Velasco. From being one of the most open
economies of the region, where the role of the state had been minimal, the
Peruvian economy became one of the most closed with one of the largest
roles for the state.[142] The closed, big-state policies continued after the transition to democratic government in 1980 and endured until the "Fujishock"
in 1990.

Policies of the period from 1960 to 1990 were not without their successes. Secondary-school and university enrollments soared to rates well
above regional averages.[143] Between 1965 and 1980, manufacturing production grew at a compound annual rate of 3.8 percent, more rapidly than
the economy as a whole.[144] It also continued to grow, albeit more slowly,
between 1980 and 1988.[145] Perhaps most important, the apparent overall

effects on income distribution were strongly positive, as reflected by dramatic improvements in the country's Gini index; Peru's income distribution became more equal than Costa Rica's or Chile's by 1985.[146] Important beneficiaries of the new economic policy pattern included peasants who became members of agrarian cooperatives, workers who became members of industrial communities, and the more than 900,000 Peruvians who were employed in Peru's public sector by 1990.[147]

Economic growth, however, was dismal. Between 1963 and 1990, Peru's economic growth rates were consistently below regional averages; between 1985 and 1990 in particular, Peru's rate was way below the regional average (see Table 6.6). Concomitantly, poverty increased, afflicting not only the traditionally most disadvantaged group, highlands peasants, but increasingly urban families as well. For various reasons, despite the mili-

Table 6.6 Economic Growth Rates, 1950–1996 (percentage of average annual real GDP growth per capita)

	Peru	Latin America and the Caribbean
By Era		
1950–1960[a]	2.9	1.9
1961–1970	2.6	3.2
1970–1980	0.9	3.5
1980–1990	–3.4	–1.1
1990–1996	3.1	1.5
By Regime		
First Belaúnde government[b]	1.5	2.4
Velasco government[b]	2.0	3.5
Morales Bermúdez government[b]	–1.2	3.0
Second Belaúnde government	–2.8	–1.6
García government	–2.8[c]	–0.4[c]
Fujimori government (1990–1996)	3.1	1.5
Post-autogolpe Fujimori government (1993–1996)	4.3[c]	1.6[c]

Sources: Unless otherwise indicated below, the annual reports of the Inter-American Development Bank, entitled *Economic and Social Progress in Latin America,* and published in Washington, D.C., by the Inter-American Development Bank, usually in the same year. For eras: for 1961–1970, *1985 Report,* p. 152; and for 1970–1980, 1980–1990, 1990–1996 (the same years as the Fujimori government), *1997 Report,* p. 221. For the second Belaúnde government (and for the region during this period), *1986 Report,* p. 394. For García, *1988 Report,* p. 20; *1989 Report,* p. 10; *1991 Report,* p. 4. For post-*autogolpe* Fujimori government (and for the region during these years), the figure averages the data in *1997 Report,* pp. 289 and 3, respectively (as well as *1994 Report,* p. 4).

Notes: a. World Tables, 3d ed. (Baltimore: Johns Hopkins Unviersity Press, 1983), vol. 1, pp. 485–488.

b. Figures are GNP per capita in Thomas Scheetz, *Peru and the International Monetary Fund* (Pittsburgh: University of Pittsburgh Press, 1986), p. 158.

c. Per capita statistic is the author's calculation from data in the Inter-American Development Bank reports.

tary government's agrarian reform, the incomes of highlands peasants declined and, in some areas, a real threat to their subsistence emerged.[148] According to the Economic Commission for Latin America and the Caribbean, the incidence of poverty in both rural and urban Peru increased from 50 percent of families in 1970 to 52 percent in 1986; after 1986, poverty increased much more.[149] By 1989, Lima's real minimum-wage level was less than one-third the level of 1963.[150] More than 94 percent of Lima's potential workforce was unemployed or underemployed in 1990.[151]

The reasons that Peru's closed, state-led economic policies did not occasion growth are numerous. Many analysts, of course, believe that such policies virtually always fail to do so; others point to particular problems in their implementation in Peru.[152] This second group of scholars suggests that, especially given the suddenness of the establishment of Peru's new state and its especially large size, the country's historical patterns of crony capitalism and administrative mismanagement were unlikely to be transformed overnight. Also, although between the mid–1960s and 1990 the overall pattern of a closed, state-led economy was constant, variations on the model were introduced by different administrations, at times provoking political uncertainty and anxiety among potential investors.

In any case, Peru returned to open, export-led economic policies under Fujimori in 1990. Especially in 1993 and 1994, growth was vigorous, based on an influx of foreign investment and exports (see Table 6.6). Relative to the 1960s, the value of agricultural exports had declined; mineral exports, in particular copper, made up almost half of Peru's total exports.[153] However, for many reasons, income inequality was likely to have worsened again; also, although per capita income, the real minimum wage, and employment were above the levels of 1990, they were not above the levels of 1980.[154] As of mid-1998, it was not clear whether or not Peruvians would come to blame these continuing problems upon the open, export-led economic model as they had in the past.

Unfortunately, the development performance of democratic governments has not been superior to the development performance of authoritarian governments in Peru. As Table 6.6 indicates, there is no clear correlation between regime type and development performance in Peru in the post–World War II era. During the 1950s, under both the authoritarian Odría regime and then the elected Prado government, Peru's economic growth rate was superior to the regional rate. But between the mid-1960s and 1990, neither democratic nor authoritarian governments achieved economic growth rates superior to the regional rates.

Many question marks remain about Peruvians' assessments of the relationship between regime type and development performance at the threshold of the twenty-first century. It is not clear whether most Peruvians will ultimately classify the Fujimori government as democratic or as authoritarian, and whether they will assess his government's development performance as superior because of robust growth and low inflation, or as inferior because of continuing unemployment and poverty as well as the sale of many Peruvian enterprises to foreign companies. If the government is judged authoritarian and the development performance judged favorable—as seems possible as of this writing—the correlation would bode badly for democratic consolidation in Peru after the year 2000. This is especially the case due to the disastrous development performance of the two preceding administrations, virtually universally labeled democratic.

International Factors

International influences have not been decisive in the rise or fall of any Peruvian government. Neither the United States nor any other nation has intervened militarily in Peru or directly fomented a Peruvian military coup. However, by approximately the time of the Leguía government (1919–1930) and the increase in U.S. loans as well as U.S. investment in mining and other extractive industries, the United States emerged as a very important actor in Peruvian politics, both in absolute terms and relative to any other nation. (Neither the Soviet Union nor Cuba played a major role in Peruvian politics during the Cold War.)

At various junctures the United States encouraged democratic transitions in Peru. Franklin Roosevelt's pro-democratic initiatives contributed to the return of civilian rule in 1939 and to the openness of the 1945 election. The Kennedy administration sharply criticized the 1962 military coup, even withholding recognition from the military regime for almost a month. In the late 1970s, in conjunction with its human rights policy, the Carter administration provided considerable moral and economic support to the Morales Bermúdez government after it had initiated a democratic opening. Most recently, the U.S. Department of State criticized Fujimori's *autogolpe* and worked with the Organization of American States to persuade Fujimori to schedule elections for a constituent assembly within five months.[155]

However, after democratic regimes have been launched in Peru, U.S. support for democratic principles was frequently tempered by its pursuit of economic interests. The first important example of U.S. prioritization of its economic interests to the detriment of the democratic cause was its relationship with the 1945–1948 Bustamante government. Although the United States was in principle sympathetic to the Bustamante government, the bilateral agenda was topped by the issue of Peru's debt service, and the United States provided no substantive support to the Bustamante government as Odría's military coup loomed.[156]

A second major example was the U.S. stance toward the 1963–1968 Belaúnde government. The Belaúnde government was widely considered to be a model Alliance for Progress government: honestly elected and reformist, but not revolutionary. However, when Belaúnde sought to fulfill a campaign pledge to gain nationalistic concessions from the IPC, the U.S. Embassy criticized the government. After President Kennedy's assassination, when a new agreement between the Peruvian government and the U.S. company still had not been reached, all U.S. aid to Peru was suspended for about a year.[157] Conflicts over fishing rights and arms sales erupted as well. In good part as a result of these tensions, U.S. aid to Peru remained relatively low during these years—only a third to a half of U.S. aid to Chile, for example.[158] U.S. policy proved very shortsighted: when the Peruvian military took over in 1968, it immediately expropriated IPC and developed military and fishing relationships with the Soviet Union.

After 1980, U.S. support for democracy in Peru has been expressed more emphatically than in the past; still, however, other policy priorities usually appeared to be at the top of the bilateral agenda. During the 1980s and 1990s, U.S. economic concerns generally appeared to be most important, but the U.S. effort to stop the flow of drugs into the United States from Peru and other Latin American nations also became very salient. To the extent that U.S. aid to Peru is an indicator of U.S. alienation or support of its incumbent government, the United States was niggardly toward the García government, which was at odds with the United States on economic policy, albeit an electoral democracy; but generous toward the Fujimori government, which adopted economic and antidrug policies convergent with U.S. preferences, albeit in many analysts' judgments not an electoral democracy. In real dollars, the annual average amount of U.S. eocnomic and military aid for Peru between 1993 and 1996 was about 60 percent more than the average between 1985 and 1989; as a percentage of total U.S. aid to Latin America and the Caribbean, the figure for 1993 to 1996 was more than three times the figure for 1985 to 1989.[159]

As the year-2000 elections loom and polarization around the question of Fujimori's quest for a third term becomes more intense, will the Clinton administration put pro-democratic concerns higher on the policy agenda? Possibly. On the one hand, as mentioned above, the U.S. State Department is obviously aware of Fujimori's strongman proclivities; the 1996–1999 U.S. ambassador to Peru, Dennis Jett, has frequently criticized Fujimori's authoritarian measures, especially those against the judiciary that affect the likelihood for free and fair elections. On the other hand, the international financial community, the U.S. Drug Enforcement Administration, and probably the Central Intelligence Agency as well are very satisfied with the performance of the Fujimori government in their respective policy areas; these agencies' leaders are loath to obstruct Fujimori, especially when there is no evident Peruvian opposition leader who advances the policy positions favored in the United States. Further, the advancement of democracy concerns is difficult given that the classification of the Fujimori regime as democratic, pseudodemocratic, or authoritarian is complex and controversial; in any case, who in the Clinton administration wanted to acknowledge that a Latin American nation has slipped from the democratic classification?

CONCLUSION AND PROSPECTS FOR THE FUTURE

In 1992, Peru's electoral democracy was derailed. This author doubts that Peru has yet returned to the democratic road. Almost certainly, however, the country will return to it; as we have seen, in the past Peruvians have increasingly chafed under authoritarian rule, and they are more politically engaged and pro-democratic now than in the past. But almost certainly the road to democracy will continue to be rocky.

Indeed, with respect to some important variables, the prospects for democratic government appeared bleaker in Peru in the late 1990s than in 1980. To an unusual degree even in Latin America, Peru's political parties were less institutionalized and more personalistic in the late 1990s than they were in 1980. The 1993 Constitution concentrates power in the executive to a greater degree than the 1979 Constitution—or indeed the 1933 Constitution. International actors' commitment to democracy in the region also seems less firm. In particular, the U.S. government appears conflicted among its various policy goals for Peru; unless the Fujimori government shifts toward a blatant dictatorship, the United States is not likely to advance democracy as its top priority.

Further, to the extent that the Fujimori regime is considered authoritarian, there are important questions about its impact on a succeeding democratic government: Would the hyperpresidentialist 1993 Constitution be retained? Would judicial, electoral, and other political institutions be able to regain the autonomy that they had lost under Fujimori? Would political polarization around Fujimori's legitimacy exacerbate the country's political tensions? In general, would the Fujimori government reinforce the traditional vicious political circles in Peru that were identified in this chapter's Theoretical Analysis? For example, would the perception that the "strong," personalistic leader governs more effectively than the more democratic leader be intensified?

Yet there are also grounds for optimism. Most important, although Peru's overlapping ethnic, class, and geographical cleavages endure—and could be among the catalysts of renewed guerrilla conflict—they are much less sharp than they were prior to the 1960s. Concomitantly, over the longer run, Peruvians' mistrust and ambivalence toward authority should become less severe, enhancing the potential for the development of democratic political institutions.

Also, in the 1970s and 1980s, many Peruvians were expecting rapid socioeconomic advancement, and Peru's political left was one of the strongest in the hemisphere. The concomitant leftist orientation of Peru's governments during the 1980s, especially the García government, put Peru at odds with global free-market trends and with the United States, and the results were catastrophic. By contrast, today Peruvians are more aware of the complexities of politics, and their expectations for their future living standards are lower; the political left is much weaker and Peru's political spectrum is similar to that in the rest of the Americas.

For this author, it is important also that the 1992 *autogolpe* was different from Peru's previous democratic breakdowns; it was not a predictable result of social, economic, or political tensions that could not be resolved through the democratic process, but rather the unpredicted choice of the country's leadership. Accordingly, to a greater degree than in the past, what is necessary for electoral democracy in Peru is "merely" the withdrawal of Fujimori and his key colleagues. In this event, given Peru's well-educated and politically engaged citizens and the sobering experiences of both the 1980–1992 electoral democracy and the Fujimori government, it could be reasonably hoped that efforts to construct truly collaborative and politically accountable political parties and other democratic institutions would be reinvigorated.

NOTES

1. "Regime" is defined as continuous government under the same constitution (or one that is consensually amended) or continuous de facto government, without a constitution that was widely perceived as legitimate. The only other Latin American nation where there has been somewhat similar oscillation between democratic and authoritarian governments is Argentina; in Argentina, however, democratic roots were stronger in the late nineteenth and early twentieth centuries than in Peru, but in most respects the polity was less democratic during the Cold War era (see chapter 2 in this volume).

2. This restriction was significant. In 1940, about 60 percent of Peruvian adults were illiterate, and in 1960 about 40 percent. See Magli S. Larson and Arlene G. Bergman, *Social Stratification in Peru* (Berkeley: Institute of International Studies, University of California, 1969), pp. 363–364. As a result, in the early 1960s Peru ranked fourteenth among twenty major Latin American nations in the percentage of the population voting, in a calculation by David Scott Palmer, *"Revolution from Above": Military Government and Popular Participation in Peru, 1968–1972*, Latin American Studies Program Dissertation Series (Ithaca, NY: Cornell University, 1973), p. 9.

3. See Table 1.3 in the introductory chapter to this volume. "Electoral democracy" is a conceptualization for political regimes that hold genuinely competitive and fair elections, but whose democratic features do not extend beyond this "minimalist" procedural criterion; the conceptualization is developed by Larry Diamond, "Is the Third Wave Over?" *Journal of Democracy* 7 (July 1996): 21–25. "Electoral democracy" is juxtaposed both to "liberal democracies" (in which there are checks and balances to executive power and in which the military or other forces not accountable to the electorate do not retain a "reserved domain" of power) and to "pseudodemocracies" (in which contestation is not sufficiently fair as to allow the ruling party to be turned out of power, although the existence of independent opposition parties is tolerated). For other thoughtful discussions of the definition of democracy, see Jonathan Hartlyn, "Democracies in Contemporary South America: Convergences and Diversities," Unpublished paper, Department of Political Science, University of North Carolina, November

1995, and David Collier and Steven Levitsky, "Democracy with Adjectives: Conceptual Innovation in Comparative Research," *World Politics* 49 (April 1997): 430–451.

4. Constitutional ruptures were threatened in Guatemala and Paraguay, but averted. In Haiti, Aristide was elected in 1990 and overthrown in 1991. Peru's "political rights" ranking by Freedom House in 1992 was 6 (only one point from the nadir ranking); see R. Bruce McColm, ed., *Freedom in the World* (Westport, CT: Greenwood Press, 1993), p. 408. Accordingly, on the six-point scale of Latin American nations' experience with democracy established in Larry Diamond, Juan J. Linz, and Seymour Martin Lipset, eds., *Democracy in Developing Countries: Latin America* (Boulder, CO: Lynne Rienner, 1989), p. xxvi, at this date Peru scored a lowly 5 ("democratic rule has broken down but there are considerable pressures and prospects for its return").

5. For the definition of the concept "pseudodemocracy," see Diamond, "Is the Third Wave Over?" p. 25, or footnote 3 above. A regime similar to Diamond's "pseudodemocracy" is described under the label "semiauthoritarian" in Thomas Carothers, "Democracy Without Illusions," *Foreign Affairs* 76, no. 1 (January-February 1997): 91.

6. The "authoritarian" label is reserved only for regimes that do not allow the functioning of opposition political parties in Diamond, "Is the Third Wave Over?" p. 25. However, many Latin American regimes—such as the military-dominated governments in El Salvador between 1931 and 1979 as well as the Somoza governments in Nicaragua—allowed considerable political-party activity, and yet most analysts consider the "authoritarian" label more appropriate than the "pseudodemocratic" classification.

7. Various labels for Fujimori's Peru have been used by scholars; its ambiguous nature is often highlighted. See, for example, Maxwell A. Cameron, "Self-Coups: Peru, Guatemala, and Russia," *Journal of Democracy* 9 (January 1998): 126; Philip Mauceri, "Return of the Caudillo: Autocratic Democracy in Peru," *Third World Quarterly* 18 (1997): 899–911; John Crabtree, "The 1995 Elections in Peru: End of the Line for the Party System?" Institute of Latin American Studies Occasional Paper No. 12, University of London, 1995, pp. 9–11. Other scholars have eschewed the question of democracy in Fujimori's regime and applied the concept of populism; see David Scott Palmer, "'Fujipopulism' and Peru's Progress," *Current History* 95 (February 1996): 70–76; Kenneth M. Roberts, "Neoliberalism and the Transformation of Populism in Latin America: The Peruvian Case," *World Politics* 48 (October 1995): 82–116; Kurt Weyland, "Neopopulism and Neoliberalism in Latin America: Unexpected Affinities," *Studies in Comparative International Development* 31 (1996): 3–31; and Bruce H. Kay, "'Fujipopulism' and the Liberal State in Peru, 1990–1995," *Journal of Interamerican Studies and World Affairs* 48 (winter 1996–1997): 55–98.

Other analysts do not tackle the classification question directly. Susan Stokes speaks of the restoration of democracy "in a formal sense"; see Susan Stokes, "Peru: The Rupture of Democratic Rule," in Jorge I. Domínguez and Abraham F. Lowenthal, eds., *Constructing Democratic Governance: South America in the 1990s* (Baltimore: Johns Hopkins University Press, 1996), p. 70. Peruvian scholars are most likely to use the authoritarian label. See Julio Cotler, *Política y sociedad en el Perú: Cambios y continuidades* (Lima: Instituto de Estudios Peruanos, 1994), pp. 222–224, and César Arias Quincot, *La modernización autoritaria* (Lima: Fundación Friedrich Ebert, 1994).

8. Magnus Morner, *The Andean Past: Land, Societies, and Conflicts* (New York: Columbia University Press, 1985), pp. 10–25.

9. Ibid., p. 32.

10. David Scott Palmer, *Peru: The Authoritarian Tradition* (New York: Praeger, 1980), pp. 36–40.

11. Ibid.

12. An excellent synthesis is Peter F. Klarén, "Historical Setting," in Rex A. Hudson, ed., *Peru: A Country Study* (Washington, DC: Library of Congress, 1993), pp. 32–34.

13. Julio Cotler, *Clases, estado, y nación en el Perú* (Lima: Instituto de Estudios Peruanos, 1978), p. 109.

14. Heraclio Bonilla, *Un siglo a la deriva* (Lima: Instituto de Estudios Peruanos, 1980), p. 172; Klarén, "Historical Setting," p. 37.

15. Dennis Gilbert, *The Oligarchy and the Old Regime in Peru,* Latin American Dissertation Series (Ithaca, NY: Cornell University Press, 1977), pp. 77–79. Gilbert carefully identifies various wealthy families, their fortunes, and social networks. See also Carlos

Malpica, *Los dueños del Perú* (Lima: Ediciones Ensayos Sociales, 1968); and Cotler, *Clases, estado, y nación,* p. 140.

16. Gilbert, *The Oligarchy,* pp. 55, 75–79.

17. A particularly nuanced analysis of the impact of the Cerro de Pasco copper mine on nearby peasant communities is Florencia E. Mallon, *The Defense of Community in Peru's Central Highlands: Peasant Struggle and Capitalist Transition, 1860–1940* (Princeton: Princeton University Press, 1983).

18. Peter F. Klarén, *Modernization, Dislocation, and Aprismo: Origins of the Peruvian Aprista Party, 1870–1932* (Austin: Institute of Latin American Studies, University of Texas Press, 1973), pp. 50–64. Water is the scarcest agricultural input on Peru's coast.

19. Morner, *The Andean Past,* p. 182. The dynamics of agro-export expansion were more varied and complex than in some Latin American nations, but the result by the late 1950s was severe land concentration.

20. Rosemary Thorp and Geoffrey Bertram, *Peru 1890–1977: Growth and Policy in an Open Economy* (New York: Columbia University Press, 1978), pp. 112–118.

21. Palmer, *Peru: The Authoritarian Tradition,* p. 63.

22. Latin American Bureau, *Peru: Paths to Poverty* (Nottingham, England: Russell Press, 1985), p. 32.

23. Particularly useful works on this era include David P. Werlich, *Peru: A Short History* (Carbondale: Southern Illinois University Press, 1978); Jane S. Jaquette, *The Politics of Development in Peru,* Latin American Studies Program Dissertation Series (Ithaca, NY: Cornell University, 1971); François Bourricaud, *Power and Society in Contemporary Peru* (New York: Praeger, 1970); Arnold Payne, *The Peruvian Coup d'Etat of 1962* (Washington, DC: Institute for the Comparative Study of Political Systems, 1968); Howard Handelman, *Struggle in the Andes* (Austin: University of Texas Press, 1975); and Klarén, *Modernization.*

24. Between 1945 and 1963, the percentage of the adult population registered to vote increased from an estimated 25 percent to 46 percent; see Cynthia McClintock, "Peru: Precarious Regimes, Authoritarian and Democratic," in Larry Diamond, Juan Linz, and Seymour Martin Lipset, eds., *Democracy in Developing Countries: Latin America* (Boulder, CO: Lynne Rienner, 1989), p. 346.

25. The 1931 turnout was about 20 percent, almost twice the percentage under the Aristocratic Republic; see Latin American Bureau, *Peru: Paths to Poverty,* p. 32; and Steve Stein, *Populism in Peru* (Madison: University of Wisconsin Press, 1980), pp. 197–198.

26. Stein, *Populism in Peru,* p. 166. Among the epithets used against Sánchez Cerro were "latent homosexual" and "Black-Indian half-caste."

27. One owner of a large sugar hacienda commented about this time: "[I hope that the repression of APRA will be] bloody, very bloody, and definitively put an end to this damned APRA . . . immediate punishment . . . without waiting for trials and other idiocies." Quoted in Gilbert, *The Oligarchy,* p. 103.

28. Frederick B. Pike, *The Politics of the Miraculous in Peru* (Lincoln: University of Nebraska Press, 1986), p. 176.

29. Ibid., pp. 158–161.

30. McClintock, "Peru," p. 346; Fernando Tuesta Soldevilla, *Perú político en cifras: Élite política y elecciones* (Lima: Fundación Friedrich Ebert, 1994, 2d ed.), p. 224.

31. John Sheahan, "The Economy," in Rex A Hudson, ed., *Peru: A Country Study* (Washington, DC: Library of Congress), p. 183; Thorp and Bertram, *Peru 1890–1977,* pp. 259–274. Social mobilization in Peru in the early 1960s is compared to social mobilization in other Latin American nations in Palmer, *"Revolution from Above,"* pp. 9–11.

32. Latin American Bureau, *Peru: Paths to Poverty,* p. 38; Thorp and Bertram, *Peru 1890–1977,* p. 259.

33. Larson and Bergman, *Social Stratification,* p. 383.

34. Thorp and Bertram, *Peru 1890–1977,* pp. 264–273.

35. Valuable studies for this period include Latin American Bureau, *Peru: Paths to Poverty;* Abraham F. Lowenthal, ed., *The Peruvian Experiment: Continuity and Change Under Military Rule* (Princeton: Princeton University Press, 1975); Cynthia McClintock, *Peasant Cooperatives and Political Change in Peru* (Princeton: Princeton University Press, 1981); Henry Pease García, *El ocaso del poder oligárquico* (Lima: DESCO, 1977); and Alfred C. Stepan, *The State and Society: Peru in Comparative Perspective* (Princeton: Princeton University Press, 1978).

36. Luigi R. Einaudi and Alfred C. Stepan, *Latin American Institutional Development* (Los Angeles: Rand Corporation, 1971), p. 56; Víctor Villanueva, *El CAEM y la revolución de la fuerza armada* (Lima: Instituto de Estudios Peruanos, 1973); Carlos A. Astiz, *Pressure Groups and Power Elites in Peruvian Politics* (Ithaca, NY: Cornell University Press, 1969), p. 143.

37. From the Manifesto of the Revolutionary Government of the Armed Forces, October 2, 1968, reprinted in María del Pilar Tello, ed., *Golpe o revolución? Hablan los militares del '68* (Lima: Sagsa, 1983), pp. 284–285.

38. For comprehensive data on the agrarian reform, see McClintock, *Peasant Cooperatives,* pp. 48–63; and Cynthia McClintock, "Why Peasants Rebel," *World Politics* 37, no. 2 (October 1984): 64–67.

39. Bernardo Sorj, "Public Enterprises and the Question of the State Bourgeoisie, 1968–1976," in David Booth and Bernardo Sorj, eds., *Military Reformism and Social Classes* (London: Macmillan, 1983), p. 78; and Richard Webb, "Government Policy and the Distribution of Income in Peru, 1963–1973," in Abraham F. Lowenthal, ed., *The Peruvian Experiment* (Princeton: Princeton University Press, 1975), pp. 79–127; and Adolfo Figueroa, "El impacto de las reformas actuales sobre la distribucíon de ingresos en el Perú," in Alejandro Foxley, ed., *Distribución del ingreso* (Mexico City: Fondo de Cultura Económica, 1974).

40. World Bank, *Social Indicators of Development 1990* (Baltimore: Johns Hopkins University Press), p. 245.

41. World Bank, *Social Indicators of Development 1988* (Baltimore: Johns Hopkins University Press), p. 187 (for Peru) and other pages for other Latin American nations; and James W. Wilkie, *Statistical Abstract of Latin America* (Los Angeles: University of California Press, 1980), p. 123.

42. About 10 to 15 percent of Peru's peasant families became members of cooperatives; see note 38 for sources. Also, approximately 6 percent of Peru's labor force—some 288,000 workers in about 4,000 enterprises—were incorporated into "industrial communities," which were to be established in most enterprises employing more than six workers; see Nigel Haworth, "Conflict or Incorporation: The Peruvian Working Class, 1968–79," in David Booth and Bernardo Sorj, eds., *Military Reformism and Social Classes* (London: Macmillan, 1983), pp. 101–102.

43. Juan Velasco Alvarado, *Velasco: La voz de la revolución,* 2 vols. (Lima: Ediciones Participación, 1972), vol. 2, p. 271.

44. The number rose from 2,318 to 4,384, according to data in Jorge Parodi, "Los sindicatos en la democracia vacía," in Luis Pásara and Jorge Parodi, eds., *Democracia, sociedad, y gobierno en el Perú* (Lima: CEDYS, 1988), p. 90; Latin America Bureau, *Peru: Paths to Poverty,* p. 13.

45. On this period, see Henry Pease García, *Los caminos del poder* (Lima: DESCO, 1979); Luis A. Abugattas, "Populism and After: The Peruvian Experience," in James M. Malloy and Mitchell A. Seligson, eds., *Authoritarians and Democrats* (Pittsburgh: University of Pittsburgh Press, 1987), pp. 130–138; and Philip Mauceri, "The Transition to 'Democracy' and the Failures of Institution Building," in Maxwell A. Cameron and Philip Mauceri, eds., *The Peruvian Labyrinth: Polity, Society, Economy* (University Park: Pennsylvania State University Press, 1997), pp. 14–36; NACLA, "Peru Today," *Report on the Americas* 14 (November-December 1980); and Latin America Bureau, *Peru: Paths to Poverty,* pp. 54–80.

46. Tuesta Soldevilla, *Perú político en cifras,* p. 201.

47. Ibid., pp. 201, 213, and 219. Percentage is of the valid vote.

48. Ibid., p. 201. Percentage is of the valid vote.

49. A. Havier Hamann and Carlos E. Paredes, "The Peruvian Economy: Characteristics and Trends," in Carlos E. Paredes and Jeffrey D. Sachs, eds., *Peru's Path to Recovery* (Washington, DC: The Brookings Institution, 1991), p. 70.

50. Ibid., p. 70.

51. "Cinco años y la opinión pública," *Debate* 7, no. 32 (May 1985): 24–28.

52. Pike, *The Politics of the Miraculous,* p. 293.

53. President Alan García's inaugural address to the Peruvian Congress, July 28, 1985, reprinted in its entirety by the *Andean Report* (August 1985). The United States was referred to as "the richest and most imperialist country on earth," p. 16.

54. For the 1985 vote, see Table 6.2; for García's approval rating, see John Crabtree,

Peru Under García: An Opportunity Lost (Pittsburgh: University of Pittsburgh Press, 1992), p. 159.

55. As Russ Graham, economics officer in USIS, said in an interview with the author on August 19, 1987: "The Treasury Department hates Peru because of its stand on the debt." See also Crabtree, *Peru Under García,* pp. 39–45.

56. Inter-American Development Bank, *Economic and Social Progess in Latin America: 1987 Report* (Washington, DC: Inter-American Development Bank, 1987), pp. 2 and 376–377.

57. Paul Glewwe and Gilette Hall, "Poverty, Inequality, and Living Standards During Unorthodox Adjustment: The Case of Peru, 1985–1990," *Economic Development and Cultural Change* 42 (July 1994): 715.

58. *Perú económico* 13 (August 1990): 1–16.

59. Cynthia McClintock, *Revolutionary Movements in Latin America: El Salvador's FMLN and Peru's Shining Path* (Washington, DC: U.S. Institute of Peace Press, 1998), p. 73.

60. See Table 6.2. In the second round, Fujimori won 62 percent of the valid vote to 38 percent for Vargas Llosa; see Tuesta Soldevilla, *Perú político en cifras,* p. 149. On the 1990 election and Fujimori's candidacy in particular, see especially Carlos Iván Degregori and Romeo Grompone, *Elecciones 1990: Demonios y redentores en el nuevo Perú* (Lima: Instituto de Estudios Peruanos, 1991); and Stokes, "Peru: The Rupture of Democratic Rule," pp. 61–62.

61. The clearest statement of the sharpness of the reversal is Stokes, "Peru: The Rupture of Democratic Rule," p. 62. For an excellent chronology of politics in the 1990–1992 period, see Henry Pease García, *Los años de la langosta: La escena política del Fujimorismo* (Lima: IPADEL, 1994).

62. *Ideele* nos. 32–33 (December 1991): 4–14; *Ideele* 34 (February 1992): 5–9.

63. The primary scholar advancing legislative-executive conflict as the most important explanation is Charles Kenney, "Por qué el autogolpe? Fujimori y el congreso, 1990–1992," in Fernando Tuesta Soldevilla, ed., *Los enigmas del poder: Fujimori 1990–1996* (Lima: Fundación Friedrich Ebert, 1996), pp. 75–104. Scholars emphasizing Fujimori's political will and a permissive structural context include Cynthia McClintock, "La voluntad política presidencial y la ruptura constitucional de 1992 en el Perú," in Tuesta, ed., *Los enigmas del poder,* pp. 53–74, above; Cameron, "Self-Coups," p. 127; Stokes, "Peru: The Rupture of Democratic Rule," pp. 63–69; and the vast majority of Peruvian scholars.

64. This point is elaborated in McClintock, "La voluntad política," pp. 65–66.

65. See especially Fernando Rospigliosi, "Las fuerzas armadas y el 5 de Abril," Working Paper No. 73 (Lima: Instituto de Estudios Peruanos, 1996).

66. *Resumen semanal* nos. 15–23 (April 1992): 1.

67. McClintock, "La voluntad política," pp. 56–60.

68. An especially cogent analysis of Fujimori's assessment of Peru's political parties is Martín Tanaka, "Los espejos y espejismos de la democracia y el colapso de un sistema de partidos: Perú, 1980–1995, en perspectiva comparada," paper presented at the Latin American Studies Association meeting, April 1997, especially pp. 40–46.

69. Hermoza was finally retired in August 1998; it had been apparent for many months that Fujimori sought his departure.

70. Richard Webb and Graciela Fernández Baca, *Perú en números 1994* (Lima: Cuánto, 1994), p. 369; and "On Line," *The Peru Report* VI (December 1992): 1–3.

71. On the points in this paragraph, see the *Andean Report* XX (December 20, 1993): 1–2, and the Latin American Studies Association, "The 1995 Electoral Process in Peru: A Delegation Report of the Latin American Studies Association," Latin American Studies Association and the North-South Center (Pittsburgh and Miami, March 1995), pp. 7–10.

72. For a detailed account of these events, see Cynthia McClintock, "The Decimation of Peru's Sendero Luminoso," in Cynthia Arnson, ed., *Comparative Peace Processes in Latin America* (Stanford and Washington, DC: Stanford University Press and the Woodrow Wilson Center Press, 1999), pp. 223–250.

73. According to the *Washington Post,* April 8, 1995, p. A22, eighty-one state enterprises were sold for a total of more than $8 billion during Fujimori's first term, primarily to foreign investors.

74. Inter-American Development Bank, *Latin America After a Decade of Reforms* (Baltimore: Johns Hopkins University Press, 1997), pp. 268–293.

75. Ibid., p. 289; and John Sheahan, "Effects of Liberalization Programs on Poverty and Inequality: Chile, Mexico, and Peru," *Latin American Research Review* 32 (1997): 7–38.

76. Roberts, "Neoliberalism and the Transformation of Populism," p. 84.

77. Ibid., p. 104; and Kay, "'Fujipopulism' and the Liberal State," pp. 63–67.

78. In this effort, the Fujimori government specifically targeted departments where its support had previously been weak. See Carol Graham and Cheikh Kane, "Opportunistic Government or Sustaining Reform? Electoral Trends and Public-Expenditure Patterns in Peru, 1990–1995," *Latin American Research Review* 33 (1998): 67–105.

79. Richard Webb and Graciela Fernández Baca, *Perú en números 1997* (Lima: Cuánto, 1997), p. 1149. The question was posed in January 1997 to more than four hundred respondents by APOYO.

80. Richard Webb and Graciela Fernández Baca, *Perú en números 1996* (Lima: Cuánto, 1996), pp. 399–400.

81. Ibid., pp. 399–400, for the 1995 results; and Tuesta Soldevilla, *Perú político en cifras,* pp. 156 and 175–176, for the 1980–1985 results. "Null" votes are ballots that are marked but invalid, purportedly because they are marked incorrectly. The extremely high percentage of "null" votes (more than four times as high as in the presidential election) reflected in part voters' and voting-table monitors' errors in the use of the "preferential vote" (indicating their preferred candidate within a political-party list). However, the "preferential vote" was also in place for the 1990 and 1985 elections, without such serious problems. Many opposition leaders and some scholars believe that ballots for opposition candidates were voided either at the voting tables or by computers.

82. According to the official results, 835,964 Peruvians voted in the presidential race but "abstained" in the congressional race. Given that null and blank votes are included in electoral tallies and that the presidential and congressional ballots were both on the same sheet of paper, the number of voters in the presidential race and the congressional race should be the same.

83. For the opinion-poll predictions, see Catherine M. Conaghan, "Troubled Accounting, Troubling Questions: Looking Back at Peru's Election," *LASA Forum* XXVI (summer 1995), p. 9; and *Latin American Weekly Report,* no. 4 (February 2, 1995): 41, and no. 11 (March 23, 1995): 124.

84. Webb and Fernández Baca, *Perú en números 1997,* p. 1149, and The Economist Intelligence Unit, *Country Report: Peru 3rd Quarter 1998* (London: The Economist Intelligence Unit, 1998), p. 6.

85. The Economist Intelligence Unit, *Country Report: Peru, 2nd Quarter 1998* (London: The Economist Intelligence Unit, 1998), pp. 5, 16; The Economist Intelligence Unit, *Country Report: Peru 1st Quarter 1999,* pp. 10, 17–18; The Economist Intelligence Unit, *Country Profile: Peru 1997–1998* (London: The Economist Intelligence Unit, 1998), pp. 14, 45. The "high" tax rate is relative to historical standards; tax revenue in 1989 was below the equivalent of 7 percent of GDP, versus about 12 percent in 1996. The lending rate was 26 percent in 1996. A thoughtful comparison of Peru's liberalization program and its effects to the Chilean and the Mexican is Sheahan, "Effects of Liberalization Programs on Poverty and Ineqaulity," pp. 7–39.

86. In a June 1998 sample of four hundred respondents in Lima, the polling firm Mayeutica found that 42 percent classified the Fujimori government as "dictatorial/authoritarian" (rather than "totally democratic," "democratic dominated by the military," or "democratic but without independent institutions"). Data provided to the author courtesy of Mayeutica. In another survey in late July 1998, 72 percent classified the regime as "dictatorial," and only 21 percent as "democratic." This survey was by Empresa Interancional Peruana de Investigación de Mercado and reported in *La República,* September 6, 1998, p. 3.

87. A plurality of Peruvians in one poll judged Montesinos more powerful than Fujimori. See *Debate* XIX (July-August 1997): 13.

88. Catherine M. Conaghan, "The Permanent Coup: Peru's Road to Presidential Reelection," LASA Forum XXIX (spring 1998), pp. 7–8.

89. For 1996 data, PromPerú, *El Perú en el Latinobarómetro 96: Un instrumento de medición comparativa de la opinión pública latinoamericana* (Lima: Apoyo, n.d.); for 1998, a preview of the Latinobarómetro survey, courtesy of Alfredo Torres, Director of Apoyo, in an interview, June 16, 1998.

90. Percentage of the population estimated as "white" from Astiz, *Pressure Groups and Power Elites,* p. 42. See also Einaudi and Stepan, *Latin American Institutional Development,* p. 56, on the social backgrounds of Peru's big businessmen.

91. Figures for population in the highlands in 1940s and language in Larson and Bergman, *Social Stratification in Peru,* pp. 299, 363.

92. Richard Webb, *Government Policy and the Distribution of Income in Peru, 1963–1973* (Cambridge, MA: Harvard University Press, 1977), p. 6. The shares to the wealthiest were larger in Peru even than in Brazil or Mexico, the two Latin American countries that are most often described as inegalitarian. See Susan Eckstein, "Revolution and Redistribution in Latin America," in Cynthia McClintock and Abraham F. Lowenthal, *The Peruvian Experiment Reconsidered* (Princeton: Princeton University Press, 1983), pp. 368–369; James W. Howe, *The U.S. and World Development* (New York: Overseas Development Council, Praeger, 1975), p. 215.

93. Daniel Martínez and Armando Tealdo, *El agro peruano, 1970–1980* (Lima: CEDEP, 1982), pp. 15–16.

94. For data on land scarcity in Peru, see Martínez and Tealdo, *El agro peruano,* p. 39. Eighty percent of the lowest quartile of Peru's income distribution in 1961 was characterized as subsistence farmers working 0.9 hectares of cropland; 63 percent lived in the southern highlands; see Webb, *Government Policy,* p. 13.

95. Orin Starn, "Missing the Revolution: Anthropologists and the War in Peru," *Cultural Anthropology* 6 (1991): 63–91.

96. Whereas in 1876 the populations of both the Cuzco and Puno departments were larger than the population of the Lima department, by 1989 the population of Lima was more than five times that in each of these departments; whereas in 1940, 58 percent of Peru's fifteen-years-and-over population had no education at all, the corresponding figure for 1981 was 18 percent. See Richard Webb and Graciela Fernández Baca, *Perú en números 1990* (Lima: Cuánto, 1990), pp. 98, 136.

97. Seymour Martin Lipset, *Political Man: The Social Bases of Politics* (New York: Anchor Books, 1963).

98. Cited by Franciso Durand, "The Growth and Limitations of the Peruvian Right," in Maxwell A. Cameron and Philip Mauceri, *The Peruvian Labyrinth* (University Park: Pennsylvania State University Press, 1997), p. 155.

99. Durand, "The Growth and Limitations," p. 155; Julio Cotler, "Traditional Haciendas and Communities in a Context of Political Mobilization in Peru," in Rodolfo Stavenhagen, ed., *Agrarian Problems and Peasant Movements in Latin America* (Garden City, NY: Doubleday, Anchor, 1970); Handelman, *Struggle in the Andes,* p. 221; McClintock, *Peasant Cooperatives,* pp. 72–83.

100. For a recent definition of "clientelism" and its applicability not only to the rural but also the urban Peruvian context, see Susan C. Stokes, *Cultures in Conflict: Social Movements and the State in Peru* (Berkeley: University of California Press, 1995).

101. McClintock, *Peasant Cooperatives,* pp. 72–83, 207. More than 80 percent of the peasants in most sites said that "you cannot trust most people in this place."

102. Daniel Goldrich, Raymond B. Pratt, and C. R. Schuller, "The Political Integration of Lower-Class Urban Settlements in Chile and Peru," in Irving Louis Horowitz, eds., *Masses in Latin America* (New York: Oxford University Press, 1970), pp. 175–214. Among a similar Chilean sample the figure was 72 percent.

103. See especially David G. Becker, *The New Bourgeoisie and the Limits of Dependency: Mining, Class, and Power in "Revolutionary" Peru* (Princeton: Princeton University Press, 1983).

104. Compare and contrast the conclusions in Becker, *The New Bourgeoisie,* and Durand, "Growth and Limitations of the Right."

105. Stokes, *Cultures in Conflict;* McClintock, *Peasant Cooperatives;* and Evelyne Huber Stephens, *The Politics of Workers' Participation: The Peruvian Approach in Comparative Perspective* (New York: Academic Press, 1980).

106. By 1980, about 80 percent of the members of coastal cooperatives favored the return to electoral politics. Cynthia McClintock, "The Peasantry and Post-Revolutionary Agrarian Politics in Peru," in Stephen M. Gorman, ed., *Post-Revolutionary Peru* (Boulder, CO: Westview Special Studies, 1982), p. 145.

107. Eighty-two percent of a nationwide Venezuelan sample chose democracy in 1983; see Enrique A. Baloyra, "Public Opinion and Support for Democratic Regimes: Venezuela, 1973–1983," paper presented at the American Political Science Association meeting, September 1985, p. 17.

108. For the three presidential elections between 1980 and 1990, turnout averaged 66 percent of the eligible population, a percentage higher than in many industrialized countries. Comparisons to most Latin American nations are not readily available as turnout is usually reported as a percentage of registered voters rather than as a percentage of eligible voters, but I consider the second figure more important as in some nations registration laws are designed to reduce participation. The 66 percentage figure in Peru was almost 50 percent more than the average for El Salvador's 1989 and 1994 elections. For further discussion and sources on this issue, see McClintock, *Revolutionary Movements,* pp. 121–122.

109. Also, in a May 1990 survey in Huancayo commissioned by the author (N = 200), 14 percent of the respondents favored this alternative; see McClintock, *Revolutionary Movements,* pp. 78–81 and appendix 1.

110. Kenneth M. Roberts, "Economic Crisis and the Demise of the Legal Left in Peru," *Comparative Politics* 29 (Oct. 1996): 69. On the vote for Izquierda Unida in the 1980s municipal contests, see Tuesta Soldevilla, *Perú político en cifras,* pp. 169, 182, and 188.

111. Peruvians' support for the *autogolpe* and belief that it was not antidemocratic are indicated in *Resumen semanal* XV (April 10–14, 1992): 2; and *Sí* (May 11–17, 1992): 22. One of the best efforts to understand this apparent contradiction is Julio F. Carrión, "Explaining Mass Support for Anti-Democratic Actions: The Case of Fujimori's Auto-Coup in Peru," paper submitted to *Comparative Political Studies,* May 1996. Carrión finds that many Peruvians endorsed what Carrión calls "plebiscitarian" definitions of democracy. It should be noted too that, just as Velasco before him, Fujimori explained his action as necessary to achieve "real" democracy over the longer term.

112. Carrión, "Explaining Mass Support," pp. 35–38. In a 1996 survey, Peruvians' interest in politics was similar to the Latin American average, but Peruvians were more likely to say that politics stimulated their interest rather than their boredom, indifference, irritation, or disgust; see PromPerú, *El Perú en el Latinobarómetro,* p. 20.

113. Cecilia Blondet, *Las mujeres y el poder: Una historia de Villa El Salvador* (Lima: Instituto de Estudios Peruanos, 1991); and Maruja Barrig, "The Difficult Equilibrium Between Bread and Roses: Women's Organizations and the Transition from Dictatorship to Democracy in Peru," in Jane Jaquette, ed., *The Women's Movement and the Transition to Democracy* (Boulder, CO: Westview, 1991). Also, an excellent discussion is Romeo Grompone, *Nuevos tiempos, nueva politica: El fin de un ciclo partidario* (Lima: Instituto de Estudios Peruanos, 1995), pp. 35–38.

114. PromPerú, *Latinobarómetro,* p. 24.

115. PromPerú, *Latinobarómetro,* p. 36.

116. On the recent scholarly debate about presidentialism, see especially Scott Mainwaring and Matthew Soberg Shugart, *Presidentialism and Democracy in Latin America* (New York: Cambridge University Press, 1997). For a discussion of the Peruvian experience, see Cynthia McClintock, "Presidents, Messiahs, and Constitutional Breakdowns in Peru," in Juan J. Linz and Arturo Valenzuela, eds., *The Failure of Presidential Democracy* (Baltimore: Johns Hopkins University Press, 1994), pp. 360–395.

117. For example, in both the 1980 and 1985 elections, the PPC won only 3 to 5 percent of the vote in most highland departments; see Tuesta Soldevilla, *Perú político en cifras,* pp. 176, 195. A 1987 public opinion poll in Lima found that it was supported by 37 percent of the wealthiest citizens, but a mere 4 percent of the poorest; see *Caretas,* June 22, 1987, p. 12.

118. The definitive analysis is Roberts, "Economic Crisis."

119. Pike, *The Politics of the Miraculous,* is an excellent analysis of these themes within the APRA party.

120. *Debate* 12 (August-October 1990): 29.

121. Tuesta Soldevilla, *Perú político en cifras,* p. 155.

122. "Collapse" is the common characterization by Peruvian scholars. Excellent discussions include Tanaka, "Los espejos y espejismos"; John Crabtree, "The 1995 Elections in Peru: End of the Line for the Party System?" Occasional Paper No. 12, Institute of Latin American Studies, University of London, 1995.

123. Webb and Fernández Baca, *Perú en números 1996*, p. 400. It should also be noted, though, that some individuals who had previously run under the banner of one of these parties competed in 1995 as candidates of Unión por el Perú. The Partido Popular Cristiano did not compete for the presidency; it won 3.1 percent of the legislative vote.

124. On various indices of electoral volatility, Peru's party system scored as the most volatile among numerous Latin American nations; see Scott Mainwaring, "Rethinking Party Systems Theory in the Third Wave of Democratization: The Importance of Party System Institutionalization," paper presented at the Latin American Studies Association meeting, Guadalajara, April 17–19, 1997, p. 21 (in an analysis of twenty-five European and Latin American countries), and Hartlyn, "Democracies," p. 51 (in an analysis of seven Latin American nations). Volatility was also high in Peru prior to 1980; see Michael Coppedge, "Freezing in the Tropics: Explaining Party-System Volatility in Latin America," paper presented at the Midwest Political Science Association meeting, Chicago, April 6–8, 1995, p. 23.

125. See, for example, Webb and Fernánedez Baca, *Perú en números 1996*, pp. 396–398, which provides results for Lima but not elsewhere.

126. For 1968–1983, see Patricia A. Wilson and Carol Wise, "The Regional Implications of Public Investment in Peru, 1968–1983," *Latin American Research Review* 21 (1986): 93–116; for 1983–1987, Instituto Nacional de Planificación, "Evaluación de la Inversión Pública 1986" and "Evaluacíon de la Inversión Pública 1987," both data sets mimeographed by the Instituto Nacional de Planificación in Lima, and author's calculation from data for 1983–1985 at the Instituto Nacional de Planificación. On the bias in public investment in agriculture, see Cynthia McClintock, "Agricultural Policy and Food Security in Peru and Ecuador," in Bruce Drury, Birol Yeshilada, and Charles Brockett, eds., *Agrarian Reform in Reverse* (Boulder, CO: Westview, 1987), pp. 110–116.

127. See, for example, Hernando de Soto, *El otro sendero* (Lima: Editorial el Barranco, 1986); and Felipe M. Portocarrero, "The Peruvian Public Investment Programme, 1968–1978," *Journal of Latin American Studies* 14 (1982): 433–445; and *The Andean Report* VI (December 1980): 221–223, and *The Andean Report* XIV (March 1987): 50–56, which reprints a critical World Bank report on Peruvian public investment policy.

128. Between 1968 and 1990, Peru's military expenditures were frequently estimated at 20 percent of total government expenditures—a percentage almost three times the average for the Latin American region. World Bank, *World Development Report* (Washington, DC: World Bank, various annual editions), and U.S. Arms Control and Disarmament Agency, *World Military Expenditures and Arms Transfers* (Washington, DC: U.S. Government Printing Office), annual editions.

129. Author's calculation from data in Luis Alberto Arias, "Fiscal Policy," in Carlos E. Paredes and Jeffrey D. Sachs, eds., *Peru's Path to Recovery: A Plan for Economic Stabilization and Growth* (Washington, DC: The Brookings Institution, 1991), p. 221. Total number of state enterprises from World Bank, *Report on Peru* (Lima: Andean Air Mail and Peruvian Times, 1986), p. 2.

130. de Soto, *El otro sendero*, p. xx.

131. Webb and Fernández Baca, *Perú en números 1996*, p. 928; Kay, "'Fujipopulism' and the Liberal State," pp. 74–78; Juan Felipe Isasi Cayo, *Cultura política y constitución 1993* (Lima: Universidad de Lima, 1997), pp. 217–220.

132. Luis Pásara, *Jueces, justicia, y poder en el Perú* (Lima: CEDYS, 1982), p. 27; "Quinta encuesta anual: El poder en el Perú," *Debate* 33 (July 1985): 56.

133. Shane Hunt, "Peru: The Current Economic Situation in Long-Term Perspective," in Efraín Gonzales de Olarte, ed., *The Peruvian Economy and Structural Adjustment* (University of Miami: North-South Center Press, 1996), p. 15. This figure is for total GDP growth; in Hunt's chapter, the per capita figure is reported as 1.5 percent, approximately the same as that provided by Thorp and Bertram, *Peru 1890–1977*, p. 321.

134. Thorp and Bertram, *Peru 1890–1977*, p. 208.

135. Hunt, "Peru: The Current Economic Situation," pp. 12–19.

136. For this period, Peru's annual per capita GDP growth averaged 3.0 percent, the same as in Mexico and considerably higher than in Brazil, Chile, Colombia, or Argentina. See Hunt, "Peru: The Current Economic Situation," p. 18.

137. Thorp and Bertram, *Peru 1890–1977*, p. 321.

138. Sheahan, "The Economy," p. 182; Webb, *Government Policy and the Distribution of Income*, p. 7.

139. Thorp and Bertram, *Peru 1890–1977,* p. 9; Webb, *Government Policy,* p. 6; E.V.K. FitzGerald, *The Political Economy of Peru 1956–78: Economic Development and the Restructuring of Capital* (London: Cambridge University Press, 1979), p. 93.

140. Charles L. Taylor and Michael C. Hudson, *World Handbook of Political and Social Indicators,* 2d ed. (New Haven: Yale University Press, 1972), p. 267.

141. Martínez and Tealdo, *El agro peruano 1970–1980,* p. 39.

142. Carol Wise, "The Politics of Peruvian Economic Reform: Overcoming the Legacies of State-Led Economic Development," *Journal of Inter-American Studies and World Affairs* 36 (spring 1994): 85. In June 1990, the average tariff rate was 66 percent and effective protection for the industrial sector averaged 82 percent (Sheahan, "The Economy," p. 169). The state-owned share of GDP was 23 percent in 1975 (see the "Historical Overview"). For rigorous comparisons to other Latin American nations, see Inter-American Development Bank, *External Debt and Economic Development in Latin America* (Washington, DC: Inter-American Development Bank, 1984), p. 182.

143. McClintock, *Revolutionary Movements,* p. 186.

144. Sheahan, "The Economy," p. 150.

145. Ibid.

146. Ibid. p. 182; and the World Bank, *World Development Report 1997* (New York: Oxford University Press, 1997), pp. 222–223. See also Hamann and Paredes, "The Peruvian Economy," p. 54.

147. Thorp and Bertram, *Peru 1890–1977,* pp. 305–307; the number of Peruvians employed in the public sector is from Daniel M. Schydlowsky, "The Peruvian Economy Circa 1990: Structure and Consequences," in Efraín Gonzales de Olarte, ed., *The Peruvian Economy and Structural Adjustment* (University of Miami: North-South Center Press, 1996), p. 112.

148. McClintock, "Why Peasants Rebel," p. 61; McClintock, *Revolutionary Movements,* pp. 180–184.

149. Sheahan, "The Economy," p. 180; Cuánto, *Ajuste y economía familiar 1985–1990* (Lima: Cuánto, 1991), pp. 32–33.

150. Richard Webb and Graciela Fernández Baca, *Perú en números 1990,* p. 714.

151. McClintock, *Revolutionary Movements,* p. 164.

152. Hunt, "Peru: The Current Economic Situation," p. 45; Thorp and Bertram, *Peru 1890–1977,* pp. 321–327; FitzGerald, *The Political Economy of Peru,* pp. 293–301.

153. The Economist Intelligence Unit, *Country Profile: Peru 1997–1998,* p. 51.

154. Fernando Eguren López, *Evaluación social del desarrollo humano en el Perú* (Lima: Acción Ciudadana, 1997), p. 51, and data in the annual editions of Webb and Fernández Baca, *Perú en números.*

155. The Bush administratation took a harsher stance against the *autogolpe* than did the International Monetary Fund or the World Bank; see Stokes, "Peru: The Rupture of Democratic Rule," p. 65.

156. Gonzalo M. Portocarrero, *De Bustamante a Odría* (Lima: Mosca Azul, 1983), p. 91.

157. Adalberto J. Pinelo, *The Multinational Corporation as a Force in Latin American Politics: A Case Study of the International Petroleum Company in Peru* (New York: Praeger, 1973), pp. 115–119.

158. See U.S. Agency for International Development, *U.S. Overseas Loans and Grants: Series of Yearly Data FY 1946–FY 1985 Vol. II Latin America and the Caribbean* (Washington, DC: AID, 1986).

159. Ibid.; and also U.S. Agency for International Development, *U.S. Overseas Loans and Grants and Assistance for International Organizations* (Washington, DC: AID, various annual editions). Real values calculated from *U.S. Department of Commerce, Statistical Abstract of the United States* (Washington, DC: U.S. Government Printing Office, various editions), table 751, p. 485.

NICARAGUA

COSTA
RICA

PANAMA

Pacific

Ocean

COLOMBIA

ECUADOR

PERU

Atlantic

Ocean

Caracas
Barquisimeto
Valencia
Maturín
Cumaná

San Cristóbal
Ciudad Bolívar
Ciudad Guayana

V E N E Z U E L A

Puerto Ayacucho

GUYANA

SURINAME

BRAZIL

BOLIVIA

VENEZUELA

7

VENEZUELA:
The Character, Crisis, and Possible Future of Democracy

Daniel H. Levine & Brian F. Crisp

Democracy in Venezuela, as both ideal and reality, has been on a roller-coaster ride over the past few decades. Four decades of uninterrupted constitutional succession and mass democratic politics have changed democracy from an impossible dream into a routine and expected state of affairs. Recent generations of Venezuelans have come to maturity knowing no other kind of political system: leftist revolution is a faint echo from the past, military rule only a distant memory. As democracy has become the norm, the issue of preserving democracy (of paramount concern in the early, shaky years after 1958) became less compelling than the goal of improving, extending, and "democratizing" the system. Praise of democracy as such has yielded to harsh and, at times, unremitting criticism. To put the matter plainly, Venezuelans' honeymoon with democracy ended some time ago. Democracy is now "the system," "the establishment." Beginning in the mid-1980s, as mounting economic, institutional, and political problems converged to create what ordinary Venezuelans refer to simply as "the crisis," many have come to see democracy Venezuelan-style as a key part of the problem.

The democratic regimes in place since 1958 have profoundly shaped the transformation of modern Venezuela, making it into the kind of country it is today. There is both light and shadow here. Presiding over a steady (and at times spectacularly increasing) flow of income from the petroleum industry, elites controlling powerful political parties built a dominant central state. This state apparatus spent oil money building roads, cities, schools, and public works in ways that turned a poor, illiterate, fragmented, sickly, and predominantly peasant society into a highly urban, mobile, literate, and media-soaked nation. When oil prices boomed in the early 1970s, the idea of a greater Venezuela (La Gran Venezuela celebrated in the speeches of then-president Carlos Andrés Pérez) seemed achievable. Shadows appeared soon after. Starting with the currency devaluation of 1983 (the first in this century), income inequality began an inexorable increase, levels of living declined, and state institutions proved incapable of delivering basic services to the population. Health and welfare indices declined sharply, malnutrition rose, and diseases such as malaria, dengue fever, tuberculosis, and cholera appeared after a long absence. Large-scale corruption became endemic, and citizen disaffection made itself known in the form of growing voter abstention, citizen movements for reform, demonstrations and protests including massive public riots, hero worship of unsuccessful military conspirators, and support for new parties and for political leaders who campaigned on "antiparty" platforms.

This brief sketch suggests the intense and sometimes confusing pattern of conflict and change that has marked the life and times of democracy in Venezuela in recent years. There has also been extensive and sometimes bitter debate among scholars concerning the causes of crisis, and the significance and viability of reform. It is difficult to strike a balance, and many have slipped too easily into an all-encompassing pessimism. One observer has gone so far as to compare the current situation to simply rearranging the deck chairs on the Titanic.[1] We take a different view here. Although there can be no doubt about the severity of the crisis of democracy in Venezuela, obituaries are premature. The "system" has been considerably more resilient than much early commentary or theorizing anticipated or allowed for. Despite sustained economic decline, civil violence and military conspiracy, institutional decay, and leadership betrayal, sufficient reserves remained in "the system" and in the population to defeat two attempted coups, to generate a host of new political movements (including one major new party), to remove and impeach one sitting president, to choose an interim successor, to hold two national elections, and to return a trusted elder statesman to the presidency—all in the space of a few years. The political elite has displayed remarkable consensus about how to proceed. A striking aspect of what one might call the "political management" of the crisis is how steady it has been, how closely constitutional norms have been followed. No government has been overthrown. Even the impeachment and removal of President Carlos Andrés Pérez in 1993—an event unprecedented in national history—was conducted with scrupulous attention to constitutional procedure. Hard times indeed, but the system did not roll over and play dead. Real human agents worked for solutions. They did not always succeed, and they may fail in the long run, but they refused to be passive captives.

The recent challenges to Venezuelan democracy would not have been possible without forty years of democratic development. We stress that the crisis that has gripped Venezuela since the late 1980s is best understood not simply as the decay of the established system, but rather as a crisis *within* democracy. The foundations of the democratic system, and the key to understanding the possibilities of democracy's transformation and survival in the future, rest on five elements that will structure our later analysis: the pattern of state-led socioeconomic development; the party and electoral systems; the evolution of state structures and interbranch relations; the emergence and possible significance of "civil society"; and the changing role of international forces. Powerful democratizing elements within Venezuelan society have generated a host of political and institutional reforms that together provide guidelines for the shape and character of a possible future democracy. Major reforms of the electoral system, combined with significant elements of decentralization, have sparked the beginnings of vigorous local and regional politics for the first time in this century. The result has been major changes in intraparty dynamics, leadership recruitment, and in the way legislatures operate. There has been a notable increase in citizen activism manifest in a range of social movements unknown in Venezuela until the 1990s. These democratizing transformations have all taken place against a backdrop of severe and unremitting economic decay, revealing the failure of the development strategy that inspired the founders of this democracy in the first place. Simultaneous political and economic reform is notoriously difficult to achieve. Whether or not Venezuelans manage the task will depend in large measure on the skills, resilience, and creativity that four decades of democratic life have created not only in the country's leaders, but also in its citizens, and in the new civil society that has emerged in recent years.[2]

Given the importance we place on the purely political, as opposed to the cultural, social, or economic, it may be helpful to begin by clarifying a few key political terms. We use "democracy" as it is defined in this series, *Democracy in Developing Countries*: that is, a national political system characterized by free and open elections, relatively low barriers to participation, genuine competition, and protection of civil liberties. We use "democratization" in two related senses, each with notable implications for democracy. The first is temporal: democratization appears as a stage in the creation and maintenance of democracy. Several phases are involved, running from inauguration through consolidation to a transformation to maturity. This is not to say that the process is irreversible or that "maturity" is an equilibrium point. As Venezuelan experience indicates, hard-won stability can be put in jeopardy by rapid social change, institutional rigidity, and organizational complacency. The second sense of democratization refers to the nature of organized social life and predominant cultural orientations. Democratization here involves the creation, nurturance, and spread of more egalitarian social relations and norms of authority and leadership. These are worked out in associational life, especially through encouraging participation, developing new sources and patterns of leadership, and creating lasting relations between group life and national politics. Ties like these under-

gird the formal legitimation of democracy with day-to-day experience of
competition and association in all walks of life, with the spread of leadership skills, the diffusion of norms of accountability, and greater openness in
the conduct of public affairs. These comments suggest that democracy in
Venezuela is not well understood as the sole creation of enlightened or supposedly "modern" leaders, whose values are gradually taken up by the
benighted masses. Quite the contrary: from the beginning, Venezuelan
democracy has rested on an alliance of middle-class leaders with poor and
peripheral groups.

We go into such detail on the meaning of democracy and democratization because we believe that the issues must be put in positive terms.
Democracy is more than just the absence of authoritarianism or military
rule: democracy has sources, dynamics, and values of its own. It is particularly important to work on the concepts of democracy and democratization
now, as the consolidation of new or restored democratic regimes throughout Latin America challenges common understandings of the process. Our
effort to make theoretical sense of the decay and crisis of democracy in
Venezuela shares many of the concerns that have driven comparative work
on democracy and democratization. We will attempt to capitalize on four
perspectives: stress on how contingent historical conditions shape processes and likely outcomes; attention to institution building, rules of the game,
and interbranch relations; focus on specific political vehicles, above all
political parties; and concern with "civil society" as generative of new
actors and more democratic rules of the game and state-society relations. In
the scholarly literature to date, each of these perspectives has stood more or
less alone: the first placing greater weight on economic forces and "political economy" issues; the second placing greater weight on politics itself,
including a new look at institutions; and the remaining two stressing social
forces and political dynamics, including organizational and leadership
issues. Our chapter underscores the need to combine these perspectives,
examining in detail the actual capabilities of civil society and social forces.
Some contribute more to our explanations than others.

Following on general analyses by Guillermo O'Donnell, Philippe
Schmitter, and Laurence Whitehead or by Ruth Berins Collier and David
Collier, Terry Karl and others have argued strongly that state structures and
historically evolving institutions (conceived broadly) in Venezuela have
been shaped by the petroleum industry, above all by the abundant, "cost-
less" revenue it has provided to political leaders and bureaucrats.[3] Oil
money paid for what Marcello Cavarozzi terms a "state centered matrix"
able simultaneously to mitigate social conflict and manage economic
growth and distribution.[4] The state is top-heavy: controlled by remote
elites, colonized by interest groups, and dependent on ever greater infu-
sions of oil money. Once revenues decline, the model is "exhausted," and
conflict comes to the surface, making crisis a part of everyday life. This

perspective views institutions as historically contingent on social and economic variables. Here, we place greater emphasis on institutions as structures that shape the incentives and behavior of politicians and citizens. This focus informs our understanding of why interest groups in Latin America interact almost exclusively with the executive branch and how presidents have evaded an inactive Congress.[5] As a result, the relative power of the branches has been skewed in favor of the executive. Excessive presidentialism has become problematic and, as we shall see, has been an important factor in institutional immobilism and the decay of legitimacy. This approach points to reform of electoral rules and constitutionally allocated powers as possible responses to the crisis. The allocation of these powers and the partisan control of branches can help explain the likelihood of interbranch stalemate and the degree of presidential dominance.

An exclusive focus on formal institutions would leave out a great deal about the political process. Comparative work on political parties has underscored the central role that institutionalized parties and party systems can play in mobilizing social forces and channeling conflict, creating and sustaining long-term loyalties, concentrating choice, and eliciting, training, and circulating generations of leaders.[6] Students of Venezuela have analyzed these issues very thoroughly.[7] In addition, a growing body of research demonstrates the powerful impact that electoral rules have on party formation and on the stability of party systems.[8]

At the same time, the emergence of "civil society" has brought active social movements of the most varied kind into the political process: business and human rights associations, neighborhood and church groups, new unions, feminist organizations, and citizen groups of all kinds. These phenomena have little place in the theoretical lexicon of the new institutionalism, and their absence makes it difficult to say much about who gets organized, in what way, and how and why they interact with politicians and policymakers. The impact of state-society relations on the creation, growth, and quality of democracy has been a staple of political analysis since Aristotle and de Tocqueville, to name only two distinguished predecessors. Seymour Lipset, Seymour Lipset and Stein Rokkan, Robert Dahl, and the contributors to this volume have stressed how a pluralistic, balanced development of social forces makes democratic politics possible.[9] Studies of social movements and "civil society" have expanded this perspective, placing greater emphasis on the democratizing impact social movements can have on political institutions and practices. So-called new social movements are widely perceived as a seedbed of more egalitarian values and practices, and a vehicle through which new social strata can be recruited into political activism.[10]

Much recent work differentiates sharply between civil society and the state, as if the groups and movements at issue were isolated and wholly autonomous from state institutions.[11] This is unrealistic and, in the case of

Venezuela, clearly untrue. Although the Venezuelan state has historically been large and wealthy, it has been neither autonomous nor totally dominant. In order to appreciate the potential of groups in civil society to affect political change, we must know both about the qualities of the groups themselves and the nature of their interaction with one another and the state. State structures contain several institutional channels for participation by organized forces. For much of the democratic era, business associations and trade unions effectively colonized the state, but a more diverse array of groups is now seeking to participate. These elements of civil society engage in regular interaction with the state—searching for access, connections, and resources and working to alter the rules of the political game in their favor. In contrast to much of the recent literature, we acknowledge that not all groups labeled as "civil society" are small in scale and egalitarian in character: traditional actors including political parties, trade unions, and business associations also constitute civil society.[12]

Elsewhere, Levine has pointed up the significance of building norms of legitimacy, and of the autonomous role of leadership and political organization.[13] Together, these create bonds and shared loyalties between elites and mass publics, which make for enduring forms of power and thus make politics effective. Political commitments can be carried out because the power of strong organization makes implementation possible. Likewise, institutions were adopted and rules of the game were agreed on and put in place that made it possible for competing groups and politicians to operate and to compete within a common democratic framework. A general willingness to play by the rules and its incorporation into routine political practice kept democratic institutions stable for more than thirty years. When the process established no longer fit the society being governed and when the policies generated benefited only the privileged few, the pace of political and economic reform picked up and efforts were made to revitalize the system. We examine these reforms and consider their significance for the way political space is structured and political authority legitimated in Venezuela.

Venezuelan experience has been enormously dynamic. For the first fifty years of this century, Venezuela stood as a model of military rule. The inauguration and surprising survival of democracy in the decades after 1958 made it a model of democracy in a continent where military authoritarian regimes became the norm. The current crisis of Venezuelan democracy has made its flaws all too evident, particularly given the contrast to hopeful new democracies being established elsewhere in the region. As we shall see, the very elements that were critical to the origins and long-term stability of the political system (strong parties, low social conflict in a "managed" civil society, and a dominant state paid for by oil revenues) are now widely taken as reasons for its decay. The challenge for the future will be to democratize Venezuelan democracy, so that it better reflects and represents the kind of society Venezuela has become in the democratic years.

HISTORICAL OVERVIEW

The modern history of Venezuela is well documented, and only a brief account is possible here.[14] It is noteworthy how much of the relevant history is contemporary: many core institutions and much of the tone and character of modern Venezuelan life are of recent origin. Indeed, in the Latin American context, Venezuela stands out precisely for how little carries over from the colonial period and the nineteenth century to shape the modern scene. There are few great families whose wealth and power span the centuries. The parties that dominated nineteenth-century politics left no trace at all. The development of the petroleum industry, from the 1920s on, reworked all aspects of national life: destroying agriculture, spurring massive internal migration, and funding an active state. Petroleum income, cycled through the central state, underwrote the creation of an urban economy that attracted large-scale immigration from southern Europe in the years following World War II. The resulting concentration of Spaniards, Italians, and, in lesser numbers, Portuguese immigrants changed the character of life in the capital, Caracas, and throughout the country in profound ways.

It may be useful to preface the discussion of recent history with brief consideration of several aspects of colonial and nineteenth-century Venezuela, if only to clarify why they survived so little. Colonial Venezuela was a quiet and unimportant backwater of the Spanish Empire. The local economy was based on ranching and plantation agriculture and was generally weak and unproductive. Religion was also weak: the ecclesiastical structures of the Catholic Church were largely absent in much of the territory. The colonial period did establish regional and population patterns that have persisted to the present, weighted to the primacy of the capital city and its surrounding area. It also set general relations of dependence on external trade.[15] In these regards, Venezuela differs little from the rest of Spanish America. Independence struggles with Spain were exceptionally costly. Many campaigns were fought on Venezuelan soil, and Venezuelan soldiers took a leading role in the fighting. The most famous of these was, of course, Simón Bolívar (The Liberator), whose statue (usefully equestrian) graces the vast majority of town and city plazas in Venezuela today. The wars of independence had several relevant effects. First, they began a series of civil wars and armed conflicts that continued throughout the nineteenth century, wrecked the basis of colonial wealth, and spurred the destruction of what passed for a local aristocracy. Continuous warfare by regional warlords also furthered notable administrative decay and regional fragmentation. Throughout the nineteenth century, the central state was, for the most part, nominal. The role of armed, regional *caudillos* began to fade only in the early twentieth century, when a central state and permanent standing army were built after the 1920s.[16]

The long independence wars furthered the decline of Venezuelan aris-

tocracies in another way. Once conflict was under way, masses of plains-
men *(llaneros)* emerged as a formidable cavalry and played a key role in
the fighting. Their initial leader, Paez, made his peace with the old elite, but
the presence of large numbers of potential military forces of popular extraction and uncertain loyalty remained a visible threat, erupting time and again
in the nineteenth century.[17] The most notable instance came in the Federal
Wars (1858–1863), which were especially bitter and destructive.[18] The
fighting and constant upheaval undermined traditional ties throughout rural
Venezuela and sparked a process of internal migration that has continued in
accelerated ways ever since. Migration initially flowed to the Andean states
of Mérida, Táchira, and Trujillo, which were relatively safe havens from
the violence endemic in the central and plains regions. The growth of
Andean states also reflected the emergence of a coffee-export economy as
production expanded onto the mountain slopes of the Andean region.

The accumulation of wealth, population, and power in the Andean
region had great significance for the future. At the turn of the century,
Venezuela was conquered by an army from the state of Táchira, led by
Cipriano Castro and Juan Vicente Gómez. Not long after, the feckless
Castro was maneuvered out of office by his lieutenant, Gómez, who
remained in power until his death in late 1935. Burgeoning oil revenues
allowed Gómez to buy weapons, build a permanent standing army, and lay
the bases for the first effective central state apparatus in Venezuelan history. Military and administrative power helped Gómez destroy the enemies of
the past, and close the books definitively on nineteenth-century political
life.[19] Traditional political parties and military *caudillos* disappeared; political opposition and protest soon began to take new tacks, working to create
mass politics and political democracy.[20]

The combination of unchecked state terror and police power with the
social changes spurred by petroleum had unexpected effects. The growth of
the oil industry created new classes and social formations and spurred
notable population movement. These new groups and forces had little connection to older elites, or to the social or political structures of the past.
Effective repression saw to that, and thus in curious and doubtless unintended ways, the Gómez autocracy laid the bases of modern political life,
leaving an open field and a growing potential clientele to the organizers of
new movements. Most significant among these were the university students
and trade unionists who emerged first in the 1920s, and later returned from
exile and prison after the dictator's death. After the death of Gómez, political history falls easily into four periods: 1936–1945, 1945–1948, 1948–
1958, and the post-1958 years of democratic rule. The democratic era can
itself be divided into three periods: beginnings and consolidation, from
1958 to 1968; stable two party rule, from 1968 to 1988; and crisis and
reform, starting in 1989 and continuing to the present. Each period has a
different dynamic, with distinct organizational principles and political

methods playing a central role. Table 7.1 summarizes some of the central features of each period.

Transitional Rule: 1936–1945

Gómez was followed in office by his designated successor, General Eleazar López Contreras, who had been his minister of war. López Contreras struggled effectively to keep the lid on change. He repressed incipient trade

Table 7.1 Regimes, Presidents, Central Political Groups, and Basic Political Methods in Twentieth-Century Venezuela

Regime Type	Executive	Central Political Groups	Basic Political Methods
Personalistic Rule	J. V. Gómez (1903–1935)	Military/police	Force, terror, bribery
"Transitional" Military	E. López Contreras (1936–1941) I. Medina Angarita (1943–1945)	Military/police, bureaucracy	Intramilitary consultation, limited suffrage
Trienio of Democracy	R. Betancourt (1945–1947) R. Gallegos (1947–1948)	Acción Democrática, mass organizations	Mass parties, elections
Military	Junta (1948–1950) M. Pérez Jiménez (1950–1958)	Military/police, bureaucracy	Intramilitary consultation, terror
Democracy Consolidation	Provisional Government (1958–1959) R. Betancourt (1959–1964) R. Leoni (1964–1969)		Competitive elections, political bargaining, mass suffrage
Stable Two-Party Rule	R. Caldera (1969–1974) C. Andrés Pérez (1974–1979) L. Herrera Campins (1979–1984) J. Lusinchi (1984–1989)	Acción Democrática, COPEI, minor parties, mass organizations	
Crisis and Reform	C. Andrés Pérez (1989–1993) R. J. Velásquez (1993–1994) R. Caldera (1994–1999) H. Chávez (1999–)	Civil society, social movements	Demonstrations

union and party organization, keeping power in the hands of the army and state machine. López Contreras was succeeded in turn by his minister of war, General Isaías Medina Angarita. Once in office, Medina began a gradual liberalization. Seeking a base of support independent from López, and perhaps influenced by the climate of democratic struggle in World War II, Medina opened the doors to union and political organization. With these changes in the air, an amalgam of groups applied for legal status, and the new party was formally constituted in September 1941 as Acción Democrática (AD).

AD immediately began to build a new kind of political party in Venezuela: a permanent organization, existing at all levels and integrating many groups into the party structure. All major (meaning long and lasting) parties in Venezuela have followed this basic pattern. They are vertically integrated, with strong links binding block and neighborhood to regional and national structures. They are also horizontally integrated, with functional groups like labor, students, professionals, or peasants represented within the party organization. These groups are themselves divided by competing party groups, a state of affairs that underscores the appeal of party as a key affiliation and enhances the independent power of party leaders, who are able to play off one group against another in the name of the party as a whole.[21]

During the Medina period, AD created a vigorous, effective, and close-knit organization. Party organizers helped mobilize and set up industrial and peasant unions; by 1945, AD had defeated competitors (e.g., from the Communist Party) and generally had the upper hand in popular organization. But the limited nature of political change frustrated the party and its leaders. Although organization had indeed grown notably, the political system continued to restrict participation. Indirect elections remained the rule, there was no female suffrage, and in general mass organization yielded little in the way of effective power. This context helps explain the party leadership's decision to join with young military officers in a conspiracy against the Medina government. They saw this as a chance to initiate rapid and far-reaching change. The coup was launched on October 18, 1945, and after a few days of fighting, a provisional junta was formed with four members from AD, two officers, and one independent civilian. The three years that followed, known in Venezuela as the *trienio,* mark the definitive introduction of mass politics into national life.

The Trienio: 1945–1948

It is hard to overstate the depth of the changes *trienio* politics brought. Organization of all kinds was encouraged and did indeed flourish, especially among labor and peasant groups. In general, barriers to participation were lowered, and suffrage was made genuinely universal, extending to all citizens over eighteen, with no restrictions by education, gender, or property. The electorate expanded from 5 percent of the population before 1945 to 36 percent immediately thereafter. Free, direct elections were instituted at all levels, from municipal councils and state legislatures to the national Congress (deputies and senators) and president. New parties were also formed, most importantly the Christian Democratic Comité de Organización Política Electoral Independiente (COPEI) and Unión República Democrática (URD), which grouped the noncommunist left wing of forces that had backed Medina.

All sorts of services were extended for the first time to poor and peripheral groups and regions. As a result, AD strengthened its mass base in spectacular and long-lasting fashion. The party dominated national politics completely, with opposition centered on the extreme right, represented by the Catholic Church, by a range of political parties (most notably COPEI), and by conservative elements in the military. Expanded participation during the *trienio* must be set against the intense and bitter conflicts that dominated national politics. Conflict stemmed from resistance to AD's radical policies, and from fear that the new regime and its supporters would destroy the previous social order entirely. It is important to realize that while many organizations had been created after 1936, these were mainly popular in composition and radical in orientation. Economic and social elites relied on control of the army and administration to guarantee power and privilege. Religious leaders also failed to build organization, depending instead on networks of elite schools and the sponsorship of other power groups to guarantee their interests.

Many sectors were threatened in symbolic and material terms by AD and its regime. There was little trust and no sense of mutual guarantees among major social and political groups. Business generally, and the oil industry in particular, contested policies favoring labor and restricting company profits. Rural interests resisted land reform and objected vehemently to measures promoting peasant unions and giving them a major voice in implementing rural policy. The Catholic Church strongly resisted educational reforms that promoted public schools and restricted the autonomy and likely appeal of church-run institutions. Church resistance generally served as a lightning rod, stimulating and drawing together a broad range of antiregime groups and activities.[22]

This brief review of *trienio* politics suggests that while AD managed in these years to build and secure a mass base, at the same time the party alienated many important power factors in Venezuela. Confident in its vast electoral majorities and secure in its alliance with the military, AD largely ignored such opposition. The party did so at its peril and on November 24, 1948, fell to a military coup: the three-year experiment in democracy gave way to a decade of bloody dictatorship.

Pérez Jiménez: 1948–1958

Under the leadership of General Marcos Pérez Jiménez, public policy was rolled back across the board: educational, labor, and agrarian reforms were rescinded, and a new deal was reached with the oil companies, with extensive concessions for exploration arranged on very favorable terms.[23] Military government relied for its public legitimacy on an image of material progress, manifest, for example, in major public-works initiatives. These initiatives gave the regime a limited number of allies in the banking, real estate, and construction sectors.[24] Attempts were made to eliminate all political opposition through a combination of bribery, fraud, and violence. A large secret police force (Seguridad Nacional) hunted down opponents and ran notorious concentration camps.[25] AD maintained an underground organization throughout the dictatorship. Nonetheless, as late as mid-1957, the combination of strong economic resources, a powerful police apparatus, and visible public backing by the United States made continued military rule seem a safe bet.[26]

Opposition grew dramatically from that point on, and things fell apart quickly. Several factors converged to undermine military rule. The Catholic Church, which had greeted military rule in 1948 as salvation and had long supported Pérez Jiménez personally, turned against the regime, legitimating opposition to the military among many of its hitherto finest supporters. At the same time, a general economic downturn combined with notorious corruption (especially in public works) alienated business and stimulated public criticism by professional societies (engineers, lawyers, and the like).

Confident of his position, Pérez Jiménez called elections for December 1957, but with no warning he scrapped election plans in favor of a plebiscite. There would be only one candidate for every office; all Venezuelans over eighteen and all foreigners with more than two years of residence were declared eligible voters. The plebiscite was a clear affront and managed to unify and stimulate the opposition. Support within the military proved surprisingly brittle. Concern about the economy, resentment over corruption, and mingled fear of and disdain for the secret police soon resulted in a failed military coup on New Year's Day, 1958. Although the attempt was put down, the dictator's invincible image had cracked. Underground political forces, now united in a Junta Patriótica, mounted a wave of demonstrations and street fighting.[27] The regime collapsed quickly, and Pérez Jiménez fled the country on January 23, 1958. A provisional government (under mixed military and civilian rule) took over: elections were scheduled and held at the end of the year.

Consolidation of Democracy: 1958–1968

Pérez Jiménez was Venezuela's last military ruler. Within the history of democracy, a further periodization is possible, marking off the *trienio:* the decade after 1958 when enemies of right and left were isolated and defeated; two decades after 1968 of transformation and maturation; and the post-1988 period of decay, crisis, and reform. We noted earlier that *trienio* democracy was characterized by sudden change, deep penetration of the party system, and extremely bitter conflict. Political change after 1958 was driven by the particular lessons political actors chose to learn from recent experience. The overthrow of Pérez Jiménez was widely seen in Venezuela as a second chance for democracy, an opportunity to correct past mistakes and thus avoid repeating the political disasters of the *trienio*. The experience of being overthrown, and the corrupt and capricious nature of military rule, had a sobering effect on democratic leaders in many camps. In AD, party elites argued that the vast electoral majorities of the 1940s had created a false sense of confidence, making the party ignore the need to bring others along. At the same time, many who had welcomed the coming of military rule (opposition parties, foreign business, and the church) also had suffered under Pérez Jiménez and now sought accommodation with AD.

Elite understandings of the *trienio* were shaped and amplified by the specific character of the transition to democracy in 1958. From the beginning, the transition was an enterprise built on coalitions. Political parties cooperated, both underground and through pacts forged among exiled leaders. Business and professional groups joined, as did key elements in the military and in popular organizations linked to the political parties. The need to hold such diverse allies together reinforced dispositions to prudent compromise. The inauguration of democracy was relatively sudden, but though the dictator was thrown out, the military institution remained intact. Great effort was expended, in 1958 and after, to woo the officer corps, purging disloyal elements while gradually bringing new generations along.

Of course, this general strategy was not inevitable. Others, pushed, for example, by the left, stressed the need for more thorough social and economic change and relied on mass mobilization to the exclusion of other methods. But in 1958 and after, key Venezuelan leaders correctly believed that without revolution and firm control of armed force, strategies of that kind were doomed. Moreover, they believed that even under the best of circumstances, democracy is not a likely result of these strategies. Either power is too concentrated in the party running the show (which thus becomes another dictatorship), or conflict is so exacerbated as to make survival simply impossible. Having failed with similar approaches in the past (i.e., dominance in the *trienio),* the political class learned from experience and opted, this time, for caution. This new stance was critical in the decade after 1958, when the democracy survived its most direct and severe challenges. Five points keyed the post-1958 settlement: (1) pacts and coalitions; (2) inter-elite consensus; (3) program limitation; (4) encouragement of participation, but controlled and channeled; and (5) exclusion of the revolutionary left.

Alliances and coalitions were central to the 1958 transition and have remained at the core of political life ever since. A few specific examples may help drive the point home. Before the 1958 elections, the major non-communist parties (AD, COPEI, and URD) signed two formal agreements. The first, known as the Pact of Punto Fijo, pledged the signatories to respect elections whatever the outcome, to maintain a political truce depersonalizing debate and ensuring interparty consultation on touchy matters, and to provide for sharing political responsibility and patronage. The stress on pacts and coalitions was carried forward after the elections, in coalition regimes led by AD. The party's specific coalition partners changed over time, but the orientation to coalition remained constant. Indeed, the use of coalitions extended beyond national politics to all levels of organized activity: trade unions and secondary associations generally began choosing leaders by proportional representation, with leadership typically shared among representatives of various parties. Competition within a single group thus replaced older patterns of parallel and conflicting organizations.

The consensus sought through pacts and coalitions was both substantive and procedural. Key political forces essentially agreed to disagree—setting difficult and potentially explosive issues aside to concentrate on more manageable areas where limited, "technical" solutions could be found. Program restriction was central to the process, and its basic outlines were enshrined in a second formal agreement, the Minimum Program of Government. Here, the parties together accepted a development model based on foreign and local private capital, subsidies to the private sector, principles of compensation for any land reform, and a generally cautious approach to economic and social reform. Other key elements of these pacts and agreements aimed at defusing potential oppositions: the military got amnesty for previous abuses and a commitment to modernize equipment and upgrade salaries; the Catholic Church got commitments to improved legal status, increased public subsidies, consultation on educational reform, and a general sense of security derived from Christian democratic participation in the coalition government after 1958.[28] For business and labor, these pacts were institutionalized into tripartite decisionmaking procedures. Throughout the democratic era, government officials continued to consult with business and labor, especially as represented by the Federation of Chambers of Commerce and Associations of Commerce and Production (FEDECAMARAS) and the Confederación de Trabajadores de Venezuela (CTV), and their support for the regime remained steadfast.

In all these ways, party elites deliberately set out to conciliate old enemies and thereby avoid the kind of intense and relentless opposition that had brought democratic government down in 1948. Reflection on the *trienio* drove two lessons home with special force. First, there is almost always something left to lose. All-out opposition costs, undermining democratic practices and paving the way for coups and dictatorship. Second, dictatorship has no virtues and, in fact, is likely to prove all the more extreme and repressive in highly mobilized societies like Venezuela. The costs of political carelessness thus grow continuously and must be taken into account at every step.

The core agreements were political: support democracy, band together to resist challenges to its legitimacy and survival, respect elections, and strive in general to institutionalize politics, channeling participation within democratic vehicles and arenas. This had immediate practical consequences, for example, in early clashes between the government and the left over what counted as legitimate political methods. Specifically, Communists and their allies argued that "the streets belong to the people" and therefore could be used for demonstrations of any kind at any time. President Betancourt's reply marks a watershed in Venezuelan politics:

> The thesis that the streets belong to the people is false and demagogic. The people in abstract is an entelechy professional demagogues use to upset the social order. *The people in abstract does not exist. . . . The people are the political parties, the unions, the organized economic sectors, the professional societies, university groups.* Whenever any of these groups seeks authorization for a peaceful demonstration, there will be no difficulty in granting it. But any time uncontrolled groups go into the streets, on whatever pretext, they will be treated neither with softness nor lenience. For a country cannot live and work, acquire culture and forge riches, if it is always threatened by the surprise explosions of street violence, behind which the ancient enemies of democracy, totalitarians of all names and colors, seek to engineer its discredit [emphasis added].[29]

Political issues and the search for operative codes of coexistence dominated elite concerns, as the political class made building legitimacy its most immediate and urgent task.[30] As created in Venezuela after 1958, democracy was both a goal and a means to other unspecified ends: an open-ended set of arrangements founded on common ways of defining "politics" and appropriate political action.

The overall strategy embodied in these pacts, coalitions, and documents was grounded partly in fear of renewed conflict leading to military intervention, but it also rested on the belief that a political order founded on consensus of this kind was good and proper. Of course, elites are not all there is to politics. Without followers, and especially without mediating structures to organize and mobilize the population, elites are helpless— mere claimants to power and legitimacy. After 1958, barriers to participation were dramatically lowered, and active political involvement facilitated and encouraged. Associational life grew, but until the 1980s was encapsulated and controlled by the major political parties. The result was levels of participation that were high, as measured for example in voter turnout, but marked by strong constraints on choice and limits to the number and kind of organizations deemed legitimate. As we shall see, both voter choice and participation in elections in general were constrained by an electoral and legal system that severely limited choice and gave parties and party leaders unquestioned sway at all stages of the process.

The left was excluded in several ways. The parties of the left were deliberately shut out of pacts and coalitions, though they joined in consensual approval of the constitution. Major party leaders excluded the left in order to reassure elements in business, the church, and the military, and reconcile them to the new democracy. In any event, the commitment to incremental change embodied in the Pact of Punto Fijo and the Minimum Program of Government obviously excluded the left's agenda of radical transformation. The left also excluded itself. Frustrated by the shrinking outlook for major change at home and inspired by the example of the Cuban Revolution, parties on the left came to believe that revolution was possible in Venezuela.[31] After 1960, they moved quickly to armed opposition, and Venezuela thus became the first major theater of guerrilla war in Latin America after the Cuban Revolution.

The insurrection was easily isolated and defeated. Further, in retrospect it is clear that this failed adventure was decisive in consolidating the coalitions being put together by AD. Pointing to the revolutionary left (and beyond to Cuba), AD's leaders painted themselves as the only real hope for stability. They also positioned Venezuela internationally as an alternative to Cuba, seeking and obtaining strong U.S. support. That support also reassured conservative elements and helped isolate diehard military groups, who on several occasions attempted coups in the years just after 1958.

Stable Two-Party Rule: 1968–1988

The post-1958 decade was thus devoted to consolidating and defending the new democracy. This was a primary goal, more primary, for example, than any specific economic reform. It was pursued both through alliances and coalitions and through vigorous efforts to isolate and defeat enemies on right and left. After 1968, the political game changed considerably, but the spirit of caution and compromise, and the broad commitment to competition and democracy as good in themselves, continued to mark the political process. The 1968 elections were the high-water mark of electoral dispersion in Venezuela in this period. Nine major parties (and countless minor groups) competed for public office, with none gaining more than 30 percent of the vote. But while competition remained high after 1968, fragmentation disappeared. Until 1993, the two dominant parties (AD and COPEI) combined to take over 80 percent of the vote and exchanged power in most elections. Figure 7.1 shows the pattern of voting for president and highlights the precipitous decline of other parties over the 1947–1988 period.

The evolution of competition warrants separate attention. In terms of the periodization sketched out earlier, the decade after 1958 was marked by

Figure 7.1   Partisan Voting Pattern, 1947–1988

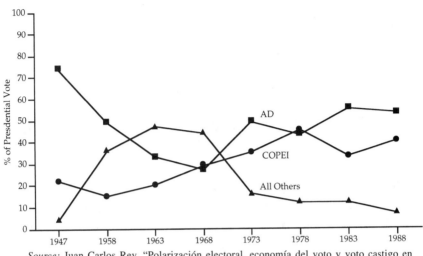

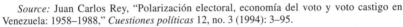

Source: Juan Carlos Rey, "Polarización electoral, economía del voto y voto castigo en Venezuela: 1958–1988," *Cuestiones políticas* 12, no. 3 (1994): 3–95.

steady decline for AD, uninterrupted growth for COPEI, and the rise and fall of a number of personalist vehicles or "electoral phenomena." During these years, elections became more competitive, but this competition lacked coherence or enduring structure. There was notable danger of fragmentation and atomization of the party system. The 1968 elections were a decisive turning point. In that year, COPEI took power—the first time an opposition party had ever defeated the government and taken office in free elections. In the subsequent decade, electoral phenomena disappeared, AD rebounded, and COPEI continued to grow, peaking in the 1978 vote. Together, AD and COPEI pushed their rivals to the political margin.[32] Their joint competition thoroughly dominated the political scene, and the two parties alternated in power until 1988, when AD's Carlos Andrés Pérez successfully sought reelection as president, succeeding AD's Jaime Lusinchi. Table 7.2 provides detailed results for presidential and legislative elections through 1988. All this took place in the context of high electoral turnout and a rapidly expanding electorate, with the number of registered voters growing in each successive election by at least 15 percent.

As noted earlier, AD was founded in 1941 and soon took a leading role in the development of mass organization. The party's early base was decisively reinforced during the *trienio,* but organization and electoral predominance decayed together in the decade after 1958. Effective competition from other parties (especially COPEI) kept AD from extending its previous

Table 7.2   Partisan Pattern of Presidential and Legislative Votes, 1947–1988
(for parties receiving at least 10% of the vote in any race that year)

Year of Election	Popular Vote for the Presidency (%)	Popular Vote for the Legislature (%)	Valid Votes Cast (Presidential Ballot)	Turnout of Registered Voters (%)
1958	AD: 49 URD: 31 COPEI: 15	AD: 49 URD: 27 COPEI: 15	2,610,833	92
1963	AD: 33 COPEI: 20 URD: 18 IPFN: 16	AD: 33 COPEI: 21 URD: 17 IPFN: 13	2,918,877	91
1968	COPEI: 29 AD: 27 MEP: 17 URD: 12 CCN: n.a.	AD: 26 COPEI: 24 MEP: 13 CCN: 11 URD: 9	3,720,660	94
1973	AD: 49 COPEI: 35	AD: 44 COPEI: 30	4,375,269	96
1978	COPEI: 45 AD: 43	COPEI: 40 AD: 40	5,332,712	88
1983	AD: 55 COPEI: 33	AD: 50 COPEI: 29	6,653,317	88
1988	AD: 53 COPEI: 40 MAS-MIR: 3	AD: 43 COPEI: 31 MAS-MIR: 10	7,315,186	82

Sources: Juan Carlos Rey, "Polarización electoral, economía del voto y voto castigo en Venezuela: 1958–1988," *Cuestiones políticas* 12, no. 3 (1994): 3–95; and Miriam Kornblith and Daniel H. Levine, "Venezuela: The Life and Times of the Party System," in Scott Mainwaring and Timothy Scully, eds., *Building Democratic Institutions: Party Systems in Latin America* (Stanford: Stanford University Press, 1995).

hegemony unchallenged to the new generations of voters now entering the electorate in large numbers. At the same time, ideological and factional disputes caused a series of damaging splits (1960, 1962, 1967) that cut deeply into AD's strength. These were mostly repaired after 1968, as successful organizational and electoral campaigns underwrote the party's remarkable rebound.[33]

COPEI was founded in 1945, as a party narrowly based on somewhat sectarian opposition to the *trienio* regime. Initially, party support was concentrated in traditionally Catholic Andean states. From these origins, COPEI grew into a genuinely national party able to compete effectively at every level. The party's steady growth reinforced democracy in several ways. It provided an alternative focus for popular mobilization, and the party's continued success showed that others could win by playing according to democracy's rules, which had long been identified with unquestioned AD hegemony. As a partner in coalition government from 1959 to 1963, and later as a loyal opposition in Congress and in the nation at large, COPEI gave solid and dependable support to the democratic system.

AD and COPEI share a few key characteristics. Each is a multiclass party that draws a varied social base together around a central party leadership. The economic and social changes of the interwar period generated enormous social and physical mobility. AD captured these transformations, building a heterogeneous but strongly integrated base. COPEI is similar in organizational structure. Indeed, of all the parties that have contested for power with AD, only COPEI managed to build a durable popular base, drawing elements from all across the social spectrum. Both AD and COPEI have survived their founders and passed leadership successfully to new generations.

Both parties have permanent professional leaders, both organize across the entire nation and at all levels, and both incorporate functional groups (such as unions, students, or professional associations) as wings in the party organization. This structural trait reinforced leadership autonomy and helps explain the success they both had in making elite pacts and coalitions and in selling them to the party faithful. Leadership autonomy was also institutionalized by formally giving the national executive committee of the party firm control over candidate selection processes and appointment to party leadership posts.

Organizational strength also included penetration of other groups in civil society. Partisan struggle for control of leadership positions was extended to the local, regional, and national levels of professional societies, labor unions, university administrations, and student groups. The members of these groups then became sources of support for AD and COPEI at the national level. While this extension of partisan competition showed organizational strength and helped generate political stability, it also showed a desire to monopolize the political space. Given this organizational penetration and the control of state resources by AD and COPEI, it was virtually impossible to be politically active without expressing partisan affiliation and making secondary the preferences of one's group to those of a major party. *Partidocracia,* or rule by parties, became a major source of frustration in Venezuelan politics and one of the primary targets of opposition groups and reformers by the late 1980s.

During this period, the left encompassed a wide range of parties and movements, most of them small and weak. The Communist Party is actually older than AD, but Communists lost the organizational struggles of the 1940s and have remained weak ever since. The post-1968 divisions reduced the Communist Party to little more than a handful of aging debaters. The banners of leftist politics and organization were carried into succeeding decades by the Movimiento al Socialismo (MAS) and La Causa R (LCR), whose visions of what a consistent leftist position should mean differed sharply from the beginning. MAS dedicated itself to becoming a party on the model created by AD, building a centralized organization and contesting elections at all levels. LCR took a different path, building an insurgent trade-union movement and working from that to secure a regional political party base. Electoral reforms that began in the late 1980s helped both parties. The separation of local and regional from national elections allowed smaller, weaker parties to gain a toehold without running the risk and cost of mounting a national campaign.

Crisis, Reform, and Uncertain Transformation: 1989 to the Present

Before getting into the particulars of the crisis, it may be helpful to recapitulate the major components of the system in its "golden age." Most observers cite consistent economic growth with improved equity, a centralized state paid for by steadily rising oil revenues, and exceptionally strong political parties that penetrated and controlled organized social life from top to bottom all across the national territory. Pacts and agreements negotiated by the parties knit the system together, and were implemented on a day-to-day basis through a vast network of formal and informal contacts. Although bipolar party competition is often noted as a key factor, this pattern only appears in the 1970s, and is best understood not as a cause but rather as a by-product of other changes. The rules of the game were simple: in *economic* terms, strong currency, low inflation, growth, and a dominant role for the central state as regulator and distributor of oil-based revenues; in *politics,* a centralized state, a dominant center, strongly organized national parties that monopolize political action and control social movements (trade unions are a prime example), a professional political class, and a subordinated military; and in *social* terms, great mobility (social as well as geographic), mass education, and gradual homogenization of national cultural and organizational life.

The preceding sketch underscores the traumatic effect of a chain of events that sparked and sustained the crisis. The first was Black Friday (February 18, 1983), when the currency collapsed, initiating the present period of depreciation, economic stagnation, and inflation. Six years later came the bloody urban riots touched off on February 27, 1989 (27-F), in a spontaneous response to the new government's structural adjustment package. Third was the attempted military coups of 1992, on February 4 (4-F) and November 27 (27-N), the first in three decades. Further shocks were produced by the impeachment and removal from office of President Carlos Andrés Pérez (the so-called coup of civil society of May 1993); followed by the December 1993 election of former president Rafael Caldera, who abandoned the party he himself had founded (COPEI) and ran a brilliant campaign to win a four-way race on an explicitly antiparty platform; followed in turn by the December 1998 presidential victory of Hugo Chávez, leader of the failed February 1992 coup, at the head of a personalist electoral vehicle and a coalition of several small parties. At each of these points, a key pillar of the system was undermined or removed: economic strength (Black Friday); social pacts, control, and civil order (27-F); a depoliticized and controlled military (4-F and 27-N); unquestioned executive dominance (the destitution of Pérez); and party hegemony (the elections of Caldera and Chavez). These events are drawn together and their impact magnified by long-term growth in public skepticism and disaffection coupled with a surge of associational life independent of parties and party-linked networks.[34]

Now we can begin to deconstruct the crisis, starting with its economic dimension. The economic crisis is severe, especially given the record compiled in the first twenty years of democratic rule. Those years witnessed gradual improvement in income distribution, declining poverty, and a steady rise in indicators of social welfare from literacy and school population to health, diet, and life expectancy.[35] The trends reverse, beginning around 1980: wages and salaries stagnate, real income declines, and services drop in quality with visible declines in services as well as access to them. The decay in social services was not a result of resource constraints. Resources continued to flow but the capacity of state institutions to deliver services crumbled under the weight of mismanagement, corruption, and politically bloated bureaucracies.[36] The proportion of households in poverty and extreme poverty grew as average real income from wages and salaries dropped.[37] When Venezuela's record is set in comparative context, the results are striking. Many Latin American countries have experienced income drops equal to or greater than Venezuela's in these years, but none, with the possible exception of Chile (1973–1976 or 1982–1984), had a greater increase in poverty. Overall economic decline was one of the most severe in modern history.[38]

The depth and pattern of economic decline is well illustrated by several macroeconomic indicators (see Table 7.3). Gross domestic product per capita had grown steadily until 1977, but by 1983 it was below 1967 levels. It fluctuated thereafter but hit a more than twenty-year low of U.S.$2,410 in 1989. The consumer price index illustrates that Venezuelans had never had to contend with significant inflation until the late 1980s, but it increased precipitously from the late 1980s through the mid 1990s. Inflation eroded purchasing power at the same time the GDP per capita was shrinking, putting Venezuelan consumers in a double bind.

Although a number of aggregate indicators had been showing signs of decline for some time, the sense of crisis was driven home to Venezuelans for the first time on Black Friday in February 1983, when the government announced that it could no longer support the exchange rate of B 4.3 (4.3 bolívares) to U.S.$1. For decades, the government had used petroleum

Table 7.3   Indicators of Economic Crisis

Year	GDP per capita (1990 U.S.$)	Consumer Price Index (1990 = 100)	Exchange Rate (bolívar per dollar)
1966	2,651	5.2	4.45
1968	2,709	5.3	4.45
1970	2,881	5.5	4.45
1972	2,865	5.9	4.40
1974	3,037	6.6	4.29
1976	3,106	7.9	4.29
1978	3,157	9.1	4.29
1980	2,937	12.4	4.29
1982	2,778	15.8	4.29
1984	2,447	18.7	7.02
1986	2,536	23.2	8.08
1988	2,678	38.5	14.50
1990	2,514	100	46.90
1992	2,793	176.4	68.38
1994	2,577	391.8	148.50
1996	2,513	1,252.3	417.33

Source: International Monetary Fund, *International Financial Statistics Yearbook* (Washington, DC: International Monetary Fund, 1997).

revenues to buy and sell foreign exchange, making foreign-made consumer and capital goods affordable. By the end of March, despite government intervention into the exchange market, the value of the bolívar had slipped to B 8 to U.S.$1. Venezuelans' ability to purchase imported goods had almost been cut in half in six weeks! During the oil booms of the 1970s, it had not been uncommon for Venezuelans to travel to Miami on shopping sprees. The rising real cost of imported goods hit not only individual consumers, but also industry, agriculture, and commerce, which all relied on foreign-made inputs and capital goods or who had foreign debts to service. The effect rippled through the economy as investment and employment in all industries dependent on foreign exchange slowed or declined. Government efforts to parse out foreign exchange at the predevaluation rate through the RECADI commission ultimately produced massive corruption and political scandal. Further devaluation became common throughout the 1990s, as ordinary Venezuelans watched their purchasing power plummet steadily (by the end of 1998, the exchange rate was around B 560 to U.S.$1).

Economic decline was accompanied by political crisis. One early sign of crisis was the long-term increase in rates of electoral abstention. High voter turnout was the norm in national elections for the first three decades of democratic rule. In 1988 voter abstention jumped to over 18 percent, jumped again in the 1993 presidential elections to almost 49 percent, but then declined in the controversial election of 1998. Despite the hopes of reformers, who bet that the introduction of separate municipal and state elections would diversify choice and spur voter interest, abstention in elections at these levels has been high from the beginning. Abstention in regional races was over 25 percent in 1979, and it had grown to over 50 percent by 1989, the first year of direct elections for governors (see Figure 7.2). In political terms, the most salient aspect of the crisis is the reduced capacity of parties and party leaders to channel conflict, control organizations, and mobilize votes. Party coherence decayed (taking Venezuela's legendary party discipline with it) and, as we shall see, a series of new organizations emerged to challenge the parties' hitherto unquestioned role as the only legitimate vehicle for public voice and representation.

Creating more elected offices at lower levels of government and giving voters more opportunity to go to the polls were also supposed to open the system to alternative forces, making the whole system hopefully more responsive and representative. Results so far have been ambiguous. The same can be said of changes instituted in the system for electing members of the Chamber of Deputies. Beginning in 1993, a mixed-member, proportional representation electoral system, with single-member districts

Figure 7.2   Abstention in National and Regional Elections

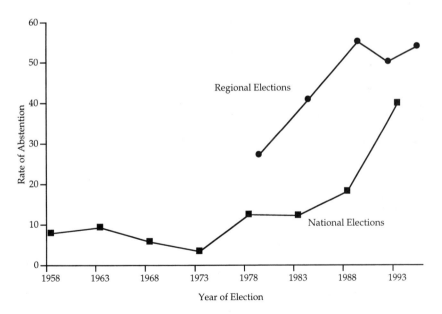

Source: Brian F. Crisp and Daniel H. Levine, "Democratizing the Democracy: Crisis and Reform in Venezuela," *Journal of Interamerican Studies and World Affairs* 40, no. 2 (1998): 27–60.

throughout the country contributing approximately half the members of the Chamber of Deputies, was instituted. The goal of introducing single-member districts was to enhance the connection between legislators and a more narrowly defined group of constituents. Continued high levels of abstention suggest that voters are as yet unconvinced by the rationale of the institutional change itself and, at best, were awaiting a change in behavior by legislators themselves. One of Chávez's popular campaign promises in 1998 was to call a Constituent Assembly in order to redesign Venezuelan political institutions, presumably including the electoral laws.

These long-term indicators of decay were punctuated and sharpened by dramatic moments of crisis. The first came with demonstrations, rioting, and extensive looting that began in Caracas on February 27, 1989. The immediate cause was protest over sudden increases in bus fares and in the cost of basic goods. The larger issue was public reaction (the Caracazo) to the sudden and unexpected adoption of a shock strategy of structural adjustment by a president (Carlos Andrés Pérez) who had been reelected on the strength of his identification with the good times of the 1970s. Pérez and his advisers made two key mistakes: they underestimated the depth of popular reaction, and overestimated the ability of traditional mechanisms of social control (such as party or trade-union networks) to contain the protests. The result was that the police were overwhelmed, and nervous and trigger-happy young soldiers unaccustomed to such duties produced hundreds of deaths. The exact number of victims remains in dispute: there were mass burials in unmarked graves and many bodies remain unaccounted for.[39] Although Venezuelans had experienced urban violence before, for example during the guerrilla insurrection of the early 1960s, the events of February 1989 constituted a major national trauma. The intensity and scope of violence were unprecedented, as was the image of troops occupying urban centers and firing on civilians. Public support for the government plummeted, and demonstrations and protests became an everyday affair. In addition, the experience of being used as an urban shock force in support of an unpopular regime brought a growing cadre of younger military officers into a circle of conspirators who would ultimately launch the coup of February 4, 1992 (4-F), the first such attempted military overthrow of a civilian government in Venezuela in almost thirty years.

Venezuela's democracy was one of the oldest in the region, and for some time its stability had been unquestioned. By the late 1960s, the long struggle between military officers and political parties for the right to control national politics seemed to have been definitively resolved in favor of the parties. The attempted coup of 4-F threw those assumptions into question. The coup was led by elite army units and missed succeeding by very little. The coup itself was a shock, but a greater shock came in the aftermath of its defeat. Massive demonstrations immediately after the coup attempt expressed open sympathy for the rebels, whose leaders became popular heroes. This was most dramatically the case for Colonel Hugo Chávez, who commanded the rebels in Caracas and was ultimately elected president in 1998; and Colonel Francisco Arias Cárdenas, who led the rebellion in the country's second city, Maracaibo, and was later elected governor of the state of Zulia.[40]

Underlying the political crisis was a slow, steady decay of two-party domination, not only in the electoral arena, but also in control over core associations such as trade unions. The complex and reinforcing power of these arrangements had provided the foundation for the whole pattern of pacts and pact making on which the operating rules of the system relied. Pacts could be effective in the past because strong party structures and party control over civil associations gave leaders the ability to bring followers along. The contrast in the months following the 4-F coup is striking. Efforts to contain protest and reconstitute the pacts and coalitions that had once guaranteed democratic stability failed utterly. The major parties no longer had the discipline and unity required to come to agreement. Even if they had, leaders could no longer be sure of their ability to keep the parties' clientele in line. The administration's estrangement from once close allies had been made clear not long after 27-F riots, when the trade-union confederation (CTV), traditionally affiliated with AD, staged a twenty-four-hour, general strike in May 1989. This was the first general strike in the country in thirty-one years and it was against a president from AD and a congress with AD pluralities. Yet, the administration did not vary from its program. It attempted to balance price increases with wage hikes, but in general it proceeded apace with its neoliberal reforms.

Although efforts were made to alleviate the impact of the crisis by distributional measures, the broad outlines of public policy remained unchanged and efforts to achieve something like a government of national unity failed utterly.[41] Public discontent grew throughout the year: the popularity of the government, and especially of President Pérez and anyone identified with him, plummeted. Demonstrations and scattered acts of violence became a part of the normal, expected routine of everyday life, particularly in Caracas. All this was prelude to the second coup attempt of the year, launched on November 27 (27-N) by elements in the high command (especially the air force) in alliance with a collection of small leftist groups. Although this time the rebels had control of television, and used it to issue calls for popular rebellion, no massive popular action of any kind ensued. The military rebels were isolated and, after bombing in Caracas for the better part of the day, either surrendered or fled the country in air force transports. In contrast to the events of 4-F, this coup brought considerable violence in its wake, most notably in the recapture of television and radio stations by loyal forces, and in a massacre of inmates in the central jail in Caracas. Public support for the 4-F rebels and apathy in the face of the 27-N stand in sharp contrast to popular reaction to coup attempts against the newly established democracy in the early 1960s. Then, citizens responded with public marches and other displays of support for the regime. By late 1992, merely not coming out in support of the coup plotters was considered an endorsement by the democratic regime.

In both 1992 coup attempts, the president declared a state of emergency and suspended constitutional guarantees, including rights to free assembly and demonstration. An attempt was made to censor the media, but this failed in the teeth of fierce opposition. President Pérez took the occasions of these suspensions of constitutional guarantees to rule by decree. This allowed him to bypass Congress not only on political or security issues, but on economic policy as well. When Pérez used decrees to institute dramatic economic changes, he also had to use them to deal with the political fallout. Pérez himself came to embody the sources of popular discontent, and many politicians became convinced that he had to be removed from office.

It was proposed to amend the constitution so that the presidential term could be shortened and new elections could be called early, but this and other constitutional reforms stalled in Congress because both AD and COPEI predicted that their electoral prospects were at a low point. Next, a proposed nonbinding plebiscite to be included in the December 1992 elections for mayors and city council members also failed to come about. Several prominent politicians repeatedly made public calls for the president's resignation. The administration, though, never varied from its neoliberal program. Opposition grew steadily, and after surviving two coup attempts, President Pérez was finally removed from office on May 21, 1993, to face trial on corruption charges. He was accused of misusing public funds, specifically, of profiting from illegal exchange transactions involving classified accounts in the Ministry of the Interior related to national security.[42] This "coup of civil society" was peaceful, and Ramón J. Velásquez was chosen by the Senate to complete the remainder of Pérez's term in office, which he did without incident. Court proceedings finally concluded in 1996 and President Pérez was found guilty of a relatively minor misuse of public funds for sending National Guard troops to Nicaragua to provide security for Violeta Chamorro during her presidential campaign. He was the first president in the democratic era who failed to complete his constitutional term.

The political upheaval of these years impacted the conduct and outcome of the 1993 national elections in powerful ways. Abstention reached new heights, and those who did vote broke the two-party monopoly, electing Rafael Caldera to a second term in office. Beginning with congressional debates after 4-F, Caldera had made himself into a major voice in opposition to the second Pérez government and to its programs. He later broke with COPEI (the party he had founded almost a half-century earlier), taking major elements of the party leadership and base with him. In alliance with

MAS and several minor parties, Caldera then established Convergencia, an electoral alliance that captured a plurality of votes for president. The elections of 1993 mark the first time in Venezuela's democratic history that a candidate from AD or COPEI did not win the presidency. The pattern of congressional representation also changed dramatically. AD emerged from these elections with a plurality of only 27 percent of the seats in the Chamber of Deputies and 32 percent of seats in the Senate. Previously, the largest party had never controlled less than 31 percent of the seats in the Chamber of Deputies and 37 percent of the seats in the Senate (see Table 7.4).

Table 7.4   The Crisis of Stable Two-Party Rule

Year of Election	Popular Vote for the Presidency (%)	Seats in the Chamber of Deputies (%)	Seats in the Senate (%)	Turnout of Registered Voters (%)
1993	AD: 23	AD: 27	AD: 32	60
	COPEI: 22	COPEI: 26	COPEI: 28	
	Causa R: 22	Causa R: 20	Causa R: 18	
	Convergencia: 17	Convergencia: 13	Convergencia: 20	
	MAS: 18	MAS: 11	MAS: 2	
1998	MVR: 40[a]	AD: 29	AD: 35	54[c]
	PRVZL: 29[b]	MVR: 26	MVR: 29	64[c]
	AD: 9[b]	COPEI: 14	COPEI: 15	
	COPEI: 2	PRVZL: 13	PRVZL: 4	

Source: Brian F. Crisp, "Presidential Behavior in a System with Strong Parties: Venezuela, 1958–1995," in Scott Mainwaring and Matthew Soberg Shugart, eds., *Presidentialism and Democracy in Latin America* (New York: Cambridge University Press, 1997).

Notes: a. Movimiento V República (MVR) and eight other parties supported Hugo Chávez, who got 56% of the vote.

b. Proyecto Venezuela (PRVZL), Acción Democrática (AD), the Christian Democrats (COPEI), and one other party supported Henrique Salas Romer, who got 40% of the vote.

c. 54% of registered voters voted in the congressional elections in November and 64% voted in the presidential elections of December.

In political terms, Caldera promised to restore the days of consultative consensus building, and in economic terms he promised to return to the days of an interventionist state. He suspended economic liberties, decreed exchange controls, and did away with the controversial value-added tax, but many other economic plans were put on hold by a serious banking crisis that escalated shortly after he took office. The bailout was extraordinarily expensive, especially given that the state was already suffering from enormous foreign debts and budget deficits. In the end, ten of the nation's biggest banks were permanently closed, and the executive received powers allowing for increased economic intervention without further congressional constraint. A number of major insurance companies also failed at this time, extending the economic crisis.

Congress and the executive clashed repeatedly over the suspension of constitutional guarantees, as the president appeared willing to rely on popular support to implement measures of doubtful constitutionality. The stand-off was resolved in the president's favor when AD withdrew its support for reestablishing the guarantees. However, the president's popularity declined, and he faced increasing popular dissent. The arrest of several hundred dissidents associated with the Movimiento Revolucionario Bolivariano (MRB-200), a movement with origins in the attempted coups against Pérez, signaled to many an increasing militarization of the regime. Caldera's administration became marked by massive demonstrations and strikes in response to austerity measures agreed to with the IMF after two years of heterodox muddling.

Adding further to the sense of crisis, the 1998 elections were rescheduled. National legislative, state legislative, and gubernatorial elections were moved up to November and municipal elections were postponed until June 1999. Only presidential elections were held as originally scheduled in December 1998. AD and COPEI orchestrated the rescheduling in Congress, reasoning that they could use momentum that their national organizational bases brought them in November to combat the powerful independent presidential candidacies of Hugo Chávez and Henrique Salas Romer in December. The move failed. After mediocre results in the legislative elections (see Table 7.4) and continued popular support for the independent presidential candidates, especially Hugo Chávez, AD and COPEI tried to remove their presidential nominees from the race during the last week of campaigning in order to back Salas Romer. Chávez won by the largest margin in the current democratic era. He campaigned on a nationalist and populist platform and promised to completely revamp the democratic system once in office.

Despite this lengthy succession of destabilizing events, all was not decay. The process of political reform and rebuilding had been undertaken before the explicit signs of severe economic and political crises were apparent. The Comisión Presidencial para la Reforma del Estado (COPRE) was created in 1984 by President Jaime Lusinchi of AD. Decentralization, broadly defined, was COPRE's overarching goal, and its proposals for change covered every level and branch of government. Reformers concentrated their energies in four areas: strengthening the checks and balances within the national government, moving decisionmaking authority to lower levels of government, decreasing the role of parties in elections, and making more transparent the internal workings of the political parties. They reasoned that increasing participation, making participation more meaning-ful, and decentralizing authority would lead to more popular or responsive outcomes and restore legitimacy to the democratic regime. Many of their proposals met with resistance, some were probably ill-conceived, but reformers also found a great deal of support from citizens' groups and achieved many successes.

Increased federalism centered on creating new elected posts at the municipal level and making governors directly elected rather than presiden-tial appointees. Efforts at national electoral reform also met with some suc-cess. A compensatory-member system styled after German elections was adopted for choosing members of the Chamber of Deputies. The partisan composition of the chamber was still determined by proportional represen-tation, but about one-half of its members were chosen from single-member districts—making their attachment to a geographically defined constituen-cy much more clear. Strengthening checks and balances was dependent upon reestablishing the autonomy of the judicial branch, and, though a new law reforming the Judicial Council (the body charged with naming most judges) was adopted, it was stripped of its most significant content by the time it got through Congress.

The area in which COPRE met with the least success was internal party reform. The commission proposed more financial accountability, less spending, greater state financing, more internal democracy, and more open nomination procedures. Given the historic strength of the parties and the strong role played by their central leadership bodies, it is no surprise that internal party reforms met with intense resistance and bogged down in Congress, where the very parties that were the objects of reform were well placed to inhibit the process of change. The importance of COPRE's pro-posals and other reform efforts will be assessed below in the section on the party and electoral systems.

THEORETICAL ANALYSIS

The analysis advanced here rests on political variables: the goals of leader-ship; leaders' ability to create and control organizations; the institutions built to regularize interaction between these organizations in civil society and the state; and the development policies that this interaction promoted. The foundations of this system, and the key to understanding the possibili-ties of democracy's transformation and survival in the future, rest on five elements: the pattern of state-led socioeconomic development; the party and electoral systems; the evolution of state structures and interbranch rela-tions; the emergence and possible significance of "civil society"; and the changing role of international forces.

State-Led Socioeconomic Development

The social foundations of Venezuelan democracy were laid in the course of the many changes the nation has undergone in this century. Since the discovery and large-scale exploitation of petroleum just before 1920, almost every aspect of national life has been altered beyond recognition. Over the last seventy years, the population has increased more than sixfold. A nation that was overwhelmingly rural and illiterate has moved to the cities and gone to school. In 1920, almost three-quarters of the labor force worked in agriculture; by 1981, less than 15 percent did. From 1941 to 1981, the literacy rate more than doubled (see Table 7.5). The population increasingly became very young (well over half are under nineteen) and urban.

Table 7.5   Indicators of Social and Economic Change, 1936–1991

	1936	1941	1950	1961	1971	1981	1991
Population (millions)	3.4	3.9	5.0	7.5	10.7	15.6	18.1
Literacy Rate (%)	—	42.5	51.2	65.2	77.1	88.1	91.0[d]
Economically Active Population by Sector							
Agriculture[a] (%)	58	51.3	40.2	29.3	20.0	14.5	10.7
Manufacturing (%)	15	16.0	10.7	11.7	13.9	17.0	14.9
Commerce and							
Services (%)	25	28.1	28.9	33.3	37.2	39.1	50.9
Gross Domestic Product by Sector							
Agriculture (%)	21	—	7.9	7.0	6.9	7.0[c]	5.5
Mining and Oil (%)	20.8	—	29.8	26.3	16.7	18.1	18.2
Manufacturing[b] (%)	11.7	—	10.0	12.5	12.9	21.5	19.6
Construction, Power,							
Commerce, Services,							
and Others (%)	46.5	—	52.3	54.2	64.5	53.4	56.7

Sources: Compendio estadístico de Venezuela (Caracas: Dirección de Estadística y Censos Nacionales, 1968), p. 10; *Noveno censo general de población: Resúmen general de la república, parte A* (Caracas: Dirección de Estadística y Censos Nacionales, 1966), pp. 12–13; *X censo de población y vivienda: Resúmen nacional características generales, tomo II* (Caracas: Dirección de Estadística y Censos Nacionales, 1974), p. 3; *Informe social 1982* (Caracas: Presidencia de la República, 1983), pp. 25, 133; Terry Lynn Karl, *The Political Economy of Petrodollars: Oil and Democracy in Venezuela,* Ph.D. diss., Stanford University, 1982), p. 132; James Hanson, "Cycles of Economic Growth and Structural Change Since 1950," in John Martz and David Myers, eds., *Venezuela: The Democratic Experience* (New York: Praeger, 1977), p. 68; *Encuesta de hogares por muestreo: Resúmen nacional,* Segundo Semestre, 1981 (Caracas: Oficina Central de Estadística e Informática, 1982), p. 65; Franklin Bustillos Galvez, *Introducción a la economía venezolana* (Caracas: Libreria Editorial Salesiana, 1978), p. 128; and *South America, Central America, and the Caribbean: 1997,* 6th ed. (London: Europa Publications Limited, 1997), pp. 661, 671, 674.

Notes: a. The figure for agriculture in 1920 was 72%.
b. Including oil-related activities.
c. This figure is for 1980.
d. This figure is for 1995.

National population has expanded by well over 400 percent since the census of 1936, and several regions have grown with exceptional speed. Two notable instances are the Federal District (Caracas) and the surrounding central states, whose population has risen by 730 percent and 673 percent over the same period. As a rule, cities have grown faster than rural areas, and bigger cities fastest of all. The countryside has emptied, allowing Venezuela to "solve" its peasant problem by eliminating the peasantry as a social group: there are hardly any peasants left. In the process, once-notable regional differences have blurred as improved transport, communications, and the development of national organizations and media combined to create a truly national society, culture, and market.[43]

There is general agreement that petroleum played a critical role in stimulating these changes and driving them forward. The oil industry shaped modern Venezuela in at least three ways, each of which contributed indirectly to democracy: (1) fiscal and administrative (including the consolidation of the state machine); (2) demographic and social; and (3) economic.

The most immediate and easily visible impact of the petroleum industry was on public finance. Once oil production and export got under way on a substantial scale in the 1920s, official revenue expanded tremendously, and the state was able to pay off foreign debt, stabilize the currency, and underwrite an extensive bureaucracy and public-works program. Indeed, since the 1920s, Venezuelan governments have depended on rising petroleum income to solve most of their problems.[44]

As we suggested earlier, the administrative unification of the country combined with the Gómez regime's elimination of old political vehicles to make new kinds of organization possible when the dictatorship finally passed from the scene. It also set in motion and reinforced the very elements of social change that later converged to undergird democracy. With systematic public-health measures, tropical disease declined, and population began the explosive growth that has continued to the present. New roads were built, making travel easier, and the elimination of internal war allowed commerce to grow. Finally, with the growth of commerce and of the public bureaucracy, new middle classes (especially civil servants and minor professionals) began to emerge. Their sons and daughters first surfaced in student politics and later appeared as founders of the political parties.

This brief account shows how hard it is to sort out the direct and indirect effects of petroleum. In the short term, oil underwrote dictatorship by providing the money to pay for a strong state and military. But over the long haul, petroleum created the gravediggers of the old system. The complex and interrelated nature of the process is well exemplified by the fate of agriculture, and by the evolving pattern of economic change generally.

An immediate effect of the oil boom was to distort the structure of agricultural prices and investment, and thus touch off a massive rural depression. Foreclosures and abandonment of farms were common, the concentration of landholdings was accelerated, and peasants—when not already pulled to oil camps and to the cities by tales of easy wealth—were pushed off the land in great numbers.[45] Until the twentieth century, Venezuela was an agricultural exporting country, but with the advent of petroleum, every line of agricultural production and export dropped sharply. Agriculture's share of GDP sank from over one-third in the 1920s to less than one-tenth by 1950: the smallest contribution in all of Latin America.[46] Manufacturing employment increased somewhat since the 1920s (dropping in the 1940s and then rebounding), while commerce and especially services have grown very sharply. The sectoral composition of Venezuela's GDP has also shifted notably since 1936: the primary sector (including petroleum) has dropped from more than two-fifths to just over 13 percent; the share of the secondary sector has more than doubled (11.7 to 26.5 percent); and the tertiary sector has grown slightly from 46.4 to 56.2 percent.[47]

Petroleum revenues accruing to the state have accounted for more than half of government revenue during the democratic era, and government expenditures have averaged more than 20 percent of GDP. One especially notable way such funds have augmented central state power is by providing the fiscal basis for a series of state corporations and public enterprises. These have grown steadily throughout the democratic period and have given public authorities a set of tools with which to shape economic development, subsidize private capital, pay off political allies, and co-opt enemies. Through a broad range of public or semipublic corporations, the state now holds substantial interests throughout the economy, from agriculture and petroleum to electricity, transport, and tourism.[48]

State funds have also been used to support development of the private sector. Both business owners and organized urban workers have been very successful at pressuring the government to make expenditures from which they would benefit. Several hundred consultative commissions and the governing boards of decentralized public bureaucracies have been used to give interest groups regular access to the policymaking process, allowing them to lobby for the adoption of preferential interest rates, forgiveness of debts, tax incentives, and direct transfers.[49] For example, between 1970 and 1980 subsidies to agricultural producers averaged 15 percent of the gross domestic product generated by the sector. Likewise, subsidies to industrial producers averaged more than 10 percent of private investment until the oil booms of the 1970s—at which point subsidies rose to an amount equal to 50 percent of private investment.[50] More workers benefited from increased public and private employment opportunities and higher wages than would have otherwise been possible.[51] In addition, government deposits supported the Banco de los Trabajadores de Venezuela, which amounted to a financial empire under the control of the largest labor union, CTV.[52]

The overall pattern reflects the emergence of an urban, service-oriented economy. It makes sense in a society that has never "taken off" industrially, relying instead on imports (ultimately paid for by oil) to fill its needs, and on semiskilled service, commerce, and construction jobs to employ its people. Oil revenues have been recycled into the economy mostly through central state expenditures.

The Party and Electoral Systems

The political impact of these socioeconomic changes began some time ago. Their impact on and interaction with the party and electoral systems is key to understanding both Venezuelan stability and instability. The political alliances present at democracy's creation were forged primarily between small-town, middle-class youth and the poor and dispossessed of Venezuela's periphery. These alliances responded to the social changes set in motion by petroleum. Once in power, democratic regimes furthered policies that undercut their own base. The continued growth of public works and education, along with relentless urban expansion, together eliminated much of the social base of the original democratic alliance. This process created a dilemma that seemed critical by the mid-1960s: the ability of political organizations to appeal to changing needs and circumstances and to incorporate new generations and groups into the political process in an orderly and enduring way.

The dilemma was resolved in several ways. Voter registration and turnout kept up with population growth. Between 1958 and 1988 the percentage of the voting-age population that was registered to vote never dropped below 83 percent, and over the same period the percentage of registered voters who actually turned out to vote never dropped below 82 percent.[53] This is no mean feat in such a young and rapidly growing country, but the effort was deliberate and consistent. Voting is easy in Venezuela, registration is simple, and barriers to participation are deliberately kept low. Until 1979, when separate municipal elections were instituted, voting for public office in Venezuela occurred only once every five years. To cast a ballot, voters had to make two choices: one for president, by selecting or marking a large card with the appropriate party color or symbol; and another by repeating the operation with a small card, thereby casting a vote for the party's slate for all legislative seats (including candidates for the Senate and Chamber of Deputies on the national level, and also for state legislative assemblies and municipal councils). But increasing numbers of participants and ease of use are not enough for stability and continuity: intense organizational effort and new political tactics have also played a central role.

Both AD and COPEI mounted major efforts to rebuild urban structures throughout the 1960s. Strong financial backing from business and government enabled these two parties to bear the heavy costs of this organizational battle.[54] They succeeded through a deft combination of effective media campaigns and a careful, deliberate organizational campaign at all levels. Competitors were driven to the margins, and beginning with the elections of 1968, electoral choice consolidated overwhelmingly around AD and COPEI, two socially heterogeneous parties that drew support from similar social bases.[55] Differences in variables such as sex, literacy, education, income, religiosity, or region had little discernible impact on partisan choice.[56] From the late 1970s through the 1980s, AD and COPEI took a share of the legislative vote that approached 80 percent. Unlike the *trienio* and even the election of 1958, the 1970s and 1980s were not wholly dominated by AD. The two parties competed evenly and in similar ways throughout the nation. The evolution of vote shares is shown graphically in Figure 7.3.

The electoral system's ease of use made it a stabilizing force, but its closed nature also made it partially responsible for dissatisfaction and instability in the 1980s and 1990s. The organization of the ballot and the process of candidate selection constrained voter choice in ways that magnified the power of national party leaders. Top leaders controlled candidate selection completely and fixed the place of each candidate on the party's slate. The lists or slates were closed: voters could not add to or alter them. Legislative voting was thus an all-or-nothing proposition centering on differences between the parties. The names of individual legislative candidates were often little known.[57] The power exercised by party elites in the nomination and election procedures resulted in highly disciplined legislative delegations. Legislators had no incentive to serve particular constituencies because it was party leaders who nominated them and determined their position on the party's slate—thus virtually determining their chances for reelection. As a result, democratically elected officials appeared unresponsive and unaccountable.

The unresponsive nature of elected officials was made even less tolerable by the overwhelming organizational capabilities of party elites. On the one hand, they successfully managed the establishment of stable democracy, but, on the other hand, they controlled elected officials, ran the parties in a highly centralized fashion, and thoroughly penetrated every other group in civil society. The centralized nature of internal party decisionmaking, including nominations, meant that party activism through primaries or caucuses was not a viable means of influencing future elected officials. The penetration of other groups meant that it was not possible to evade party elites by joining autonomous groups. The political space was monopolized by parties, and the parties were run by a small group of leaders (*cogollos*).

Given parties' penetration of other groups in civil society and the highly disciplined manner in which partisans were expected to behave, there

Figure 7.3　Legislative Vote Shares, 1947–1988

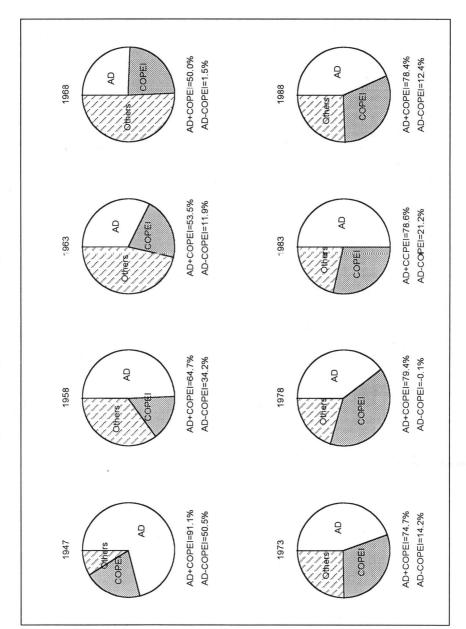

was a widespread sense that Venezuela was governed by the parties (*partidocracia*), not the people who elected them. Prior to the 1993 elections, the electoral system was revised so that approximately one-half of the Chamber of Deputies were elected from single-member districts. The rationale behind this change was that legislators from single-member districts would be more accountable and responsive to their constituents, thus generating legitimacy for the regime. There are a number of reasons this reform has not had the expected consequences. The mobility of the Venezuelan population and the indirect form of representation that had predominated for so long meant that many people originally registered in and continued to vote in districts other than those in which they lived, thus undermining the intended sense of representation and connection between legislator and constituent. Moreover, the candidate selection process has not changed, so the candidates in single-member districts are still beholden to party elites. In any case, the deputies elected through the new system are only one-half of the chamber, the partisan makeup of the legislature is still determined by the closed-list PR portion of the vote, and the Senate continues to be elected entirely under the old system. Given these limitations, further electoral reform remains on the table, along with more general constitutional reform.

Direct election of executives at the state and municipal level embodies an important change in the philosophy of representation and governance. The power to appoint state governors had been concentrated in the hands of the national executive, and the position of mayor did not exist prior to 1989. In 1995 citizens elected 22 state governors and 330 mayors—opportunities for representation they did not have under the constitution adopted in 1961. However, the results of these reforms were more ambiguous than proponents of decentralization and increased participation might have hoped. First, newly elected officials at the state and municipal level still confronted a national government with a preponderant number of political responsibilities. It was difficult for regional and local officials to be responsive when their powers were limited. This was particularly apparent in their limited ability to collect taxes and distribute government budgets. Second, public response to the electoral innovations was muted. As Figure 7.2 illustrates, from the outset abstention rates in these races were higher than national rates, and they remained higher as abstention rates in all elections increased dramatically. Either voters did not see decentralization as critical or they did not believe that the direct election of governors and mayors would give them increased control over political outcomes. The discussions surrounding reforms made it clear that many hoped they would break the stranglehold of AD's and COPEI's national electoral machines. However, the traditional parties continued to perform well in these races. Combined, AD and COPEI won 90 percent of the governorships in 1989, 70 percent in 1993, and 66 percent in 1995. At the municipal level, they won 94 percent of the mayoral races in 1989, 51 percent in 1992, and 59.2 percent in

1995.[58] Still, victories by other parties gave them valuable governing experience and served as springboards for launching individual political careers that might have been stymied by national party elites.

State Structure and Interbranch Relations

A federalist terminology is one of the few visible heritages the nineteenth century left to Venezuelan political discourse. But the nomenclature of states and territories should not obscure what is in practice a highly centralized system of government and public administration. This centralization of administrative and political life stirred much critical commentary in Venezuela, and the Comisión Presidencial para la Reforma del Estado was charged with crafting proposals to improve public administration and promote citizen involvement in ways that would make Venezuelan democracy more efficient, more accountable, and ultimately more participatory.[59] Its list of accomplishments is lengthy, including the direct election of mayors and governors and the creation of single-member districts for one-half of the lower house. While power has devolved to some degree, reformers have been unable to break the national dominance, the hold of party elites over individual legislators, and the basic relations between the executive and Congress.

The electoral and party systems promoted party discipline, and party discipline led to an institutionally underdeveloped Congress, interest-group interaction exclusively with the executive branch, and presidential dominance of the legislative agenda. Because legislators have no motivation to listen to groups in civil society or to serve geographically small districts (where they could claim credit for their actions), Congress as an institution is internally underdeveloped and is marginalized in the policymaking process. Congress lacks sufficient professional staff and physical facilities. A structure of permanent legislative committees exists, but legislators often change committee assignments annually—so they do not accumulate expertise or seniority. Thus, while virtually all bills are referred to committee, committee consideration rarely involves serious scrutiny by legislators, and it is not used as an opportunity for legislators to hear from concerned interest groups.

Given that legislators were bound by strict party discipline and therefore had no incentive to develop an institutional structure to interact with pressure groups, these groups focused their attention on the executive branch. Between February 1959, when the first elected president of this democratic era took office, and December 1989, the Venezuelan government created 330 advisory commissions with participants representing interest groups or entire socioeconomic sectors. Presidents used consultative commissions to institutionalize interaction between their appointees and important interest groups. Consultative commissions regularized business and labor influence, enabling the latter to promote an import-substitution industrialization strategy that made them the beneficiaries of the petroleum-funded government spending outlined in the section on state-led socioeconomic development. Interaction with the executive branch allowed interest groups to influence the legislative agenda because the vast majority of legislation was drafted in and proposed by the executive branch.

The partisan makeup of the legislature also influenced its relationship with the executive. The concurrent nature of presidential and legislative elections promotes a large partisan contingent for the president in Congress. The proportional representation system scheme makes it difficult for any single party to gain control of the legislative branch. Together, these features have ensured that if there is a majority party in Congress, it is the president's party. The pull effect of presidential elections then encourages a legislative vote that also coalesces behind the major parties who have a realistic chance of winning the presidency. The proportional representation system that characterizes seat allocations in legislative elections, on the other hand, does not mechanically underrepresent small parties and, as a result, it does not psychologically encourage voters to endorse one of the two major parties either. Given this combination, it is not surprising that the president's party tends to do well (pull effect) but any party finds it difficult to win an outright majority in Congress (proportional representation)—the best recipe for an inactive legislature. In the Venezuelan system from 1958 to 1998, the president's copartisans were usually able to prevent the legislature from censoring and removing his ministers, and when they were a majority, they increased his power by delegating him decree authority.

Strong disciplined support for the president has led to both a failure to check executive-branch activities and a willingness to cede powers to the president in the form of delegated decree authority. Decree authority in economic and financial matters has been delegated to five different presidents. In the first three cases, this authority was requested by the executive branch and was used to enact much of the president's program. Every Congress where one party has had a majority has delegated decree authority to the president for one year. In each case, congresses where AD had a majority delegated authority for a year to their presidents—Betancourt in 1961, Pérez in 1974, and Lusinchi in 1984. The disciplined party delegations in Congress were willing to cede power to the executive branch and the interest groups that influenced it. The next two times in which decree authority was delegated, it was less clearly an opportunity for the president to enact his program. Carefully circumscribed power was briefly delegated to President Ramón J. Velásquez in 1993 and Rafael Caldera in 1994.

In addition, by suspending any of the individual, social, economic, and political guarantees in the constitution, the president can assume powers that are normally reserved for the Congress. Most decrees issued on these grounds are related to the right to economic liberty (Article 96), which has been restricted or suspended for nearly the entire democratic era. This guarantee calls for protection against monopolies, usury, and unduly high prices. Presidents have used this power to control prices, fix currency exchange rates, offer differential rates of foreign exchange, and to influence the production of "goods of basic necessity." Between 1961 and 1994 this power was used to issue at least 194 decrees.

Party discipline led to a relatively inactive Congress that was willing to acquiesce to presidents despite their comparatively weak constitutional powers. Presidents initiated the vast majority of legislation and issued decrees of various kinds. Given this balance of power, interest groups focused their attention on the executive branch. As a result, the locus of policymaking is highly centralized around a single elected official who is not eligible for immediate reelection. These interbranch dynamics diminish accountability both as a result of the marginal role of most elected representatives and the lame-duck status of the sitting president.

Social Cleavages, Associational Life, and the Emergence of Civil Society

The relation between cleavage patterns and political loyalties or outcomes is rarely simple and direct. This is particularly so in Venezuela, where the social changes of this century have shaped a remarkably homogeneous national constituency. Politically significant linguistic, ethnic, racial, religious, or class divisions are absent. The strong religious motives that characterized opposition to AD during the *trienio* faded long ago. Religion is no longer a distinguishing factor in voter choice, ideological argument, or political life generally. There are also no major religious minorities. Single-class, especially working-class, political parties have rarely made much headway, losing ground to populist parties such as AD that prospered early by creating socially heterogeneous organizations with nationalist appeal.

Regionalism is an interesting case of once powerful cleavages that seemed to disappear, only to be reborn in recent years. In the nineteenth and early twentieth centuries, regional differences played a key role in shaping political forces and coalitions. The Andean domination of national life that began with Cipriano Castro and Gómez illustrates the point well. Regional variation has also served as a stand-in for other dimensions. Consider the case of the initial democratic alliance. The marriage between small-town youth and the poor masses of the nation's periphery is best understood as a convergence of social groups, not regions. In any event, the nationalization of Venezuela's economy, culture, and political life that we noted earlier in this chapter helped wash out the impact of region, especially as a political variable. The rebirth of region as a political factor is the result of the decentralization and related political and electoral reforms beginning in the late 1980s. Uncoupling local and state levels from national elections made it possible for smaller parties to get started and gain a secure political base without having to fight costly national campaigns. Cases in point include the early success of La Causa R, rooted in a base in the eastern state of Bolívar, and the success that MAS experienced through the 1990s, when it expanded, capturing a number of governorships. These reforms may be spurring the creation of a different model of political party. For example, MAS could be viewed increasingly as more of an umbrella organization for several strong regional leaders than as a centralized party.[60]

Associational life and the role of "civil society" have undergone dramatic changes since the mid-1980s. Through much of the democratic period, associational life in Venezuela was tightly linked to the structure of the major political parties and controlled by them. Parties made a deliberate, continuous effort to penetrate social organizations (and areas of potential organization), to incorporate leaders and members into party networks, and to bring them under the authority of party leaders. One was organized into the party, and in the same measure brought under party control and subject to party discipline. The result was reminiscent of what Susan Eckstein has called the "irony of organization." Commenting on Mexico's Partido Revolucionario Institucional (PRI), she pointed out that "organizations do not necessarily serve as instruments of political power if their members gain no institutionalized access to authorities, if the groups lack economic resources of their own, and if informal processes inhibit members from using the groups to serve their collective interests."[61] Elsewhere we have shown that the overwhelming power of party organizations became a source of weakness as society began to change.[62]

When societies change more rapidly than political institutions, old ways of doing politics are outpaced, and often outflanked. The changes experienced in Venezuelan society during the democratic period (including urbanization, mass education, economic and geographical mobility) meant that established groups became less representative of their constituencies, and new groups sometimes appeared to challenge them. New groups sprang up around the edges of conventionally "legitimate" channels of action and new forms of action were tried out. Diego Urbaneja states that groups aspiring to voice and representation soon learned that working with the established parties carried too high a price. As a result, groups began to emerge outside the parties and to work to forge new kinds of ties with the state.[63] The new trade-union movement is a case in point.

Beginning in the 1980s, insurgent groups began seeking a voice in labor unions, most notably in the steel industry of the state of Guayana, in eastern Venezuela. In the face of opposition from goon squads, a pliant Ministry of Labor, and national labor federations controlled by the main parties, insurgents finally gained legitimate status, and took control of the steel unions in the late 1980s. This was the origin of what soon became a major new political movement on the left, La Causa R (LCR). If attention is confined to electoral statistics, LCR's rise to prominence appears truly meteoric (as does its subsequent decline following factionalism and division). The party emerged suddenly from obscurity to win a major state governorship (Bolívar) in 1989, took the mayoralty of Caracas in 1992, and garnered over 20 percent of the vote for president along with a strong congressional representation in the 1993 elections.[64] This spectacular electoral success makes it easy to forget the long years activists spent "in the wilderness" working in obscurity to build a movement against seemingly insurmountable odds. The real origins of this party lie outside the great institutions of "the system." La Causa R grew out of the same divisions in the Communist Party that spawned the Movimiento al Socialismo (MAS). LCR's guiding spirit, Alfredo Maneiro, led a small group of supporters in rejecting MAS's decision to adapt to the political system by organizing on the AD model and competing in elections and organizations on the same terms as all parties. Instead they opted to build a movement with three components: neighborhood groups in the barrios of Caracas, university students, and working-class organization in the steel mills of Guayana.[65] The first two failed, but against all odds the effort to build an alternative union succeeded, giving the new party what appeared to be a strong and reliable political base. However, after succeeding in its union activities, building an independent base of support, and becoming a major force in national elections, LCR divided in February 1997, diminishing its electoral prospects.

Challenges to the old system not only took the form of alternative parties, business groups, and unions, but were also embodied in the mobilization of organizations hitherto unknown in Venezuela. Beginning in the early 1980s, groups identifying themselves as "civil society" pressed with growing vigor for a change in the rules of the game. The very term "civil society" only came into wide use in Venezuela in the last decade or so.[66] Party domination was thorough and party-controlled networks were the privileged venue for the expression of most organized social life. As used in Venezuela, "civil society" embraces groups that are nationally organized as well as a host of regional and local associations. Even a short list would have to include barrio and neighborhood movements, insurgent trade unions, cooperatives, human rights organizations, NGOs, private foundations, new business associations, as well as a range of groups working to promote coordination and common action among all of the above. Self-conscious efforts by elements of "civil society" to present a common front, join forces, and reach beyond specific concerns to achieve a voice in policymaking and politics are one of the really new features Venezuelan politics displays in recent years.[67]

Civil society, in Venezuela or anywhere, is more than a simple defensive reaction against the intrusions of an impersonal world. The movements we refer to under the rubric of "civil society" have done more than resist and protest; they have proposed and constructed alternatives, campaigned for their incorporation into law, and maintained steady pressure on public opinion and institutions. The women's movement was energized by the reform of the civil code, and grew subsequently through the 1980s to establish networks of national coordination. A number of human rights organizations established in the 1980s began as responses to specific abuses (PROVEA, COFAVIC, Red de Apoyo para la Justicia y la Paz, etc.).[68] Cooperatives, by all accounts the most widespread and best rooted of the civil associations, began in most instances as efforts at economic self-defense by small groups of citizens desiring better prices, more accessible capital or credit, better transportation, etc. The neighborhood movement, in all its many manifestations, began as uncoordinated efforts by urban middle-class citizens to resist unplanned city growth and to defend their neighborhoods.[69] One need not agree that such new, nonparty movements are the seed of a potential new political culture to accept their importance as a sign of the demystification of politics.[70] Increasingly, the tools of association are in many hands, and politics is no longer the exclusive province of political leaders.[71] In the context of Venezuelan politics, it is important to note the extent to which the emergence of civil society involved an activation of social and cultural energies outside the party-related network of associations.[72] Indeed, it is a peculiarity of the discourse of civil society in Venezuela that political parties tend to be explicitly excluded, doubtless in reaction against past party domination of any organized expression of social interests.

The experience of the neighborhood movement, or *vecinos,* illustrates well the growing presence and possible impacts civil society has had in Venezuela in recent decades. These impacts are best understood not in narrowly political or partisan terms, but rather as part of a broad movement to redefine what is "political" and to open new spaces for legitimate citizen action. Although the movement has spawned a range of organizations and pursued a variety of goals, from neighborhood preservation and local political action to major institutional changes, municipal reforms (and related changes in the electoral system) have been central to their agenda from the start. The movement began in the early 1970s as neighborhood associations popped up in a series of middle-class areas of Caracas.[73] In 1971, the Federación de Asociaciones de Comunidades Urbanas (FACUR) was established as a coordinating body and subsequently provided a model for associations and similar regional federations throughout the country. By the early 1990s, approximately 15,000 associations were gathered in federations in every state.

The impact of the movement has been sharpened and extended by the school for neighborhood groups, the Escuela de Vecinos de Venezuela (EVV). The EVV arose out of classes within FACUR, and consolidated on a national level in the mid-1980s, with important support from business and from national and international NGOs. Since that time, the EVV has established regional offices, and mounted a regular program of courses for associations and local public officials. The EVV also provides a range of correspondence courses, organizes periodic meetings, and most recently has reached into the mass media with weekly radio programming and a daily television show, all intended to find and diffuse news about community projects and groups. There is no easily identifiable national movement, no single leadership group or voice. Instead, we find a loose collection of organizations and networks, some local, some providing services to local organizations that together help focus energies and generate new issues. The leadership of the Escuela de Vecinos de Venezuela has resisted pressure to form groups structured on the conventional party model: instead, a series of organizations has been spun off, each dedicated to a specific issue. Examples include Queremos Elegir (We Want to Elect), a group devoted to electoral reform, Fiscales Electorales de Venezuela (Electoral Officials of Venezuela), dedicated to promoting citizen involvement in supervision of voting sites, and, most recently, Venezuela 2020, an organization that promotes workshops and round tables concerned with the shape of the country's future—in other words, not a party but something more like "civil society." The efforts of these and related groups are directed above all at shaping opinion and creating conditions for long-term institutional change. The single most important instances of such changes are the transformation of city government and municipal politics and a series of related changes in electoral laws. These stemmed from initiatives promoted by the *vecinos,* beginning in 1987 with a petition drive (a little-used technique in Venezuela) that gathered 140,000 signatures in favor of reform of the basic law governing municipalities (Ley Orgánica del Regimen Municipal, or LORM). This was one of the most important nonviolent mobilizations in contemporary Venezuelan history. Changes to the law ultimately included the direct popular election of governors and mayors, the creation of parish councils, and the possibility of recalling officials. These reforms have been at the heart of institutional and political changes since the late 1980s.

The evolution of grassroots groups in Venezuela illustrates both the strengths and limitations of civil society as a vehicle for transforming politics in Venezuela. Strengths include the capacity to mobilize opinion and place new issues on the national agenda. Notable successes have included campaigns to change electoral laws and to begin effective decentralization, with states and municipalities gaining new status and taking on new responsibilities. Weaknesses are also evident. With the exception of La Causa R, few of the new movements generated from civil society have consolidated in enduring political form. For La Causa R itself, the transition from insurgent movement to major party has been difficult and costly. Finding themselves all of a sudden in the surprising position of running state and local governments and occupying positions of power in the

Congress, LCR leaders encountered pressures to act like a party, making electoral alliances and closing deals in ways that run against the participatory and egalitarian ethos of the movement. There have been notable failures at local government, factions emerged, and the party split in 1997. The experience of the neighborhood organizations is also ambiguous. The *vecinos* movement is flexible and its leaders brilliant at mounting campaigns and mobilizing opinion. Their strength lies in civil society. On the other hand, because they cannot and do not want to govern, they remain vulnerable to penetration from parties who do want to govern and pressure from the state itself. They need the state not only for access to decisional arenas, but also for resources and guarantees for access to the media. The effectiveness of the *vecinos* movement lies in a demonstrated capacity to regroup and muster resources for new issues with minimum sunk costs. In the search for more conventional political solutions, it is easy to dismiss effectiveness of this sort.[74] The kind of power and political capacity being created here fits only with great difficulty into the standard categories that the system has to offer. Explicitly political vehicles are not the only, and perhaps not even the most effective means for acquiring voice, shaping debate, and changing the rules of the game. The experience of civil society suggest that no clear and unequivocal solution exists: no single "right" answer can provide a reliable formula for future organizations.

Much commentary on Venezuela's political "crisis" attributes the problems of the system and the surge of new groups to what is loosely called "the exhaustion of the model": that is, the collapse of the formula that underwrote modern economic and political life. In this view, once the money ran out, the patronage networks on which the system depended decayed rapidly, and the institutions that managed the system fell of their own weight, ossified and rigid victims of excess and old age.[75] The difficulty with this position is that conceptualizing crisis purely in terms of decay ignores the role that new forces play in creating pressures for change and exploiting openings. To be sure, institutional and political decay play a role, if only by weakening elite capacity to reach and control, but change cannot be understood merely as a passive result of that decline. New forces, groups, and the effort to change the agenda of public discourse are the work of real women and men, active subjects whose efforts began as challenges from inside the established order, or at its margins.[76]

Both decay and the emergence of new alternatives are best understood not as the exhaustion of the model, but rather as a product of democracy itself. They are the expression of a generation with no direct experience of military rule, a generation that in the democratic years became more urbanized, educated, and integrated into mass communications than any in national history.[77] These transformations had the effect of diffusing skills of organization and communications (once monopolized by state agents or political parties) into the population, creating a kind of citizenry that was not dreamed of when the main lines of the model were laid down almost fifty years ago. They gained strength from an organized civil society that simply did not exist when the party system and the state took their original forms. The groups now emerging in civil society and reaching for political expression have many strengths. They are organizationally flexible, are innovative, and have daring and creative leaders. They have few sunk costs, and in any case are rooted in a general disposition to organize that makes for great flexibility—defeated in one form they can quickly shift terrain and emerge again elsewhere. The reforms they have helped set in motion provided invaluable flexibility and resilience to the Venezuelan political system in the time of its greatest crisis. But there are important weaknesses too, and success will not be easy. Although the decay of parties sets groups free, in the same measure it sets them adrift and leaves them with dwindling resources, easy prey to manipulative leaders and personalist politics. The task at hand is not just to represent, but rather to do so in a way that provides reasonable order and governability to democratic politics.

International Factors

The impact of international factors, both political and economic, and the way that Venezuela's political system has been situated in the international arena, have all changed substantially since the inception of democratic politics in 1958. In the early years, Venezuela seemed like a hard-won success story—a notable exception to the trend toward military rule and bureaucratic authoritarianism that swept the continent from the mid-1960s on. The strength of the country's core political institutions allowed Venezuelan elites and mass publics to defeat extremes on both right and left. By the late 1960s, a solid two-party system emerged that was to dominate the national scene for more than two decades. Internal political strength provided the underpinnings of a foreign policy that combined anticommunism with a consistent rejection of dictatorships of the right.

The arrangement of Venezuela's relation to the international economic system worked to support the consolidation of democracy by financing a powerful state sector, directing public spending to key political groups, and fostering the incorporation of business and labor into the day-to-day operations of the state. The availability of a constantly increasing income from petroleum allowed Venezuela to continue import-substitution policies and a dominant state sector long after these options had lost their viability elsewhere in the region. Revenues from petroleum, channeled through the national state, provided incentives to local capital while at the same time paying for a vast expansion in education, health services, and social mobility, including urbanization.

Throughout this period, in political and economic as well as in military terms, influence from the United States played a central role. Believing that

military rule provided a stable and reliable guarantee for U.S. economic
and strategic interests, the Eisenhower administration had backed the country's last military regime (that of Pérez Jiménez) openly and strongly. All
this left a bitter taste in Venezuela and contributed strongly to Vice
President Richard Nixon's hostile reception in Caracas in early May
1958.[78] With the advent of the Kennedy administration, and the inception
of the Alliance for Progress, U.S. policy changed, giving strong political
and diplomatic backing to the new democracy. This support helped allay
conservative fears and restrain potential military conspirators, above all
during the shaky early years of the Rómulo Betancourt government. U.S.
fear of the Cuban Revolution was also important. Betancourt and his party
had long been firmly anticommunist, but Fidel Castro's emergence as a radical leader helped them distinguish their program and general orientation
all the more firmly from those on the left. Cuba provided a convenient foil,
a telling argument for swaying potential allies. When the likely alternative
to AD was no longer the military, but rather something like Castro and his
revolution, AD must have seemed considerably more acceptable to conservatives, both at home and in the United States. In later years, although U.S.
policy grew more critical of corruption and was opposed to the Venezuelan
pattern of state management of the economy, U.S. policy remained consistently opposed to military intervention. This position was an important element in reinforcing opposition to attempted coups in 1992.

Venezuela's economic dependence on petroleum exports means that
the country and its governments, regardless of leadership preference or
party ideological stances, are closely tied to world economic fluctuations.
Crises in other petroleum-exporting countries (e.g., the Iran-Iraq War, or
sanctions on Iraq) are good for Venezuelan policymakers. The tremendous
expansion of the state sector and plans for La Gran Venezuela that came
with President Carlos Andrés Pérez's first term were made possible by the
worldwide surge in oil prices that began in the mid-1970s. By the same
token, as oil prices began to weaken, the costs of maintaining this vast and
inefficient apparatus became impossible to meet, and political coalitions
that depended on payoffs from it began to lose their coherence and viability. Beginning with the currency crisis of 1983, income distribution worsened, welfare levels declined, and the capacity of bloated institutions to
manage resources and deliver services decayed sharply.[79] When international economic pressures and an impending financial crisis forced a sudden change of course on the new government of Carlos Andrés Pérez, as we
have seen, political crisis erupted in riots and sustained public discontent,
attempted coups, and significant challenges to the country's dominant political parties, and in general to the way elite-mass relations were managed.

The preceding observations underscore how different Venezuela looks
in the international arena of the 1990s as compared to the early 1960s. As
public policy elsewhere in Latin America turned with remarkable consen-

sus to privatization and structural adjustment, Venezuelan leaders and mass publics resisted, and in 1993 elected a leader pledged to maintain the central, distributive role of the state intact. With the restoration of democratic politics throughout the region, Venezuela can no longer stand as a model. Moreover, a surge of concern throughout the region over human rights, the incorporation of social movements and an active citizenry into governance, and the revitalization of local and regional politics have made the classic Venezuelan pattern of powerful national parties and dominant central governments less attractive. International criticism has been especially sharp in the area of human rights, with the penal and judicial systems coming under particular scrutiny.[80] Looked at from the point of view of other countries in the area, Venezuelan politics has often seemed like a film run in reverse: instead of economic reform, we find entrenched resistance; instead of consolidation, we see institutional decay and decomposition of democracy; instead of a military withdrawing from government, we observe armed forces emerging from the barracks to popular acclaim.[81] Nonetheless, as we have argued above, and in more detail elsewhere, excessive pessimism is misplaced.[82] Elements pressing for reform in Venezuela also take strength from international political and economic connections, which provide them with models and signposts just as Venezuela's lonely democracy did for others in the dark years when authoritarian regimes dominated the rest of the continent, and seemed destined to remain in power indefinitely.

FURTHER REFLECTIONS AND FUTURE PROSPECTS

How can both the successes and shortcomings of Venezuelan democracy be explained in ways that shed light on its own future, and on the implications Venezuelan experience holds for other countries? Our analysis has attributed success above all to the combination of strong party organization, effective leadership, an evolving democratic political culture, and effective institutions.[83] Because of these political strengths, Venezuelans successfully addressed a series of difficult challenges. For just some of the more noteworthy examples, recall the early isolation and defeat of military oppositions from right and left; the strong move to a disciplined, two-party system after 1968, which laid to rest fears of party atomization, vote dispersion, and political fragmentation; and the survival of virtually simultaneous economic crisis, coup attempts, and impeachment proceedings in the early 1990s. To be sure, these political strengths are not without their downsides. Effective political leadership also entailed centralized decisionmaking within parties, and strong parties penetrated other groups in civil society. Effective institutions channeled participation, limiting voters' choices and privileging a limited set of interest groups. These overdoses of control and caution led to growing electoral abstention and fragmentation of the party system (most evident in 1993 and after). They also led to the continuation of a development strategy that had long proven itself incapable of transforming the Venezuelan economy into one less dependent on government deficits, foreign borrowing, and international demand for primary products.

The preceding summary suggests that the moderating characteristics that made a successful transition from authoritarian rule possible have also doomed Venezuela to a limited and unstable form of democracy made all the more shaky by an outdated development strategy. In recent years, a mounting chorus of critics and commentators have painted a similarly grim picture of the future of Venezuelan politics. They have argued that the political system had ossified into a rigid party oligarchy *(partidocracia),* opposing this to a somehow more genuine "real" democracy. The parties were dismissed as rotten machines for peddling influence and patronage; governments were attacked for their corrupt mismanagement (especially of the economy); and the electoral system was ridiculed for its emptiness and carnival atmosphere. As the late Enrique Baloyra noted, "Judging from these apocalyptic descriptions, one may imagine that the Venezuelan regime survives by an unparalleled act of political will and/or the sheer imbecility of the population."[84] What these doomsayers failed to appreciate was the ongoing process of democratization within democracy itself. It should surprise no one that the democracy that emerged in Venezuela after 1958 would undergo further changes, some of them very painful and destabilizing. What long-standing democracy has not? Thus far, rather than proving to be insurmountable bottlenecks, these crises have pointed out challenges that Venezuelans have then set out to overcome. Many see the electoral victory of coup-plotter Chávez in 1998 as an indicator of democratic failure. On the other hand, he came to power through constitutional means, and although he made vague promises of radical changes, it is too soon to evaluate the impact of his efforts on the quality and nature of democracy.

Our explanation of Venezuelan democracy underscores some variables as more important than others, and we have specified the relationships among the remaining causes. First, "historical factors" is not in and of itself a causal concept, but rather cautions us to think about the remaining factors (culture, institutions, associational life, etc.) as variables whose value may change over time, and whose previous character may help explain contemporary events even while undergoing change in the contemporary era. For example, the conflict-avoidance aspects of elite political culture in the 1960s help explain the logjam of demands that burst onto the political scene in the late 1980s and 1990s. Once out in the open, the repeated and insistent public expression of the demands triggered changes in the operating style and overall political culture of the very elites whose rigid arrangements had helped generate these demands in the first place. Likewise, as used in this chapter, "the military" and "economic policies and performance" are not theoretical dimensions. The military is an important actor whose preferences, resources, institutional structure, and relationship to other actors warrants attention. We have tried to account for the preferences of the military in both the analysis of democratic inauguration and in more recent coup attempts. Economic policy is an outcome of political struggle, a process deserving of analysis, and we have given attention to the choices made and the process used in our discussion of consultative commissions and the decentralized public administration. Finally, "international factors" are important but only as they affect other theoretical dimensions on the list. The impact of the changing international milieu (especially the Cold War) on the viability of socialist alternatives, for example, influenced the political culture and associational life in Venezuela. Likewise, the changing international petroleum market affected the state strength and socioeconomic development patterns. We prefer to place attention on the Venezuelan aspects of these relationships, not the international ones.

The preceding exercise still leaves us with a long list of variables that are related to one another in complex ways. "Political leadership," "civil and associational life," and "political culture" were all influenced by the failed attempt at democracy during the *trienio*. Given another chance, political elites attempted to minimize conflict and work collectively to protect democracy as a process. Their success in doing so and in making their commitment to democracy a priority are only understandable through attention to the associations they worked so hard to construct and lead (parties, unions, and chambers of commerce). These cultural and mobilizational characteristics were made concrete and self-perpetuating through the construction of a set of "political institutions" (electoral laws and constitutional allocation of powers, for example) and a "state structure" (a large bureaucracy and consultative commissions infiltrated by interest groups) that privileged party elites, certain business interests, and some labor leaders over challengers from both within their sectors and outside them. The importance of the state and access to its decisionmaking processes and resources was magnified by Venezuela's pattern of "socioeconomic development." The state controlled petroleum revenues, and these revenues were distributed to business and labor through a highly protectionist set of policies. Gaining access to the state and partaking in the spoils that came with it became the primary political end for many actors. This development pattern did not resolve "inequality and class cleavages." Instead, it created a highly urbanized and mobile population that depends on state development policies without having much access to the process through which those policies were determined.

The civil and associational life that characterized Venezuela when democracy was inaugurated and consolidated did not remain frozen in time. The civil liberties and human rights provided by the democratic regime and the socioeconomic development funded by petroleum allowed society to evolve. On the other hand, the strong state and rigid institutions constructed in the ensuing years allowed elites to protect their privileges. The resulting lack of fit led to crises. Parties lost their grip on other associational forms, and the failure to present new ideas led interest in electoral politics to decline. Powerful interest groups were ensconced in privileged decision-making positions, and remained there despite diversification in their own sectors and in civil society more generally.

This lack of fit means that Venezuelan democracy faces four principal challenges in the future: maintaining organizational strength while opening the political space; reforming institutions to better reflect a more pluralistic civil society; stemming the decline in living standards and reversing the trend of growing inequality; and dealing effectively with the ups and downs of the international economy, on which Venezuela depends so heavily. Organizational rebuilding and diversification continue. As the once dominant parties retrench to face the challenges of Chávez's Movimiento V República (MVR), La Causa R, Convergencia, and MAS, other organizations have found it possible to evade party penetration. As noted earlier, neighborhood associations, human rights groups, cooperatives, and others are gaining their political voices and looking for ways to interact with the state while avoiding political parties as mediators.

Electoral reforms have begun to chip away at the dominant role of national party leaders. Direct election of governors and mayors decentralized the locus of decisionmaking, and while the powers of these offices rivaled that of the president, they have allowed local interests to target their efforts to pressure for change. The adoption of a mixed-number electoral system for the Chamber of Deputies did not lead to dramatic changes in legislator behavior in the short run, but it did signal an effort to respond to popular discontent through institutional change. President Chávez, elected in December 1998, has promised even more profound changes in electoral rules, interbranch relations, federalism, and decentralization. It is unlikely that all these changes would follow previous trends.

Has democracy brought democratization, in the sense of greater equity and participation? The extent of democratization in Venezuela in these terms must be assessed in the context of notable continuing social and economic inequalities and strong class barriers. If average people remain very poor and thus heavily dependent on government and party leaders, what does this suggest about the quality of democracy? The issue has immense practical as well as theoretical significance. In practical political terms, increased inequality, declining standards of living, and institutions that seem remote and out of touch have all clearly contributed to the decay of political legitimacy, and hence to the "crisis" that Venezuela has experienced since the late 1980s. For a long time, questions such as *who governs?* and *how do they govern?* held little interest for many students of Latin American politics. The theoretical sway exercised by issues of dependency and analyses of bureaucratic authoritarianism made "material" or "substantive" democracy (*for whose benefit?* or *for whom does government act?*) seem more urgent than matters of democratic process. Certainly one of the lessons we have learned from past dictatorships is that protecting public liberties, guaranteeing rights, and choosing leaders through free and competitive elections deserve the highest attention. But today the major threat to democracy in Venezuela, and throughout Latin America as well, is not disinterest in these questions. The primary danger now lies elsewhere: in forgetting that even though democracy has an undeniable intrinsic value, at the same time democracy should also be considered a fundamental tool that people use to pursue their goals—not only for liberty, but also for justice and well-being. In other words, the questions of *who governs?* and *for whose benefit?* are not unrelated.

Perhaps the area in which Venezuela has made the least progress is establishing a policymaking process to design and implement a development strategy that avoids the deficits and debts of the past. Economic reforms have been implemented in the late 1980s and the 1990s. The sudden shift by Pérez was repudiated, but several more years of decline and discussion made a similar neoliberal package more tolerable under Caldera. However, even if the economic policy changes are successful, which is far from guaranteed, they have not resulted from an agreed-upon consultative process to rival the former tripartite, consensus-seeking system of old. Venezuelan policymakers must find a means to accommodate the interests of economically powerful but numerically small groups—such as domestic capitalists and organized workers in the modern sector. It may be that constitutional reform, including electoral reforms that encourage constituency service, might also free legislators to respond to sectoral demands as well. The electoral reforms that would free individual legislators from excessive party discipline would also give them incentives to become more active participants in the policymaking process. As a result, the number of elected officials involved in policymaking would increase and the diversity of opinions represented could also rise.

What does all this add up to in policy terms? On the basis of Venezuelan experience, what lessons can be learned? Extracting reproducible "lessons" from Venezuelan experience is difficult. Structures and strategies cannot simply be transplanted in a mechanical way from one setting to another. Without real social bases and commitments that make sense in context, they are likely to produce little but frustration and failure. In any case, social and political systems of this kind cannot be created by fiat. Attempts to build parties by decree will produce just empty shells with no power to move the population. Parties of this kind collapse at the first sign of trouble or simply disappear once a particular sponsoring leader passes from the scene. The short and unlamented life of the much-vaunted organizations created by the Peruvian military, after 1968, are a good case in point.

The same holds true for pacts and coalitions. Making pacts in a mechanical fashion will surely fail without prior agreement that pacts should be honored, and that compromise and coalitions are proper ways of arranging the business of political life. A choice for political methods of this kind at the very least makes it possible to create new ways of acting politically. Transitions in Brazil and Spain, and the coalitional efforts of the democratic opposition in Chile, suggest the broad appeal of this lesson—a lesson once rejected with scorn by the Chilean left. Venezuelan experience also suggests that managed transitions that focus on both electoral and con-sultative institution building may be more durable. Controlling the scope and pace of change soothes the fears of powerful groups. Establishing respected institutions influences behavior by assuring actors that they will be forced to interact with one another again in the future. If institutions are carefully wrought, momentary victory will not give one the right to exclude other actors from the game. Once again, events in Brazil and Spain confirm this impression, and a sympathetic look at the program of El Salvador's Christian Democrats shows how much their strategy was modeled on an interpretation of Venezuelan experience. Early success, however, does not mean that traumatic growing pains will not be experienced in the future, as Venezuela is demonstrating in the late 1990s.

The role that strong political parties exercised in the establishment and consolidation of democracy in Venezuela underscores the value of powerful organization, effective leadership, and institutions that reinforce a disposi-tion toward conciliation and compromise. At the same time, however, Venezuelan experience points up the danger of organizations becoming ends in themselves, and concern for short-term stability outweighing evolu-tionary change with the times. Agreements that made sense in the early democratic years, as means of stabilizing shaky institutions, became frozen in place. The result was rigid institutions and top-heavy structures that eventually lost touch with a changing society. Trends of this kind are hard to counter. Michels's "iron law of oligarchy" works itself out in the most varied ways, as entrenched interests are created, and then defended against newcomers and efforts at reform. As we have seen, one way to break the logjam is to create conditions for free associational life and to lower barri-ers to citizen organization. We should not forget that the current proponents of further democratization would probably not exist in Venezuela if not for its long history of democratic rule—even with its imperfections. There would be no neighborhood groups, no cooperatives, no human rights orga-nizations, no "minor" parties, and no COPRE without the political space to organize that democratic rule provided. On the other hand, the pressure these groups have brought for change since the mid-1980s indicates that political parties cannot monopolize political space to the exclusion of other organized groups. Groups other than parties should be provided with institutional means to lobby and persuade, and parties should be required to democratize internally. In Tocqueville's words:

> A certain nation, it is said, could not maintain tranquillity in the community, cause their laws to be respected, or establish a lasting government if the right of association were not confined within narrow limits. These blessings are doubtless invaluable, and I can imagine that, to acquire or preserve them a nation may impose upon itself severe temporary restrictions: but still it is well that the nation should know at what price these blessings are purchased. I can understand that it may be advisable to cut off a man's arm in order to save his life; but it would be ridiculous to assert that he will be as dexterous as he was before he lost it.[85]

The critical issue for Venezuelan politics at this time is less a choice between democracy or authoritarianism than it is the kind and quality of democracy the country can build. The ongoing transformations we have detailed here suggest that the crisis of Venezuelan democracy has brought opportunity along with danger. Venezuela's years of acute and visible crisis have also been years of citizen pressure for change and a host of reforms. The changes of the past fifty years have created a kind of citizenry in Venezuela that was undreamed of when "the model" and its core institutions were first established. The growing capacity and public presence of this active citizenry has spurred institutional changes and political reforms that incorporate a different understanding of politics from the one enshrined in the model and its working rules of the game.

Consider the matter of governability and legitimacy. Analyses that rely on ideas about the "exhaustion of the model" all too often frame these issues in a top-down fashion. The model decays, control and decisional capacity decline, institutions crack open, elites divide, and so forth. But this is a political/economic manager's point of view. Governability is defined in terms of control and capacity to manage. Legitimacy is defined as an elite formula, projected from above and accepted or rejected from below. Suppose we invert the question and ask what governability means and how legitimacy looks when viewed from outside the system, from below, or, more precisely, from the margins of established channels and forums. Governability and legitimacy take on new meaning in the context of an active if still constrained and controlled citizenry. From this vantage point, governability and legitimacy depend less on control and order than on connection, predictability, and accountability.[86] Connection, predictability, and accountability require access to a game and rules of that game that are more flexible, less thoroughly mediated by central structures. The effort to construct new sources of governability and legitimacy will be strengthened as costs of organization are lowered and the arenas created over the last decade are really used.[87]

Democratizing Venezuelan democracy will require continual changing of the rules of the game that organize political life. The overwhelming power of national party structures and the autonomy of their leaders, the unquestioned dominance of the central state, and the institutionalized division of representation and spoils among political parties, business, and labor over the commitment to maintaining democracy itself, ensuring equity, and responding to local and sectoral interests are all expressions of a system that lost its effectiveness and its capacity to create and sustain legitimacy. Success in the effort to replace one set of rules of the game with another will require time. The obvious question is whether the balance of decay and change is positive enough to yield the time required to make the change. The evidence is ambiguous, but the very fact of reform gives grounds for hope. Reform has been in the air and was evident on the ground throughout the 1980s. Once in motion, reforms provided a point of reference of action, a context for nonviolent citizen action, and a set of arenas that attracted new leaders and made a place for working with new norms of accountability. To be sure, reform is no panacea. Reformers have not achieved all their goals, and some of the changes they did implement have not had the intended consequences. What is more, reform can undermine existing institutions before alternatives are in place. It can also generate expectations and create hopes that are impossible to fill. But at the very least, reform can extend a bridge from one "model" to another.

Crossing the bridge will not happen all at once. The legitimacy of a system and its capacity to provide for governability is negotiated and worked out in specific arenas. The present generation of leaders and activists will have to figure out how to combine the virtues of looseness and stimuli to diffused, scattered participation with the advantages of coherent leadership and unified organization. Success in the effort will require a commitment to keeping arenas open while expanding their boundaries and changing the rules that determine access—who gets into the game. The question for the future is whether changes in the formal structure of representation now on the table can capture and channel social energies. What the future of democracy in Venezuela will look like, and how Venezuelans will get there, will depend on the capabilities and commitments of democracy's children: the new generations of leaders and active citizens that have come to maturity and moved onto the public scene in the democratic years.

NOTES

1. Aníbal Romero, "'Rearranging the Deck Chairs on the Titanic': The Agony of Democracy in Venezuela," *Latin American Research Review* 32, no. 1 (1997): pp. 7–36.

2. Daniel H. Levine discusses the nature of democracy and democratization, and their

implications for group and institutional life, in "Paradigm Lost: Dependence to Democracy," *World Politics* 40, no. 3 (April 1988): 377–394.

3. Guillermo O'Donnell, Philippe Schmitter, and Laurence Whitehead, eds., *Transitions from Authoritarian Rule: Prospects for Democracy* (Baltimore: Johns Hopkins University Press, 1986); Ruth Berins Collier and David Collier, *Shaping the Political Arena: Critical Junctures, the Labor Movement, and Regime Dynamics in Latin America* (Princeton: Princeton University Press, 1991); Terry Lynn Karl, "Petroleum and Political Pacts: The Transition to Democracy in Venezuela," *Latin American Research Review* 22, no. 1 (1987): 63–94; and Terry Lynn Karl, "The Venezuelan Petro-State and the Crisis of 'Its' Democracy," in Jennifer McCoy, Andrès Serbin, William C. Smith, and Andrès Stambouli, eds., *Venezuelan Democracy Under Stress* (New Brunswick, NJ: Transaction Publishers, 1995), pp. 33–55.

4. Marcelo Cavarozzi, "Beyond Transitions to Democracy in Latin America," *Journal of Latin American Studies* 24 (1992): 665–684.

5. Barry Ames, "Electoral Rules, Constituency Pressures, and Pork Barrel Bases of Voting in the Brazilian Congress," *Journal of Politics* 57 (1995): pp. 324–343; Scott Mainwaring and Matthew Soberg Shugart, eds., *Presidentialism and Democracy in Latin America* (New York: Cambridge University Press, 1997); and Matthew Soberg Shugart and John. M. Carey, *Presidents and Assemblies, Constitutional Design, and Electoral Dynamics* (New York: Cambridge University Press, 1992).

6. Atul Kohli, *Democracy and Discontent: India's Growing Crisis of Governability* (New York: Cambridge University Press, 1990), and Scott Mainwaring and Timothy Scully, eds., *Building Democratic Institutions: Party Systems in Latin America* (Stanford: Stanford University Press, 1995).

7. John D. Martz, *Acción Democrática: The Evolution of a Modern Political Party in Venezuela* (Princeton: Princeton University Press, 1966); Juan Carlos Rey, "El sistema de partidos Venezolanos," *Politeia* 1 (1972): 175–230; Daniel H. Levine, *Conflict and Political Change in Venezuela* (Princeton: Princeton University Press, 1973); Michael Coppedge, *Strong Parties and Lame Ducks: Presidential Partyarchy and Factionalism in Venezuela* (Stanford: Stanford University Press, 1994).

8. José Enrique Molina, *El sistema electoral venezolano y sus consecuencias políticas* (Valencia: Vadell Hermanos, 1991); Miriam Kornblith and Daniel H. Levine, "Venezuela: The Life and Times of the Party System," in Scott Mainwaring and Timothy Scully, eds., *Building Democratic Institutions: Parties and Party Systems in Latin America* (Stanford: Stanford University Press, 1995), pp. 37–71; and Miriam Kornblith, "Elecciones 95: Nuevos actores, reglas y oportunidades," *Debates IESA*, no. 3 (1995): 3–7.

9. Seymour M. Lipset, *Political Man* (Baltimore: Johns Hopkins University Press, 1981), and Seymour M. Lipset and Stein Rokkan, *Party Systems and Voter Alignments* (New York: The Free Press, 1968).

10. Arturo Escobar and Sonia Alvarez, eds., *The Making of Social Movements in Latin America: Identity, Strategy, and Democracy* (Boulder, CO: Westview, 1992); Alberto Melucci, *Nomads of the Present Social Movements and Individual Needs in Contemporary Society* (Philadelphia: Temple University Press, 1988); Susan Eckstein, ed., *Power and Popular Protest: Latin American Social Movements* (Berkeley: University of California Press, 1989); Philip Oxhorn, *Organizing Civil Society: The Popular Sectors and the Struggle for Democracy in Chile* (University Park: Pennsylvania State University Press, 1995); Jonathan Fox, "How Does Civil Society Thicken? The Political Construction of Social Capital in Rural Mexico," *World Development* 24, no. 6 (1996): 1089–1103; and Luis Gómez Calcaño, "Organizaciones sociales autónomas y reconstrucción de la legitimidad democrática en Venezuela, 1992–1996," paper presented at a symposium on "La crisis de legitimidad de la democracia en Venezuela," Universidad Simón Bolívar, Caracas, 1996. However, for warnings about romanticism see Judith Adler Hellman, "The Study of New Social Movements in Latin America and the Question of Autonomy," in Arturo Escobar and Sonia Alvarez, eds., *The Making of Social Movements in Latin America: Identity, Strategy, and Democracy* (Boulder, CO: Westview, 1992), pp. 52–61; Sidney Tarrow, *Power in Movement* (New York: Cambridge University Press, 1994); and Sherry Ortner, "Resistance and the Problem of Ethnographic Refusal," *Comparative Studies in Society and History* 37, no.1 (1995): 173–193.

11. See, for example, Escobar and Alvarez, eds., *The Making of Social Movements*.

12. Gomez Calcaño, "Organizaciones sociales"; Margarita López Maya, "El ascenso en

Venezuela de la Causa R," *Revista venezolana de economía y ciencias sociales* 2–3 (April-September 1995): 205–239; and Margarita López Maya, "Nuevos actores en la crisis de legitimidad del sistema político venezolano: La Causa R, Convergencia, y el MBR-200," paper presented at a symposium on "La crisis de legitimidad de la democracia en Venezuela," Universidad Simón Bolívár, Caracas, 1996.

13. In particular, see Levine, *Conflict;* Daniel H. Levine, "Venezuela Since 1958: The Consolidation of Democratic Politics," in Juan J. Linz and Alfred Stepan, eds., *The Breakdown of Democratic Regimes* (Baltimore: Johns Hopkins University Press, 1978), pp. 82–109; and Daniel H. Levine, "The Transition to Democracy: Are There Lessons from Venezuela?" *Bulletin of Latin American Studies* 4, no. 2 (1985): 47–61.

14. Important sources in English include Robert Bond, ed., *Contemporary Venezuela and Its Role in International Affairs* (New York: New York University Press, 1977); Martz, *Acción Democrática;* and Franklin Tugwell, *The Politics of Oil in Venezuela* (Stanford: Stanford University Press, 1975). Karl, "Petroleum and Political Pacts," sets Venezuelan experience in the framework of the political-economy school. Judith Ewell's *Venezuela: A Century of Change* (Stanford: Stanford University Press, 1984) is a convenient but flawed overview of contemporary history.

15. John Lombardi explores the nature and impact of colonial history in "The Patterns of Venezuela's Past," in John D. Martz and David Myers, eds., *Venezuela: The Democratic Experience* (New York: Praeger, 1977), pp. 1–26. For a more detailed treatment, see John Lombardi, *Venezuela: The Search for Order, the Dream of Progress* (New York: Oxford University Press, 1982). The development of city hierarchies and demographic patterns is discussed in John Friedmann, "The Changing Pattern of Urbanization in Venezuela," in Lloyd Rodwin et al., *Planning Urban Growth and Regional Development: The Experience of the Guayana Program of Venezuela* (Cambridge, MA: MIT Press, 1969), pp. 40–59.

16. See R. L. Gilmore, *Caudillism and Militarism in Venezuela 1810–1910* (Athens: Ohio University Press, 1964).

17. On the bases and broad implications of coffee's growth and later decline, see Luise Margolies, "Urbanization and the Family Farm; Structural Antagonism in the Venezuelan Andes," and William Roseberry, "On the Economic Formation of Boconó," both in Luise Margolies, ed., *The Venezuelan Peasant in Country and City* (Caracas: EDIVA, 1979), pp. 92–114; and also Roseberry's fine *Coffee and Capitalism in the Venezuelan Andes* (Austin: University of Texas Press, 1983). Roseberry shows that the Andean region's share of total national population grew from 10.6 percent at independence in 1873 (date of the first official census), to 14.5 percent by the 1890s and 17.9 percent by 1926. See *Coffee and Capitalism,* p. 76. It has dropped steadily ever since.

18. Antonio Arraiz, *Los días de la ira: Las guerras civiles en Venezuela, 1830–1903* (Valencia: Vadell Hermanos, 1991).

19. See Gilmore, *Caudillismo.* Ramón J. Velásquez discusses the social basis of nineteenth-century militarism and of the Andean triumph in his *La caída del liberalismo amarillo* (Caracas: Ediciones Roraima, 1973). See also Domingo Alberto Rangel, *Los andinos en el poder* (Caracas: Talleres Gráficos Universitarios, 1964).

20. Useful sources on the origins of organization include: for peasants, John Powell, *Political Mobilization of the Venezuelan Peasant* (Cambridge, MA: Harvard University Press, 1971); for labor, Steve Ellner, *Los partidos políticos y sus disputas por el control del movimiento sindical en Venezuela, 1936–1948* (Caracas: Universidad Católica Andres Bello, 1980); and Charles Bergquist, *Labor in Latin America: Comparative Essays on Chile, Argentina, Venezuela, and Colombia* (Stanford: Stanford University Press, 1986); on students, Maria de Lourdes Acedo de Sucre and Carmen M. Nones Mendoza, *La generación venezolana de 1928: Estudio de una elite política* (Caracas: Ediciones Ariel, 1967); and for a general overview, Levine, *Conflict,* especially chapters 2, 3, and 8. Juan Bautista Fuenmayor's *1928–1948: Veinte años de política* (Madrid: Editorial Mediterraneo, 1968) reviews early events from the perspective of a founder of the Communist Party.

21. The critical point to bear in mind here is that party ties cut across and dominate those derived from social class alone. This relation of party to class has been criticized by some (e.g., Bergquist, *Labor in Latin America)* who see it as a betrayal of revolutionary potential. For more detail on the origins of party organization, see Rómulo Betancourt's *Venezuela: Política y petróleo,* rev. ed. (Caracas: Ediciones Senderos, 1967), and Levine, *Conflict.*

22. Details on the quality of conflict and oppositions during the *trienio* can be found in Glen Kolb, *Democracy and Dictatorship in Venezuela, 1945–1958* (Hamden, CT: Shoestring

Press, 1974); Andres Stambouli, *Crisis política Venezuela 1945–58* (Caracas: Editorial Ateneo de Caracas, 1980); and Levine, *Conflict.*

23. On the ideology of the Pérez Jiménez regime, see Freddy Rincón, *El nuevo ideal nacional y los planes económicos-militares de Pérez Jiménez, 1952–1957* (Caracas: Ediciones Centaurs, 1982). On the events leading to its fall, see especially Kolb, *Democracy and Dictatorship,* and Stambouli, *Crisis política.*

24. See Clemy Machado de Acedo, Elena Plaza, and Emilio Pacheco, *Estado y grupos económicos en Venezuela* (Caracas: Editorial Ateneo de Caracas, 1981).

25. See José Vicente Abreu, *Se llamaba SN* (Caracas: Editor José Augustín Catalá, 1964). The regime's most infamous concentration camps were located in the Orinoco Delta area, especially at Guasina. See José Vicente Abreu, *Guasina donde el Rio Perdió las 7 estrellas relatos de un campo de concentración de Pérez Jiménez,* ed. José Augustín Catalá (Caracas: Ediciones Centauro, 1997); or the collection, *Documentos para la historia de la resistencia Pérez Jiménez y su regimen de terror* (Caracas: Editor José Augustín Catalá, 1969).

26. Pérez Jiménez received the Legion of Honor from the Eisenhower administration in 1954. The full citation of the award is reproduced in Kolb, *Democracy and Dictatorship,* p. 142. It is lavish in praise for the dictator and his regime.

27. Kolb's account of the January 1958 events brings out the depth of popular opposition: "In dramatic intensity and popular violence, the events of January 21 and 22 in Caracas, Venezuela, can find a proper comparison only in such a heroic uprising as that of the Hungarian Freedom Fighters of Budapest in 1956 against their Communist overlords. It was a true popular revolution of Venezuelan citizens of all ages and social classes, armed with rocks, clubs, home-made grenades, and Molotov Cocktails against a ferocious and well-trained police force equipped with armored vehicles, sub-machine guns, rifles, revolvers, machetes, and tear gas." *Democracy and Dictatorship,* p. 175.

28. For further detail, see Karl, "Petroleum and Political Pacts," which argues forcefully that postwar changes in the Venezuelan economy created new interests and opportunities *for* a structural place for democratization after 1958. She gives special emphasis to the economic underpinnings of the 1958 agreements.

29. Rómulo Betancourt, *Tres Años de Gobierno Democrático* (Caracas: Imprenta Nacional, 1962), p. 245.

30. After 1958, Venezuelan politics have been guided by four operative norms that set the "game" for elites and the organizations they controlled: freedom for leaders; respect for the fragility of politics; agreement to disagree; and concentration of politics in a narrow and predictable range of vehicles. For further details and general comments on the nature of legitimacy in Venezuela, see Levine, *Conflict,* chapters 8–10.

31. Levine explores the left's revolutionary goals in *Conflict,* pp. 47ff. In part, these generational conflicts, pitting exiled leaders against those who had run clandestine party networks during the dictatorship. The former tended to support pact-making, conciliation, and the Communists from post-1958 arrangements. The latter had worked closely with Communists in mobilizing opposition to Pérez Jiménez and backed broad alliances and more radical transformations. The Cuban Revolution had a major impact on this process, spurring divisions and convincing leftists generally that revolution was indeed possible.

32. The relevant names of the minor parties are as follows: On the left are the Partido Comunista de Venezuela (PCV); the Movimiento Electoral del Pueblo (MEP), the largest of the groups derived from divisions in AD; and the Movimiento al Socialismo (MAS). The most significant of the "electoral phenomena" were the Frente Nacional Democrático (FND), Democrática Popular (FDP), and the Cruzada Cívica Nacionalista (CCN). The first was backing Arturo Uslar Pietri, a well-known writer; the second gathered around Larrazábal; and the last was organized by supporters of ex-dictator Pérez Jiménez.

33. A brief overview of AD's divisions and of party fragmentation generally in the early 1960s is in John D. Martz, "The Evolution of Democratic Politics in Venezuela," in Howard Penniman, ed., *Venezuela at the Polls* (Washington, DC: American Enterprise Institute, 1980), pp. 1–29; Levine discusses the matter in "Venezuela," in Myron Wiener and Ergun Ozbudon, eds., *Competitive Elections in Developing Countries* (Durham, NC: Duke University Press, 1987), pp. 248–282.

34. On the evolution of public opinion, see Andrew Templeton, "The Evolution of Public Opinion," in Louis Goodman et al., eds., *Lessons of the Venezuelan Experience* (Washington, DC: Woodrow Wilson Center Press, Johns Hopkins University Press, 1995), pp. 79–114. For a very pessimistic account see Romero, "Rearranging the Deck Chairs." See also the chapters by

Friedrick Welsh and José Vicente Carrasquero, "Democratic Values and the Performance of Democracy in Venezuela," pp. 149–165, and Valia Pereira Almao, "Venezuelan Loyalty to Democracy in the Critical 1990s," pp. 139–148, in Damarys J. Canache and Michael R. Kulisheck, eds., *Reinventing Legitimacy: Democracy and Political Change in Venezuela* (Westport, CT: Greenwood Press, 1998).

35. Luis Pedro España, *Democracia y renta petrolera* (Caracas: Universidad Catolica Andres Bello, 1989), and Luis Pedro España and Francisco Vivancos, *La crisis que nos falta recorrer* (Caracas: ILDIS–Nueva Sociedad, 1993).

36. Moises Naím, *Paper Tigers and Minotaurs: The Politics of Venezuela's Economic Reform* (Washington, DC: Carnegie Endowment for International Peace, 1993); Juan Carlos Navarro, "Reversal of Fortune: The Ephemeral Success of Adjustment in Venezuela Between 1989 and 1993," working paper (Washington, DC: World Bank, Governance and Successful Adjustment Conference, 1994); and Alan Angell and Carol Graham, "Can Social Sector Reform Make Adjustment Sustainable and Equitable? Lessons from Chile and Venezuela," *Journal of Latin American Studies* 27 (1995): 189–219.

37. V. Cartaya and Y. D'Elia, *La pobreza en Venezuela: Realidad y políticas* (Caracas: CESAP-CISOR, 1991); Brian F. Crisp, Daniel H. Levine, and Juan Carlos Rey, "The Legitimacy Problem," in Jennifer McCoy, Andrés Serbín, William Smith, and Andres Stambouli, eds., *Venezuelan Democracy Under Stress* (New Brunswick, NJ: Transaction, 1995), pp. 139–170; and Gustavo Marquez, *Escaleras y ascensores: La distribución del ingreso en la década de los ochenta* (Caracas: IESA Working Paper, 1991).

38. Asdrúbal Baptista, "¿Crisis en Venezuela? Elementos para ayudar a entender los tiempos del país," *Economía hoy* (Caracas, May 30, 1995) [special edition on La Crisis].

39. PROVEA (Programa Venezolano de Educación y Acción en Derechos Humanos), *Situación de los derechos humanos en Venezuela* (Caracas: PROVEA, selected years).

40. Daniel H. Levine, "Goodbye to Venezuelan Exceptionalism," *Journal of Inter-American Studies and World Affairs* 36, no. 4 (1994): 145–182; and Angela Zago, *La rebelión de los ángeles* (Caracas: Fuentes Editores, 1992).

41. Juan Carlos Rey, "La crisis de legitimidad en Venezuela y el enjuiciamiento y remoción de Carlos Andrés Pérez de la presidencia de la república," *Boletín electoral latinoamericano* IX (January-June 1993): 67–112.

42. The funds in question were supposedly changed at preferential rates for approximately U.S.$17 million. Only days after this illegal transaction was alleged to have occurred, the government ended the differential exchange rate, calling it a source of "permanent corruption." According to the constitution, the Senate can vote to put a sitting president on trial if the Supreme Court determines that there is merit to the charges against him. While on trial, the president is relieved of his duties. The court made this determination on May 20, and the Senate voted unanimously the next day to remove the president from office (Rey, "La crisis de legitimidad," pp. 102–103).

43. Population data are derived from the sources cited in Table 7.5, and in note 10 above. For a more detailed account of demographic transformation, see C. Y. Chen, *Desarrollo regional-urbano y ordenamiento del territorio mito y realidad* (Caracas: Universidant Católica Andres Bello, 1978).

44. Tugwell details the state's overwhelming dependence on petroleum revenue in *The Politics of Oil*. See also Terry Karl, "The Political Economy of Petrodollars: Oil and Democracy," Ph.D. diss., Stanford University, 1982.

45. On the agricultural depression, see Margolies, "Urbanization and the Family Farm"; Roseberry, *Coffee and Capitalism;* and Powell, *Political Mobilization.* The decline of rural life and the pull of cities and oil towns is a staple of Venezuelan literature of the period.

46. Karl, *Political Economy,* p. 84.

47. The relative percentage share of these sectors over time breaks down as follows:

	1936	1950	1960	1970	1980
Primary	41.8	38	36.0	26.2	13.8
Secondary	11.7	17	19.8	19.7	26.5
Tertiary	46.4	45	44.2	44.1	56.2

Figures for 1936 from Rodwin, *Planning Urban Growth,* p. 63. Figures for 1950, 1960, and 1970 from Franklin Bustillos Gálvez, *Introducción a la economía venezolana* (Caracas: Librería Editorial Salesiana, 1978), p. 128. Figures for 1980 calculated from data in Ewell, *Venezuela,* p. 233.

48. On the growth of public enterprises, see especially Janet Kelly de Escobar, "Las empresas del estado: Del lugar común al sentido común," in Moises Naím and Ramón Piñango, *El caso Venezuela: Una ilusión de armonía,* 2d ed. (Caracas: Ediciones IESA, 1985), pp. 122–151; and Gene E. Bigler and Enrique Viloria, "State Enterprises and the Decentralized Public Administration," in John Martz and David Myers, eds., *Venezuela: The Democratic Experience,* rev. ed. (New York: Praeger, 1986), pp. 183–217.

49. On interest group participation in consultative commissions and governing boards, see Brian F. Crisp, *Control institucional de la participación en la democracia venezolana* (Caracas: Editorial Jurídica Venezolana, 1997).

50. See Comisión de Estudio y Reforma Fiscal (CERF), *Análisis de los efectos económicos y sociales del gasto público en Venezuela* (Caracas: República de Venezuela, 1987).

51. On the petroleum rent component of workers' salaries, see Asdrúbal Baptista, "Gasto público, ingreso petrolero, y distribución del ingreso," *Trimestre económico* XLVII, no. 2 (April-June 1980): 431–464; Asdrúbal Baptista, "Gasto público, ingreso petrolero, y distribución del ingreso: Una nota adicional," *Trimestre económico* LII, no. 1 (January-March 1985): 225–236; and Asdrúbal Baptista and Bernard Mommer, "Renta petrolera y distribución factorial del ingreso," in Hans-Peter Nissen and Bernard Mommer, eds., *¿Adios a la Bonanza?* (Caracas: ILDIS-CENDES and Editorial Nueva Sociedad, 1989), pp. 15–40.

52. Margarita López Maya, *El Banco de los Trabajadores de Venezuela: ¿Algo más que un banco?* (Caracas: Universidad Central de Venezuela, 1989).

53. See Miriam Kornblith and Daniel H. Levine, "Venezuela: The Life and Times of the Party System," in Scott Mainwaring and Timothy Scully, eds., *Building Democratic Institutions: Party Systems in Latin America* (Stanford: Stanford University Press, 1995).

54. The cost of politics rose sharply after 1968, as traditional reliance on mass meetings, parades, and block and precinct work yielded to stress on regular polling and to very lengthy national media campaigns. Both have been packaged and programmed following campaign-management pamphlets and outlines, many of them from the United States. For a more complete discussion of costs, see Howard Penniman, ed., *Venezuela at the Polls* (Washington, DC: American Enterprise Institute, 1980); and Levine, "Venezuela."

55. While the end result is clear enough, great care is needed in tracing the dynamics of change and, in particular, in drawing inferences about group or individual choice from aggregate electoral or demographic data. We cannot be sure that change is occurring within identical groups, or if (as suggested here) it stems primarily from the incorporation of new voters. Conclusions about changing bases of individual or group voting decisions are thus unwarranted. The data do not allow us to be certain whether shifts are grounded in changing working-class attitudes, middle-class orientations, or the like.

56. For the 1978 elections, Robert O'Connor comments, "Demographic variables do not account for the voting intentions of the Venezuelan electorate. If one were to select at random 100 Herrera [COPEI] supporters and place them in a room, and then repeat this procedure with Piñerua [AD] supporters, the two groups would look very similar." O'Connor, "The Electorate," in Howard Penniman, ed., *Venezuela at the Polls* (Washington, DC: American Enterprise Institute, 1980), pp. 56–90.

57. In mid-1988, after a lengthy period of study and intense national debate, two important political reforms were adopted. Beginning in 1989, mayors and state governors (hitherto appointed by the national executive) would be elected in separate elections. These changes would make it possible for opposition parties to build independent local and regional bases more effectively. Further changes included a move to open party lists, giving voters a chance to select candidates by name. If implemented fully, these and other reforms proposed by the Presidential Commission for the Reform of the State would have changed the way power is organized in the state, in the political parties, and in the electoral process. The whole package of reforms proposed by this commission was intended to spur the decentralization and deconcentration of power, and to make citizen participation easier and more meaningful at all levels. The early experience with these reforms was promising. Governors and mayors became important political figures in their own right, and these offices provided the bases for national

campaigns. Recent examples include Claudio Fermín and Andrés Velásquez in 1993, and Enrique Salas Romer in 1998. The advent of a Constituent Assembly, proposed by candidate and now President Hugo Chávez, and approved by the voters in a referendum on April 25, 1999, throws these reforms, and all matters of institutional design, into question.

58. Angel Alvarez, "Venezuelan Local and National Elections, 1958–1995," in Henry Dietz and Gil Shidlo, eds., *Urban Democratic Elections in Latin America* (Washington, DC: SR Books, 1998), pp. 239–274.

59. On the Presidential Commission for the Reform of the State, see Juan Carlos Rey, *El Futuro de la Democracia en Venezuela* (Caracas: IDEA, 1989). Janet Kelly de Escobar, "Reform Without Pain: The Commission on State Reform in the Lusinchi Administration," paper presented at the 13th International Congress of the Latin American Studies Association, Boston, October 1986; and COPRE, *La reforma del estado: Proyecto nacional de nuestro tiempo* (Caracas: COPRE, 1994).

60. Alvárez, "Venezuelan Local and National Elections," p. 260.

61. Susan Eckstein, *The Poverty of Revolution* (Princeton: Princeton University Press, 1976), p. 101 and chapter 3 passim.

62. Brian F. Crisp and Daniel H. Levine, "Democratizing the Democracy: Crisis and Reform in Venezuela," *Journal of Interamerican Studies and World Affairs* 40, no. 2 (summer 1998): 27–60; Levine, "Goodbye to Venezuelan Exceptionalism"; Daniel H. Levine, "Beyond Exhaustion of the Model: Survival and Transformation of Democracy in Venezuela," in Damarys J. Canache and Michael R. Kulisheck, eds., *Reinventing Legitimacy: Democracy and Political Change in Venezuela* (Westport, CT: Greenwood Press, 1998), pp. 187–214; Coppedge, *Strong Parties and Lame Ducks;* or Diego Bautista Urbaneja, *Pueblo y petroleo en la política venezolana del siglo XX* (Caracas: CEPET, 1992).

63. Urbaneja, *Pueblo y petroleo,* p. 345.

64. LCR lost the governorship of Bolívar to AD in 1995, in a hotly contested election marked by allegations of fraud.

65. On Maneiro and the early strategy of LCR, see Alfredo Maneiro, *Notas políticas* (Caracas: Ediciones del Agua Mansa, 1986); Farruco Sesto, *Tres entrevistas con Andrés Velásquez, 1986, 1990, 1991* (Caracas: Ediciones del Agua Mansa and Sesto, 1992); and Farruco Sesto, *Pablo Medina en entrevista* (Caracas: Ediciones del Agua Mansa, 1992).

66. Gomez Calcaño, "Organizaciones sociales"; Edgardo Lander, *Neoliberalismo, sociedad civil, y democracia: Ensayos sobre América Latina y Venezuela* (Caracas: Universidad Central de Venezuela, Consejo de Desarrollo Científico y Humanístico, 1995); Daniel H. Levine, "Beyond the Exhaustion of the Model: Survival and Transformation of Democracy in Venezuela," in Eli Diniz, ed., *Os desafios da democracia na America Latina* (Rio de Janeiro: IUPERJ, 1996), pp. 367–397.

67. Juan Carlos Navarro, "Venezuela's New Political Actors," in Louis Goodman et al., eds., *Lessons of the Venezuelan Experience* (Washington, DC: Woodrow Wilson Center Press, Johns Hopkins University Press, 1995), pp. 115–135.

68. PROVEA (Programa Venezolana de Acción y Educación en Derechos Humanos, or the Venezuelan Program for Action and Education on Human Rights) documents human rights issues and conducts courses and campaigns on human rights. COFAVIC (Comité de Familiares de Víctimas de los Sucesos del 27 de Febrero, or Committee of Family Members of Victims of the Events of February 27) was established by relatives of those dead or disappeared and unaccounted for as a result of the violence surrounding the riots of February 27, 1989. The Red de Apoyo para la Justicia y la Paz (Network in Support of Justice and Peace) is an independent citizens' movement that monitors human rights, above all at local levels. These and other organizations have targeted abuses and called for greater public and police accountability. All are of recent creation. Cf. Kathryn Sikkink, "Human Rights, Principled Issue Networks, and Sovereignty in Latin America," *International Organization* 47, no. 3 (summer 1993): 411–441, on the growth of human rights movements in Mexico and Argentina.

69. Nelson Geigel Lope-Bello, *La defensa de la ciudad* (Caracas: Universidad Simón Bolívar, Instituto de Estudios Regionales y Urbanos, 1979); Rexene Hanes de Acevedo, *El control político en tiempos de crisis: Estudio del caso de una asociación de vecinos en Venezuela* (Caracas: Ediciones IESA, 1991); Lander, *Neoliberalismo, sociedad civil;* Levine, "Beyond Exhaustion"; Maria Luisa Ramos Rollón, *De las protestas a las propuestas: Identidad, acción, y relevancia política del movimiento vecinal en Venezuela* (Caracas: Editorial Nueva Sociedad, 1995); Elias Santana, *El poder de los vecinos* (Caracas: Tropykos, 1983).

70. Daniel H. Levine, *Popular Voices in Latin American Catholicism* (Princeton: Princeton University Press, 1996); and Scott Mainwaring and Eduardo Viola, "New Social Movements, Political Culture, and Democracy: Brazil and Argentina in the 1980s," *Telos* 61 (1986): 17–52.

71. The point extends to the character of protest. Public actions are no longer monopolized by parties. Street demonstrations and coordinated actions involving banging of pots and pans (*cacerolazos*) or blowing of whistles or car horns (*bocinazos*) are now common. Cf. the 1991 Annual Report of PROVEA, a major human rights group, which states: "In contrast to earlier years, and basically during and after the National Protests of February 1989 it was possible to confirm that *the social spectrum participating in protests is widening. Now participation in organized protests has opened fields of action for new groups: along with students and workers one finds a range of professional associations and social groups: doctors, nurses, peasants, Indians, firemen, police, cultural workers, housewives, and neighborhood groups actively joining in movements in defense of basic rights* (italics in original) (from "Informe Anual, Situación de los Derechos Humanos en Venezuela" (Caracas: PROVEA, selected years).

72. Levine, *Popular Voices,* chapter 3.

73. Geigel Lope-Bello, *La defensa de la ciudad;* and Santana, *El poder de los vecinos.*

74. Cf. Christian Smith, *Resisting Reagan: The U.S.–Central America Peace Movement* (Chicago: University of Chicago Press, 1996) for an account of the Central American peace movement in the United States that acknowledges the movement's failure to achieve its policy goals while underscoring the capacity of the "submerged networks" at its roots (churches and local organizations of all kinds) to regroup and mount campaigns with limited resources and few sunk costs. A related and even clearer example comes from the history of the civil-rights movement in the United States. Did these movements fail because they failed to achieve all their policy goals? A better question is what capacities are left behind, and how the agenda of politics looks once the specific issues that motivated these activists have passed from the scene.

75. Coppedge, *Strong Parties and Lame Ducks;* Terry Lynn Karl, *The Paradox of Plenty: Oil Booms and Petro States* (Berkeley: University of California Press, 1997); Romero, "'Rearranging the Deck Chairs.'"

76. Gómez Calcaño, "Organizaciones sociales"; Levine, "Beyond Exhaustion."

77. Asdrúbal Baptista, "Mas allá del optimismo y del pesimismo: Las transformaciones fundamentales del país," in Moises Naím and Ramón Piñango, eds., *El caso Venezuela: Una ilusión de armonía* (Caracas: Ediciones IESA, 1985), pp. 20–41; and Baptista, "¿Crisis en Venezuela?"

78. On Nixon's visit, see Kolb, *Democracy and Dictatorship,* pp. 182–184.

79. The best accounts of the relation of economic factors to state structure, policies, and political outcomes are Karl, *Paradox of Plenty;* Naím, *Paper Tigers and Minotaurs;* Coppedge, *Strong Parties and Lame Ducks;* Diego Bautista Urbaneja, *Pueblo y petróleo;* and Juan Carlos Rey, "La democracia venezolana y la crisis del sistema populista de conciliación," *Revista de estudios políticos* 74 (1991): 553–578. For general reviews of this literature, see Levine, "Goodbye to Venezuelan Exceptionalism" and "Beyond Exhaustion."

80. On human rights and the judicial system, see the 1992 report issued by the Andean Commission of Jurists, *Venezuela: Administración de justicia y crisis institucional* (Lima: Comisión Andina de Juristas, 1992). On the development of human rights groups regionally, and their relation to domestic politics and social movements, see Sikkink, "Human Rights, Principled Issue Networks."

81. On this point, see Levine, "Goodbye to Venezuelan Exceptionalism," and the sources reviewed there.

82. Crisp and Levine, "Democratizing the Democracy."

83. This is not to say that petroleum played no role. It brought about enormous social changes and supplied the state with revenues, but its effects are only understandable in conjunction with the political characteristics noted above.

84. Enrique Baloyra, "Public Opinion and Support for Democratic Regimes, Venezuela, 1973–1983," paper presented at the 1985 Annual Meeting of the American Political Science Association, New Orleans, August 29–September 1.

85. Alexis de Tocqueville, *Democracy in America* (New York: Schocker Books, 1961), pp. 143–144.

86. Constructing a realistic theory of representation will be vital to the whole effort. It will not do simply to assume that the system was so tainted at birth that no "true" representation was possible. This exaggerates the social base of alternatives excluded in the early years and reduces the survival of the system to little more than an act of will (aided by deceit) on the part of its leaders. For works that appear to exaggerate the absence of representation, see Daniel Hellinger, *Venezuela: Tarnished Democracy* (Boulder, CO: Westview, 1991); Richard S. Hillman, *Democracy for the Privileged: Crisis and Transition in Venezuela* (Boulder, CO: Lynne Rienner, 1994); and Karl, "Petroleum and Political Pacts."

87. Although decentralization is no panacea, it can provide resilience and multiple sources of leadership for future versions of "the model."

8

COSTA RICA:
The Roots of Democratic Stability

John A. Booth

Democracy involves citizen participation in making and implementing public decisions, but there are many kinds of democracy. Since 1949, Costa Rica has had a constitutional, representative, republican (liberal) government with a high correspondence between the actual governance of the system and the formal political arrangements described in its constitution. Electoral probity has remained a hallmark of the system, and all changes of administration have occurred in accord with the law. Citizens enjoy a degree of participation in public decisions equal to or greater than that in most other Western, liberal constitutional regimes. One may, therefore, justly characterize Costa Rica as a liberal, representative, constitutional democracy.[1]

John Peeler correctly observes that liberal democracy denotes "a system very far from true 'rule by the people' [and is] a liberal political system legitimated by the appearance of democracy."[2] Liberal democracy, in Carl Cohen's terms, permits considerable breadth of citizen participation with rather little depth or range[3]; that is, many vote for leaders, but significant, direct popular influence on policy is modest. In some respects, the depth and range of participation by Costa Ricans are greater than one might expect in a liberal democracy, but recent pressures, mostly external, have somewhat reduced both the range and depth of popular influence on public policy.

HISTORICAL DEVELOPMENT[4]

Costa Rica's national myth holds the country unique among Latin American nations because its contemporary political institutions have

COSTA RICA

evolved from a colonial tradition of egalitarian rural life, civilian rule, relatively equal land distribution, ethnic and racial homogeneity, and long-standing electoral integrity. History reveals a more complex reality, substantiating only parts of the myth.[5]

Spanish conquest of Costa Rica began in 1561, and the colony began to develop after 1575. Colonists settled mainly in the elevated valleys of the nation's center (*meseta central*); they were largely isolated from both coasts by inhospitable terrain, and from the colonial seat of the Kingdom of Guatemala by great distance. Smaller population centers remained marginal: settlers in Guanacaste (the northwest) were oriented toward Nicaragua; Atlantic coastal cacao plantations eventually failed completely. Spain's Costa Rican colony never developed significant exportable agricultural or mineral wealth and thus received little attention from the metropolis and colonial bureaucracy.

Costa Rican colonists imported few slaves to work in the paltry mines and on the plantations of Guanacaste and the Atlantic region. The small indigenous population, heavily exploited for forced labor in the sixteenth century, quickly shrank to low levels, and thus barred development of large haciendas. In the absence of sufficient cheap labor, more land than a family itself could work was generally wasted; land ownership was not a source of great wealth and remained rather equally distributed in comparison to other Spanish colonies.[6] By the later colonial era, most Costa Ricans—regardless of their social standing—were subsistence farmers. Much of the wealth and capital that accumulated came from commercial enterprises.

The leveling effect of this poverty and isolation did not prevent status differences. Noble lineage, race, commercial wealth, and ethnicity intertwined to define a status hierarchy topped by a highly self-conscious Creole aristocracy.[7] This limited wealth differentiation contributed a certain egalitarianism among lower-status Costa Ricans, but the colony was far from democratic. Participation in governance through the *cabildos* (municipal councils) of Cartago and Heredia (and later Alajuela and San José) was restricted mainly to a political class drawn from the aristocracy. Early liberal and conservative factions, forerunners of later political parties, emerged within this political class.

Two characteristics of colonial Costa Rica—contrasting with most of Latin America—contributed to later democracy. First, Costa Rica did not develop a quasi-feudalistic hacienda system in which a Creole aristocracy controlled highly concentrated land holdings and exploited Indians and black slaves as elements of plantation economic production. Without haciendas, economic elites never came to depend on armed force to ensure cheap rural labor, a practice that elsewhere bred militarism and authoritarianism. Disease and forced labor decimated the indigenous populace, and extensive racial mixing largely absorbed the remaining Indians.[8]

Second, the colonial era ended without the wars that wracked much of

Latin America. Costa Rica, as Guatemala's most remote province, was a dependency of the Viceroyalty of New Spain (Mexico). When Mexico won its independence in 1821, the Central American colonies came with it but declined to join the Mexican empire. Instead, in 1823 they formed the Central American Republic, a five-province federation. Its four northern provinces were so torn by civil conflict between liberals and conservatives that the federation collapsed by 1839. Costa Rica largely escaped this civil war because conservatives took control there early on. Internal political conflict remained low in the federal and early national periods, and the first several governments were civilian. By the time a politicized army developed, Costa Rican political elites had already acquired a habit of civilian rule.

The introduction and rapid expansion of coffee cultivation with the opening of the European market in 1845 brought profound socioeconomic change. Expanding coffee production forged and rapidly expanded a class of smallholding farmers. Simultaneously, the progressive concentration of coffee exporting, milling, and land ownership consolidated a strong class of coffee planters and importer-exporters (*cafetaleros*).[9] As land ownership became more concentrated, a new class of landless agricultural workers appeared, but the agricultural labor shortage kept rural wages high until the 1880s and protected landless Costa Rican peasants from poverty. José Luis Vega Carballo argues that this interdependence among rural classes reinforced the egalitarianism of social values that had developed in the colonial era. "Because peasants and artisans . . . were not mere servile employees or passive instruments of exploitation, . . . it was therefore necessary to elaborate a series of subtle psycho-social, symbolic, and normative ('soft') mechanisms in order to guarantee that they could be persuaded to work."[10]

The social and political aristocracy (most now *cafetaleros*) continued to dominate national politics, largely excluding the general public. A brief period of direct elections and expanded popular suffrage (1844–1847), plus the passage of early laws establishing electoral rolls (1848, 1861), revealed an early "preoccupation for organizing the electoral process with great care."[11] Throughout much of the nineteenth century, however, literacy and property ownership requirements and the exclusion of women barred all but about 10 percent of citizens from voting. Most elections were indirect. Those with the franchise voted only in the first round of elections to choose electors (usually from the coffee aristocracy), who in turn would choose the officeholders. Liberal and conservative elite political factions struggled for power using manipulated elections, fraud, and even military force. By mid-century, military institutions had appeared and they became more politically active after the Central American War of 1857. The military and its budget expanded greatly after 1870.[12] From 1824 to 1899, the average Costa Rican presidency lasted only 2.4 years, 37 percent of the presidents resigned before completing their terms, and another fifth were deposed by coups d'état. From 1835 to 1899, Costa Rica was under military rule over half the time—the generals in the presidency were almost always coffee aristocrats (see Table 8.1).

Table 8.1   Characteristics of Costa Rican Presidencies, 1824–1998

Characteristic	1824–1889	1890–1920	1921–1950	1951–1998
Average years per presidency	2.4	3.4	3.8	4.0
Civilian presidents only	1.5	3.6	3.8	4.0
Military presidents only	5.8	2.0	—	—
Percentage of period under military rule	44	7	—	—
Percentage of interim presidencies (not including those resulting from brief absences of constitutional president)	30	11	—	—
Percentage of presidents serving less than one year (excluding interims resulting from absences)	37	22	—	—
Percentage of presidencies ended by resignation	19	22	13	—
Percentage of presidencies ended by coup d'état	19	11	13	—
Average voter turnout as percentage of population	n.a.	14	15	34

Sources: John A. Booth, "Representative Constitutional Democracy in Costa Rica: Adaptation to Crisis in the Turbulent 1980s," in Steve C. Ropp and James A. Morris, eds., *Central America: Crisis and Adaptation* (Albuquerque: University of New Mexico Press, 1984), table 5.1; updated with data from Inter-American Development Bank, *Economic and Social Progress in Latin America: 1987 Report* (Washington, DC: IADB, 1987), p. 270; Carlos F. Denton and Olda M. Acuña, *La elección de un presidente: Costa Rica, 1982* (San José: Instituto del Libro del Ministerio de Cultura, Juventud, y Deportes, 1984); Roberto Tovar Faja, *Partido Unidad Social Cristiana: Bosquejo histórico* (San José: Litografía e Imprenta LIL, 1986); and John A. Booth, *Costa Rica: Quest for Democracy* (Boulder, CO: Westview, 1998), p. 46.

Note: n.a. = not available.

Further social differentiation came with the development of interest groups and labor organization during the nineteenth century. At first, the government organized certain workers and professionals to regulate key trades and protect wider societal interests. Between 1830 and 1865, for example, the Costa Rican state created mandatory guilds of miners, or drovers, port and dock workers, and boatmen. The government chartered guilds of medical practitioners and lawyers in the 1850s. Mutual-aid societies proliferated in the last quarter of the nineteenth century as the economy increasingly suffered from international market forces and the novelty of under- and unemployment. Between 1890 and 1902, there appeared a third type of organization in the cities—multitrade self-help guilds. Numerous but short-lived, they mobilized artisans and laborers directly into politics by promoting their education and supporting presidential candidates.

The dictatorship of Liberal Party chief Tomás Guardia (1870–1882) and his two Liberal successors (1882–1890) laid important foundations for later democratization of Costa Rican politics by greatly expanding public education. Growing literacy and an expanding urban middle class also brought many more Costa Ricans into the political arena.[13] In addition, several new political parties were formed. By the late nineteenth century, such changes and forces had brought into politics a broader public than ever before, much of it dissatisfied with the political elite's decisions.

In the late nineteenth century, economic change accelerated with the construction of a railroad to the Atlantic port of Limón from the capital, San José, and with the accompanying cultivation and exportation of bananas. The railroad and banana industries spread Costa Rica's settlement outside the *meseta central*. The new industries also brought many Caribbean black and Chinese immigrants, whose presence elicited racial discrimination and gave rise to labor conflict. Costa Rica's first recorded labor unrest was a strike by Chinese laborers in 1874. Later came a mutiny by Jamaicans in 1879, and a major strike by Italians in 1888. Native Costa Ricans (telegraph workers) struck for the first time in 1883. From 1890 to 1901 there followed a series of strikes by Costa Rican artisans and craftsmen in different industries.

After 1900, Costa Rica's social class system evolved markedly. The system of yeoman farming ceded further to export agriculture (though the rural middle class persisted). Commerce, services, and manufacturing grew, and urbanization began to accelerate. The *cafetalero* bourgeoisie of large coffee farmers, millers, and exporters expanded its investments into commercial and industrial enterprises, while successful new entrepreneurs from outside the coffee industry bought coffee farms. Thus the economic/political elite diversified somewhat but remained generally dominant in politics and strongly opposed to redistributive social reforms.[14] Simultaneously, the growth of new industry created more proletarians, working conditions in traditional trades deteriorated, and the first true labor unions emerged. The banana industry absorbed many workers displaced by coffee production but also bred sharp regional and class tensions and provided fertile ground for labor organization. The increase of popular political participation that had begun in the late nineteenth century accelerated in the early twentieth century.

Political Liberalization

Costa Rica's first modern political parties arose in the last quarter of the nineteenth century. A key event was the 1889 presidential race, occurring after two decades of Liberal dictatorship by Guardia and his successors. The 1889 contest was between the Liberal Progressives and the new Catholic Union Party, which the Catholic Church had mobilized to fight the Liberals' anticlerical policies. Electors chose Catholic Union candidate José J. Rodríguez by a wide margin, but a pro-Liberal military rebelled to block Rodríguez from office. The church then incited Costa Ricans to riotous protest, prompting the plotters to back down and permit Rodríguez to become president. This marked the first opposition victory and successful power transfer in Costa Rican history, as well as the first major popular impact on an election. Its impact was short-lived, as the Liberals returned to power in 1893 and suppressed the Catholic Union Party. In subsequent elections, the Liberal movement fragmented and gave rise to several personalistic parties/factions that eventually included the National Union Party (Unión Nacional) and the Republican Party (Partido Republicano), which between them would dominate the next several decades of Costa Rican politics.

In 1905, a heated election campaign (with over half the populace now literate and able to vote for electors) brought the National Union Party's Cleto González Víquez to the presidency on the crest of higher voter turnout. In 1909 González Víquez broke with tradition when he allowed his opposition to campaign freely. This permitted Ricardo Jiménez Oreamuno to win the presidency by appealing for votes to local peasant leaders (*gamonales*) outside the aristocracy. Once elected, Jiménez Oreamuno secured a constitutional amendment (1913) that instituted direct popular election of public officials, and municipal reforms that permitted the election of *gamonales* to municipal councils.[15] These actions by González and Jiménez (each of liberal orientation and with coffee bourgeoisie backing), between 1905 and 1914, extended the franchise, political participation, and access to public office beyond the aristocracy and convinced more and more of the general public to vote.

The expansion of liberal democratic institutions and processes in the late nineteenth and early twentieth centuries has been generally attributed to the coffee aristocracy's efforts to consolidate and to protect its political power. Facio and Aguilar Bulgarelli, for instance, argue that the Liberal dictatorship of Guardia led *cafetalero* politicians to promote parties, elections, and suffrage in order to protect their political influence from new dictatorships.[16] Vega Carballo contends that because "visible, frontal, domination 'from above' was inappropriate" under Costa Rica's long-standing condition of relative class equality, the expansion of suffrage in the late nineteenth and early twentieth centuries helped the *cafetaleros* to retain political power as class inequality grew.[17]

> This made possible the implantation in the society of an egalitarian ideology, reinforced by the rhetoric with which the rulers pretended to obtain consensus (and . . . credited themselves for their moderate use of violence

and force), in order to continue building the modern Costa Rican Nation-State . . . Thus it was that, with the passage of time, there emerged "rules of the game" . . . that helped maintain and validate the established order, that regulated and oriented toward defined goals the conduct of the subordinated classes.[18]

These authors erroneously attribute the liberalization of Costa Rican politics to concerted, self-conscious actions by a unified national bourgeoisie. There was a *cafetalero* class, but it was fragmented among anticlerical Liberals, various personalistic factions, and pro-Catholic elements. What really democratized Costa Rica was that an increasingly complex class structure widened the distribution of power resources throughout society and produced new class and political forces. The diverse and burgeoning new civil society intensified political conflict, further divided the bourgeois political elite, and eventually forced the adoption of new, liberal democratic rules of the game via the 1948 civil war and 1949 constitutional reform.[19]

Economic crisis brought on by World War I led President Alfredo González Flores to impose economic reforms, new taxes, and austerity measures that sharply expanded the state's economic role. This so angered certain *cafetaleros* that they promoted yet another coup and two years of military rule under the Tinoco brothers. The highly repressive Tinocos, however, failed to solve economic problems. Popular protest against the regime and an invasion from Nicaragua by other, exiled Costa Rican elites toppled the Tinoco regime. Costa Ricans had thus rejected the military experiment and loudly demanded civilian constitutional rule.

During the 1920s and 1930s, expansion of suffrage and tinkering with the electoral system continued, in part, because of divisions within the national bourgeoisie and the persistence of class "interdependence." This permitted burgeoning middle- and working-class groups to expand and win "access to political and economic influence, without by so doing . . . undermining the general system of oligarchic domination."[20] A first national election agency, the Consejo National de Elecciones, was established (1925); parties were given a monopoly on the nomination of candidates for office (1932); the vote became both secret (1928) and obligatory (1936); and the legislature received authority to scrutinize and validate elections (to reduce executive-branch manipulation and fraud). Despite such steps, fraud and executive manipulation of elections continued.[21]

From 1910 to 1950, the number and types of organizations—community groups, cooperatives, labor unions, professional and trade associations, school groups, and many others—expanded rapidly. They mobilized ever more Costa Ricans into the political arena, and conveyed a proliferating array of demands to the political system. Marxist labor activists formed a Worker's Society in 1909 and helped forge Costa Rica's first central labor organization, the Confederación General de Trabajadores (CGT) in 1913.

The CGT sought to develop working-class consciousness, promoted other unions, supported many strikes, and lobbied the government for accident protection, social security, and retirement programs.

Another important movement began with social-Christian activism and eventually merged with the CGT to form Jorge Volio's Reformist Party in 1923. Volio, a devout Catholic, populist, social worker, and supporter of unions, failed in his 1923 bid for the presidency but paved the way for later cooperation between the church and the communist unions and influenced the nascent social-democratic movement. Meanwhile, Ricardo Jiménez Oreamuno, running for a second term on the Republican Party ticket, defeated Volio for the 1924–1928 presidential term. The rapidly fading Reformists united with the National Union Party and nominated Cleto González Víquez for the 1928–1932 presidential term, which he won. Ricardo Jiménez then led the increasingly dominant Republican Party to victory again in 1932 (his third term), to be succeeded in 1936 by Republican León Cortés Castro.[22]

Considerable labor turmoil in the 1920s, the emergence of a leftist intelligentsia, U.S. intervention in Nicaragua (1927–1933), and the onset of the Great Depression in 1929 spawned numerous political and labor groups, the most significant of which was the Communist Party. When labor unrest spread in the banana fields, Communists organized the workers and led the great 1933 strike. Its success rapidly expanded the Communist Party's influence. The Communists founded the Confederación de Trabajadores Costarricenses (CTCR), which quickly became the nation's dominant labor group. The CTCR and Communist Party reached their apogee of influence between 1942 and 1948 when the CTCR participated in two governments in coalition with social-Christian forces represented by Archbishop Victor Manuel Sanabria and populist Republican coffee aristocrat and president Rafael Angel Calderón Guardia.

Calderón Guardia—a charismatic physician who soon dominated the Republican Party—advocated a social-Christian reformism as appealing to depression-impoverished workers as it was alienating to his former bourgeois allies. Calderón pushed a social-security system through the legislature in 1941 and with the aid of Communist deputies enacted a labor code in 1943. The Calderón-Communist alliance, and their reformist policies, engendered several foci of opposition to the government in the early 1940s. The coffee aristocracy, a traditional enemy of redistributive reforms, quickly turned against Calderón. There also developed both conservative and progressive middle-class opposition movements—both strongly anti-Communist. When Republican Teodoro Picado Michalski succeeded Calderón in 1944, he continued the alliance with the Communists. Conservative opposition rallied behind newspaper publisher Otilio Ulate Blanco, who formed a new National Union Party to support his bid for the presidency in 1948. Under the leadership of José Figueres Ferrer, other middle-sector forces advocated a revolutionary program of anti-Communist but reformist social-democratic policies.

Partisan violence and terrorism by the social democrats escalated after 1946, as did labor unrest caused by the post–World War II economic slump. In the 1948 election, fraud by both sides and a problematic tally by the opposition-dominated electoral tribunal led the government bench in the legislature to invalidate the opposition win in the presidential race. This would have returned Calderón Guardia to the presidency, a prospect that convinced the opposition it would lose its chance to govern. This gave Figueres's social democrats a long-awaited pretext to rebel. Progovernment Calderonist and Communist forces fought a short, bloody civil war with Figueres's National Liberation insurgents. Aid and arms from Guatemala and other prodemocracy forces throughout the Caribbean tipped the balance and the rebels won.

The victorious National Liberation junta ruled for eighteen months. It dissolved many unions, outlawed the Communist Party, and enacted economic reforms such as the nationalization of all banks and a major tax on wealth. The junta called a Constituent Assembly to revise the 1871 Constitution and establish what Figueres called the Second Republic. The coffee aristocracy and other conservative elements, angered by the junta's revolutionary-reformist pretensions, won a majority of seats in the Constituent Assembly, blocked the social democrats, and preserved most of the 1871 Constitution. The Assembly enacted little change save one remarkable act; it abolished the armed forces and prohibited a standing army. The new constitution also established the Tribunal Supremo de Elecciones (TSE) in an effort to guarantee honest elections, and extended full suffrage to previously excluded women and blacks.

Having seen its backing shrink and having failed to implement its revolutionary goals, the frustrated National Liberation junta in 1949 relinquished power to the victor of the 1948 election, Otilio Ulate. The National Liberation leaders then transformed their own movement into a political party, the Partido de Liberación Nacional (PLN). Its platform was influenced by founder Figueres's links to Peruvian Victor Raúl Haya de la Torre's APRA, and by the reformism of Volio's 1920s Reformist Party. The PLN accepted most of the social reforms of the Calderón era and promoted increased governmental participation in the economy.

The 1948 Liberation victory and the PLN's eventual rise to power together transformed the Costa Rican political elite by incorporating into it urban and rural middle-sector representatives. The PLN's presidential candidate, José Figueres, won the 1953 election, and for three decades thereafter the party would virtually dominate Costa Rican politics. The PLN usually controlled the Legislative Assembly even when it had lost the presidency. By relinquishing power to Ulate in 1949, and again after its 1958 election loss to the Unidad ("Unification" or "Union") party coalition, the

PLN reinforced the integrity of elections in Costa Rica. More important, it contributed to the consolidation of what Peeler calls the "democratic regime," an agreement among major political forces to accommodate each other and abide by liberal democratic rules.[23] By 1958, the PLN and a group of conservative parties had thus established an effective working arrangement among major middle-sector political actors and representatives of the national coffee/commercial/industrial bourgeoisie that for decades afterward constituted the essence of the contemporary Costa Rican regime. Despite losing presidential elections five times from 1953 through 1998 (see Table 8.2), only twice (1990–1994, 1998–2002) did the PLN simultaneously lose both the presidency and its Assembly majority. Thus the PLN imposed and protected its social and economic policies by rarely being out of power.

POLITICAL INSTITUTIONS, BEHAVIOR, AND BELIEFS

Election Administration and Voting Rights

Peeler contends that liberal democracy in Costa Rica (and Venezuela) could not have survived without something "most untypical of Latin America: honest elections. . . . The establishment of liberal democracies . . . included the creation of powerful, independent agencies to administer the electoral process, agencies carefully structured to assure that neither the government nor any party could covertly control an election."[24]

The 1949 Constitution gave the TSE "exclusive responsibility for the organization, direction, and vigilance of acts relative to suffrage, [as well as] independence in carrying out its responsibility."[25] The TSE normally consists of three magistrates and six *suplentes* (substitutes) who are appointed to staggered six-year terms by the Supreme Court of Justice. During election periods the TSE expands to five magistrates by temporarily incorporating two of the *suplentes*. The TSE maintains voter lists and operates the national Civil Registry (which issues the mandatory national identity cards that also serve as voter registration documents).[26] The TSE may investigate charges of political partiality by public employees, file criminal charges against persons violating electoral laws, scrutinize and validate election results, and control the police and other security forces during election periods so as to "assure that electoral processes develop in conditions of guarantees and unrestricted liberties."[27] It also regulates campaign organizations' compliance with electoral law, monitors executive branch campaign neutrality, and disburses governmental campaign subsidies. So effective is the TSE in its conduct of elections that it "has all but eradicated the incidence of fraud in Costa Rican elections. Costa Rica's reputation for fairness and honesty in elections is one of the highest in the world."[28]

Table 8.2   Election Results, 1948–1998

Year	Candidates	Party	Vote (thousands)	Percentage of Vote	Turnout as % of Populace
1948	Otilio Ulate B.	Unión Nacional	55	54	12.4
	R. A. Calderón G.	Republican Nacional	45	44	
	Other		3	2	
1953	José Figueres F.	Liberación Nacional	123	65	21.0
	Fernando Castro C.	Democrático	67	35	
1958	Mario Echandi J.	Unión Nacional	103	46	19.8
	Francisco Orlich B.	Liberación Nacional	95	43	
	Jorge Rossi Ch.	Independiente	24	11	
1962	Francisco Orlich B.	Liberación Nacional	193	50	29.7
	R. A. Calderón G.	Republicano	136	35	
	Otilio Ulate B.	Unión Nacional	52	14	
	Other		3	1	
1966	José J. Trejos F.	Unificación Nacional	223	51	29.4
	Daniel Oduber Q.	Liberación Nacional	219	49	
1970	José Figueres F.	Liberación Nacional	296	55	31.6
	Mario Echandi J.	Unificación Nacional	222	41	
	Others		17	4	
1974	Daniel Oduber Q.	Liberación Nacional	295	43	34.0
	Fernando Trejos E.	Unificación Nacional	206	30	
	Jorge González	Nacional Independiente	74	11	
	Rodrigo Carazo O.	Renovación Democrática	62	9	
	Others		41	7	
1978	Rodrigo Carazo O.	Unidad	419	50	39.5
	Luis A. Monge A.	Liberación Nacional	363	44	
	Others		49	6	
1982	Luis A. Monge A.	Liberación Nacional	568	59	42.5
	R. A. Calderón F.	Unidad	325	34	
	Others		72	7	
1986	Oscar Arias S.	Liberación Nacional	620	52	46.8
	R. A. Calderón F.	Unidad Social Cristiana	542	46	
	Others		22	2	
1990	R. A. Calderón F.	Unidad Social Cristiana	695	51	46.2
	C. M. Castillo	Liberación Nacional	637	47	
	Others		17	2	
1994	J. M. Figueres O.	Liberación Nacional	739	50	45.9
	M. A. Rodríguez E.	Unidad Social Cristiana	711	48	
	M. Salguero	Fuerza Democrática	28	2	
	Others		14	1	
1998	J. M. Corrales B.	Liberación Nacional	655	45	39.7
	M. A. Rodríguez E.	Unidad Social Cristiana	685	47	
	Others		116		

Sources: Harold H. Bonilla, Los presidentes, vol. 2 (San José: Editorial Universidad Nacional Estatal a Distancia, Editorial Costa Rica, 1979), pp. 823–825; John A. Booth, "Representative Constitutional Democracy," in Steve C. Ropp and James A. Morris, eds., Central America: Crisis and Adaptation (Albuquerque: University of New Mexico Press, 1984), table 5.2; Carlos F. Denton and Olda María Acuña, La elección de un presidente: Costa Rica 1982 (San José, Costa Rica: Instituto de Libro del Ministerio de Cultura, Juventud, y Deportes, 1984), pp. 117–128; Roberto Tovar Faja, Partido Unidad Social Cristiana: Bosquejo histórico (San José, Costa Rica: Litografia e Imprenta LIL, 1986); Inter-American Development Bank, Economic and Social Progress in Latin America: 1987 Report, p. 270, and Inter-American Development Bank, Economic and Social Progress in Latin America: 1995 Report (Washington, DC: IADB, 1995), p. 262; Rubén Hernández Valle, "Costa Rica: 4 de febrero de 1990," Boletín Electoral Latinoamericano 3 (Jan.-June 1990): 13; Jorge Rovira Mas, "Costa Rica: 6 de febrero de 1994," Boletín Electoral Latinoamericano 3 (Jan.-June 1990): 51; John A. Booth, Costa Rica: Quest for Democracy (Boulder, CO: Westview, 1998), pp. 46, 67.

Costa Rican citizens eighteen years old or older are required to vote, under mild (but seldom imposed) penalties for not voting. The 1949 Constitution requires the government to register all citizens, to provide representation for minorities, and to make effective guarantees of "liberty, order, purity, and impartiality on the part of government authorities."[29] Almost all eligible Costa Ricans register to vote. Except in 1998, when only 71 percent of those registered voted, turnout in elections since 1960 has exceeded 80 percent.[30]

Political Parties[31]

Costa Rica's multimember districting and proportional representation have encouraged the survival of small parties, but after 1986 only two groups vied effectively for the presidency: the social-democratic PLN and the Partido de Unificación Social Cristiana (PUSC). The PUSC formed in the mid-1980s from the centrist and conservative parties of the Unidad coalition that had pulled together for most elections after 1950. The PLN and the PUSC/Unidad coalition have alternated in power several times. Peeler argues, "It is inconceivable that liberal democracy could have been maintained in [Costa Rica] without . . . the regular practice of alternation of parties in the presidency."[32]

The PLN is the largest and strongest party. Founded in 1951 by José Figueres from his 1948 rebel movement, the PLN became a highly organized, multiclass, permanent party committed to social-democratic ideology and policies. The PLN's major base is in the middle class; it has important links to organized labor through the Confederación Costarricense de Trabajadores Democráticos (CCTD). All PLN presidents until 1986 came from the National Liberation junta of 1948–1949: José Figueres (1953–1958, 1970–1974), Francisco Orlich (1962–1966), Daniel Oduber (1974–1978), and Luis Alberto Monge (1982–1986). A new PLN leadership generation ascended when Oscar Arias Sánchez, a young leader groomed in several top party and government posts, won the PLN presidential nomination and the presidency in 1986. José Figueres's son, José María Figueres Olsen, won the presidency for the PLN in 1994. Ideological dissensus arose within the PLN during the late 1980s and early 1990s as some business-linked leaders pushed the party to repudiate social democracy and embrace neoliberalism.

The opposition coalition of center-right parties and personalities, including remnants of Calderón Guardia's Republican Party, merged into the Partido de Unificación Social Cristiana in 1983. The PUSC's constituent parties included supporters and activists from various classes, and the new party drew from a broad base that included working-class support once attracted by the charismatic Calderón Guardia. In its previous incarnations under the banners of Unidad, Unión, and Unificación, the coalition had won the presidency three times: Mario Echandi (1958–1962), José

Joaquín Trejos (1966–1970), and Rodrigo Carazo (1978–1982). In 1986 the newly minted PUSC lost its first election with Rafael Angel Calderón Fournier heading its ticket. But in 1990 the PUSC prevailed with Calderón F. again its nomineee, and also took a majority in the Assembly. In 1998 the PUSC's Miguel Angel Rodríguez Echeverría won the presidency, but with a smaller percentage and a smaller total vote than he had lost with in 1994 (Table 8.2).

Another significant party group has been the leftist coalition known as the Partido Pueblo Unido (PPU) consisting of the old pro-Soviet Popular Vanguard (Communist) Party, the Socialist Party, and the People's Revolutionary Party. Despite involvement in labor unrest during the 1970s and 1980s, the leftist parties generally made moderate, reformist (rather than revolutionary) demands. Electoral support for the left came mainly from the Gulf Coast banana regions around Golfito, San José's working-class neighborhoods, and from some intellectuals and students. Electoral support for the left grew slowly but steadily throughout the 1970s, then declined steadily after 1982. Factors driving the left's electoral decline included its ties to organized labor and the disastrous 1984 banana strike, anticommunism in the press, the split of the Popular Vanguard Party in 1985, Costa Rica's tensions with revolutionary Nicaragua during the 1980s, and the loss of external support upon the demise of the Soviet bloc.

Costa Rica's political party system has apparently become more fragmented since the 1950s as the number of parties contesting elections and the number of presidential candidates have steadily increased. However, the number of parties winning Assembly seats grew only slightly between the 1950s and the 1990s. In presidential elections the combined PLN and PUSC/Unidad vote has exceeded 90 percent in nine of the twelve elections between 1953 and 1998. The PLN/PUSC vote total averaged 96.5 percent from 1986 through 1998. In sum, the party system has become strongly two-party dominant.

State Structure and Strength

Costa Rica differs notably from other Latin American nations in its distribution of authority among branches of government. There exist important checks on executive power, and both the Legislative Assembly and the judiciary enjoy unusual strength and independence relative to the executive. The absence of a standing army greatly strengthens the authority of civil government, and extensive and generally respected social, economic, and civil guarantees provide a framework that facilitates citizen political participation.[33]

The Costa Rican state is unitary, dominated by a highly legitimate central government. The powers and attributes of the nation's seventy-five municipal (county) governments are modest; the provincial governments are ephemeral. State power is widely dispersed among the branches of government.

The president serves a single four-year term, and may not be reelected.[34] The president heads the executive branch, but shares administrative, treaty-making and other foreign-policy, budget-writing, appointment, legislative initiative, and veto powers with his cabinet ministers.[35] The president alone names and removes cabinet members, and is commander in chief of the security forces (police and Civil Guard).[36] The president must have the approval of the Legislative Assembly to leave the country. Countering these executive weaknesses, economic crises and external lender pressures beginning in the 1980s shifted power markedly toward the presidency. Presidents have greatly increased issuing decrees and regulations to set economic policy while legislative power has retreated.[37]

Costa Rica circa 1980 had almost two hundred autonomous administrative agencies, created independently from the central ministries in order to free them from undue political manipulation and increase their technical capacity. They were typically run by independent, appointed boards not subject to presidential removal. Many provided key public services such as electrification, telephones, water and sewer service, agrarian reform, and municipal and community development assistance. Once fiscally autonomous, the decentralized agencies borrowed prodigiously, driving the runaway public debt in the 1970s and contributing to the resulting currency crises. The Assembly reined them in during the 1980s (but also made them more subject to political manipulation). Structural adjustment programs, including privatization, cut the number of autonomous agencies to 118 by 1994.

The unicameral Legislative Assembly (Asamblea Legislativa) has fifty-seven seats elected (proportionally to population) from Costa Rica's seven provinces; legislators' terms coincide with the president's terms. The Assembly's powers include the following: to amend the constitution;[38] legislate; declare war and peace; approve the national budget; levy taxes; ratify treaties; authorize the suspension of civil liberties; impeach and censure high officials; require information from government ministers; and appoint the national comptroller and the magistrates of the Supreme Court of Justice and the TSE. The Assembly may override an executive veto by a two-thirds vote. In comparison to other Latin American legislatures, the Assembly is quite powerful. Because it makes key national policy decisions and provides extensive pork-barrel funding, citizens and special interests heavily lobby its members. As executive power grew in the 1980s, the Assembly lost influence. Under the pressure of external lenders, presidents used emergency decree powers and other executive authority deriving from the very real national economic straits to take over much fiscal policy. The

Assembly sharply reduced its overall legislative output and increasingly preoccupied itself with funding small local projects (a tradition) as its effective control over the budget and other public policy shrank.

The seventeen magistrates of the Supreme Court of Justice (Tribunal Supremo de Justicia), appointed by the Legislative Assembly, automatically serve two, eight-year terms unless specifically rejected by the Assembly after their first. The court's powers include judicial review of extant and proposed legislation, hearing appeals from lower courts, and appointing lower-court judges. The Supreme Court has largely escaped the corruption and lack of independence of other Latin American high courts; it frequently rules against the government and strongly defends individual rights. One example of judicial independence came when the court overruled the José Figueres administration's granting of a passport to notorious fugitive financier Robert Vesco in the mid-1970s, despite the popular president's personal involvement on Vesco's behalf. However, lower Costa Rican courts lack the reputation for honesty and impartiality of the Supreme Court. Costa Rica has experienced an explosive growth of litigation since the 1960s and has expanded the number and types of its courts to accommodate the caseload.[39]

Overall, the Costa Rican state has considerable political resources when compared with its Central American neighbors: (1) the absence of a large, politicized army frees fiscal resources, promotes continuity of policy application, and permits political flexibility; (2) a high level of state legitimacy and the political culture's emphasis on compromise and conciliation tend to prevent or reduce the alienation of many interest groups and to ameliorate social cleavages; and (3) policy innovativeness. Some critics fear that recent shifts in power toward the executive and away from the legislature have sacrificed democracy for efficacy in policymaking and externally imposed economic liberalization. Once subject to executive-legislative policy stalemates and a heavily regulated economy with considerable state ownership, Costa Rica in the 1990s saw its presidents gain economic policy influence, shrink the public sector, and liberalize and privatize the economy.

There are also important constraints upon state power and resources: (1) Trimming government and the public payroll in the 1990s has reduced the power of public-sector unions, but organized citizens often protested (sometimes violently) and successfully pressured the government for policy concessions that undermined public-sector economic discipline. (2) Costa Rica remains a relatively poor country whose structurally adjusted state has fewer policy instruments to bring to bear on policy problems. (3) Costa Rica's dependency on exporting price-elastic bananas and coffee was diminished by booming tourism and nontraditional exports, but finding a niche in the world economy will likely remain a continuing challenge. Although the grave debt crisis of the 1980s eased with greater fiscal discipline and renewed economic growth, external debt in 1994 nevertheless remained a very high 53 percent of GDP.[40]

Church and Media

Throughout the nineteenth century the sociopolitical role of the church was limited by Costa Rica's isolation and poverty. In the late nineteenth century, the church increased its political role under the leadership of an activist Jesuit bishop, Monsignor Bernardo Thiel, who advocated fair wages for workers and mobilized a short-lived Catholic party in response to anticlerical reforms by Liberal governments. This led to the expulsion of the Jesuits from Costa Rica, further weakening the church. In the 1940s, activist Archbishop Sanabria promoted labor unions and supported the administration and sociopolitical reforms of populist president Calderón Guardia and his Communist allies. Later, Sanabria tried but failed to head off the conflict that led to the 1948 civil war. After the war, however, the church cooperated somewhat with the National Liberation movement's efforts to break up the Communist-dominated union movement. Under more conservative later archbishops, the Costa Rican Catholic Church has remained consistently less influential than in the 1940s.[41]

The press in Costa Rica generally functions freely and without government censorship. Paid newspaper advertisements are a major form of political discourse in Costa Rica. The state regulates the practice of journalism through a state-sanctioned professional association and restricts ownership of the mass media to Costa Rican citizens. A leftist shortwave radio station broadcasting to South America was closed in 1980 after protests from the Argentine government. Debate and discussion in the printed press is vigorous, and Costa Ricans have unrestricted access to a prodigious array of ideological and political viewpoints. Ownership of major media is concentrated among a few persons with conservative political leanings and with business links to major concentrations of national capital. Media owners consistently articulate such conservative positions as support for economic neoliberalism and anticommunism.[42]

Political Culture

Costa Rica is a participatory society.[43] Although Costa Ricans often characterize themselves as uncooperative, individualistic, and difficult to mobilize, they in fact frequently vote, join and take part in organizations, electioneer and do other party activities, engage in communal self-help activities, discuss politics and community affairs, and contact public officials. They do so at levels often higher than in other Third World and Latin American nations, and at levels only slightly lower, if at all, than in the United States and Europe. Although Costa Ricans view themselves as

pacific, the country regularly experiences unconventional and confrontational political participation (demonstrations, strikes, riots). Political violence, however, is low by Central American standards.

Costa Rican political culture has the previously noted egalitarian traits,
reinforced by the nineteenth century's scarcity of agricultural labor. In
much of the Hispanic world, long-standing semifeudal agrarian traditions
resulted in elaborate cultural systems of deference. In contrast, Costa Rica's
relative economic equality imbued mass culture with a sense of the fundamental worth of each citizen; such beliefs have survived despite the subsequent development of great economic inequality.[44] Contemporary Costa
Ricans manifest little reticence about expressing their opinions to persons
of greater status, wealth, or influence. A political scientist colorfully illustrated this point, "El Tico trata de 'vos,' 'mierda,' e 'hijueputa' hasta con el
presidente!"[45]

Costa Ricans tend to behave in a democratic fashion in collective settings, painstakingly hearing all points of view and voting to make decisions. Recent surveys have shown that Costa Ricans generally support
democratic civil liberties, though they tend to be intolerant of certain types
of participation by critics of the political system. In particular, Costa Ricans
generally disapprove of participation by "communists" despite the long-
standing involvement in the nation's politics of the Popular Vanguard Party
and its communist predecessors.

Anticommunism has been prominently present in Costa Rica's political
culture since the late 1940s, in part because of resentment of certain abuses
of power and electoral fraud during the Communist Party's participation in
power from 1942 to 1948. The PLN dismantled much of the Communist-
led CTCR and developed competing unions and confederations in order to
prevent consolidation of a conflict-oriented labor movement. The radical
left, once able to elect a few legislators, had lost most of its electoral clout
and legislative seats by the 1990s.

A 1995 survey of Costa Rican urban dwellers revealed certain patterns
of political culture: low levels of interpersonal trust, high life satisfaction
(despite recent economic problems), religious fundamentalism, and anticommunism. Most identified with the political center or moderate right (73
percent), expressed high levels of diffuse support (pride in national institutions—81 percent), and felt "completely free" to take part in politics (77
percent). About half expressed medium levels of political efficacy. Large
majorities supported democratic norms and rejected such political methods
as coups d'etat, civil disobedience, and radical change rather than reform.
Even Costa Ricans with relatively lower democratic norms scores (communal activists, youths, and ideological extremists) tended to support democratic liberties.[46]

Mario Carvajal's intriguing 1971 survey found some significant differences between mass and elite political values.[47] More elites were dissatis-

fied with the government's management of public affairs (74 percent) than ordinary citizens (30 percent). More elites (84 percent) than ordinary citizens (28 percent) saw a need for basic changes in the Costa Rican political system. Elites were more ideological than ordinary citizens. Elites disagreed that parties should alternate in office (66 percent opposed it), whereas 59 percent of the citizen sample favored it. Strong majorities of both samples expressed satisfaction in voting, and few in either sample favored revolutionary change. A 1995 urban survey, in contrast, found little difference between masses and elites with regard to preferring radical change, diffuse support, or democratic norms.[48]

Costa Rican political culture also promotes compromise and consensus. Parties to a dispute tend to seek mutually acceptable solutions rather than to hold unswervingly to initial principles or positions, permitting compromise and face-saving on both sides. As practiced by the political elite since 1948, this value has often contributed to innovative public policy designed to co-opt the disgruntled into the system, rather than to defeat and exclude them from it. For example, the victorious National Liberation junta in 1948 retained two of Calderón Guardia's most criticized policies, the labor code and social-security system, in order to mollify the defeated left.

Despite predominantly peaceful political intercourse since 1948, Costa Ricans sometimes resort to violence. Those employing violent political demand-making since 1980 have included banana workers, residents of the depressed Atlantic zone, landless peasants, informal-sector vendors, housing activists, ideological extremists, and citizens protesting utility rate increases. The violence (sometimes including gunplay) has on occasions been premeditated, both by protesters and by police.

Unlike neighboring nations, however, government response to confrontation and protest has generally been moderate. The Costa Rican government tends to employ force cautiously and to seek compromise. Such moderation has usually defused violence and contained conflict to the original issue. Although political violence rose in the 1980s, the press and most parties' politicians have tended to disavow violence. Thus, even when violence occurs, it is rarely extolled even by extremist parties and is generally regarded as exceptional and warranting special efforts to resolve its causes.

Even though both parties to the 1948 conflict employed terrorism, it had so long been absent from the national scene that several terrorist incidents during the 1980s shocked Costa Ricans. Stimulated by large immigrant communities, revolution in the isthmus, and foreign espionage, terrorist activity rose in the 1980s but abated in the 1990s as the region's geopolitical temperature declined.[49] Despite this surge, terrorism remained limited in Costa Rica, especially compared to other Central American societies. Neither rightist nor leftist terrorist groups enjoyed a significant popular base.

Even during periods of unrest, popular support for national political institutions has remained strong and widespread. In 1971, Carvajal found broad support for the Costa Rican governmental system and for elections, regardless of levels of political activity or education, a finding confirmed by subsequent surveys.[50] Even more interesting, Mitchell Seligson and Edward Muller tracked Costa Ricans' levels of diffuse or general support for their political system through a national crisis in the early 1980s.[51] They reported that before Costa Rica's severe 1980 economic crisis (which prompted a 70 percent devaluation of the currency and very high inflation), "levels of system support were very high by any standard of comparison, [and] fell from 79.7 percent in the high category to 70.2 percent." However, the percentage expressing "low support" for the system barely increased (from 2.3 to 3.7 percent), "even though negative incumbent evaluations had more than tripled between 1978 and 1980." Three years later and after a new government had responded to the economic crisis, "positive incumbent evaluations had risen from less than one-third in 1980 to over two-thirds in 1983, and negative evaluations had dropped from one-third to only 5 percent.[52] This constitutes clear evidence of the legitimacy that has enabled the Costa Rican system to remain stable through political and economic crises.

State, Socioeconomic Structure, and Development

The social-democratic premise shaping Costa Rican economic development from 1948 through 1982 was that unfettered capitalism causes undesirable socioeconomic dislocations and inequalities. The state would therefore constrain markets through regulation of business, public ownership of certain enterprises, joint public-private ventures, tariffs, currency controls, and social guarantees that would redistribute income to the middle class and poor. The 1980s economic crisis gave international lenders and domestic conservatives enough leverage to force Costa Rica to abandon this strategy and adopt a neoliberal development model.

The social-democratic development model steadily expanded the state's economic role until the 1980s. Public-sector monopolies included banking, insurance, telephone and electrical service, railroads, ports, and refineries. The state invested in mass transit and alcohol and banana production, and regulated the currency, exports, imports, consumer prices, agricultural production, and the environment. The government subsidized health care, higher education, and housing. The government's budget as a percent of GDP ranged from 11 to 12 percent from 1970 through 1985. The overall public-sector share of GDP (government spending plus state-owned enterprises) reached 28 percent in 1983. The government's share of the workforce trebled from 6.1 percent in 1950 to 19.1 percent in 1985.[53]

Costa Rica's large public sector, long criticized by conservatives as inefficient and excessively costly, entered a profound crisis in the early 1980s. A regional recession began in the 1970s and deepened in the 1980s, prompting the government and autonomous agencies to borrow heavily to maintain their spending. Costa Rica eventually borrowed so much that it had to default on its foreign debt (which peaked at 147 percent of GDP in 1983). In order to resolve the resulting crisis, Costa Rica made a series of structural-adjustment agreements with the International Monetary Fund, Interamerican Development Bank, and the U.S. and European governments. These accords required a dramatic liberalization of the economy and reduction of the government's budget and workforce. As it unfolded through a series of economic policy reforms taken in exchange for bailout loans, the new neoliberal development strategy had profound effects. The government budget's share of GDP fell from 11.1 to 8.6 percent from 1985 to 1994. The public sector's share of the total workforce declined by one-seventh between 1980 and 1989. Education spending dropped 35 percent and health spending fell almost 50 percent for the same period. Public-sector infrastructure investment shrank sharply. Taxes shifted away from incomes and to sales and imports. The state divested most of its enterprises. Living standards declined because of the severe recession and public-sector cutbacks, and many Costa Ricans angrily took to the streets in protest. To ameliorate these problems, the government almost doubled social-assistance programs and boosted spending on housing by half between 1980 and 1989.[54]

Costa Rica's 1950–1980 social-democratic development model produced steady and broadly felt improvement of popular well-being. Income redistribution and public services for the poor and middle classes increased living standards and decreased income inequality. As Table 8.3 reveals, from 1961 to 1971 income shifted away from the wealthiest quintile (20 percent) of the population (its share dropping from 60 to 51 percent), moved markedly toward the middle three quintiles (from 34 to 44 percent), and declined somewhat for the poorest quintile. From 1971 to 1983 the middle three quintiles' share remained static, while the richest quintile recovered a bit and the poorest quintile fell below 4 percent.

The economic crunch of the 1980s and dramatic shifts in public policy drove down real incomes and living standards. Intriguingly, social assistance programs to ameliorate these problems worked—they helped all four bottom quintiles of Costa Ricans gain income share from 1983 through 1992. In contrast, the richest quintile lost further ground. While no big jump in income inequality had occurred by early 1992, the new economic model's privatization, public-sector job layoffs and reduced social welfare, education, and health spending seem certain to negatively affect income distribution for the poor in the long term. Costa Rican public policy in the 1990s managed—despite contrary external pressures—to ameliorate inequality and poverty by usually keeping wages ahead of inflation and by occasional surges in deficit spending to stimulate the economy.

Because of the Costa Rican state's economic role and the national

Table 8.3   Income Distribution in Costa Rica, 1961–1992 (as percentage of national income earned by quintiles of income earners)

Quintiles	1961	1971	1977	1983	1992
Poorest 20 percent	6.0	5.4	3.6	3.9	4.9
Second quintile	7.8	9.3	8.4	8.5	9.4
Third quintile	9.8	13.7	13.5	13.8	14.5
Fourth quintile	16.4	21.0	21.1	20.3	22.1
Fifth quintile	60.0	50.6	53.4	53.0	49.1

Sources: Victor Hugo Céspedes S., "Evolución de la distribución del ingreso en Costa Rica" (Ciudad Universitaria Rodrigo Facio: Universidad de Costa Rica, Instituto de Investigaciones en Ciencias Económics, November 1979), table 6; Victor Hugo Céspedes, Alberto di Mare, and Ronulfo Jiménez, *Costa Rica: La economía en 1985* (San José: Academia de Centroamérica, 1986), p. 73; and Mitchell A. Seligson, Juliana Martínez F., and Juan Diego Trejos S., *Reducción de la pobreza en Costa Rica: El impacto de las políticas* (San José: United Nations Development Program, draft ms. dated 11/11/1995).

elites' consistent promotion of social welfare, Costa Ricans have the lowest infant mortality and disease rates and the highest literacy and life expectancy of all Central American countries.[55] These measures of well-being significantly improved during the 1960s and 1970s (see Table 8.4). In addition, a land-reform program in the 1960s and 1970s distributed some land to landless peasants, but it appears to have had little impact on the substantial inequality in the countryside reflected in the poorest quintile's declining income share (Table 8.3).

GDP in Costa Rica during the 1960s and 1970s grew at an average rate of over 6 percent per year (the third fastest in Latin America). GDP per capita (in constant dollars) nearly doubled during the same period, reflecting substantially better growth than in any other Central American country.[56] But in the 1980s, the Costa Rican economy entered a severe economic crisis from which it was still recovering in the late 1990s. Declining terms of trade, high levels of imports, and excessive foreign public debt brought about a default on foreign obligations, a dramatic devaluation of the *colón,* and more than a decade of recession.

In order to refinance its crushing debt, the Costa Rican government acceded to the pressures of international lenders (allied with key domestic economic interests) to reduce public spending, lower tariffs, permit private banking, and privatize public enterprises. The Luis A. Monge and Oscar Arias administrations (1982–1990) dragged their feet, reluctant to abandon the PLN's distinctive development model. Necessity and the international bankers prevailed, however, and reforms accelerated after 1990. By the mid-1990s, the net impact of this restructuring was a revolutionary redesign of the national economic development model from a redistributive, social-democratic approach to a less redistributive, neoliberal development one. The promotion of nontraditional agricultural and industrial

Table 8.4   Selected Indicators of Socioeconomic Change

| Indicators | Costa Rica | | | | Other Lower-Middle Income Countries |
	1927	1960	1980	1994	ca. 1994
Per capita GDP (U.S.$)[a]	—	1332	2222	2283	1488
Percentage of literate adults	66	84[b]	90	95	80[c]
Infant mortality (per 1,000 births)	—	83	20	13	36
Life expectancy at birth (years)	—	62	73	77	67
Percentage of economically active population in:					
Agriculture	63	51	35	26	36
Industry	12	19	23	27	27
Services	7	30	48	47	37
Percentage of urban dwellers	20	37	44	49	56

Sources: Unless otherwise specified, drawn from World Bank, *World Development Report 1983* (New York: Oxford University Press, 1983), statistical appendix, and World Bank, *World Development Report 1996* (Oxford: Oxford University Press, 1996), statistical appendix.

Notes: a. Estimate based on Inter-American Development Bank, *Economic and Social Progress in Latin America: 1987 Report* (Washington, DC: IADB, 1987), p. 426; and Inter-American Development Bank, *Economic and Social Progress in Latin America: 1995 Report* (Washington, DC: IADB, 1995), tables B1, B2.

b. Estimate from Mavis Hiltunen de Biesanz et al., *Los costarricenses* (San José: Editorial Universidad Nacional a Distancia, 1979), p. 399.

c. Estimate based on data in World Bank, *World Development Report 1996* (New York: Oxford University Press, 1996).

export goods and tourism had replaced previous emphasis on traditional exports (coffee and bananas) and on import-substitution industrialization. Under these policies, external debt declined and recovery began, but public services in infrastructure, health, education, and welfare had been sharply curtailed.[57]

Observers have long credited some of Costa Rica's political stability to the effects of the social-democratic development model that elevated citizens' living conditions well above those in other developing nations (Table 8.4). The new neoliberal development model, if it proves successful, may continue to improve Costa Ricans' well-being. If unsuccessful, however, neoliberalism may diminish both, increase inequality, and perhaps challenge the long-term stability of the political system.

Organizational Demands[58]

High levels of formal organization distinguish Costa Rica. Citizens take part in many groups, and through them make demands of the government.

A 1973 national survey found that family heads reported a mean of 1.5 organizational memberships each. Two-thirds of the sample reported having held office in some group, and about 60 percent attended with medium frequency. About 56 percent reported having engaged in at least one project to improve their communities, an activity that frequently brought people into contact with public officials. A 1995 survey of urban Costa Ricans reported even higher levels of activity in school, communal, and other kinds of organizations. These findings suggest that Costa Ricans remain active organizational participants.

The tendency to organize is not new in Costa Rica. The government organized guilds of key artisans as early as the 1830s; independently organized guilds of professionals and mutual-aid societies appeared in the 1850s, community improvement groups in the 1880s, and modern labor unions in the early twentieth century. Government-promoted cooperatives and health, nutrition, and community improvement groups proliferated after 1950. Various new social movements—groups seeking housing, land, and even foreign policy changes—sprang up after 1970. The Ministry of Labor and Social Security in 1977 estimated there to be 417 unions with 132,000 members, and 327 cooperatives in Costa Rica.[59] Except for labor unions, which had lost some ground, there appeared to be even more organizations by the mid-1990s. Costa Rica thus abounds with organizations, and most of them—especially business and producer groups, unions, cooperatives, and self-help groups—make demands on the government. The Costa Rican government has traditionally responded favorably to group pressure. A 1973 nationwide survey of organizations and their projects in over a hundred communities found that a substantial majority had received some form of outside assistance, usually from the national or municipal governments.[60] A 1995 survey reported that 35 percent of urban Costa Ricans had contacted at least one public official.

Costa Rican organizations usually initiate their demand by contacting the competent authority through regular channels, sometimes with the help of someone with political contacts or prestige, later followed by higher appeals if unsuccessful. When such efforts fail, groups sometimes escalate demands through confrontational tactics such as demonstrations, civil disobedience, or consumer or employee strikes. The government generally responds to such confrontation with study and compromise to defuse the conflict.

Organized labor constitutes an important but divided interest sector.[61] Government policies have fragmented, and restrictive laws hobbled, organized labor since the 1948 defeat of the Calderón-Communist populist alliance. Overall, only about 19 percent of the workforce was organized in unions and professional associations in 1977, a moment at which membership was near its historic peak. In the late 1970s, 40 percent of Costa Rica's unions (teachers, health/hospital employees, telephone and electrical system workers, and other government and autonomous agency employees) remained independent from the several labor confederations. The independent unions generally pressed middle-sector demands and often won benefits for public employees.

Four major confederations divided the rest of the unionized workforce. The Christian Democratic Confederation had about 4 percent of the organized workforce. The social-democratic Confederación Costarricense de Trabajadores Democráticos—affiliated with the American Institute for Free Labor Development and the Interamerican Regional Labor Organization—had about 16 percent, and a CCTD splinter known as the Confederación Auténtica de Trabajadores Democráticos (CATD) another 8 percent.[62] CATD and CCTD leaders have close links to the National Liberation Party.

The Communist-dominated Confederación General de Trabajadores Democráticos—built since the CTCR was dismantled in 1948—and other Communist-led unions united in 1980 into the Confederación Unitaria de Trabajadores (CUT), which represented about a third of the organized workforce.[63] Strongly oriented toward class struggle, the CUT promoted several violent banana-worker strikes that failed to win higher wages, but prompted United Fruit to leave Costa Rica. A subsequent leadership struggle split the CGT. Union membership has declined ever since, partly due to the recession. In 1986 a new coalition of independent federations arose, Consejo Permanente de Trabajadores (CPT).

Another type of labor organization is "solidarity associations," which had some 40,000 members in about 230 groups as of the early 1980s—around 8 percent of the total workforce. Solidarity-association employers make modest profit-sharing contributions to the associations, which employees use mainly as credit unions. Solidarity associations arose out of a private-sector initiative informed by conservative social-Christian theory in the late 1940s. The PLN also backed them in order to weaken organized labor. Dominated by the enterprises rather than workers, their principal political objective is "helping detain the advance of the popular movement directed by the Popular Vanguard [Communist] Party."[64] Solidarity associations thus undercut class-conscious labor organizations, reduce labor conflict, and raise productivity by promoting patron-employee "cooperation." They have grown rapidly since the mid-1980s.

Another class of interest/pressure groups is the associations (colleges) of professionals, which are much more widespread than in the United States. These state-chartered groups (rather like U.S. state bar associations) officially represent their members' professional interests in the public-policy arena. They act as pressure groups for their members and have been important vehicles representing middle-sector interests.

Business pressure groups are numerous, and several exercise great influence over national economic policy. The Costa Rican Management

Association, the National Association for the Promotion of Enterprise, the Chamber of Commerce, the Chamber of Industries, and the National Union of Chambers represent private capital (or important subsectors of it). They strongly support business interests. Many, for instance, ardently lobbied the executive and legislature for neoliberal reforms. Business interests consistently exert considerable policy influence, apparently because entrepreneurs contribute to and otherwise support PLN and PUSC candidates, and because they often serve in public posts.

In summary, Costa Rica has numerous clearly articulated pressure groups making demands on the government, endorsing and backing candidates, and even placing members in administration. Associational cleavages have tended to be crosscutting, rather than mutually reinforcing. This has permitted the state and elites to reduce overt interclass competition for influence and benefits, despite the existence of effective political organizations representing lower-class, middle-class, and bourgeois interests. The recession of the 1980s, however, intensified class conflict and mobilization of demands as the national economic pie shrank. The government, though deprived of some resources, struggled to ameliorate some problems, but interclass conflict seemed likely to grow under the new neoliberal development model.

Class Structure

Costa Rica's social structure has evolved rapidly since the onset of coffee exportation in the mid–nineteenth century. The population, one of the most rapidly growing in Latin America for much of the period since independence, rose from 60,000 in 1821 to 472,000 in 1927 to 3,604,300 in 1997. The capital city grew during the same period from a village to a modern city with over one-fourth of the nation's population. The overall percent of the populace residing in urban areas climbed from 37 to 49 percent between 1960 and 1997.

Seligson shows that the expansion of coffee production drove rapid urban growth and land ownership concentration by displacing small farmers from the land. Coffee also caused peasants displaced from the *meseta central* to colonize open peripheral lands, beginning the dispersion of the population throughout the national territory. By the 1970s this process exhausted cultivable public land available for colonization.[65]

The growth of exporting and importing and of urban centers brought increases in the service, manufacturing, and other sectors of the economy in the late nineteenth and early twentieth centuries. By 1927, one worker in eight labored in industry, and one person in nine lived in San José. As towns and new economic activities developed, multiple new interests mobilized into politics in conflict with the politically dominant coffee aristocracy, especially when the economy suffered from world recessions. Industrial and service sectors have continued to expand throughout the twentieth century. By the mid-1990s, 27 percent of the workforce labored in manufacturing, but only 26 percent remained in agriculture (see Table 8.4).

The assumption of new roles by the state during the 1940s at the beck and call of the burgeoning labor movement—roles expanded by the post–civil war governments—swelled the government and made public employees a key political and economic force. By the early 1980s, the service sector made up almost half the workforce, and two persons in seven lived in San José. The public sector (government employees) grew from about 6 percent of the workforce in 1950 to peak at around 19 percent in 1980. Public-sector employment subsequently contracted under structural adjustment to only 16.2 percent by 1989.[66]

The benefits of the expanded political power of the middle class since 1950 are compellingly reflected in the data on the changing distribution of income between 1961 and 1971 (see Table 8.3). The middle 60 percent of income earners increased its share notably between 1961 and 1971, while the share of the poorest fifth declined only modestly. The segment benefiting the most was the middle quintile, whose 1971 share of national income increased by 40 percent. The middle three quintiles include much of the populace represented by the labor unions, professional associations, and professional colleges discussed above. Most heavily represented in the poorest quintile are landless and land-poor peasants.

As in most developing countries, income inequality coincides with the huge gap between town and country. The social groups earning higher incomes disproportionately reside in the metropolitan area of San José and in the larger towns and cities. Citizens residing in the San José metropolitan area enjoy incomes several times greater than others, and have greater access to all manner of public services.[67] A 1979 study reported that three-fourths of Costa Rica's poorest families lived in rural areas, and that about two-thirds of these were rural nonfarm families (landless peasants).[68] While real progress in service distribution had been made by the 1990s, significant inequities remained.

Rural inequality remains the most extreme. The spread of coffee cultivation in the mid–nineteenth century created a large population of small-holding peasants, but in the late nineteenth and early twentieth centuries there occurred a great concentration of land ownership, coffee production, milling, and exportation in the hands of the emergent class of coffee capitalists. This greatly increased the percentage of landless peasants. Since then, the proportion of landless peasants has increased further. Some of the excess rural populace has been absorbed in the cities, but even so three-quarters of 183,000 persons working in agriculture in 1963 either had no land at all or less than two acres.

Despite government land redistribution efforts since the 1960s, land concentration and the impoverishment of peasants continued. Inequality in the ownership of land increased at least until the early 1980s. The lack of an agrarian census since 1983 obscures more recent trends, but other information provides certain clues. Continued rural economic deterioration of the 1980s caused a boom in peasant organizations that mobilized thousands of smallholder and landless campesinos. The most prominent of the 142 peasant groups identified in 1990 was the Unión de Pequeños y Medianos Agricultores (UPA Nacional), which demanded land reform and other public assistance.[69] Seligson's observations from the 1970s retain currency today because agriculture remains a mainstay of the economy:

> [I]t is the peasantry that bore the cost of economic development in the past and continues to do so in the present. Therefore, it is on the peasants' back that the coffee aristocracy and growing middle class ride. . . . To the extent that there has been economic development in Costa Rica, it has been a product of the ability of the elites to extract an even greater surplus from the underlying peasantry, while at the same time restricting the peasantry from partaking of the benefits of that developed society.[70]

These two trends—the shrinkage of the peasantry and increasing rural inequality and poverty—offer challenges for Costa Rican democracy. On one hand, the relative decline of the peasantry might be expected to reduce the overall significance of peasants as a potential political force. On the other hand, increasing rural poverty has driven unrest and peasant rebellion in many places, including neighboring Central America.[71] Although the Costa Rican peasantry did not rebel, serious economic strains represent a potential problem for political stability.

By way of summary, the breakdown of social classes described by Mavis Hiltunen de Biesanz and colleagues in the late 1970s is useful:[72]

• Half the upper class consists of an elite of roughly 1 percent of the population, earning about 10 percent of the national income and made up of aristocratic families descended from the conquerors. The other half consists of 1 percent of the population, earning a like amount of income but lacking aristocratic family connections. The wealth and income of both groups derive from large land holdings, especially in coffee production, from import-export and other commercial enterprises, and from industrial investments.

• The upper middle class, perhaps 5 percent of the population, includes merchants, industrialists, larger landholders, and prosperous professionals, whose earnings make up 10 percent of national income.

• The lower middle class, or perhaps 15 percent of Costa Ricans, consists of small-business owners, poorer professionals (such as most teachers), upper-level white-collar employees, and "relatively prosperous small farmers."[73] I estimate that their share of national income is roughly 20 percent.

• Roughly 50 percent of Costa Ricans fall into the working class, which earns between 40 and 45 percent of national income. In this class are steadily employed proletarians, some white-collar and most blue-collar public employees, manual laborers, smallholding peasants, and service workers.

• The lower class, made up of roughly one-quarter of the population, earns only about 7 percent of the national income. Among its members are landless and very land-poor peasants (except banana workers), domestic servants, unskilled urban laborers, street vendors, and others in the urban informal sector, including beggars, prostitutes, and bootblacks.

Racial and Religious Cleavages

Costa Rica is fairly homogeneous racially, culturally, and religiously because its original indigenous and black populations were almost completely assimilated into the predominant mestizo population.[74] However, there is some tendency to overstate racial and ethnic homogeneity and to overlook discrimination in Costa Rica.

About one-third of the Atlantic coastal area's population (and 3 percent of the nation's) is of African origin. Most blacks descend from Jamaicans hired as railroad and banana workers in the nineteenth century. The Atlantic zone developed pronounced racial discrimination and marked tensions between blacks and whites. The United Fruit Company moved its operations to the Pacific coast in the 1930s, but blacks were prohibited from following the company and their jobs there. Since then, the Atlantic region and its people have been mired in poverty.

In the 1990s, many blacks still spoke much English, did not share the culture of Latin Costa Rica, and resented the Hispanization of their education since 1948. Average income, economic status, employment, service delivery, and educational attainment of Atlantic-zone residents remained below national averages.[75] De jure discrimination no longer existed in Costa Rica, but cultural biases against blacks were common. Such reinforcing racial, religious, linguistic, cultural, and economic cleavages—aggravated by discrimination—may well contribute greatly to the riots that periodically shake the Atlantic port city of Limón.

Other significant minority groups include Costa Rica's indigenous people and a rapidly growing community of evangelical Protestants. Protestants, especially Pentecostals, increased from only 3 percent of the populace in the 1960s to over 11 percent by the 1990s.[76] The indigenous constituted less than 1 percent of Costa Ricans, but during the 1980s mobilized politically to demand more protections and rights.

International Pressures and Constraints

Costa Rica, without a standing army, has pursued a foreign policy of pacifism and qualified neutrality since 1950.[77] On the one hand, this has meant advocating peaceful resolution of international disputes, mediating between other Central American states in conflict, seeking international assistance (especially from the Organization of American States) when its national security was threatened, and resisting repeated U.S. pressures to expand its national security forces.[78] On the other hand, throughout the Cold War Costa Rica has generally aligned itself with the United States in international organizations and supported the Western alliance.

During the 1970s, Costa Rica acted somewhat more independently of the United States than previously (though it remained quite friendly). It renewed diplomatic ties with Cuba and overtly supported the insurrection against the Somoza regime in neighboring Nicaragua. But this pro-Sandinista stance (1977–1979) brought very real costs in terms of "important allies and links in the international environment."[79]

President Rodrigo Carazo reversed field and cooled Costa Rica's relations with Nicaragua after 1980 as the revolutionary government's Marxism and growing military power became evident. Under President Monge (1982–1986) relations with Nicaragua mixed official declarations of formal neutrality with practical cooperation with many U.S. anti-Sandinista efforts. Monge experienced heavy domestic pressure from the left (pro-Nicaragua groups and pacifists) and right, each mobilizing both within the government and in the streets.[80] Rather than seek to alter the constitution and build a costly army—and break with the country's most distinctive tradition—the Monge administration took a middle path of accepting escalated U.S. military assistance for its Civil Guard, including U.S.-run training. U.S. military assistance to Costa Rica rose from zero in 1980 to $2.5 million in 1983, and to $10 million in 1985.[81] Costa Rica also harbored anti-Sandinista guerrilla forces (Contras) backed by the United States, and permitted U.S. authorities to set up a Voice of America radio transmitter to broadcast into Nicaragua. This precarious policy package placated Washington, garnered vital increases in U.S. economic assistance, and provided a modest security counterweight against the Nicaraguan armed forces. But it also risked losing control over national territory to the Contras and brought escalated conflict with Nicaragua.

These changes had three main effects: First, Costa Rican democracy became less secure both from without (through increased regional turmoil and Nicaragua's growing military strength) and from within (because of the Contras and their domestic impact). Second, the strengthened Civil Guard and various paramilitary groups that sprang up appeared to threaten the security of civilian governments by introducing a new power contender into the Costa Rican polity. Terrorism by both leftists and rightists, inspired by regional geopolitical conflict and involving both foreign and domestic actors, became a serious problem. The resulting political turmoil, militarization, and escalating border tensions with Nicaragua generated considerable public anxiety about Costa Rica's future. When Oscar Arias adopted a pro-peace platform in his presidential campaign, he came from behind to win the 1986 election. Continuously monitoring public opinion, Arias subsequently pushed hard for the Central American peace accord signed in Guatemala in August 1987. Ultimately this agreement facilitated a cease-fire in Nicaragua and eased Costa Rican–Nicaraguan tensions. In 1990 Nicaraguans voted the Sandinistas out of power as the Cold War ended. Relations with Nicaragua quickly improved, and Costa Rica's domestic paramilitary groups, terrorism, and turmoil swiftly subsided. The democratic regime thus weathered largely intact the geopolitical hurricane of the 1980s, but not without some anxious years for Costa Ricans and outside observers.

Another international effect on Costa Rican democracy involved economic policy. From 1946 to 1975, Costa Rica received $208.5 million in U.S. economic assistance. From 1970 to 1981 foreign assistance was $523 million.[82] This aid and extensive public borrowing from foreign private lenders boosted the growth rate in the 1970s but built up $2.25 billion in public external debt by 1981 (a seventeenfold increase over the 1970 level)—an amount almost equal to a year's GNP.[83] Deteriorating terms of trade, a decline in the Central American Common Market, regional political tensions, and capital flight brought on the 1980 default on foreign obligations and caused a severe economic slump. In 1986, after three years of slow recovery, real GDP remained 8.3 percent below its 1980 level.[84]

In order to weather this crisis, Costa Rica required massive balance-of-payments aid, new credit, and a reorganization of its gargantuan foreign debt. The U.S. Agency for International Development and the IMF successfully pressured Costa Rica to implement a radical economic austerity program (curtailed imports and reduced deficit spending), and in return restructured the debt package. Although successive governments resisted many of the requisites contained in a series of structural-adjustment deals, the foreign lenders and key domestic allies eventually prevailed. In addition to causing Costa Rica to replace its social-democratic development model with a new, neoliberal one, foreign pressure had two negative effects on Costa Rican democracy. First, Costa Rica lost autonomy over its economic destiny. The exigencies of the debt and its repayment permitted foreign actors not accountable to Costa Rican voters to impose key economic policies. Second, the economic crisis forced the presidency to usurp (through executive decrees) much of the economic policymaking power of the popularly elected Legislative Assembly. Power thus shifted away from the people's representatives, and from domestic institutions to foreign ones.[85]

In sum, Costa Rica's economic development options (especially redistributive programs) were curtailed by the debt crisis and the resulting structural adjustment. Four decades of social-democratic development policy created and co-opted a substantial middle and working class, but the 1980s crisis and neoliberal structural reforms stripped the state of many policy instruments. Under neoliberalism, redistributive mechanisms and human capital investment policies were curtailed or dismantled, the economy made more open to foreign competition, and the government reduced in size. These changes had potential to invigorate the economy if successful, but they also risked increased income inequality and poverty. Such changes, should they occur, could sharply increase class conflict in Costa Rica and, perhaps, increase long-term instability.

THEORETICAL ANALYSIS

Liberal democracy in Costa Rica has roots that go back centuries, but the regime consolidated itself only in the aftermath of the 1948 civil war. During the colonial era and nineteenth century, many Latin American nations developed export-oriented economies based on militarily enforced, feudal, or forced-labor systems that exploited Indians and blacks. Their polities were dominated by the beneficiaries of that system—a landowning aristocracy that ruled by military power. In contrast, Costa Rica's isolation, emergent racial homogeneity, and poverty bred much less economic inequality while building a habit of civilian rule, weak military institutions, and egalitarian social values, when coffee production eventually permitted the Costa Rican social aristocracy to accumulate capital. Economic inequality therefore grew in the late nineteenth century, but did so during a labor shortage that made landowners dependent on scarce rural workers. This circumstance restrained the bourgeoisie's political and economic power. This interdependence among economic classes was reinforced by the organization, enfranchisement, and political mobilization of emergent middle-class and working-class interests.

Two remarkable political leaders (Ricardo Jiménez Oreamuno and Cleto González Víquez) developed elections and expanded popular suffrage as mechanisms for the *cafetaleros'* accommodation of growing popular demands in the first third of the twentieth century. As evolving class structures and economic crises impoverished many Costa Ricans after 1910, an ethic of social reformism (informed by social-Christian, social-democratic, *aprista,* and Marxist movements) developed within parts of the Costa Rican political elite. Calderón Guardia's populist reformism, burgeoning class conflict, and electoral fraud led to the 1948 civil war. Eventual accommodation between José Figueres's victorious middle-class National Liberation movement and the upper-class opponents of Calderón eventually bound both electoral integrity and social reformism into the modern Costa Rican political system.

From 1948 until the early 1980s, the commitment of the political elite (now expanded to include middle-class elements) to a social-democratic political philosophy expanded the economic role of the state, redistributed income toward the middle sectors, ameliorated some of the effects of poverty, and strongly supported electoral probity. Political institutions also promoted democratic consolidation. The 1949 Constitution decentralized the state, limited executive authority, and gave the courts and legislature more power than those of most Latin American polities. The abolition of the army in 1949 strengthened civilian institutions and freed economic resources for the state. The social democratic development model increased the size of the national economic pie and markedly increased the middle sectors' share of it for several decades. Two major, moderate, multiclass parties—the PLN and the PUSC (formerly the Unity coalition)—alternated in power and manifested commitment to the post-1949 constitutional rules of the game.

Costa Rican citizens have been politically mobilized, but associational cleavages have tended to crosscut one another. Deliberate elite and governmental efforts have divided and hamstrung organized labor. Extreme inequality has marked differences between the landed and landless in agriculture, between the capital and hinterland, and between the poor and middle/upper classes in urban areas. The lower classes, both urban and rural, recieved some attention from the state in the form of social welfare and land reform programs. A large middle sector (about half the population) benefited from redistributive public policies and programs. Neoliberalism, however, significantly undermined some redistributive programs after 1990.

Costa Rica's political culture has contributed significantly to the maintenance of democracy. Costa Ricans and their organizations have tended toward pacific demand making, and the state has traditionally acquiesced to such demands. Political elites and masses have shared a commitment to the system of alternating parties and clean elections. Even through hard times, Costa Ricans have usually remained loyal to the political system, regardless of their disapproval of momentary incumbents. Political confrontation and violence have been more common than usually recognized, but remained mild by regional standards. The state has reacted to them with moderation and conciliation.

Costa Rican political culture developed a preference for civilian rule and a drive for consensus and conciliation, while the configuration of the class system required upper-class co-optation of increasingly mobilized middle- and working-class elements. The resolution of the 1948 political crisis generated both electoral democracy and redistributive social policies. The high degree of political organization and participation among the populace and special interests is modulated by crosscutting allegiances and by a wide dispersion of effective power within and outside the state. One can hardly overstate the importance of this situation, variously described by Costa Rican scholars as the "neutralization of classes"[86] or the "interdependence of classes."[87]

CONCLUSIONS AND
PROSPECTS FOR COSTA RICAN DEMOCRACY

Costa Rica's class structures, state institutions, public policy, and popular and elite political culture have created a system of stable liberal democracy without parallel in Latin America. The economic crisis of the early 1980s demonstrated the short- and middle-run stability of the polity. Despite a plunge in economic activity and employment and soaring inflation that sharply lowered the standard of living of most Costa Ricans, and despite dramatically increased, geopolitically driven conflict and terrorism during the 1980s, the five national elections between 1982 and 1998 transpired normally. Ruling power passed peacefully from Carazo's National Unity government to two successive PLN administrations, then to the PUSC's Calderón Fournier, back to the PLN's Figueres Olsen, and back again to the PUSC's Rodríguez. Costa Rica's liberal democracy, however, is probably not invulnerable. Uruguay and Chile provide grim reminders that neither age nor tradition guarantees the survival of liberal democracies. Several potential threats to the stability of Costa Rican democracy can be identified.

The social-democratic public ideology that prevailed in Costa Rica from 1948 through 1982 has been replaced by neoliberalism. The state's role in the economy has diminished, and social-welfare programs have shrunk. The Costa Rican state thus became weaker in domestic resources and now enjoys less autonomy vis-à-vis external actors than it did before the onset of the crisis.

These changes have begun to reverse a decades-old trend of reducing income inequality and improving popular living standards. In the short run, public support for the political system remained high, but as of this writing it was too early to assess the implications of increasing poverty and inequality stemming from structural adjustment. One may reasonably surmise that eroding benefits for organized middle- and working-class groups could increase class conflict. Growing rural inequality and the potential for further erosion of services for and living standards of the urban poor might also provoke increased political conflict. On balance, the ability of a diminished Costa Rican state to contend with intense competing policy demands or a policy stalemate has eroded, unless economic growth should surge in the wake of recent reforms. (Poor economic performance in 1996 and 1997, however, suggests that a clear turnaround had not yet occurred.) Over the long run, escalated conflict could in turn increase governmental or private repression to curtail demands. Such increases in either conflict or repression could weaken public support for national institutions.

In the 1980s, Costa Rican animosity toward Nicaragua, encouraged by the United States, exploited by domestic actors for their own political reasons, and fed by old rivalries, also raised a potential threat to Costa Rican democracy. By 1985, anticommunist rhetoric in the press had risen to unprecedented levels, anti-Nicaraguan sentiment was intense, and rightist groups had attacked peace demonstrators and the Nicaraguan Embassy. There were discussions of "anti-Costa Ricanism " (strikingly similar to 1950s commentary about "un-Americanism" in the United States). Despite all this, little official persecution of suspected subversives occurred, and the election of Oscar Arias and the Central American peace accord of 1987 eventually ameliorated such troubling trends.[88]

Distaste for Sandinista rule and a fear of growing Nicaraguan military power contributed to some strengthening of Costa Rican military and paramilitary forces. The expansion and partial militarization of the Civil Guard sounded alarms for Costa Rican democratic and constitutional stability. By the end of the 1980s, however, the Arias administration had largely contained these problems. The end of the Cold War and the 1990 electoral defeat of the Sandinistas in Nicaragua eased Costa Rican and U.S. geopolitical anxieties about the threat of communism to the region and thus eliminated the impetus for militarization.

Finally, one can posit a possible worst-case scenario for Costa Rican democracy, yet one informed by the recent behavior of certain elites: In a moment of increased class conflict, popular unrest, or terrorism, elites from the right or center could overthrow the government in an effort to restore order and pursue particular policy objectives—as occurred in the 1948 civil war. Such events could, especially if popular organizations resisted, engender considerable violence, and democracy could be damaged or destroyed.

How likely is such a scenario? Among Costa Rican economic and political elites there are those who might profit from reduced democracy, curtailed political participation, and reduced benefits for the working and middle classes. Indeed, Daniel Oduber in 1979 publicly revealed that, while president, others had several times encouraged him to suspend the constitution and impose certain desired, but frustrated, policy initiatives through a dictatorship. During the Monge administration a decade later, certain entrepreneurial elites issued thinly veiled public threats to oust Monge should he fail to adopt a more belligerent posture toward Nicaragua. That none of these threats bore fruit indicates that the political values and skills of Costa Rica's leaders contribute to institutional stability. Such incidents made manifest, however, that not all elites hold democratic beliefs.[89]

External actors and forces can influence the Costa Rican liberal democratic regime. Costa Rica's huge foreign debt was managed, after 1980, largely by rescheduling, new borrowing, and austerity. The United States, European nations, and various intergovernmental lenders provided aid that ameliorated economic threats to Costa Rican democracy in the 1980s. But in exchange they required Costa Rica to adopt a new development model that has both short-term and long-term implications for democracy. These outside pressures eroded elected domestic actors' influence over economic policy and ballooned executive power within the political system. They thus arguably reduced the depth of democracy. The neoliberal economic model may also have increased the long-term risk of conflict and instability by decreasing the state's capacity to co-opt the middle and working classes.

Despite the enormous geopolitical strains placed upon Costa Rican democracy during the 1980s, the nation ultimately retained its institutional integrity. Regional and great-power forces made the country a geopolitical pawn and for a time seemed to threaten Costa Rican democracy in order to "save" it. These pressures eventually diminished, lowering their threat. As the fifth decade of its democracy ended, Costa Rica found itself among peaceful and newly democratic neighbors. Major external actors favored democracy in the region. These factors clearly enhance Costa Rica's democratic prospects. The range and breadth of participation in politics in Costa Rica remained extensive, but its depth has lessened. Should some future political or economic crisis harm the interests of major mobilized groups in Costa Rica, one might reasonably expect citizens to demand help from the government as they have so often done in the past. That could put them in conflict with extant elites, sharpen interclass conflict, increase political turmoil, and once again strain the pillars of liberal democracy in Costa Rica. The country's democratic edifice and culture weathered similar threats in the 1980s, and may well have the strength and resiliency to repeat this success.

NOTES

1. See John A. Booth, "Representative Constitutional Democracy in Costa Rica: Adaptation to Crisis in the Turbulent 1980s," in Steve C. Ropp and James A. Morris, eds., *Central America: Crisis and Adaptation* (Albuquerque: University of New Mexico Press, 1984), pp. 153–188.

2. John A. Peeler, *Latin American Democracies: Colombia, Costa Rica, Venezuela* (Chapel Hill: University of North Carolina Press, 1985), pp. 5–6.

3. Carl Cohen, *Democracy* (New York: Free Press, 1983), pp. 8–27.

4. This section is drawn mainly from Booth, "Representative Constitutional Democracy," pp. 158–176; and John A. Booth, "Costa Rican Labor Unions," in Gerald W. Greenfield and Sheldon L. Maram, eds., *Latin American Labor Unions* (New York: Greenwood Press, 1987), pp. 213–242.

5. Lowell Gudmundson discusses the myth in detail in his *Costa Rica Before Coffee: Society and Economy on the Eve of the Export Boom* (Baton Rouge: Louisiana State University Press, 1986), pp. 1–24.

6. Elizabeth Fonseca, *Costa Rica colonial: La tierra y el hombre* (San José: Editorial

Universitaria Centroamericana, 1984); see also Gudmundson, *Costa Rica Before Coffee,* pp. 25–87.

7. See Carlos Meléndez, "Bosquejo para una historia social costarricense antes de la independencia," in V. de la Cruz et al., *Las instituciones costarricenses del siglo XIX* (San José: Editorial Costa Rica, 1985), pp. 42–43 (my translation).

8. By 1800, among Costa Rica's 52,591 persons, only 16 percent were Indian (down from about 80 percent in 1700), 67 percent "Spanish and Mestizo," and 17 percent black (up from 7 percent in 1700). See de la Cruz et al., *Las instituciones,* p. 44. See also Mavis Hiltunen de Biesanz et al., *Los costarricenses* (San José: Editorial Universidad National a Distancia, 1979), ch. 2.

9. Deborah J. Yashar, *Demanding Democracy: Reform and Reaction in Costa Rica and Guatemala, 1870s–1950s* (Stanford: Stanford University Press, 1997) discusses how this trait of Costa Rica's export agriculture influenced state formation and behavior in comparison to Guatemala.

10. José Luis Vega Carballo, *Poder político y democracia en Costa Rica* (San José: Editorial Porvenir, 1982), p. 30 (my translation).

11. Ibid., p. 88; see also Johnny Alfaro Ramos et al., *La evolución del sufragio en Costa Rica* (Licenciatura thesis in Law, Facultad de Derecho, Universidad de Costa Rica, 1980), pp. 39–40.

12. Orlando Salazar Mora, *El apogeo de la república liberal en Costa Rica* (San José: Editorial de la Universidad de Costa Rica, 1990), pp. 275–280; and Astrid Fischel, *Consenso y represión: Una interpretación socio-política de la educación costarricense* (San Josæ: Editorial Costa Rica, 1987).

13. Fischel, *Consenso y represión.*

14. Jacobo Schifter, "La democracia en Costa Rica como producto de la neutralización de clases," in Chester Zelaya et al., *¿Democracia en Costa Rica? Cinco opiniones polémicas* (San José: Editorial Universidad National Estatal a Distancia, 1978), pp. 197–200.

15. Vega Carballo, *Poder político,* p. 96; and Samuel Stone, *La dinastía de los conquistadores* (San José: Editorial Universidad de Costa Rica, Editorial Universitaria Centroamericana, 1975), p. 223.

16. See Oscar Aguilar Bulgarelli, "Evolución histórica de una democracia," in Chester Zelaya et al., *¿Democracia en Costa Rica? Cinco opiniones polémicas* (San José: Editorial Universidad National Estatal a Distancia, 1978), pp. 42–46.

17. Vega Carballo, *Poder político,* p. 30.

18. Ibid., p. 30.

19. Variants of this theory about Costa Rican democratization are laid out in the first edition of this chapter and in John A. Booth, *Costa Rica: Quest for Democracy* (Boulder, CO: Westview, 1998), chapter 3; Dietrich Rueschemeyer, Evelyne Huber Stephens, and John D. Stephens, *Capitalist Development and Democracy* (Chicago: University of Chicago Press, 1992); and Bruce M. Wilson, *Costa Rica: Politics, Economics, and Democracy* (Boulder, CO: Lynne Rienner, 1998), pp. 29–35. Yashar's *Demanding Democracy* makes a similar argument, despite overlooking much of the growth of Costa Rican civil society prior to the 1930s.

20. Vega Carballo, *Poder político,* p. 95.

21. Ibid., pp. 97–98; and Booth, *Costa Rica: Quest for Democracy,* chapter 3.

22. Harold H. Bonilla, *Los presidentes,* vol. 2 (San José: Universidad Nacional Estatal a Distancia, Editorial Costa Rica, 1979), pp. 823–825.

23. Yashar's *Demanding Democracy* has the best account of these events, pp. 179–182.

24. Ibid., p. 113.

25. *Constitución política de la República de Costa Rica* (San José: Asamblea Legislativa, 1978), Article 99 (my translation).

26. Ibid., Article 104.

27. Ibid., Article 102.

28. Charles D. Ameringer, *Democracy in Costa Rica* (New York: Praeger, 1982), p. 51.

29. *Constitución política,* Article 95.

30. Only convicted felons are excluded from voting. Ibid., Articles 90–95: Ameringer, *Democracy in Costa Rica,* p. 58; Mitchell A. Seligson and Edward Muller, "Democratic Stability and Economic Crisis: Costa Rica, 1978–1983," *International Studies Quarterly* 31 (1987): 307–309, fig. 1; Booth, *Costa Rica: Quest for Democracy,* p. 46.

31. See Burt English, *Liberación Nacional in Costa Rica: The Development of a*

Political Party in a Transitional Society (Gainesville: University of Florida Press, 1971); Peeler, *Latin American Democracies*, pp. 43–142; Jorge Rovira Mas, "Costa Rica: 6 de febrero de 1994," *Boletín Electoral Latinoamericano* (January-June 1994): pp. 40–53.

32. Peeler, *Latin American Democracies,* p. 113.

33. See, for example, U.S. Congress, *Country Reports on Human Rights Practices* (Washington, DC: U.S. Government Printing Office, February 2, 1981), pp. 391–396.

34. The provision for no reelection does not affect presidents elected prior to 1969. It was for some years the object of an unsuccessful push for constitutional amendment by Daniel Oduber Quirós, who became president after 1969.

35. At least one cabinet member must also veto a bill for the veto to take effect.

36. *Constitución política,* Articles 130–140.

37. Carlos José Gutiérrez, "Cambio en el sistema jurídico costarricense," in Juan Manuel Villasuso, ed., *El nuevo rostro de Costa Rica* (Heredia, Costa Rica: Centro de Estudios Democráticos de América Latina, 1992), pp. 359–384. On structural adjustment and the executive branch and autonomous agencies, see Wilson, *Costa Rica: Politics, Economics,* pp. 51–58.

38. Amendment occurs by a two-thirds vote of total membership in each of two successive annual sessions of the Legislative Assembly.

39. *Constitución política,* Articles 152–167; Ameringer, *Democracy in Costa Rica,* p. 53; and Carlos José Gutiérrez, *El funcionamiento del sistema jurídico* (San José: Editorial Juricentro, 1979), pp. 150–239.

40. Based on data in Inter-American Development Bank (hereafter, IADB), *Economic and Social Progress in Latin America: 1987 Report* (Washington, DC: IADB, 1987); Booth, *Costa Rica: Quest for Democracy,* chapter 8; and Mary A. Clark, "Transnational Alliances and Development Policy in Latin America: Nontraditional Export Promotion in Costa Rica," *Latin American Research Review* 32, no. 2 (1997): 71–97; Wilson, *Costa Rica: Politics, Economics,* pp. 124–134.

41. James Backer, *La iglesia y el sindicalismo en Costa Rica* (San José: Editorial Costa Rica, 1978), pp. 83–220; Phillip Williams, *The Catholic Church and Politics in Nicaragua and Costa Rica* (Pittsburgh: University of Pittsburgh Press, 1989), chapters 5–7; and Miguel Picado, "Cambios dentro del catolicismo costarricense en los últimos años," in Juan Manuel Villasuso, ed., *El nuevo rostro de Costa Rica* (Heredia, Costa Rica: Centro de Estudios Democráticos de América Latina, 1992), pp. 45–54.

42. María Pérez Y., "Costa Rica: Las comunicaciones al ritmo del mundo" (pp. 209–250), and Eduardo Ulibarri, "Los medios de comunicación: Diversidad con desafíos" (pp. 251–262), both in Villasuso, ed., *El nuevo rostro de Costa Rica* (Heredia, Costa Rica: Centro de Estudios Democráticos de América Latina, 1992), and the author's personal observations and conversations with Costa Rican scholars, August 1985 and August 1987.

43. Booth, "Representative Constitutional Democracy," table 5.3; Booth, *Costa Rica: Quest for Democracy,* chapter 6.

44. See Biesanz et al., *Los costarricenses,* pp. 30–39.

45. "The Costa Rican says 'vos' [*thou*—the familiar second-person pronoun], 'shit,' and 'son of a whore' even to the president." All are common locutions in Costa Rica.

46. Biesanz et al., *Los costarricenses,* chapter 7.

47. Mario Carvajal Herrera, *Actitudes políticas del costarricense* (San José: Editorial Costa Rica, 1978), pp. 137–173. He sampled 100 party and group leaders and 305 citizens from three municipalities.

48. Booth, *Costa Rica: Quest for Democracy,* chapter 7.

49. Martha Honey, *Hostile Acts: U.S. Policy in Costa Rica in the 1980s* (Gainesville: University Presses of Florida, 1994); Booth, *Costa Rica: Quest for Democracy,* chapters 6 and 9.

50. Carvajal Herrera, *Actitudes políticas,* pp. 166–167; Booth, *Costa Rica: Quest for Democracy,* chapter 7.

51. Seligson and Muller, "Democratic Stability."

52. Ibid., pp. 319–322.

53. This section is drawn mainly from Booth, *Costa Rica: Quest for Democracy,* chapter 8; and Victor Hugo Céspedes et al., *Costa Rica: La economía en 1985* (San José Academia de Centroamérica, 1986), pp. 59, 78.

54. Booth, *Costa Rica: Quest for Democracy,* chapter 8, especially tables 8.4–8.6; Wilson, *Costa Rica: Politics, Economics,* chapter 5.

55. Booth, *Costa Rica: Quest for Democracy,* appendix, table A.2.

56. Victor Bulmer-Thomas, "Economic Development over the Long Run—Central America Since 1920," *Journal of Latin American Studies* 15 (November 1983): 269–294.

57. Clark, "Transnational Alliances"; and Booth, *Costa Rica: Quest for Democracy,* chapter 8.

58. Booth, *Costa Rica: Quest for Democracy,* chapter 6; Booth, "Costa Rican Labor Unions"; and John A. Booth, "Democracy and Citizen Action in Costa Rica: The Modes and Correlates of Popular Participation in Politics," Ph.D. diss., University of Texas at Austin, 1975.

59. E. Lederman et al., "Trabajo y empleo," in Chester Zelaya, ed., *Costa Rica contemporánea,* vol. 2 (San José: Editorial Costa Rica), tables 26, 27, 30.

60. John A. Booth and Mitchell A. Seligson, "Peasants as Activists: A Reevaluation of Political Participation in the Countryside," *Comparative Political Studies* 12 (April 1979): pp. 29–59; and Booth, *Costa Rica: Quest for Democracy,* table 6.1.

61. Material on labor drawn from Backer, *La iglesia,* pp. 13–28, 135–207; Booth, "Costa Rican Labor Unions"; Lederman et al., "Trabajo y empleo," table 27; Schifter, "La democracia," pp. 171–240; and Manuel Rojas B., "Un sindicalismo del sector público," in Villasuso, ed., *El nuevo rostro de Costa Rica* (Heredia, Costa Rica: Centro de Estudios Democráticos de América Latina, 1992), pp. 181–189.

62. Lederman et al.'s 1988 statistics (table 29) from the Ministry of Labor and Social Security vary somewhat from these, taken from 1979 Ministry of Labor data summarized in Booth, "Costa Rican Labor Unions."

63. Booth, "Costa Rican Labor Unions"; see also Lederman et al., "Trabajo y empleo," table 29.

64. Gustavo Blanco and Orlando Navarro, *El solidarismo: Pensamiento y dinámica social de un movimiento obrero patronal* (San José: Editorial Costa Rica, 1984), p. 298; Oscar Bejarano, "El solidarismo costarricense," in Villasuso, ed., *El nuevo rostro de Costa Rica* (Heredia, Costa Rica: Centro de Estudios Democráticos de América Latina, 1992), pp. 203–208.

65. Mitchell A. Seligson, *Peasants of Costa Rica and the Development of Agrarian Capitalism* (Madison: University of Wisconsin Press, 1980), chapter 2.

66. Ibid.; statistics on the public sector from Lederman et al., "Trabajo y empleo," tables 7 and 8; and Céspedes et al., *Costa Rica: La economía,* p. 79; Castro Valverde, "Sector público y ajuste estructural en Costa Rica (1983–1992)," in Trevor Evans, ed., *La transformación neoliberal del sector público* (Managua, Nicaragua: Latino Editores, 1995).

67. Booth, "Democracy and Citizen Action," figures 2.2, 2.3, and 2.4.

68. Biesanz et al., *Los costarricenses,* p. 247; Mitchell A. Seligson, Juliana Martínez F., and Juan Diego Trejos S., "Reducción de la probreza en Costa Rica: El impacto de las políticas públicas," draft manuscript, United Nations Development Programme, San José, Costa Rica, November 11, 1995.

69. Seligson, *Peasants of Costa Rica,* pp. 23, 147; workforce data from Lederman et al., "Trabajo y empleo," table 4; Jorge Mora A., "Los movimientos sociales agrarios en la Costa Rica de la década de los ochenta," in Villasuso, ed., *El nuevo rostro de Costa Rica* (Heredia, Costa Rica: Centro de Estudios Democráticos de América Latina, 1992), p. 155; Leslie Anderson, "Mixed Blessings: Disruption and Organization Among Peasant Unions in Costa Rica," *Latin American Research Review* 26, no. 1 (1991): 111–143; and Leslie Anderson, *The Political Ecology of the Modern Peasant* (Baltimore: Johns Hopkins University Press, 1994).

70. Quote from Seligson, *Peasants of Costa Rica,* p. 48 and chapter 6.

71. John A. Booth, "Socioeconomic and Political Roots of National Revolts in Central America," *Latin American Research Review* 26, no. 1 (1991): 33–73.

72. Biesanz et al., *Los costarricenses,* pp. 245–251.

73. Ibid., p. 246.

74. Ibid., p. 274.

75. John A. Booth et al., *Tipología de comunidades, Tomo 2: Estudio para una tipología de comunidades* (San José: Dirección Nacional de Desarrollo de la Comunidad—Acción Internacional Técnica, 1973).

76. Booth, *Costa Rica: Quest for Democracy,* chapter 5.

77. Francisco Rojas Aravena, "La percepción de la crisis centroamericana y la administración Monge Alvarez," occasional paper series (Heredia, Costa Rica: Escuela de Relaciones Internacionales, Universidad Nacional Autonóma, 1984), pp. 69–70.

78. *CRISIS* 1 (spring 1985): 2–6.

79. Rojas Aravena, "La percepción," p. 61.

80. Luis Guillermo Solís, "Costa Rica: La política exterior y los cambios en el sistema internacional en los ochenta," in Villasuso, ed., *El nuevo rostro de Costa Rica* (Heredia, Costa Rica: Centro de Estudios Democráticos de América Latina, 1992), pp. 341–356; Honey, *Hostile Acts;* Carlos Sojo, *Costa Rica: Política exterior y sandinismo* (San José: Facultad Latinoamericano de Ciencias Sociales, 1991).

81. *CRISIS* 1 (spring 1985): 4.

82. World Bank, *World Development Report: 1983* (London: Oxford University Press, 1983), table 15.

83. Ibid., table 16.

84. Victor Bulmer-Thomas, *The Political Economy of Central America Since 1920* (New York: Cambridge University Press, 1987), table 11.6.

85. Booth, *Costa Rica: Quest for Democracy,* chapters 9–10.

86. Schifter, "La democracia."

87. Vega Carballo, *Poder político.*

88. Author's observations based upon visits to Costa Rica in August 1985 and 1987, and on an informal survey of Costa Rican press for several decades.

89. Daniel Obuder Quirós, lecture series, Escuela de Relaciones Internacionales, Universidad Nacional Autónoma, Heredia, Costa Rica, August 1979; Sojo, *Costa Rica: Política exterior.*

9

THE DOMINICAN REPUBLIC: The Long and Difficult Struggle for Democracy

Rosario Espinal & *Jonathan Hartlyn*

Political democracy has been scarce in the Dominican Republic. Unmistakably one reason is due to its past, which has weighed heavily on current political practices in the country, although we believe this requires careful analysis rather than overly broad generalizations. Similarly, the country's obvious international vulnerability must be considered along with the paradoxical inability of international actors to shape specific political outcomes in the country. In particular, we reject reductionist interpretations that identify the Spanish colonial experience or the role of the United States or of other international actors as the predominant factor explaining the country's limited democratic evolution. Although the negative implications for democracy of "organic-statist" ideology, and of many of the actions of foreign powers, are real, often too much explanatory weight is attached to these factors. In general, the country's experience highlights the negative impact on democracy of certain kinds of historical sequences on democratic developments, as well as the difficulty of constructing democracy in countries with highly unequal social structures, weak civil societies, porous states incapable of imposing the rule of law, and political leaders dedicated more to remaining in power than furthering democratic practices.

The historical evolution of the Dominican Republic proved particularly inimical to democratic development. It deviated significantly from patterns viewed as optimal for the development of democracy. Robert Dahl has argued that sequences in which successful experiences with limited liberalization are followed by gradually greater inclusiveness appear to favor democracy. In turn, Eric Nordlinger has asserted that the nature and sequence of key crises in a country's political evolution regarding national identity, authority, and participation are essential: the pattern most promising for the development of democracy is one in which national identity

469

FLORIDA

A t l a n t i c

THE BAHAMAS

O c e a n

CUBA

DOMINICAN REPUBLIC

HAITI

Puerto
Rico

JAMAICA

Santo Domingo

C a r i b b e a n   S e a

PANAMA

COLOMBIA

V E N E Z U E L A

THE DOMINICAN REPUBLIC

emerges first, then legitimate and authoritative state structures are institutionalized, and then mass parties and a mass electorate emerge with the extension of citizenship rights to non-elite elements. Dankwart Rustow's "genetic" model of democracy is similar, having as a background condition national unity, and then proceeding through phases of inconclusive struggle, compromise on democratic rules to resolve conflict, and then habituation to these rules.[1]

The pattern followed by the Dominican Republic was very different from any of the above. National integration was truncated first by a Haitian occupation (1822–1844) and then by the attempts of some Dominican elites to trade nascent Dominican sovereignty for security by having foreign powers annex the country, while enriching themselves in the process. State building also suffered under the dual impact of international vulnerability and unstable, neopatrimonial authoritarian politics. Both integration and state building were also impaired by bitter regional struggles based on different economic interests and desires for power that accentuated the *caudillo* politics of the country during the second half of the nineteenth century and the early twentieth century.

Indeed, a Dominican state arguably did not emerge until the late nineteenth century or even the era of Rafael Trujillo (1930–1961); Trujillo's emergence, in turn, was unquestionably facilitated by changes wrought by the eight-year U.S. occupation of the Dominican Republic in 1916–1924. Trujillo's pattern of rule could not have been more hostile to democratic rule. However, his remarkable centralization of power, monopolization of the economy, destruction or co-optation of enemies, and constitutional hypocrisy were combined with the forging of national integration, the establishment of state institutions, and the beginnings of industrialization, however distorted.

Thus, the country essentially had no history of democratic rule prior to 1961, though it did have a liberal constitutional tradition, often evanescent political parties, and frequently fraudulent elections. In the context of contradictory and extensive U.S. actions both to foster democracy and to block perceived communist threats, efforts toward democratic transition following the death of Trujillo ultimately failed. The short-lived democratic regime of Juan Bosch was followed by unstable governments and ultimately by U.S. intervention out of a fear of a "second Cuba." A key figure from the Trujillo era, Joaquín Balaguer, was to govern the country for twenty-two of the next thirty years, from 1966 to 1978 and again from 1986 to 1996, combining political stagnation with dramatic socioeconomic transformation. The Dominican Republic is entering the twenty-first century bolstered by potential changes in political leadership, though with weak party structures and the possibility of excessive political factionalism and polarization; it is also doing so at a time when the international context is more favorable to political democracy, though that same context also provides challenges in terms of difficult economic adjustments, and concerns about negative impacts from problems such as drug trafficking and environmental degradation.

HISTORICAL REVIEW AND ANALYSIS

The Struggle for Formal Sovereignty

Dominican history has been marked by the recurrence of different kinds of neopatrimonial, and sometimes neosultanistic, regimes, which have left a historical legacy difficult to overcome. These types of regimes base their rule on the extension of personal patronage networks, heavily centralizing authority in the hands of a single leader and blurring the distinction between the state and his private affairs.[2] We argue that the lack of democracy in the Dominican Republic should be traced less to its colonial heritage (though this played a role) and more to the consequences of its protracted, violent, and often unsuccessful efforts to consolidate formal sovereignty, construct a viable state, and achieve national integration in the nineteenth century. These efforts led to cycles of "failed liberalism,"[3] leading authoritarian leaders to turn to the cultural repertoire of neopatrimonialism from the country's past in the context of a social structure favorable to its emergence, fostering a pernicious constitutional hypocrisy that has deeply marked Dominican history. These patterns, in turn, were deeply affected and often reinforced by the country's economic marginality, existence of distinct regions, and marked inequalities combined with weakly organized socioeconomic or other national-level actors (such as the Catholic Church or the military) and by the consequences of the country's international vulnerability.

What was to become the Dominican Republic provides another tragic example of the effects of brutal Spanish rule and of disease. When the Spanish landed on Hispaniola in 1492, an estimated 400,000 indigenous inhabitants on the island were soon enslaved to work in gold mines. As a consequence of mistreatment, forced labor, hunger, disease, and mass killings, by 1535 only a few dozen were still alive. Eventually, the French settled the newly unpopulated western areas of the island, where they established a plantation society based on the exploitation of slave labor so that what is today Haiti became the wealthiest colony of the seventeenth century. In contrast, the Spanish colony remained poor and unprotected.[4]

The nineteenth-century struggle for independence was an incredibly difficult process for the Dominican Republic. In 1791, inspired by the French Revolution, a rebellion emerged in the French colony (known as Saint-Domingue), which was far more prosperous than the Spanish one of Santo Domingo. The Spanish colony was ceded first to France in 1795 and then it was invaded by the English in 1796. Five years later black slaves in rebellion invaded from Saint-Domingue. The devastated colony was then occupied by the French in 1802, in spite of the dramatic defeat of Napoleon's forces at the hands of the former French slaves who proclaimed the independent republic of Haiti in 1804. Santo Domingo was invaded again by Haitians in 1805 and then by the English anew in 1809. The Spanish reclaimed it later that year, but found the colony in economic ruins and demographic decline.[5]

In December 1821, Dominicans rose up in rebellion against the Spaniards, declaring themselves the Independent State of Spanish Haiti, only to hand over authority to the Haitian ruler Jean-Pierre Boyer in February of the next year. The twenty-two-year Haitian occupation that followed is recalled by Dominicans as a period of brutal military rule, though the reality is more complex. It led to large-scale land expropriations (particularly against the church and absentee landlords) and failed efforts to force production of export crops, impose obligatory military service, restrict use of the Spanish language, and eliminate traditional customs. It reinforced Dominican perceptions of themselves as different from Haitians in "language, race, religion and domestic customs."[6] Yet, this was also a period that definitively ended slavery as an institution in the eastern part of the island.

A potential turning point in 1844 was soon lost. A successful independence (or secession) effort producing what became known as the First Republic (1844–1861) was unable to construct an effective state or constitutional order in the Dominican Republic. Trying to construct republican, constitutional rule in the context of a devastated economy, an impoverished and regionally divided population, and a polity without functioning institutions would have been difficult under any circumstances. Beyond this, national security concerns remained paramount, enhancing the role and the value of militarism; unscrupulous leaders negotiated away Dominican sovereignty out of a belief that defense from Haiti required it and for their own personal gain.

The seven decades from 1844 to 1916 were characterized by bewilderingly complex interactions among Dominican governing groups, opposition movements, Haitian authorities, and representatives of France, Britain, Spain, and the United States. Juan Pablo Duarte and the liberal merchants who had led the initial independence effort were soon swept out of office and into exile, and the independent tobacco growers and merchants of the northern Cibao valley, who tended to favor national independence, were unable to consolidate control of the center. Government revolved largely around a small number of *caudillo* strongmen, particularly Pedro Santana and Buenaventura Báez (initially allies who became rivals), and their intrigues involving foreign powers.[7]

Support from foreign powers was pursued in defense against Haiti,

eventually leading to Spanish reannexation during 1861–1865. Protracted
war against Spain ended with renewed Dominican independence in July
1865. Shortly thereafter a complex battle over the potential annexation of
the country to the United States ensued, driven by an interest in Samaná
Bay as a naval station, which ultimately failed. This would be one of the
first of many subsequent episodes in which Dominican political struggles
would be battled out by Dominicans in Washington as much as in their own
country.[8]

The effort to regain independence in 1865 left the country devastated
again by war, with vast sectors of the population both armed and politically
and regionally fragmented. Once the Spanish were vanquished, the military
and guerrilla leaders began to fight among themselves. Indeed, the Second
Republic (1865–1916) resembled the first in that violence and force prevailed over democratic means to achieve and retain power. Elections were
frequently used simply to settle conflicts surrounding the distribution of
political power. Gradually, Baecistas (those loyal to Báez) revolved around
what came to be known as the Partido Rojo, and the anti-Báez forces, more
fragmented, mostly northern interests, formed the Partido Azul. Although
Báez managed to serve as president briefly in 1865–1866, and for longer
periods in 1868–1874 and again in 1878–1879, in the period from 1865 to
1879 there were twenty-one different governments and at least fifty military uprisings.[9]

The country was in almost continual civil war until the end of the
1870s. Gradually the key national political struggle following the founding
of the second republic in 1865 came to revolve around the "Rojos" and the
"Azules," a division that approximated that between conservatives and liberals elsewhere in the region. The struggle combined economic, regional,
and personalistic motivations. The Rojos were a centralized movement,
concentrating the more conservative powerholders of the northwest, south,
and east, who tended to identify with Buenaventura Báez. The basis of their
wealth was predominantly large livestock haciendas and the export of pre-
cious woods such as caoba. In turn, the Azules were composed primarily of
the more liberal, smaller tobacco growers and merchants of the northern
Cibao, with some of Santana's former supporters from the east. Although
the Azules were more imbued with liberal predilections, they also often
came to power through conspiracy and rebellion, only to be overthrown in
the same fashion. Regionalism based in part on the structurally different
societies of the east and the north was superimposed over personalistic
rivalries for power.[10] The central state was incapable of defeating the
regional uprisings. Thus, a clear national identity and authoritative state
structures were still lacking.

The century ended with the increasingly neosultanistic seventeen-year
reign of Ulises Heureaux (1882–1899), an able military leader and a
shrewd, despotic political leader, who reached out to the country's emerg-

ing sugar interests.[11] During his rule and in the subsequent decades, aided by rising international demand, the country's economic structure began undergoing more substantial change. With favorable state policies, modern sugar estates began to replace cattle-ranching estates, even as exports of coffee and cacao expanded; domestic financing of the state shifted from the more liberal tobacco merchants of the north to the producers of the south. A Dominican bourgeoisie was begun, involving both the enrichment of old families and new immigrants. The first railroads were completed and other basic infrastructure built. Initial attempts at professionalizing the army and bureaucratizing the state were made, and educational reforms were introduced.

Two other legacies of Heureaux were debt and instability, both of which led to even greater intromission of the United States in Dominican affairs (and those of many of its Caribbean neighbors). Following Heureaux's assassination in 1899, the country again experienced political chaos, with four revolts and five presidents over the subsequent six years. Weak proto-parties and clientelistic politics built around *caudillo* figures and regional uprisings furthered economic chaos and political instability. National politics revolved primarily around the conflict between the followers of Juan Isidro Jiménes and Horacio Vázquez (Jimenistas and Horacistas), both involved in plots against Heureaux. The only long-term presidency of this period was by Ramón Cáceres (1906–1911), whose assassination led to another period of political turmoil, as the country's economic disorganization facilitated U.S. intervention.

Gradually, control of Dominican affairs by its northern neighbor grew. Pressures by European creditors on the Dominican Republic (as well as the Anglo-German blockade of Venezuela in 1902–1903) led to President Theodore Roosevelt's "corollary" to the Monroe Doctrine. Anxious to preclude European intervention in the Caribbean because of debt problems, Roosevelt unilaterally declared that the United States would assume police powers necessary to ensure adequate repayment. By 1905, Dominican customs was headed by a U.S. appointee, a relationship that became formalized in a 1907 treaty that also paid off all previous loans with a new one converting private U.S. bankers into the country's only foreign creditor. U.S. investments in sugar lands and sugar mills also gradually expanded, becoming dominant during the period of U.S. military occupation. U.S. interest in the Dominican Republic (and in neighboring Haiti) expanded both for commercial reasons and for strategic reasons, including fear of Germany establishing a foothold in the region.[12]

Although Heureaux's dictatorship and economic growth helped generate more coherent social groups and a more coherent state toward the end of the nineteenth century, Abraham Lowenthal's broad generalization about the country on the eve of the U.S. intervention remains valid: "the Dominican Republic was not characterized by a powerful triad of oligarchy, church and military, but rather by exactly the reverse: an insecure grouping of elite families, a weak and dependent church, and no national military institution."[13] This combination of weak social forces and national institutions proved strongly congruent with neopatrimonial politics, and helped delay and distort the process of state formation in the country.

The United States' occupation of the Dominican Republic (1916–1924) was a critical turning point in Dominican history, though not for the reasons intended by the occupying force. Programs were enacted in education, health, sanitation, agriculture, and communications, roads were built, and other public works were carried out. In addition, other programs crucial to strengthening state structures and a market economy were begun, including both a census and a cadastral survey, the latter allowing land titles to be regularized and U.S. sugar companies to expand their holdings dramatically, even as infrastructure to facilitate exports was developed.[14]

The most significant measure was the establishment of a new Dominican constabulary force. In the Dominican Republic as elsewhere in Central America and the Caribbean, U.S. officials hoped that the establishment of new constabulary forces initially under U.S. tutelage would permanently depoliticize the armed forces in these countries, serving to bolster stable constitutional government. The result was totally the opposite. The United States helped establish a relatively effective national military institution where one had previously not existed and in which traditional power-holders were weak. It also improved transportation and communication infrastructure, which also benefited whoever controlled the central state. Thus, largely unintentional but predictable consequences of the occupation, combined with continuing patterns of Dominican domestic politics and shifts in U.S. policy toward noninterventionism, provided an opportunity for the head of the country's newly established military force, Rafael Leónidas Trujillo Molina, to take power and consolidate his grip on it.

The Era of Trujillo

Trujillo emerged from being an obscure minor officer in a newly formed constabulary force to head of the country's army over a ten-year period. As was soon to be discovered, he harbored strong sentiments of social rejection and of animosity against the country's elite families, the so-called *gente de primera,* whom he would force to work for him and often humiliate, and whose homage and admiration he actively pursued.[15] At the same time, the country's neopatrimonial political patterns—based on personalistic and clientelistic rule, questionable constitutional maneuverings, intrigue, and occasional rebellion, all of which predated the U.S. occupation—continued. Trujillo soon proved his political adeptness, and arranged his own election as president in 1930; he remained in power, if not always formally as president, until his assassination in 1961.

Trujillo's regime quickly moved beyond the traditional Dominican *caudillo* regimes of the nineteenth century, and by the end of his first presidential term (if not sooner) its neosultanistic tendencies were clear.[16] By the end of his second term, it was evident this regime's despotic and totalitarian features went beyond those of Heureaux, its historical predecessor in the country. There would be occasional partial liberalizations in response to international pressures, particularly following the Haitian massacre of 1937 and in the immediate post–World War II era. But Trujillo's accumulation of wealth and power would continue, reaching a peak in 1955. The regime's deterioration began shortly thereafter, accelerating in 1958.

How was Trujillo able to maintain such nearly total control over the country for as long as he did? Five sets of factors are important. First are background *historical* factors of geographical isolation, weak traditional power-holders or potential challengers from other social groups, and the more effective repressive apparatus created by the United States. Related to these are how he built upon and enhanced *state structures,* especially those related to repression. Yet his prolonged rule did not rely on repression alone. He employed *ideological* arguments, revolving initially around economic nationalism, anti-Haitianism, Catholicism, order, and progress, to project himself domestically and to justify his vast financial empire. Various *economic and political* means meshed strategies of repression, co-optation, and corruption while permitting him to enhance his own personal wealth and power. Finally, *international* factors played a central role, given the country's dependence on the United States. Trujillo pursued an active policy toward the United States, and he was helped initially by his strong contacts with the U.S. military and by the U.S. Good Neighbor policy of noninterventionism and then by the U.S. focus on anticommunism. Indeed, a dramatic shift in U.S. attitude toward Trujillo in the late 1950s was crucial in the denouement of his regime.

Central to Trujillo's domination of the country was control over an expanding armed forces and police, which were clearly Trujillo's personal instrument rather than a national institution. Trujillo remained as commander in chief of the armed forces even when he was not formally president. In spite of a sharp drop in the overall government budget in the 1930s due to the effects of the Great Depression, the military budget grew substantially. In subsequent decades, as the economy improved, the military portion expanded even more dramatically. By the mid-1950s, the best troops and weapons (even tanks) had been transferred to a military service known as the Dominican Military Aviation, controlled by Trujillo's son Ramfis.[17]

Yet, Trujillo's regime was not based purely on repression, though over time it did so increasingly. Trujillo articulated certain ideological positions with the collaboration of several leading intellectuals that resonated across different social sectors of the population. His was the first prolonged period in the country's history when the country suffered no direct intervention by

Spain, the United States, or Haiti. Trujillo built upon the country's antipathy to Haiti to help articulate a nationalist ideology appealing to traditional Hispanic and Catholic values. Especially in the 1930s, he also articulated a vision of discipline, work, peace, order, and progress. As these became embodied in a number of large-scale public-works and construction projects, particularly as the economy began moving out of the depression in the late 1930s, they almost certainly gained him respect—if not support—among some elements of the population, as he also presented himself in a messianic form. By the 1950s, and particularly after signing a concordat with the Vatican in 1954, Trujillo would often attack "international communism" as a threat to the country's traditional values he claimed he was seeking to uphold.[18] Yet, Trujillo never articulated a fully formulated ideology; indeed, even his espousal of anticommunism changed dramatically in his final, desperate days.

Trujillo also waved the ideological banner of economic nationalism, although it sometimes cloaked his own personal accumulation of wealth. This was facilitated by the country's abject dependency on the United States and tragic history. In fact, many of his economic measures were inferior to those taken by other Latin American states in the same period. Yet in seeking to legitimize his rule, Trujillo could argue that he ended U.S. administration of Dominican customs, retired the Dominican debt, and introduced a national currency to replace the dollar.

Thus, ideologically Trujillo portrayed himself with some success as a forger of the Dominican nation, builder of the state, and defender of its economic interests. As he amassed a sizable fortune, Trujillo also built up the Dominican state, reduced the extent of direct control by foreigners over the economy, and stimulated an incipient process of industrialization. He and his propagandists, though, exaggerated the efficacy of measures and the role of his regime in restoring the country's financial independence and sovereignty while downplaying the tremendous costs of his economic measures.

Economically, Trujillo eventually became the single dominant force in the country by combining abuse of state power, threats, and co-optation. Although some of the country's economic elite maintained a degree of individual autonomy, there was no possibility for independent organization. Trujillo enjoyed humiliating those who previously possessed both social prestige and economic wealth; they intensely disliked him but were forced to conform. Only in Trujillo's last two years did any concerted opposition emerge from within the economic elite. Indeed, Trujillo's economic holdings at the time of his death were staggering. Almost 80 percent of the country's industrial production was controlled by him; and nearly 60 percent of the country's labor force depended directly or indirectly on him, 45 percent employed in his firms and another 15 percent working for the state.[19] Thus, Trujillo's domination of the country was increasingly economic, as well as military and political. The only organization that retained any degree of autonomy was the Catholic Church; yet, until the very end of his rule it remained abjectly loyal to him.

Politically, Trujillo combined guile, cynicism, ruthlessness, and co-optation. There was cynical deployment of constitutional norms and legal requirements that were ostensibly followed faithfully, a single-party apparatus totally dominated by Trujillo, and byzantine manipulation of individuals, who were shifted around public offices in disconcerting fashion as personal rivalries were promoted and tested. At its apogee, the Dominican Party had branches throughout the country, helping to keep Trujillo apprised of local realities, needs, and potential threats to his rule. The party's charitable activities, homages to Trujillo, and campaign efforts were financed largely by a percentage taken from the salaries of public employees. Although the Dominican Party played no role in either political recruitment or policy formulation, in certain periods of the Trujillo era it did help to legitimize his rule. Trujillo made voting mandatory (and not voting could be risky), and in 1942 he expanded the suffrage to women.[20]

If these various domestic factors were critical in sustaining Trujillo's grip on power, international ones were as well. Early in his rule, Trujillo found strong support among military contacts he had forged during the U.S. occupation, which counterbalanced an often hostile State Department. Trujillo employed public relations firms and assiduously cultivated his military contacts and individual politicians in the United States to enhance his reputation and sustain U.S. support. He went to elaborate lengths to demonstrate domestically that he retained support from the United States, and in some periods U.S. diplomats expressed their frustration at being manipulated by Trujillo even as U.S. military personnel openly praised his rule. At the same time, his complex web of conspiracy, intrigue, and violence extended well beyond Dominican borders, as he provided support for various regional dictators and plotted against perceived foreign enemies, some of whom provided support for exile groups plotting against him.

By the late 1950s, though, Trujillo was facing multiple challenges, even as the country's economy was suffering and his own mental acuity was declining. Domestic opposition, exile activities, and international pressures all began to reinforce each other. A failed invasion attempt in June 1959 helped spawn a major underground movement, itself brutally crushed in January 1960. But domestic opposition continued to grow, the Catholic Church finally began to distance itself from the regime, and with concerns mounting about the Cuban Revolution, the United States did so as well. The end came for Trujillo in May 1961, when conspirators who had largely been former supporters of the regime—with at first vigorous and then ambivalent encouragement from the United States—assassinated him.[21]

The Immediate Post-Trujillo Period

Given the nature of Trujillo's regime, and the lack of other factors commonly associated with successful democracy, it is not surprising that democracy ultimately failed to take root in the Dominican Republic in the 1960s. In November 1961, some six months after the despised dictator was assassinated, Dominicans celebrated wildly as it became clear that his family would not retain power. But five years later, in July 1966, Trujillo's puppet president in 1961, Joaquín Balaguer, assumed the presidential office that he was then to occupy for twenty-two of the subsequent thirty years.

The period from 1961 to 1966 was a convulsive one for the country. The preexisting political institutions and practices from the Trujillo regime were clearly inimical to a successful democratic transition. Yet, a clear break with the Trujillos was achieved as the old regime collapsed and a provisional government was formed in 1962. The potential risks of this kind of transition process—of a provisional government subverting democratic elections either because it represents the old regime or a new radical leadership—were averted, and democratic elections were successfully organized.[22] However, democratic elections in 1962 were facilitated by the extraordinary degree of U.S. involvement, which was able to meld its anti-communist and democratic promotion objectives together in the absence of any serious revolutionary threat in the country. The upper-class opposition to Trujillo was organized in the Unión Cívica Nacional (UCN). They dominated the provisional government and expected to win the elections. To their surprise, they were defeated by Juan Bosch, one of the founders of the Partido Revolucionario Dominicano (PRD) in exile in the late 1930s, and the UCN soon disappeared. The PRD was successfully converted into a mass party as Bosch campaigned as the candidate of the poor. Ultimately, the conservative socioeconomic forces coalesced with political, military, and church figures to overthrow President Bosch only seven months after he assumed office in 1963, as U.S. support for his government also weakened. The institutional changes that Bosch, his new constitution, and his proposed reforms represented, in a situation in which his party possessed an absolute majority, were perceived as too threatening, even though middle-sector and popular-sector groups remained relatively weak and unorganized. If Bosch's regime was overthrown in 1963 ostensibly because of its alleged communist nature, weak radical leftist elements were in fact strengthened by the coup and the country experienced further polarization over the next several years.

Thus, the 1963 coup was to lead to another U.S. intervention. On April 25, 1965, the Dominican government attempted to put down a civil-military conspiracy that sought to return Bosch to power. This provoked a series of events leading to the "constitutionalist" uprising in support of Bosch and then resulted in the U.S. intervention three days later as the "loyalist" Dominican military was unable to control the growing civil-military rebellion. That intervention was the result of an exaggerated fear on the part of the United States regarding a potential "second Cuba."[23]

Ultimately, negotiations during 1965–1966 arranged a peaceful surrender of the constitutionalist forces surrounded by foreign troops in downtown Santo Domingo, prevented a new outbreak of hostilities, and provided for elections in 1966. However, these elections, which permitted the United States to extricate its troops from the country, were viewed as tainted by many Dominicans. Bosch and Balaguer were the two main candidates. Bosch felt betrayed by the United States, which had blocked his possible return to power and turned on his military supporters, and he ran a lackluster campaign. Balaguer, in turn, at the head of his own conservative Reformist Party, campaigned skillfully and energetically, promising peace and stability. Balaguer was clearly the candidate favored by most conservative business interests and by the officer corps that retained control of the armed forces; most Dominicans also were convinced he was the candidate strongly favored by the United States. Although the civil war had been contained to urban areas, it left some 3,000 dead and the country polarized. Thus, for many Dominicans, Balaguer's administration lacked legitimacy.

Authoritarian Modernization: Joaquín Balaguer, 1966–1978

In the period from 1966 to 1978, Balaguer governed in an authoritarian and neopatrimonial, but not sultanistic, fashion. In his predilection for grandiose public-construction projects and his emphasis on the country's Hispanic and Catholic essence, Balaguer resembled Trujillo. However, in his treatment of economic, military, and political power Balaguer differed from the strongman under whom he had served, in part due to changes both in Dominican society and in international circumstances. Economically, a business sector developed during this period that was linked to, but still somewhat autonomous from, the state. Militarily, Balaguer was unmistakably a civilian figure, if still an authoritarian one. Politically, opposition parties were never totally banned or eclipsed. All these factors played a central role in explaining how a democratic transition could occur in the country in 1978. In that year, a more moderate PRD, without the presence of Bosch (who had left to found a new party in 1973), won the elections and assumed power.

The Balaguer period from 1966 to 1978 was one of rapid economic growth, averaging 7.6 percent in real GDP for the whole period and 11 percent from 1968 to 1974. Growth was based upon increased export earnings, import-substitution in consumer goods promoted by generous tax incentives, and public investment projects. It was facilitated by the U.S. sugar quota and generous economic assistance, particularly in the early Balaguer years. Balaguer was the central axis around which all other major political and economic forces revolved. The centerpiece of his new developmental model was import-substitution industrialization. In 1968, the government passed Law 299 of Industrial Protection and Incentives, providing industrialists with tax benefits and foreign exchange advantages. Thus, in contrast to Trujillo, he eventually undermined his position by promoting the development of business groups separate from, even if dependent upon, the state. Balaguer also aided industrialists by repressing union activists, curtailing union activities, and repressing wages. Soon after taking office, Balaguer announced the Wage Austerity Law, which froze the monthly minimum wage and banned collective bargaining.[24]

Balaguer had a commanding presence within the military as a result of his ties to the Trujillo period, his anticommunism, his statesmanlike *caudillo* figure, and his acceptance of military repression as well as large-scale corruption. However, unlike Trujillo, he was not a military figure. He sought to manage the military by playing off the ambitions of the leading generals and shifting their assigned posts. Yet he occasionally confronted serious challenges, such as a coup effort in 1971 that he successfully dismantled.

The initial Balaguer years were a period of relative polarization, with repression from government and sporadic terrorist activities by opposition groups. Some 2,000 additional Dominicans were killed in a six-year period after the 1965 occupation. Following his electoral victory in 1966, Balaguer ran again and won in elections in 1970 and 1974. In these elections, the military placed strong pressure on the opposition, most of whom ultimately withdrew prior to election day. Balaguer also assiduously practiced a policy of co-optation, but the extent and nature of repression, particularly after 1976, was considerably less than in the Trujillo years.

As the 1978 elections approached, Balaguer had alienated a number of his former supporters due to his drive for power, reelectionist aspirations, and policy decisions. An economic downturn finally affected the country around 1976, when the sugar boom that had offset oil price increases faded. In addition, the country's substantial growth, industrialization, and urbanization had created new business sectors and expanded middle-sector and professional groups who were increasingly disgruntled by Balaguer's neopatrimonial style of rule, which appeared to favor more-established interests with close ties to the regime. In the absence of any "threat" from below, some of these new groups were supportive of democratization and a few of the PRD directly.[25] Furthermore, with President Jimmy Carter in the White House, pressure to hold free and fair elections was considerably stronger than it had been in 1970 or 1974.

At the same time, for these elections the PRD also sought to project a more moderate image and to strengthen its international contacts, particularly with the U.S. government and the Socialist International. It purposefully selected a moderate figure, S. Antonio Guzmán, as its candidate. The

PRD's ability to project itself as a less threatening alternative to Balaguer in 1978 was facilitated by the decision of Bosch in 1973 to abandon his party and establish another, more radical and cadre-oriented one, the Partido de la Liberación Dominicana (PLD). Bosch's exit built upon his disillusionment with liberal democracy following the 1965 U.S. intervention, though in the 1980s he was to lead his party back into the electoral arena.

Electoral victory for the PRD in 1978 was not to come easily. As it became evident early in the morning after election day that the party was winning by a wide margin (see Table 9.1), a military contingent stopped the vote count. In the end, the effort to thwart the elections was dismantled, due to firm opposition by the Carter administration, other Latin American and European governments, and domestic groups. In the tense period between the election and the inauguration, congressional electoral results were "adjusted" to provide the exiting Balaguer with guarantees, principally a majority in the Senate (which appointed judges, and thus was key to successful prosecution of corruption charges). The succession ultimately went through, though fulfillment of the country's many democratic aspirations was not to be fully realized.

A Missed Opportunity: The PRD, 1978–1986

Unlike Balaguer, the leaders of the PRD promoted a democratic agenda. During the electoral campaign of 1978, the PRD conveyed the image of being the party of change (*el partido del cambio*). This meant a commitment to improve the living standards of the less privileged, political inclusion of those who felt underrepresented, the modernization of state institutions, and the rule of law. These were campaign promises stated in the party platform around which the PRD built a broad base of social support. As a result, the PRD's rise to power generated expectations for socioeconomic and political reforms among the Dominican people, many of which were not achieved.

One threat to democracy that did begin to recede in 1978 was that of military incursion into politics. The armed forces have remained under civilian control, though more through personalized relations with the president and divided political loyalties within the organization than through their consolidation as a corporate, professional organization. Like most government institutions in the Dominican Republic, the military has been affected by low salaries and poor morale and plagued by corruption and disregard for the rule of law. The initial crucial step in controlling the Dominican military came under President Guzmán, who in 1978 dismissed many of the key generals associated with repression. Even when Balaguer returned to power in 1986, the military never regained the level of importance and influence they had had during his first twelve years in office.

484 ESPINAL & HARTLYN

Table 9.1   Official Results for Elections, 1978–1998 (various years)

	1978	1982	1986	1990	1994	1996 1st round	1996 2nd round	1998
Parties and Party Alliances (% of vote)								
PRSC	42.2	39.2	40.5	33.5	n.a.	15.0		16.6
PRSC and allies			41.5	35.0	42.3			16.8
PRD	51.7	46.7	33.5	23.0	n.a.			48.9
PRD and allies			38.8	23.2	41.5	45.9	48.7	51.6
PLD	1.1	9.9	18.4	33.8	n.a.	38.9	51.3	
PLD and allies				33.9	13.1			31.3
PRI				7.0	2.3			
Valid votes[a] (thousands)	1,658	1,818	2,112	1,934	3,016	2,904	2,861	2,094
Null votes (%)[b]	5	3	4	3	5	1.5	.1	4.3
Observed votes (%)[b]	3	3	1	1	1	.0	.0	
Total votes (thousands)	1,744	1,922	2,195	1,973	3,082[c]	2,951	2,879	2,184
Abstention (%) (electoral registry)	24	26	28	40	14est[c]	21	23	49
Abstention (%)[d] (est. population over 18)	26	31	38	51	24	37	38	55

Sources: Julio Brea Franco, "Cuando el pasado volvió a tener futuro: Las elecciones dominicanas de 1990" (Santo Domingo: unpublished ms., 1991), various pages; F. D. Monción, *Estadísticas electorales de 1986* (Santo Domingo: n.p., n.d.), various pages; Junta Central Electoral, "Boletín Electoral No. 22," in *Listín Diario,* May 20, 1994; *Gaceta Oficial,* November 10, 1996. Estimated population over 18 for 1994 of 4.07 million from *El Siglo,* September 9, 1993; 1996 population estimates from Instituto de Estudios de Población y Desarrollo.

Notes: n.a. = not available.

For 1978–1996, based on official presidential election results; for 1998, based on official congressional results.

a. Party vote percentages based on valid vote totals.

b. Based on preliminary vote count for 1978–1996; subsequently, some observed and null votes are validated for specific parties. In 1998, null votes are also calculated as a percent of valid votes.

c. Based on preliminary and incomplete vote count.

d. This rough estimate also includes individuals legally ineligible to vote such as foreigners, military and police personnel, and convicted criminals (for 1998, based on an assumption of 2% population growth per year from 1996).

Full party names and presidential candidates: PR, Partido Reformista (1978, 1982), PRSC, Partido Reformista Social Cristiano (1986, 1990)—Joaquín Balaguer (1978, 1982, 1986, 1990, 1994), Jacinto Peynado (1996); PRD, Partido Revolucionario Dominicano—S. Antonio Guzmán (1978), Salvador Jorge Blanco (1982), Jacobo Majluta (1986), José Franciso Peña Gómez (1990, 1994, 1996); PLD, Partido de la Liberación Dominicana—Juan Bosch (1978, 1982, 1986, 1990, 1994), Leonel Fernández (1996); PRI, Partido Revolucionario Independiente—Jacobo Majluta (1990, 1994).

Further, in 1996 President Leonel Fernández dismissed the head of the air force, General Juan Bautista Rojas Tabar, when the general challenged the president's authority.[26]

In many respects, not all of them of their own making, the PRD administrations turned out to be acute disappointments. The Guzmán administration (1978–1982) was viewed as transitional and limited in its reform agenda, facing a Senate controlled by Balaguer's party and growing intraparty rivalry in the PRD. Initial hopes that the administration of Salvador Jorge Blanco (1982–1986) could be an important example of a less personalistic, more institutional, reformist presidency fell short as well under the impact of the country's economic crisis, executive-congressional deadlock now driven by intraparty factionalism, and the reassertion of customs of patronage and executive largesse. By the end of Jorge Blanco's term, the PRD was a factionalized organization that had been forced to oversee a brutal economic adjustment and that confronted widespread accusations of corruption and mismanagement. Although civil liberties had generally been respected during the PRD years, there were no significant advances in democratic institutionalization or participation nor reforms of a social or economic nature. Rather than leaving a legacy of lasting political and economic changes implemented by a social-democratic party, the period of PRD rule was one of persistent patronage politics, followed by a complex up-and-down process of wrenching economic stabilization involving extensive negotiations with the International Monetary Fund (IMF) and other international creditors. Bitter party wrangling and eventually division of the PRD resulted.[27]

The country's economic crisis resulted from a complex web of international and domestic constraints compounded by policy errors. Internationally, oil prices sharply increased following the second OPEC oil shock, interest rates skyrocketed, exports declined, and sugar prices fell in 1977–1979 to rebound in 1980 and then fall sharply again even as the U.S. sugar quota was being reduced, and prices of other Dominican exports also declined. Policy moves by the Guzmán administration, including expansionist fiscal policies, large-scale increases in public-sector jobs, exchange-rate policy, and the structuring and financing of public enterprises, all came under heavy criticism. Similarly, Jorge Blanco's management of negotiations with the IMF, and his turn to a clientelistic style of governing, were harshly criticized, as corruption charges swirled around some of his top officials (and eventually himself). At the same time, business groups were able to thwart fiscal measures and shift the burden of adjustment onto other groups in society even as the struggle for state spoils further fueled political fragmentation.

Significant steps toward economic stabilization were taken under the Jorge Blanco administration, though not without difficulty. In April 1984, the government imposed price increases on fuel, food, and other items as part of a package of measures negotiated with the IMF to renew international credit flows. Protests against these measures escalated into full-scale "IMF riots," which were tragically mismanaged by the armed forces, leading to scores of deaths and the suspension of the measures. In the face of growing international constraints, however, the administration did successfully comply with an IMF standby program during 1985 and 1986. However, the program of devaluation, tight monetary policy, and control of public-sector expenditures induced a sharp recession in the country; the country's GDP declined in 1985 for the first time since the 1965 civil war and U.S. intervention, while inflation reached 37.5 percent, a record until it was superseded in subsequent years.

In his final months in office, Jorge Blanco lowered fuel charges by more than the drop in international prices, increased public employment and food subsidies, and granted massive numbers of tax exemptions for the importation of automobiles and other goods. Dominican observers surmised that these efforts were intended to position the president for a potential electoral comeback in 1990, while enriching his close associates, whether for personal or future political use.

Joaquín Balaguer, Again (1986–1996), and a Transition, Again

Economic decline and divisions within the PRD paved the way for the unexpected presidential comeback of Joaquín Balaguer in 1986. A captive electorate, especially among older, less educated, rural, and women voters, and splits within and between the opposition parties, permitted Balaguer to win the 1986 elections; also because of measures of electoral fraud, Balaguer was also able to eke out narrow victories in 1990 and 1994 as well. However, international pressure and domestic protest in 1994 forced Balaguer to reduce his term to two years and accept a number of constitutional reforms, including the prohibition of immediate presidential reelection. As a consequence, the eighty-eight-year-old Balaguer finally exited from power in 1996, handing power over to the PLD's Leonel Fernández, whom Balaguer had tacitly supported and then openly endorsed (for presidential election results for 1978–1996, see Table 9.1).

In 1986, Balaguer won a narrow plurality victory over the PRD. In preparation for this election, he merged his Reformist Party with several smaller existing Christian-Democratic parties to create the Partido Reformista Social Cristiano (PRSC); this provided him with a veneer of ideology as well as support from the international Christian Democratic Union as a counterpart to the support the PRD received from the Socialist International. Balaguer's victory was aided by the fact that many disgruntled supporters of the PRD and some new voters turned to Juan Bosch and the PLD, which received 18 percent of the vote, doubling the percentage it had received four years earlier.

Balaguer began his term in office by denouncing mistakes and irregularities carried out by his predecessors, leading ultimately to the arrest of former president Jorge Blanco on corruption charges. Yet, the administration did nothing to remove factors that foster corruption. In the end, Balaguer's campaign of moralization primarily had a political impact, helping to further discredit the PRD and particularly Jorge Blanco, and adding fuel to preexisting bitter internal disputes within the PRD. At the same time, the fact that the trial of Jorge Blanco dragged on into Balaguer's subsequent term, and the appeals for years after that, helped demonstrate the poor state of Dominican judicial structures and the political motivations behind the accusation (as of 1998, Jorge Blanco's appeal of his conviction was still under consideration by the judiciary).

In an additional effort to boost his popularity, Balaguer also sought to revive the economy quickly, principally by carrying out a number of large-scale public-investment projects. He pursued a policy of vigorous monetary expansion, fueling inflationary pressures and eventually forcing the government to move toward a system of exchange controls. Inflation, brought down to around 10 percent in 1986, steadily climbed through Balaguer's first term. Through a patch-quilt of policies, the administration was able to limp through the 1990 elections without a formal stabilization plan.

In spite of the country's serious socioeconomic problems, Balaguer was able to win a narrow plurality victory in 1990.[28] In elections marred by irregularities and charges of fraud, the eighty-three-year-old incumbent edged out his eighty-year-old opponent, Juan Bosch, by a mere 24,470 votes. José Franciso Peña Gómez, the PRD candidate, emerged as a surprisingly strong third candidate. By 1990, the PRD was irreparably split along lines that had formed during the bitter struggle for the 1986 presidential nomination between Peña Gómez, supported by then president Jorge Blanco, and Jacobo Majluta. Peña Gómez had stepped aside for Majluta to be the presidential nominee in 1986, but had vowed not to do so again. Peña had primarily concerned himself with developing the PRD's institutional base and its international links with the Socialist International. The failure of numerous efforts since 1986 to settle internal disputes, as well as extensive legal and political wrangling, eventually left Peña Gómez in control of the PRD apparatus. Majluta, a more conservative and "machine-style" politician than Peña Gómez, hinted that he would be interested in serving as Balaguer's running mate. In the end, Majluta ran at the head of a new party and came in a distant fourth (see Table 9.1).

The electoral disputes that ensued in 1990 were never resolved adequately, and the closeness of the race between Balaguer's PRSC and Bosch's PLD made the race even more controversial. The PLD alleged voting by members of the armed forces and Haitians, vote buying, and tampering with electoral tallies at the polling stations. The electorate was suspicious of the results, especially since the polls had shown the PLD ahead in previous months and Balaguer was known for using fraud to remain in power. No firm evidence of rigging emerged, however, and after several weeks of controversies, Balaguer was declared the winner by a razor-thin margin.[29]

Once Balaguer had secured his reelection, he focused on resolving growing tensions between his government and business and the international financial community. Business discontent with Balaguer's economic policy had grown considerably as a result of Balaguer's commitment to massive investments in public works, budget deficits, exchange controls, and his refusal to negotiate with the IMF during the 1986–1990 presidential term, even as the country fell considerably behind in its debt payments. Pressures from importers and exporters to liberalize the economy mounted in 1990. In August, Balaguer called a dialogue with business that prompted the signing of a solidarity pact. In this context, Balaguer was forced to curtail (but not abandon) his state-led developmentalism in favor of more austerity and market liberalization. That is, Balaguer gave in to international and domestic pressures to reduce public spending, negotiate the foreign debt, and liberalize the exchange rate, but not to privatize state-owned enterprises. Balaguer's new economic strategy consisted of increasing selected taxes to fund his construction programs, while keeping government finances in line with IMF stipulations. An agreement with the IMF was reached in 1991 that ultimately helped lead to a dramatic decline in what had been historically high rates of inflation in the country (59 percent in 1990 and 54 percent in 1991, according to official figures).

In addition to growing business discontent, Balaguer also faced increasing social unrest in the late 1980s. Numerous strikes took place between 1987 and 1989, and in 1990 Balaguer faced two general strikes in the summer and two others in the fall.[30] Initially, these were led by the Coordinadora de Luchas Populares (CLP), which soon became the Conferencia Nacional de Organizaciones Populares (CNOP) and then in 1990 the Colectivo de Organizaciones Populares (COP). These groups played a key role in promoting social mobilization in the midst of a rapid decline of trade union membership, increasing segmentation of the labor movement, and labor's failures to sustain agreements with business and the government reached in the context of tripartite pacts mediated by Catholic Church representatives. The COP was never acknowledged by the government, business, the church, and even labor unions as a legitimate partner to negotiate with, yet it was able to gather the support of the discontented masses on several occasions when they called for national or regional strikes.

Balaguer's pact with business in August 1990, his IMF agreement and the subsequent decline in inflation by late 1991, the electoral reforms instituted in 1992 to secure fair elections in 1994, and the marginalization of the COP due to its increasing radicalization led to a decline in social mobilization by 1992. While Balaguer barely changed his neopatrimonial style of leadership, it appeared after 1992 that the Dominican Republic was heading in the direction of holding fair elections in 1994. Both opposition parties (the PRD and the PLD) were vigilant and hoped for a fair election; Dominican civil society was becoming increasingly organized and also vigilant of the electoral process; and, the United States had decided to make a major investment in the democratization (and cleaning) of Dominican elections through substantial aid provided by the United States Agency for International Development (USAID).

However, the 1994 campaign was to result in even more crisis-ridden elections than the 1990 ones.[31] In the context of a reformed electoral code that established greater financial independence for the Junta Central Electoral (JCE) and increased the number of electoral judges from three to five to make it more representative, the Electoral Board embarked on establishing a new voting-registration system. As the elections drew nearer, doubts mounted about the Electoral Board's ability to conclude voting registration successfully and hold fair elections, leading to increased offers of international assistance and efforts by church leaders to seek agreements among leading political figures.

The main contenders in the elections were Balaguer of the PRSC and Peña Gómez of the PRD, with Bosch of the PLD running a distant third. In spite of suspicion and controversies, hopes ran high that with international help to the Electoral Board, a consensus document signed by the leading parties in place, and international monitoring, the 1994 elections would be fair, ending a long sequence of disputed elections in the Dominican Republic. Much to the surprise of many Dominicans and international observers, irregularities in voter registry lists were detected early on election day, which prevented large numbers of individuals from voting. As was documented later, those disenfranchised appeared to be largely PRD followers in what turned out to be extremely close elections, thus potentially affecting the outcome. The prolonged postelection crisis included harsh criticisms from international observer missions,[32] calls from the PRD to annul the elections, extensive pressure from the United States, and OAS mediation.

Almost two months of uncertainty passed before an agreement (known as the Pact for Democracy) was reached among the three major parties on August 10, 1994. The agreement reduced Balaguer's presidential term to two years, after which new presidential elections would be held, and called for appointment of a new Electoral Board, as well as numerous constitutional reforms, including banning consecutive presidential reelection, separating presidential and congressional-municipal elections two years apart, a runoff election if no presidential candidate wins a majority of the votes, reforms to the judicial system, and dual citizenship.

The Pact for Democracy proved to be a satisfactory solution to all parties involved. Balaguer secured at least two more years in office, the PRD avoided violent confrontations with the government or the possibility of remaining ineffective in the midst of obvious fraud, the PLD played a key role in the negotiation even though it had done very poorly electorally, and the United States secured a constitutional exit of Balaguer.

Between 1994 and 1996, the political efforts of opposition parties, Dominican civil society (including substantial elements of the business community), and the international community (the United States in particular) focused on how to secure the holding of fair elections in 1996, while blocking any effort by Balaguer to extend his term in office, either unconstitutionally or by modifying the constitution. In 1996, unlike in previous crisis-ridden elections, presidential reelection was not an issue, and the Central Electoral Board was staffed by professional nonpartisans. Furthermore, in addition to several high-profile missions of international observers, civil society mobilized far more extensively in support of free and fair elections. The Red Ciudadana de Observadores Electorales was organized to monitor the elections, and USAID and other international organizations provided financial assistance to an array of civil-society organizations engaged in civic education, electoral promotion, and consensus building in the formulation of a national agenda for reform.[33]

None of the three main contenders in 1996 received the absolute majority necessary to win in the first round. Peña Gómez of the PRD reached the highest percentage with 45.9 percent, followed by Leonel Fernández of the PLD with 38.9 percent (age and illness had led to Bosch's retirement following the 1994 elections), and Jacinto Peynado of the PRSC with 15 percent. With a renewed PRD under his tight leadership, Peña was able to perform well again in 1996. Balaguer, in turn, did not endorse his party's candidate (indeed, he did not even vote in the first round), instead providing his implicit support to Fernández during the first round. For the second round, Balaguer and the PRSC officially endorsed the candidacy of Fernández in a "Patriotic Pact" calling for the preservation of national sovereignty and Dominicanness, against the candidacy of Peña Gómez (and by so doing, articulating racial and anti-Haitian themes relevant to Peña Gómez's Haitian ancestry). With this endorsement, Fernández was able to defeat Peña in the second round. Yet, Fernández's party had a very small representation in Congress due to its poor performance in the 1994 elections, and soon after Fernández's electoral victory, the PRSC negotiated a pact with the PRD to secure leadership positions in Congress.

Without congressional support, the Fernández administration has faced serious difficulties. The legislative attempt to reform the economy in late 1996 failed when Congress refused to agree on a set of policy proposals to liberalize the economy, including lower tariffs and a higher value-added tax. Congressional deadlock even prevented an agreement over the national budget for 1997, which led President Fernández to withdraw the budget bill from Congress and use the 1996 budget agreement to apply in 1997, as stipulated by the constitution when no agreement is reached between the executive and the legislative over revenues and expenditures.

Fernández has nonetheless governed in a more democratic fashion than Balaguer. As of mid-1998, the Fernández administration had two major political successes. One was the appointment of a new Supreme Court—widely viewed as comprising many distinguished jurists—in a much more open process through a Council of the Judiciary established by the constitutional reform of 1994; another was the securing of fair congressional and municipal elections on May 16, 1998. The death of Peña Gómez on May 10, 1998, and the results of these elections, however, indicate the state of flux of Dominican politics at the close of the twentieth century. The PRD won by an even wider margin than polls had suggested, gaining most congressional seats and municipal governments (80 percent of senate seats, 56 percent of deputy seats, and 83 percent of mayoral races). Although Fernández's own PLD improved its congressional representation compared to 1994, it was not nearly to the level expected by the party; the PRSC, in turn, did very poorly (see Table 9.1).

The 1998 voting results showed that as a unified force, the PRD had regained a majority of the vote in a three-way split (which accounts for its overwhelming electoral success in the congressional and municipal elections). The death of Peña Gómez just a few days before elections may have encouraged PRD sympathizers to go to the polls, adding to their successful performance in elections with a record high abstention rate for the country of 49 percent. The decline of PRSC support without Balaguer running was evident, both from the 1996 and 1998 electoral results, and the PLD, which benefited through the 1980s and 1990s from the misfortunes of the PRD or the PRSC, failed to capitalize on the PRSC's weakness in 1998 because of the high abstentionism.

In 1998, for the first time, political parties received public funding established by an electoral law (Law 275-97) approved in December 1997. This law also instituted a 25 percent quota for female candidates, which contributed to improve women's representation in the Chamber of Deputies, from 8.6 percent in 1994 to 16.1 percent in 1998, and in the municipal councils, from 14.7 in 1994 to 26.5 percent in 1998.

THEORETICAL ANALYSIS

The Dominican Republic has had a limited history of democratic politics, and many factors identified as important by scholars in explaining this have

been present in the country. Of particular relevance are the country's historical evolution given the nature of its international relations, its state and
social structure, and political patterns. Recent changes in the country's
socioeconomic structure and in the role of the United States with regard to
political democracy and human rights, and more limited shifts in terms of
the country's state structure and political patterns, permit a somewhat more
optimistic vision regarding the possibilities for strengthening political
democracy in the country in the near future. At the same time, other features of the country's tangled relations with the United States, and continuing challenges in each of the other areas, highlight the many problems that
continue to confront democracy in the country.

Historical Sequences

The historical evolution, socioeconomic development, and political-
institutional patterning of the Dominican Republic were all inimical to
democratic development and favorable to the emergence of neopatrimonial
and authoritarian rule. We believe it is most appropriate to analyze this in a
"path-dependent" fashion, which sees the links from the colonial era to the
failures of Dominican democracy not as inevitable, but as mediated by
other factors. In particular, it is important to focus on the consequences of
the country's history in the nineteenth century, in which warfare, economic
destitution, and insecurity were bred by the country's relationship with foreign powers and with Haiti, and whose effects were exacerbated by the
actions of unscrupulous leaders. This perspective may be contrasted with a
type of political culture approach for Latin America, which in a rather
reductionist fashion sees an inevitable "destined" pathway from the authoritarian past—Spanish colonial rule—to the present. Howard Wiarda, a
noted scholar on the Dominican Republic, has argued that the Spanish colonial system, a "rigid, top-down, hierarchical, and authoritarian system,"
was imposed on the island of Hispaniola in the sixteenth century, and lasted

> through three centuries of Spanish colonial rule, on into the independence
> rule of the nineteenth century, and even to the present. For even now, the
> sixteenth-century Spanish model of a bureaucratic-authoritarian state
> serves as an alternative to the liberal one, a top-down system that has by
> no means disappeared from the Dominican consciousness.[34]

There are at least two problems with this perspective. One is that it
does not explain how the cultural tradition was effectively transmitted
given that colonial institutions nearly disappeared as did most elements of
the original colonial settlers. Another is that differing arguments about the
consequences of being a colonial backwater have been made. Wiarda notes
(and historians concur) that by the mid–sixteenth century Hispaniola had
become an unimportant and largely ignored part of the Spanish colonial

empire, and that traditional institutions of Spanish colonialism, particularly a landed oligarchy based on the hacienda system and the church, were notoriously weak by the early nineteenth century and in fact remained so over the century. Indeed, one can concur with his judgment that the country lacked any institutions at all (viewing institutions as formal organizations) on which to base a viable sociopolitical order. However, this means that what was to become the Dominican Republic had little of the reality of effective Spanish colonial political and social governance present elsewhere on the continent. If the Spanish colonial system was most notorious in the Dominican Republic for its weakness, it is difficult to see how that "tradition" could be the principal causal factor explaining subsequent authoritarianism. Furthermore, this kind of approach also cannot explain why the country was incapable of developing institutions (formal organizations) subsequently.

The other major problem is that others have argued that being a backwater of Spanish colonialism *favored* subsequent democratic evolution, such as in the cases of Costa Rica or Chile.[35] If we accept that the Chilean case may have been marked both by more traditional colonial domination and by institutional discontinuity, as Arturo Valenzuela argues, then it is more clearly the Costa Rican example that complicates arguments that authoritarianism in the Dominican Republic stems essentially from a legacy or a tradition established during Spanish colonial rule. That is because there are impressive similarities between the two in terms of their colonial eras: both were colonial backwaters that experienced leveling effects due to poverty and isolation, and neither economy was based on large-scale export agriculture based on forced labor or slavery. Yet, this did not favor democracy in the Dominican Republic as it did in Costa Rica.

The way out of this puzzle is to analyze how the link to the colonial era was mediated by other critical factors affecting historical sequences. In our view, the role of ideas in political action needs to be understood within their social setting and in terms of the institutions and social groups that promote and sustain them.[36] The failure of "liberal ideas" in the Dominican Republic was rooted also in the failure of the social and political forces that supported them to become politically hegemonic, and in the ability of authoritarian rulers eager to justify their rule in a structural setting favorable for neopatrimonialism to employ a "cultural solution" that was available to them from a repertoire of ideas from the country's past history.

It is more fruitful to view Dominican history not as predetermined by Spanish colonial rule but rather in a "path-dependent" fashion to understand what links there may have been between the colonial era and subsequent critical moments in Dominican development. In doing so, it is also important to examine the confluence of domestic structural factors and international geopolitical ones. Indeed, one obvious critical difference between Costa Rica and the Dominican Republic is the absence of war, economic devastation, and international vulnerability in the former. In Costa Rica, a modest economic prosperity built upon relatively greater social and economic equality was able to emerge. And, unlike its northern Central American neighbors that were wracked by bitter civil conflict between liberals and conservatives emerging out of the colonial era, in Costa Rica (in contrast to Chile) there was a greater degree of institutional continuity, albeit dominated by aristocratic, civilian conservatives that avoided militarization. In the Dominican case, chronic warfare, shaped by international vulnerability, helped generate a pattern of economic destitution, regionalism, new struggles for power, and the lack of effective national integration or an effective central state, until a military *caudillo* could accumulate sufficient military and administrative power to impose a brutal order.[37] Additional geographic and ethnic factors may have contributed to the country's concerns about national security and willingness to trade sovereignty for protection. The territorial division of the small island of Hispaniola into two countries with ethnic, linguistic, and cultural differences, and the manipulation of racial and ethnic fears, intensified distrust and militarization.

We also reject excessively reductionist arguments that view Dominican authoritarianism as an imposition by imperialist powers.[38] International vulnerability has different meanings, but the most significant loss is unquestionably that of national sovereignty. Of the Spanish colonies that gained their independence in the early to mid nineteenth century, the Dominican Republic is certainly at the extreme in the extent of its loss of sovereignty and its perceived vulnerability throughout the nineteenth century. One does not need to condone the actions of foreign powers or of unscrupulous foreign speculators to emphasize that it is critical to understand the domestic consequences of this vulnerability. The historical narrative above indicates the country's international vulnerability helped lead to an emphasis on leadership based on military might, to a willingness to seek out foreign protectors, and to the renewed loss of national independence. At the turn of the century, the United States sought dominance of the Caribbean and Central America for its own economically and security-oriented motives, dominance which it largely achieved and which unquestionably had a number of often negative and unforeseen consequences for these countries. Thus there is an intimate link between international vulnerability and the country's authoritarian history, though not in an automatic fashion. It is not possible to blame occupation by foreign forces, alone, for the lack of subsequent Dominican democracy: neither U.S. intervention in the country's economic affairs nor its military occupation of the country in the 1916–1924 period, or the earlier nineteenth-century Haitian or Spanish occupations, truncated what would otherwise have been a smooth democratic evolution.

In this context, perhaps the most important turning point for the country came during the period of 1916–1930. As in Nicaragua and Haiti, U.S. military occupation strengthened a national military institution where none had previously existed and enhanced the value of the state where other sources of power and wealth were still few. With the shift in U.S. foreign policy toward nonintervention, these new factors facilitated the rise to power of Trujillo, who had a profound effect on Dominican institutions and psyches. Under Trujillo, a central state was built and national integration was achieved, but under a perverted discretional neopatrimonial rule that inhibited the development of independent political or social organizations or institutions.

State Structures

As the previous section has highlighted, the process of state formation was long and difficult in the Dominican Republic. Modern nation-states are usually articulated in terms of the market as well as the political arena. This proved difficult to achieve in the Dominican Republic, where capitalist relations of production were poorly developed. As a result, the precepts and practices of the liberals for much of Dominican history, like the constitutional guidelines, were quite irrelevant to the actual exercise of political power. Such a society provided no secure foothold for democracy. Consequently, the constitutions of this period were viewed more as statements of principles than as concrete political blueprints for organizing the nation-state.[39]

As we have argued above, functional state institutions developed during the U.S. occupation of 1916–1924.[40] While the period of occupation was important in laying the grounds for the development of state structures, the process of state formation lacked a national reference. In the context of a foreign occupation, the latter was simply impossible to achieve. The occupation suppressed factional fighting as local *caudillos* became subordinate to the authority of the U.S. military government. But instead of helping to institutionalize democracy, this period paved the way for the lengthy authoritarian Trujillo regime, while laying the bases for this to be the first Dominican government to assume control over the means of violence in the country.

It was during the Trujillo dictatorship that the Dominican nation-state was fostered and consolidated. Trujillo took hold of the administrative state that had developed during the occupation and infused it with a sense of the truly Dominican, based on the shared destiny of Dominicans striving for peace and progress. His plan was to salvage national values under the tutelage of an authoritarian state. The forging of a collective identity around notions of work and discipline played a key role in Trujillo's plan to consolidate the Dominican state and its capacity to regulate the economy, control the populace, and eventually become the source of enrichment for the dictator. State structures were vital to perform these functions.

With the rise of Balaguer to power in 1966, state institutions played a similar role, facilitated by the fact that all of Trujillo's vast holdings had been expropriated and were now state "patrimony." With disdain and distrust of the state, Balaguer essentially focused on using public resources for construction and public-works projects, largely forgoing investment in education or health; in campaign periods, he freely employed state resources and personnel in pursuit of his reelection. He may not have amassed wealth personally, but he did allow many others to amass large fortunes in a complex patronage system that ranged from meager handouts to the poor to generous commissions in construction projects and valuable import privileges. The rule of law was of little significance to a neopatrimonial president who openly stated that constitutions were mere pieces of paper.

With the process of democratization that began in 1978, the state underwent some changes, although the PRD failed to deliver on its reform agenda. Most significantly, the repressive apparatus changed considerably. Violations of human rights still occurred sporadically and police abuse of suspected criminals was common, but outright massive repression was not a common practice. However, state structures have remained inefficient and ineffective. Civil service laws are weak and public employees are generally underprepared and underpaid; their desire (and also need) to improve their salaries has led to a variety of corrupt practices. In the absence of transparent processes of competitive bidding for procurement or construction projects, irregular deals were commonplace.

These processes not only continued, but were exacerbated when Balaguer returned to office in 1986. Balaguer initiated his new period in office using corruption charges against Jorge Blanco and several other former public officials associated with the PRD as a means of destroying the former president as a political threat and of seeking to distinguish his own government. However, Balaguer continued to collect and to use state resources in a highly discretional fashion, and to employ state resources for campaign purposes. In his subsequent terms in office, major corruption scandals emerged in different areas of public administration that were never properly investigated or prosecuted. The deterioration of the state, combined with economic decline and increasingly disputed elections, served to awaken Dominican civil society and led them to promote a reform agenda.

Domestic and international pressure helped lead to important electoral, constitutional, and judicial reforms in the 1990s, and to hopes that further state reforms would follow when Balaguer stepped down from office in 1996. There has been some reorientation of state expenditures toward health and education, important advances in the management of elections, and more modest ones in the judicial branch; and, as of mid-1999, there have been no major corruption scandals under the Fernández administration as under the previous one. However, practically all state institutions continue to operate with high inefficiency and opportunities for corruption remain high. The attempts to reform the civil service, the Central Bank, the financial system, and the Congress, and to further reform the judiciary, have continued to face major political obstacles as the Congress controlled by the opposition has blocked passage of key bills.

Political Culture

Given the colonial experience and then particularly the historical evolution of the Dominican Republic in the nineteenth century, it is hardly surprising that liberal ideas did not penetrate deeply into the country. Constitutions and formal-legal institutions were often either ignored or ex post facto rationalizations; they kept liberal doctrines alive but at the cost of hypocrisy and cynicism, although by 1880 one could assert that the liberal constitutional *doctrine,* though of course not the practice, emerged triumphant in the country against constitutional texts that were openly authoritarian.[41]

The Trujillo dictatorship played a key role in promoting and reinforcing authoritarian beliefs and practices. The subsequent process of democratization has helped to promote democratic ideals in Dominican politics, but even today authoritarian views prevail among many Dominicans. According to the results of two recent political-culture surveys (DEMOS-1994 and DEMOS-1997), these views are especially found among Dominicans who live in rural areas, have lower levels of education, and are from lower socioeconomic strata.[42] The surveys found that women, on average, held more authoritarian values, except with regard to the family, and that younger and especially older groups in the sample did as well (though to what extent these findings would decline once education was controlled for is not clear).[43] The two surveys also found substantial majorities of those surveyed agreed with the statement that a good president should be like a father on whom you rely to solve your problems (76.4 percent in 1994 and 81.8 percent in 1997); concurred that they value order over democracy (66.5 percent in 1994 and 64.7 percent in 1997); and indicated that a strong leader could do more good for the country than all the existing laws (50.4 percent in both 1994 and 1997).

These findings indicate the existence of substantial attitudinal support for authoritarian and neopatrimonial practices. However, rather than viewing political culture as the central independent variable inhibiting democracy in the country, we view it more as an intervening variable (providing a cultural "space" for certain kinds of political leaders such as Balaguer) or as a dependent variable (amenable to change). We see the pattern of the country's democratic evolution as ultimately shaped more by socioeconomic and political structures and political leadership. With a political leadership committed to enhancing democracy, and with socioeconomic changes and mobilization from civil society, authoritarian attitudes can change in a democratic direction. Thus, political-cultural change is not a *pre*condition for making democracy work in the Dominican Republic; rather, we see democracy working as the best way to change these types of attitudes.[44]

Another potential source of political-cultural change may be returning migrants, who often bring new economic and political skills. Indeed, President Fernández is himself a return migrant. Dominican migration abroad has not been a permanent, one-way step, but a much more fluid process of travel and return, with the maintenance of complex transnational ties between Dominican communities in the diaspora and their home country and communities.[45]

Socioeconomic Structure and Development Performance

Neopatrimonial polities and clientelist practices rest on and reinforce societal situations of high levels of inequality and weak levels of formal organization, especially among poorer sectors of society, both of which also help explain authoritarian attitudes such as those presented above.[46] The Dominican Republic has been marked both by vast inequalities of wealth and income and by substantial percentages of its population living in poverty; relative to the other eight countries discussed in this volume, it has also had substantially lower levels of per capita income.[47] As seen above, the country historically did not have a powerful, wealthy oligarchy, which facilitated the emergence of a dictator like Trujillo who was able to amass considerable power from the state and also become the country's dominant economic force. Similarly, the levels of organization of popular-sector groups have also been extremely low even by comparison to other Latin American countries.

For most of this century, the Dominican Republic's economy has been centered around the export of primary products, especially sugar cane, though also tobacco, coffee, cocoa, and ferronickel. As with other countries of the Caribbean and Central America, the Dominican Republic initiated its process of import-substitution industrialization in the 1940s, which was facilitated by the surplus from foreign trade. However, when Trujillo died in 1961, the country was still largely rural and isolated, with almost 70 percent of its 3 million people living in rural areas and over 60 percent of its labor force in agriculture. There were essentially no independent organizations in society, and efforts at labor organization had been brutally repressed.[48]

Over the next three decades, the country became much more urban (60 percent in 1990), and industry and especially services expanded dramatically. In the early and mid-1960s, political turmoil hampered economic growth, yet workers saw their salaries and benefits improve initially in the midst of business opposition to any labor gains. The resulting tensions made unviable a democratic reform plan that contemplated significant redistribution of wealth as proposed by the PRD in 1962, and helped lead to Bosch's overthrow.[49] When Balaguer came to office in 1966, he immediately implemented a program of economic development centered around helping the private sector expand import substitution in consumer goods, containing labor demands, and implementing extensive public investment projects.

The PRD came to power in 1978 promising a reformist overhaul of the Dominican economy. Yet, during their period in office, the dramatic changes that took place in the country's economy were not the ones they had intended. Traditional exports, especially of sugar, declined sharply, and protected industry oriented to the domestic market stagnated.

In a dramatic reorientation of the country's economy, the country's foreign exchange from the 1980s on was increasingly generated from three new sources: export-processing or free-trade zones, tourism, and remittances from overseas Dominicans. Free-trade zones were a response to preferential market-access schemes, especially to U.S. markets, whereby the country could export certain quota-affected consumer goods (such as clothing and footwear) from free-trade zones, with duties being charged primarily on the value added by labor. By the mid-1990s, more labor was employed in these areas than by traditional industry. The factories in these areas tended to employ predominantly women and to resist union organizing; thus, following a surge in collective bargaining with the 1978 transition, an already weak labor movement eventually fragmented further organizationally and was largely unable to make inroads into a key area of the economy. This changed somewhat with the enactment of a new labor code in 1992, which finally replaced Trujillo's 1951 labor code. The new legislation was enacted under the threat of U.S. trade sanctions promoted by U.S. labor unions. The growth of tourism was also dramatic. By the middle of the 1990s, net foreign exchange earnings from tourism were equivalent to those of sugar exports.

Finally, the country's economy became increasingly dependent upon the remittances of overseas migrants. Following the 1965 civil war and U.S. intervention, the United States facilitated migration of Dominicans to the United States, many of whom could be considered "political migrants" as they came from disgruntled urban middle sectors. However, from the late 1970s and especially since the mid-1980s, there was a dramatic jump in overall migration levels, motivated increasingly by economic reasons and facilitated by family ties. Around 7 to 14 percent of those born in the Dominican Republic currently live overseas.[50]

The dramatic changes in the country's socioeconomic structure over these past several decades have not centrally affected the country's high levels of inequality and they have had contradictory effects on the extent and nature of organization in society, weakening many popular-sector groups and enhancing other types of predominantly middle-sector organizations. Into the 1980s, migration served to remove potential dissidents from the country, while the country's economic restructuring helped fragment key parts of Dominican civil society, especially among working-class and other popular sectors.

Changes in the country's political economy, though, did place new limits on the state and thus on the ability of presidents to abuse and manipulate state resources. When he returned to office in 1986, Balaguer repeated his strategy of massive investments in public works to the extent possible, largely ignoring investments in health and education. However, as the fiscal crisis became more serious over the 1980s and 1990s, the state was forced increasingly to subsidize state enterprises rather than to draw resources from them. Although difficult to prove, politicians and observers alike have argued that awareness of tourism's sensitivity to political stability almost certainly has helped to constrain protest activities, especially by leading political actors.

By most indicators the Dominican economy performed poorly in the 1980s. Total consumption dropped from an annual average rate of growth of 7 percent in 1970–1980 to 1.1 percent in 1981–1989. Gross domestic investment also declined, from 10 percent in 1971–1980 to 4.4 percent in 1981–1989. The average rate of growth of the GDP declined both in general and in per capita terms, from 7 percent in 1971–1980 to 2.6 percent in 1981–1989, and from 4.4 percent in 1971–1980 to 0.2 percent in 1981–1989, respectively.[51] Following the implementation of a stabilization program in 1990, which led to a decline in GDP of over 5 percent, growth rates have improved in the 1990s relative to the 1980s. Adding to the depth of the economic problems was the lack of commitment of different administrations to consult and democratize the decisionmaking process. In managing the economic difficulties, the president (whoever the incumbent) and a few cabinet members made the decisions.

Overall, societal changes since 1961 have tended to be favorable for democracy. As domestic firms became more diversified and the country's economy expanded, the possibilities for more independent elements within civil society to emerge also increased, though principally within business and middle-sector groups. This phenomenon emerged under Balaguer's first twelve-year period, playing a role in the 1978 transition. It became evident again, and played an even more important role, in the 1996 transition from Balaguer. Ultimately, though, the quality of democracy and perhaps even the consolidation of political democracy depend upon strengthening civil society further and ameliorating the country's sharp inequalities, which help to feed clientelist politics and limit effective citizenship.

Ethnic Cleavages

Dominican nationality was constructed around the notion of rejecting the Haitian presence. Although the country is overwhelmingly mulatto, Trujillo and Balaguer sought to project an image of the country built around a Catholic, Hispanic, white essence, in contrast to a "pagan," African, black Haiti.[52] The indigenous population died off soon after the Spaniards arrived. Yet Dominicans have continued to make references to an indigenous past that was short-lived and prefer to be identified as Indians over black. Dominicans, like other societies in the Caribbean, see a racial continuum, including white, black, and mixed.[53] Under the mixed category, various terms are used to refer to those who approximate white or black. The term "Indian" is frequently used to define those in the mixed category: *indio claro, indio oscuro;* another term used for the same purpose is *trigueño.*[54]

Waves of migrants have defined the ethnic composition of the Dominican Republic. The indigenous populations, the Spaniards, and the African slaves constituted the ethnic foundation of Dominican society. Thus, historians have emphasized the presence of Europeans, Africans, and to a more limited extent indigenous people. Since the late nineteenth century, however, other groups arrived in the Dominican Republic, making the society more diverse ethnically. Many European and Lebanese immigrants eventually achieved positions of higher social status in business and the professions. By the 1970s, they constituted a large segment of the upper and upper middle class of Dominican society.

Migration from Haiti to the Dominican Republic has been steady, particularly after the fall of Trujillo in 1961, supplying low-paid workers to the growing but highly inefficient sugar economy. The process of labor migration from Haiti has never been regulated in a satisfactory manner, in spite of international pressures to improve working conditions of Haitians in the Dominican Republic. With the decline of the sugar economy in the 1980s, Haitians have found jobs in coffee and rice plantations, in construction and tourism. Ultranationalists have claimed that 1 million or more Haitians reside in the Dominican Republic. Academic experts, in turn, estimate the number of Haitians and of Dominicans of Haitian descent (whose citizenship rights have commonly been denied) in the country to be around 500,000 to 700,000.[55]

Because Dominicans hold deep-seated prejudices against Haitians, as well as because of their illegal status and poverty, the integration of Haitians into Dominican life has been extremely difficult. Haitians have constituted a very useful card for conservative politicians to use when they wish to mobilize Dominicans and gather their support on patriotic terms. Balaguer, who allowed the massive migration of Haitians to supply cheap labor to sugar producers in the 1970s and to construction crews in the 1980s, consistently expressed racist (anti-Haitian) views in his speeches and writings, and he was also known for his policy of deporting Haitians when he needed to appeal to the patriotic sentiments of many Dominicans. Prejudice against Haitians played an important role in the strategy employed by Balaguer against Peña Gómez in the 1994 campaign, given his Haitian origins. Similarly, in 1996, Balaguer and the ultranationalists, eventually with the support of the PLD, mounted a racist campaign against Peña Gómez.

While race is frequently used by conservative politicians to separate Haitian Afro-blackness from what is Dominican, race has not provided a basis for progressive politics in the Dominican Republic. Because of the three-tiered division, dark blacks (mostly identified as Haitians) are, in ideological terms, separated from the rest of the population that is defined as truly Dominican. With this social construction of race,[56] Dominicans hardly identify blackness as their own, and even if they are phenotypically black, race is redefined with the use of another term, such as *indio, trigueño,* or *mulatto* in the case of darker blacks. Thus, cross-ethnic labor alliances—for example, in the sugar cane fields—never succeeded, while the ability to hyperexploit Haitian labor precluded the need to treat Dominican workers as harshly.

Dominican social construction of race is therefore based on black denial. Blackness is reserved for Haitians, who Dominicans claim they reject not because they are black, but because they are Haitians who have wanted to dominate the island ever since they achieved independence from France in 1804.[57] Haitian occupation of the Dominican Republic in 1822–1844 provides the historical proof to this argument. It is when Dominicans migrate abroad, to the United States in particular, that they must confront their blackness. In the United States, the social construction of race is based on a two-tiered system that clearly differentiates between whites and blacks,[58] with other groups being defined more in terms of ethnicity than race (Hispanics, Asian Americans, Native Americans). Since most Dominicans are mulattos (who in the U.S. two-tiered racial system are blacks), they face the daunting task of redefining themselves racially. The implications of this for racial relations in the Dominican Republic are still not clear.

What is clear is that it is difficult to conceive of consolidating democracy in the Dominican Republic without ensuring that basic human rights and citizenship rights of a substantial minority of the population are respected. At the same time, given the complex historical, cultural, economic, and political dimensions of the problem, building democratic coalitions across the Dominican Republic and Haiti to address this issue is likely to be a difficult and protracted process.

Political Parties

In spite of the lack of a history of democratic politics, during the 1960s and 1970s a surprisingly strong party system with substantial roots in society was constructed in the country.[59] Throughout the nineteenth century, a weak two-party system prevailed in the style of a conservative-liberal party split. However, these were easily swept away by the Trujillo dictatorship, which established one-party rule from the state.[60] In the post-Trujillo period, a moderate multiparty system has gradually emerged.

In the early 1960s, three major political forces defined the political field. One was the Unión Cívica Nacional (UCN), an elite party that was formed by the Dominican oligarchy opposed to the Trujillo dictatorship. Another was the PRD, a party formed in the late 1930s by exiles opposed to the Trujillo dictatorship that quickly became a mass party after the fall of Trujillo. The third was the Movimiento Revolucionario 14 de Junio (MR-14J), which embraced a revolutionary ideology (with other Marxist organizations forming in subsequent years). The electoral defeat of the UCN in the first democratic elections of the post-Trujillo period held in 1962 led to its quick demise. The winner of the 1962 elections, the PRD, in turn was to become one of the country's leading parties. The discourse of its leader, Juan Bosch, was also crucial in defining the PRD as the party of the underprivileged. Using a class-based discourse, Bosch differentiated between the privileged Dominicans (the *tutumpotes*) and the deprived Dominicans (the *hijos de machepa*).[61] This discourse was instrumental to the PRD as it evolved into a mass-based, catchall party.

The PRD was unable to establish its credibility as a democratic party in the early 1960s, in the context of a weak and insecure business class, strongly anticommunist church and military institutions, and a United States deeply fearful of "another Cuba." Moreover, the overall fragility of state structures, indeed of any political or economic organization in the country (in addition to the adverse international factors), made it impossible for democracy to flourish and process societal demands. However, the de facto governments that followed the coup of 1963, which overthrew Bosch's government, failed to institute a workable repressive system, leading to the civil war of 1965 and the subsequent U.S. intervention. These events, following on the heels of the 1963 coup, helped to consolidate the heroic image of the PRD as a protagonist of democratization and a base of mass support. They also infused the party with a revolutionary ideology, though many of its leaders remained committed to political struggle within the parameters of liberal democracy (one important exception was Juan Bosch).

Starting in 1966, the party system was redefined. Balaguer returned from exile, where he had founded the Reformist Party. He ran in 1966 and won the elections under allegations of unfair competition by the PRD. With Balaguer in office, the Reformist Party gathered the support of the conservative electorate across social classes, though it was particularly strong in rural areas. Thus, between 1966 and 1978, the Dominican party system was characterized by two dominant, catchall parties: one with a conservative-authoritarian agenda (the Reformist Party) and the other with a populist-democratic one (the PRD). Balaguer was reelected in 1970 and 1974 in elections that were unfair; had military pressure and, in the end, were uncontested by the PRD. In 1973 Bosch left the PRD, expressing his discontent with what he viewed as its ineffective liberal-democratic bent, creating the PLD. Unlike the PRD and the Reformist Party, the PLD did not seek to become a mass-based party. It was a leftist cadre party that appealed mostly to middle- and lower-middle-class professionals.

During the twelve-year-long presidency of Balaguer (1966–1978), the heroic image of the PRD was further consolidated as the party suffered persecution and defeats in its attempts to reinstitute democracy. The PRD finally succeeded in 1978 in its efforts to force Balaguer to hold free elections. The new realities of the transition to democracy in 1978 led to further changes in the party system. Electoral competition as the only "game in town" to achieve power, and the ability of the electorate to throw out of office inefficient governments, led the PLD to enter the electoral arena, where it saw its votes increase dramatically over the 1980s.

Thus, by 1986 the Dominican party system was characterized by three major parties, all with the ability to win an election: the PRD, the PLD, and the Reformist Party, now renamed the Partido Reformista Social Cristiano (PRSC). To a remarkable extent, the three parties penetrated society and together mobilized high percentages of the population on election day. In spite of a myriad of smaller parties and movements, these three parties have together received over 90 percent of the vote in each election since 1978; and, with the exception of the 1990 elections when the PRD was emerging from a bitter split, electoral participation rates during this period have fluctuated between 62 and 76 percent of the estimated population eligible to vote (see Table 9.1).

However, these Dominican parties are plagued by weak links to organized groups in civil society and by the inability of the party leadership to abandon clientelism, personalism, and, in some cases, factionalism. These problems contribute to the centrifugal and counterorganizational tendencies in the party system. Parties are held together essentially around loyalty to charismatic leaders and the expectations of clientelistic rewards when a particular party is in power. The economic difficulties that characterize highly dependent economies such as the Dominican one aggravate the struggle among party elites to control resources and patronage, frequently leading governing parties to abandon their campaign promises, and raising serious questions of accountability. As a consequence, the country has not advanced in terms of more formal, regularized forms of institutionalization.[62]

In the PRSC and the PLD, dissidence was also severely punished by the party leader, thus preventing deep factionalism; Balaguer was further able to maintain loyalty through pursuit of reelection. In the PRD, where charismatic leadership is combined with a traditional rejection of presidential reelection, and there is a strong party machine of many organizational units with positions filled by numerous party leaders, factionalism has been an endemic problem. As factional strife was leading to a potentially disintegrating split of the party in the late 1980s, Peña Gómez took tight control of the party and reasserted his charismatic leadership over that of other party leaders in 1990. With this formula, Peña Gómez prevented further divisions within the PRD, but this was accomplished at the expense of party democracy and institutionalization.

While in office, both the PRSC and the PRD established clientelistic systems that encouraged corruption and retarded the democratic institutionalization of state and party structures. The first government of the PLD, inaugurated in August 1996, has not yet relied on extensive corruption to foster political clienteles. The PLD being a small (cadre) party mostly of middle-class professionals, President Fernández has appointed most of the party leadership to cabinet positions with significantly improved salaries assigned to those positions. As a relatively young politician who witnessed how corruption charges derailed former president Jorge Blanco's career, Fernández is aware of the potential damage he can do to his future political career should he rely on outright corruption to gather political support. Thus, he has been consistently tough on corruption, and through the first three years of his term no major corruption scandal had exploded in the media.

The three-party system has been functional to Dominican democracy in the narrow sense that it has provided stability. However, the stability of the party system—the ability of the three parties to monopolize voter support—had relied primarily on the charismatic and strong leadership of Joaquín Balaguer (PRSC), Juan Bosch (PLD), and José Francisco Peña Gómez (PRD). As of mid-1999, only the PRSC had not yet made the transition from tight control by its aging traditional leader, even as it experienced historically low levels of voter support in the 1996 and 1998 elections. Without these charismatic leaders, though, all three Dominican parties face the problem of managing leadership succession and party survival. Furthermore, the party system and the regime as a whole confront the crucial issue of how to achieve the representation of societal interests in accountable and democratic fashion, rather than through personalistic-charismatic rule as has been the norm to date.

Political Structures

The relationships across the presidency, Congress, and the judiciary have been long-standing problems in Dominican politics. The presidency has had significant formal power, and historically vast informal powers, especially due to the absence of any effective check from the country's judiciary and the inability or the unwillingness of the legislature to assume its constitutional responsibilities in lawmaking and in oversight of the executive.[63] And, when Congress has chosen to act, it has usually been to restrain the president for narrow personal or sometimes partisan purposes rather than to seek alternative policies.

Authoritarian governments have ruled with disregard for Congress, and congressional representatives usually endorsed the executive agenda for narrow political or for personal gain. The weakness of the rule of law has permitted the use and abuse of state resources throughout the state. President Balaguer simply spent a large portion of the national budget through the office of the presidency at his discretion, and he was quick to rule by decree when he did not find support in Congress for his initiatives. This was facilitated by the fact that he retained majorities (often very slim) in Congress, and by the fact that the judiciary was unwilling to provide any check on his actions.

After the democratic transition, Congress has also played the opposite role: namely, opposing executive initiatives in order to undermine presidential plans, principally obstructing rather than proposing alternatives, but failing to exercise effective scrutiny over executive branch functions. During the eight-year rule of the PRD (1978–1986), factions within the PRD made it extremely difficult for the incumbent presidents (Guzmán in 1978–1982 and Jorge Blanco in 1982–1986) to rely on the support of their own party in Congress. Since 1996, congressional opposition to PLD president Fernández has undermined his ability to promote economic, political, and social reforms. Deadlock and immobilism have therefore defined the administrations of the PRD and the PLD (though for somewhat different reasons). This has been particularly unfortunate because the PRD and the PLD are the parties better positioned to promote reforms aimed at consolidating Dominican democracy.

The judiciary remained unchanged, underfunded, and largely forgotten until the early 1990s. The notion of judicial independence is not entrenched in Dominican institutions or mentality. Balaguer's disregard for the law was well-known and was coined in his statement: "Fortunately, constitutions in countries like ours have been, are, and will be for many years simple pieces of paper. In every country, in every era, at any moment in history, men, not principles, are most important."[64] The law was applied arbitrarily based on political preferences or on the payment received by a judge to make a decision. Political maneuvering and corruption permeated the judicial system.

With the increasing modernization of Dominican society and business, this constitutional and judicial legacy and its neopatrimonial bases are under growing challenge. The constitutional reform of 1994 established a Council of the Judiciary to appoint a new Supreme Court based on judicial criteria and outstanding professional credentials. The new Supreme Court was appointed in 1997, but further implementing legislation must be approved for the Supreme Court to appoint other judges, and a vast reform of the organization of the judiciary is needed. Insufficient funding for the courts, inadequate preparation and training for the judges, and continued corruption make the administration of justice arbitrary, inefficient, and untrustworthy.

Political Leadership

Political leadership can sometimes help establish new patterns of expectations and behavior, helping to forge a more democratic politics. In the Dominican Republic, though, leadership has frequently been highly authoritarian and willing to abuse state resources for its own narrow purposes, while also being largely charismatic and personalistic. Trujillo monopolized the use of political and economic resources to an unprecedented extent. His was an authoritarian and personalistic leadership, but he also cultivated his charisma as a tough leader. Balaguer, with a fragile physical appearance, used his intellect to weaken opponents and keep his associates under fear of political revenge. Indeed, revenge and co-optation were key to Trujillo and Balaguer as mechanisms to secure the support of their collaborators.[65] They appealed to the masses as fatherlike figures who knew best how to develop the country and lead its people to peace and prosperity. Active opponents were simply repressed. For almost fifty years, from 1930 to 1978, co-optation, repression, and revenge were the key components of neopatrimonial political leadership of the Dominican Republic.

Briefly, after the fall of Trujillo, with democratic aspirations on the rise, a new charismatic leader emerged to guide the nation toward democracy. Juan Bosch replaced Trujillo as the father figure, albeit with a contrasting political agenda. Whereas Trujillo had attempted to fuse society into a great silent mass, Bosch's message focused on inequalities and social distinctions between the oligarchy and the people. Working with these ideas, Bosch led the PRD to become a multiclass party with a democratic ideal and a populist orientation. Bosch was nicknamed "The Professor"; speaking a simple language, he patiently instructed the people throughout the experiment with democracy. His failed attempt to establish democracy in the early 1960s, in the midst of harsh opposition by the military, the Catholic Church, business, and the United States, turned him into a national hero.

If Bosch instructed the masses, Peña Gómez captivated them with a more radicalized discourse in the post–coup d'état period. Thus, in the late 1960s and early 1970s, the PRD had two charismatic leaders that helped to consolidate the largest and best organized mass party in Dominican history. As Bosch grew increasingly discontented with the political situation in the country in the late 1960s, Peña Gómez gained more prominence as the party leader. When Bosch left the PRD in 1973 to form the PLD, he devoted his energy to build a party of enlightened cadres, tutored under Bosch's notions of politics and society (*el boschismo*).

The rise of Balaguer to power in 1966 was the product of a profound social and political crisis. The brief interval following the Trujillo era had been a time when democratic ideals had coexisted with political chaos and the persistent call for authoritarianism. In this context, Balaguer took advantage of the cultural space available for appeals built around the promise of order and progress based on social, economic, and political discipline and loyalty to the Catholic Church. This had a strong appeal across social sectors, among upper-class sectors within the society that feared the PRD and its proposed changes, and within the lower classes among rural and less-educated groups that could embrace a leader who promised to set the house in order. Like Trujillo, Balaguer held up a vision of the rule of law as the key to full harmony and the path to civilization, though the law did not acquire any real status and responded instead to his personal dictates. Balaguer arrogated himself a place among the few Dominicans with an unselfish concern for the nation, setting himself up on a pedestal of self-sacrifice in a society afflicted with unpatriotic selfishness.[66] With this discourse, Balaguer frequently sought to justify his need to stay in power and the exclusionary nature of his rule.

There was a missed opportunity to establish a new pattern of more democratic leadership over the 1978–1986 period of PRD rule. Guzmán's government was widely viewed as riddled with nepotism. Guzmán's bitter enmity with Jorge Blanco (even though they were of the same party), concerns about corruption charges against his family, isolation from former political associates, and depression led to his suicide a few weeks before the end of his term. Also tragic was the outcome of Jorge Blanco's presidency. It had begun with hopes that it would establish a new pattern of rule and style of leadership, but saddled with economic crisis, it ended with bitter intraparty factionalism and growing charges of corruption.

Bosch, Peña Gómez, and Balaguer constituted the pillars of Dominican politics in the post-Trujillo period. The end of their leadership posed daunting tasks to their parties. While the PLD resolved the question of leadership succession when Bosch retired from active politics in 1994 and Leonel Fernández was chosen to run for president in 1996, the party lacks its own social basis of support and a clear ideology around which to mobilize the electorate. As a result, Leonel Fernández relies on contingencies to remain popular and sustain his power.[67] They range from clientelistic strategies to consensus-building experiments such as the National Dialogue in March 1998, when President Fernández and his cabinet listened for several days to hundreds of organizations of civil society as they proposed multiple proposals for administrative, socioeconomic, environmental, political, and other types of reforms.

The death of Peña Gómez in May 1998 found the PRD without a clear succession. Since 1990, Peña had maintained tight control over the party to prevent factionalism, yet the factions, while contained for a few years, have reemerged after his death. The PRD's sweeping victory in the 1998 congressional and municipal elections has helped it to remain unified in the hope of winning the presidency in the year 2000, yet a small group of PRD deputies joined the opposition parties in the House of Representatives and were as a result expelled from the PRD. Presidential elections, scheduled for the year 2000, are likely to aggravate intraparty rivalry in the PRD as the different factions struggle to dominate the party and the candidate nomination process. In turn, the poor performance of the PRSC in the 1996 presidential and the 1998 congressional and municipal elections is an indication that without Balaguer as candidate, and with no succession allowed by Balaguer, the PRSC is unlikely to reemerge as a strong electoral contender.

International Factors

Throughout its history, the Dominican Republic has been extremely vulnerable to international influence. In the nineteenth century, the actions of foreign powers and unscrupulous foreign speculators fostered an emphasis on leadership based on military might, a willingness to seek out foreign protectors, and the renewed loss of national independence. At the turn of the century, U.S. intervention in the country's economic affairs eventually led to military occupation, which helped facilitate Trujillo's accession to power. Thus, there are links between the country's international vulnerability and its authoritarian history.

In the last half-century, U.S. actions have wavered between greater or lesser involvement in the country's internal affairs, and greater or lesser focus on democracy promotion as opposed to concerns over communism or other issues.[68] Following the Cuban Revolution in 1959, the United States became extensively involved in the domestic affairs of the Dominican Republic; indeed, democracy advanced further after the death of Trujillo than may have been expected, aided by U.S. pressure against Trujillo's remaining family members. Ultimately, though, U.S. policy was driven more by Cold War fears of "another Cuba" than by any perceived interest in democracy promotion. A summary of U.S. policy intentions during this period is provided in President John Kennedy's dictum that, in descending order of preferences, the United States would prefer a democratic regime, a continuation of the Trujillo regime, or a Castro regime, and that it should aim for the first, but not renounce the second until it was sure the third could be avoided.

If there is no necessary relation between U.S. actions and authoritarianism in the past, the same may be said about U.S. actions and democracy in the present, even as certain U.S. policies have more clearly advanced democratic politics in the country. In 1978, there were no perceived U.S. national security threats in the Dominican Republic. In that year, President Carter's human rights policy was crucial in ensuring that the results of the elections would be respected and that Balaguer would step down from the presidency. Between 1990 and 1996, the United States played a key role through its embassy and its USAID mission in Santo Domingo in seeking free and fair elections. Assistance to the Electoral Board in 1993–1994 to improve its technical capability was important. After the fraud of 1994, U.S. diplomats in Santo Domingo lobbied for fair elections in 1996. USAID in Santo Domingo provided financial assistance to civil society organizations that aimed at putting pressure on the government to comply with the terms of the 1994 Pact for Democracy and that closely monitored the 1996 electoral process. The result was a highly successful election essentially free of disputes, unlike any other in the country's history. Thus, over the decades, democratization in the Dominican Republic has sometimes been impaired and sometimes advanced by U.S. actions. However, given the country's geographic location and size and the extent of U.S. involvement over the years, even the favorable actions have helped to reinforce an international dimension to political conflict in the country that complicates democratic consolidation.

At present, a number of international factors may be viewed as having a positive impact on processes of democratization in the Dominican Republic. These include the international shift to a focus on democracy and respect for human rights in this post–Cold War era. Also, both the U.S. government and international financial institutions have retreated somewhat from extreme expressions of neoliberalism to recognize the importance of constructing strong state institutions that can enhance efficiency and accountability and improve the rule of law.

Other international factors may be viewed as having a more questionable or negative impact on democracy in the country. The country remains extraordinarily vulnerable economically, both to shifts in trends and policies by leading countries, and to conditionalities attached to loan and aid programs. The access of Dominican products to the U.S. market is challenged by NAFTA (the North American Free Trade Agreement); indeed, all the small economies of the Caribbean are likely to suffer an extremely difficult transition away from the preferential trade agreements that they have had to the markets of industrialized countries, and they have responded slowly to the challenges and opportunities of economic integration.

The country also remains vulnerable to U.S. pressure on issues that are of concern in domestic U.S. politics, pressure that is often expressed in a unilateral fashion. Illegal Dominican migration to U.S. territory and the connection that the U.S. government is making between migration, crime, and drug trafficking are two of these issues. The extradition of Dominicans residing in Dominican soil who have committed crimes in the United States is likely to remain a contested issue between the two governments, even as the deportation of Dominicans convicted of crimes in the United States back to the island republic has stirred concern over their impact on growing crime in the Dominican Republic.

As elsewhere in Latin America, one may currently consider the international system to be providing important political-ideological support for at least a minimal version of political democracy centered on free elections and the respect for basic human rights. At the same time, the international system is the source of important pressures for dramatic socioeconomic changes, which in the short term have been extremely difficult to manage politically even as they have tended to exacerbate poverty and inequality and to weaken many previously organized groups in civil society. At least in the Dominican Republic, the reforms have yet to be fully implemented, and it remains to be seen whether they will exacerbate income concentration and further weaken the state or instead lay the foundation for sustained growth, while diffusing resources away from the state and more equally within society, in a way that produces a stronger, leaner, more efficient state.

FUTURE PROSPECTS

As this chapter has demonstrated, the Dominican Republic's historical evolution has largely been inimical to the development of political democracy. Beginning with the death of Trujillo in 1961, in an uneven process, there have been significant—if still modest—advances toward democracy. Yet, at least until 1996, it appeared that the country was experiencing political stagnation as a consequence of the ability of President Balaguer to retain power and the inability of his political opposition to enact democratic reforms, even as the country was also undergoing rapid socioeconomic transformation. Democratic advances under the governments of the PRD (1978–1986) were limited, and upon Balaguer's return to power the country experienced increasingly problematic elections and democratic decline.[69] The mobilization of groups from an emerging civil society and international support facilitated what can be considered a new transition in 1996, helping to strengthen key state electoral institutions and to usher in a new president. Thus, as the Dominican Republic enters a new century, it also faces an opportunity to forge more formal, regularized, accountable, and democratic institutions. We see four key challenges the country will face over the next several years.

One relates to pressures to enact more far-reaching market-oriented structural reforms in the face of economic globalization and integration. Implementing such reforms through a consensual, negotiated political process is difficult, requiring some combination of an effective political-party system, exceptional leadership, and public acquiescence. Some countries have suffered policy stasis and economic decline, and others have enacted reforms through unilateral executive action (as has President Fujimori in Peru), weakening democratic accountability in the name of governability. If either of these scenarios prevails in the country, the temptation for the Dominican Republic to return to strong presidentialism, especially if the party system becomes more fragmented, could be strong, with negative implications for democratic institutionalization.

The country's current constitutional framework and electoral calendar point to a second, alternative risk. The current institutional framework combines a single four-year presidential term with no immediate reelection with congressional and local elections being held at the midterm of the presidential term, rather than concurrently. As comparative research examining the effects of electoral cycles and timing indicates, this calendar is likely to lead to a situation where presidents may never achieve effective governing majorities.[70] If the president has scant legislative support, he or she is also open to the threat of rapid ouster (as occurred with President Bucaram in Ecuador). Under President Fernández to date, because of the constitutional and electoral changes, his political volition, and the current makeup of Congress, the executive has not displayed excessive discretionary control of economic and political resources; however, Congress has not shown its ability to compromise and negotiate sound policies and is plagued by corruption and narrow partisanship. Thus, constructive opposition and reciprocal accountability between the legislature and the executive are lacking. The result thus far has been ineffective government, which Dominicans are not likely to tolerate indefinitely. In seeking the appropriate balance between democracy and governability, it will almost certainly be necessary to rethink the electoral calendar while implementing other kinds of reforms, such as democratizing party nomination procedures and campaign finance reform.

This points to a third challenge. The Dominican party system is now clearly in flux as a result of the aging, retirement, or death of the three leaders that defined the political field in the post-Trujillo period: Balaguer, Bosch, and Peña Gómez. As of mid-1999, only the PLD had managed a leadership succession. All the parties that were highly dominated by their charismatic figures face the difficult challenge to modernize and democratize internally, while at the same time they are expected to promote similar processes in society at large. During the 1980s and 1990s, Dominican civil society grew increasingly impatient with the inability of different governing parties to promote democracy, end corruption in government, be accountable, and deliver economic growth. The pressures on the political parties can only be greater now that they face the dual task of maturing internally and governing effectively.

Thus, a fourth key issue will be increasing the efficiency, accountability, and transparency of the country's major governing and state institutions. The 1996 and 1998 elections indicate that the Dominican electoral system can work well; a return to conflict-ridden elections would have to be the result of blatant political maneuvering, as major technical difficulties have been resolved. If electoral institutions need to be consolidated, nascent judicial reform must advance. In addition, the ability of the Dominican state to move beyond public-works programs to implement effective social policy programs must also be constructed.

In sum, the country still confronts many of the same types of difficulties it faced in preceding decades—from the international economic arena, from domestic societal actors with vastly unequal levels of organization and access to resources, from political dynamics and informal norms, and from weak state institutions. The specific challenges it confronts over the next several years at the level of the polity, the political parties, and the state are difficult, but not insurmountable. They highlight not only the difficult historical legacies the country must continue to overcome, but the fragile democratic advances it has achieved as well.

NOTES

1. Robert Dahl, *Polyarchy: Participation and Opposition* (New Haven: Yale University Press, 1971); Eric Nordlinger, "Political Development, Time Sequences and Rates of Change," in Jason L. Finkle and Robert W. Gable, eds., *Political Development and Social Change*, 2d ed. (New York: John Wiley, 1971), pp. 455–477; Dankwart Rustow, "Transitions to Democracy: Toward a Dynamic Model," *Comparative Politics* 2 (1970): 337–363. For a critical review of Rustow's arguments with respect to Dominican democratization, see Rosario Espinal, "Dominican Republic: Electoralism, Pacts, and Clientelism in the Making of a Democratic Regime," in Carlene Edie, ed., *Democracy in the Caribbean: Myths and Realities* (London: Praeger, 1994), pp. 147–161. See also the discussion in the introduction to this volume and in Arturo Valenzuela's chapter 4.

2. These concepts build upon Max Weber's arguments about patrimonialism as a type of government based on traditional authority that was organized more or less as a direct extension of the royal household; because legitimacy of authority is no longer based on traditional appeals, we refer to *neo*patrimonialism in the Dominican Republic. The extreme form of this type of traditional authority, which Weber called "sultanism," is based even more on the discretion of a personal ruler, who exercises personal power almost without restraint; to maintain consistency, because of the presence of elements of legal-rational order and of a legitimizing ideology, we refer to *neo*sultanism. For a more detailed discussion of these terms and an extended analysis of the establishment and legacy of neopatrimonialism and neosultanism on Dominican politics, see Jonathan Hartlyn, *The Struggle for Democratic Politics in the Dominican Republic* (Chapel Hill: University of North Carolina Press, 1998); this section and the next one are based in part on text drawn from chapter 2 of that book. See also Guenther Roth and Claus Wittich, eds., *Max Weber Economy and Society: An Outline of Interpretive*

Sociology (New York: Bedminster Press, 1968), vol. 1, pp. 231–232; see also H. E. Chehabi and Juan J. Linz, eds., *Sultanistic Regimes* (Baltimore: Johns Hopkins University Press, 1998).

3. For an extensive discussion of liberalism in the nineteenth century, see Mu-kien Adriana Sang, *Una utopía inconclusa: Espaillat y el liberalismo dominicano del siglo XIX* (Santo Domingo: Instituto Tecnológico de Santo Domingo, 1997).

4. Frank Moya Pons, *El pasado dominicano* (n.p.: Fundación J. A. Caro Alvarez, 1986), pp. 15–19, 29–32.

5. Frank Moya Pons, "Haiti and Santo Domingo, 1790–c.1870," in Leslie Bethell, ed., *Cambridge History of Latin America* (Cambridge: Cambridge University Press, 1985), vol. 3, p. 248.

6. Ibid., p. 266.

7. See Harry Hoetink, "The Dominican Republic, 1870–1930," in Leslie Bethell, ed., *Cambridge History of Latin America, c. 1870 to 1930* (Cambridge: Cambridge University Press, 1984), vol. 5, pp. 287–298; and Frank Moya Pons, *The Dominican Republic: A National History* (New Rochelle, NY: Hispaniola Books, 1995). Santana, the country's first military *caudillo,* served as president from 1844 to 1848, for a few months in 1849, 1853–1856, and, after overthrowing Báez in coalition with forces from the Cibao (who Santana eventually marginalized), over 1858–1862, a period during which Spain reannexed the country with Santana's urging. Báez served as president a total of five times, including 1849–1853 and 1856–1858.

8. See Luis Martínez-Fernández, "The Sword and the Crucifix: Church-State Relations and Nationality in the Nineteenth Century Dominican Republic," *Latin American Research Review* 30 (1995): 69–93; and William Javier Nelson, *Almost a Territory: America's Attempt to Annex the Dominican Republic* (Newark: University of Delaware Press, 1990).

9. Moya Pons, "Haiti and Santo Domingo," p. 274; on Báez more generally and on why Hispanophile Dominican historians have tended to favor Santana over the mulatto Báez, see Mu-Kien Adriana Sang, *Buenaventura Baéz: El caudillo del sur (1844–1878)* (Santo Domingo: INTEC, 1991), pp. 187–199. See also Martínez-Fernández, "The Sword and the Crucifix," on the failure of Cibao leaders to control the central government.

10. Moya Pons, *El pasado dominicano,* pp. 178–180; Julio A. Cross Beras, *Sociedad y desarrollo en la República Dominicana, 1844–1899* (Santo Domingo: INTEC, 1984), pp. 111–141.

11. On the concept of neosultanism, see note 2. On Heureaux, see Cross Beras, *Sociedad y desarrollo,* pp. 145–153, and Howard J. Wiarda, *Dictatorship, Development and Disintegration,* 3 vols. (Ann Arbor, MI: Xerox University Microfilms, 1975), p. 221; for a somewhat less harsh assessment and periodization of his rule, see Mu-Kien Adriana Sang, *Ulises Heureaux: Biografía de un dictador* (Santo Domingo: INTEC, 1996). For an argument that a capitalist state first emerged in the Dominican Republic during the Heureaux dictatorship, see Emelio Betances, *State and Society in the Dominican Republic* (Boulder, CO: Westview, 1995), p. 4.

12. See Bruce Calder, *The Impact of Intervention: The Dominican Republic During the U.S. Occupation of 1916–1924* (Austin: University of Texas Press, 1984), p. 4; Sumner Welles, *Naboth's Vineyard: The Dominican Republic 1844–1924,* 2 vols. (Mamaroneck, NY: Paul Appel Publisher, 1966), pp. 1005–1111 for the text of the 1907 convention; Martin Murphy, *Dominican Sugar Plantation: Production and Foreign Labor Integration* (New York: Praeger, 1991), pp. 19–22; and Franklin W. Knight, *The Caribbean: The Genesis of a Fragmented Nationalism,* 3d ed. (New York: Oxford University Press, 1990), p. 223.

13. Abraham F. Lowenthal, "The Dominican Republic: The Politics of Chaos," in Robert Kaufman and Arpad von Lazar, eds., *Reform and Revolution: Readings in Latin American Politics* (Needham Heights, MA: Allyn and Bacon, 1969), p. 53.

14. See Calder, *The Impact of Intervention,* p. xix; on U.S. expansion into sugar, see Murphy, *Dominican Sugar Plantation.*

15. See Robert Crassweller, *Trujillo: The Life and Times of a Caribbean Dictator* (New York: Macmillan Company, 1966), pp. 39–51, 104.

16. Of all the country cases considered in a recent comparative volume on sultanistic regimes (including Batista in Cuba, the Somozas in Nicaragua, the Duvaliers in Haiti, Marcos in the Philippines, and Ceaușescu in Romania), the Trujillo regime is probably the closest approximation to the ideal type discussed in the introduction to Chehabi and Linz, eds., *Sultanistic Regimes;* see also the discussion in Jonathan Hartlyn, "The Trujillo Regime in the

Dominican Republic," in H. E. Chehabi and Juan J. Linz, eds., *Sultanistic Regimes* (Baltimore: Johns Hopkins University Press, 1998), pp. 85–112.

17. The relationships between Trujillo and the military are examined in Valentina Peguero, "Trujillo and the Military: Organization, Modernization, and Control of the Dominican Armed Forces, 1916–1961," Ph.D. diss., Columbia University, 1993.

18. The role of these ideological factors in helping to consolidate the Trujillo dictatorship is emphasized by Rosario Espinal, *Autoritarismo y democracia en la política dominicana* (San José, Costa Rica: CAPEL/IIDH, 1987; Santo Domingo: Editorial Argumentos, 1994), pp. 51–77 (1987 edition). Other analyses of the major themes of "Trujillo's ideology" and of the key intellectuals behind them include Andrés L. Mateo, *Mito y cultura en la era de Trujillo* (Santo Domingo: Librería La Trinitaria e Instituto del Libro, 1993); Frank Moya Pons, "The Dominican Republic Since 1930," in Leslie Bethell, ed., *Cambridge History of Latin America* (Cambridge: Cambridge University Press, 1990), vol. 7, p. 517; José Luis Sáez, S.J., "Catolicismo e hispanidad en la oratoria de Trujillo," *Estudios sociales* 21 (July-September 1988): 89–104; and Murphy, *Dominican Sugar Plantation,* pp. 129–144.

19. Wiarda, *Dictatorship,* pp. 370–374; Moya Pons, "The Dominican Republic Since 1930," p. 515.

20. Universal male suffrage had legally existed in the Dominican Republic since 1865, with some exceptions regarding property (but never literacy) under some of the constitutions in force during the nineteenth century. Trujillo first permitted women a symbolic vote in two elections in the 1930s. Julio A. Campillo Pérez, *Elecciones dominicanas: Contribución a su estudio,* vol. 49, Academia Dominicana de la Historia (Santo Domingo: Relaciones Públicas, S.A., 1982), pp. 316–329.

21. Bernardo Vega has compiled many volumes highlighting Trujillo's international relations. Among other works, see Bernardo Vega, *Trujillo y las fuerzas armadas norteamericanas* (Santo Domingo: Fundación Cultural Dominicana, 1992); and Bernardo Vega, *Eisenhower y Trujillo* (Santo Domingo: Fundación Cultural Dominicana, 1991). See also Charles Ameringer, *The Caribbean Legion: Patriots, Politicians, Soldiers of Fortune, 1946–1950* (University Park: Pennsylvania State University Press, 1996). For a valuable account of Trujillo's assassination and the conspirators involved, see Piero Gleijeses, *The Dominican Crisis: The 1965 Constitutionalist Revolt and American Intervention* (Baltimore: Johns Hopkins University Press, 1978), esp. pp. 302–304.

22. See Hartlyn, *The Struggle for Democratic Politics,* pp. 61–67; and Juan J. Linz and Alfred Stepan, *Problems of Democratic Transition and Consolidation: Southern Europe, South America, and Post-Communist Europe* (Baltimore: Johns Hopkins University Press, 1996), pp. 44–45, 51–65.

23. See Piero Gleijeses, *The Dominican Crisis: The 1965 Constitutionalist Revolt and American Intervention* (Baltimore: Johns Hopkins University Press, 1978); and Abraham F. Lowenthal, *The Dominican Intervention* (Cambridge, MA: Harvard University Press, 1972).

24. Rosario Espinal, "Labor, Politics and Industrialization in the Dominican Republic," *Economic and Industrial Democracy: An International Journal* 8, no. 2 (1987): 183–212.

25. For an analysis of business conflicts over economic policy, see Rosario Espinal, "Business and Politics in the Dominican Republic," in Francisco Durand and Eduardo Silva, eds., *Organized Business, Economic Change, and Democracy in Latin America* (Miami: North-South Center Press, 1998), pp. 99–121; and Frank Moya Pons, *Empresarios en conflicto* (Santo Domingo: Fondo para el Avance de las Ciencias Sociales, 1992).

26. See Hartlyn, *The Struggle for Democratic Politics,* pp. 146–149.

27. Useful discussions of intraparty rivalry in the PRD appear in José Oviedo and Rosario Espinal, *Democracia y proyecto socialdemócrata en República Dominicana* (Santo Domingo: Editora Taller, 1986); and Jacqueline Jiménez Polanco, "El Partido Revolucionario Dominicano (PRD): La faccionalización de un partido carismático," in Lourdes López Nieto, Richard Gillespie, and Michael Waller, eds., *Política faccional y democratización* (Madrid: Centro de Estudios Constitucionales, 1995), pp.155–176; for a discussion of how informal and formal rules and institutions helped shape this rivalry, see also Hartlyn, *The Struggle for Democratic Politics,* pp. 149–188. An assessment of the electoral consequences of intraparty rivalry appears in Rosario Espinal, "The Defeat of the Dominican Revolutionary Party in the 1986 Elections: Causes and Implications," *Bulletin of Latin American Research* 9, no.1 (1990): 103–115.

28. For accounts of the 1990 elections, see Rosario Espinal, "The 1990 Elections in the

Dominican Republic," *Electoral Studies* 10, no. 2 (1991): 139–144; and Jonathan Hartlyn, "The Dominican Republic's Disputed Elections," *Journal of Democracy* 1, no. 4 (1990): pp. 92–103.

29. For a discussion of electoral observation in the 1990 elections, see Rosario Espinal, "Electoral Observation and Democratization in the Dominican Republic," in Kevin Middlebrook, ed., *Electoral Observation and Democratic Transitions in Latin America* (San Diego: Center for U.S.-Mexican Studies, University of California at San Diego, 1998), pp. 93–114.

30. A discussion of social unrest in the midst of economic decline is found in Rosario Espinal, "Economic Restructuring, Social Protest, and Democratization in the Dominican Republic," *Latin American Perspectives* 22, no. 3 (1995): 63–79.

31. An assessment of the 1994 elections is found in Jonathan Hartlyn, "Crisis-Ridden Elections (Again) in the Dominican Republic: Neopatrimonialism, Presidentialism, and Weak Electoral Oversight," *Journal of Interamerican Studies and World Affairs* 36, no. 4 (1994): pp. 91–144.

32. For an assessment of international observation in the 1994 elections, see Espinal, "Electoral Observation and Democratization."

33. For an analysis of the key differences between the 1996 elections and the previous ones, as well as a critical comparison of the 1978 and 1996 elections as democratic transitions for the country, see Hartlyn, *The Struggle for Democratic Politics,* pp. 259–273. For an account of national and international electoral observation in the 1996 elections, see Espinal, "Electoral Observation and Democratization."

34. See Howard Wiarda, "The Dominican Republic: Mirror Legacies of Democracy and Authoritarianism," in Larry Diamond, Juan J. Linz, and Seymour Martin Lipset, eds., *Democracy in Developing Countries: Latin America,* 1st ed. (Boulder, CO: Lynne Rienner, 1989), pp. 426–427.

35. See chapter 8 in this volume by John Booth on Costa Rica; on Chile, see Tina Rosenberg, *Children of Cain: Violence and the Violent in Latin America* (New York: Penguin Books, 1991), pp. 17–19, 336–338. Chapter 4 in this volume by Arturo Valenzuela disputes this view for Chile.

36. See the discussion in Brian Downing, *The Military Revolution and Political Change: Origins of Democracy and Autocracy in Early Modern Europe* (Princeton: Princeton University Press, 1992), p. 8; and Carlos Waisman, *Reversal of Development in Argentina: Postwar Counterrevolutionary Politics and their Structural Consequences* (Princeton: Princeton University Press, 1987), pp. 104–106.

37. Indeed, as discussed in this volume's chapter 7 by Daniel Levine and Brian Crisp, much more analogous is the experience of Venezuela. Venezuela was also an unimportant area during the colonial era, with weak traditional institutions such as the church. However, many wars were fought on what was to become Venezuelan soil, and military prowess and leadership became highly prized, leading to the neopatrimonial—if not neosultanistic—regime of Juan Vicente Gómez.

38. For one of the best analyses of this type, focusing on the "overdetermining influence of imperialism" on the Dominican Republic, see Roberto Cassá, *Modos de producción, clases sociales y luchas políticas en la República Dominicana, siglo XX* (Santo Domingo: Alfa y Omega, 1979), quote on p. 17; for his own subsequent critical self-reflection of the need to "overcome reductionist explanations," see Roberto Cassá, "Reescritura veinte años después," *Estudios sociales* 29 (October 1996): quote on p. 25.

39. Ramonina Brea, *Ensayo sobre la formación del estado capitalista en la República Dominicana y Haiti* (Santo Domingo: Editora Taller, 1983).

40. Betances argues, however, that a state bureaucracy began to develop in the late nineteenth century during the Heureaux dictatorship, *State and Society,* p. 19.

41. Moya Pons, *El pasado dominicano,* pp. 182–183.

42. Isis Duarte, Ramonina Brea, Ramón Tejada Holguín, and Clara Báez, *La cultura política de los dominicanos: Entre el autoritarismo y la democracia (*Santo Domingo: Pontificia Universidad Católica Madre y Maestra, 1950), p. 11; and Isis Duarte, Ramonina Brea, and Ramón Tejada Holguín, *La cultura política de los dominicanos: Entre el paternalismo y la participación* (Santo Domingo: Pontificia Universidad Católica Madre y Maestra, 1998), p. 18.

43. Given these findings, it is not surprising that the core of Balaguer supporters were to be found among rural, older, and women voters. See Bill Hamilton and Ray Strother, "The Comeback Geezer: How Constant Polling and Finely-Tuned Messages Won a Dominican Republic Presidential Race," *Campaigns and Elections* (August 1994): 43–44, 67.

44. See the discussion on political culture in the introduction to this volume; see also Terry Karl, "Dilemmas of Democratization in Latin America," *Comparative Politics* 23 (October 1990): 5.

45. See, among other works, Sherri Grasmuck and Patricia Pessar, *Between Two Islands: Dominican International Migration* (Berkeley: University of California Press, 1991); Pamela Graham, "Re-Imagining the Nation and Defining the District: The Simultaneous Political Incorporation of Dominican Transnational Migrants," Ph.D. diss., University of North Carolina at Chapel Hill, 1996; Luis Guarnizo, "The Emergence of a Transnational Social Formation and the Mirage of Return Migration Among Dominican Transmigrants," *Identities* 42, no. 2 (1997): 281–322; Peggy Levitt, "Transnationalizing Civil and Political Change: The Case of Transnational Organizational Ties Between Boston and the Dominican Repubic," Ph.D. diss., Massachusetts Institute of Technology, 1996; and Silvio Torres-Saillant and Ramona Hernández, *The Dominican Americans* (Westport, Conn.: Greenwood Press, 1998).

46. Indeed, in these respects, the Dominican Republic is comparable to many African countries; for a valuable discussion of neopatrimonialism in the African context and how it has inhibited democratic politics and practices throughout that continent, see Michael Bratton and Nicholas van de Walle, *Democratic Experiments in Africa: Regime Transitions in Comparative Perspective* (Cambridge: Cambridge University Press, 1997).

47. According to the Inter-American Development Bank, the percentage of the Dominican population considered to be in moderate poverty in 1990 was 42.4 percent, and in 1995 it was 36.6 percent; that in extreme poverty in 1990 was 15.6 percent, and in 1995 it was 11.6 percent (of the eight other countries discussed in this book, only Brazil had a worse population estimate for moderate poverty and substantially worse population estimates for extreme poverty, and Mexico and Peru had comparable ones for extreme poverty). The IADB estimated the country's GDP per capita in 1995 to be $928 (the other eight countries discussed in this book ranged from $5,983 for Argentina to $1,720 for Colombia); see Inter-American Development Bank, *Latin America After a Decade of Reforms: Economic and Social Progress in Latin America, 1997 Report* (Washington, DC: IADB, 1997), pp. 18, 221.

48. For more detail, see Rosario Espinal, "The Dominican Working Class: Labour Control Under Trujillo and After," in Malcolm Cross and Gad Heuman, eds., *Labour in the Caribbean* (London: Macmillan, 1988), pp. 176–194.

49. For an analysis of business politics under authoritarian and democratic governments, see Espinal, "Business and Politics."

50. See Hartlyn, *The Struggle for Democratic Politics,* p. 142, for more details and sources.

51. Inter-American Development Bank, *Economic and Social Progress in Latin America* (Baltimore: Johns Hopkins University Press, 1990).

52. A detailed analysis of this topic is found in Ernesto Sagás, "A Case of a Mistaken Identity: Antihaitianism in the Dominican Republic," *Latinamericanist* 29, no. 1 (1993): 1–5; and Ernesto Sagás, "The Development of Antihaitianism into a Dominant Ideology During the Trujillo Era," in Juan Manuel Carrión, ed., *Ethnicity, Race, and Nationality in the Caribbean* (San Juan: Institute of Caribbean Studies, University of Puerto Rico, 1997), pp. 96–121.

53. For a discussion of this topic, see Jorge Duani, "Reconstructing Racial Identity: Ethnicity, Color, and Class Among Dominicans in the United States and Puerto Rico," *Latin American Perspectives* 25, no. 3 (1998): 147–172.

54. For a brief discussion of *indianismo* and racism in the Dominican Republic, see Harry Hoetink, *Santo Domingo y el Caribe: Ensayos sobre cultura y sociedad* (Santo Domingo: Fundación Cultural Dominicana, 1994).

55. See Wilfredo Lozano, ed., *La cuestión haitiana en Santo Domingo: Migración internacional, desarrollo y relaciones inter-estatales entre Haití y República Dominicana* (Santo Domingo: FLACSO, Centro Norte-Sur de la Universidad de Miami, 1992); and André Corten and Isis Duarte, "Five Hundred Thousand Haitians in the Dominican Republic," *Latin American Perspectives* 22, no. 2 (summer 1995): 94–110.

56. The social construction of race is well-argued theoretically by Michael Omi and

Howard Winant, *Racial Social Formation in the United States* (New York and London: Routledge & Kegan Paul, 1986). See also Howard Winant, *Racial Conditions: Politics, Theory, Comparisons* (Minneapolis: University of Minnesota Press, 1994).

57. For a concise account of this tension, see Ernesto Sagás, "Haiti and the Dominican Republic: Socio-Economic Dimensions of a Historically Conflictive Relationship," *International Journal of Group Tensions* 25, no. 3 (1995): 247–268.

58. For more on this comparison, see Duani, "Reconstructing Racial Identity."

59. A valuable analysis and review of the literature on issues of political parties and institutions is Ramonina Brea, Isis Duarte, Ramón Tejada Holguín, and Clara Báez, *Estado de situación de la democracia dominicana (1978–1992)* (Santo Domingo: Pontificia Universidad Católica Madre y Maestra, 1995); for a careful analysis of charismatic leadership and organizational types of Dominican political parties, see Jiménez Polanco, *Los partidos políticos en la República Dominicana: Actividad electoral y desarrollo organizativo* (Santo Domingo: Editora Centenario, 1999).

60. For more on the argument that the Trujillo dictatorship can be considered one-party rule, see Espinal, *Autoritarismo y democracia;* for an argument that the dictatorship should be viewed as an antiparty system, not a one-party system, see Jiménez Polanco, *Los partidos políticos.*

61. Espinal, *Autoritarismo y democracia.*

62. These arguments appear in Catherine Conaghan and Rosario Espinal, "Unlikely Transitions to Uncertain Regimes? Democracy Without Compromise in the Dominican Republic and Ecuador," *Journal of Latin American Studies* 22, part 3 (1990): 553–574. For a discussion of the links across neopatrimonialism, electoral rules, and Dominican political parties, see Hartlyn, *The Struggle for Democratic Politics,* pp. 149–159, 219–257.

63. For an extensive analysis of neopatrimonialism and presidentialism in the Dominican Republic from 1978 to the present, see Hartlyn, *The Struggle for Democratic Politics,* chapters 5–9. On presidentialism, see also Rosario Espinal, "The Dominican Republic: An Ambiguous Democracy," in Jorge Domínguez and Abraham Lowenthal, eds., *Constructing Democratic Governance: Latin America and the Caribbean in the 1990s* (Baltimore: Johns Hopkins University Press, 1996), pp. 118–134.

64. *Listín Diario,* December 6, 1966.

65. These comments about Balaguer refer more to his leadership style until 1978. When Balaguer returned to power in 1986, in the postdemocratic transition, he relied less on repression and fear to rule.

66. Rosario Espinal, "Joaquín Balaguer: El eterno retorno de la política dominicana," *Revista Nueva Sociedad,* no. 118 (1992): 109–115.

67. Jacqueline Jiménez Polanco calls this new style of leadership *"liderazgo contingente,"* meaning a leadership that, unlike charismatic leadership, is not firmly rooted in society and relies on a variety of pacts, agreements, and events to gather the support of the people. It is also a leadership that is not strongly rooted in a specific ideology or governing platform. See Jacqueline Jiménez Polanco, "El pactado ascenso al poder de Leonel Fernández en la elección presidencial de 1996: La emergencia del liderazgo contingente y la construcción de una poliarquía consultiva," in Ramonina Brea, Rosario Espinal, and Fernando Valerio Holguín, eds., *La República Dominicana en el umbral del siglo XXI: Cultura, política y cambio social* (Santo Domingo: Pontificia Universidad Católica Madre y Maestra, 1999, forthcoming).

68. For a review and for additional sources, see Jonathan Hartlyn, "The Dominican Republic: The Legacy of Intermittent Engagement," in Abraham F. Lowenthal, ed., *Exporting Democracy: The United States and Latin America* (Baltimore: Johns Hopkins University Press, 1991), pp. 175–214.

69. During the 1986–1996 period, there was unquestionable slippage in political rights, as the country became something of a hybrid regime with both authoritarian and democratic characteristics. For example, Freedom House indicators reflect the growing decline of political rights in the country, from a 1 in 1989 (the highest possible score) to a 2 in 1990, a 3 in 1993, and a 4 in 1994; see the discussion in Hartlyn, *The Struggle for Democratic Politics,* pp. 228–229.

70. See Matthew Soberg Shugart, "The Electoral Cycle and Institutional Sources of Divided Presidential Government," *American Political Science Review* 89, no. 2 (June 1995): 327–343.

10

MEXICO:
Sustained Civilian Rule and the Question of Democracy

Daniel C. Levy & Kathleen Bruhn

Alone among the Latin American countries examined in this comparative project series (*Democracy in Developing Countries*), Mexico has had no significant experience with democratic rule. Mexican politics long disdained the public competition and accountability integral to liberal democracy. Despite substantial increases in the level of competition and the cleanness of elections, Mexico has yet to pass the ultimate test of democratic governance: acceptance of alternation in power. Instead, with its victory in the 1994 presidential election, Mexico's Partido Revolucionario Institucional (PRI) became the longest-ruling party on the planet. However, the PRI's loss of the Mexico City mayor's position and of majority control of the Congress in the 1997 federal congressional elections is a significant step toward alternation, and forces the PRI to share power with opposition parties to an unprecedented degree in Mexican history.

Despite lacking a democratic legacy, Mexico merits inclusion in our comparative study for three reasons: (1) the nation's overall importance, (2) theoretical insights distinguishing the bases of democratic and stable civilian rule, and (3) notable democratizing developments in recent years. The first reason is obvious; this chapter focuses on the others.[1] A dichotomy between fully "authoritarian" and fully "democratic" fails to capture the recent past or especially present of Mexican reality, which has evolved much more slowly and irregularly than the cases of transition from military rule. Arbitrary focus on the "great moment of transition" risks missing very important realities and changes in the political system.

The dominant historical theme that runs through this chapter is that many factors commonly associated with good prospects for democracy have long persisted in Mexico without producing democracy. Moreover, the very achievement of Mexico's major political success—stable civilian

MEXICO

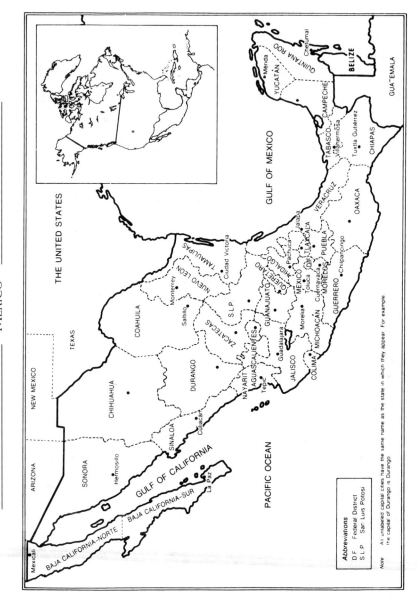

rule—presented obstacles to democratization, and probably delayed democratization far longer than most theorists of democracy would have expected. Moreover, the country's nondemocratic legacy continues to condition further Mexican democratization; indeed, concerns about how democratization might undermine the historic achievement of stable civilian rule have been important sources of resistance and fear. Finally, even if some of the same trends and variables thought important in other cases of democratization now seem to have contributed to the erosion of Mexican authoritarianism, the extraordinary length of this delay raises serious questions about the difference between how these factors affect "democracy" and how they affect "stability." Naturally, observers have long realized that democracy and stability are empirically and analytically separable, but a strong tendency lumps the two together as one desired outcome. Many of the hypotheses initially orienting this comparative project illustrate that tendency; although distinct measures are developed for democracy and stability, democratic stability appeared as the key dependent variable.

Authors writing about different countries have had to assess the difficulty of achieving democracy and stability together, and the reasons democracies often fall. For other nations discussed in this volume, but not Mexico, one can analyze democratic periods, democratic breakdown, and "redemocratization." Another line of inquiry concerns the conditions under which authoritarian regimes become democratic.[2] But the literature on that process deals overwhelmingly with military regimes—typically very exclusionary and coercive—and to a limited extent with narrow personalistic regimes. Unlike either military authoritarian or personalistic rule, Mexico's authoritarianism has had much of the institutionalization, breadth, forms, pacts, and legitimacy often associated with democratic government.

In fact, in Mexico many factors associated with democratic stability promoted a civilian authoritarian rule that managed the most impressive political stability in all of Latin America regardless of regime type. No other major Latin American nation has sustained civilian rule throughout the postwar period; Mexico's predates that period. No regime in the region matches Mexico's in durability and legitimacy built through periods of change, conflict, and challenge. Despite recent evidence that support and legitimacy have declined substantially (including stronger electoral opposition, increased nonpartisan identification, a more vigorous civil society, major corruption scandals, and even the emergence of an armed guerrilla movement in the southern state of Chiapas in 1994), Mexico has ranked in the category of stable polities, albeit bordering on partially stable. Unlike Latin American systems that are partially stable because they have not consolidated new democratic regimes, Mexico's main difficulty concerns erosion of consolidated authoritarianism.

Assessments of stability have been clearer than assessments of democracy in Mexico. The latter have been influenced excessively by dominant paradigms in comparative politics in general and in Latin American studies in particular. An irony is that interpretations of Mexican politics changed so much while the system itself remained remarkably stable. In line with burgeoning literature on political development, Mexico was typically depicted in the 1950s and most of the 1960s as incompletely but increasingly democratic. Probably the most cited work emphasized an evolution toward Western democracy in rising interest-group activity, participation, inclusiveness, national identity, legitimacy, and functional specialization, along with declining personalism. Mexico fell short on its citizenship base and leadership selection largely because the regime had pursued "suitable social and economic conditions" before democratic goals, but those conditions had made Mexico ready for democracy.[3] Subsequently, however, Mexico was almost consensually depicted as authoritarian, with democratic tendencies not ascendant. Juan Linz's seminal work on authoritarianism was widely employed by Mexicanists, and Mexico was even tied overzealously to "bureaucratic authoritarianism." More recently, interpretations of complex blends of authoritarianism and pluralist forces have developed.[4]

From 1945 to 1985, while many Latin American countries suffered military rule, Mexico ranked between third and seventh among twenty nations on the best-known, if controversial, ratings for Latin American democracy.[5] Mexico ranks lower today, primarily because most other cases currently fit our basic definition of democracy; however, this should not obscure the fact that in an absolute sense, Mexico was clearly more democratic in 1997 than in 1985.

Three elements have limited Mexico's classification as democratic: (1) Mexico has lacked meaningful and extensive competition among organized groups for major government office; (2) participation has not reliably extended to leadership selection through fair elections, although elections have always been regular; and (3) civil and political liberties have been insufficient to guarantee the integrity of competition and participation. But recent changes in all three elements have weakened the traditional case for classifying Mexico as nondemocratic. Competition for major government offices has become more widespread and increasingly results in acknowledged PRI defeats, even when this means the loss of executive power in key states and cities or the loss of PRI majority control in the national Congress. Although some civil and political liberties remain fragile, with violations severely undermining competition in some areas of the country, advances in media freedom in particular have significantly improved opposition access. These changes increase democratic space considerably, although Mexico still falls into the lowest category (failure/absence) in the Democracy in Developing Countries six-part "summary scale" of democratic experience because there has been no extended period of democracy as yet.

At least until the recent democratic advances, Mexico could be classified as a "hegemonic party" system. The dominant party did not tolerate genuine challenges (i.e., alternatives) to its rule, it claimed almost all sub-federal posts, and it engaged in widespread electoral fraud, a practice that is not dying quickly or easily. Still, the party no longer regularly claims the high vote percentage cited for hegemonic systems: In 1994, for the first time, the ruling party acknowledged receiving less than 50 percent of the presidential vote. In 1997, it accepted that its support had fallen even further. More broadly, this volume's overall definition of democracy is heavily weighted toward electoral dimensions, long a weak area for Mexico. Even before recent democratization, the Mexican case suggests that hegemonies are not necessarily the least democratic of authoritarian nations.

In terms of the study's overall typology, we would currently classify Mexico as a "semidemocracy" making major but uneven progress toward democracy. It remains to be seen how much the new Congress will develop the capacity to challenge effectively the power of the president; whether newly elected opposition mayors and governors will win more autonomy and resources to carry out their campaign promises or be hamstrung by the central PRI executive; whether advances in civil and political liberties at the national level and in many urban areas will be generalized to Mexico's poorer and more marginalized zones; whether the threat of rural violence can be contained without massive military intervention; and—perhaps most of all—whether PRI acceptance of opposition victories in lesser positions truly signals a willingness to accept alternation in power at the national level. Until then, scholars should be uncomfortable labeling Mexico "democratic." At the same time, however, traditional classification of Mexico as "authoritarian" obscures significant change. Although democracy is not yet manifest in all elections, all areas of government, or all important decisionmaking in society, it is wise to remember that democracy remains partial or incomplete in *many* Latin American countries. Despite continued aspirations for a "democracy without adjectives,"[6] scholars must routinely apply qualifying language to the democracy they find, including terms such as "delegative democracy," which imply a participation that is too limited alongside hierarchical power that is too great.

On the stability dimension, Mexico comes near the editors' concept of "partially stable," though no clear trend emerges. On the one hand, traditional sources of stability have clearly eroded. On the other, new sources of stability—including increasingly legitimate and credible elections—have emerged. Overall, economic and political uncertainty is higher than it was in the early 1990s, not to mention most of the postwar decades, with increased local violence (including the activities of right-wing vigilante groups, several guerrilla forces, and the military) and mounting concerns about drug cartel penetration of the Mexican state; related to all this is a preoccupying social instability, epitomized by soaring crime rates. However, focusing on the political system, Mexico still appears closer to stable than unstable. To some extent, higher unpredictability in Mexico is actually a healthy sign of democratic change, replacing the deadly certainty of outcomes under authoritarian rule.

This chapter identifies basic roots and characteristics of Mexico's complex system of sustained civilian rule without democracy and, more specifically, considers the editors' hypotheses about stable democracy and their increasing relevance for understanding political change in Mexico. Finally, it analyzes prospects for democratization and the role the United States might play.

AN UNDEMOCRATIC PAST: REVIEW AND ANALYSIS

Mexico's political heritage is overwhelmingly authoritarian. There is less democratic precedent to analyze than in the other Latin American countries considered in this volume; viable democratic rule has been virtually absent. As in the Dominican Republic, so in Mexico, democratic experiments have historically proved ineffective, in contrast to certain authoritarian periods.

Great precolonial civilizations, such as the Aztec, presaged a pattern of relatively strong authoritarian rule. Spain's centuries-long rule was similar in that respect. Some observers see not only precedent but causal roots in these experiences. According to Octavio Paz, the Aztec *tlatoani* introduced impersonal, priestly, institutional rule, and colonialism introduced Arabic-Hispanic reverence for the personal *caudillo:* "I repeat: there is a bridge that reaches from tlatoani to viceroy, viceroy to president."[7] Much also has been made of the contrast between authoritarian and "liberal" colonization by Spain and England, respectively.

Independence (1821) brought neither democracy nor stability. Federalist-centralist conflicts were among the most important. The lack of stability crippled hopes for economic growth, which in turn contributed to further instability. Despite examples of autonomous local rule, liberal projects were weak. Liberal rule was extremely short-lived until the Reform (La Reforma, 1855–1876), probably the closest Mexico has come to democracy until recent times. It featured a belief that democracy, however restricted, was compatible with stability and growth; a liberal constitution; substantial liberties; some significant elections; and some socioeconomic mobility and educational expansion along with attacks on large landholders, including the Catholic Church. On the other hand, the Reform was limited in mass inclusiveness and was hostile to Indian communitarianism. Yet democracy often begins with public contestation restricted to certain groups. Mexico's liberal experiment failed because it could not build sufficient strength. French imperial intervention, although eventually beaten back, was debilitating. Mostly, liberal democratic forms were used by antidemocratic forces. Regional *caciques* used decentralized authority to block reform. As it often has in Latin America, Congress represented *cacique* and other oligarchic interests in conflict with a liberal executive.[8] The weakness of liberal experiments with decentralized political authority did not go unnoticed by twentieth-century leaders.

Always fragile, the Reform faded after leader Benito Juárez's death in 1872. A split over the 1876 presidential succession opened the way for a military coup, and Porfirio Díaz became supreme dictator. The regime was repressively authoritarian: gone were free elections, diminished was freedom of the press. As is common for Latin America, some democratic formalities were preserved, but Díaz's reference to Congress as his herd of tame horses was indicative of the basic realities. Nevertheless, under the *porfiriato* independent Mexico achieved political stability and economic growth for the first time. In its positivist notions of progress through permanent evolution, its support for development through foreign trade and investment, its preference for rational administration by *científicos,* and, most of all, its model of economic growth without distribution and political stability without democracy, the *porfiriato* offers broad historical parallels to the regime that would dominate Mexico in the last years of the twentieth century.

Among factors that ultimately brought down the *porfiriato* (1910), contemporary optimists about democracy might speculate on both repressiveness and economic growth leading to calls for democracy. However, the main reason for the regime's fall was its unwillingness to allow political mobility among the elite.[9] Representatives of the new national bourgeoisie, such as northerner Francisco Madero, demanded access to power. When Díaz reneged on his pledge not to seek reelection in 1910 and then attempted electoral fraud, Madero called for a popular uprising in support of his claim to have won. Díaz fell within a few months, and Madero became president. Madero's agenda envisioned a relatively limited form of political democracy, basically "a return to '57," the Reform Constitution, and "free suffrage, no reelection." Congress was autonomous from the executive and was the scene of powerful debates among very antagonistic forces. True division of power (federalism) and separation of power (including judicial review) became priorities.

But such democratization proved largely irrelevant for Mexico. Democratic structures did not lead to the destruction of Porfirian forces, including *caciques,* governors, bureaucrats, the military, and a partially revitalized church. Madero even appointed former Díaz aides to government positions, whereas he tended to exclude revolutionary groups. In other words, this democratic leader, so popular in 1911, neither destroyed the old order nor constructed a viable new one. Achieving a democracy is much harder than simply kicking out the old—as contemporary opponents of the PRI would do well to remember. Although a good deal of the literature on transitions to democracy stresses the need for pacts among elites, probably the major weakness in Madero's approach was his reluctance to address socioeconomic problems and popular demands (especially for land) and his consequent failure to strengthen democratic forces by adding a mass base. Of course, whether Madero could have successfully done so is unknown. After his assassination by reactionary forces (covertly aided by the United States), other leaders would incorporate the masses—undemocratically.

Revolutionary warfare among various armies broke out again, bringing mass mobilization and, especially, death and destruction. By 1916, a million Mexicans had died and nearly as many had emigrated from a population of just under 14 million in 1910. Compared with Emiliano Zapata's peasant army and its demands for land reform, Venustiano Carranza's ultimately victorious constitutionalists were not committed to fundamental socioeconomic change. In subsequent years, some observers would even question whether a real revolution had occurred. Nevertheless, the revolution became a symbol of mass involvement, progressive change, and nationalism, skillfully manipulated by the regime to bolster its legitimacy. By 1940, the revolution was "institutionalized," the fragile stability forged since 1916 safely deepened.

Two crucial factors in building this postrevolutionary stability were pacts among those elites not destroyed by the revolution and the organized integration of mass groups.[10] President Carranza only partly recognized these two necessities, but he accepted provisions that gave the 1917 Constitution strong mass appeal as a legacy of the revolution. These included a minimum wage, an eight-hour workday, workers' compensation, land reform, and notable nationalist measures. Equally significant, the constitution ambiguously blended democratic aspirations with authoritarian realities, on the one hand stressing popular sovereignty, free elections, guarantees for individual rights, federalism, and separation of powers, but on the other hand laying the basis for a potent central government in general and a strong presidency in particular.

Between them, Carranza's two powerful successors—Alvaro Obregón and Plutarco Elías Calles—extended the state's ties to and control over mass agrarian and urban labor interests. Yet when their terms ended (1928), the regime's stability was still much in doubt. All three presidents had plotted to rule beyond their constitutional terms; two had been assassinated. Major groups still competed violently, and none was powerful enough to end the nation's political stalemate.

At this point, Mexico experienced three moments of great political leadership, the kind associated in many ways with democratic consolidation. However, the leadership that stabilized Mexico's civilian rule would be undemocratic not only in means, but also in ends. First, Calles engineered a grand pact among elite power-holders. Convincing them that without compromise they faced defeat, renewed armed conflict, or endless uncertainty, he brought them to support the creation of a civilian institution (the party) that would centralize authority for the regime on the basis of bargains, including elite circulation through peaceful means. Second, Calles's successor, Lázaro Cárdenas, fortified the party by creating and incorporating mass organizations within it. He did so in large part to block Calles's personalistic attempt to perpetuate his rule from behind the scenes. Cárdenas used his personal influence within the mass organizations to counteract Calles's edge among elites—in the process winning their allegiance not only to himself but also to the regime.[11] Critically, however, Cárdenas stressed the leadership of the state rather than the formation of autonomous organizations of masses. His modes were corporatist, and he openly opposed bourgeois democracy.

Finally, the immensely popular Cárdenas peacefully relinquished power to a moderate successor in 1940, ending the succession of presidents who had tried to dominate the country beyond their constitutional terms and setting a valuable precedent. By this time the regime was sufficiently institutionalized to pave the way for more than a quarter-century of maximum strength and stability, before a continuing period of greater turmoil opened new demands and prospects for democracy.

CIVILIAN RULE WITHOUT DEMOCRACY

The following sections analyze four topics identified as crucial to democratic development. For each, the analysis explores how basic features evolved, how they served civilian stability but not democracy, and how popular challenges and reforms altered these traditional bases of support for the system.

State-Society Relations

State relations with mass groups have approximated "state corporatism" much more than pluralism.[12] The regime has had significant control over organizations that bring the masses into the system. Through unions and other organizations affiliated with the ruling party, the state has had the capacity to influence strike behavior, restrain wage demands, and mobilize support for the system. In fact, despite increasingly autonomous participation, much of the Mexican population remains unorganized and politically "marginal"; it rarely expresses discontent, and tends to ask for help from political mediators in clientelistic fashion, without demanding rights. Even formal, organized groups often react to, more than participate meaningfully in, policy formation.[13]

The state's encapsulation of mass organizations had obviously antithetical effects on the chances for democracy. It greatly limited the democratizing option available in Venezuela's *trienio* when the AD (Accíon Democrática) party organized peasants and workers in opposition to the military rulers. Those groups had already been organized in Mexico into a single undemocratic party controlled by the state. On the other hand—also as in Venezuela—the early incorporation of mass groups (especially labor) promoted stability and civilian rule.[14] It gave the regime a wide base, which helped counterbalance the armed forces and which in some periods was used to boost the regime's autonomy from business. Mainly, however, incorporation protected the state from organized dissent on the left by making the formation of popular alliances extremely difficult. The Mexican regime has repeatedly been able to effect austere economic policies that would bring revolt in other nations. Thus, the regime's undemocratic control of a mass base has sustained civilian rule and stability.

This dominant pattern of state-controlled incorporation was never absolute or unchallenged, however. By the 1990s, moreover, state-society relations had become considerably more complex and problematic for the regime. In part, this resulted from the deterioration of traditional corporatist institutions, particularly key peasant and labor unions, which gradually lost much of their power to mobilize support for the regime. On the one hand, economic development tended to reduce the centrality of unions, as Mexico became an increasingly urban society with a large informal sector and an ever more mobile workforce. By the early 1980s, only about 20 percent of the economically active population was unionized.[15] On the other hand, the regime's insistence on control and union sacrifices tended to delegitimize the unions' leadership. A classic example is the fate of the dominant union within the labor sector, the Confederación de Trabajadores de México (CTM), and its leader-for-life Fidel Velázquez, a member of the CTM leadership since Cárdenas created it and grafted it onto the PRI. Velázquez and the CTM came to symbolize everything that was wrong with the Mexican labor movement: its capture by leaders with absolute and seemingly perpetual dominance, its flourishing corruption and personalism, and its tendency to sacrifice the interests of union members at the president's behest. Such labor leaders helped make Mexican unions "moderate" but neither autonomous nor democratic.[16] Occasionally, when independent labor movements threatened to become powerful, the regime resorted to severe repression (as in the late 1950s), but it has usually relied on the undemocratic internal structure of organized labor and its ties to the regime.[17]

For a long time, economic growth allowed the regime to use these controls sparingly. Carefully funneled benefits to organized labor helped sustain the relationship. However, the economic crisis of the 1980s compelled unprecedented sacrifices from labor. To control inflation, President Miguel de la Madrid initiated the first of several pacts that put a freeze on both wages and some prices—a major reason wages rose slower than inflation during the 1980s. Real minimum wages fell by 40 to 50 percent between

1982 and 1988.[18] Despite some bargaining, complaints, and threatened strikes, the labor movement seemed remarkably docile.[19] Not surprisingly, this affected popular support for labor unions: 31 percent of the labor candidates appointed by the CTM lost to opposition candidates in the 1988 election.[20]

Into this context came renewed activity from independent labor movements and dissident factions of official movements. The death of Fidel Velázquez in 1997, at the age of ninety-seven, may accelerate the breakdown of traditional corporatism; no other CTM leader can boast his blend of personal political networks and unquestioned corporate leadership. After his death, several unions banded together publicly in a new union "central" called the Unión de Trabajadores de México (UTM), while the struggle within traditional unions like the CTM to replace Velázquez may further undermine their cohesion and strength. For the PRI, the erosion of its labor base may affect both its political support and its traditional methods of economic management. The consequences for Mexican democratization are less clear, and depend on whether unions become fragmented, marginalized, and subject to new forms of undemocratic control, or whether they develop the independence, internal democratic accountability, and legitimacy to participate in a more pluralist and autonomous civil society.

Another significant part of such a society are the relatively autonomous popular-sector organizations, which have become increasingly common and significant as formulators of demands and forums for popular participation. The growth of these organizations has been fostered in part by general disenchantment with government, particularly given the consequences of repeated economic crises. A second, more specific catalyst was the earthquake of 1985, to which the government failed to react effectively. A third factor has been political organization by activists from leftist currents who saw little hope in electoral opposition, preferring self-organization of the masses to deal with urgent problems. Individuals have formed associations to deal with urban problems such as tenant conditions, schooling, environmental pollution, and the lack of basic public services. Recent behavior can be contrasted to Richard Fagen and William Tuohy's well-known depiction of "depoliticized" urban life, where management substitutes for politics and most people believe government should or will handle their political affairs.[21] The new vibrancy in Mexican politics alters traditional state-society patterns associated with stability; indeed, it has resulted both from the state's success in modernizing and diversifying society and from its declining legitimacy.

However, the tendency to use the increasing democratic space has been greatest among more-privileged groups, particularly the middle class, intellectuals, and business. State-business relations have long epitomized a pattern of state-society relations in which the state is less dominant, and the social sector more influential than in state-labor relations. Some "peak" business associations established by the government were mandatory and dependent on government in matters ranging from subsidies to leadership selection. But even these older associations, such as the Confederation of Industrial Chambers and the National Chamber of Manufacturing Industry, long worked with the government because of mutual self-interest and "inducements" more than coercion and "constraints," and were politically able to influence regulatory, trade, and other policies.[22] In any case, this view in which pluralist features are clearly at play (though not exclusive of corporatist features) clearly holds for newer associations, such as the Entrepreneurial Coordinating Council and the Mexican Employers' Confederation. Two developments in particular raised the level of business activism: the economic populism of President Luis Echeverría in the early 1970s and the nationalization of the banking system by President López Portillo in 1982. The bank nationalization impressed many business elites with their own vulnerability to presidential authority and encouraged them to take a more active and critical role in politics, even to the point of supporting the conservative opposition, Partido Acción Nacional (PAN).

Under the administration of Carlos Salinas (1988–1994), the government-business relationship improved considerably. His decision to open up the economy and to seek a free-trade agreement with the United States did not please many of the business sectors that had benefited extensively from state protection and subsidies, but the Mexican government developed close cooperation and communication with those business groups able to take advantage of—and support—the economic opening. Nevertheless, these groups never abdicated their independent judgment, and never entirely reversed their political activism, even during the high point of the Salinas years. In the aftermath of the 1994 peso crisis, business groups criticized government responses and contributed policy ideas to the debate over how to restore economic growth. Business groups have both the financial and organizational resources to contribute to the strengthening of pluralism and civil society. However, they also have the potential to dominate civil society, to the detriment of poorer organizations, representative pluralism, and broad democratic accountability.

The juxtaposition of business and labor relations with the state illustrates how social class affects the balance between freedom and corporatist controls. Similarly, the state's relative tolerance has usually extended to middle-class groups. Middle-class dependence on the state goes far beyond what is found in the United States in terms of employment opportunities and professional associations, but intellectuals and other professionals have been much freer than workers to control their affairs and even to criticize the government. Despite depending heavily on the state for income, Mexico's public universities have had substantial autonomy from the government. Furthermore, groups within the public universities have considerable freedom of expression and power to affect institutional policies, as the massive student demonstrations against academic reforms proposed in 1986 illustrate.[23] Private institutions, roughly one in five of the nation's more than 1 million enrollments, add significantly to state-society pluralism.[24]

Even these groups have been targets of repression, as in the infamous events of 1968, when the government killed hundreds of protesting university students. The slaughter was a watershed in views about Mexican democratization, convincing many of the regime's unalterably repressive nature. The events of 1968 serve as a chilling and restraining reminder of the state's potential for violent response to protest, a response much more commonly visited on poorer groups.[25] However, limits on protests have varied; behavior that lies within the "logic" of this authoritarian system is not inevitable behavior, and at times, other Mexican leaders have been more tolerant.

One rule central to Mexico's exclusion from the democratic category has been the restrictions against organized dissent that posed a realistic alternative to the regime. Violations brought harsh repression along with co-optation. Even this formidable restriction left some room for pluralism, especially at the level of individual freedoms.[26] Religion provides an example of both the restrictions and the possibilities. After the revolution finally broke the church's tremendous political-economic power, a modus vivendi allowed it considerable autonomy in religious-cultural-educational affairs—beyond what the constitution ostensibly permitted. In turn, the church was not allowed the opposition voice heard in Brazil, Chile, Nicaragua, and elsewhere in Latin America—although individual Mexican church leaders have supported opposition party calls for democratization, and some priests support popular struggles. Meanwhile, individuals were generally free to worship (or not) as they pleased.

While this rule no doubt remains the first preference of the regime— still exercised whenever an organization is isolated enough to make operation against it feasible—outright repression has become increasingly costly for the regime. This reflects both the growth of popular organizations, as well as greater communication among them. Actions against one group now tend to become widely known, and other groups more frequently mobilize in their defense. One well-known example of this is the case of Chiapas. Initially, the Mexican government responded to the emergence of the Ejército Zapatista de Liberación Nacional guerrilla army (usually referred to as the EZLN, or the *zapatistas*) with military force, but the guerrillas made skillful use of the national and international media to publicize their cause, and within weeks, popular mobilizations all over the country in support of the EZLN had forced the government to the bargaining table.

These points about societal freedom—its limits and its growth—are further illustrated by analysis of the media and public debate. Outright repression and censorship exist. Reporters have been intimidated and even

killed. More often, there has been self-censorship, encouraged by overlapping elite interests in "macro" orientations such as growth and stability and
reinforced by "micro" tools such as dependence on government advertising
revenue, control over the supply of inputs such as paper, and supplemental
state stipends to friendly reporters. In the past, these methods gave the government an ability to count on favorable reporting and the ability to restrict
or manipulate information about critics of the regime. As a result, citizens
often lacked the basic information needed to ensure responsible democracy
with accountability. Typically, the most independent outlets have reached
the most limited audiences. The print media, for instance, long enjoyed a
relatively wide range of freedom. Yet, partly because they are expensive,
and partly because of the limited education of much of the populace, their
circulation is rather small. Electronic media usually remained safer in content. Television's conservative banality has been crucial. Additionally,
while the government allowed rather abstract, if fundamental, critiques of
the state, it reacted more strongly to specific critiques of policy alternatives, or investigative reporting of police and government officials.[27]

Violence against reporters continues, and may even have increased as
traditional methods of censorship have weakened, leaving targets of journalistic investigation dependent on overt threats to block negative reports
about them. Nevertheless, economic changes have brought significantly
greater media freedom. In part, these changes reflect competition among
proliferating news outlets. Neoliberal policies weakened the government
monopoly over the supply of paper for printing, for instance. New papers
such as *Reforma* won a reputation for investigative reporting—strengthened by their refusal to accept government advertising. In the television
industry, though government influence remains strong (among other things,
the state awards all new television station concessions), reporting is noticeably less obsequious than in the past, due to partial privatization, an
expanded number of stations, and more competition among stations for
viewers. Weaker control over the media also reflects international influence. With the expansion of cable and Internet connections, information
from foreign outlets such as CNN, the *New York Times,* or the *Wall Street
Journal* reaches news-watchers in Mexico and is frequently picked up by
domestic news coverage. A third factor is legal reform, and particularly
electoral reform, which has expanded opposition-party access to television.
In the 1997 election, opposition parties ran ad campaigns that would have
been impossible only three years earlier. Finally, a dramatic growth in
public-opinion polls has given Mexicans new information about themselves. All of this has contributed to a new era of democratic expression
and challenge.

Government efforts to contain this upsurge have, in established PRI
fashion, fallen back on a mixture of co-optation and repression, but with a
twist: with state resources for co-optation strained as never before by budget cuts, the PRI has sought to do more with less, to target benefits more

precisely and to design programs that both maximize political returns and are compatible with the basic market models being implemented in the economic sector. For example, noting the strong showing of leftist presidential candidate Cuauhtémoc Cárdenas in 1988, by his electoral alliance with many of the new popular movements, and by the manifest inability of the corporatist unions to mobilize sufficient votes for the PRI, Carlos Salinas moved to mend fences between the state and civil society. No sooner had he been inaugurated than he announced the creation of the National Solidarity Program to "repair the tattered social safety net . . . inherited from the economic crisis and austerity" but also to effect the "rearrangement of state-society relations, and of the coalition supporting the ruling [party]."[28] Under Salinas, "Solidarity" was the umbrella for well over twenty separate programs, most of which concentrated on infrastructure improvement, welfare, and support for productive activities. Like many previous government spending programs, Solidarity was intended to win political support for the regime. However, its design attempted to differentiate it from populism in terms of its fit within a neoliberal market economy. Broad subsidies were cut back and replaced with direct aid targeted at specific populations (allegedly, the most poor; practically, also certain disaffected political groups). Specific programs attempted to raise productivity and economic integration as well as relieve suffering. Material contributions and participation were solicited from beneficiaries themselves. Additionally, old PRI channels were bypassed in favor of direct links between the federal government and local populations.

Some observers viewed this approach as contributing to democratic discussion and grassroots organization.[29] Others denied that Solidarity committees had truly become a counterweight to the state or the PRI; links to the PRI appeared relatively common and participation often affected only a small proportion of the population. Solidarity may also have undermined the strength of opposition parties. In part, these different perceptions may simply reflect genuine variation depending on the nature and strength of Mexico's diverse civil society and local institutions across Mexico's diverse regional landscape.[30] Yet regardless of its impact at the local level, Solidarity at least began as an effort to "modernize" co-optation, and met with some success until negative popular reaction to the government's handling of economic policy overwhelmed the image of social concern. The later absorption of Solidarity into a cabinet-level ministry of social development may have institutionalized this trend toward targeting and productive welfare investment, though further research remains to be done.

Government Centralization

In turning now from state-society relations to the structure of the government itself, we deal less with elements intrinsic to democracy and more with elements hypothetically associated with democracy. That is, a system with widespread freedoms and pluralism is more democratic than one in which state corporatism rules society, whereas decentralized governments can exist in undemocratic systems and centralized governments can exist in democratic systems.

The editors have hypothesized a strong association between decentralization and democracy. The Mexican case historically supports this hypothesis, but indirectly, as it combines centralization with the absence of democracy. Much clearer is that centralization—geographically and in the presidency—has been crucial to civilian stability. As Pablo González Casanova's classic analysis showed, Mexico City–based presidentialism with a hegemonic party ended military and legislative conspiracies as well as divisively unstable rule by regional and other *caudillos*. "Respect for the balances of power would have been respect for the conspiracies of a semi-feudal society."[31]

The construction of central authority and national identity is a major problem for new nations. Mexico failed to establish stable central government until the late nineteenth century under Porfirio Díaz. Following the turmoil of the revolution and even into the 1930s, regional and village strongmen ruled outside the grasp of Mexico City. Such decentralized power had nothing to do with democracy but reflected local fiefdoms. Overcoming centrifugal antidemocratic forces is often a prerequisite to democratic consolidation. In Mexico, the centralization of power by key political leaders (Obregón, Calles, and Cárdenas) proved crucial to stability but not democracy.

Mexico formally has a federalist structure with thirty-one states (plus the Federal District), which in turn are divided into over 2,000 supposedly free municipalities. State political structures parallel the national structure except that their legislatures are unicameral. In practice, a range of daily and other activities are handled by states, and the federal government usually intervenes only when conflicts are not locally contained. However, the very infrequency of explicit interventions reflects (as we saw in state-labor relations) ongoing national government control over basic policy. In essence, presidents appoint the official party's gubernatorial candidates and depose troublesome PRI governors. National cabinet ministries have delegates in each state, and stationed military officers represent national authority. States have limited funds and depend on the national government for most of their income. Similarly, municipalities depend on states and the national government for leadership and funds. Most municipalities lack independent income beyond very small appropriations and fees from licenses and fines. Political careers have been made in Mexico City, not at the grassroots.

Because centralization limits the power of subnational governments, opposition victories were first accepted at the (less risky) local level. Only after 1989 did this include governorships. More common have been municipal opposition gains. Although the PRI still governs the vast majority of all municipalities, it has lost power in most of the largest and economically significant cities, including the two largest cities in Mexico: Guadalajara (to the PAN) and Mexico City (to the PRD).[32] The regime has used violence to oust municipal opposition, particularly in rural areas, but like other traditional practices, this has become more costly and less routine. More often, the government has relied on the limited resources and authority of municipal governments themselves to make it hard for the opposition to use local wins to consolidate their electoral strength and prove its capacity to govern. Because this is a relatively passive strategy, it carries less political risk. It remains to be seen whether the new opposition mayors in high-profile cities will be able to do any better than their predecessors in more humble positions. This is the challenge facing Cuauhtémoc Cárdenas, who won control of Mexico City in 1997, as well as PAN governors such as Vicente Fox in Guanajuato, who hope to prove by their administration that they would be the best candidate for president in the year 2000. Nevertheless, the existence of opportunities to govern at the local level, however frustrating their limitations, may make democratization more stable and viable in the long run, by bringing public attention to opposition parties, by offering them some administrative experience, and by encouraging competing parties to pay attention to citizen demands.

Centralization of power in Mexico City has also long meant centralization of power in the presidency. Constitutional provisions about the separation of powers within the federal government have had no more impact than provisions about the division of powers between federal and state governments. Mexico achieved stability not by defying authoritarian tendencies toward the enormous concentration of authority in one leader but by limiting the leader's term. Apt are references to Mexico's "king for six years." The president has been central to policymaking, agenda setting, conflict resolution, government appointments, control over the party, and so forth. Fernando Henrique Cardoso—later elected president of Brazil—once called the Mexican president more powerful than any Southern Cone military president.[33]

Even prior to the 1997 congressional election, such assessments probably underestimated four factors. One involves the comparative limits of the Mexican state's control over society; the Mexican president can be no more powerful than his government. Second are the terrible disorders, rivalries, and duplications rampant in the Mexican federal bureaucracy. Third, presidential immunity from criticism has eroded in the past two decades, reaching an unprecedented low under President Ernesto Zedillo, whose competence and personality have been repeatedly attacked.

Most important, however, are long-term trends that have slowly increased the combativeness of subnational actors (such as state and local governments), as well as more effective separation of powers. Although

Mexico's president is constitutionally a very strong one, with the explicit right to present initiatives, exercise a line-item veto, and freely name and remove most state employees, including cabinet secretaries, without congressional approval, Congress does have more powers than it has usually exercised. It can, for instance, override a presidential veto by a two-thirds vote in both chambers, raise and lower taxes, and approve the issue of public debt. It must also approve many actions taken by the president, including treaties and the naming of judges, routinely approved by the PRI-controlled congresses of the past. The failure of the PRI to win majority control of Congress in 1997 puts the president and PRI party leaders in the unprecedented position of having to negotiate with opposition parties in order to pass even such ordinary legislation. Since the 1970s, political reforms intended to keep opposition parties interested in legal participation have gradually expanded opposition representation in Congress. This has led to more vigorous debates, some limited investigations of government action, and even examples of cross-party legislative coalitions. Nevertheless, until recently, a disciplined PRI majority could ensure the passage of presidential initiatives. This lent executive action a stamp of legitimacy, actually bolstered by the presence of opposition parties, that it would otherwise have lacked. Even in 1995 and 1996, the PRI vote made it possible for Zedillo to pass harsh and unpopular measures to restore Mexico's international credit, such as a 50 percent hike in the value-added tax. After 1997, an opposition coalition with a congressional majority threatened to repeal this and other measures, eliminate large presidential discretionary spending budgets, and subject Zedillo's initiatives to more critical scrutiny. It is not clear whether the role of Congress will remain more reactive than proactive, or more oriented toward criticizing and amending executive action than independent policymaking. Moreover, the opposition "majority" is divided among two major and two minor parties, on different ends of the ideological spectrum. This will make cooperation on substantive issues quite difficult. Nevertheless, the 1997 election raises the possibility of fundamental changes in the balance of power in the Mexican central government. It seems likely that the importance of coalition building will increase, and that executive wishes may not automatically become Mexican policy. Meanwhile, even the PRI delegation may learn to exercise more autonomy from its own executive-branch leader, as party activists realize that unconditional obedience to the president can have negative electoral effects.

The judiciary has played a more important role than the legislature until recently, but also a limited one. It has been a place for privileged actors to protect their interests even against executive initiatives, particularly in the case of landlords working against land reform. Although it has handled disputes among citizens, it has not limited executive authority by interpreting the constitution or executive actions. Little parallel has emerged for the liberalization occurring in the legislature. Except for the special electoral court, which in 1994 demonstrated its new independence by reversing several PRI congressional victories, "judicial reform" has usually referred to speeding up the decisionmaking process, not increasing autonomy from the executive.

Presidential power depends ultimately on a rarity in Latin American politics (and in Mexican history from independence until roughly the 1930s): subordination of the military to civilian government. In the postwar era, only Costa Rica—which abolished its standing army—has enjoyed similar immunity from military interference. Outside Mexico, military subordination is generally associated with the establishment and defense of democracy. Mexico produced no democratic rule. Nonetheless, as in Costa Rica, skilled political leadership was crucial in establishing civilian supremacy.

Presidents Obregón, Calles, and Cárdenas, themselves revolutionary generals, like all presidents until 1946, adeptly timed and executed measures to subordinate the military. These included purges and other forced retirements and transfers of top commanders (which limited the development of personal loyalties to specific officers), welcoming opportunities for corruption within the service and for business employment outside it, social security, professionalization, cuts in military funding, creation of a viable political party, and incorporation of mass organizations into civilian structures. Since 1946, all presidents have been civilians.

Since the institutionalization of the regime, there have been no coups or serious threats of coups. The military has not been a powerful interest group blocking policies it does not like and insisting on others. Its share of government expenditures has been famously low. The military has not been integrated with the civilian right. All these factors distinguish Mexico from most of Latin America and help us understand the nation's stability.

Some signs of increasing military strength and activism have recently appeared.[34] Most troubling is an increasing tendency for the regime to call on the military to resolve domestic political problems. The military has not only taken an active role in pursuing guerrilla forces, and occupied areas where guerrillas are operating—a precursor of military coups in many South American nations—but has also been called on for domestic policing in Mexico City, and action against drug traffickers. Several military officers have been implicated in investigations of drug-related corruption. In connection with these new responsibilities, the military increased its budget and modernized its forces, with assistance from the United States. Nevertheless, to this point, the Mexican military has loyally sustained rather than threatened stable civilian rule. Its loyalty has not been to democracy, and it would probably not intervene on behalf of democratic forces against threatened repression. However, as long as the civilian regime remains basically stable, a major expansion of military involvement in politics is not predicted.

Centralization and presidentialism have recently come under increasing attack. Disaffection runs especially high in the industrial north, although Mexico does not face the separatist threats that undermine stability in some nations. Many Mexicans consider decentralization necessary for increased participation and democratization. Decentralization or limits on presidential power could lower the stakes enough for the ruling party to accept alternation in power, as well as give opposition parties more opportunities to acquire experience in governing. Decentralization in implementation and, more controversially, in decisionmaking is increasingly linked to regime effectiveness and stability as well. Even some regime supporters back decentralization as a means of improving government efficiency and legitimacy. President de la Madrid initiated reforms in the 1980s to expand municipal autonomy and increase access to local resources. Salinas also made decentralization and local participation a theme, particularly through programs like Solidarity. Their support was often more rhetorical than practical, but some change occurred.

More effective limits to centralization and presidential power include the rising presence of opposition parties and popular movements in particular regions, extensive privatization, and neoliberal trade opening. In the early 1980s, the president headed a vast network of federal agencies and state-owned companies (parastatals) employing 17 percent of the nation's workforce. By 1991, the number of parastatals had fallen from over 1,000 to 269.[35] Major companies, including telephones, airlines, and banks, passed into private hands. Moreover, with entrance into the General Agreement on Tariffs and Trade (GATT, which became the World Trade Organization [WTO] in January 1995) and the negotiation of the North American Free Trade Agreement (NAFTA), the Mexican government constrained its ability to use traditional economic instruments like tariffs and import controls. Decisions formerly subject to executive approval could now be made in boardrooms.

But obstacles to decentralization remain enormous. Centralization goes beyond the political and into economic and social realms. Politically, decentralization means taking away resources and privileges, such as the power of appointment, from entrenched union-party leaders and state administrators, who therefore resist. Moreover, since the ruling party has held together largely on the basis of patron-client networks anchored by presidential power, decentralization or limits on presidentialism could cause the party to split and thus threaten stability. Decentralization or less presidentialism could also endanger national policy coherence, and this engages resistance from technocrats. Furthermore, many modernizers have not renounced the idea of an influential state. Slimming down the state also streamlines policymaking, restores presidential control in what had become an overbureaucratized system, and allows top technocrats to distribute subsidies on the basis of evaluated performance.[36]

Overall, decentralization involves substantial risks. Even if over-centralization blocks democracy and threatens stability, sudden decentralization might threaten stability more. Nevertheless, the president is decreasingly able to control the pace and extent of decentralization. Much will depend on the will and commitment of opposition parties, especially now that they may be on the brink of winning national power, to push for decentralizing reforms.

The Party and Electoral Systems

The dominance of the Institutional Revolutionary Party has been integral to both state corporatism and centralization. The editors hypothesize that deeply institutionalized competitive parties are conducive to stable democracy. The PRI has been deeply institutionalized. As it held power longer than any other currently ruling party in the world, it reached widely into society. Yet this has been conducive to a distinctly undemocratic stability. The PRI has helped encapsulate groups and preclude alternative institutionalized parties. Until recently, it has done all this effectively.

From independence until the revolution, parties were mostly political clubs. The elections in which they participated "were not a mechanism of popular voting but a legitimization of military force."[37] Of seventy-one governments (1823–1911), only seventeen were elected by constitutional norms. Even these involved indirect elections, open balloting, and so forth. The elected president almost always came from the incumbent party or group. Nonetheless, all new governments felt obliged to seek popular-constitutional legitimization through elections. Again, democratic ideology was juxtaposed with undemocratic reality.

Even after the revolution, parties continued to be weak, transitory, dependent on a single leader, without mass bases, and multitudinous. Then the new party, continually juggled and deepened from 1929 to 1946 (when it became the PRI), replaced anarchic conflict and made elites play by institutionalized and legal rules. From 1929 to 1933, the number of parties dropped from fifty-one to four.[38] Mass organizations were incorporated. Civilian rulers built a strong institution that could organize and distribute resources, thus helping to subordinate the military. Such developments are often associated with transitions to democracy, but in Mexico competition among elites did not encompass open public contestation, and mass incorporation was corporatist.

Not surprisingly, then, the PRI has not concentrated on the functions expected of democratic parties. Its main mission has been neither to aggregate nor to articulate demands. It has not truly competed for power.

Although it has always been "in power," the PRI has not had a major role in policymaking. Instead, it has concentrated on other party functions, directed to the service of the government of which it is really a part (although party and government personnel are formally distinct). These functions included mobilizing support for the regime, suppressing dissent, gathering and manipulating information, distributing welfare and patronage, engaging in political socialization and recruitment, handling particularistic grievances, and providing an ideological rationale for government action. Unlike what one expects of democratic party systems, the PRI's hegemonic rule has sustained socioeconomic inequalities, but the PRI has won its largest vote from the least-privileged groups.

Over time, however, the PRI's performance of these functions became less effective. Popular movements criticized the state's performance of welfare distribution, organizing self-help networks and demanding better deals from the government. Independent union organizers complained about the suppression of dissent and the lack of democratic accountability in the PRI union sector, and the ability of peasant and labor organizations to deliver popular support (especially votes) diminished. Independent media defied intimidation and repression to circumvent the government's control over information. The imposition of austerity during Mexico's repeated economic crises also generally undermined popular support for and confidence in the PRI's management. Under these conditions, the ritualized elections traditionally used by the PRI to justify and legitimize its continued governance unexpectedly became an avenue for angry voters to express their feelings. Opposition parties saw the opportunity to challenge the government's monopoly over political recruitment, most dramatically in the 1988 presidential election, when Cuauhtémoc Cárdenas—son of one of the party's founders—officially won 31 percent of the vote in a disputed and dirty election. As Jorge Domínguez and James McCann note, these electoral changes reflected changes in the political education, interest, and loyalties of an increasingly independent Mexican electorate.[39] They also reflected the breakdown of traditional mechanisms of elite co-optation and control. The experience of 1988 further shook political expectations: no longer was it impossible to imagine the PRI losing. Although economic recovery in the early 1990s temporarily shored up the PRI's electoral position, political loyalties to the PRI never fully recovered (see Table 10.1).

The PRI's crisis generated difficulties for stability but increased hopes that democratic competition might replace traditional methods of gathering and mobilizing support, engaging in political socialization and recruitment, and distributing services and information. The inverse relationship between stability and democracy during periods of transition is a source of both strength and weakness for the PRI. On the one hand, fear that alternation in power would mean a loss of stability was probably one of the key factors behind the PRI's victory in one of the cleanest and most-watched elections

Table 10.1   Electoral Support and Legislative Representation, 1946–1994

| | Percentage of Congressional Vote[a] | | | | Percentage of Congressional Seats | | | |
Year	PRI	PAN	Left[b]	Other	PRI	PAN	Left	Other
1946	73.5	2.2	0.5	23.8	94.3	2.7	0	0
1949	93.9	5.6	—	0.5	96.6	2.7	—	0
1952	74.3	8.7	15.9	1.5	93.8	3.1	1.2	1.9
1955	89.9	9.2	—	1.0	94.4	3.7	—	1.9
1958	88.2	10.2	—	1.5	94.4	3.7	—	1.2
1961	90.2	7.6	—	1.7	96.6	2.8	—	0.5
1964	86.2	11.5	—	2.1	83.3	9.5	—	7.1
1967	83.3	12.3	—	4.2	84.0	9.0	—	7.1
1970	83.2	14.2	—	2.4	83.6	0.4	—	7.0
1973	77.4	16.3	—	6.0	81.8	10.8	—	7.4
1976	84.8	9.0	—	5.8	82.3	8.4	—	9.3
1979	74.0	11.5	5.3	9.1	74.0	10.8	4.5	10.8
1982	69.3	17.5	5.9	7.3	74.5	12.8	4.3	8.3
1985	68.1	16.3	6.3	9.2	72.3	10.3	6.0	11.5
1988	51.1	18.0	29.6	1.3	52.0	20.2	27.8[c]	—
1991	61.5	17.7	8.9	12.0	64.0	17.8	8.2	10.0
1994	50.3	25.8	16.7	7.2	60.0	23.8	14.2	2.0
1997	39.1	26.6	25.7	8.5	47.8	24.2	25.0	3.0

Sources: Contienda electoral en las elecciones de diputados federales (Mexico City: Instituto Federal Electoral, 1991); Silvia Gomez Tagle, *Las estadísticas electorales de la reforma política* (Mexico City: Colegio de México, 1990); *Relación de los 300 Distritos Federales Electorales* (Mexico City: Instituto Federal Electoral, 1991); *Elecciones federales 1994* (Mexico City: Instituto Federal Electoral, 1994); Mireya Cuellar and Nestor Martinez, "Profundas Inequidades," *La Jornada* 23 (October 1994): 1; *Elecciones federales 1997* (Mexico City: Instituto Federal Electoral, 1997).

Notes: a. For comparability, congressional vote is used for all years, including presidential election years (1946, 1952, 1958, etc.). Presidential vote corresponds closely to congressional vote, except for 1976, when the PAN did not run a candidate. Figures reflect percentage of valid vote and may not sum to 100% because of rounding and the omission of votes for non-registered candidates.

b. "Left" refers to the independent left, not the "parastatal" parties allied for all practical purposes to the PRI. Dash marks indicate no legal independent left parties in that year. For each year, the specific parties included in the "independent left" total are as follows: (1) in 1952, the congressional vote associated with the candidacy of Miguel Henríquez Guzmán; (2) in 1979, the vote of the Mexican Communist Party; (3) in 1982, vote of the Partido Socialista Unificada Mexicana (PSUM, 2.8%), the Trotskyist Revolutionary Workers Party (1.3%), and the Social Democratic Party (0.2%); (4) in 1985, vote of PSUM (3.4%), Revolutionary Workers Party (1.3%), and Mexican Workers Party (1.6%); (5) in 1988, vote of the Cárdenas coalition plus the Revolutionary Workers Party (0.6%); (6) in 1991, vote of PRD (8.3%) plus the Revolutionary Workers Party (0.6%); (7) in 1994, vote of the PRD; and (8) in 1997, vote of the PRD.

c. Seats won by the Cárdenas coalition. Only the Mexican Socialist Party (4.5% of seats) joined the PRD.

in Mexican history—the 1994 presidential election—despite its candidate's manifest inability to arouse popular enthusiasm.[40] On the other hand, so integral is the PRI to the regime that all of the *regime* difficulties already cited, such as decentralization and the beleaguered presidency, are PRI problems as well. It is therefore difficult for the PRI to accept changes in the rules of the regime without undermining the very features that helped it manage Mexico's postrevolutionary conflicts and maintain its hegemonic position. Similarly, it is difficult for the PRI to make a transition to an electoral party competing for popular support when it has always operated on the assumption that its control of power was not fundamentally in question, and that one of its primary functions was to help the government manage conflict and maintain political stability. In the interest of stability, for example, PRI leaders have supported unpopular government policies, declined to mobilize their union bases against the government, and accepted sacrifices. If the PRI chooses to abandon this tradition in favor of more electorally popular positions, it might undermine the president and presidential policy so much that political and economic stability would be endangered—and as long as the president is a PRI member, voters would likely blame the PRI anyway. Thus, whether the PRI supports or opposes the president, it risks negative electoral consequences. To date, the party has tended to support the president because he still controls vast resources that represent the party's best electoral hope.

The PRI has also been slow to adapt itself to a democratizing climate because of institutional inertia, and because almost any adaptation is fraught with danger. It has been difficult for a party built to handle a basically rural and uneducated society to fit its structure and practices to modern Mexico. It has been even harder for a party established without true democratic functions—indeed, to avoid the risks of intra-elite competition—to compete openly for citizen support. Efforts to reform the PRI naturally produce tensions within the party and so far have had relatively little impact.[41]

If democracy has been weak within the PRI, it has also been weak in the party system overall. Opposition parties have existed, and some have expressed considerable dissent. But until recently, they served mostly to legitimize PRI rule by providing a facade of competition. In fact, many opposition parties were largely government-sponsored and cooperated with the PRI. However, since 1988, most of these pseudoparties have lost positions to the much more independent and now more powerful opposition parties: PAN and PRD.

On the left, independent parties have enjoyed legal registry only since the electoral reform of 1977. Whether clandestine or participating in elections, left parties have traditionally been handicapped by government hostility and by the lack of a trade union or a peasant base (already captured by PRI corporatism) and have generally had little mass appeal.[42] The left also suffered from intense internal conflicts that led to the formation of countless parties, quasi parties, and currents. Since its legalization in 1977, however, the left has undergone a process of moderation and unification, which culminated in the formation of the Partido de la Revolución Democrática

(PRD) in 1989. The PRD represented the convergence of ex-communist and socialist currents with the traditional left wing of the PRI, known as the *cardenista* left. These groups were brought together by the Cárdenas presidential candidacy in 1988. Initially, his coalition won broad popular support, though his campaign was primarily oriented toward protest against the negative social consequences of the economic crisis of the '80s, and benefited considerably from nostalgic remembrance of his immensely popular father, radical president Lázaro Cárdenas. As it attempted to consolidate a party structure, the PRD suffered from severe government persecution, as well as debilitating internal divisions, weak local organization, a vague and even contradictory ideological program, and a tendency toward personalism.[43] In addition, as the economy improved under Salinas, levels of protest began to decline. These trends undermined electoral support for the PRD, which fell from 31 percent achieved by the Cuauhtémoc Cárdenas coalition in 1988, to just 8.2 percent in 1991. The return of Cárdenas as a candidate in 1994 improved the party's performance to 17 percent, but most observers still felt that the PRD's prospects were poor, particularly compared to those of the better organized, more pragmatic, and more consolidated right party: PAN.

Nevertheless, even before the PRD's surprising 1997 comeback, the PRD (and the ghost of its 1988 threat) had lifted the left's political profile and influence. The percentage of congressional districts in which leftist parties came in first or second increased between 1985 and 1994 from 5.3 percent (and no first-place finishes) to 30.7 percent of all districts; in 1997, this percentage rose to 51.6 percent.[44] In several states the left could beat the PRI on at least a municipal level. Moreover, with the ideological convergence of the Salinas PRI and the right, the PRD was the only sustained critic within the party system of the government's fundamental economic and social policies. Although the left's confrontational stance and its reluctance to negotiate with the government frustrated some opportunities to advance electoral reform, it served a purpose as a voice of popular protest. In this sense, the PRD contributed to the development of multiparty democracy.

In 1997, the high-profile Cárdenas campaign for the mayorship of Mexico City—the first election for a position that had previously been filled by presidential appointment—not only resulted in an overwhelming victory for Cárdenas personally, but also in an improvement of the PRD's image on a national level. The PRD elected nearly twice as many congressional representatives in 1997 as in 1994, displacing the PAN as the second-largest congressional bench. When the opposition parties formed a coalition to wrest formal control of the Congress from the PRI, they elected a PRD member, Porfirio Muñoz Ledo, as the first opposition head of Congress. Yet despite this apparent improvement, the PRD still faces the daunting challenge of fulfilling its new responsibilities, and of consolidating the votes it won in 1997. Regardless of whether it succeeds, the existence of *two* strong competitors for protest votes against the PRI probably encourages the development of responsible opposition parties, a positive sign for democratization.

This is especially relevant because, despite the PAN's disappointment at not winning more of the protest vote in 1997, it remains a party to reckon with; indeed, it probably still has a stronger organization and clearer political identity than the PRD, and partisan loyalties at least as deeply rooted. Indeed, until 1997, as Table 10.1 shows, the main beneficiary of electoral opening was not the left but the conservative PAN, founded in 1939. The PAN has not attracted a major portion of labor or the peasantry, as Christian democratic parties have in nations such as Chile and Venezuela. Its strongest bases have been historically limited to certain regions, particularly the north and urban areas, and to privileged groups. Like the left, the PAN functioned primarily as a symbolic counterweight to the PRI for most of its history. But beginning in the 1980s, a growing portion of the party favored all-out competition in a democratic setting and resorted increasingly to civil disobedience and mobilization to protest electoral fraud. Unlike the PRI, PAN selects candidates rather openly. In recent years, however, ideological and programmatic distinctions between the PRI and the PAN narrowed, especially in the area of economic reform, as the PRI moved steadily to the right during the 1980s.

At the same time, the PAN's attractiveness to sectors alienated by the 1982 bank nationalization contributed to a marked business orientation and some movement away from the party's roots in Catholic social thought. The PAN's increasing cooperation with the PRI was particularly important because since 1988 the PRI has lacked a sufficient majority to pass constitutional amendments unaided. The PAN even supported passage of a 1990 electoral reform that many observers (and some PAN legislators) felt would hurt the PAN, largely in order to deter the left's advance after 1988. Its more cordial relationship with the PRI led to serious problems within the party, including several public resignations by party leaders and accusations of selling out. Nevertheless, accommodation brought results. The government accepted electoral wins by the PAN—including governorships of several important states, such as Baja California and Jalisco—when less than six years earlier it had denied PAN municipal victories. In the view of the PAN leadership, the gradual expansion of local opposition power would ultimately further the goal of national democratization. Yet the PAN also took the opportunity to portray itself as the only "safe" opposition (compared with the "unsafe" left opposition), in order to attract a larger share of the protest vote.

The PAN also benefited from electoral reforms that made fraud more difficult and improved the competitive position of opposition parties. Most of these reforms were PRI efforts to maintain a delicate balance in which elections did not jeopardize PRI control, yet were clean enough and offered enough access to power to encourage opposition-party participation— therefore bolstering legitimacy. These reforms were not intended to alter the fundamental rules of the game or allow the genuine democratization of free competition for power. Yet despite intentions, successive reforms did chip away at PRI control over the electoral process, beginning with the 1977 reforms that legalized the left, allowed parties to register more easily, and granted public funds and free media time. More dramatically, they greatly expanded opposition representation in the Chamber of Deputies. Although three hundred seats were still allotted to plurality winners in each district, first one hundred (1977) and then two hundred seats (1986) were reserved for distribution according to proportional representation (PR), though only parties winning at least 1.5 percent of the vote were eligible for PR seats. Clauses requiring overrepresentation of the largest party remained in subsequent versions of the electoral law.

A salient feature of the 1994 reforms was replacement of party representatives on the board of the Federal Electoral Institute with "citizen councilors" elected by at least two-thirds of the Congress. The reforms also made it illegal for parties to transport groups to the polls on election day, a long-standing PRI practice. For the first time, the PRI lacked an automatic majority on the governing electoral board, although it retained effective control.[45] The old voter-registry system was replaced with a photo ID, though complaints persisted that opposition voters had been unfairly removed from voter rolls and "false" PRI voters substituted. Next, the 1996 reforms, adopted after multiparty negotiation, limited PRI control over the Federal Electoral Institute even further, and significantly expanded the public resources (including financing and access to media) available to opposition parties. This immediately made possible much more technically sophisticated and mass-based campaigns than in the past. Even critics on both the left and the right have generally acknowledged that the electoral system now provides more freedom, information, exposure, and checks against fraud and manipulation than in the past, though much remains to be done.

Mostly, reforms responded to declining legitimacy, opposition threats to boycott the electoral system, or nonelectoral threats. They were intended to stabilize the regime and to make sure dissent would be institutionalized and channeled.[46] Thus, at various times "reform" provisions aimed at ensuring the PRI a legislative majority and at guaranteeing continued PRI dominance on the electoral body that supervises elections (reduced to de facto veto power over the selection of those who serve). The new law still overrepresented the largest party: with 39 percent of the 1997 vote, the PRI would control nearly 48 percent of the seats in Congress. PRI leaders have also blocked measures imposing reform on some states.[47] Federal financial support and media access remained partly proportional, by law, to each party's previous electoral strength. Perhaps most important, the PRI retained the backing of the state.

Yet increasing reliance on electoral legitimacy carries certain vulnerabilities for the traditional PRI regime. First, by stressing its ability to win elections, the regime has raised the cost of blatant electoral fraud. Improved opposition organization and heightened international attention to Mexican politics (stemming in part from deeper economic integration under the North American Free Trade Agreement [NAFTA]) have also contributed to raise the costs of fraud. If opposition parties threaten to defeat the PRI, the regime must weigh more carefully than ever the costs of using its weapon of last resort. Second, for many in Mexico the only truly credible election is an election the PRI loses. This results in part from long experience with PRI "electoral wizards," in part from disbelief that a party regarded with such widespread cynicism could actually win, and in part from self-serving opposition attempts to question the legitimacy of elections it loses. Protests of fraud now mention not only traditional methods such as ballot stuffing but also more sophisticated manipulation of voters and above all—and with justification—"structural fraud," referring to the PRI's massive advantages in resources, organization, media attention, and state connections. So a contradiction emerges: the purpose of reform is to legitimate PRI victories by making electoral competition credible, but convincing electoral competition increases the possibility of losing—of genuine democratic alternation in power. The PRI has tried to avoid this by accepting the tremendous economic costs of winning elections "cleanly," including lavish campaigns, two new national voter registries in five years, an extensive mobilization program, and manipulation of government social programs for electoral purposes, as well as continued traditional fraud on a more limited, targeted, and local scale. This in itself implies that even when the PRI wins, it is now forced to use more traditional democratic and competitive tactics, including *responding* to popular demands and attempting to persuade as well as coerce.

Increasingly, however, elections have become a purgatory for the PRI—an arduous and exhausting process in which victories are met with protests and only losses win praise. Whereas electoral protest was once confined to PAN states, it now affects even states like Chiapas and Oaxaca, where the PRI won 80 to 90 percent of the official vote as recently as 1988. Hunger strikes, roadblocks, demonstrations, boycotts, occupation of government buildings, and repeated denunciations have become common. More than appeasing the opposition, concessions and reforms have increased pressure for free and honest elections. In no other way can one explain the government's willingness to spend so lavishly to win the 1994 presidential election credibly. The Federal Electoral Institute estimated spending about U.S.$730 million on the 1994 electoral registry alone, "equivalent to having built 48,000 new classrooms."[48] In sum, prospects for clean elections are good, but prospects for elections with equal conditions for competition appear still uncertain.

Performance and Support

Until the 1970s, Mexico's strong civilian rule brought widely envied economic success and societal support. Like many nations in Latin America, Mexico relied heavily on import substitution. Unlike others, Mexico achieved average annual economic growth of over 6 percent from 1940 to 1970 and held its inflation low (under 5 percent annually) in the latter half of the period. Given the repeated economic crises of recent times, these earlier sustained achievements are especially worth remembering.

Economic growth promoted enormous social change. Only about one-fourth of the labor force remains in agriculture. A middle class has developed, although it is still clearly outnumbered by the lower class. Mexico has pulled itself to an average position among the larger, relatively developed Latin American nations with its 69.7-year life expectancy at birth, its infant mortality rate of 56 per 1,000 live births, its 87 percent adult literacy, and its dramatic improvements in caloric intake, access to primary schools, and energy consumption.[49] The regime also used economic growth to promote selective social modernization. Historical comparisons often seem impressive, even if largely because of how poor Mexico had been. For example, the percentage of Mexicans over fifteen years old with at least six years of schooling more than doubled, to 62 percent, from 1970 to 1990.[50]

Of course, even official national figures show not just progress but also underdevelopment. Moreover, these figures often obscure regional and class inequality, both tragically high in Mexico. Such outcomes have been consistent with Mexico's striking internal contrasts in the distribution of power and freedom. In fact, government policies have contributed to inequalities. Promotion of capital-intensive industrialization has brought severe problems for rural Mexico and for employment of the less privileged. Hyperurbanization often means urban dwellers also suffer from a lack of piped water and sewage systems and from increasing water, soil, and air pollution. Government social expenditures and services have been very unequally directed, in ways that co-opt and reward some groups while repressing and marginalizing others. Social services for unionized workers are a good example. Consistent with Mexico's elite pluralism, a wide network of private organizations, including schools, universities, and hospitals, is available for the privileged.[51] Consequently, economic successes under civilian rule have been compatible with what the World Bank called one of the world's worst profiles of income distribution.[52] As Table 10.2 shows, the profile did not improve even during decades of growth and selective mobility.

Table 10.2   Income Distribution in Mexico, 1950–1992 (percentage of income earned[a])

Income group (deciles)	1950	1963	1977	1984[b]	1992
1–2 (lowest 20 percent)	4.7	3.5	3.3	4.8	4.3
3–5	12.7	11.5	13.4	16.0	14.1
6–8	23.7	25.4	28.2	29.7	27.4
9–10 (highest 20 percent)	58.9	59.6	55.1	49.5	54.2

Sources: Daniel C. Levy and Gabriel Székely, Mexico: Paradoxes of Stability and Change, 2d ed. (Boulder, CO: Westview, 1987), based on data from ECLA for 1950 and 1963, and Mexico's Secretaría de Programación y Presupuesto for 1977. Figures for 1984 calculated by Diana Alarcón González, based on government figures, in Changes in the Distribution of Income in Mexico and Trade Liberalization (Tijuana: El Colegio de la Frontera Norte, 1994), p. 87. 1992 data from Encuesta nacional de ingresos y gastos de los hogares (Mexico, DF: Instituto Nacional de Estadística, Geografía, e Informática, 1992), p. 39.

Notes: a. Estimates may vary slightly due to calculations by different sources. Similar estimates for 1963 and 1977 appear in Enrique Hernández-Laos and Jorge Córdoba, La distribución del ingreso en México (Mexico, DF: Centro de Investigación para la Integración Social, 1982). Slightly less-favorable data are reported in Werner Baer, "Growth with Inequality," Latin American Research Review 21, no. 2 (1986): 198.

b. Alarcón's data may reflect improvement between 1977 and the onset of the economic crisis in 1981–1982. However, her estimates for 1989 come quite close to government estimates for 1992, and confirm a deterioration during the crisis of the 1980s.

Nevertheless, careful manipulation of the fruits of economic success was long associated with political strength and high support levels. That manipulation helped sustain a myth of continual progress, which provided legitimacy. In fact, Mexicans took pride in their political system and credited it for many of the social and personal material successes they have seen, despite cynicism about politicians and low evaluations of the daily performance of government.[53] Even much of the left granted legitimacy to the regime's progressive record in some socioeconomic and particularly nationalist matters.

Until the 1980s—or in other words, for at least forty years—hypotheses linking economic growth to the development of democratic government were not supported in Mexico. Nor did Mexico fit the notion that dependent industrialized development leads at a certain point to instability followed by military rule. Instead, Mexican economic and social modernization reinforced stable, undemocratic civilian rule. Indeed, it was the economic reversals of the 1980s and 1990s that most clearly brought pressures on the regime and contributed to increased electoral opposition.

Many have blamed Mexico's recurrent economic crises on policies designed for political, not economic, efficiency. In the 1970s, the costs of creating jobs and subsidies for a coalition that included business, the middle class, organized labor, and even less-privileged groups drove the government to borrow heavily; this, combined with a plunge in revenue as world oil prices fell sharply, caused a balance-of-payments crisis that led to eight years of blocked and even negative growth, inflation rates of roughly 100 percent, socially devastating declines in employment and real wages, and rising political protest. In the 1990s, economic crisis was attributed less to deep-seated structural problems (many of which were addressed in a decade of major economic reforms) and more to specific policy mistakes, especially in fiscal management, but still tied in part to the government's unwillingness to risk the political consequences of devaluing the peso before the 1994 election. In the period between 1989 and 1994, however, economic recovery did bolster support for the PRI, though this did not necessarily imply support for authoritarian values.

Significant government corruption also tarnished the regime's legitimacy. Perhaps a more modernized society has decreasing tolerance for corruption. Certainly, the increased availability of alternative sources of information, often characteristic of more modernized societies, has raised public awareness of corruption. In any case, the struggle against corruption has become part of the struggle for democratic accountability. Both de la Madrid and Salinas felt the need to mount public campaigns against corruption. Salinas even arrested the powerful and notoriously corrupt head of the petroleum workers' union. However, these efforts appeared less calculated to change political practices than to move against symbols, with whom, in addition, Salinas in particular had personal quarrels.

President Zedillo's arrest of Raúl Salinas, brother of the former president, as "intellectual author" of the 1994 murder of a top PRI official broke a tradition of immunity for presidents and their families. The former president has even been questioned in the case, and there is also evidence lending credence to claims that Raúl Salinas used his influence with his brother on behalf of businessmen and possibly drug cartels. However, the investigation's meager results did little to improve public confidence in the government. Less dramatic but probably more substantial was the arrest of the government's newly named "drug czar" (General Jesús Gutiérrez Rebollo) for taking money to protect the Juárez drug cartel, as well as a number of cases involving prosecution of wealthy Mexican businessmen for tax fraud. While the drug czar incident was highly embarrassing for the government, its willingness to prosecute anyway suggests a departure from past practice, as does its refusal to ignore tax evasion by the rich.

As with so many other aspects of Mexico's democratization process, the fight against corruption has double-edged effects, undermining sources of traditional stability even as it attempts to replace them with new, more-democratic ones. We have already seen that opportunities for corruption helped bring the military under civilian control. Additionally, corruption has provided some flexibility in an often unresponsive bureaucracy. It has given major and minor actors incentives to seek rewards within the system and to rely on the peaceful turnover of personnel. It has been the glue for many implicit political pacts among elites and has been integral to patron-client and state-society relationships.

But corruption on the Mexican scale is not compatible with democracy and its need for accountability. Corruption, therefore, joins the list of factors that may have promoted stability in nondemocratic Mexico yet could now undermine stability as well as democratization.

THEORETICAL ANALYSIS

We have tried to show how several factors commonly associated with democratic stability have in Mexico long contributed to stable civilian rule that is not democratic. We now turn more fully and explicitly to an examination of this study's hypotheses about democracy. Many of these hypotheses have come to seem more prescient in the light of recent developments in the country. However, even if Mexico becomes clearly democratic in the near future, the Mexican case would remain an important warning about the limitations of these hypotheses. Factors hypothesized to contribute directly to democracy contributed instead to the stability of undemocratic politics for decades. The length of this stability, the depth of its institutionalization in nondemocratic organizations, and even the effects of an authoritarian legacy in shaping the current course of democratization all render facile a "big picture" conclusion that democracy was inevitable and PRI authoritarianism merely delayed it. A system that lasts for well over sixty years is a political regime in its own right, not a minor aberration.

Political Culture and Legitimacy

Despite growing data from studies and public opinion polls, evidence on the impact of political culture on democracy in Mexico remains inconclusive. On the one hand, works on Mexico's "national character" have often depicted hierarchical, authoritarian, submissive, and other undemocratic inclinations. They suggest that such character traits help promote Mexico's authoritarian politics; political culture both explains and legitimizes the political system. Certainly, Mexicans have been remarkably accepting of their political system. Whether because of a national trait of stoicism, or the fear of disorder, or belief in the regime's positive orientations, Mexicans have at a minimum not rebelled even when their aspirations were long frustrated, and many maintained pride in their system.[54]

On the other hand, most social scientists have been either skeptical or hostile to cultural arguments. They point out that political culture may result primarily from political learning in an authoritarian institutional framework, and add that it is "striking how much of Mexican politics can be comprehended by a model of the rational political actor."[55] Still others argue that the political culture is basically at odds with the political structure, not supportive of it.[56] They find that Mexicans support participation and dissent and oppose censorship.

If evidence on deep values remains inconclusive, evidence on behavior is not. Mexico's regime was not precariously superimposed on a society filled with democratic practices. The society never was so constituted, and the revolution brought new and strong but mostly undemocratic institutions. State corporatism went hand in hand with hierarchical, authoritarian rule inside mass institutions such as unions. It also went hand in hand with limited mass participation, encapsulated and restricted to official channels; patrimonial networks; and petitions rather than aggregated demands. Efficacy increased with socioeconomic status, however.[57] Participation by elites was much freer and more influential, but elite institutions (media, intellectual publications, businesses, private schools, and universities) often operated undemocratically. Pluralism exceeded democracy.

Yet elites did display a behavioral norm hypothesized (in this book and elsewhere) to be powerfully associated with democracy. This is the disposition to compromise. Postrevolutionary politics provide ample evidence of flexibility, bargaining, moderation, restraint, and pacts that avoid "fights to the finish."[58] In Mexico, acceptance of such norms contributed to regime consolidation and stability without democracy. First, although elite pacts in democracies often limit mass participation, Mexico's corporatist mass inclusion has been distinctly antidemocratic. Second, the restraint in the elite pacts has also excluded open, organized competition for rulership by even a significant minority of the public.

However, both this long-standing elite propensity to compromise and undemocratic forms of incorporation now face grave challenges even from within the PRI. Analysts have worried about the consequences of increasing "technocratization" of Mexican administrations since the late 1970s, and a consequent breakdown of understanding between technocrats and traditional PRI politicians.[59] Whatever their origins (and a *técnico/político* division is admittedly too simplistic to explain all of them), divisions within the PRI have become more public. The 1994 assassination of PRI presidential candidate Luis Donaldo Colosio in Tijuana, which marked the first murder of a president or heir apparent since the founding of the governing party after the murder of president-elect Obregón, led to widespread public suspicion of PRI involvement. Investigation of the later murder of a top PRI functionary not only resulted in the arrest of the president's brother and accusations against ex-president Salinas himself, but also raised concerns about the influence of narco-politics on the Mexican political elite. As norms of complicity break down, norms of compromise may face more severe tests.

At the same time, the growth of autonomous grassroots organizations challenges the traditional patterns of demand making. Organizations speak not only of rights to government aid (instead of individual petitions) but rights to participation and democracy. This may well indicate a shift in political culture at the mass level. Nevertheless, political culture is too complex and contradictory to yield strong evidence that confirms or disconfirms project hypotheses.

Historical Sequences

Mexico scores low on the historical dimensions associated with democracy. Mexico lacks sustained, successful democratic precedents or even many experiments with democratic government. If the present regime has precedents, they are chiefly authoritarian. Where it democratizes, it innovates.

Moreover, Mexico did not follow Robert Dahl's favored route of early liberal contestation followed by mass incorporation.[60] Rather, Calles, Cárdenas, and others adeptly incorporated mass organizations into a corporatist system that excluded them from democracy. Mexico's pacts attempted to control masses mobilized by the revolution and establish viable, ingenious alternatives to open elite contestation for power. However, if one highlights the persistent marginality of unorganized Mexico, or if one reserves "inclusiveness" for independent mass participation, Mexico might rank low historically on that dimension. In that case, recent political reforms expanding contestation, coupled with longer-standing and expanding personal freedoms, might give some sense of liberalization preceding inclusiveness.

Class, Ethnic, and Religious Cleavages

Key hypotheses on class structure and cumulative cleavages do not suggest favorable conditions for democracy in Mexico. The distribution of wealth is terribly unequal. Despite massive land reform (now officially terminated), big agribusiness and a large impoverished peasant population divide the land very unequally in terms of both the size and desirability of plots. Mexican agriculture is not characterized by middle-class farming. Moreover, many cleavages are cumulative. A profile of the most disadvantaged commonly fits the low-income Indian peasant living in the rural south.

"Indians" form the largest ethnic minority, perhaps 10 percent of the population (depending on definition), although the percentage is much higher in some regions. The revolution brought some respect for Indian identity, and pockets of self-governance exist, with some direct democratic selection of leaders and policies. Mostly, however, the indigenous population continues to be either marginalized or integrated into a servile underclass, despite some mobility for individuals. In turn, the "rule of law" and the state often arrive as oppressive alien forces in Indian communities.

Traditionally, Indian distinctiveness and marginalization served the interests of the PRI, rather than forming the basis for pluralist politics. Since the emergence of a guerrilla rebellion lead by the *zapatistas,* a largely indigenous force, not only have ethnic issues risen to the top of the national agenda, but ethnically based popular organizations have often taken the lead in pressuring the government to respond to demands for democracy, dignity, and respect—demands central to but certainly not limited to the ethnic communities themselves. The *zapatista* army has encouraged the formation of a broad political coalition between civil society groups with common goals, held national "plebiscites" in 1996 and 1999 to demonstrate wide support for democracy and human rights, and won official government agreement to grant greater autonomy to indigenous communities, although as of early 1998 the government had not lived up to most of the commitments it made. Ethnic cleavages are both more salient and contribute more to democratic pluralism than in the past.[61] However, they also contain the potential for violent clashes with local elites (a problem that has become serious in Chiapas and Oaxaca), as well as with the national government.

To defuse the destabilizing potential of great societal diversity and cumulative cleavages, the regime tacitly respected spheres of influence and autonomy to groups that avoided mainstream politics. This fits Juan Linz's classic notion of authoritarian regimes.[62] The regime also handled politics in ways that cut across class cleavages—not on basic distributive policies but on symbolic and organizational ones. Symbolically, it successfully used nationalism even if the concept means different things to different groups. Organizationally, it structured itself on vertical patron-client relationships. This reinforced hierarchy and other undemocratic societal norms. The "formation of horizontal alliances based on common class interests is impeded," and the relationships serve "to maintain the separation between ideology and its social base."[63]

As noted earlier, the regime has been sophisticated in managing privileged groups differently from other groups. State relationships with elite groups have been much more pluralist than those with mass organizations, though even autonomous elite organizations have not usually been run democratically, or demanded democratization. Instead, they have normally accepted a stable nondemocracy that has granted them considerable advantages over other Mexicans in material rewards and personal freedom.[64]

However, class-based politics may be an arena where prospects for democracy have actually worsened, according to the editors' hypotheses. Even their supporters expect neoliberal economic programs to result in worsening income distribution at least in the short term. Repeated economic crises have fragmented the middle class and pushed many toward the poverty line. The ethnic cleavages that have become more politically active also have a class base. While most of the reaction to these problems has so

far been increased demand for democracy rather than revolution, they raise
more questions about the fragility and future of democratic reforms than
about their causes. Increasing democratization has coincided with continuing and even increasingly unequal patterns of distribution. In the long run,
these patterns of inequality may pose grave challenges for the stability of
democracy. Thus, for many critics of neoliberalism, Mexican democratization is at best elite democratization rather than a broader and fairer societal
democratization.[65]

State Structure and Strength

Although state strength is a necessary condition for democratic stability, it
is not sufficient. Lack of strength may doom a democratic experiment, but
in Mexico state strength has meant the stability of an undemocratic system.
In fact, the advance of democratization has followed the weakening of state
power on several fronts.

Building authority was a historic accomplishment of the postrevolutionary regime. The regime centralized power, maintained order, and preserved civilian rule. It created an adept political class while controlling
mass groups and excluding organized challenges to its rule. Nonetheless,
the state was rarely the almost omnipotent political force much of the literature on Mexican authoritarianism depicted. Its power has been limited by
business and the middle class, and it has had to work out deals and make
compromises with organized labor and even with less privileged groups.
The state has often lacked the capacity to tax enough to pay for the political
bargains it struck.

Moreover, the neoliberal shrinking of the state may further weaken its
capacity to control and direct political activity. One element in the regime's
political strength was its early and sustained control over key parts of the
economy. Because state power was often used for partisan political purposes, such statism hypothetically diminishes prospects for democracy; lower
dependence on state permits and the generation of resources outside the
state would then hypothetically improve prospects for democracy. But this
has yet to be shown empirically, particularly since these autonomous
resources may not be shared evenly enough to support broad political participation.

What is clearer is that statism promoted civilian stability. It provided
populist legitimacy; the nationalization of oil (1938) is a notable example:
it gave the regime tremendous political leverage. Even though the Mexican
economy was long mostly privately owned, the state owned such sectors as
oil, mining, electricity, railroads, and, for several years in the 1980s, banks.
It was heavily involved in regulation, subsidies, public investments, public
credits, and so forth. It established institutions such as the Central Bank
(1925), the National Development Bank (1934), and a tremendous network

of parastatal agencies. Measures such as the public-expenditures share of GDP show an expanded state role as recently as 1982 (from 22 percent in 1970 to 44 percent in 1983).[66] But de la Madrid undertook a reversal, and his successors made the reversal more extreme. These presidents repeatedly cut state expenditures, employment, and subsidies. They sold off many state enterprises and brought Mexico first into the GATT and then into NAFTA. The state remains powerful but is no longer as important a gate-keeper to economic wealth.

Political Structure and Leadership

The structural reality of Mexico's undemocratic civilian rule has been over-whelmingly centralized. Mexico's has been a presidential system with only limited roles for the judiciary, the legislature, and state and local govern-ment. More liberalism, although still restricted, existed regarding freedom of the media, and some civil liberties. But the party system was long char-acterized by PRI hegemony and integration with the regime. Generally pragmatic, the PRI was at least somewhat inclusionary and built a multi-class base. It kept the vote for extremist parties very small. Yet as with other successes of the centralized party regime, these served civilian stabil-ity without democracy. Earlier interpretations of a political structure pur-posefully or ineluctably evolving into liberal forms proved naive and pre-mature. On the other hand, the recent ineffectiveness of centralized forms has raised interesting speculations about future changes in Mexico's politi-cal structure.

Like the political structure, political leadership in postrevolutionary Mexico has proven unusually effective, and this effectiveness has been cru-cial to sustaining civilian rule without democracy. In fact, leadership and structure have been intertwined. Leaders have created and respected struc-tures strong enough to condition behavior but flexible enough to allow for change and continual leadership.

Mexico took second place to no nation in the skill and will of leader-ship to build a viable civilian system out of a past characterized mostly by weak political rule. We have highlighted the formative leadership acts of Carranza, Obregón, Calles, and Cárdenas in establishing legitimate, inclu-sive, centralized, civilian rule. Their acts provide powerful evidence for those political scientists who have championed the resurgence of "politics" and "choice" as major variables in studies of development. For example, Gabriel Almond and Robert Mundt write that a rational prediction from coalition theory would have pointed toward a military coup in the 1930s, but Cárdenas pulled off the "most striking" leadership success discussed in their volume featuring choice in a number of nations.[67] But unlike leaders in the Venezuelan case or in contemporary Argentina, Brazil, and other Latin American nations, Mexico's civilian leaders did not generally act out of a democratic commitment. On the contrary, some Mexican leaders have been hostile to democracy as a foreign, unworkable model, whereas others have been indifferent, and still others see democracy as too risky. Yet another view, however, is that realities have changed to where *blocking* democratization has become too risky.

Political learning was crucial to Mexico's civilian success, but most leaders did not set competitive democracy as their goal, and the lessons they learned were undemocratic ones. Again, unlike Venezuela, with its *trienio,* not to mention Argentina, Brazil, and (at an extreme) Uruguay, Mexico has not had a modern liberal experiment that lasted. Mexico would have to look back to the Reform for even a mixed record with liberal politics; the Madero interlude at the beginning of the revolution represents more recent failure. Most of the nineteenth century and the first two revolutionary decades suggested to elites the impracticality of decentralized systems and the dangers of excessive competition among elites. The revolution also impressed on them the need for elite pacts to forestall devastating actions by the masses.

In essence, the institutionalization of the system institutionalized these attitudes, converting the PRI into a school for nondemocratic political managers. They became very good at their jobs, forming a political class that could boast many of the traits of successful professions, including comparative autonomy, status, authority, and power, as well as control over training and rites of entry. Since the 1940s (with due qualifications for the deterioration elaborated previously), Mexico's leaders shaped politics in ways largely associated with democracy. Yet for each aspect, the shaping has been distinctly undemocratic. The party incorporated and legitimized but also encapsulated. Sexennial rule guaranteed mobility, turnover, renewal, and flexibility, but not public choice of leaders. Leaders denounced disloyalty to the system and violence against the system but regarded some democratic dissent as disloyal and used violence against peaceful dissenters. They contained conflicts and managed crises enviably, but their tools have been predominantly undemocratic. Formative leaders shrewdly forged pacts among conflicting elites, and subsequent leaders continually bargained, compromised, and disciplined themselves and their followers to accept less than optimal outcomes. Such procedures excluded democratic opponents, limited mass participation, and often worked against mass material interests. Leaders also subtly varied their approaches (depending on time, place, policy field, and constituency) in ways that show a greater sensitivity to and understanding of the public than most authoritarian regimes have, but such sophistication is not synonymous with democracy. Thus, Mexico experienced corporatism mixed with pluralism, repression with co-optation and acquiescence, and continuity with flexibility. Where Mexico may more closely approach the expectations of current democratic theory is

in the relevance of negotiation, bargaining, and strategy among leaders of
the democratic opposition and the PRI. Successive political reforms, while
largely pushed by growing popular pressure for change, have made conditions for political competition significantly easier.

Economic Development

Political leadership also played a major role in establishing Mexico's
decades of high growth with low inflation, one of the regime's key sources
of legitimacy and stability. Social and demographic changes associated
with development contributed to raise the interest and ability of Mexicans
to push for more competitive democracy and political freedoms. Yet even
high and sustained growth did not produce democracy for many years—
over forty, by any count. Why did this transformation not occur sooner?

One explanation concerns Mexico's failure to attain the kind of sustained growth hypothesized to promote democracy, growth whose fruits are
well distributed. Mexico's have been horribly maldistributed. A middle
class grew, but with a debatable commitment to democracy (as in comparative politics generally) and substantial dependence on the state. Moreover,
the rise of the middle class has not been part of a generalized equalization
of wealth or a broad movement involving coalitions with mass groups. In
fact, a second possible explanation for the lack of democratization is that
the growth argument is by itself irrelevant to democracy or even that
growth may serve the interests of reigning undemocratic regimes. In
Mexico, growth contributed to the legitimacy and power of such a regime.
It allowed it to manipulate, reward, and claim credit, and in the aftermath
of 1988, economic recovery and stabilization went along with the PRI's
electoral recovery, at least through 1994.

A third explanation, compatible with the first two, distinguishes growth
from economic development. In Mexico, sustained growth brought about
considerable changes in social structure that eventually promoted pressures
for broad democratization and liberalization. Growth per se may also provide some opposition forces with resources needed for democratization. In
short, there is much to conventional development theses about an association between growth and social change and between both and the chances
for democracy.[68] Still, chances are far from certainties. The record shows
that decades of growth produced comparatively limited pressures for
democracy in Mexico and more limited results. The strongest calls for
democratization came when growth was reversed—although they did not
go away with renewed growth.

To sum up, economic growth may increase the chances for democracy
eventually but for a long time may shore up almost any regime. After all,
the fall of Latin American authoritarian regimes, like Latin American

democracies, has been tied to economic failure more than success. In Mexico, growth long proved integral to the stability of civilian authoritarian rule.

International Factors

As with so many other variables in this comparative study, international factors hypothesized to be conducive to democratic stability have, in Mexico, long contributed to stability without democracy. First, Mexico has not been a significant target of external subversion since the regime consolidated power. But such fortune is much more likely to sustain than to create democracy. Second, the major source of diffusion—given realities of geography, back-and-forth migration, trade, investment, and cultural and media might—has been the United States, a democracy. Third, Mexico has received extraordinary foreign assistance from the United States and other democracies, although the emphasis is recent. Indeed, historically Mexican leadership deliberately limited contacts with the United States, primarily in order to limit U.S. economic influence, but also limiting the potential political effects of contact.

For example, Mexico followed a progressive foreign policy, largely in order to protect itself from leftist subversion. The only Latin American nation not to break diplomatic relations with Communist Cuba, Mexico was never targeted the way Bolivia, Venezuela, and others were. Comparatively sympathetic to the Sandinistas and the guerrillas in El Salvador, Mexico achieved at least tacit agreement that leftists outside Mexico would not encourage independent leftists inside.[69]

In the past, such progressivism also enhanced domestic political legitimacy by demonstrating independence from the United States. Given a historical legacy of U.S. military conquest—costing Mexico about half its national territory—and an ongoing contrast of wealth and culture, it is not surprising that Mexicans would feel alienation as well as respect for their neighbor. While liberal democracy was defined as a U.S. model, many Mexicans viewed it with considerable suspicion. Even defenders of democracy stressed the need for democracy "Mexican style," although they also have recognized that the regime used the nationalist card to discredit basic democratic concepts associated with the United States. Moreover, U.S. leverage gave priority to stability, not democratization. Thus, even though Mexico typically depended on the United States for almost two-thirds of its imports and exports, roughly 80 percent of its tourism, and roughly 70 percent of its foreign investment, Mexico maintained a notable degree of independence from U.S. influence.

Economic crisis and neoliberal reform in Mexico have altered this traditional situation. Instead of the import-substitution model and its focus on expanding domestic consumption, the neoliberal model would depend heavily on both foreign investment (to replace dried-up sources of domestic investment) and foreign markets (to replace the dried-up domestic demand that had vanished with the loss of state contracts and the crisis itself). These policies were consolidated with the signing in 1993 of NAFTA, which committed Mexico and the United States to an ongoing process of deepening interdependence. Import-substitution industrialization had been compatible with attempts to hold the United States at arms length. Neoliberalism is not.

The effects of these changes on the prospects for democracy are complex, and do not all point in the same direction. On the negative side, the exposure of Mexican business and agriculture to international markets means people will lose jobs, lose their business or their land, and be forced to migrate to the cities or even abroad. This could cause protest and demands for redistribution that are typically difficult for democracies to handle. The timing of the Chiapas rebellion, on the very day NAFTA took effect, was rightly seen as a protest by the *zapatistas* against the effects of NAFTA on the life chances of the Indian peasants. Violent or highly confrontational protests may undermine both economic recovery and political stability. Greater interdependence also brings the risk of greater vulnerability to international trends and decisions. An example of this problem was the 1994 peso crisis, when Mexico's decision to devalue the peso in order to avoid default on its dollar-denominated debt led to a crash of the Mexican stock market as foreign investors quickly pulled out. The subsequent fall of the peso was, in the view of some, more extreme than it might have been because Mexico had become more dependent on foreign investors with little commitment to Mexico. Mexico had to accept harsh conditions, including yet another emergency austerity program and putting its oil income up as collateral, in order to get U.S. help to stem the run on the peso. Such programs could undermine the credibility and legitimacy of any government, even after fuller democratization.

However, on the positive side, the expanded interchange implied by NAFTA has also contributed to greater deference to foreign sensibilities, including support for elections. The attention paid to Mexican elections by the U.S. press makes any temptation to use fraud much more costly, resulting not only in *domestic* political unrest, but in shaken investor confidence due to fears that Mexico will not remain politically stable. Domestic opponents of the regime know this, and use protests to attract international attention. The strongly positive reaction of Wall Street to the election of a leftist mayor and an opposition majority in Congress confirms international preferences for democracy and puts more pressure on the regime to accept its losses.

Domestic opponents of government policies also reach out to international actors beyond the media, both within and outside foreign governments. The Chiapas rebels, for example, built a network of international as well as domestic allies—NGOs, human rights organizations, and assorted progressive movements—in order to pressure the Mexican government to negotiate instead of using force. Opponents of NAFTA have formed coalitions with U.S. and Canadian unions, environmental groups, and U.S. congressmen, among others, in order to demand attention to labor rights and environmental concerns that were not addressed in the original agreement. The resources, aid, and advice available through international NGOs also underwrite the budgets of new civil-society actors in Mexico, such as the Civic Alliance, which has monitored recent elections. Thus, not only democratic ideals but actual resources cross the border, intended to contribute to democratization in Mexico.

PROSPECTS AND POLICY IMPLICATIONS

However much these cited variables may have contributed to sustaining civilian stability without democracy, Mexican politics has changed. Of course, one of the strengths of the system and its leaders has been their flexibility, their ability to adapt to change with reforms that kept them in power. Our view is that contemporary changes do add up to more than modest adaptation within a nondemocracy. However, these changes remain fragile. The current situation is probably not a stable equilibrium, something we can expect to stay at approximately the present level of democratization indefinitely, but a dynamic and changing one with the potential for further deepening and consolidation on the one hand, or regression on the other. On the whole, especially given the growth of civil society and international rejection of antidemocratic regression, we are inclined to anticipate more progress toward democracy, at least in the near term. In the long term, however, the stability of democratic reforms will depend, ironically, on Mexico's ability to count on some of the very factors that for so long reinforced *un*democratic stability: economic growth, shared at least to some extent; a willingness to compromise; and the construction of institutionalized channels of participation. Part of this process will involve an increase in general levels of uncertainty about *outcomes,* but also a decrease in uncertainty about the *rules* of political competition. Still, uncertainty about the rules probably has to increase before it can decrease; one could not say yet that Mexico has a genuine national consensus about the rules accepted by popular as well as partisan actors of all stripes.

Positive Prospects for Democratization

Numerous political uncertainties represent some hope for democratization. First, the erosion of undemocratic practices widens the possibility for democratic alternatives and strengthens opposition voices. Second, the regime's realization that traditional bases of stability are endangered stimulates positive moves for democracy even though they are aimed chiefly at protecting stability. Third, some of the uncertainties themselves involve a degree of opening. To be sure, the second and third points have often involved liberalization rather than transformation toward a democracy, as defined here. Nevertheless, continued liberalization seems to have increased the pressure for free elections among truly competitive alternative parties.

The following recapitulates some of the major recent political changes that involve uncertainties. Regarding state-society relations, the vitality of civil society and some freedoms (e.g., media freedom) have expanded. Middle-class, business, and even grassroots popular groups have organized more autonomously and become more critical of the regime, and a "third sector" of private, nonprofit organizations or nongovernment organizations is developing. Regarding centralized regime power, the presidency has been tarnished, the legislature is increasingly a forum of debate and dissent, and perceptions are widespread that geographical centralization is excessive and that significant decentralization must somehow be achieved. Regarding the party system, the PRI (like the political class overall) has lost support and its aura of invincibility, whereas both an independent left and an independent right have grown substantially. Although many recent elections have been times of delegitimation more than popular affirmation, pressures for honest elections continue to be strong, probably undeniably so. Electoral reforms have opened the system significantly and made it easier to monitor fraud. Regarding the regime's performance, the economic crises of the 1980s and 1990s have eroded the regime's legitimacy, perhaps permanently. Economic opening, even if ultimately successful in purely economic terms, might well reduce the regime's tools of control.

Political reform, uncertainty, and regime weakness have contributed to increased calls for democratization. Such calls are not new, of course. For years, some observers argued that democratization was necessary for socioeconomic development and, therefore, for political stability. These observations did not fare well historically, but the balance of power appears to have shifted in their favor. Previous calls for democratization were not nearly as widespread and sustained as today's, nor did they enjoy the degree of political space that later dissenters have.

Naturally, proponents of democratization are not united. They do not hold identical views of what democracy means or of how to pursue it. Voices on the right argue in terms partly consistent with major hypotheses of this project: a highly centralized state with massive power concentrated in an unchecked presidency, which exercises extensive corporate controls over society and the economy, is incompatible with democracy. By contrast, most of the left argues that democratization requires a revitalized state assuming a central role in economic policy and social change, although a

significant part of the modern left emphasizes not only increased autonomy
and democratization within societal organizations, but also the potential for
decentralization to create democratic spaces for these groups and to
empower civil society. Finally, one may question the sincerity of certain
democratic banners on both the right and the left. For some, such banners
are but a tool in the play for power. For others, democracy is a worthy pursuit but principally a means toward higher priorities. Thus, some business
leaders see democracy largely as a way to weaken government and achieve
growth and profits, and others want a revitalized state to suppress labor and
grant concessions to business; at the same time, some intellectuals see
democracy as a means of mass mobilization to achieve better socioeconomic distribution.

Another way to see hopeful signs for democratization is to focus on the
many ways in which Mexico ranks high on variables associated with
democracy. We have argued that Mexico shows that many of these variables are compatible with civilian rule that is effective, stable, and undemocratic. That thesis has allowed, however, that Mexico's high standing on
some of the variables may have built pressures for democratization. The
notion of "zones" of lower and higher probabilities for democracy may be
useful in assessing Mexico's future. Economic growth, industrialization,
urbanization, the growth of a middle class, increased education and other
indices of rising expectations among even the poorer classes, the persistence of at least formal structures of liberal government, growing if still
inconclusive evidence of some political-cultural support for democracy—
these and other factors put Mexico in a higher zone of probability for
democracy than would have been the case even a decade ago.[70]

Research on transitions to democracy also suggests some hopes for
democratization in Mexico, although Guillermo O'Donnell rightly labeled
Mexico "a type by itself" (largely because the regime was so institutionalized). First, authoritarian regimes constantly evolve. Second, transitions
usually occur through evolution, not sudden overthrows. Third, democracy
usually results from stalemate and disagreement, not from a clear plan
based on consensus. Fourth, successful transitions usually begin with elite
calculations and initiatives, not independent mass mobilization. When the
regime initiates liberalization, it runs risks of losing the initiative amid rising expectations and mobilizations, but it can sometimes control the pace
of change, experiment, retreat, and so forth. Even where, as in Mexico,
changes in popular behavior motivate and encourage elites to change their
strategies, its process of transition has been marked by a notable degree of
elite control over the pace and content of reform, with many popular initiatives (such as approval of referendums and independent candidacies) finding little or no echo in successive electoral laws. This process is best seen
as an interactive dynamic, in which changes at the mass level motivate but
also reflect elite initiatives. Fifth, democratization often emerges from situ-

ations with seemingly low initial probabilities for it.[71] In sum, the slow and meandering path toward democracy, including reverses as well as progress, does not preclude democratization. The experimental, evolutionary, regime-led transition has allowed significant societal liberalization involving press freedom and criticism, as well as party and electoral reform. Expanded representation for oppositions, and opposition victories in localities and even states, have now occurred without immediate threat to Mexican stability, and even evoked strong international support. It is now possible to speculate about the transfer of national government to the opposition, although some skepticism naturally remains.

The Brazilian case is particularly interesting for speculations on Mexico.[72] Brazilian authoritarian rule was comparatively long and economically successful on its own terms, with massive inequalities. Repression was comparatively limited in the years prior to transition. In fact, constitutional forms persisted almost throughout the dictatorial period, and the limited term of the presidency proved significant. Elections took on increasing importance even as the regime manipulated the rules. Transition was stimulated by long-term factors, but an economic downturn critically undermined support for the regime. Nonetheless, unlike some other cases, democratization was not precipitated by mass mobilizations but by elite accommodations. In short, the Brazilian case illustrates how democratization need not be an all-or-nothing proposition. This fact can make the prospect less threatening for the Mexican regime, which realizes that some political changes are necessary.

Negative Prospects for Democratization

Despite these positive signs, Mexico's democracy is far from assured. Some factors continue to point away from stable democracy. Mexico remains a deeply unequal country, a problem for democratic systems that depend on the ability of all, or at least most, citizens to participate effectively and to compromise on their interests. Mexico has also embarked on a course of economic restructuring that will almost certainly disrupt and divide the country further in the short term, even as hopes persist that, in the long run, restructuring will make possible the creation of more and better jobs to employ Mexico's young and growing population.

In addition, Mexico lacks any significant experience with democratic government. Ironically, the slow pace of liberalization may make democracy more viable in the end, by giving the opposition important experience in governing before it has to take full responsibility. Despite its declining legitimacy, the regime has not been discredited in the dramatic way that sometimes leads to democratic transitions (e.g., in Argentina), although the economic crisis of the 1990s—often laid at the feet of Salinas and his successor—comes close to such a turning point. Yet not all criticism of the

Mexican regime concerns its lack of democracy. The political-cultural attachment of the masses to democracy is questionable, and elites have given uncertain evidence of such attachment. Opposition parties have not yet developed strong and deeply rooted organizations. Corporatist controls have precluded both independent mass-based institutions (unions or parties) and mobilization of the unorganized. The state retains a large role in politics and the economy, even after neoliberal reforms. These factors help explain why democratization has taken so long—and why it remains unsatisfactory to so many Mexicans.

Prospects for democratization have also been constrained by the risks of transition.[73] Fear is a central notion in the relevant literature; in Mexico, the fear of transition has long dominated the perceived need for or benefits of transition. To be sure, even before the 1988 elections some in the regime, as well as critics, believed the system required major changes. President de la Madrid spoke repeatedly of how changes in demographics, urbanization, education, communications, and class structure had created a greatly expanded "civil society" that required political changes. As in Colombia, there is a widespread perception that conditions that called for structures of restricted, stable civilian rule have been superseded. But also as in Colombia, powerful political incentives are built into the status quo. Even "soft-liners" within the Mexican regime have usually focused on modernizing measures (including liberalizing ones) that would not produce a liberal democracy. To many in the PRI, at least, "democracy" still means the PRI as the "party of majorities," with opposition voice allowed. Some even argue that a return to economic normalcy would basically return politics to normal. And many, whatever their ultimate hopes, believe that times of great economic change, and of some inevitable political change, require steadying reliance on established political structures and practices.

Crucially, fear of transition is not limited to the PRI or even the elites overall. As Carlos Monsiváis has emphasized, the regime largely succeeded in portraying alternatives to it as disasters, as fascism, communism, or anarchy.[74] Anarchy is particularly frightening to many Mexicans, perhaps because of the nation's history, and many have felt they could little afford democracy, which has been associated with some of Mexico's greatest social disorder.[75] Their system has provided them with relative social peace and political tranquillity, economic growth, mobility, selective rather than pervasive repression, a degree of political liberty, and substantial national pride. Perhaps the slow progress of democratization will convince such people that nothing terrible will happen if an opposition mayor, governor, or Congress, or even president is elected. However, much depends on the success of these administrations, and neither presidentialism nor the interests of the PRI in seeing the opposition disappoint voters favor their success.

In sum, the prospects for political business as usual in Mexico are more uncertain than at any time since the consolidation of the postrevolutionary political regime. The emergence of yet another economic crisis brought on by fiscal mismanagement has again led some of the regime's erstwhile business allies to consider alternatives publicly. Mexico now faces a substantial likelihood of democratic transition, or, should that tendency collapse, authoritarian regression. The contrast reflects the fact that the unraveling of Mexico's undemocratic political system implies risks to stability, to which some may respond in a reactionary fashion, while others seize the opportunity to promote democratic compromise. One should not underestimate the resilience of the Mexican political system, or its capacity to handle even the severe challenges to its legitimacy that it now confronts. Much may depend on whether any opposition force (democratic or anti-democratic) can constitute itself as a credible, viable alternative, but in the past, Mexico's version of sustained civilian authoritarianism derived its longevity from its highly effective methods to prevent precisely this development. The difficult task of democratic reformers will be to relax some of these constraints and allow the growth of democratic alternatives, without provoking crippling concern about political instability, chaos, or reactionary violence by supporters of an authoritarian peace.

U.S. Policy

If democratization merits increasing attention but remains uncertain, what should the United States government do? The conventional scholarly wisdom has been: not much. We concur, although that view has come under increasing attack by U.S. public opinion and political leaders in both parties.

Not all attempts by one nation to encourage democracy in another are wrong, but several demanding criteria ought to be present. They usually are not. First, a viable alternative to the present regime must exist. Second, that alternative should be more democratic than the present regime. Third, a rather limited role by the foreign nation should have a high probability of having a substantial positive impact.

None of these conditions has characterized the case of Mexico and the United States. Leading opposition parties and groups have yet to prove their governing ability or democratic credentials. More important, even if both of the first two conditions were met, official U.S. efforts might have an insignificant or a negative impact. The Mexico-U.S. relationship is particularly sensitive, given historical, geographical, economic, and cultural realities. Repeated military interventions and threats have contributed to turmoil, not democracy, and left a legacy of mistrust about the democratic giant to the north. In the early 1980s, perceptions that the U.S. ambassador and Republican Party leaders supported the PAN probably hurt that opposition party, as the PRI successfully identified it among some voters with a still arrogant, interfering neighbor. Efforts by the United States to close down the safety valve of immigration probably increase the difficulties for democracy in Mexico. Pressure to cooperate in the antidrug effort has contradictory effects on Mexico. On the one hand, it gives the Mexican government needed aid against a trade that undermines state authority. On the other hand, it makes drug cartel efforts to buy protection ever more necessary (thus increasing the impact of corruption on the Mexican government) and undermines the government's popular legitimacy by putting it in the position of appearing to "knuckle under" publicly to the United States and permit incursions on Mexico's sovereign right to make and enforce its own laws.

None of this is to deny the U.S. government a right to express critical opinions about Mexican politics, including its most undemocratic aspects, but advocacy and heavy pressure are different matters. A far more useful strategy is simply to allow the continued development of international cooperation between U.S. and Mexican civil-society organizations. Increased foundation aid to academic institutions and scholarship recipients seems legitimate and hopeful, as do the greatly expanded exchanges of information and resources between nongovernmental organizations in the United States and Mexico, improving the capacity of Mexican organizations to make demands and monitor their own elections. As long as U.S. donors and partners bear in mind the importance of allowing Mexican organizations to define their own goals, such contact can encourage democratization by building institutions with autonomy from the government.

Moreover, fundamental changes in Mexico's economic and foreign policy have made Mexico far more integrated than before with international trends, largely U.S.-led. From 1980 to the present, the U.S. share in Mexico's total imports increased from 65.6 percent to 70.6 percent and its share in Mexico's exports grew from an already impressive 63.2 percent to 80.4 percent. Meanwhile, Mexico had become the second largest market for U.S. goods, surpassing Japan in the first part of 1998.[76] This percentage increase masks an even more substantial growth in Mexican exports, from $22 billion in 1986 to $117 billion by 1998, over half of this growth during the post-NAFTA period.[77] Total Mexico-U.S. trade grew at an average of 18.5 percent every year after NAFTA took effect, a period that includes the serious Mexican recession of 1995.[78] U.S. foreign direct investment in Mexico has also increased substantially: in 1980, $1.1 billion flowed into Mexico; in 1995 (a recession year) $4.2 billion flowed in. Mexican figures indicated that by the end of the second quarter of 1996, as the economy began to recover, more than twice that amount had already come in. The total stock of U.S. direct investment thus has accumulated at a rapid rate, resulting in the extensive integration of production processes. Nearly 60 percent of total FDI in Mexico comes from the United States.[79]

At the same time, flows of legal and illegal immigration have increased, with corresponding effects on flows of money and resources, including remittances from Mexican migrants working in the United States. Thus, the United States has gained enormously in influence over Mexico, including pro-democratic influence, without the need for direct political pressure.

If Mexico continues to liberalize and even democratize without shattering its stability, it will have achieved a truly historic and magnificent political feat. Our understanding of the conditions for Third World democracy would be profoundly affected. For most of the twentieth century, however, Mexican reality has shown how many conditions conducive to sustained civilian rule can have neutral or even negative implications for democracy.

NOTES

1. Mexico's population, roughly 90 million, ranks second in Latin America; combined with the size of its economy and of course its geography, it is vital for the United States. We use "democracy" in the sense of a desired result (defined earlier in this volume), "democratization" as movement in that direction, and "liberalization" as movement in terms of increased civil liberties without actual changes in the breadth of access to decisionmaking. See also Guillermo O'Donnell and Philippe Schmitter, *Transitions from Authoritarian Rule: Tentative Conclusions About Uncertain Democracies* (Baltimore: Johns Hopkins University Press, 1986), pp. 7–8.

2. On breakdown, see Juan Linz and Alfred Stepan, eds., *The Breakdown of Democratic Regimes* (Baltimore: Johns Hopkins University Press, 1978). On democratization, see Guillermo O'Donnell, Philippe C. Schmitter, and Laurence Whitehead, eds., *Transitions from Authoritarian Rule: Latin America* (Baltimore: Johns Hopkins University Press, 1986).

3. Robert Scott, *Mexican Government in Transition* (Urbana: University of Illinois Press, 1964), pp. 16, 300–301.

4. See, for example, the citations and analysis in Daniel C. Levy and Kathleen Bruhn, with Emilio Zebadúa, *Mexico: The Struggle for Democratized and Internationalized Development* (forthcoming).

5. Kenneth F. Johnson and Philip L. Kelly, "Political Democracy in Latin America," *LASA Forum* 16, no. 4 (1986): 19–22. According to James Wilkie, Carlos A. Contreras, and Christof Anders Weber, eds., *Statistical Abstract of Latin America* (henceforth, *SALA*), vol. 30, part 1 (Los Angeles: UCLA, 1993), p. 276, Mexico ranked number 5 in Latin America (as of 1985); the 1990 Freedom House Ratings, however, gave Mexico only a 4 on political rights and a 4 on civil rights, with 1 the most-free score and 7 the least.

6. Enrique Krauze, *Por una democracia sin adjetivos* (Mexico City: Editorial Joaquín Mortiz, 1986).

7. Octavio Paz, *The Other Mexico: Critique of the Pyramid,* trans. Lysander Kemp (New York: Grove Press, 1972), pp. 102, 111.

8. See, for example, Juan Felipe Leal, "El estado y el bloque en el poder en México: 1867–1914," *Latin American Perspectives* 11, no. 2 (1975): p. 38.

9. For an analysis of elite composition and circulation (or lack of it) during the *porfiriato,* see Peter Smith, *Labyrinths of Power* (Princeton: Princeton University Press, 1979).

10. A standard work on the integration is Arnaldo Córdova, *La formación del poder en México,* 8th ed. (Mexico City: Serie Popular Era, 1980). See also John Higley and Richard Gunther, eds., *Elites and Democratic Consolidation in Latin America and Southern Europe* (Cambridge: Cambridge University Press, 1992).

11. Two major accounts are Tzvi Medín, *Ideología y praxis político de Lázaro Cárdenas*

(Mexico City: Siglo XXI, 1976); and Wayne A. Cornelius, "Nation Building, Participation, Distribution: Reform Under Cárdenas," in Gabriel A. Almond, Scott C. Flanigan, and Robert J. Mundt, eds., *Crisis, Choice, and Change: Historical Studies of Political Development* (Boston: Little, Brown, 1973), pp. 394, 429, 462.

12. We use the terms as elaborated in Philippe C. Schmitter's widely cited "Still the Century of Corporatism?" in Frederick Pike and Thomas Stritch, eds., *The New Corporatism* (Notre Dame, IN: University of Notre Dame Press, 1974), pp. 93–105.

13. On political marginality, see Pablo González Casanova, *Democracy in Mexico,* trans. Danielle Salti (London: Oxford University Press, 1970), pp. 126–134; on reacting, see Susan Kaufman Purcell, *The Mexican Profit-Making Decision: Politics in an Authoritarian Regime* (Berkeley: University of California Press, 1975).

14. On the consequences of early incorporation, see Ruth Berins Collier and David Collier, *Shaping the Political Arena* (Princeton: Princeton University Press, 1991); Robert R. Kaufman, "Mexico and Latin American Authoritarianism," in José Luis Reyna and Richard S. Wienert, eds., *Authoritarianism in Mexico* (Philadelphia: ISHI, 1977), pp. 220–221; and Kevin Middlebrook, *The Paradox of Revolution: Labor, the State, and Authoritarianism in Mexico* (Baltimore: Johns Hopkins University Press, 1995). See Evelyn Stevens, *Protest and Response in Mexico* (Cambridge, MA: MIT Press, 1974), pp. 276–277, on how activists have been unable to attract mass followings.

15. Pablo González Casanova, *El estado y los partidos políticos en México* (Mexico City: Ediciones Era, 1985), p. 48.

16. See, for example, Jesús Silva Herzog, *La revolución mexicana en crisis* (Mexico City: Ediciones Cuadernos Americanos, 1944), pp. 22–34; and for a similar point on peasants, see Gerrit Huizer, "Peasant Organization in Agrarian Reform in Mexico," in Irving Louis Horowitz, ed., *Masses in Latin America* (New York: Oxford University Press, 1970), pp. 445–502.

17. Raúl Trejo Delarbe, "El movimiento obrero: Situación y perspectivas," in Pablo González Casanova and Enrique Florescano, eds., *México, hoy,* 5th ed. (Mexico City: Siglo XXI, 1981), pp. 128–130.

18. Total wage income fell a cumulative 40 percent between 1983 and 1988, whereas the real minimum wage fell 48.5 percent. See Nora Lustig, *Mexico: The Remaking of an Economy* (Washington, DC: Brookings Institution, 1992), pp. 68–69. For other representative estimates, see Sidney Weintraub, *Transforming the Mexican Economy* (Washington, DC: National Planning Association, 1930), p. 13; and Ruth Berins Collier, *The Contradictory Alliance* (Berkeley: University of California Press, 1993), p. 128.

19. Kevin Middlebrook makes this point in his article "Dilemmas of Change in Mexican Politics," *World Politics* 41 (October 1988): 120–141.

20. See Juan Reyes del Campillo, "La selección de los candidatos del Partido Revolucionario Institucional," in Juan Felipe Leal, Jacqueline Peschard, and Concepción Rivera, eds., *Las elecciones federales de 1988 en México* (Mexico City: Universidad Nacional Autónoma de México [UNAM], 1988), p. 96.

21. Richard Fagen and William Tuohy, *Politics in a Mexican Village* (Stanford: Stanford University Press, 1969).

22. However, the business class was comparatively distinct from the nation's economic elites, despite these overlapping interests. See Smith, *Labyrinths of Power.* Needler compared the Mexican political elite to the East European "new class" described by Milovan Djilas, *The New Class: An Analysis of the Communist System* (New York: Praeger, 1957), except that it was more legitimate and effective in its ownership of state power. See Martin C. Needler, *Mexican Politics: The Containment of Conflict* (New York: Praeger, 1982), pp. 131–133. On general business-state relations, see also Dale Story, *Industry, the State, and Public Policy in Mexico* (Austin: University of Texas Press, 1986); John J. Bailey, *Governing Mexico: The Statecraft of Crisis Management* (London: Macmillan, 1988), chapter 6; and Sylvia Maxfield and Ricardo Anzaldúa, *Government and Private Sector in Contemporary Mexico* (La Jolla: University of California at San Diego, Center for U.S.-Mexican Studies, 1987).

23. On intellectuals, see Roderic A. Camp, *Intellectuals and the State in Twentieth-Century Mexico* (Austin: University of Texas Press, 1985); on public universities, see Daniel C. Levy, *University and Government in Mexico: Autonomy in an Authoritarian System* (New York: Praeger, 1980). However, neoliberal reforms have had their impact in higher education.

Especially outside the National University, students have decreasingly blocked reforms aimed at greater academic and economic competition; see Daniel C. Levy, "Fitting In? Making Higher Education Part of the New Development Model," *Mexican Studies/Estudios Mexicanos* 14, no. 3 (summer 1998): pp. 407–440.

24. One prominent view of democratization is that it requires democratizing society's associational life. See, for example, Lynn Stephen, "Democracy for Whom? Women's Grassroots Political Activism in the 1990s, Mexico City and Chiapas," in Gerardo Otero, ed., *Neoliberalism Revisited: Economic Restructuring and Mexico's Political Future* (Boulder, CO: Westview, 1996), pp. 167–186. Mexico's mass-based organizations have been notoriously undemocratic. Both labor and peasant elections are controlled and corrupt. Practice varies among the associations of more-privileged classes, but many media, intellectual, and student associations are far from open and free. See, for example, Camp, *Intellectuals and the State*, p. 225.

25. See Sergio Zermeño, *México: Una democracia utópica: El movimiento estudiantil del 68* (Mexico City: Siglo XXI, 1978); and Levy, *University and Government,* pp. 28–33, 39–41.

26. In Brandenburg's apt label for the regime, "liberal Machiavellian," "liberal" refers to tolerance more than to the Dahl/O'Donnell-Schmitter sense of contestation. Frank Brandenburg, *The Making of Modern Mexico* (Englewood Cliffs, NJ: Prentice-Hall, 1964), pp. 141–165. Disturbing evidence of intolerance has long come from brutal repression of peasant actions as well as from continuing reports about human rights abuses, including torture, disappearances, and unpunished assassinations of popular and opposition leaders.

27. Daniel C. Levy and Gabriel Székely, *Mexico: Paradoxes of Stability and Change,* 2d ed. (Boulder, CO: Westview, 1987), chapter 4.

28. Wayne Cornelius, Ann Craig, and Jonathan Fox, "Mexico's National Solidarity Program," in Wayne Cornelius, Ann Craig, and Jonathan Fox, eds., *Transforming State-Society Relations in Mexico* (La Jolla: University of California at San Diego, Center for U.S.-Mexican Studies, 1994), p. 3.

29. By official figures, Solidarity led to the formation of 150,000 community-based committees in the first five years of the program, perhaps one-third of which "were fully functional, had real presence in their communities, and were capable of making some demands upon government." Ibid., p. 20.

30. Jonathan Fox, "The Difficult Transition from Clientelism to Citizenship," *World Politics* 46, no. 2 (January 1994): 151–185.

31. González Casanova, *Democracy in Mexico,* p. 68.

32. In addition, the PAN won control of six states: Baja California, Chihuahua, Jalisco, Guanajuato, Queretaro, and Aguascalientes, though it lost Chihuahua in the next gubernatorial election. Whereas some observers found local political participation minimal, others saw competition that leads to citizen support for political wings within the PRI, or for candidates proposing popular policies (e.g., improvement of water or electrical systems). Alvaro Arreola Ayala, "Elecciones municipales," in Pablo González Casanova, ed., *Las elecciones en México: Evolución y perspectivas* (Mexico City: Siglo XXI, 1985), pp. 330–336. More recent analyses focus on innovative opposition efforts as well. See Victoria Rodríguez and Peter Ward, eds., *Opposition Government in Mexico: Past Experiences and Future Opportunities* (Albuquerque: University of New Mexico Press, 1995); Victoria Rodríguez and Peter Ward, *Political Change in Baja California: Democracy in the Making?* Monograph Series No. 40 (San Diego: Center for U.S.-Mexican Studies, 1994); Alicia Ziccardi, ed., *La tarea de gobernar: Gobiernos locales y demandas ciudadanas* (Mexico City: UNAM, 1995); Mauricio Merino, ed., *En busca de la democracia municipal: La participación ciudadana en el gobierno local mexicano* (Mexico City: El Colegio de México, 1995).

33. Fernando Henrique Cardoso, "On the Characterization of Authoritarian Regimes in Latin America," in David Collier, ed., *The New Authoritarianism in Latin America* (Princeton: Princeton University Press, 1979), pp. 42–43.

34. A prominent recent source on the military is Roderic Camp, *Generals in the Palacio: The Military in Modern Mexico* (New York: Oxford University Press, 1992).

35. *El nuevo perfil de la economía mexicana* (Mexico City: Secretaria de Hacienda y Crédito Público, 1991), p. 15.

36. See John Bailey, "Centralism and Political Change in Mexico," in Wayne Cornelius,

Ann Craig, and Jonathan Fox, eds., *Transforming State-Society Relations in Mexico* (La Jolla: University of California at San Diego, Center for U.S.-Mexican Studies, 1994), pp. 117, 102; Daniel C. Levy, "Mexico: Towards State Supervision?" in Guy Neave and Frans van Vught, eds., *Government and Higher Education Relationships Across Three Continents* (Oxford: Pergamon, 1994), pp. 241–263.

37. Gustavo Ernesto Emmerich, "Las elecciones en México, 1808–1911: Sufragio electivo, no reelección?" in Pablo González Casanova, ed., *Las elecciones en México: Evolución y perspectivas* (Mexico City: Siglo XXI, 1985), p. 64.

38. Luis Javier Garrido, *El partido de la revolución institucionalizada 1929–45* (Mexico City: Siglo XXI, 1982); González Casanova, *Democracy in Mexico*, p. 34.

39. Jorge Domínguez and James McCann, *Democratizing Mexico: Public Opinion and Electoral Choices* (Baltimore: Johns Hopkins University Press, 1996).

40. At least for the 1988 and 1991 elections, Domínguez and McCann (ibid.) argue that the choice about whether or not to support the PRI was the first choice made by voters, rather than choices about which of the three parties to support. Their evidence generally fits views about the importance of fear of change.

41. Implemented reforms have been limited to measures such as selecting candidates with local appeal and varying selection methods, always leaving the PRI leadership with the choice of method. Usually, they chose not to implement possible democratic primaries.

42. On leftist weaknesses and platforms, see, for example, Barry Carr, "Mexico: The Perils of Unity and the Challenge of Modernization," in Barry Carr and Steve Ellner, eds., *The Latin American Left* (Boulder, CO: Westview, 1993).

43. For an analysis of the formation and subsequent struggles of the PRD, see Kathleen Bruhn, *Taking on Goliath: The Emergence of a New Left Party and the Struggle for Democracy in Mexico* (University Park: Pennsylvania State University Press, 1997).

44. Data from official voting results, from Mexico, Registro National de Electores, computer printout furnished by Juan Molinar Horcasitas; 1991–1997 figures calculated by this author, from Mexico, Instituto Federal Electoral, *Relación de los 300 distritos federales electorales* (Mexico City: IFE, 1991); Mexico, Instituto Federal Electoral, *Elecciones federales 1994* (Mexico City: IFE, 1994); and Mexico, Instituto Federal Electoral, *Elecciones federales 1997* (Mexico City: IFE, 1997). Calculations for 1985 add the vote of the two independent left parties (PMT and PSUM) that merged into the Mexican Socialist Party in 1987, and into the PRD in 1989.

45. The head of the board was still a presidential appointee (the secretary of the interior); the PRI kept the power to veto any citizen councilor, since no combination of opposition votes could reach two-thirds; and at least two board members represent the majority party in the House and Senate, respectively. In 1996, the executive board was removed from the supervision of the secretary of the interior.

46. Juan Molinar, *El tiempo de la legitimidad* (Mexico City: Cal y Arena, 1991); Kevin Middlebrook, "Political Liberalization in an Authoritarian Regime," in Paul W. Drake and Eduardo Silva, eds., *Elections and Democratization in Latin America, 1980–1985* (La Jolla, CA: University of California at San Diego, Center for Iberian and Latin American Studies, 1986), pp. 73–104.

47. Some states then chose reform anyway; most recently, those under PAN control led the way in many reforms later adopted at a national level, such as the picture ID. See Jorge Madrazo, "Reforma política y legislación electoral de las entidades federativas," in Pablo González Casanova, ed., *Las elecciones en México: Evolución y perspectivas* (Mexico City: Siglo XXI, 1985), pp. 293–302.

48. Packet of information for foreign observers, provided by the Instituto Federal Electoral, 1994.

49. Table 1.1 herein; Inter-American Development Bank (IADB), *Economic and Social Progress in Latin America, 1986 Report* (Washington, DC: IADB, n.d.), p. 314; *Anuario estadistico de los Estados Unidos Mexicanos* (Mexico, DF: INEGI, 1993), pp. 20, 39, 124; and World Bank, *Social Indicators of Development: 1991–1992* (Baltimore: World Bank, 1992), p. 204.

50. *Perfil socioeconomico: XI Censo general de poblacion y vivienda, 1990* (Mexico City: INEGI, 1993), p. 38.

51. See, for example, Daniel C. Levy, *Higher Education and the State in Latin America:*

Private Challenges to Public Dominance (Chicago: University of Chicago Press, 1986), pp. 114–170.

52. World Bank, *World Development Report, 1980* (Washington, DC: World Bank, 1980), pp. 156–157.

53. Gabriel A. Almond and Sidney Verba, *The Civic Culture* (Boston: Little, Brown, 1963); Ann L. Craig and Wayne A. Cornelius, "Political Culture in Mexico: Continuities and Revisionist Interpretations," in Gabriel A. Almond and Sidney Verba, eds., *The Civic Culture Revisited* (Boston: Little, Brown, 1980), p. 375. See also Fagen and Tuohy, *Politics in a Mexican Village,* pp. 38–39, 136–137.

54. The three respective explanations of acceptance are emphasized in, for example, Paz, *The Other Mexico;* Fagen and Tuohy, *Politics in a Mexican Village;* and Almond and Verba, eds., *The Civic Culture Revisited.*

55. Susan Kaufman Purcell and John F. H. Purcell, "State and Society in Mexico: Must a Stable Polity Be Institutionalized?" *World Politics* 32, no. 2 (1980): 204–205. See Craig and Cornelius, "Political Culture in Mexico," pp. 341, 385–386 (note 35), on the different positions. A prominent example of the causal political-cultural approach, denounced in Mexico, is Alan Riding, *Distant Neighbors: A Portrait of the Mexicans* (New York: Knopf, 1985).

56. John Booth and Mitchell Seligson, "The Political Culture of Authoritarianism in Mexico: A Reexamination," *Latin American Research Review* 19, no. 1 (1984): 110–113. The authors report uniformly strong democratic values, although less among women, the less educated, and the working class than in the middle class. But their data come from developed urban areas known for dissent from the PRI regime. Also, expressed values do not seem quite so at odds with the system when one acknowledges that it permits some degree of free expression, demonstration, etc.; it does not permit organized alternatives, and the one issue on which the authors report a majority of undemocratic responses was on critics seeking office. See also the discussion of democratic values—where Mexico has changed, and where it has not—in Domínguez and McCann, *Democratizing Mexico,* especially chapter 2. Craig and Cornelius, "Political Culture in Mexico," pp. 348–350, report conflicting data regarding "working-class authoritarianism."

57. Rafael Segovia, *La politicización del niño mexicano,* 2d ed. (Mexico City: El Colegio de México, 1982); Craig and Cornelius, "Political Culture in Mexico," p. 369. Family socialization and interrelations are often described as intolerant and undemocratic. However, the introduction of more participatory educational practices (e.g., Montessori schools) may have a democratizing influence. See also the findings of Domínguez and McCann, *Democratizing Mexico,* about the relative importance of class cleavages on both voting behavior and values.

58. In a sense, then, elites developed a degree of "trust" in their pacts even though interpersonal trust is low. On the generally low degree of trust in Mexican society, see Craig and Cornelius, "Political Culture of Mexico," p. 372.

59. Intertwined with the official party, the political class lacked career service and merit characteristics, but its strength has been tied to its politicization and social ties formed often during education at the National University. Since the 1970s, however, its coherence has been weakened by a surge of technocrats who rise to high posts based on special educational credentials rather than apprenticeship with the party, elective office, public universities, mass organizations, and so forth. See, especially, Roderic Camp, "The Political Technocrat in Mexico and the Survival of the Political System," *Latin American Research Review* 20, no. 1 (1985): 97–118; Miguel Angel Centeno, *Democracy Within Reason* (University Park: Pennsylvania State University Press, 1994).

60. Robert Dahl, *Polyarchy: Participation and Opposition* (New Haven: Yale University Press, 1971).

61. Guillermo Bonfil Batalla, "Los pueblos indígenas: Viejos problemas, nuevas demandas," in Pablo González Casanova and Enrique Florescano, eds., *México, hoy,* 5th ed. (Mexico City: Siglo XXI, 1981), pp. 100–107. On the rebellion itself, see also George Collier, with Elizabeth Lowery Quaratiello, *Basta! Land and the Zapatista Rebellion in Chiapas* (Oakland, CA: Food First, 1994); and Neil Harvey, *Rebellion in Chiapas,* Transformation of Rural Mexico Series, No. 5 (La Jolla: University of California at San Diego, Center for U.S.-Mexican Studies, 1994).

62. Juan J. Linz, "Totalitarian and Authoritarian Regimes," in Fred I. Greenstein and

Nelson W. Polsby, eds., *Handbook of Political Science,* vol. 3 (Reading, MA: Addison-Wesley, 1975).

63. Respective quotations from Larissa Lomnitz, "Social Structure of Urban Mexico," *Latin America Research Review* 16, no. 2 (1982): 69; and Purcell and Purcell, "State and Society," p. 226.

64. Mexico's elite autonomous organizations have not usually served as "training grounds" for democracy. The public university is the best example of a substantially autonomous organization that has trained most of Mexico's (undemocratic) political elite. Relevant skills are the ability to mobilize and manipulate mass groups, bargaining, and leadership.

65. See, for example, Ilán Semo, "The Mexican Political Pretransition in Comparative Perspective," in Gerardo Otero, ed., *Neoliberalism Revisited: Economic Restructuring and Mexico's Political Future* (Boulder, CO: Westview, 1996), p. 109. On Mexico's inequality and economic policy in comparative perspective, see John Sheehan, "Effects of Liberalization Programs on Poverty and Inequality: Chile, Mexico, and Peru," *Latin American Research Review* 32, no. 3 (1997): 7–38. Among the many recent works linking changed economic policy to political and social aspects of development are: Gerardo Otero, ed., *Neoliberalism Revisited: Economic Restructuring and Mexico's Political Future* (Boulder, CO: Westview, 1996); Judith Teichman, *Privatization and Political Change in Mexico* (Pittsburgh: University of Pittsburgh Press, 1995); Laura Randall, ed., *Changing Structure of Mexico: Political, Social, and Economic Prospects* (Armonk, NY: M. E. Sharpe, 1996); Maria Lorena Cook, Kevin Middlebrook, and Juan Molinar, eds., *The Politics of Economic Restructuring* (San Diego: Center for U.S.-Mexican Studies, University of California, 1994).

66. Bailey, *Governing Mexico,* table 6.1.

67. Gabriel A. Almond and Robert J. Mundt, "Crisis, Choice, and Change: Some Tentative Conclusions," in Gabriel A. Almond, Scott C. Flanigan, and Robert J. Mundt, eds., *Crisis, Choice, and Change: Historical Studies of Political Development* (Boston: Little, Brown, 1973), pp. 635, 637.

68. Perhaps Mexico's unequal socioeconomic development has facilitated autonomous political participation for some privileged groups alongside mobilized participation by mass groups. See Samuel P. Huntington and Joan Nelson, *No Easy Choice* (Cambridge, MA: Harvard University Press, 1976). Such a view appears consistent with this chapter's corporatist-pluralist contrasts.

69. Daniel C. Levy, "The Implications of Central American Conflicts for Mexican Politics," in Roderic A. Camp, ed., *Mexico's Political Stability: The Next Five Years* (Boulder, CO: Westview, 1986), pp. 235–264.

70. Joe Foweraker, *Popular Mobilization in Mexico* (Cambridge: Cambridge University Press, 1993); Daniel C. Levy, "Fuera de la universidad: Una perspectiva comparativa de los centros de investigacion en México," in Sylvia Ortega Salazar and David Lorey, eds., *Crisis y cambio de la educacion superior en México* (Mexico City: UNAM-Azcapotzalco, 1997), pp. 119–134.

71. Guillermo O'Donnell, "Introduction to the Latin American Cases," pp. 5, 15, and Luciano Martins, "The 'Liberalization' of Authoritarian Rule in Brazil," p. 72, both in Guillermo O'Donnell, Philippe C. Schmitter, and Laurence Whitehead, eds., *Transitions from Authoritarian Rule: Latin America* (Baltimore: Johns Hopkins University Press, 1986); and especially O'Donnell and Schmitter, *Transitions from Authoritarian Rule: Tentative Conclusions,* pp. 48–72; also, Alfred Stepan, "Paths Toward Redemocratization: Theoretical and Comparative Considerations," in Guillermo O'Donnell, Philippe C. Schmitter, and Laurence Whitehead, eds., *Transitions from Authoritarian Rule: Comparative Perspectives,* (Baltimore: Johns Hopkins University Press, 1986), pp. 72–74.

72. See chapter 3 by Bolívar Lamounier in this volume, and also Martins, "The 'Liberalization,'" pp. 72–74.

73. The theoretical argument is developed in Adam Przeworski, "Some Problems in the Study of the Transition to Democracy," in Guillermo O'Donnell, Phillipe C. Schmitter, and Laurence Whitehead, eds., *Transitions from Authoritarian Rule: Prospects for Democracy* (Baltimore: Johns Hopkins University Press, 1986), pp. 47–63; and in O'Donnell and Schmitter, *Transitions from Authoritarian Rule: Tentative Conclusions,* pp. 7–16, 48–49.

74. Carlos Monsiváis, "La ofensiva ideológica de la derecha," in Pablo González

Casanova and Enrique Florescano, eds., *México, hoy,* 5th ed. (Mexico City: Siglo XXI, 1981), p. 315. This underscores Przeworski's point ("Some Problems," pp. 50–53) that perceptions of alternatives as well as of the present regime are critical to choices about pushing for transition.

75. It is curious that Mexico's most democratic presidents—Juárez and Madero—are also associated with the outbreak of armed conflicts: Juárez with the Conservatives and the French, and Madero with the Mexican Revolution.

76. Christen Jamar and Angelo Young, "NAFTA @ 5," *MB* (formerly *U.S./Mexico Business*), April 1999, p. 30.

77. Ibid., p. 28.

78. From the website, www.canada.org.ms/trade.

79. From the website, dgcnesyp.inegi.gob.mx; Jamar and Young, "NAFTA @ 5," p. 32.

Acronyms

AD	Acción Democrática (Democratic Action, Venezuela)
AD M-19	Alianza Democrática M-19 (M-19 Democratic Alliance, Colombia)
ANAPO	Alianza Nacional Popular (National Popular Alliance, Colombia)
ANUC	Asociación Nacional de Usuarios Campesinos (National Association of Peasant Users, Colombia)
AP	Acción Popular (Popular Action Party, Peru)
APRA	Alianza Popular Revolucionaria Americana (Popular American Revolutionary Alliance, Peru)
ARENA	Aliança Renovadora Nacional (Alliance for National Renewal, Brazil)
BA	bureaucratic authoritarian regime
CADE	Conferencia Anual de Directores de Empresas (Annual Business Executives' Conference, Peru)
CAEM	Centro de Altos Estudios Militares (Center for Advanced Military Studies, Peru)
CATD	Confederación Auténtica de Trabajadores Democráticos (Authentic Confederation of Democratic Workers, Costa Rica)
CCD	Congreso Constituyente Democrático (Democratic Constituent Congress, Peru)
CCP	Confederación de Campesinos del Perú (Peruvian Peasants Confederation, Peru)
CCTD	Confederación Costarricense de Trabajadores Democráticos (Costa Rican Democratic Workers Confederation)
CGT	Confederación General de Trabajadores Democráticos

(General Democratic Confederation of Workers, Costa Rica)

CGTP Confederación General de Trabajadores del Perú (General Confederation of Peruvian Workers)

CLP Coordinadora de Luchas Populares (Coordinator of Popular Struggles, Dominican Republic)

CNA Confederación Nacional Agraria (National Agrarian Confederation, Peru)

CNOP Conferencia Nacional de Organizaciones Populares (National Conference of Popular Organizations, Dominican Republic)

COP Colectivo de Organizaciones Populares (Collective of Popular Organizations, Dominican Republic)

COPEI Comité de Organización Política Electoral Independiente (Committee for Independent Political Electoral Organization, Venezuela)

COPRE Comisión Presidencial para la Reforma del Estado (Presidential Commission for the Reform of the State, Venezuela)

CPT Consejo Permanente de Trabajadores (Permanent Workers Council, Costa Rica)

CRS Corriente de Renovación Socialista (Current of Socialist Renovation, Colombia)

CTC Confederación de Trabajadores de Colombia (Confederation of Colombian Workers)

CTCR Confederación de Trabajadores Costarricenses (Costa Rican Workers' Confederation, Costa Rica)

CTM Confederación de Trabajadores de México (Confederation of Mexican Workers)

CTV Confederación de Trabajadores de Venezuela (Confederation of Venezuelan Workers)

CUT Confederación Unitaria de Trabajadores (Unitary Confederation of Workers, Costa Rica)

DAS Departamento Administrativo de Seguridad (Administrative Department of Security, Colombia)

DINA Dirección de Inteligencia Nacional (National Intelligence Bureau, Chile)

ECLAC Economic Commission for Latin American and the Caribbean

ELN Ejército de Liberación Nacional (Army of National Liberation, Colombia)

EPL Ejército Popular de Liberación (Popular Liberation Army, Colombia)

EZLN Ejército Zapatista de Liberación Nacional (Zapatista Army of National Liberation, Mexico)

FARC	Fuerzas Armadas Revolucionarias de Colombia (Revolutionary Armed Forces of Colombia)
FREDEMO	Frente Democrático (Democratic Front, Peru)
FREPASO	Frente por un País Solidario (Front for a Solidary Country, Argentina)
GATT	General Agreement on Tariffs and Trade (became the WTO in 1995)
GDP	gross domestic product
GNP	gross national product
IADB	Inter-American Development Bank
IMF	International Monetary Fund
IPC	International Petroleum Company (Peru)
IU	Izquierda Unida (United Left, Peru)
LCR	La Causa R (The Radical Cause, Venezuela)
M-19	Movimiento del 19 de Abril (Movement of the 19th of April, Colombia)
MAS	Movimiento al Socialismo (Socialist Movement, Venezuela)
MDB	Movimento Democrático Brasileiro (Brazilian Democratic Movement)
MEP	Movimiento Electoral del Pueblo (People's Electoral Movement, Venezuela)
Mercosur	Mercado Común del Sur (Common Market of the South)
MR-14J	Movimiento Revolucionario 14 de Junio (Revolutionary Movement 14th of June, Dominican Republic)
MRL	Movimiento Revolucionario Liberal (Liberal Revolutionary Movement, Colombia)
MRTA	Movimiento Revolucionario Túpac Amaru (Túpac Amaru Revolutionary Movement, Peru)
MSN	Movimiento de Salvación Nacional (Movement of National Salvation, Colombia)
MST	Movimento dos Sem-Terra (the Landless Movement, Brazil)
MVR	Movimiento V República (Fifth Republic Movement, Venezuela)
NAFTA	North American Free Trade Agreement
NGOs	nongovernmental organizations
OAS	Organization of American States
PAN	Partido Acción Nacional (National Action Party, Mexico)
PCV	Partido Comunista de Venezuela (Communist Party of Venezuela)
PDS	Partido Democrático Social (Democratic Social Party, Brazil)
PFL	Partido da Frente Liberal (Liberal Front Party, Brazil)
PJ	Partido Justicialista (Justicialist Party-Peronist Party, Argentina)

PLD   Partido de la Liberación Dominicana (Party of Dominican Liberation, Dominican Republic)

PLN   Partido de Liberación Nacional (National Liberation Party, Costa Rica)

PMDB   Partido do Movimento Democrático Brasileiro (Party of the Brazilian Democratic Movement)

PPC   Partido Popular Cristiano (Popular Christian Party, Peru)

PPD   Partido por la Democracia (Party for Democracy, Chile)

PPU   Partido Pueblo Unido (United People's Party, Costa Rica)

PR   proportional representation

PRD   Partido Revolucionario Dominicano (Dominican Revolutionary Party, Dominican Republic)

PRD   Partido de la Revolución Democrática (Party of the Democratic Revolution, Mexico)

PRI   Partido Revolucionario Institucional (Institutional Revolutionary Party, Mexico)

PRN   Partido da Reconstrução Nacional (National Reconstruction Party, Brazil)

PRSC   Partido Reformista Social Cristiano (Reformist Social Christian Party, Dominican Republic)

PRT   Partido Revolucionario de los Trabajadores (Workers' Revolutionary Party, Colombia)

PSD   Partido Social Democrático (Social Democratic Party, Brazil)

PSDB   Partido da Social-Democracia Brasileira (Brazilian Social Democratic Party, Brazil)

PSUM   Partido Socialista Unificada Mexicana (Unified Mexican Socialist Party, Mexico)

PT   Partido dos Trabalhadores (Workers' Party, Brazil)

PUSC   Partido de Unificación Social Cristiana (Social Christian Unity Party, Costa Rica)

RN   Renovación Nacional (National Renovation, Chile)

SIN   Servicio de Inteligencia Nacional (National Intelligence Service, Peru)

SINAMOS   Sistema Nacional por Mobilización Social (National System for the Support of Social Mobilization, Peru)

SODE   Solidaridad y Democracia (Solidarity and Democracy, Peru)

TSE   Tribunal Supremo de Elecciones (Supreme Electoral Tribunal, Costa Rica)

UCN   Unión de Pequeños y Medianos Agricultores (Union of Small and Medium Farmers, Costa Rica)

UCR   Unión Cívica Radical (Radical Civic Union, Argentina)

UDI   Unión Democrática Independiente (Independent Democratic Union, Chile)

UDN	União Democrática Nacional (Democratic National Union, Brazil)
UP	Unidad Popular (Popular Union, Chile)
UP	Unión Patriótica (Patriotic Union, Colombia)
UPP	Unión por el Perú (Union for Peru, Peru)
URD	Unión República Democrática (Democratic Republican Union, Venezuela)
USAID	United States Agency for International Development
UTC	Unión de Trabajadores de Colombia (Union of Colombian Workers)
UTM	Unión de Trabajadores de México (Union of Mexican Workers)
WTO	World Trade Organization (replaced GATT in January 1995)

THE CONTRIBUTORS

John A. Booth is Regents Professor of Political Science at the University of North Texas. He is the author of *Costa Rica: Quest for Democracy* and *The End and Beginning: The Nicaraguan Revolution,* coauthor of *Understanding Central America,* and coeditor of *Elections and Democracy in Central America* and *Elections and Democracy in Central America, Revisited.*

Kathleen Bruhn is assistant professor of political science at the University of California, Santa Barbara. Her research has focused primarily on the Mexican left. She is the author of *Taking on Goliath: The Emergence of a New Left Party and the Struggle for Democracy in Mexico,* about the creation of the Partido de la Revolución Democrática (PRD).

Brian F. Crisp is associate professor of political science at the University of Arizona. He is the author of *Democratic Institutional Design: The Powers and Incentives of Venezuelan Politicians and Interest Groups,* as well as of numerous articles and book chapters on issues of democratic institutional design and political economy.

Larry Diamond is senior research fellow at the Hoover Institution, coeditor of the *Journal of Democracy,* and codirector of the International Forum for Democratic Studies of the National Endowment for Democracy. His most recent book is *Developing Democracy: Toward Consolidation.* He is editor or coeditor of many books on democracy, including *The Self-Restraining State, Democracy in East Asia,* and *Consolidating the Third Wave Democracies.*

John Dugas is assistant professor of political science at Kalamazoo College. He is the editor of *La constitución de 1991: ¿Un pacto político viable?* and coauthor of *Los caminos de la descentralización.*

Rosario Espinal is associate professor of sociology and director of the Latin American Studies Center at Temple University. She is the author of *Autoritarismo y democracia en la política dominicana* and more than forty articles published in English, Spanish, and French.

Jonathan Hartlyn is professor of political science and director of the Institute of Latin American Studies at the University of North Carolina at Chapel Hill. He is author of *The Struggle for Democratic Politics in the Dominican Republic; The Politics of Coalition Rule in Colombia,* which has also been published in Spanish; and numerous other articles and book chapters.

Bolívar Lamounier is cofounder and research director of IDESP (Instituto de Estudos Econômicos, Sociais e Políticos de São Paulo). Among his many works are *Parties and Elections in Brazil* (with Fernando Henrique Cardoso) and "Democracy and Economic Reform in Brazil" (with Edmar Bacha), which was included in *A Precarious Balance,* edited by Joan Nelson.

Daniel H. Levine is professor of political science at the University of Michigan at Ann Arbor. He has published widely on religion and politics and on social change, politics, and democracy in Latin America. His most recent books are *Constructing Culture and Power in Latin America* and *Popular Voices in Latin American Catholicism.*

Daniel C. Levy is professor at the University at Albany, SUNY. His latest book, *Building the Third Sector,* won the 1997 prize for best book on non-profit and voluntary action research. With Kathleen Bruhn and Emilio Zebadúa, Levy is currently writing *Mexico: The Struggle for Democratized and Internationalized Development.*

Juan J. Linz is Sterling Professor of Political and Social Science at Yale University. He is the author or coauthor of numerous books and articles, among them: "The Breakdown of Democratic Regimes"; "Totalitarian and Authoritarian Regimes"; "Presidentialism and Parliamentarism: Does It Make a Difference?"; *Conflicto en Euskadi* on the Basque problem in Spain; *Problems of Democratic Transition and Consolidation: Southern Europe, South America and Post-Communist Europe;* and *Sultanistic Regimes,* on a form of nondemocratic rule. He was awarded the Spanish

Premio Príncipe de Asturias in the Social Sciences, and the Johan Skytte prize in Political Science (at Uppsala University).

Seymour Martin Lipset holds the Hazel chair of Public Policy at the Institute of Public Policy, George Mason University, and senior fellow at the Hoover Institution, Stanford University. He is the author or coauthor of numerous books on democracy and comparative sociology, including *Political Man, The First New Nation, Union Democracy, Revolution and Counterrevolution, The Confidence Gap, Consensus and Conflict,* and, most recently, *American Exceptionalism: A Double-Edged Sword.* He is the only person ever elected president of both the American Political Science Association and the American Sociological Association.

Cynthia McClintock is professor of political science and international affairs at George Washington University. She is the author of *Peasant Cooperatives and Political Change in Peru* and *Revolutionary Movements in Latin America,* among numerous other works. She is continuing to research the issue of democratization in Peru and is coauthoring (with Peter F. Klaren) a textbook on Latin American politics. She was president of the Latin American Studies Association in 1994–1995.

Arturo Valenzuela is special assistant to the president and senior director for inter-American affairs on the National Security Council. He is on leave as professor of government and director of the Center for Latin American Studies at Georgetown University. His works include *The Breakdown of Democratic Regimes: Chile* and *A Nation of Enemies: Chile Under Pinochet* (with Pamela Constable). With Juan J. Linz, he coedited *The Crisis of Presidential Democracy.*

Carlos H. Waisman is professor and chair of the Department of Sociology, University of California, San Diego. He is the author of *Modernization and the Working Class: The Politics of Legitimacy; From Military Rule to Liberal Democracy in Argentina* (coedited, with Monica Peralta Ramos); *Reversal of Development in Argentina; Institutional Design in New Democracies* (coedited with Arend Lijphart); and numerous other articles and book chapters.

INDEX

Acción Democrática (AD) (Venezuela), 26, 28, 35, 376, 377, 379, 380, 382–386, 392, 393, 394, 399–400, 401, 402–403, 404, 405
Acción Popular (AP) (Peru), 320, 321, 322, 326, 345, 347
Aguirre Cerda, Pedro, 200
Alessandri, Arturo, 36, 199, 200, 201, 218
Alfonsín, Raúl, 37, 98–100
Aliança Renovadora Nacional (ARENA) (Brazil), 134, 136, 137
Alianza Nacional Popular (ANAPO) (Colombia), 271, 275
Alianza Popular Revolucionaria Americana (APRA) (Peru), 26, 309, 310, 316–322, 325, 326, 328, 329, 330–331, 345, 346
Allende, Salvador, 37, 193, 201, 204, 218–219, 221
Alliance for Work, Education, and Justice (Argentina), 103
Andean Pact, 324
Argentina: agrarian elites, 48, 76, 78, 79–82, 84, 86, 93, 94, 108; authoritarianism, 83, 84; and Brazil, 100–101; capitalist revolution, 103–107; civil society, 114–116, 122, 123, 124; class structure, 73, 75, 77, 81, 84, 85, 86–87, 92–93, 110–111; cleavages, 73, 76–77, 81, 84, 85–87, 90, 92–93, 101, 111, 112–113; colonial legacy, 76; communism, 91, 92–93; Congress, 82, 83, 113; corporatism, 55, 83, 85–86, 87–90, 91, 94, 97; corruption, 103; cultural integration, 111–113; democracy, 44, 71, 76, 82–84, 94, 97–103, 107–121; democratic breakdown, 16, 82; democratic prospects, 122–124; development poli-

cy, 73 76, 77–78, 84; dualization tendencies, 123–124; economy and economic policy, 17–18, 37, 71, 74, 75, 76, 77, 80, 84, 85, 93, 94, 96, 97, 98–99, 100–102, 103, 104–105, 113–114; elections, 100, 102; electoral practices and reform, 75, 77, 78, 79, 80; as elite democracy, 74–75, 77–80; ethnicity, 113; fascism, 92–93, 120; immigrant population, 73, 76, 79–80, 83, 111; international influences, 119–121; judiciary, 33, 103, 113; labor, 78–80, 81, 83, 84, 85–90, 91, 92–93, 94, 100, 101, 106–107, 115; military coups, 74, 75, 82, 83, 84, 86, 89, 94, 95, 121; military rule, 75, 84–85, 94, 95, 96–97; military's delegitimation and subordination, 96–97, 99; mobilization, 78–79, 80, 87, 94–95; neomercantilism, 71, 100, 103; participation, 75, 78, 84, 109; parties and party system, 78, 83, 97, 99–100, 102, 113, 117–119; Peronism, 26, 27, 91, 95, 97–98, 99–100, 102, 108, 109, 117–118; personalistic leadership, 119; political culture, 108–109; political-institutional gender equality, 32; political legitimacy/illegitimacy, 80–81, 82, 83, 86–87; populist-corporatist regime (Peron), 75, 83, 85–86, 89; poverty and unemployment, 101, 102; presidency, 33, 113, 122; protectionism, 84, 87–88, 89, 91, 94; radical intelligentsia, 94–95; Reform of 1912, 35, 78, 80, 119; repression and terrorism, 94, 95–96, 99; restrictive democracy, 82–84, 94; and rule of law, 101, 122; social mobility, 102, 103; and Soviet Union, 120, 121; state structure and strength, 71,

77, 90–91, 93, 100, 103–107, 113–117, 122; and the United States, 121
Arias Sánchez, Oscar, 441, 450, 459, 463
Associational life. *See* Civil society
Authoritarianism, 24, 40, 55–56. *See also specific countries*
Aylwin Azocar, Patricio, 191, 193, 232–234

Báez, Buenaventura, 473, 474
Balaguer, Joaquín, 45, 471, 480–483, 486–490, 496, 499, 500, 501–502, 503–504, 506, 507, 508, 509, 511, 512
Balmaceda, José Manuel, 198
Barco, Virgilio, 251, 271–272, 278–280, 281, 296
Barrantes, Alfonso, 329, 346
Batlle y Ordóñez, José, 36
Belaúnde, Fernando, 36, 320–322, 323, 326–328, 331, 345, 353
Benavides, Oscar, 318–319
Bentacur, Belisario, 37, 271, 276–278
Betancourt, Rómulo, 381, 404, 412
Billinghurst, Guillermo, 315
Bolívar, Símon, 8, 10–11, 373
Booth, John A., 419
Bosch, Juan, 471, 480–481, 483, 487, 499, 503, 507, 508, 512
Boundary conflicts, 11–12
Brazil, 45; authoritarianism, 131, 133, 134, 135, 137, 153, 563; civil society, 149, 151; class structure, 144–145, 156–158; colonial legacy, 12–13, 149; Congress, 134, 136–137, 141, 146, 151, 171, 174–176, 183; constitutions, 140, 141, 144, 152, 157, 176; *coronelismo,* 141; corporatism, 151, 176; Cruzado Plan, 171; democracy, 61, 132, 149–167, 172–178; democratic consolidation prospects, 168–171; democratic failure, 27, 38, 145–147; democratic opening (*abertura*), 132–137, 153; economy and economic policies, 135, 152–154, 167, 170–173, 177–179; elections and electoral process, 132, 133–135, 136, 137, 139, 140, 142–143, 165, 166; elites, 43, 138, 166, 167; entrepreneurial class, 158; Estado Novo, 43, 144, 145; ethnic and national cleavages, 159; First Republic, 140–142, 159; gubernatorial elections (1994), 179; international factors, 167; judiciary, 141; legitimacy, 153; military, 140, 148, 150–151, 167; military-authoritarian rule (1964–1985), 151, 153; mobilization, 153, 157; New Republic period (1985–1990), 50–51, 169–176; parliamentary monarchy, 138–140; parties and party system, 134–135, 136–137, 146–147, 148, 162,
173–174, 175 (Table 3.4), 176, 179–180, 182; political culture, 144–145, 163–166; political elites, 43, 138; political-institutional gender equality, 32; political leadership, 163; political structure, 24, 159–162; population and socioeconomic change, 155 (Table 3.1); poverty and income inequality, 50–51, 154–156, 158; presidency, 144, 146, 148, 162, 179–180, 181, 182–183; Real Plan, 171, 179, 181, 183; reforms, 181–182; regional cleavages, 142, 144, 145; representative system, 137–138, 142–145, 148, 162; repression and human rights violations, 133, 148, 151; Revolution of 1930, 142, 149, 159, 162; social mobility, 158, 166; state building, 137–148; state-centered industrialization model, 179; statist ideology, 173
Bruhn, Kathleen, 519
Bulnes, Manuel, 34, 195, 213
Bustamante, José Luis, 319, 353

Cáceres, Ramón, 475
Caldera, Rafael, 386, 392–394, 404, 417
Calderón Fournier, Rafael Angel, 442
Calderón Guardia, Rafael Angel, 437, 438, 445
Cali cartel, 279, 284, 285–286, 291
Calles, Plutarco Elías, 526–527, 537
Carazo, Rodrigo, 442, 458
Cárdenas, Cuauhtémoc, 535, 537, 540, 543
Cárdenas, Francisco Arías, 391
Cárdenas, Lázaro, 527, 528, 537, 543, 555
Cardoso, Fernando Henrique, 28, 132, 171, 177–183, 535
Carranza, Venustiano, 526
Carter administration, 60, 121, 353, 482, 483
Catholic Church, 26, 40; in Argentina, 86, 91, 115; in Chile, 197, 201, 207–208; in Colombia, 250, 256, 258, 264–265, 266; in Costa Rica, 435, 445; in Dominican Republic, 479, 508; in Mexico, 524, 531; in Venezuela, 373, 377, 378, 380
Center-periphery conflicts, 11, 196, 199
Central American peace accord, 459, 463
Central American Republic, 432
Chávez, Hugo, 387, 390, 391, 394, 414
Chile: citizenship rights, 207, 214–215, 225, 226, 241n5; civil society, 54; class structure, 199, 201, 208, 210–211; cleavages, 194–196, 199, 201; coalition government, 203–204, 216–219, 232, 237, 238, 240; colonial legacy, 205–207; Congress, 192, 193, 195, 200, 203, 204, 216–217, 221, 225, 226, 231, 239; constitutions, 194, 195, 199, 206, 224, 225–226, 231; democracy and redemocratization, 3, 30,

61, 191–193, 213–214, 216–222, 230–240; economy and economic policy, 17–18, 196, 200, 201, 226, 227, 229, 232–233, 235; elections, 196–197, 199, 200, 201, 202, 204, 209, 217, 228–230, 232, 233, 234–235, 236–237; electoral process and reforms, 35, 195, 197, 198, 215, 216–217, 239; elites, 48, 209, 210, 214, 218; labor movement, 199, 200; left, 201, 217, 218, 222, 224, 226, 227, 228, 230, 234, 236, 237, 238–239; military, 213–214, 219, 225, 230, 231, 233–234; military rule, 192–193, 199, 222–230, 231; mobilization, 217, 219–220, 227; national identity, 212–213; parliamentary government, 198–199; parties and party system, 26, 196–197, 198, 199, 200–204, 220, 226, 227–228, 231, 232, 239–240; political culture, 202–203, 204, 210; political leadership, 34, 213–214; poverty and inequality, 233; presidentialism, 30, 195, 197, 200, 207, 217, 220–222, 223, 226, 231, 239–240; repression and human rights abuses, 222–223, 224, 225, 227, 233, 238–239; secret police, 224; Senate, 226, 231, 234, 236, 239; socioeconomic development, 44; state autonomy and authority, 16, 196, 213–214; unconstitutional rule, 98, 199; United States' intervention in, 220

Christian Democratic Party (Chile), 201, 202, 216–219, 221, 227, 228, 232, 234, 236, 237–238

Christian Democratic Party (El Salvador), 418

Christian Democratic Party (Venezuela), 377

Citizenship and suffrage, 192, 207, 214–215, 241n5

Civilista Party (Peru), 313, 314, 315

Civil society, 27, 54–57, 64, 369–370, 371–372. *See also specific countries*

Class structures and cleavages, 48–51. *See also specific countries*

Clinton administration, 285–286, 353–354

Collor de Mello, Fernando, 131, 169, 176, 177

Colombia: authoritarianism, 252, 253; broker clientelism, 289–290; civilian rule, 254; civil society, 293; civil wars, 255, 256; class structure, 293–295; coalition rule, 251, 265, 266–268, 274, 275, 278–279; Congress, 251, 256, 257, 262, 267, 280, 282, 283, 286, 287, 289, 291; consociationalism, 251, 252–253, 255, 256, 265–268, 274, 288; constitutions, 249, 251, 252, 255, 256, 267, 272, 280, 281–283, 289; criminal violence, 250,

252, 283; culture of violence, 294, 295; democracy, 61, 249, 251–252, 253, 281–283, 287, 295; democratic prospects, 297–299; dictatorial rule, 256, 262–264; drug trafficking, 273, 274, 279–280, 283–286, 291, 294, 297, 298; economy and socioeconomic development, 257, 262, 268–273, 279, 296–297; elections, 260–261, 262, 263 (Table 5.2), 265, 274, 275, 276, 277, 280, 281, 283, 287, 288–289; elite pacts, 35; guerrilla movements, 273, 276–277, 283, 286, 287; historical development, 250, 253–256; industrialization, 257, 258, 269; international factors, 296–297; judiciary, 33, 251, 252, 282, 291; labor, 258–260, 261, 269, 273, 275–276; *la violencia* (1945–1958), 260–265; left-wing political movement, 277–278; media, 292–293; military, 255, 266, 273, 290; military rule, 264; National Constituent Assembly, 280, 281–283, 291, 293, 295; oligarchical democracy, 257–262, 288; opposition parties and movements, 273, 275–276, 290; paramilitary groups, 286, 298–299; parties and party system, 26, 251, 255, 256–258, 267, 274–275, 283, 288–289, 293; political crisis, 249–250, 265, 277–280; political culture, 294–295; political leadership and statecraft, 295–296; political violence and repression, 249, 251, 252, 253, 254, 255, 256, 257, 260–265, 273, 278, 279–280, 283, 286; poverty and socioeconomic disparities, 49, 249, 257, 269, 272, 293–294; presidency, 251, 254, 257, 266, 267, 273, 282, 289–290; producer groups, 291–292, 294; reforms, 36, 272, 277, 278–279, 281, 282–283; regionalism, 256; state structure and authority, 16, 252, 256, 261–262, 290–291; and the United States, 269, 285–286, 297

Colonial-continuity theory, 205–207

Colonialism, 2, 7–13. *See also specific countries*

Colosio, Luis Donaldo, 551

Comisión Presidencial para la Reforma (COPRE) (Venezuela), 394

Comité de Organización Política Electoral Independient (COPEI) (Venezuela), 377, 380, 382–386, 392, 393, 399–400, 401, 402–403

Communist Party (Argentina), 92

Communist Party (Chile), 199, 201, 232

Communist Party (Costa Rica), 437, 438

Communist Party (Venezuela), 385, 407

Competitive politics, 14, 25–29

Concertación de Partidos por la Democracia (Chile), 232, 233, 234, 236, 237, 238

Confederación de Trabajadores de México (CTM), 528, 529
Confederación de Trabajadores de Venezuela (CTV), 380, 391, 399
Confederación de Trabajadores de Colombia (CTC), 260, 261
Confederación General de Trabajadores (CGT) (Costa Rica), 436–437
Confederación Unitaria de Trabajadores (CUT) (Costa Rica), 452–453
Conservative Party (Argentina), 75, 81, 82, 108, 113
Conservative Party (Chile), 196, 197, 198, 201, 214
Conservative Party (Colombia), 251, 254–255, 256, 257–258, 260, 261–262, 264, 266, 274, 278, 279, 281, 287
Constitutions, 6, 29–33, 39. *See also specific countries*
Contreras, Manuel, 233
Corruption, 204. *See also specific countries*
Costa Rica: civil society, 54, 433–434, 436–437, 442, 451–454; class structure and cleavages, 50, 431, 432, 434, 435–436, 454–457, 461; colonialism, 431, 493–494; communism/anticommunism, 436–437, 442, 446; constitutions, 435, 438, 439; democracy and democratic prospects, 3, 429, 462–464; economic and political elites, 432, 434, 436, 437, 438; economy and economic policy, 433, 434, 436, 444–445, 448–449, 450–451, 460, 462–463; education, 434, 449; egalitarian social culture, 49; elections and electoral systems, 429, 432, 434–435, 436, 438–442; foreign policy of pacifism, 458; historical development, 429–434, 460–461; indigenous population, 431, 457; international factors, 458–460; judiciary, 444; labor organizations, 452–455; Legislative Assembly, 443–444; Liberal Republic, 35; media, 445; military, 432, 438, 442; military rule, 436; National Liberation junta (1948–1949), 438, 441; neoliberalism and structural adjustment, 450–451, 459–460, 462, 464; and Nicaragua, 458–459, 463; participation, 429, 431, 435, 445–446, 461–462; parties and party system, 434, 435, 437–439, 441–442, 461; political culture, 41, 42, 445–448; political-institutional gender equality, 32; political leadership, 34–35; political liberalization, 36, 434–439; political violence and terrorism, 446, 447, 458–459, 461; poverty and income inequality, 431, 449, 450 (Table 8.3), 455–457, 460, 462; presidency, 432–433, 443, 444; racial and religious cleavages,
434, 457; Second Republic, 438; social-democratic movement, 437–438, 448–449, 450–451, 459, 460, 461; socioeconomic development, 432–434, 449–450; state structure and strength, 442–445, 462; and the United States, 450, 458
Costa Rican Workers' Confederation (CTCR), 437, 446
Crime, 16, 250, 252, 283. *See also* Drug trafficking
Crisp, Brian F., 367
Cuba, 3, 24, 458, 558
Cuban Revolution, 58, 120, 382, 412, 479
Cultural homogeneity, 53–54

Dahl, Robert, 14
Decentralization, 18–19, 534
Deconcentration, 50, 170
de la Madrid, Miguel, 528, 539, 549
da Silva, Luís "Lula" Inácio, 176, 177, 178, 181
Democracy: comparative, 60, 61, 62 (Table 1.2); concept and definition, xi-xiii, 369; cultural obstacles to, 43; and democratic values, 43; liberal, 429; and political legitimacy, 4–5; as political subsystem, 131; and prospects, comparative, 60–65; proto-democracies, 13; qualified, 523; restrictive, 82–84, 94
Democratic consolidation, 3–7, 168–169
Democratization: colonial-continuity thesis, 205–207; criteria and optimal patterns, 469–470, 561–562; defined, 369–370; economic-class-structure thesis, 210–211; and economic performance, 46–48; political-culture thesis, 207–210; political-determinants thesis, 211–216; political variables in, 250; and socioeconomic development, 44–46
Díaz, Porfirio, 525
DINA (Dirección de Inteligencia Nacional) (Chile), 224
Dominican Republic, 38, 45, 55, 56, 60; authoritarianism, 492–494, 495–496, 497–498; civil society, 54, 489, 496, 500, 504, 512–513; class structure, 475; colonialism and independence, 9, 472–474, 492–494; Congress, 506; constitutions, 497, 506; corruption, 487, 496; democracy, 3, 469–471, 480, 481, 491–492, 496, 497–498, 500, 503, 506, 507; democratic prospects, 511–512; development performance, 498–500; economy and economic policy, 481–482, 485–486, 487, 488, 498–500; elections, 474, 480, 481, 482–483, 484 (Table 9.1), 486, 487–488, 489, 491, 504–505, 509,

513; elites, 478; ethnic and racial cleavages, 501–502; First and Second Republics, 473–474; historical development, 471–476; international context, 471–472, 473–474, 477, 478, 479, 494, 509, 511; judiciary, 506–507, 513; labor, 482, 488, 499; migration and diaspora, 498, 499–500; military, 476, 477, 481, 482, 483–485; nationalism, 478; neopatrimonial leadership, 472, 476–477, 481–483, 495, 497, 507; parties and party system, 25, 475, 478–479, 480, 481; political culture, 41, 497–498; political-institutional gender equality, 32; political leadership style, 33, 507–509; political violence, 474, 486; poverty and income inequality, 49, 498, 499–500; PRD rule (1978–1986), 483–486, 508, 511; reforms, 496–497, 499; repression and human rights violations, 477, 482, 496, 507; slavery, 472–473; social mobilization, 488–489; socioeconomic development, 471, 498–500; state and political structures, 471, 477, 495–497, 506–507, 513; state building, 471; Trujillo era, 476–479; and the United States, 474, 475–476, 477, 479, 480–481, 482, 489, 509–511; United States's occupation (1916–1924), 475–476, 494–495
Drug trafficking, 16, 253, 273, 274, 279–280, 283–286, 291, 294, 297, 298
Dugas, John, 249

Echeverría, Luis, 530
Economic Commission on Latin America and the Caribbean (ECLAC), 51
Economic crises, 36–37, 46–47. *See also specific countries*
Economic globalization, 58–59
Economic performance, 46–48, 557–558. *See also specific countries*
Economic restructuring, 16–18
Eisenhower administration, 412
Ejército de Liberación Nacional (ELN) (Colombia), 276–277, 279, 283
Ejército Popular de Liberación (EPL) (Colombia), 277, 281
Ejército Zapatista de Liberación Nacional (EZLN) (Mexico), 531
Electoral reform, 31
Elite behavior and values, 41–42
Elite pacts, 35
Escuela de Vecinos de Venezuela (EVV), 408–409
Espinal, Rosario, 469
Ethnic cleavages, 53–54. *See also specific countries*

Fascism, 24, 40, 92–93, 120, 145
Federalism, 11, 525, 534
Fernández, Leonel, 485, 486, 490–491, 497, 498, 505, 506, 508–509
Figueiredo, João Baptista, 134, 135–136, 172
Figueres Ferrer, José, 34–35, 437
Figueres Olsen, José Maria, 441
Figueroa, Emiliano, 199–200
Franco, Itamar, 131, 177
Frei Ruiz-Tagle, Eduardo, 191, 201, 217, 234, 235–236, 238, 239
Frente Democrático (FREDEMO)(Peru), 329, 330, 331, 345
Frente por un País Solidario (FREPASO) (Argentina), 102, 103
Fuerzas Armadas Revolucionarias de Colombia (FARC), 276, 277–279, 281, 282, 283
Fujimori, Alberto, 310, 329–337, 347, 348, 349, 355, 356

Gaitán, Jorge Eliécer, 260, 261
Galán, Luís Carlos, 280
García, Alan, 105, 328–329, 331, 346, 354, 356
GATT, 555
Gaviria, César, 36, 272, 281, 283–284, 295, 296
Geisel, Ernesto, 132, 134, 135, 167
Gender equality, political-institutional, 32
Gómez, Alvaro, 278
Gómez, Juan Vicente, 374
Gómez, Laureano, 260, 261, 262–264, 265
González Flores, Alfredo, 436
González Videla, Gabriel, 201
González Víquez, Cleto, 35, 435, 437
Goulart, João, 38, 147, 162, 163
Governability/ungovernability, 16, 29, 419
Gran Colombia federation, 10–11, 254, 255
Guardia, Tomás, 434, 435
Gutiérrez Rebollo, Jesus, 549
Guzmán, Abimael, 334
Guzmán, S. Antonio, 482, 483, 485, 508

Haiti, 3, 471, 478, 501–502
Hartlyn, Jonathan, 249, 469
Haya de la Torre, Víctor Raúl, 316–321, 325, 326, 328, 346
Heureaux, Ulises, 474–475, 477
Human rights violations, 16, 23. *See also specific countries*

Ibañez, Carlos, 200, 201
Immigration, postindependence, 9
Indigenous population, 7–8
Inequality. *See* Poverty and inequality
Institutionalization, 6–7
Internationalism, 57–59. *See also specific*

countries
International Monetary Fund (IMF), 270, 325, 330, 394, 449, 459, 485, 486, 488
International Petroleum Company (IPC), 322, 323
Irarrazaval, José Manuel, 197
Izquierda Socialista (Peru), 329, 346
Izquierda Unida (IU) (Peru), 326, 328, 329, 345–346

Jiménez Oreamuno, Ricardo, 36, 435, 437
Jorge Blanco, Salvador, 37, 485–486, 487, 505, 506, 508
Juárez, Benito, 525
Judiciary, 31, 32. *See also specific countries*

Kennedy administration, 59, 353, 412, 509–510
Kubitschek, Juscelino, 153, 163, 167

Labor movements, 50. *See also specific countries*
La Causa R (LCR) (Venezuela), 385–386, 406, 407, 409–410
Lagos, Ricardo, 234, 237–238
Lamounier, Bolívar, 131
Legislatures, power and effectiveness of, 32
Legitimacy, political, 4–6, 419. *See also specific countries*
Leguía, Augusto, 36, 311, 315–316, 353
Leigh, Gustavo, 223, 224–225
Letelier, Orlando, 233
Levine, Daniel H., 367
Levy, Daniel C., 519
Liberal Party (Colombia), 251, 254–255, 256, 257–258, 260, 261–262, 264, 266, 274, 275, 278, 279, 281, 284, 287
Liberal Party (Costa Rica), 434, 435
Lleras, Alberto, 261, 265–266
Lleras, Carlos, 268, 270–271
López, Alfonso, 275
López Contreras, Eleazar, 375–376
López Michelsen, Alfonso, 271
López Portillo, José, 530
López Pumarejo, Alfonso, 257–260
Lusinchi, Jaime, 303, 394

Madero, Francisco, 525–526
Majluta, Jacobo, 487
Malvinas/Falklands War, 96
Maneiro, Alfredo, 407
Mariátegui, José Carlos, 316–318
Maurras, Charles, 40
McClintock, Cynthia, 310
Medellín cartel, 279–280, 284, 291, 298
Media, 56–57, 292–293, 445
Médici, Emílio Garrastazu, 135, 153
Medina Angarita, Isaís, 376

Menem, Carlos, 33, 61, 84, 100–103, 119
Mercosur (Mercado Común del Sur), 58, 100, 121
Mexico, 45; authoritarianism, 521, 522, 524, 526, 531, 550–551, 553–554; business-state relations, 529–530; Chiapas rebellion, 531, 559–560; civil and political liberties, 522, 523; civil society, 54, 529, 551–552, 560–562; class, ethnic, and religious cleavages, 552–554; colonial and precolonial rule, 7, 524; Congress, 523, 525, 536, 543, 545; constitutions, 525, 526; co-optation of popular groups, 527–528, 532–533, 540, 551; corruption, 549–550; democracy, 3, 61, 519, 523, 525, 527–528, 531, 533–534, 537–539, 549–560; democratization prospects, 560–565; drug trafficking, 537, 549; economic restructuring, 17–18, 547, 548–549, 557–558; elections and electoral system, 517, 522, 529, 532–533, 534–535, 536–537, 539–547, 559, 561; elites and elite pacts, 525, 526, 527, 540, 547, 551, 553, 556; federalism, 525, 534; foreign policy, 558; government centralization, 533–539; indigenous population, 552–553; international factors, 558–560; judiciary, 536–537; labor, 528–529; La Reforma, (1855–1876), 524–525; left, 542–544, 548; liberalization, 561, 563; military role, 537–538; mobilization, 526, 527, 531; participation, 522, 527, 551; parties and party system, 523, 527, 536, 539–547, 561; peso crisis, 559; political culture, 521, 548–549, 550–552, 554, 563; political leadership, 33–34; political violence, 523, 526, 531, 532; popular movements, 531–532, 538, 540; presidential power, 535, 536–538; religion, 531; repression and co-optation, 528, 531–532; social instability, 523; socioeconomic development and social welfare, 533, 547–548, 557; Solidarity program, 533; state corporatism, 527–528, 529, 530, 539, 551, 552, 564; state-society relations, 527–533; state structure and stability, 521–522, 523–524, 525, 526, 527, 528, 534, 539, 549–550, 554–555; student demonstrations, 530–531; subnational governments, 534–535; and the United States, 558–559, 565–567
Military, 12–13; amnesty for, 23; coups, 65; and democratic consolidation, 19–23. *See also specific countries*
Mobilization, 49–50; populist, 12; in state-building sequence, 14–15. *See also specific countries*
Monge, Luis Alberto, 441, 450, 458, 463

Montt, Manuel, 195, 196, 213
Morales Bermúdez, Francisco, 311, 314, 352–353
Movimiento del 19 de Abril (M-19) (Colombia), 276–277, 278, 281
Movimiento al Socialismo (MAS) (Venezuela), 385–386, 406, 407
Movimiento Revolucionario (Dominican Republic), 503

NAFTA. *See* North American Free Trade Agreement
National Action Party (PAN) (Mexico), 542, 544–545, 565
National Commission for Truth and Reconciliation (Chile), 223, 233
National Democratic Front (Peru), 319
National Front (Colombia), 251, 252, 253, 260, 264, 265–268, 274, 275, 288, 290, 292, 293, 295
National Intelligence Service (SIN) (Peru), 332, 336
Nationalism, 12, 40, 49, 212–213, 478
National Security Council (Chile), 225–226, 231
National System for the Support of Social Mobilization (SINAMOS) (Peru), 324
National Union Party (Costa Rica), 435, 437
Neves, Tancredo, 131, 136, 172
Nicaragua, 456–459, 463
Nixon, Richard, 412
North American Free Trade Agreement (NAFTA), 510, 555, 559–560, 566
Núñez, Rafael, 256

Obregón, Alvaro, 526, 537
Odría, Manuel, 311, 319–321
Oduber, Daniel, 441, 463
Oligarchical democracies, 9, 13–14, 42, 257–262, 288
Organization of American States (OAS), 58
Ospina Pérez, Mariano, 260–261, 262, 264

Pardo y Barreda, José de, 315
Parliamentary systems, 29, 138–140, 241n3
Participation, 27, 429; and popular organizations, 54; in state-building sequence, 14–15. *See also specific countries*
Partido do Frente Liberal (PFL)(Brazil), 176, 180
Partido da Social-Democracia Brasileira (PSDB), 179, 180
Partido de la Liberación Dominicana (PLD), 483, 487–488, 489, 490, 491, 502, 504–505, 506, 508, 512
Partido de la Revolución Democrática (PRD) (Mexico), 542–544
Partido de Liberación Nacional (PLN) (Costa

Rica), 26, 438–439, 441, 442, 453, 461
Partido de Unificación Social Cristiana (PUSC) (Costa Rica), 441, 442, 454, 461
Partido do Movimiento Democrático Brasileiro (PMDB), 176
Partido dos Trabalhadores (PT, Workers' Party) (Brazil), 176, 177, 178, 181, 182
Partido por la Democracia (PPD) (Chile), 232, 236, 237
Partido Pueblo Unido (PPU) (Costa Rica), 42
Partido Reformista Social Cristiano (PRSC) (Dominican Republic), 486, 487–488, 490, 491, 504–505, 509
Partido Revolucionario Dominicano (PRD), 28, 480, 481, 482, 483–486, 487, 489, 490, 491, 496, 503–509
Partido Revolucionario Institucional (PRI) (Mexico), 519, 522, 523, 528, 531, 532, 534, 535, 536, 537, 539–547
Partido Social Democrático (PSD) (Brazil), 136, 147, 162
Parties and party systems, 25–29. *See also specific countries*
Pastrana, Andrés, 251, 284, 287
Pastrana, Misael, 271
Peña Gómez, José Francisco, 487, 489, 490, 491, 505, 507–509, 512
Pérez, Carlos Andrés, 368, 383, 386, 390, 391, 392, 394, 404, 412
Pérez de Cuéllar, Javier, 335–336, 347
Pérez Jiménez, Marcos, 378
Perón, Isabel, 95
Perón, Juan, 13, 49, 76, 83, 84, 85, 89, 91, 93, 94, 95, 119
Peru: agrarian reform, 322, 323; Aristocratic Republic, 36, 311, 314–315; authoritarianism, 309, 311, 316, 331, 336; *autogolpe* (April 1992), 310, 331–332, 353, 356; bicameral legislature, 345; and Chile, 313–314; civil society, 55, 56, 342–343; colonialism, 7, 312, 338, 339–340; Congress, 310, 320, 331; constitutions/constitutional structure, 310, 311, 325–326, 333, 343–345, 355; coups, 319, 323, 325; debt crisis, 325, 327, 328, 330; democracy, 3, 61, 309, 325–326, 343, 352–353; democratic failure, 310–311, 337–338; democratic prospects, 337, 355–356; development performance, 349–353; economy and economic policy, 17–19, 315–316, 320, 321, 325, 326–327, 328–329, 330, 331, 332, 335, 336, 349–353; education, 324, 350; elections and electoral system, 309, 310, 313, 314, 315, 316, 317 (Table 6.1), 318–319, 320–321, 325, 326, 328, 332–334, 335, 336–337, 346, 347; electoral democracy

(1980–1992), 326–332; elites, 309–310, 339–342; export-oriented growth, 315, 349–350, 352; guerrilla movement (Shining Path), 326, 327–328, 329, 331, 332, 334; historical development, 311–316; human rights, 329; import-substitution industrialization policies, 319, 322, 350; Inca Empire, 312; indigenous population, 309–310, 312, 313–314, 315, 339–341; international context, 332, 338–339, 353–355; judiciary, 310, 348–349; labor, 319, 320, 325; leftist military regime (Velasco), 322–325; Marxism, 326, 327, 329, 331, 343; military, 322–323; military rule, 311, 313–319; oligarchy, 314, 316, 318, 319, 320, 322, 323; parties and party system, 309, 313, 314, 315, 316–318, 325, 326, 329, 333 (Table 6.3), 334 (Table 6.4), 335, 338, 339, 345–348; peasantry, 321; political culture, 41, 338–339, 341–343; political-institutional gender equality, 32; political violence, 318; populism, 335; poverty and income distribution, 51, 331, 340–341, 350–351, 352; presidency, 331, 338, 339, 344; presidential elections, 317 (Table 6.1), 327 (Table 6.2); reforms, 321–322, 323–325, 341; regime type preferences, 342–343; repression, 318, 328; socioeconomic development and cleavages, 309–310, 335, 336, 338, 339–341; state, 16, 313, 348–349; and the United States, 316, 320, 323, 328, 339, 353–355
Peru-Bolivia Confederation, 194, 212
Piérola, Nicolás de, 313–314
Pinochet Ugarte, Augusto, 3, 24, 40, 42, 193, 222–230, 234, 238
Pizarro, Francisco, 312
Political culture: concept, 39; and foreign influences, 40; political development role of, 38–43; and social structure, 41; sources, 39–41. *See also specific countries*
Political institutions, 5, 6, 23–33. *See also specific countries*
Political leadership, 33–38; in democratic founding, 34; in economic and political crises, 36–38; style and effectiveness, 33–34. *See also specific countries*
Political reforms, 35–36, 64
Popular Front (Chile), 201
Popular sovereignty, 192
Popular Unity coalition (Chile), 201, 219, 221
Portales, Diego, 206
Poverty and inequality, 5–6, 48–53. *See also specific countries*
Prado, Manuel, 36, 313, 319, 320, 345

Presidential Commission for the Reform of the State (COPRE) (Venezuela), 403
Presidentialism, 29–31, 338. *See also specific countries*
Prieto, Joaquín, 194, 195
Protodemocracies, nineteenth-century, 13

Quadros, Jânio, 147, 150, 163

Radical Party (Argentina), 28, 75, 78–79, 80, 81, 82, 83, 97, 98, 102, 103, 108, 109, 113, 117–118, 209
Radical Party (Chile), 196, 197, 199, 200, 201, 203–204, 209, 215, 217, 218, 221, 232
Reagan administration, 60, 328
Reformist Party (Costa Rica), 437
Reformist Party (Dominican Republic), 503–504
Regional cleavages, 50, 53–54, 142, 144, 145, 405–406
Renovación Nacional (RN) (Chile), 231, 232
Republican Party (Costa Rica), 435, 437, 441
Revolution on the March (Revolución en Marcha) (Colombia), 258
Reyes, Rafael, 256
Rodríguez, José J., 435
Rodríguez Echeverría, Miguel Angel, 442
Rojas Pinilla, Gustavo, 264–265, 275
Roosevelt, Franklin, 353
Roosevelt, Theodore, 475
Rule of law, 33, 101, 122

Sáenz Peña, Roque, 35
Salas Romer, Henrique, 394
Salinas, Carlos, 533, 549
Salinas, Raúl, 549
Samper, Ernesto, 38, 251, 272–273, 284–286, 295, 297
Sánchez Cerro, Luis, 316, 318
Santa Cruz, Andrés, 194
Sarney, José, 136, 170–171, 175–176, 179
Sendero Luminoso (Shining Path) (Peru), 326, 327–328, 329, 331, 332, 334
Serpa, Horacio, 286, 287
Socialist International, 482, 486, 487
Socialist Party (Argentina), 75
Socialist Party (Chile), 228, 230, 232
Social structure, and political culture, 41
Socioeconomic conditions, 41, 44–46, 168. *See also specific countries*
Soviet Union, 120, 121
State building: historical legacies in, 7–9; political development sequences in, 13–15; and postindependence politics, 10–13
State expansion, democratic impact of, 16–18
State structure and strength, 6, 15–23

Statism, 15, 17, 173

Tomic, Radomiro, 201, 218
Trejos, Joaquín, 442
Trujillo Molina, Leónidas, 471, 476–479,
  495–496, 501, 503, 507, 509
Túpac Amaru II, 312
Turbay, Julio César, 271, 275–276

Ulate Blanco, Otilio, 437, 438
União Democrática Nacional (UDN) (Brazil),
  145, 146, 162, 163
Unidad Party coalition (Costa Rica), 438,
  441–442
Unidad Popular (UP) (Chile), 201, 219, 221
Unión Cívica Nacional (UCN) (Dominican
  Republic), 503
Unión Demócrata Independiente (UDI)
  (Chile), 232, 237
Unión de Trabajadores de Colombia (UTC),
  261
Unión de Trabajadores de México (UTM),
  529
Unión Patriótica (UP) (Colombia), 277–278,
  279, 281
Unión República Democrática (URD)
  (Venezuela), 377, 380
United States: and Argentina, 121; and Chile,
  220; and Colombia, 269, 285–297; and
  Costa Rica, 450, 458; and Dominican
  Republic, 474, 475–476, 477, 479,
  480–481, 482, 489, 494–495, 509–511;
  Latin American policy, 59–60; and
  Mexico, 558–559, 565–567; as model of
  democracy, 39, 57; and Peru, 316, 320,
  323, 328, 339, 353–355; and Venezuela,
  378, 382, 411–412. See also U.S. Alliance
  for Progress
United States Agency for International
  Development (USAID), 489, 510
Uruguay, 24; democracy, 3, 44, 50, 61; economy, 17; political culture, 42–43; reforms,
  36; state capacity, 16, 17
U.S. Alliance for Progress, 321

Valencia, Guillermo León, 265, 270
Valenzuela, Arturo, 191
Vargas, Getúlio, 13, 43, 142, 144–145, 146,
  163, 176
Vargas Llosa, Mario, 329, 345
Velasco Alvarado, Juan, 36, 311, 322–325,
  341
Velásquez, Ramón J., 392, 404
Velázquez, Fidel, 528, 529
Venezuela: associational life and civil society,

56, 369–370, 371–372, 381–382,
  406–411, 415–416, 418; civil wars,
  373–374; cleavages and regionalism, 50,
  405–406; coalition politics, 379, 380–382,
  418; colonial and nineteenth-century, 9,
  373–374; Congress, 371, 392, 394,
  403–405; coups and attempted coups,
  376, 377, 378, 386, 390–392; crisis and
  reforms, 367, 368, 370–371, 386–395,
  410–411; democratic consolidation and
  rule, 61, 374, 375 (Table 7.1), 376–386,
  414; democratic prospects, 369, 413–420;
  economic crisis and reform, 387–388,
  393–394; elections and electoral system,
  369, 376–377, 378, 381–382, 383, 386,
  388–390, 392, 393, 399–403; elites and
  elite pacts, 35, 377, 379, 380, 381, 400,
  414, 415; human rights violations, 413;
  international factors, 411–413, 415; labor
  unions, 406–407; left, 382, 385, 406–407;
  military, 414–415; military rule
  (1936–1945), 372, 375–376, 378; mobilization and movements, 374, 379, 384;
  neighborhood movement (vecinos),
  408–410; participation, 381–382, 413;
  parties and party system, 28, 369, 376,
  377, 379, 382–383, 389, 399–403, 406,
  407, 413–414, 416, 417, 418–419; personalistic rule, 374; petroleum industry,
  367, 370, 373, 374, 377, 378, 397–398,
  411, 412, 415; political culture, 42; political legitimacy, 372, 378, 381; political
  protests and violence, 390, 391; presidency, 371, 404–405; private sector development, 398–399; proportional representation, 389–390, 404; socioeconomic development, 396–399, 414, 415, 417; state
  structure and interbranch relations, 367,
  370, 371–372, 373, 374, 403–405, 413;
  state terror and police power, 374, 378;
  trienio politics (1945–1948), 376–377,
  383, 384; two-party rule, 382–386, 391;
  and the United States, 378, 382, 411–
  412
Volio, Jorge, 437

Waisman, Carlos H., 71
War of the Pacific (1879–1883), 12, 198, 212,
  313–314
Wars, interstate, 11–12
Wiarda, Howard, 38

Yrigoyen, Hipólito, 35, 119

Zedillo, Ernesto, 535, 536, 549

About the Book

Extensively revised since the first edition was published in 1989, this analytically balanced and empirically rich volume thoroughly examines the historical, cultural, social, economic, political, and international factors that affect both the prospects for and the nature of political democracy in Latin America.

The book reflects improvements in democratic trends in some countries, but also the erosion of democratic advances in others, with substantial malaise regarding key political actors and institutions and continuing concerns about the impact on democratic consolidation of economic constraints, weak states, judicial inefficacy, and high degrees of inequality. A comprehensive introduction precedes the nine country chapters, which follow a similar format to facilitate comparisons.

Larry Diamond is senior research fellow at the Hoover Institution. **Jonathan Hartlyn** is professor of political science at the University of North Carolina at Chapel Hill. **Juan J. Linz** is Sterling Professor of Political and Social Science at Yale University. **Seymour Martin Lipset** holds the Hazel Chair of Public Policy at George Mason University.